OUR AMERICAN MUSIC

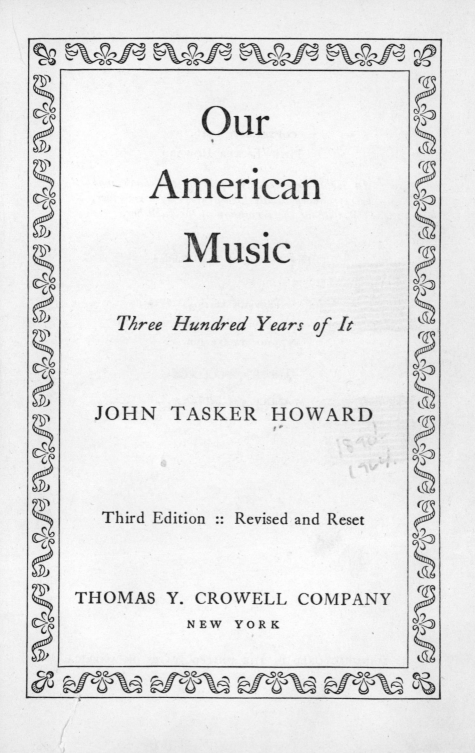

Our
American
Music

Three Hundred Years of It

JOHN TASKER HOWARD

Third Edition :: Revised and Reset

THOMAS Y. CROWELL COMPANY
NEW YORK

TO

THE TWO

MRS. JOHN TASKER HOWARDS,

MY WIFE AND MY MOTHER,

this book is lovingly inscribed

PREFACE

THE author of a book on American music may well approach his task with fears as to the outcome, knowing that no matter how thorough he may try to be, his work will be incomplete in many respects. Yet it has seemed that a book like this is called for, to bring information about the music that has been written in this country; one that will be both historical and contemporary, look facts fairly in the face, avoid chauvinism, and present the honest opinion of the writer. This book is an account of the music that has been written in America; not a history of musical activities, except, of course, where we must have some idea of the conditions that have produced the composers of each era.

The student of American music will find many paths open to him. There is an abundance of source material, gathered by such tireless research workers as Oscar G. Sonneck and others who have worked in our libraries and historical societies. Mr. Sonneck's source books on our early secular music, concerts, and opera, though written a quarter of a century ago, are still surprisingly complete. While discoveries have been made since his books were published, little has been found that would prove any of his findings wrong. Mr. Sonneck carried his studies up to 1800, and beyond that date the student must do his own research, in newspapers, musical journals, diaries, from concert programs, and from printed music. It is of interest to note that a fund has been established as a memorial to Mr. Sonneck, which, it is hoped, will provide for a complete compilation of all musical records of New York, Boston, and Philadelphia for the years 1800 to 1850; a mammoth task, but one that will be of inestimable value.

Material for the present volume has been gathered from a wide variety of sources, as listed in the bibliography. Mr. Sonneck's compilations were, of course, invaluable. Private collectors have generously opened their collections, and descendants and relatives of our early composers have been kind in showing material that has added fresh data to the information previously available. Contemporary musical journals of various periods have likewise yielded an amazing wealth of information.

An outline serialization of much of the material in this book has appeared in *Voice of the Air;* and other material has appeared in the form of articles in *The Musical Digest* and *The Musical Quarterly*. I acknowledge the kindness of their editors in granting permission to include this matter.

Many individuals have also been helpful in my task. Among the descendants and relatives of composers—Mr. Edward Hopkinson, great grandson of Francis Hopkinson; Mr. Hobart Hewitt and Miss Carrie W. Hewitt, grandson and great granddaughter of James Hewitt; Mrs. James Spurr Whitman, granddaughter of Oliver Shaw; Mr. Howard Van Sinderen, husband of the late Minna Mason Van Sinderen, who was the daughter of William Mason and grand-daughter of Lowell Mason and George James Webb; Mrs. Edward MacDowell; Mrs. Ethelbert Nevin; Mrs. Horatio Parker; as well as many friends and associates of MacDowell, Parker, Nevin, Paine, and others, who have given valuable information, impressions, and anecdotes.

Those in charge of the libraries to which I have gone for reference and study have done much to make my work pleasant and easier. Dr. Otto Kinkeldey, who was head of the Music Division of the New York Public Library until he became librarian of Cornell University; Miss Dorothy Lawton and her assistants at the 58th Street Music Library in New York; Mr. Walter R. Whittlesey, and Mr. W. Oliver Strunk of the Library of Congress; Mr. Richard G. Appel, of the Public Library of the City of Boston; as well as those at the many state libraries who have helped me in finding books referring to music and musicians in their states.

Among the private collectors who have given access to their treasures, I am particularly grateful to Mr. Arthur Billings Hunt of Brooklyn, Mr. Joseph Muller of Closter, New Jersey, and Mr. George Fischer of New York City.

I wish also to acknowledge the kindness of the book publishers who have granted me permission to quote from their copyright publications, as indicated in the text.

Music publishers have been helpful in supplying information about the composers of the music in their catalogues; and I should like to save a large portion of my gratitude for the contemporary composers, who have responded most graciously to requests for data. If I have failed to put any of them in the place they feel they should have, I hope they will forgive me and credit it to ignorance rather than to malice.

And lastly I wish to acknowledge my debt to many friends who have helped in suggestions and criticism, and in many cases with recollections of the happenings chronicled in these pages; among them my erstwhile music teacher and lifelong friend, Paul Tidden; my friend and neighbor, Osbourne McConathy; Professor Homer A. Watt of New York University, who has been helpful in introducing me to specialists in several fields; J. Walker McSpadden, who has been my friend and adviser as well as my publisher's editor. Many others, too, whom I should like to mention; but space forbids.

So here is the book. I let it go from me with misgivings, but at least I know that I have tried to state the case of the American composer honestly. And I have the feeling that his music is better qualified to speak for him than any single writer of a book on American music.

J. T. H.

Glen Ridge, New Jersey.
January, 1931.

PREFACE TO SECOND
REVISED EDITION

In 1939, when *Our American Music* had been in circulation for eight years, two supplementary chapters were added to tell briefly of the developments and the many new composers that had appeared in that comparatively short time. And now, after six more years, it is not only desirable, but necessary, to revise the book completely, to adjust certain viewpoints to changing conditions, to re-evaluate, to add to the discussion of composers included in the original volumes the many works they have composed more recently, and also to include the several hundred composers who became recognized after 1931.

Since the first appearance of *Our American Music* many specialists have been busy with research into the early days of America's music life, some of them carrying on the work of Oscar G. Sonneck in examining the beginnings of our secular music and concert life; others in the backgrounds of the psalmody and hymnology of New England, some into folk music, many into regional history, and a dozen or more into jazz and contemporary manifestations of twentieth-century phenomena. Consequently, our scholars know infinitely more about the backgrounds of American music than was known even fifteen years ago. Evidence of this is in the addition of more than three hundred titles to the Bibliography at the end of our book, most of them of works published in recent years.

In order that *Our American Music* might have the benefit of this varied research, certain chapters and sections of the book have been submitted to specialists in several fields, who have checked the accuracy of all statements in the light of recent discoveries, and have suggested additional text material to amplify what was already presented in the book. Accordingly, my thanks and sincere appreciation for invaluable assistance go to Henry Wilder Foote for his contributions on early New England psalmody, the later hymn-tune composers, and on certain phases of our contemporary church music; to William Treat

Upton for his help in the sections on early secular music and on Anthony Philip Heinrich and William Henry Fry; to Richard S. Hill for the latest information on the origins of our national airs, particularly *The Star-Spangled Banner;* to Hans Nathan for the benefit of his studies in Negro minstrel shows, Negro minstrel music, singing families of the mid-nineteenth century, and for material on David Decatur Emmett; to George Pullen Jackson for his contribution on the "White Spirituals" and folk hymnody and their effect on the present-day gospel songs; to Fletcher Hodges, Junior, for a review of the chapter on Stephen Foster; and to Sigmund Spaeth for amplifying the material on popular songs to cover more adequately the period between the Civil War and the 1890's.

Several institutions and individuals have been particularly helpful. The Americana Collection of the Music Division of the New York Public Library, of which the author is curator, has naturally been a rich mine of information, and a clearing ground for many matters which required examination and sifting. The staff of the Music Division has had an indispensable part in the preparation of these pages. My thanks are due to them and particularly to Miss Anita Goldstein, who has given unsparingly of her time in attending to innumerable details of preparation.

Likewise, the staff of the Music Library on 58th Street have been highly co-operative and helpful in locating information on many individuals included in these pages. Thanks are due also to Mr. Daniel McNamara of the staff of the American Society of Composers, Authors and Publishers for supplying information on composers who are members of that society.

It is a pleasure further to express my appreciation of the willingness of my publishers to spare no pains in making this revised edition of *Our American Music* as thorough and comprehensive as it could be made, and of the interest and sympathetic co-operation offered by Mr. Robert L. Crowell and his editorial staff. And lastly, but by no means least, my heartfelt thanks are offered to Miss Ava Yeargain, for her invaluable assistance in research and in the actual preparation of several chapters, as well as in proofreading.

J. T. H.

Glen Ridge, New Jersey, 1946.

Contents

List of Illustrations

INTRODUCTION

BEFORE beginning this account of Our American Music, it will be wise if the reader and the author agree as to just what American music is and, likewise, who is an American composer. It may be argued that all such classifications are arbitrary, and that the author is privileged to make his own distinctions. Nevertheless, we will get along much better, and be happier, if we can agree.

Shall we insist that music must be nationalistically American? We shall have to settle this at the start, for it will make a vast difference in our contents. And if we limit ourselves to those things that we can agree are American, we probably will need to write no book at all; for even though we may each have our own ideas on the subject, I doubt if any two of them are alike. And, moreover, even if we do agree, we must omit all composers who have written principally in the manner of other nations, and perhaps whatever may be considered *universal* or *cosmopolitan* in its style or idiom. Under such a rule, Tschaikowsky might conceivably be barred from a book on Russian music. So why not say right here that music written by Americans will be our American music, at least for the purpose of our discussion? Then, if we are careful to point out Americanisms as we find them, we can give the composers responsible for them an A double plus, or whatever merit mark we choose.

Then who is the American composer? Many think he must be born in this country; that those who urge the adoption of foreign residents as Americans, do so because we have so few natives. That a French-born composer is always a Frenchman; a German-born, a German. Maybe so, and the day may come when we no longer lengthen our list with foreigners. But our case is a little different. We have all adopted America, even those of us who let our ancestors do our immigrating for us. And shall we be like college boys in treating new-comers as freshmen, just because our ancestors had the idea first?

You may say that the Constitution requires the president of the country to be a native-born citizen; but there can be only a few presidents, and we have room for many composers. You and I know many native Americans whose families have been here for generations, but whose temperaments and points of view are as foreign as those of their cousins who stayed at home. Of course, it is obvious that mere residence will not make an American, and we cannot call a composition American merely because its composer has had a part of his physical existence in this country. If that were allowable, the *New World* Symphony would have been written while Dvořák was an American composer. No; visitors are welcome, but they are not Americans.

It must be a case of extended residence, to all intents permanent; the adopted composer may go home to visit, but he mustn't stay away too long. And it must be something more subtle and subjective than citizenship. Legal naturalization may make a citizen, but it does not in itself make an American. The foreigner must become one of us, become identified with our life and institutions. And also he must make his reputation here. He must come to us in his formative years, not as an established artist.

Try this definition: a composer is an American if, by birth or choice of permanent residence, he becomes identified with American life and institutions before his talents have had their greatest outlet; and through his associations and sympathies he makes a genuine contribution to our cultural development.

These specifications would admit Charles Martin Loeffler, who came here at the beginning of his career; Ernest Bloch, who received his first important recognition in this country; and Percy Grainger, who came to us well established as a pianist, but with his most important composing yet to be accomplished. The definition obviously does not include many of those who have become citizens in recent years, men who were widely discussed and internationally known composers abroad in the years before racial persecution drove them from Europe. Arnold Schoenberg, Igor Stravinsky, Darius Milhaud, Sergei Rachmaninoff, Ernst Křenek, Kurt Weill, and dozens of others have become Americans by naturalization, and our nation may well be proud of the fact, but it does not seem appropriate to include them in this volume as the musical product of the United States.

The music of America's three hundred years seems naturally to fall into three periods, but not according to centuries. Dating its existence in this country from the settlement of Plymouth in 1620, the first period would include the one hundred and eighty years to 1800, to a time when our independence was established and we had begun to be a nation, and we were beginning to absorb the first immigration of those foreigners who came to our land of freedom after we had become the United States of America. There were the early psalmodists in New England, but none who were known to have written music of their own until the time of William Billings, in the latter part of the eighteenth century. There was secular music in New York, Philadelphia, and the South, but no composers we know of until Francis Hopkinson appeared. Yet we shall find that there were certain factors in our early musical life, barren as it was, that have had an influence on the music of our day. Euterpe did indeed come to a wilderness, but she made the best of her situation.

The next period, in which Euterpe seems to have made up her mind to stay with us, extends from 1800 to 1860. The foreigners who had come in the 1780's and 1790's, because of the French revolution and because they had heard of America's freedom, were becoming Americans. The native composer, who had been forced to the background by the coming of skilled Europeans, came forward again with more confidence. Lowell Mason appeared, with his contemporary hymn writers. Concert life and operas became more firmly established. The new Western cities demanded some music. The minstrel show became a favorite diversion, and Stephen Foster wrote melodies that have become folk songs.

Then another tide of immigration swept our shores, which had the same effect that the latter eighteenth-century coming of foreigners had had fifty years before. The revolutions in Central Europe made America a refuge for hundreds of Germans in the years around 1848. When they came here they took over a large part of our musical life, and many Americans were content to sit back and listen rather than put their less developed talents in competition with the foreigners. And so the second period ended, as the first had finished, with aliens in the foreground.

The third period reaches from 1860 to the present day. Euterpe makes a home with us. As at the beginning the century, in the second period, most of the foreigners became Americans. Moreover, we were beginning to be nationally conscious in our music. And we began to produce composers who were important: John K. Paine and Dudley Buck among the first. Then MacDowell—Chadwick, Foote, Parker, and the rest of the Boston group; Ethelbert Nevin, with his lilting tunes and his *Rosary*. All of this right down to our own day, when we are arguing about musical nationalism, and trying to determine what American music is, as far as its idiom is concerned. To a time when we have produced jazz, and are wondering how important it really is. To a period when our musical life is on a par with that of any other country in the world; when we have the finest of symphony orchestras in our large cities; the finest teachers of the world in our conservatories or in their own private studios; and, what is most important, to a day when we may really be on our way to becoming a musical nation; when our public schools are giving musical training to pupils equal to that offered by conservatories twenty-five years ago.

How much of this external music can make us musical in our inner depths is another question. But we have the desire, anyway. And if the desire is sincere enough and strong enough the rest will follow. We cannot buy a musical soul with our money, but we can wish for a musical soul and get it. And I think that we are wishing for it.

But more of this in its proper place. The division into periods has been arbitrary, and there has been some chronological overlapping. For example, the first national airs are included in the second section, yet two of them—*Yankee Doodle* and *Hail Columbia*—first appeared in the eighteenth century. It has seemed better to include all of these national songs in one chapter, and to consider that the earliest of them bridged the century and the first two periods.

And now we go to the first act of our pageant. There will be much to amuse us, and, I trust, to interest us. But I ask one favor of you: smile and laugh if you wish, but *with* not *at* the friends we shall meet. For when we think of their handicaps, the few tools they had to work with, talent rises to genius. But enough of the sermon. Raise the curtain and meet Euterpe in the Wilderness.

PART ONE

1620–1800

EUTERPE IN THE WILDERNESS

CHAPTER ONE

Early Days

I. NEW ENGLAND PSALMODY

THE history of American music, meaning the music of what is now the United States, should logically start with the psalm singing of the New England colonists, not because it was the first music known on the North American continent, but rather because it was the earliest music of which we have any satisfactory record, and of which any extended account can be written.

The folk music of the American Indians was probably in existence long before the coming of the colonists, and no doubt the Negroes who were brought from Africa in the first slave ship in 1619 used song as an outlet for their emotions; but recognition of folk music has been a comparatively modern fashion, and it seems more appropriate to discuss it in other than a chronological place which is wholly problematical. The earliest European music to be heard upon either coast of North America north of the Spanish settlements was the French psalmody sung by the Huguenots on the Carolina Coast in 1572, before their brief settlement was wiped out by the Spaniards; and the English psalmody sung by Drake's seamen during their stay of several weeks in June, 1579, at what is now known as Drake's Bay on the California Coast, as described in Francis Fletcher's *The World Encompassed by Sir Francis Drake.*

Aside from these brief episodes the first recorded use of music on this continent, north of the Spanish domain, was that of the Pilgrims at Plymouth. The settlement at Jamestown preceded that at Plymouth by eleven years, it is true, but the Virginia planters have left no record of singing, though it is not unreasonable to assume that in spite

3

of the miseries they endured they may at times have plucked up courage to sing popular "catches" round their campfires, and psalms in their houses of worship. In contrast to our lack of information about the Jamestown settlement, we do have definite knowledge of the music the New England settlers brought with them from England, and contemporary documents tell of their methods of singing. We are, therefore, able to follow the course of musical development in the Northern colonies from the earliest days.

The first century of New England's history was in many respects a musical wilderness, but probably little if any more so than in the other colonies. The England from which the first settlers emigrated was a land noted for its singing, and there is no reason to suppose that only those persons emigrated who were unmusical. The Puritans, of course, held strictly to psalmody as the only music suitable for use in worship, and discountenanced lewd and indecent songs, of which there were plenty in the seventeenth century, as tending to "the nourishment of vice and the corruption of faith," but there is adequate evidence that many of them appreciated good music and that some brought musical instruments with them to this country.[1]

But the hard conditions of pioneer life, with its heavy labor, left no leisure for the fine arts, and in all the colonies the second and third generations grew up without the cultural background their English fathers had enjoyed. This was undoubtedly the principal cause of the musical impoverishment that existed until more stable conditions made possible the revival of interest in music early in the eighteenth century.

When the Pilgrims crossed from Holland in the *Mayflower* in 1620 they brought with them Henry Ainsworth's *Book of Psalmes*, prepared by him in 1612 for the congregations of Separatists who fled from England to Holland. His book included thirty-nine psalm-tunes, about half being taken from English psalm books, the rest being the longer and finer French and Dutch tunes in a considerable variety of meters. Ainsworth's *Psalter* was superior, musically, to any English psalm book then available.[2]

[1] H. W. Foote, *Three Centuries of American Hymnody*, chap. III (1940); also Foote, "Musical Life in Boston in the Eighteenth Century," *Proceedings of the Antiquarian Society, New Series*, XLIX, 293–313.
[2] Waldo S. Pratt, *The Music of the Pilgrims*, Boston, 1921.

The Plymouth Pilgrims undoubtedly had a love for music, for a contemporary account of their sailing from Leyden tells of the ceremony that attended their departure. In *Hypocrisie Unmasked* Edward Winslow wrote:

They that stayed at Leyden feasted us that were to go at our pastor's house . . . ; where we refreshed ourselves, after tears, with singing of Psalms, making joyful melody in our hearts as well as with the voice, there being many of our congregation very expert in music; and indeed it was the sweetest melody that ever mine ears heard.

Ainsworth's *Book of Psalmes* remained in use at Plymouth until 1692, when it was abandoned in favor of the *Bay Psalm Book,* because the children of the emigrant generation were no longer able to sing the longer and more involved tunes their fathers had loved.

The Puritans of the Massachusetts Bay Colony brought with them the psalm book that had been produced by English Protestant exiles in Geneva on the model of the *French Genevan Psalter* of 1562. The English book was first printed in the same year by John Day under the title *The Whole Booke of Psalmes, collected into English Meter by T. Sternhold, I. Hopkins and others; conferred with the Ebrue, with apt Notes to sing them withal, Faithfully perused and alowed according to th' ordre appointed in the Queenes maiesties Iniunctions: Very mete to be used of all sortes of people privately for their solace and comfort; laying apart all ungodly Songes and Ballades, which tende only to the nourishment of Vyce & corruption of Youth.*

It is necessary to know something about this book, and its various editions, if we are to understand the Psalmody of New England. Commonly called *Sternhold and Hopkins* and later known as the *Old Version*—after the appearance in 1696 of Tate and Brady's *New Version* of the metrical psalms, the book had been quickly adopted into popular and universal use in Elizabethan England. Its verse, which later generations came to regard as crude and barbarous, was cast in the popular ballad meters and was probably as good as England could have produced at the period. At any rate, it pleased the people for whom it was written. Sternhold and Hopkins' book was promptly introduced into the worship of the Church of England, and only slowly gave way to the *New Version* nearly a century and a half later.

Musically it was inferior to the *French Genevan Psalter*. Yet at times it has a simple dignity and solemnity, often combined with sweetness. Three other musical editions followed John Day's first *Sternhold and Hopkins;* Damon's in 1579; Este's in 1592; and Allison's in 1599. Este printed his tunes in four-part settings arranged by distinguished musicians, and Allison's collection of psalm-tunes has been called by a competent authority, "on the whole the best that ever appeared." They were followed by Thomas Ravenscroft's *Psalter* in 1621, containing ninety-seven tunes, by far the best English selection available in the seventeenth century, with which the Puritans in New England were quite familiar, as will presently appear. Ravenscroft acknowledges his indebtedness to outstanding musicians of his own or the immediately preceding generation, including Dowland, Farnaby, Morley, Tallis, and Tomkins.

The only early psalm-tune that appeared in these books which is still familiar to churchgoers is the *Old Hundredth*. This melody is attributed to Louis Bourgeois, the music editor of Calvin's *Genevan Psalters,* and first appeared in 1551, set to the 38th Psalm. It was taken over by the English Puritans and was attached to William Kethe's version of the 100th Psalm in John Day's edition of *Sternhold and Hopkins,* with a slightly different ending from the Genevan form, and so passed into all the later psalm books. The original words began,

> All people that on earth do dwell
> Sing to the Lord with cheerful voyce;
> Him serve with mirth, his praise forth tell,
> Come ye before Him and rejoice.

Our forefathers called it a "lively and jocund tune," because they sang it with some quick notes which well expressed the sentiment of the words—not with the slow and solemn tread of even notes into which the tune was flattened out in the eighteenth century, and to which we are accustomed when we sing the *Doxology*. Some modern hymnbooks have revived the original form of the tune, to the original words. A few other psalm-tunes from the sixteenth and seventeenth centuries have also been restored to recent hymnbooks, notably *St. Florian, Dundee, Dunfermline, Windsor,* and *Old 120th* from Eng-

lish and Scottish sources; and *Toulon* (*Old 124th*), *L'Omnipotent*,
Donne Secours, and *St. Michael* from Genevan sources.

⌐ In John Day's edition of *Sternhold and Hopkins*, and in Ainsworth,
the music of the psalms was printed with the words, a single melody
line to be sung in unison, a single note to each syllable, after the Ge⌐
nevan fashion. A large proportion of the tunes are in the minor key,
which our forefathers do not appear to have found depressing, as so
many moderns do.⌐

But to return to New England: the Puritans brought with them to
the Massachusetts Bay Colony copies of *Sternhold and Hopkins*,
probably in most cases with Ravenscroft's settings.[3] But they were
dissatisfied with the words they found in it. To understand their dis-
satisfaction we must go back to Calvin's teaching. He held that the
only words suitable for singing in worship were those taken from
Scripture, the inspired Word of God, put into metrical verse in the
most accurate translation possible. But the New England ministers
were good enough Hebraists to realize that in many places the metrical
versions they found in *Sternhold and Hopkins* were quite inaccurate.
As Cotton Mather puts it in his Magnolia:

About the year 1639, the New English Reformers, considering that their
churches enjoyed the ordinances of Heaven in their spiritual purity, were
willing that the ordinance of singing Psalms should be restored among them
unto a share in that purity. Though they blessed God for the religious en-
deavors of them who translated the psalms into the metre usually annexed,
at the end of the Bible, yet they beheld in the translation, variations of, not
only the text, but the very sense of the Psalmist, that it was an offence unto
them.

They therefore appointed a committee of thirty divines to prepare
a new and more "close-fitting" translation, each of whom "took a portion to be translated." The work, however, appears to have been done
almost entirely by the Reverend Richard Mather of Dorchester, and
the Reverend Thomas Welde and the Reverend John Eliot of Roxbury, all of whom had studied at Emmanuel College, Cambridge.
This is indicated by Cotton Mather, who says that they "were of so

[3] John Endicott's copy of Ravenscroft's *Psalter*, with his autograph, is now owned
by the Massachusetts Historical Society.

different a Genius for their Poetry that Mr. Shephard of Cambridge on the Occasion addressed them to this Purpose,

> You Roxbury Poets, keep clear of the Crime
> Of missing to give us a very good Rhime;
> And you of Dorchester, your verses lengthen,
> But with the Text 's own words, you will them strengthen.

Today the verses of these Roxbury and Dorchester "poets" seem uncouth enough, although careful examination reveals lines of rugged beauty. But it is essential to remember that their aim was not smoothly flowing verse so much as close accuracy of translation. In that they succeeded well. Their book was printed in 1640 in the little press at Cambridge, and was the first book to appear in the English-speaking colonies of North America. It was popularly known as the *Bay Psalm Book*, but its actual title was *The Whole Booke of Psalmes faithfully translated into English Metre. Whereunto is prefixed a discourse declaring not only the lawfullnes, but also the necessity of the heavenly Ordinance of Singing Scripture Psalmes in the Churches of God.* Richard Mather wrote the preface in which he states the case for psalm singing. "The singing of Psalmes, though it breathe forth nothing but holy harmony, and melody; yet such is the subtilty of the enemie, and the enmity of our nature against the Lord, and his wayes, that our hearts can find matter of discord in this harmony and crochets of dirision in this holy melody." And he concludes: "If . . . the verses are not always so smooth and elegant as some may desire or expect, let them consider that God's Altar needs not our pollishings . . . for we have respected rather a plaine translation, and so have attended Conscience rather than Elegance, fidelity rather than poetry, in translating the Hebrew words into English language, and David's poetry into English meetre: that soe we may sing in Sion the Lord's songs of praise according to his own will; until hee take us from hence, and wipe away all our tears, and bid us entre our masters joye to sing eternall Halleluiahs."

Only ten copies of the original edition survive, not three of them perfect. In 1651 a revised edition was brought out, edited by Henry Dunster and Richard Lyon, with considerable improvements in the versification. This revised edition bore the title *The Psalms, Hymns*

*and Spiritual Songs of the Old and New Testaments, faithfully trans-
lated into English meter for the use, edification and comfort of the
Saints, in publick and private, especially in New England.* The two
books have been commonly regarded as successive editions of what was
universally called *The Bay Psalm Book.*

The early edition contained no music, probably for lack of anyone
capable of engraving the plates, but all included an "Admonition"
about the tunes to which the psalms might be sung, which reads (in
part) as follows:

The verses of these psalmes may be reduced to six kinds [metres], the first
whereof may be sung in very neere fourty common tunes; as they are
collected out of our chief musicians, by Tho. Ravenscroft. The second kinde
may be sung in three tunes, as Ps. 25, 50 and 67 in our English psalme books.
The third may be sung indifferently, as ps. the 51, 100, and ten command-
ments, in our English psalme books, which these tunes aforesaid, comprehend
almost this whole book of psalmes, as being tunes most familiar to us. . . .

Altogether some fifty tunes are referred to in either Ravenscroft's
Psalter or other English psalm books. It is important to remember
that although the editors were unable to print music in the *Bay Psalm
Book,* they did recommend to its users the best collections of tunes
which the time afforded.

The ninth edition, 1698, inserted thirteen tunes at the back of the
book and is the earliest known book with music printed in the English
colonies. The tunes were doubtless those in frequent use at the time—
*Oxford, Litchfield, Low-Dutch, York, Windsor, Cambridge, St.
David's, Martyn, Hackney, 119th Psalm Tune, 100th Psalm Tune,
115th Psalm Tune,* and *148th Psalm Tune.* Most are in common
meter, but *Cambridge* is short meter, the *100th Psalm Tune* is long
meter, and the *148th Psalm Tune* is six, six, six, six, four, four, four,
four.

The music was copied inaccurately from some unidentified English
source. It was crudely engraved on wood in diamond-shaped notes in
two-part harmony, without bars except at the end of each line. In later
editions, well-made copper plates were used.

The *Bay Psalm Book* soon came into wide use, not only in New
England but, in its 1651 form, as far south as Philadelphia. It even

had some use in England and Scotland where, according to the historian Thomas Prince, it was well esteemed. Twenty-seven editions were printed in New England, the last in 1762, and some twenty more in Great Britain, the last in 1754. Of the many versions of metrical psalms, only those of *Sternhold and Hopkins*, of *Tate and Brady*, the *Scottish Psalter*, and that of *Watts* were reprinted and used more widely.

Evidently not all of the early Bostonians favored singing, even of psalms, for in 1647 the Reverend John Cotton found it advisable to publish a treatise entitled:

Singing Psalms a Gospel Ordinance: or a Treatise wherein are handled these 4 particulars:

1. Touching the duty itself.
   (Singing of Psalmes with a lively voyce, is an holy Duty of God's Worship now in the dayes of the New Testament)
2. Touching the Matter to be Sung.
   (We hold and believe that not only the Psalmes of David, but any other spirituall songs recorded in Scripture, may lawfully be sung in Christian Churches)
3. Touching the Singers.
   1. Whether one be to sing for all the rest; or the whole congregation?
   2. Whether women; as well as men; or men alone?
   3. Whether carnall men and Pagans may be permitted to sing with us, or Christians alone, and Church members?
4. Touching the Manner of Singing.
   (It will be a necessary helpe, that the words of the Psalme, be openly read beforehand, line after line, or two lines together, so that they who want either books or skill to reade, may know what is to be sung, and joyne with the rest in the duties of singing.)

This document shows the nature of the discussions that were taking place in regard to music. Some complained that psalms should not be sung because the tunes were uninspired by God, and that God could not take delight in praises when sinful man had had a hand in making the melody. Some even went so far as to scoff at the Puritan ministers who called on the people to sing one of "Hopkins Jiggs, and so hop into the Pulpit." Cotton replied by calling all such "Cathedrall Priests of an Anti-Christian spirit," and by pointing out that "they that had

THE

VVHOLE

BOOKE OF PSALMES

Faithfully
TRANSLATED *into* ENGLISH
Metre.

Whereunto is prefixed a difcourfe declaring not only the lawfullnes, but alfo
the neceffity of the heavenly Ordinance
of finging Scripture Pfalmes in
the Churches of
God.

Coll. III.

Let the word of God dwell plenteoufly in
you, in all wifdome, teaching and exhort-
ing one another in Pfalmes, Himnes, and
fpirituall Songs, finging to the Lord with
grace in your hearts.

Iames v.

If any be afflicted, let him pray, and if
any be merry let him fing pfalmes.

Imprinted
1640

Title Page of the *Bay Psalm Book* (1640)
(See pages 7–10)

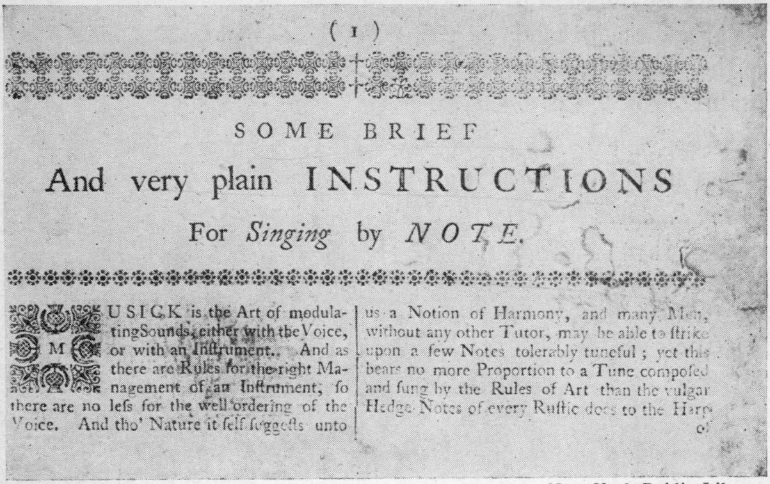
(1)

SOME BRIEF

And very plain INSTRUCTIONS

For *Singing* by *NOTE*.

MUSICK is the Art of modulating Sounds, either with the Voice, or with an Inſtrument. And as there are Rules for the right Management of an Inſtrument, ſo there are no leſs for the well ordering of the Voice. And tho' Nature it ſelf ſuggeſts unto us a Notion of Harmony, and many Men, without any other Tutor, may be able to ſtrike upon a few Notes tolerably tuneful; yet this bears no more Proportion to a Tune compoſed and ſung by the Rules of Art than the vulgar Hedge-Notes of every Ruſtic does to the Harp of

New York Public Library

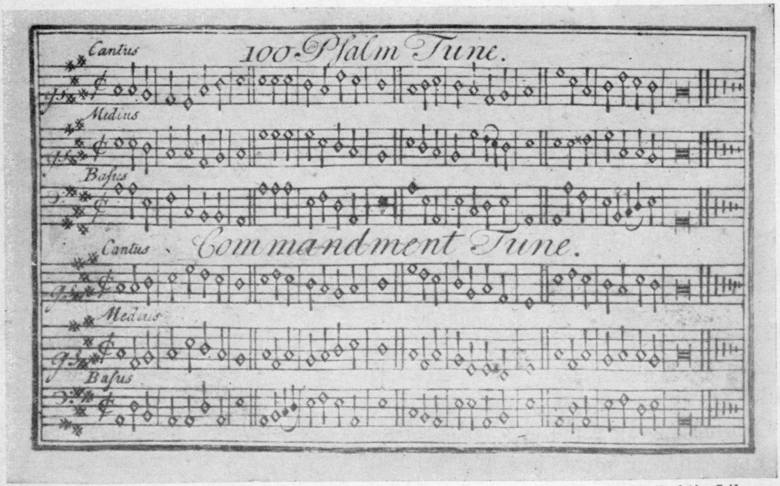

New York Public Library

Two Pages from Thomas Walter's Singing Book (1721)

(See page 13)

a hand in making Melody of the English *Psalms* were men of a better spirit than the Ahab."

The lack of music in the *Bay Psalm Book*, the inability of many in the congregations to read not only music but printed English as well, led to the continuation of the earlier English practice of "lining out" the psalms, which was done in England by the parish clerk. In New England it was led by a deacon acting as precentor, whose duty it was to "set the tune," and who would sing the psalm, line by line, pausing for the congregation to repeat the line he had just sung. If the precentor had a good ear for music, and a good sense of pitch, well and good; otherwise the results were far from musical. It was probably this practice, more than any other factor, that brought congregational singing to its deplorable condition at the beginning of the eighteenth century. Tunes would be pitched too high or too low; the leader would take it upon himself to alter the tune, to add embellishments. By the end of the seventeenth century there was great confusion in regard to the tunes themselves, and in the manner of singing them.

George Hood, in his *History of Music in New England*, gives a vivid description of conditions at this time:

When the Puritans first came to their wilderness-home, they cultivated music even in their College. [Harvard, founded in 1636.] Their songs of praise were conducted with decorum, if not with ability; and a laudable pride, if such can be, inspired them still to improve their purity and excellence. . . .

But soon after their settlement, the Colonies were disturbed by contentions and party strife. . . . Troubles came upon troubles in rapid succession. The genius of discord settled upon the land. . . .

Music dwells not in scenes of contention; she flies the abode of anarchy and confusion, and seeks a home in the land of peace. . . .

The few music-books, that had from time to time found their way into the Colonies, were rapidly decreasing; and the few they had were unlike. The cultivation of music was neglected, until in the latter part of the seventeenth, and at the commencement of the eighteenth century, the congregations throughout New England were rarely able to sing more than three or four tunes. The knowledge and use of notes, too, had so long been neglected, that the few melodies sung became corrupted, until no two individuals sang them alike. . . .

The declining state of music had been so gradual and imperceptible, that the very confusion and discord were grateful to their ears; and a melody sung in time and in tune, was really offensive. At this stage of affairs, some of the best men of the day, seeing the need of reform, resolved to set about the work. This they did; and about the year 1720, several excellent and spirited discourses from the best divines, were published and scattered among the people. . . .

One might think, that a duty so obvious and practical, would find none but friends to its best performance. But it was not so. No sooner had the cry for reform been heard, than it was opposed by a large party in almost every church; and opposed with a virulence of feeling, and tenacity of attachment to their old customs, that seemed to defy their best efforts. Objections were urged even by serious, well informed persons, which, however trifling and pitiful they may seem to us, were to them important and solemn. The idea of learning to sing by note, or to sing a melody correctly, had something in it little less fearful in itself, or in its effects, than witchcraft and its scenes, through which they had just passed.

The principal objections were:

1. That it was a new way;—an unknown tongue.
2. That it was not so melodious as the usual way.
3. That there were so many tunes, one could never learn them.
4. That the new way made disturbances in churches, grieved good men, exasperated them and caused them to behave disorderly.
5. That it was popish.
6. That it would introduce instruments.
7. That the names of the notes were blasphemous.
8. That it was needless, the old way being good enough.
9. That it was only a contrivance to get money.
10. That it required too much time to learn it, made the young disorderly, and kept them from the proper influence of the family, &c., &c.

Here was a controversy as violent as that between the fundamentalists and the modernists in the Protestant Church of our day. That which had been good enough for their fathers was good enough for the New Englanders of the early eighteenth century. The agitation among the ministers for improvement in singing did not actually commence until 1720, but previous to that time the Reverend John Tufts, a minister of Newburyport, had published *A very plain and easy introduction to the whole Art of Singing Psalm Tunes*. There is evidence that the first edition of this work was published in 1712, though no copies appear to be in existence. The book must have had a wide circulation, for the edition of 1744 is marked as the eleventh printing. This was the first instruction book on singing compiled in the English colonies. The author endeavored to give a musical notation that would be simpler to read and to understand, but really succeeded only in making it more complicated and difficult. Letters instead of notes were used on the staff, and the time was marked by placing one or more dots on the right side of the letter. The tunes were given in three parts, *Cantus, Medius,* and *Base.* Thirty-seven tunes were included in the book, in arrangements possibly copied from John Playford's *Whole Book of Psalms,* published in England in 1677.

John Tufts's book was followed in 1721 by another instruction book —*Grounds and Rules of Musick explained: or an introduction to the Art of Singing by Note,* by the Reverend Thomas Walter of Roxbury, Massachusetts. In addition to the instructions for singing by note, Walter's book contained some "Rules for Tuning the Voice." Some of the directions were a bit vague; especially the guide for distinguishing between "flat" and "sharp" keys. The author obviously refers to *minor* and *major* modes:

Tunes are said to be upon a flat Key, or a sharp Key. To know whether your Tune be upon a flat Key or a sharp Key, this is the general Rule. If the two Notes above the last Note of your Tune be whole Notes [evidently meaning whole *tones*] it is upon a sharp Key; but if the two Notes above, be one an whole Note, and the other an half Note, then it is a flat Key.

In Walter's book the tunes were given in three parts, in arrangements probably taken from Playford. The work enjoyed a number of editions.

The Reverend Thomas Symmes of Bradford, Massachusetts, was one of the parsons who fought for better singing. He published two sermons and an essay: *The Reasonableness of Regular Singing, or Singing by Note* (1720); *Prejudice in Matters of Religion* (1722); and *Utile Dulci; or Joco-Serious Dialogue* (1723). In these discourses the Reverend Doctor Symmes argued the case in detail, and sought to answer the objections of those who wanted the "old way" of lining out psalms. In the *Dialogue* he disputes the statement that reading by note is a "new way":

That which is now called the *Usual* way, in opposition to singing by note, is but a defective imitation of the *regular* way. . . . Your usual way of singing is but of yesterday, an upstart novelty, a deviation from the regular, which is the only scriptural good way of singing; much older than our fathers or fathers' grandfathers.

The beauty and harmony of singing consists very much in a just timing and turning the notes; every singer keeping the exact pitch the tune is set in, according to the part he sings. Now you may remember, that in our congregation we us'd frequently to have some people singing a note or two, after the rest had done. And you commonly strike the notes not together, but one after another, one being half way thro' the second note, before his neighbor has done with the first. Now this is just as melodious to a well-tuned musical ear, as Æsop was beautiful to a curious eye.

The author then proceeded to refute the argument that reading by note would lead to the use of instruments, and the accusation that it was a scheme to get money:

Since you make a noise (Tho' no pleasant one) about instrumental musick, I'll give you an unanswerable argument, that may put you out of all pain about it: And that is, that, truly, it's too chargeable a piece of worship ever to obtain amongst us; and you may depend upon it, that such as are not willing to be at the cost of a bell, to call the people together on Lord's day, and of a man to ring it . . . will never be so extravagant as to lay out their cash . . . to buy organs, and pay an artist for playing on them. . . . And in the mean time, pray be easy and assure yourself, that singing by Rule (note), wont in our day introduce instrumental musick, much less Quaker-ism and Popery. I promise you, your usual way of singing would much sooner dispose me to fall into them. Because the Quakers don't sing at all and I should be out of the noise of it; and the Papists sing much better when they sing by Rule.

As to getting money by it—why the singing master is not worthy of his reward for his pains in teaching our children to sing, as well as the School Dame or school master for teaching our children to read, write and cypher, I can't device. For Musick is as real and lawful and ingenious an art as either of the others.

In 1723 a tract was issued anonymously, entitled:

Cases of Conscience about singing Psalms, briefly considered and resolved. An Essay by several ministers of the Gospel, for the satisfaction of their pious and conscientious brethren, as to sundry Questions and Cases of Conscience, concerning the singing of Psalms, in the public worship of God, under the present Evangelical constitution of the Church-state.

Such questions as the following were discussed:

Whether you do believe that singing in the worship of God ought to be done skilfully?

Whether you do believe that skilfullness in singing may ordinarily be gained in the use of outward means, by the blessing of God?

Is it possible for Fathers of forty years old and upward to learn to sing by rule? And ought they to attempt at that age to learn?

Do you believe that it is Lawful and Laudable for us to change the customary way of singing, for a more uniform and regular way of singing the Psalms?

Whether they who purposely sing a tune differently from that which is appointed by the pastor or elder to be sung, are not guilty of acting disorderly, and of taking God's name in vain also, by disturbing the order of the sanctuary?

Fortunately, the progressive spirits in the clergy eventually won their battle. Singing societies were gradually established throughout New England, in which the meager instruction that was available was faithfully given. Finally, some of the churches allowed the first seats in the gallery to be reserved for the best singers, who were to lead in singing the psalms, and from this, church choirs eventually developed. Many pastors later found that these choirs grew into something more than they had bargained for. The singers' sense of their importance was often troublesome.

The lining out of psalms was not abandoned without many a bitter struggle, and in some cases the deacons whose functions were usurped by singing from note refused to give up their duties. Some of them had literally to be sung down by the congregations.

The *Bay Psalm Book* reigned supreme in the New England churches for three generations, as did *Sternhold and Hopkins* among the Presbyterians and Episcopalians in the other colonies, but with the revival of singing towards the end of the first quarter of the eighteenth century, other influences began to seep into colonial church life which brought a slow decline in the popularity of both books. This decline was caused by the appearance of Tate and Brady's *New Version* of the psalms in 1696, followed in 1711 by Watts's *Hymns* and in 1719 by his *Psalms of David Imitated*. The literary quality of the psalms and hymns in these books was far superior to that of the earlier version, more pleasing to ears which had become accustomed to the style of Addison and Pope. And with the words came new tunes which were fresh and interesting in contrast to the well-worn old psalm-tunes.

On March 16, 1720–21, Samuel Sewall noted in his *Diary*,

At night Dr. Mather preaches in the School-House to the young musicians from Rev. 14.3,—no man could learn that Song. House was full, and the singing extraordinarily Excellent, such as has hardly been heard before in Boston. Sang four times out of Tate and Brady.

This entry refers to the first singing school established in Boston. Tate and Brady provided words and tunes which were not yet admitted to the churches but were permissable in the schoolhouse. But it was inevitable that they should eventually gain admission to the churches, not only in Boston but elsewhere, though often against opposition.

Watts was well known in Boston as a theologian as well as a religious poet, and corresponded with Cotton Mather, who approved of his verses for private devotional reading. But it was George Whitefield, the English religious leader, who chiefly promoted the use of Watts's *Hymns and Psalms*. Whitefield made his great evangelistic tour of the colonies from 1739 to 1741. He was a great believer in singing. When Jonathan Edwards returned to his charge at Northampton, Massachusetts, after an absence, he found that his congregation, under Whitefield's influence, had turned to Watts's hymns "and sang nothing else, and neglected the Psalms entirely." A compromise was arranged, which included the use of both the older psalms and of Watts's hymns. In Virginia the noted preacher, the Reverend Samuel Danes, who in 1753, at the age of thirty, succeeded Jonathan Edwards as president of the College of New Jersey (Princeton), was also an ardent advocate of Watts. From the middle of the century on, the use of Watts's hymns and psalms spread rapidly, superseding the use of the *Bay Psalm Book* and of *Sternhold and Hopkins*, until by 1800, Watts completely dominated the hymnody in most churches.

In 1755 there was issued in Newburyport an American edition of William Tans'ur's *A Complete Melody in Three Parts* (1755). Tans'ur was a contemporary English psalmodist and musician of probable German origin. The publication of his work in the colonies was important, for it was the authority used by many of our early composers. Tans'ur helped to introduce some of the fine English hymntunes that were contained also in Watts, among them Crofts's *Hanover* and *St. Anne*. Tans'ur's own tune *St. Martin's* is still sung at Harvard commencements to a version of the 78th Psalm based on *Tate and Brady*, and is included in a few modern hymnbooks. By the end of the century a considerable number of the new English tunes were well established, of which Hatton's *Duke Street*, Knapp's *Wareham*, Miller's *Rockingham*, and the anonymous *Truro* are still in common use.

One more of the eighteenth-century colonial psalm books should be mentioned, if only because it was engraved by Paul Revere. This was *A Collection of the Best Psalm Tunes*, which was published by Josiah Flagg of Boston in 1764. The tunes were announced as "from the most approved authors, fitted to all measures, and approved by the best masters in Boston, New England; the greater part of them never before printed in America." Whether any of the new tunes were composed by Americans we cannot know, for the names of the authors are not given. Flagg was active in other fields than psalmody; he formed and trained a military band and often organized concerts. We shall meet him again in later pages.

2. EARLY CHURCH ORGANS

Organs had been unknown in the colonies in the seventeenth century, and even in England were to be found only in cathedrals, college chapels, and the larger parish churches, so that probably the majority of the colonists of the early period, coming from rural districts or small towns, had but slight acquaintance with them. Furthermore, organs were costly, cumbersome to ship, and it may be doubted if there were any persons in the colonies prior to 1700 capable of playing one. At the Smithsonian Institution there is an organ said to have been imported in 1700 for St. Peter's Church at Port Royal, Virginia, but the claim cannot be substantiated, and this particular instrument probably dates from at least a half a century later. The German Pietists who settled in the Wissahickon Valley, now a part of Philadelphia, had a small organ which in 1703 was borrowed for use in *Gloria Dei* (Swedish) Church in Philadelphia. A year later they were joined by an English organ builder, Dr. Christopher Witt, who built one or more organs for private use, the first to be constructed in this country. One of these was probably the instrument purchased in 1728 for Christ Church in Philadelphia. The first organ constructed by a native-born colonist was the work of young Edward Bromfield, Junior, of Boston, who was graduated from Harvard in 1742 and died in 1746 at the age of twenty-three. He left it not quite complete, but his contemporaries greatly admired his skill and ingenuity.

The first organ imported into New England was that owned by Thomas Brattle of Boston. He procured the organ as early as 1711, for on May 29 of that year the Reverend Joseph Green noted in his *Diary:*

I was at Mr. Thomas Brattle's; heard ye organ and saw strange things in a microscope.

When Brattle died in 1713 he bequeathed the organ to the Brattle Square Church, of which he was a leading member, but, foreseeing a possible, or probable, rejection of his gift, he provided that in such case it should go to King's Chapel. He further stipulated that the church which accepted the organ should "procure a sober person that can play skilfully thereon with a loud noise." The organ went to King's Chapel where it was set up a year later, and Mr. Sustone was imported from London to play it. It was supplanted by a better organ in 1756, and was sold to St. Paul's Church, Newburyport, Massachusetts, whence it went eighty years later to St. John's Church, Portsmouth, New Hampshire, where it still exists in usable condition.

Brattle's organ, when set up in King's Chapel, was the first to be permanently installed in a colonial church. The second church in the colonies to install an organ seems to have been the Dutch Reformed Church of New York; to which Governor Burnet gave an organ in 1724; the third was Christ Church, Philadelphia, already referred to; the fourth was Trinity Church, Newport, Rhode Island, which in 1733 received one from Bishop Berkeley. In 1736, Trinity Church and Christ Church, Boston, each imported an organ. In 1737, Trinity Church, New York, set up an organ built for it by Johann Gottfried Klemm, a Moravian organ builder. Bruton Parish Church at Williamsburg, Virginia, got one in 1755, and St. Michael's, Charleston, South Carolina, imported one in 1768. It will be noted that most of these organs were installed in Episcopal churches. Their congregations generally included a large proportion of newcomers from England, and their clergymen, if not of English birth, had gone to England for ordination, and naturally sought to introduce the latest Anglican practices. Even with them, however, the increase in the number of organs was slow, because of the cost of the instruments and the difficulty of procuring organists.

Other Protestant groups moved even more slowly. An anonymous writer who signed himself "A Presbyterian" in 1763 printed a tart pamphlet in Philadelphia deploring the low state of singing, and arguing that it could be improved by the introduction of organs. The Congregational Church in Providence, Rhode Island, set up an organ in 1770, as noted by Ezra Stiles in his *Diary*, July 10:

Last month an Organ of 200 Pipes was set up in the Meeting-house of the first Congregational Church in Providence; and for the first time it was played upon in Divine Service last Ldsday, as Mr. Rowland the pastor tells me. This is the first organ in a dissentive presby. Chh. in America except Jersey College, [Princeton] or Great Britain.

And under date of May 16, 1785, Ezra Stiles notes:

They have lately determined to set up an Organ in Dr. Chauncey's Meetghouse being the old Brick or first Chh. in Bo. founded in 1629. The Doctor was against it, but Mr. Clark, his colleague, and the Congregn. in general were for it. This spring the Meetghouse was repaired and Dr. C. preached a consecrn. and farewell sermon on acct. of his great age. The people eager to get an organ waited on the Dr. who told them that it would not be long before he was in his grave,—he knew that before his head was cold there they would have an organ—and they might do as they pleased.

The venerable Dr. Chauncey reflects the conservatism of old age, resisting innovations. But in his own lifetime he had seen the slow change from very poor singing without any instrumental accompaniment, to the use of tuning forks for the benefit of choirs, and then to the introduction of the bass viol which came into fairly general use by the end of the eighteenth century, and was to linger in some churches down to nearly the middle of the nineteenth. As late as 1800 there are said to have been less than twenty church organs in all New England, and no more, in proportion to the population, in other parts of the country.

3. EARLY SECULAR MUSIC IN NEW ENGLAND

Secular amusements did not have much chance to flourish in early New England. In the diary of Samuel Sewall, one of the first justices of Boston, we find an entry under the date of *Thorsday, Novr. 12, 1685:*

. . . the ministers of this Town (Boston) Come to the Court and Complain against a Dancing Master who seeks to set up here and hath mixt Dances; and 'tis reported he should say that by one play he could teach more Divinity than Dr. Willard or the Old Testament. Mr. Moodey said 'twas not the time for N.E. to dance. Mr. Mather struck at the Root, speaking against mixt dances.

This dancing master intended to fight it out, for on December 17:

. . . Mr. Stepney, the Dncing Master, desired a Jury, so he and Mr. Shrimpton Bound in 50 lbs. to Janr. Court. Said Stepney is ordered not to keep a Dancing School; if he does will be taken in contempt and be proceeded with accordingly.

The odds were too great, and on the following July 28:

. . . Francis Stepney the Dancing Master runs away for Debt. Several attachments out after him.

Evidently Stepney had a poor reputation on other grounds than wanting to open a dancing school.

Another quotation from Sewall refers to dancing (Friday, May 27, 1687):

. . . Between 5 and 6 Father Walker is taken with a Lethargy. . . . His speech came to him something between 6 and 7. . . . He overheard some discourse about the May-Pole, and told what the manner was in England to dance about it with Musick, and that 'twas to be feared such practices would be here . . .

Early in the next century dancing schools were permitted.

There was little instrumental music in New England in the seventeenth century. Drums and trumpets were used to summon people to church until bells became available—or to sound an alarm or in connection with military training. Jew's-harps were imported in quantities for trade with the Indians who delighted in them. A few of the early emigrants brought music books and small musical instruments with them, but most of them had to turn their possessions into cash in England to pay for their voyage and for equipment for pioneer life. Moreover, shipping space was too limited to allow transportation of luxuries. But Nathaniel Rogers of Rowley, dying in 1664, left a "treble Violl" and the Reverend Edmund Browne, who died in 1678, left a "bass vyol," some books of music, and the reputation of being a good musician. Tutor Wigglesworth of Harvard, about 1650, caught an idle student "in the forenoon with ill company playing musick, though I had solemnly warned him but yesterday of letting his spirit go after pleasures." The implication is that the boy was idling with undesirable companions when he ought to have been studying.

Seaborn Cotton, son of the Reverend John Cotton, who himself became a minister, left a student's commonplace book in which he copied out the words of several well-known English ballads and a bar of music jotted down as a memorandum of a tune. In 1661 the Reverend Leonard Hoar wrote from London to his nephew Josiah Flynt, a freshman at Harvard, who had asked him for a fiddle. The letter contains sensible advice and ends:

Musick I had almost forgot. I suspect you seek it both to soon and to much. This be assured of that if you be not excellent at it its worth nothing at all. And if you be excellent it will take up so much of your mind and time that you will be worth little else: and when all that excellence is obtained your acquest will prove little or nothing of real profit to you unless you intend to take upon you the trade of fidling. Howbeit hearing your mother's desires were for it for your sisters, for whom it is more proper and they also have more leizure to look after it: For them I say I had provided the instruments desired. But I cannot now attend to sending them being hurrying away from London.

The writer of this letter clearly did not disapprove of music as such, but he knew that his nephew had to earn a living in the world and that the "trade of fidling" would not suffice, though music would be a pleasant pastime for the girls.

By the end of the seventeenth century people were beginning to import larger instruments. On December 1, 1699, Samuel Sewall, always a lover of music, notes in his *Diary* that he went to a shop to inquire about repairs to his wife's virginals. In 1716, Edward Eustace, the recently arrived organist for King's Chapel, advertised in the *Boston News-Letter*:

This is to give notice that there is lately just come over from England a choice collection of Instruments, consisting of Flageolets, Flutes, Haut-boys, Bass-Viols, Violins, Bows, Strings, Reeds for Haut-Boys, Books of Instruction for all these Instruments, Books of Ruled Paper. To be sold at The Dancing School of Mr. Sustone in Sudbury Street near The Orange Tree, Boston. Note: Any person may have all instruments of Musick mended, or Virginalls and Spinnets Strung and Tuned at a reasonable Rate, and likewise may be taught to Play on any of these instruments above mentioned; dancing taught by a true and easier method than has been heretofore.

The growing interest in instrumental music led to public concerts by groups of amateur musicians. It should be remembered that concerts to which the public was admitted for a price did not occur even in London until late in the seventeenth century, and were at first held in taverns. The first authentic record of a public concert in any of the English-speaking colonies is an advertisement which appeared in the *Boston News-Letter* of December 16 and 23, 1731, as follows:

On Thursday, the 30th of this instant December, there will be performed a "concert of Music" on Sundry instruments At Mr. Pelham's great Room, being the house of the late Doctor Noyes near Sun Tavern. Tickets to be delivered at the place of Performance at "Five Shillings" each. The concert to begin exactly at Six o'clock, and no Tickets will be delivered after Five the day of Performance. N.B. There will be no admittance after Six.

This concert antedates by only three and a half months the first concert given in Charleston, South Carolina, and it is, of course, possible that there were earlier concerts in either place of which no record has survived.

The Mr. Pelham, in whose "great Room" the concert was held, was Peter Pelham, the engraver, who had emigrated to America from

London in 1726. He was an excellent maker of mezzotints and a painter of sorts, but the demand for such work was too limited to support him, and he resorted to teaching and other occupations to gain a livelihood. He later married the widow Copley, and thus became the stepfather of John Singleton Copley.

In 1732 or 1733 the first European musician of note visited Boston. He was Karl Theodor Pachelbel, son of a noted German organist related to the family of Johann Sebastian Bach, and himself well trained. It would be pleasant to believe that he was the first European artist to be heard in Boston, but there is no record of the programs or the performers at the two concerts which were held in the town in each of the two years mentioned. When Pachelbel left he took with him Peter Pelham's son by his first wife, Peter Junior. He went to Newport, where he assisted in setting up the organ which Bishop Berkeley had given to Trinity Church, and thence to New York and Charleston, where he stayed for some years. We shall learn presently of his giving New York its first recorded concert. Peter Pelham Junior did not return to Boston till 1743, and advertised on May 30 of that year in the *Boston Evening Post* that after "nine years under the Tuition of an accomplish'd Professor in the Art of Musick" he was prepared to give lessons on the harpsichord and in the "Rudiments of Psalmody, Hymns, Anthems, etc." He became the first organist of Trinity Church in Boston, where he remained until 1749. He then went to Virginia and in 1755 became the first organist at Bruton Parish Church in Williamsburg, where he served with distinction for forty years.

A few years after Pelham Senior's concert, the Boston selectmen felt justified in according the use of Faneuil Hall to such gentlemen as William Sheafe, Samuel Deblois, and Thomas Hancock for "concerts of Musick." By 1754 the city had a Concert Hall at the corner of Hanover and Court streets, where concerts of "Vocal and instrumental Musick to consist of Select Pieces by the Masters" were given. There is evidence that Thomas Dipper may have inaugurated a regular series of subscription concerts in the late fifties or early sixties, and it has been definitely established that Boston enjoyed such affairs in 1766.

Boston was not friendly to theatrical entertainments. As early as 1686 a play had been suppressed, and Increase Mather had published his "Testimony against profane and superstitious customs." Again, in 1714, we hear of Judge Sewall protesting against the acting of a play in the Council Chamber. In 1750, two young Englishmen, assisted by amateur friends, gave a performance of Otway's *Orphan* in a Boston Coffee House. This so horrified the good citizens that a law was passed absolutely prohibiting "public stage plays, interludes and other theatrical entertainments," as "tending to discourage industry and frugality, and greatly to increase impiety."

And yet, as the days of the Revolution approached, New England was growing artistically, and slowly acquiring cultural traits that made its life richer. It was in such a scene that New England's first composer made his appearance—the tanner-musician William Billings, the first American composer to make music his profession.

4. PHILADELPHIA, NEW YORK, AND THE SOUTH

It is to be regretted that records of musical life during the early years of the Southern colonies, and of Pennsylvania and New York, are not as complete as those of New England, for further information would help in estimating the relative importance of each colony's contribution. The New England psalmodists, and their successors in the latter eighteenth century, have probably exerted a deeper influence on one branch of our present music—hymnology—than any of the Pennsylvania Germans, the Dutch in New York, or even the few professional musicians who migrated to this country before 1750. Nevertheless, it seems unwise to dismiss altogether, as some historians have done, certain elements in our early music, even though they have had no obvious influence on the future of the nation. The Germans and Swedes who came to the neighborhood of Philadelphia when William Penn first proclaimed his "glorious new world," and the Moravians who later settled in Bethlehem, enjoyed a musical life far in advance of anything in contemporary New England. These were settlements established for religious motives, and many of their beliefs were fanatical, yet there was not the suspicion that any kind of music was the invention of the devil, to be shunned as worldly and frivolous. Good singing in church was required, and insisted upon. One pastor, the Reverend Andreas Sandel (Swedish), imposed a fine of six shillings on certain members of his congregation for "untimely singing."

It was in 1694 that a German band of pietists took up their dwelling beside the Wissahickon River, eight miles from Philadelphia. These people were German mystics who believed that the end of the world was near at hand, and who renounced marriage as sinful, believing that their one love should be the Lord Jesus Christ. The leader of the hermits was Johann Kelpius, a highly educated man, the son of a pastor at Dendorf, Germany. Not only did these Germans sing hymns, but they accompanied their singing with instrumental music, and brought instruments with them when they first landed in this country. As early as 1708, Kelpius wrote abroad for two clavichords "with additional strings."

The Wissahickon hermits evidently acquired a reputation for singing soon after their arrival, for in 1700 they were invited to act as choristers and to furnish instrumental music at the dedication of the new Swedish church *Gloria Dei* near Philadelphia. Kelpius is mentioned as the composer of nineteen of the hymns used by the hermits, but he probably was the author of only the words, for the same writer who mentions his authorship speaks of another as the first "composer" on American soil.

The *Gloria Dei* Church is important musically, as it may have been the first American church equipped with an organ.[1] Some authorities believe that Kelpius brought with him from Europe the organ that was installed in that church. At any rate, it was present three years later when Justus Falckner was ordained as its minister, and not only was music supplied by Jonas, the regular organist, but the neighboring mystics furnished music on the viol, hautboy, trumpets, and kettledrums. Falckner was the first German minister ordained in this country, and was the author of several of the fine hymns of his congregation.

Two years before he was awarded the pastorate of the *Gloria Dei* Church, Falckner wrote a letter to Heinrich Muhlen of Holstein, asking for assistance for his church. The letter tells of conditions in the colony, and provides an interesting contrast to the attitude of New Englanders regarding music:

[1] See pages 17–18.

. . . I will take occasion to mention that many others besides myself, who know the ways of the land, maintain that music would contribute much towards a good Christian service. It would not only attract and civilize the wild Indians, but it would do much good in spreading the Gospel truths among the sects and others by attracting them. Instrumental music is especially serviceable here. Thus a well-sounding organ would perhaps prove of great profit, to say nothing of the fact that the Indians would come running from far and near to listen to such unknown melody, and upon that account might become willing to accept our language and teaching, and remain with people who had such agreeable things; for they are said to come ever so far to listen to one who plays even a reed-pipe: such an extraordinary love have they for any melodious and ringing sound. Now as the melancholy, saturnine, stingy Quaker spirit has abolished all such music, it would indeed be a novelty here, and tend to attract many of the young people away from the Quakers and sects to attend services where such music was found, even against the wishes of their parents. This would afford a good opportunity to show them the truth and their error.

. . . And it may be assumed that even a small organ-instrument and music in this place would be acceptable to God, and prove far more useful than many hundreds in Europe where there is already a superfluity of such things.

There are in Europe masters enough who would build such instruments, and a fine one can be secured for 300 or 400 thalers. Then if an experienced organist and musician could be found, who would undertake so far a journey, he would be very welcome here. In case this could not be, if we only had an organ, some one or other might be found who had knowledge thereof.

Robert R. Drummond, in *Early German Music in Philadelphia*, claims that CONRAD BEISSEL was the first composer of music in America. This statement seems plausible, for Beissel was associated with the *Ephrata Cloister* in the early part of the century. At this famous sisterhood they sang hymns and chorals in four, five, six, and seven parts, while congregations in other parts of the country were singing in unison. The first edition of the *Ephrata* hymn collection was published by Benjamin Franklin in 1730. Over a thousand of these hymns have been attributed to Beissel.

The history of music in Philadelphia is a record of continual struggle with the Quakers in the early years, for the Friends were opposed to music of any sort. Plays, games, lotteries, music, and dancing were classed alike, and the meetings advised all members against either attending such diversions or being in any way connected with them. Arrayed against the Quakers and the Presbyterians were the members of the Church of England, who consistently championed lighter amusements. Though musical entertainments, and especially dramatic offerings, were often presented in an apologetic tone, they nevertheless existed. As early as 1710 there is record of a dancing master in Philadelphia, and dancing was taught in boarding schools in 1728. Although the earliest public concert of which there is record was given by John Palma in 1757, it seems hardly possible that some were not given before this time. Before 1750, Philadelphians enjoyed no theatrical diversions, except for an "agreeable comedy or tragedy" which Benjamin Franklin's *Pennsylvania Gazette* (our *Saturday Evening Post*) advertised in 1742 as acted "by changeable figures two feet high" every evening "at the Sign of the Coach and Horse, against the State House"; and a performance by live actors of Addison's *Cato* in 1749.

In 1750 (the year of Boston's antitheatre law), the Kean and Murray Company from London tried to give a performance in Plumstead's Warehouse, but the Recorder of the city reported that

certain persons had lately taken upon them to act plays in this city, and he was informed intended to make a frequent practice thereof, which, it was feared, would be attended with very mischievous effects.

Whereupon the Philadelphia authorities requested the Magistrates "to take the most effective measures for suppressing this disorder." The Kean and Murray Company departed for New York and the Quaker element was undisturbed by such shocking possibilities for about four years. In 1754 a company headed by Lewis Hallam, which had already entertained New York and several Southern cities, and which was later to be known as the famous American Company, attempted a Philadelphia season, lasting from April to June. The Quaker city then had its first opportunity to hear ballad-operas. Even though the players obeyed the condition that "nothing indecent or immoral should be presented," the season ended in failure, and no regular players appeared again for five years. In 1759, David Douglass, manager of the reorganized Hallam Company, obtained the Governor's permission to erect a theatre on "Society Hill," and a season of plays and ballad-operas was offered which lasted from June to December. In the meantime, however, the Quakers, Lutherans, and Presbyterians forced through the local Assembly an act against "the idle persons and strollers who have come into this Province from foreign parts in the character of players." The Governor was forced to sanction the measure, and though the King set it aside in Council less than a year later, Philadelphia heard no more operas· until 1766.

Douglass returned in that year, and from then until the Revolution, the Southwark Theatre on Society Hill saw regular seasons by the American Company, unmolested by the authorities, even though attacks by its opponents were at times insulting. In 1767, Douglass announced for performance a work that would have been the first American Opera, had it been given. This was advertised as "a new comic opera *The Disappointment, or The Force of Credulity,*" but withdrawn "as it contains personal reflections." It seems that certain prominent Philadelphians had been hunting for treasure reputed hidden by a Captain Blackbeard, and either the gentlemen themselves, or their friends, had convinced Mr. Douglass that it would be wiser not to present the satire. The libretto was subsequently printed, and copies are still in existence. The composer of the music is unknown, and the librettist used a pen name, Andrew Barton.

Bethlehem, Pennsylvania, was settled in 1741 by the Moravians, and since its first year to the present day it has been a musical center which few cities of its size can rival. It is claimed that the first copies of many of Haydn's quartets and symphonies to reach this country were brought to Bethlehem. It is believed that *The Creation* and *The Seasons* had their American premières in the little Pennsylvania town. In 1742 the first *Singstunde* was held in Bethlehem, and a few years later the *Collegium Musicum* was founded, remaining in existence until 1820, when it was succeeded by the Philharmonic Society. In the Moravian Archives at Bethlehem are manuscript copies of six trios and three symphonies by Mozart, dated 1785, when the composer was only twenty years old.

A letter from a little girl attending the boarding school at Bethlehem in 1787, states that she was taught music, vocal and instrumental. "I play the guitar twice a day; am taught the spinet and forte piano, and sometimes I play the organ"—an exceedingly well-rounded musical education for eighteenth-century America.

If a group of manuscripts now in the Archives of the Moravian Church had been dated, we would know exactly where to place a group of Bethlehem composers chronologically. These men lived in Bethlehem in the latter part of the eighteenth century, and their works show a musicianship far in advance of composers in other parts of the country. Most of the works are for instrumental combinations beyond the facilities or ability of colonial contemporaries.

One of the composers, JOHN ANTES, was born in 1740 at Fredericktop, Pennsylvania, where the Moravians had established a preaching station. He made an intensive study of music, and learned to perform on all the stringed instruments. Later in life he went abroad, and was dispatched as a missionary to Egypt. On his return to Europe he became acquainted with Haydn, who is said to have performed some of his works.

Another, DAVID MORITZ MICHAEL (1751–1825), was born and died in Germany but lived for many years at Bethlehem and Nazareth. Some of his works are in the Archives at Bethlehem: A *Parthie*, for wind instruments—two clarinets, two horns, and bassoon; a Suite, for wind instruments (for the same combination); and *Die Wasserfahrt* (The Boat Ride), a programmatic Suite for two clarinets, two bassoons, two horns.

JOHN FREDERICK PETER (1746–1813) left behind him six quintets, for two violins, two violas, and violoncello. These interesting quintets are "the oldest known chamber music works composed in the States." Peter was an organist and violinist of the Moravian congregation.

From an American standpoint, it must be admitted that these composers and their works are not of importance, even though they are superior in workmanship to those of our first native composers. That the works themselves were influenced entirely by the German school would not in itself make them unimportant, but the fact that they were not known very far beyond Bethlehem's limits prevents the possibility of their exerting any marked influence on our musical life. The Moravians at Bethlehem were complete unto themselves, and well might they be musically; there was little mingling with other colonies with whom they would have little in common. Consequently, the most advanced musical settlement did the least for the cultural advancement of the country as a whole.

Several of the Southern cities have claims as pioneers in musical activity. Charleston, South Carolina, not only runs a close second to Boston in fostering the first public concert in America, but enjoys the distinction of having what is generally considered the first musical society formed in America—the St. Cecilia Society, founded in 1762, and remaining in existence until 1912.

The activities of the St. Cecilia Society may be judged from entries in Josiah Quincy's *Journal of a Voyage to South Carolina* (1772). His accounts show that the society was in the habit of engaging professional musicians at good-sized fees:

The concert-house is a large, inelegant building, situated down a yard. . . . The music was good—the two bass viols and French horns were grand. One Abercrombie, a Frenchman just arrived, played the first violin, and a solo incomparably better than any one I ever heard. He cannot speak a word of English, and has a salary of five hundred guineas a year from the St. Cecilia Society. There were upwards of two hundred and fifty ladies present, and it was called no great number. In loftiness of headdress, these ladies stoop to the daughters of the North,—in richness of dress, surpass them,—in health and floridity of countenance, vail to them. In taciturnity during the performances, greatly before our ladies; in noise and flirtation after the music is over, pretty much on a par.

Another item tells of a musical evening in Charleston:

Dined with the Sons of St. Patrick. While at dinner six violins, two hautboys, etc. After dinner, six French horns in concert:—most surpassing music. Two solos on the French horn, by one who is said to blow the finest horn in the world. He has fifty guineas for the season from the St. Cecilia Society.

Charleston witnessed, in 1735, the first recorded performance of an opera in America, the ballad-opera *Flora, or Hob in the Well*. This inaugurated three regular theatrical seasons in the South Carolina city, after which the theatre was turned over to dancing masters for a number of years. It was reopened for plays and opera in 1754.

Williamsburg, Virginia, presented a gay contrast to bleak New England. While the Boston divines were arguing the case of church singing, a real playhouse was in use in Williamsburg, the first known to have existed in America. Records show that it was there as early as 1722, possibly earlier. It was here that George Washington, ever a lover of the theatre, saw his first play on Virginia soil, and the little city also had the honor of being the first to welcome Lewis Hallam's London Company of comedians (1752), which later became the American Company. Williamsburg was treated to regular seasons by the best players in the country.

When the Kean and Murray Company opened the new theatre in Upper Marlborough, Maryland, with *The Beggar's Opera* (1752), an orchestra was used for the first time in an American performance of the opera. The South was by no means behind in its share of musical development during the eighteenth century. If it should be disproved that Johann Kelpius brought with him the organ that was used in the *Gloria Dei* Church, the Episcopal church at Port Royal, Virginia, has the distinction of owning the first pipe organ brought to this country from Europe (1700).

Though it lagged behind the South in musical development, New York at least kept pace with other important cities. Its first concerts date from 1736, according to existing records, though some may have been given which antedate the *"Consort* of Musick, Vocal and Instrumental, for the benefit of Mr. Pachelbel, the Harpsichord Part performed by himself. The songs, Violins and German Flutes by private Hands" (January 21, 1736). Mr. Pachelbel, of course, was the Karl Theodor Pachelbel who came to Boston in 1732 or 1733, and after moving to Newport and to New York, lived for a number of years in Charleston.

Ballad-operas were probably performed in New York from 1732 on, and when the Kean and Murray Company opened a theatre in Nassau Street in 1750, music lovers of the city were treated to a repertory that included seven of them. After this troupe had played two seasons in New York, the Hallam Company arrived and opened the first theatre built for the purpose in the city. According to custom the patrons were entertained with dancing and singing between the acts of such favorites as *Damon and Phillida* and the *Conscious Lovers*. The young Hallams would perform a *Punch's Dance* or sing *As Chloe Came into the Room*, Mr. Hulett would oblige with a hornpipe, and

Mr. Love with *The Quaker's Sermon* on the violin and a solo on the hautboy. As the years passed, New York experienced some opposition to the theatre. Personal possessions brought by the audience had a habit of disappearing, and rather than blaming the unknown sneak thieves who came with the audience, the public turned against the management and the actors. In 1764 a mob wrecked a theatre that David Douglass, successor to Hallam as manager of the American Company, had built in Chapel Street.

In 1767, Douglass brought the American Company back to New York and opened the new John Street Theatre. There was still considerable antagonism to the theatre, and the actors, many of them musicians, were forced to add to their incomes by giving concerts. The theatrical season of 1773 was the last the colonial cities enjoyed until after the Revolution, for in October, 1774, the newly formed Continental Congress, because of the coming struggle with England, found it advisable to pass a resolution which was respectfully observed:

That we will discourage every species of extravagance and dissapation, especially horse-racing, and all kinds of gaming, cock-fighting, exhibition of shows, plays and other expensive diversions and entertainments.

Following Mr. Pachelbel's recital in 1736, New Yorkers were treated to increasingly frequent concerts. Such musicians as Charles Love, of Hallam's theatrical company; William Hulett, an actor, dancing master, and musician who was one of Hallam's violinists; Alexander Dienval, who taught the "violin, German Flute, hautboy, French horn, bass violin, tenor violin, etc., in the newest and best method" offered concerts for their own benefit and for charity. In 1760 the Messrs. Hulett and Dienval established New York's first series of subscription concerts, which were held regularly each season until 1767, when they were discontinued for six years. In 1765, Hulett, in association with a Mr. Leonard, established New York's first open-air summer concerts in Ranelagh Gardens, where "after the concert a small firework will be play'd off, which will continue 'till ten: the whole to be managed with the utmost regularity." Competition soon appeared in concerts in the "King's Arms Garden in the Broadway," and in the biweekly concerts of vocal and instrumental music in the "Vaux Hall Gardens," "newly fitted up with a very good long Room, convenient for a ball or turtle entertainment." A *Harmonic Society* existed in New York in 1774, and its members were active in concerts both for the society and for themselves. In that year New Yorkers had their first glimpse of French and Italian *virtuosi*. The star of the occasion was a Mr. Caze, who had the assistance of the "gentlemen of the Harmonic Society." (Amateurs were designated "gentlemen.") The program was as follows:

1ST ACT

A grand Orchestry's Symphony
A French Ariette will be sung accompanied with the guitar and violin.
Mr. Caze will play his own composed music, on the violin with Mr. Zedtwitz.
A Concert on the Flute
A Sonada on the Spanish Guitar
The first Act to end with a March

2ND ACT

A Grand Orchestry's Symphonie
A French Ariette accompany'd with the Mandolin and Violin
A Solo on the Violin
A Duo on Mandoline and Violin
A Sonada of the Salterio; and d'Exaudet's Minuet with echoes.
The Concert to finish with a March of the grand Orchestry.
After the Concert there will be a ball.

Music lovers of early Gotham were often troubled by disturbing elements at concerts. Frequently protests would appear in the press, and one who signed himself "X.Y.Z." wrote to the New York *Weekly Post Boy* (1764):

It is a very just observation that a gentleman is to be known by his politeness—this qualification, wherever it is to be found, convinces us that it's possessor has seen the world and has had his manners formed by a good education. . . .

I am led into this short reflection by a circumstance, I can scarcely think of without indignation. What I mean is the strange behaviour at the Concert, of a certain set of males and females to whom . . . I will give the soft appelation of gentlemen and ladies. I am a dear lover of music and can't bear to be disturbed in my enjoyment of an entertainment so polite and agreeable.

How great then is my disappointment and vexation, when instead of a modest and becoming silence nothing is heard during the whole performance, but laughing and talking very loud, sqawling, overturning the benches, etc. Behaviour more suited to a *broglio* than a musical entertainment.

What is meant by so ill-timed an interruption I know not: for . . . I cannot conceive that either the audience or the gentlemen performers are under any obligations to bear these impertinences—and I have authority to assure those offenders against decency that . . . the managers and performers will be forced . . . to the disagreeable necessity of insisting on their absenting themselves from a place where they do nothing but give offence or . . . of hiring the adjacent room for the convenience of such whose conduct will not bear the eye of the public. . . .

In 1753 a man who was to exert a profound influence on the city's musical life came to New York: WILLIAM TUCKEY (1708–1781), an Englishman who had been Vicar Choral of the Bristol Cathedral, and clerk of the Parish. Tuckey not only established himself in New York as an organist, choirmaster, concert artist, and composer, but he made the great contribution of organizing and directing the first performance of Handel's *Messiah* in America. In 1770 he led an orchestra and chorus in the overture and sixteen numbers from the oratorio. *The Messiah* was not performed in Germany until 1772, two years after Tuckey brought it to New York.

When Tuckey first came to New York he was appointed a clerk of Trinity Church at a salary of twenty-five pounds per annum. (Small pay in comparison with the reputed salaries of the St. Cecilia Society in Charleston.) His next step was to convince the vestry of Trinity that music should be taught to the pupils of the Charity School, which the church had established in 1739. In this way he developed a choir to sing in the church services. Before long the Trinity Choir was famous, even outside of New York. In 1762, Tuckey resolved to extend his choral efforts beyond the church, and he advertised for volunteers for a chorus. Four years later the newspapers contained an account of one of Mr. Tuckey's *rehearsals* and the announcement of a forthcoming concert.

The musician was sometimes considered worthy of his hire in early New York, for Tuckey was paid fifteen pounds for playing the organ at the dedication of the "new Episcopal Chapel called *St. Paul's*" in 1766. He was active as a concert artist, and two years after coming to America announced a concert in conjunction with William Cobham, musician and dealer in "bear skins, spotted ermin, white and yellow flannels. . . ." The concert was announced in the New York *Weekly Post Boy*, December 15, 1755:

> For the benefit of Messrs. Cobham and Tuckey, at the New Exchange on Monday the 29 instant; will be a *Concert* of Vocal and Instrumental musick. Among a variety of select pieces, both vocal and instrumental, will be performed, the celebrated dialogue between *Damon and Chloe*, compos'd by Mr. Arne. A two part song, in praise of a Soldier, by the late famous Mr. Henry Purcell. *An Ode on Masonry* never perform'd in this country, nor ever in England, but once in publick. And a Solo on the German flute, by Mr. Cobham.
>
> Tickets to be had of Mr. Cobham, in Hanover Square; of Mr. Tuckey near Mr. Willet's, at the New York Arms; and at the King's Arms; and at the new Printing Office in Beaver Street at 5 *s* each.
>
> To begin precisely at six o'clock. After the concert there will be a *Ball* for the ladies.

The *Ode on Masonry* may have been a composition by Tuckey. Although his only works extant today are those in psalm collections, we know that his music was widely known in his time. His *Thanksgiving Anthem* was sung before His Excellency General Amherst, on his return to New York from the conquest of Canada, in 1760. His *Anthem from the 97th Psalm* was performed at a "Grand Concert of Sacred Music for the benefit of the Pennsylvania Hospital and the Poor," and again in 1787 at the First Uranian Concert in Philadelphia. This anthem, subsequently known as *Liverpool*, was anonymously included in James Lyon's *Urania*, a collection of psalm tunes discussed in a later chapter.

It is through his advertisements for subscriptions that we know what Tuckey wrote. In the *New York Mercury* of March 11, 1771, appeared the following:

> *Proposals* for publishing Two select pieces of Church music.
> 1st. An Hymn (by way of an anthem) consisting of Solos, Duets, one Trio and Chorus; together with a Psalm Tune, adapted for any charitable church collection. . . .

2nd. A performance adapted for a *funeral*, consisting of three Dirges (for chorus), the words part of the burial service; together with an Anthem and a Psalm Tune suitable on the solemnity of a funeral or interment of any person of note, etc. The whole never yet perform'd being very lately set to music by *William Tuckey*. . . .

Although Tuckey labored hard to establish regular choral singing in America, the time was not yet ripe for his efforts. He accomplished some very remarkable things, when we consider what he had to contend with, but the tools he needed were not yet at hand.

An account of early music in the colonies must necessarily be superficial in a book that aims to deal with the whole subject of American music. The student who wishes to study closely the conditions in the pre-Revolutionary days must seek works that deal more specifically with those times. It has been necessary to review this period as thoroughly as space will allow, so that as we approach the work of our first native composers—Hopkinson, Lyon, and Billings—we will know what lies back of them, and what equipment their musical public possessed for receiving their work. Unless we are familiar with the conditions that produced these first makers of music, our attitude toward their efforts will be wholly unsympathetic. O. G. Sonneck, one of the foremost authorities on our early musical life, wrote that nobody composed in a musical wilderness, no matter how valueless the compositions may be, if not forced to do so by latent creative powers. With this warning, and apology if you must, we turn our attention to those believed to be the first of our composers born in America.

CHAPTER TWO

Our First Composers

I. FRANCIS HOPKINSON (1737-1791)

IT IS only from circumstantial evidence that we are able to determine who may have been our *first* native composer. Just as Francis Hopkinson was unknown to our first music historians, so may some forgotten composer be overlooked by those writing about American music today. John Antes of Bethlehem may be a possible candidate, should any manuscripts of his be discovered that bear a date prior to 1759; but the only works by Antes of which we know definitely are the string quartets he is said to have written in Europe. Some think that the problematical connection of John Barnard with the tune *Mear* gives him a claim. This matter is discussed in the section on James Lyon.

As matters stand, the evidence that Hopkinson's manuscript song *My Days Have Been So Wondrous Free* was written in 1759, and that James Lyon's psalm collection *Urania* was issued at the earliest in 1761, establishes Hopkinson as the first native composer whose works are extant today. It is altogether fitting that Hopkinson should be our first composer, for this charming musical amateur was one of the signers of the Declaration of Independence, an intimate friend of George Washington, and a man who lent his talents and best efforts to helping our nation establish itself. Among the public offices that Hopkinson held were those of the first Secretary of the Navy, and Judge of the Admiralty from Pennsylvania. In addition to his musical talents, he was a satirist, poet, inventor, and painter. Throughout the War of the Revolution he wrote satirical articles in support of his political faith. *The Battle of the Kegs* is a famous historical document. During the Constitutional Convention, his *History of a New*

37

Roof influenced some of the most distinguished men of the time. In one of his letters to his wife, John Adams thus described Hopkinson:

He is one of your pretty, little, curious, ingenious men. His head is not bigger than a large apple. I have not met with anything in natural history more amusing and entertaining than his personal appearance, yet he is genteel and well bred, and is very social.

Hopkinson was born in Philadelphia, September 21, 1737. Little is known of his childhood, except that the love of music was traditional in the Hopkinson family, and the young Francis must have been introduced to its delights at an early age. He was a member of the first class to receive the Bachelor's degree from the College of Philadelphia in 1757 (now the University of Pennsylvania), and he was later awarded degrees of Master of Arts and Doctor of Laws. He was admitted to the Bar in 1761.

His first public office was that of secretary to a conference between the Governor and the Indians of the Lehigh region. He was made secretary of the Library Company of Philadelphia in 1759. In 1766 he visited England, and in 1768 he married Ann Borden of Bordentown, New Jersey. His house in Bordentown is still standing.

He was always active in public affairs. He was made Collector of the Port of Newcastle in 1772, and in 1774 he was appointed to a seat in the Provincial Council of New Jersey. In 1776 he resigned all offices that would demand allegiance to King George III, and became a delegate to the Continental Congress. He signed the Declaration of Independence, and he was appointed by Congress to "execute the business of the navy under their direction."

In 1779 he was made Judge of the Admiralty from Pennsylvania. He was active in the debates of the convention of 1787 that framed the Constitution of the United States. According to some authorities he was the designer of the United States flag. George E. Hastings, his most comprehensive biographer, presents an interesting discussion of this claim.[1] Hopkinson lived until 1791, when he died of apoplexy on May 9.

[1] George E. Hastings, *The Life and Letters of Francis Hopkinson*, Chicago: The University of Chicago Press.

Conjecture must supply the names of Hopkinson's music teachers, for there were several with whom he could have studied in early Philadelphia. John Beals, "musick master from London," was in Philadelphia from 1749 to 1758. Charles Love, the musician from Hallam's theatrical company, gave music lessons; and in 1757, John Palma's services may have been available. A piece by Palma—*Lesson*—was copied in Hopkinson's own handwriting in his manuscript book. It is fairly certain that Hopkinson studied later with James Bremner, who came to Philadelphia in 1763 and became an active influence in the musical life of the city. When Bremner died in 1780, Hopkinson composed an *Ode* to his memory.

From his own correspondence we may guess that Hopkinson was the center of the musical life in Philadelphia. A talented harpsichordist, he was a member of a group of amateurs and professionals who met at each other's houses, and also gave subscription concerts in public. Hopkinson conducted at the harpsichord; James Bremner, Stephen Forrage, and John Schneider would play the strings in company with Governor John Penn; and wind instruments were furnished by Schneider, Ernst Barnard, George D'Eissenburg (French horn), and John Stadler (German flute). From Hopkinson's library, which is still in the possession of his descendants in Philadelphia, we learn something of the music played at these concerts. The works of Handel were well represented. The Italians, Pergolesi, Giardini, Scarlatti, Corelli, Vivaldi; the English Arne and Purcell were favorites. The group was familiar with the best music of its day.

Philadelphia enjoyed a musical life that extended to the home; households that wished to enjoy music could do so undisturbed by Quaker influences. In this respect the Pennsylvania capital was distinctive. *Soirées* of chamber music were frequent occurrences, and music for its own sake was not disturbed by the virtuoso influence that was later to dominate America's musical life.

Hopkinson's career as a composer started when he was seventeen, when he wrote an *Ode on Music*, the words later printed anonymously in the *American Magazine*. He was always closely associated with the College of Philadelphia, even after graduation, for at various of the commencements he accompanied the choruses and instrumental music on the harpsichord, and on several occasions composed the Odes. When

his teacher James Bremner temporarily relinquished the post of organist at Christ Church, Hopkinson filled the vacancy. The vestry minutes
(1770) contained the following entry:

Mr. church-warden Hopkinson having been so obliging as to perform on
the organ at Christ Church during the absence of Mr. Bremner, the late
organist, the vestry unanimously requested of him a continuance of this kind
office, until an organist should be appointed, or as long as it should be convenient and agreeable to himself. Mr. Hopkinson cheerfully granted this
request.

His musical activities in the church were not confined to playing the
organ, for he was familiar with the best of the psalmodists and taught
singing to the children of the church.

As an inventor, he is chiefly known for his improved method of
quilling the harpsichord. There are several references to this invention in his correspondence with Thomas Jefferson, whom he asked to
introduce the idea to foreign manufacturers; and in his letters to
Robert Bremner, the noted English music publisher, probably a relative of James Bremner.

A work that was probably the most important of Hopkinson's efforts
was *The Temple of Minerva*—undoubtedly from his pen—although
no record has been found of the musical setting. Since this "oratorial
entertainment" was somewhat operatic in type, it has claim to consideration as the first American opera. The libretto was first printed
anonymously in *Freeman's Journal* in Philadelphia, December 19,
1781, and the work was performed in the same year "by a company
of gentlemen and ladies in the hotel of the minister of France in the
presence of his Excellency General Washington and his lady." When
the libretto was again printed six years later in the *Columbian Magazine* it was signed "H.," and this fact, added to Sonneck's discovery of
a fragment of the manuscript in the second volume of Hopkinson's
collected poems and prose, seems to establish the authorship.

The Temple of Minerva was in effect an allegorical-political opera
or dramatic cantata, consisting of an overture, arias, ensembles, and
choruses in praise of the American alliance with France.

The earliest of Hopkinson's works are contained in a manuscript
book of *Songs*, which was in the possession of the Hopkinson family

until it was acquired by the Library of Congress in Washington. In addition to *My Days Have Been So Wondrous Free*, there are three other songs composed by *F. H.* in the volume: *The Garland, Oh! Come to Mason Borough's Grove*, and *With Pleasure Have I Past My Days*, as well as two religious compositions: *The 23ᵈ Psalm* and *An Anthem from the 114ᵗʰ Psalm*. Possibly there are also unsigned works of his.

Hopkinson was probably the compiler of *A Collection of Psalm Tunes with a Few Anthems, Some of them Entirely New for the use of the United Churches of Christ Church and St. Peter's Church in Philadelphia.*

His most ambitious published work was the collection of *Seven Songs* (actually eight), *for the harpsichord or forte piano*, which was issued in Philadelphia in 1788. An advertisement in the *Federal Gazette* states:

These songs are composed in an easy, familiar style, intended for young practitioners on the harpsichord or forte piano, and is the first work of this kind attempted in the United States.

The collection was dedicated to the composer's friend George Washington, then about to enter upon his first term as President. In his letter to Washington, Hopkinson shows himself to be a thoroughly modest person, with no exalted ideas of his greatness as a composer. He was aware of the fact that he was probably the first American composer:

. . . With respect to this little Work, which I now have the honor to present to your notice, I can only say, that it is such as a Lover, not a Master, of the Arts can furnish. I am neither a profess'd poet, nor a Profess'd Musician; and yet venture to appear in those characters united [Hopkinson wrote the words as well as the music of the songs]; for which I confess, the censure of Temerity may justly be brought against me.

If these Songs should not be so fortunate as to please the young Performers for whom they are intended, they will at least not occasion much Trouble in learning to perform them; and this will, I hope, be some Alleviation of their Disappointment.

However small the Reputation may be that I shall derive from this Work, I cannot I believe, be refused the Credit of being the first Native of the

United States who has produced a Musical Composition. If this attempt should not be too severely treated, others may be encouraged to venture on a path, yet untrodden in America, and the Arts in succession will take root and flourish amongst us. . . .

To which Washington replied with his characteristic humor and good grace:

. . . But, my dear Sir, if you had any doubts about the reception which your work would meet with—or had the smallest reason to think that you should meet with any assistance to defend it—you have not acted with your usual good judgment in the choice of a coadjutator, for, . . . what alas! can I do to support it? I can neither sing one of the songs, nor raise a single note on any instrument to convince the unbelieving.

But I have, however, one argument which will prevail with persons of true estate (at least in America)—I can tell them that *it is the production of Mr. Hopkinson.*

The titles of the songs, as well as their poetic and musical content, show the influence of the contemporary English style: *Come, fair Rosina, come away; My love is gone to sea; Beneath a weeping willow's shade; Enraptur'd I gaze, when my Delia is by; See, down Maria's blushing cheek; O'er the hills far away, at the birth of the morn; My gen'rous heart disdains, the slave of love to be;* and the eighth of the group, added after the title page announcing *seven* had been engraved, *The trav'ler benighted and lost, o'er the mountains pursues his lone way.* Hopkinson thought that the last song, "if played very slow, and sung with Expression," was "forcibly pathetic—at least in my Fancy." Its pathos was corroborated by Thomas Jefferson in acknowledging receipt of the songs:

I will not tell you how much they have pleased us, nor how well the last of them merits praise for it's pathos, but relate a fact only, which is that while my elder daughter was playing it on a harpsichord, I happened to look toward the fire & saw the younger one all in tears. I asked her if she was sick? She said "no; but the tune was so mournful."

Hopkinson's dedication of his *Seven Songs* to George Washington was altogether appropriate, even though Washington replied that he could "neither sing one of the songs, nor raise a single note on any instrument to convince the unbelieving." By that statement he contradicted the later belief that he was himself a musician, but he was

Francis Hopkinson
(See pages 37–44)

Frontispiece of Billings' Sixth and Last Book, *The Continental Harmony* (1794), Showing a "Tune" Engraved on a Circle

(See page 53)

nevertheless an active patron and friend of music. He loved the fine
things of life, and as a gentleman of culture he had the rare gift of
knowing how to get the most from his leisure. He was a frequent
attendant at concerts, and he was a lover of the theatre, where he heard
the ballad-operas of the day. At Mount Vernon there is still preserved
the harpsichord he bought for Nelly Custis. The music books which
belonged to Martha and Nelly Custis, some now at Mount Vernon
and others in private hands, contain the standard music of the time,
and also the work of some of the composers resident in America.

During the Revolutionary War, Hopkinson had penned another
musical tribute to George Washington—a *Toast*, which celebrated the
fact that Washington was commander-in-chief of the Continental
Forces, and expressed confidence that "Our arms shall in battle with
conquest be crowned, While virtue and he's on our side." The words
of the *Toast* were printed in the *Pennsylvania Packet* of April 8, 1778,
and twenty-one years later, in 1799, Benjamin Carr published both
words and music in a music-sheet that contained also "a favorite new
patriotic song in favor of Washington" entitled *Brother Soldiers All
Hail*. The latter was not a work by Hopkinson, however. Prior to the
bicentennial celebration of Washington's birth in 1932, a manuscript
book in Hopkinson's handwriting came to light, which contained the
Toast, words and music, and also the *Ode* to James Bremner which
Hopkinson had composed when Bremner died in 1780. The words
of this *Ode* appeared in the *Miscellaneous Essays* of Hopkinson,
volume III, page 184.

At about this time, in 1931 and 1932, Hopkinson manuscripts began
to appear in amazing numbers in Philadelphia. Many works described
by Sonneck, but never before found, began to appear. Musical numbers from the *Temple of Minerva*, and odes of which only the words
were known but which presumably had had musical settings, came to
light in the possession of dealers and in the hands of private collectors
who had enthusiastically purchased them. Several manuscript copies
of *My Days Have Been So Wondrous Free* appeared in various collections. Careful examination of the newly discovered manuscripts
revealed several matters that aroused suspicion. One was the dedication of one of the compositions to Benjamin Carr, who actually had
come to this country in 1793, two years after Hopkinson's death. An-

other startling discovery was that the melody of one of the composi-tions was almost identical with that of Rubinstein's *Melody in F*. It was highly improbable that Hopkinson could have written such a melody, for its interval structure was entirely unlike that of the char-acteristic style Hopkinson used. A number of the suspected manuscripts were submitted to experts who pronounced them forgeries, basing their decision on the fact that they were made with a steel pen. Only quill pens were used in Hopkinson's day.

Eventually the manuscripts were traced to the same source, and it became apparent that they were the work of a convicted forger, a man who has since served prison sentences on other charges. Unfortunately, there are probably a number of these forgeries still in the hands of private collectors who bought them in good faith and are unaware of their origin. It is my opinion, however, that the manuscript book con-taining the *Toast* and the *Ode to the Memory of James Bremner* is genuine, and that even though this book came to light in Philadelphia at about the same time the forged manuscripts were appearing, it is in no way connected with the spurious items. The source of the genuine book has been satisfactorily traced to Hopkinson's time, having once been the property of Michael Hillegas (1729–1804), the first Treas-urer of the United States.

It is, of course, as students of history, rather than as music critics, that we should view Hopkinson's works, though they are possessed of a freshness and ingenuous point of view that lends them consider-able charm. Their importance lies not in any impress they may have had on later composers, for they did not have enough originality to exert any influence in themselves. It is rather as an indication of the existing vogue in the colonies that they are interesting, and to the his-torian, important. A study of Hopkinson's life and writings shows that music was appreciated and enjoyed in the colonies; and that the people of that time had access to the best of contemporary music literature.

2. JAMES LYON (1735–1794)

Like Hopkinson, our second native composer, was also an amateur. James Lyon was chiefly a psalmodist, and he runs Hopkinson a close race as first composer. In fact, those who claim that he is the first are able to make a fairly good case. Yet when Hopkinson claimed to be the first American composer he was undoubtedly not only aware of Lyon's existence, but was well acquainted with him, and it is not to be supposed that a man of Hopkinson's standing would make such a claim lightly without being sure of his ground.

Lyon was a mild-mannered Presbyterian minister, who was so color blind that once when he journeyed a considerable distance to procure some black cloth for a ministerial frock, his wife discovered that the cloth was as scarlet as the coats of the British officers. He was born in Newark, "East New Jersey," July 1, 1735, during the turbulent days when the colony was under a royal governor, and just a few years before it was redivided into east and west sections. It is known that his father was Zopher Lyon, "Yeoman of the Town of Newark," and that he was orphaned at an early age. In 1750, Isaac Lyon and John Crane were appointed "guardians of the Body and Estate of James Lyon above fourteen years of age until he shall be the age of twenty-one."

It was during his college days that Lyon first left record of being a composer, for at the Commencement of 1759 at Nassau Hall (now Princeton), when President Samuel Davies had delivered a Latin oration that won the "applause of his numerous and learned auditors," and the "young gentlemen" had "performed the customary exercises with uncommon Facility and Correctness, the whole ceremony concluded with an ODE, set to music by Mr. James Lyon, one of the students."

Next, we hear of him as a candidate for a Master's degree at the College of Philadelphia, and in 1761 we learn of one of his works performed on the same program with an *Ode* by Hopkinson. The Pennsylvania *Gazette* (1761) stated:

On Saturday last the public COMMENCEMENT was held in the College of this City, before a vast Concourse of People of all Ranks. Besides the usual Exercises (which gave great satisfaction to the Audience) there was performed an elegant Anthem composed by James LYON, of New Jersey College, and in the afternoon an *Ode,* sacred to the Memory of our late Gracious Sovereign George II, written and set to Music in very grand and Masterly Taste by Francis Hopkinson, Esq. A.M. of the College of this City.

It was while Lyon was in Philadelphia that he produced his *Urania, or A Choice Collection of Psalm-Tunes, Anthems and Hymns,* although he may have left the city before it was finally published. He became a Presbyterian minister and went first to Nova Scotia; but, unable to support himself and his family on the meager salary the frontier church afforded, he accepted a call to the new settlement of Machias, Maine, where he remained, with a few brief interruptions, until his death, October 12, 1794.

That he returned to New Jersey at least once is indicated by the diary of a Southerner named Fithian, who spent his vacations in Cohansie, New Jersey. Fithian's diary affords a meager portrait of the minister-composer. Under date of April 22, 1774:

Rode to the stage early for the Papers, thence I went to Mr. Hunter's where I met with that great master of music, Mr. Lyon. He sung at my request, & sings with his usual softness and accuracy—he is about publishing a new book of Tunes which are to be chiefly of his own Composition.

And on the following day:

At home drawing off some of Mr. Lyon's Tunes, & revising my Own Exercises. . . . Afternoon according to Appointment I visited Mr. Lyon at Mr. Hunter's. He sings with great accuracy. I sung with him many of his Tunes & had much conversation on music, he is vastly fond of music & musical genius's. We spent the Evening with great satisfaction to me.

After Lyon's first year in Machias, the parish invited him to remain, and raised his salary to eighty-four pounds per annum, with a hundred pounds as an additional settlement. When we learn later that the parish was at one time in arrears some nine hundred pounds of the dominie's salary, we can appreciate what devotion to the cause persuaded Lyon to remain. Sometimes he and his family had to live almost entirely on fish that he caught with his own hands in the waters of Machias Bay.

Because of his residence in Nova Scotia, Lyon was familiar with the geography of the country, and when the Revolution broke out, he wrote to Washington asking permission to lead an expedition for conquering the province. With his offer he outlined a wholly practical plan of attack. The Canadian historian J. J. Bulmer admits that it was fortunate for the British that Washington rejected the scheme.

There is at hand convincing evidence to contradict the early historians who stated that *Urania* was a failure which almost ruined its publishers. Comparison of the few copies in existence today shows three separate editions, with a fourth possibly printed in New England. In many ways the collection was the most progressive of any that had yet been issued in the colonies. It was printed first in 1761, and contained six original works by Lyon, in addition to what may have been the first appearance in the colonies of the tune of our *America*, the English *God Save the King*. In *Urania* it was called *Whitefield's Tune*, to be sung to the words, "Come, Thou Almighty King."

The first tune in the book was the famous *Mear*. Some have claimed that this is an American tune, composed by a pastor of Marblehead, Massachusetts—John Barnard—in 1727. If this were true, Barnard would be the first American composer of whose works we have definite knowledge; but evidence seems to show that it was probably an English tune. There is no definite proof that Barnard was a composer of music, though he did publish a psalm book in 1752, with his own metrical version of the psalms and a neatly engraved collection of forty-nine tunes. The confusion probably arises from the fact that there was another John Barnard, an Englishman, who published a psalm book (presumably in England) in 1727. *Mear* is a fine old tune and it has come down to our own time through eighteenth- and nineteenth-century hymnbooks, set to a variety of texts. If it could be proved that it was of American origin it would be most important, for it is one of the few tunes sung in the early days that has survived to our time.

The other tunes in *Urania* were psalm-tunes, hymns, and anthems by such English writers as Arnold, Green, Knapp, and Evison. William Tuckey's *Liverpool* was included. The original works by Lyon were settings of the 8th, 23rd, and 95th Psalms; *Two Celebrated Verses by Sternhold and Hopkins*; an *Anthem taken from the 150th Psalm;* and the *104th Psalm* [translated] *by Dr. Watts*.

The fact that Fithian referred to a new book of tunes by Lyon, *chiefly of his own composition*, indicates that Lyon did not stop composing when he went to Maine, even though his later work was evidently never published. Possibly the later tunes were the ones that found their way into the collections of other psalmodists. *A Marriage*

Hymn by James Lyon appears in Daniel Bayley's *New Universal Harmony;* Simeon Jocelin's *Chorister's Companion* (1788) contained *Psalm 17th, Lyon;* the fourth edition of Andrew Law's *Rudiments of Music* (1792) included *Psalm 19, Lyon.* John Stickney's *Gentleman and lady's musical companion* (1774), and Elias Mann's *Massachusetts collection of sacred harmony* (1807), contained an ode, *Friendship: the words from Dr. Watts' lyric poems—set to music by the Rev. James Lyon.*

Frédéric L. Ritter, one of the first historians of American music, in his *Music in America,* takes occasion to be somewhat patronizing in his review of *Urania.* While Lyon's work is undoubtedly crude and primitive, it certainly is in advance of its few predecessors, and superior to some that came later. After quoting Lyon's *directions for singing,* Ritter exclaims sarcastically: "A great help that must have been to inexperienced singers!"

Well, here are the directions, and while it must be admitted that they give little technical help, they contain much common sense, and lay down some principles which were shamelessly disregarded by eighteenth-century singers:

1. In learning the 8 notes, get the assistance of some person well acquainted with the Tones and Semitones.
2. Choose that part which you can sing with the greatest Ease, and make yourself Master of that first.

(Surely Mr. Ritter could not quarrel with such a sound principle!)

3. Sound all high Notes as soft as possible, but low ones hard and full.

(True, exceptions could be found to this rule, but its observance would at least prevent the "Squeaking above, or Grumbling below" that the *Bay Psalm Book* deplored.)

4. Pitch your Tune so that the highest and lowest Notes may be sounded distinctly.

(Thoroughly sound—the obviousness of this rule was made necessary by the contemporary manner of singing.)

Lyon's exposition of the *Keys in Music* was much clearer than that

of Thomas Walter. The rules of transposition are correct as far as they
go, but less complete. Lyon had at least familiarized himself with the
best sources available in his time. He did not copy from the faulty,
incorrect Tans'ur, who had led other colonial psalmists astray. He
was an able musician for his time and surroundings, a scholar, and a
man who exerted a wholesome and thoroughly dignified influence not
only on his contemporaries but on those who were to follow in the
immediate future.

3. WILLIAM BILLINGS, AND HIS "FUGUING PIECES"
(1746–1800)

In 1770, the year in which Beethoven was born, and when Bach
had been at rest for twenty years, William Billings of Boston produced
The New England Psalm Singer, and announced his musical declaration of independence from the chafing restrictions of simplicity in
psalm tunes and hymns. For, as he proclaimed in a later work, this
collection contained some of his "fuguing pieces . . . more than
twenty times as powerful as the old slow tunes. Each part striving for
mastery and victory. The audience entertained and delighted, their
minds surprisingly agitated and extremely fluctuated, sometimes declaring for one part and sometimes for another. Now the solemn bass
demands their attention; next the manly tenor; now the lofty counter;
now the volatile treble. Now here, now there, now here again! O
ecstatic! Rush on, you sons of harmony!"

Such an imagination, and such enthusiasm should surely have produced masterworks, but alas, no—merely the crude attempts of a
tanner to produce something different, a striving for effects he could
imagine, but for which he lacked the necessary equipment. A picturesque character was Billings, blind in one eye, an arm withered, legs of
different length, and a rasping voice to add color to his slovenly appearance. And yet here was the musical enthusiast who was so wrapped
up in the making of melody that he gave up his business of tanning
to become the first American composer to make music his profession.
And as a result died in poverty. He did have the satisfaction of recognition, however, for contemporary New England had never seen the

like of him before, and as he devoted the major part of his efforts to music of the church, he was not set aside as a freak, but became a man honored in his own time, and hailed by many as a genius.

Billings was born in Boston, October 7, 1746. Music secured an early hold on him, and no doubt his tannery suffered because so much of his time was spent in chalking music exercises on the walls and on the hides with which he worked. He was self-taught, and most of his knowledge in music was gained from faulty treatises by Tans'ur and others. Like many another novice, Billings refused to be daunted by his lack of technique. Rules hampered him, and he was frank in saying so. And though, when he rushed into print with his *New England Psalm Singer*, he was loud in the praises of his brain-child, or "Reuben" as he called it, he found occasion to apologize for his first-born when he issued his second book *The Singing Master's Assistant* some eight years later.

In the Preface to the first book, Billings thus addressed his patrons:

To all musical Practitioners:

Perhaps it may be expected by some, that I could say something concerning rules for composition; to these I answer that *Nature is the best Dictator*, for all the hard dry studied rules that ever were prescribed will not enable any person to form an Air any more than the bare knowledge of the four and twenty letters, and strict Grammatical rules will qualify a scholar for composing a piece of Poetry. . . . It must be Nature; Nature must lay the Foundation, Nature must give the Thought. . . .

I have read several Authors Rules on Composition, and find the strictest of them make some exception, as thus, they say that two 8vos or two 5ths may not be taken together rising or falling, unless one be Major and the other Minor; but rather than spoil the Air, they will allow that Breach to be made, and this Allowance gives great Latitude to young Composers, for they may always make that Plea and say, if I am not allowed to transgress the Rules of composition I shall certainly spoil the Air, and cross the Strain that Fancy dictated. . . .

For my own part, as I don't think myself confined to any Rules for Composition laid down by any that went before me, neither should I think (were I to pretend to lay down rules) that any who comes after me were any ways obligated to adhere to them any further than they should think proper: so in fact I think it is best for every composer to be his own learner. Therefore, upon this consideration, for me to dictate, or to pretend to prescribe Rules of this Nature for others, would not only be very unnecessary but also a very great piece of Vanity.

The Motto of the book left no doubt as to its merits:

> Out of the mouths of babes and sucklings
> Hast Thou perfected praise.

Eight years tempered the composer's estimate, and in his second book, which became known as *Billings' Best*, he set forth this confession:

KIND READER—

No doubt you (do or ought to) remember that about eight years ago, I published a Book entitled, *The New England Psalm Singer*, &c. And truly a most masterly and inimitable performance, I then thought it to be. Oh! how did my foolish heart throb and beat with tumultuous joy! With what impatience did I wait on the Book-Binder, while stitching the sheets and putting on the covers, with what extacy did I snatch the yet unfinished Book out of his hands, and pressing to my bosom, with rapturous delight how lavish was I in enconiums on this infant production of my own Numb-Skull. Welcome, thrice welcome, thou legitimate offspring of my brain, go forth my little book, go forth and immortalize the name of your Author; may your sale be rapid and may you speedily run through ten thousand Editions, may you be a welcome guest in all companies and what will add tenfold to thy dignity, may you find your way into the Libraries of the Learned. Thou art my Reuben, my first born; the beginning of my Strength, the Excellency of my Dignity, and the Excellency of my power. But to my great mortification I soon discovered it was Reuben in the sequel, and Reuben all over, for unstable as water, it did not excel: and since I have begun to play the Critic, I will go through with my Criticisms, and endeavour to point out its beauties as well as deformities, and it must be acknowledged, that many of the pieces are not so ostentatious, as to send forth their own praises; for it has been judiciously observed, that the oftener they are sounded, the more they are abased. After impartial examination, I have discovered that many pieces were never worth my printing or your inspection; therefore in order to make you ample amends for my former intrusion, I have selected and corrected some of the Tunes which were most approved of in that book and have added several new peices [sic] which I think to be very good ones. . . .

Billings did not take kindly to one particular criticism of his "Reuben." It seems that some of his readers had considered the arrangement of tunes too simple; the constant succession of thirds and sixths proved cloying. There was none of the seasoning of discord. This criticism annoyed Billings, and in his second book he resolved to go all the way and show his critics what he could do in the field of dissonance. He included his *Jargon*, which we may consider the first of our present *modernistic* compositions, antedating Schoenberg and Stravinsky by at least a century and a half, and in one respect altogether worthy of them. There was a complete absence of concord, and the composer accomplished exactly what he was after. The words commence, "Let horrid Jargon split the air, And rive the nerves asunder—." *Jargon* also shows that Billings, sometimes given to literary bombast, could upon occasion be a humorist. It was accompanied by a *Manifesto* to the *Goddess of Discord*, which read:

In order to do this piece justice, the concert must be made of vocal and instrumental music. Let it be performed in the following manner, viz: Let an Ass bray the base, let the filing of a saw carry the tenor, let a hog who is extremely weak squeal the counter, and let a cart-wheel, which is heavy-loaded, and that has long been without grease, squeak the treble; and if the concert should appear to be too feeble you may add the cracking of a crow, the howling of a dog, the squalling of a cat, and what would grace the concert yet more, would be the rubbing of a wet finger upon a window glass. This last mentioned instrument no sooner salutes the drum of the ear, but it instantly conveys the sensation to the teeth; and if all these in conjunction should not reach the cause, you may add this most inharmonious of all sounds, "Pay me what thou owest."

To which his critics replied by hanging two cats by their tails to the sign—BILLINGS MUSIC—which swung outside his door.

Billings's best-known tune was *Chester*. It was popular in his own time, and was in wide use well into the nineteenth century. Always an enthusiast, he became one of the most fervent patriots during the War of the Revolution, and used his gifts for patriotic songs. He wrote new words for *Chester*, and the song became the *Over There* of the Revolution, with its fiery verses shouted by every soldier:

> Let tyrants shake their iron rod,
> And Slav'ry clank her galling chains,
> We fear them not, we trust in God,
> New England's God forever reigns.

Howe and Burgoyne and Clinton, too,
With Prescott and Cornwallis join'd,
Together plot our overthrow,
In one Infernal league combin'd.

When God inspired us for the fight,
Their ranks were broke, their lines were forc'd,
Their Ships were Shelter'd in our sight,
Or swiftly driven from our Coast.

The Foe comes on with haughty Stride,
Our troops advance with martial noise,
Their Vet'rans flee before our Youth,
And Gen'rals yield to beardless boys.

What grateful Off'ring shall we bring,
What shall we render to the Lord?
Loud Hallelujahs let us Sing,
And praise his name on ev'ry Chord.

Not only did Billings claim God exclusively for New England, but
he paraphrased the Scriptures, and changed the locale of some of the
psalms. The 137th Psalm became his *Lamentation over Boston,* when
the city was occupied by British troops:

By the rivers of Watertown, we sat down;
Yea we wept as we remembered Boston.

Billings published six collections altogether. In addition to the first
two there were: *Music in Miniature* (1779); *The Psalm Singer's
Amusement* (1781); *The Suffolk Harmony* (1786); and *The Continental Harmony* (1794). The last lays down the rudiments of music
in the form of a dialogue between *Scholar* and *Master.* Again we find
major and minor discussed as *sharp* and *flat* keys, but this time in an
exposition of the relations of the keys to the two sexes:

Scholar: Sir, I do not well understand you, for you have but just given it as
    your opinion, that the two keys were to most equally pleasing.
Master: When I spoke in that manner, I meant to confine the observation
    to the male sex: but you may take it for granted that the female part of
    the creation are much the greater lovers of music: for I scarcely ever
    met with one but what was more or less entertained with musical
    sounds, and I am very positive that nine-tenths of them are much more

pleased with a flat, than a sharp air; and I make no doubt, but that the musical world (if upon reading what I have now asserted, they should be induced to make some observations that way) must unavoidably fall into my opinion.

Among Billings's secular works was a choral piece entitled *Modern Music*. As a rhymster he proved himself something of a predecessor of W. S. Gilbert:

> We are met for a concert of modern invention
> To tickle the ear is our present intention
>
> .   .   .   .   .   .
>
> Through common and treble we jointly have run
> We'd give you their essence compounded in one;
> Although we are strongly attached to the rest,
> Six-four is the movement that pleases us best.
> And now we address you as friends to the Cause
> Performers are modest and write their own laws.
> Although we are sanguine and clap at the Ban,
> 'Tis the part of the hearers to clap their applause.

Billings's works were widely used and his reputation extended throughout the states, for programs of concerts in Philadelphia and other cities show his anthems in abundance. His anthem from the second of Solomon's Songs, *The Rose of Sharon*, seems to have been a favorite. At the First Uranian Concert in Philadelphia (1787), Billings was represented with three works; Lyon and Tuckey with one each. In Boston, at a *Concert of Sacred Musick* "projected by the Musical Societies" to rebuild the Hollis Street Meeting House, two of Billings's anthems were sung, and the concert concluded with the *Hallelujah* Chorus from *The Messiah*, "accompanied by kettle-drums."

Although he was respected, Billings was often the object of practical jokes. Probably his deformities provoked the jibes of the thoughtless. Once a local jokester called on him, and after a long preamble in which he flattered the composer by assuming that he could answer any musical question, asked whether snoring was to be classed as vocal or instrumental music. In spite of the fact that he was the protégé of Governor Samuel Adams and Dr. Pierce, and was termed an "extraordinary genius" by many a contemporary writer, Billings found it difficult to provide for his wife and six children. There are records of several attempts to improve the finances of the needy Billings family. *The Columbian Centinel* of December 8, 1790, announced its gratification

in hearing that a number of benevolent characters are determined to bring forward a Concert of Sacred Musick for the benefit of Mr. William Billings of this town—whose distress is real, and whose merit in that science, is generally acknowledged.

The pieces to be performed will consist of a great, and, it is expected, a pleasant variety, and whilst the charitable will rejoice in this opportunity to exercise their benevolence, the amateurs of musick, will no doubt be abundantly gratified.

Again, in 1792, when Billings was about to publish his last volume, the *Massachusetts Magazine* stated:

The distressed situation of Mr. Billings' family has so sensibly operated on the minds of the committee as to induce their assistance in the intended publication.

When he died on the twenty-ninth of September, 1800, there was no money to provide a tombstone. He lies in an unmarked grave in the little graveyard on the Boston Common.

Billings made a lasting contribution to our musical life by his activities in forming singing societies and church choirs. He was the chief agent in the second revival of singing in New England, midway between that of the 1720's and that led by Lowell Mason a little more than a century later. The singing class that he formed in Stoughton, Massachusetts, became in 1786 the Stoughton Musical Society, and continued an active existence until it grew into the oldest singing society in America. Billings's introduction of the pitch-pipe eventually did away with the faulty pitching of tunes that had caused so much poor singing in churches. His use of the violoncello in church services was a daring innovation.

Those who look for real fugues in Billings's "fuguing" pieces will be disappointed, for they are, of course, not fugues at all—they are merely primitive attempts at imitative counterpoint. It is to be doubted whether any contemporary musicians in the colonies knew what a fugue really was. Tans'ur, one of the accepted authorities of the time, thus explained the *canon* and *fugue:*

To compose a Canon, you must first prick down your Fuge (or such a Quantity of Notes as you would have to lead your Point) in *one* Part; and then carry the same Notes forward, and prick them down in another Part, either in the Unison, 3rd, 4th, 5th, or 6th etc. above, or below the leading Part.

A Canon is a perpetual Fuge, i.e. Parts always flying one before another; the following parts repeating the very same Notes (either in Unison, or higher, or lower) as the leading Part, and because it is carried on by so strict a Rule, it is called a Canon; which is the superlative, or highest Degree of Musical Composition.

A single Fuge or Imitation, is when Parts imitate one another.

A Double Fuge, is when two or several Points, or Fuges fall in, one after the other.

No indeed, we must not be too hard on Billings if this was the extent of his training. And while he was undoubtedly clumsy and crude, Billings exerted an influence on music in New England, and the other colonies too, that has had a lasting effect. The man was vital, and while he probably copied the forms of contemporary English church musicians, he did have a spark of originality. He fanned into life the smouldering musical interest of New England, and consequently really established in the young United States of America a definite interest in music, crude and imitative though it was.

In 1790 his career was at its peak. There were scarcely any psalm collections published which did not contain many of his works. His music was more popular with Americans than that of foreign composers—chauvinism was unnecessary to secure appreciation of this American composer. After 1790 his influence outside of the church lessened. The coming of foreign musicians after the Revolution exposed the primitive character of Billings's music, and as the years progressed, his name appeared less frequently on concert programs. His Revolutionary song *Chester* survived to the latter part of the nineteenth century, but to the early twentieth century he was largely a legendary figure, except in isolated instances. George Pullen Jackson found that Billings's "fuges," and those of his contemporaries and followers, had remained very much alive for a century and a half among the numerous "Sacred

Harp" singers in the rural South, but music lovers and churchgoers in the urban centers of the East and North knew of him only by reading about him.[1]

In recent years there has been renewed interest in Billings's music, and something in the nature of a revival has occurred, bringing with it modern publications of many of his tunes and some of his "fuguing" pieces. They are sung in concert and on radio programs, particularly on those designed to show the early history of American music. And modern music lovers have found that there is indeed something vital in this music of our early composer—something sincere, rugged, and altogether expressive of the age in which he lived.

[1] Cf. George Pullen Jackson, *White Spirituals in the Southern Uplands*, Chapel Hill, N.C.: University of North Carolina Press, 1933.

CHAPTER THREE

The Latter Eighteenth Century

I. NEW ENGLAND

THE closing years of the eighteenth century were somewhat more friendly to music in New England, for Puritanism was relaxing its fear and hatred of lighter diversions. Piety was still demanded by churchmen, yet music had firmly established itself as a proper part of divine worship. Secular music was gaining a foothold.

The Revolution halted musical progress less in New England than in other sections of the country, for after the field of military operations moved from Boston, musicians resumed their activities. Concerts were frequent occurrences, and as music teachers became more numerous, the audiences grew more discriminating. Owing to the difficulty of travel, there was not the opportunity for keeping in close touch with musical events in other cities; each musical center was a unit which had to rely principally on its own resources. The stagecoach, springless and uncomfortable, was about the only mode of travel by land for those who could not go on horseback. So it was something of an event when our colonial cities had a chance to become acquainted with each other's musicians. Only ten per cent of the population of the colonies lived in cities when Washington was inaugurated; the rest were farmers. Land was abundant, while money and labor for manufacturing were scarce.

There were two distinct groups among the contemporaries and successors of William Billings: those who caught the spirit of his lively "fuguing pieces," and others who were violently opposed to their style as trivial and undignified. Clergymen were often in sympathy with the latter group, for they began to realize that the pendulum in favor of popular music had swung a little too far, and that some of the music

58

sung in church was little suited to divine worship. It must be admitted that the parsons who took this stand were probably right. Had their opposition been against true contrapuntal choral music, against the lofty part-writing of a Bach or Handel, the controversy would have been a different matter. But we can well sympathize with those who hated to see their worship halted by the meaningless repetitions of Billings's "fuges." It is difficult to see how his florid anthems could have been conducive to worship.

John Hubbard, a professor at Dartmouth College, a number of years later (1807) crystallized the sentiment against frivolous church music. In one of his essays he wrote:

From the midnight revel, from the staggering bacchanal, from the pro-fane altar of Comus, they have stolen the prostituted Air, and with sacri-legious hands have offered it in the Temple of *Jehovah*. . . . Such profanation must wound every feeling heart. Devotion ever assumes a dignity. It cannot delight in the tinkling bustle of unmeaning sounds. The air of a catch, a glee, a dance, a march, a common ballad is very improper for the worship of the Most High. . . .

This, of course, is one side of a time-honored controversy which sur-vives to our own day. Nonliturgical worship has frequently allowed of the introduction of music that seems to sensitive ears unsuitable. Bach made *Chorales* of airs of questionable origin, but when he chose them, and passed his magic hands over their stately phrases, it was impossible to question their adaptability to sacred uses. In our generation evangeli-cal hymns, and many of the tunes of our hymnbooks are open to the same charge leveled against the music of Billings's time.

Among Billings's contemporaries was ANDREW LAW (1748–1821), a man of good education, and a church music composer of taste and discrimination. Law was opposed to the overflorid style, and because of his comparatively simple arrangements of his own and others' tunes, he never achieved the popularity of Billings. He spent his life in various parts of the country; some of his publications were issued in Philadel-phia, but he was born and died in Connecticut, and belongs primarily to New England.

Law was one of our first writers on music. In a series of *Essays on Music* he announced his intention of publishing reviews of contempo-rary music publications. In one of these he vigorously attacked a work which had had the boldness to designate itself as a collection of *Classical Church Music.* "What," asked the critic, "is implied by the word classical? . . . Can music, published in an altered and mutilated state, contrary to the true principles of the art . . . be called classical? Can the use of terms derived from foreign languages make it classical? . . . Or can turning churches into theatres, and ministers into comedians, make the music classical?"

Law published his first collection, a *Select Number of Plain Tunes,* in 1767, but his first works to attract much attention were his *Select Harmony* (1778), and *Collection of Best Tunes and Anthems* (1779). In his works he attempted two innovations, one of which was successful. This was setting the melody in the soprano rather than in the tenor. The idea was borrowed from English arrangers of the time, but Law was its principal exponent in this country. The other experiment was the substitution of "character notes" for the usual symbols. Character notes had four differently shaped heads—square, oval, triangular, and diamond shaped, and corresponded respectively to the four old English note names, *fa, sol, la,* and *mi,* then in general use in this land. (The *do-re-mi* system had not yet arrived on these shores.) At first Law used these notes without any staff lines at all, placing them merely on different levels relative to an imaginary line or lines. This shape-note system did not survive long in New England, but it did spread to other parts of the country, to the Midwest and the South. We shall hear more of it in the discussion of folk hymnody in Chapter XIII.

The most popular tune that Law composed was *Archdale.*

In one important respect OLIVER HOLDEN (1765–1844) should be considered the outstanding composer of this time: he was the first American to produce a melody that has been used continuously from his own time to the present day. This is *Coronation,* set to the words *All Hail the Power of Jesus' Name,* which has needed no discovery by historians, no revival, to make it known to later generations. If lasting value is the criterion by which music is to be judged, the palm goes to Holden, and an account of American music which has survived on its own merits must start with him.

He was born in Shirley, Massachusetts, in 1765, and at an early age moved to Charlestown, where he first became a carpenter. He spent his leisure hours in composing, and finally became a singing teacher. As a musician, he was about equal to Billings in equipment, but because of his associations, and more cautious nature, he did not go as far afield as his older contemporary.

A year after his first publication *The American Harmony* (1792), Holden announced an ambitious scheme which does not seem to have met with enough response to warrant starting—the publication of *The Massachusetts Musical Magazine*. An advertisement in the *Massachusetts Spy* (Worcester, March 14, 1793) gave the details:

Proposal, for printing by Subscription, in monthly numbers, a new work, to be entitled *The Massachusetts Musical Magazine*, intended principally to furnish Musical Societies and other Practitioners in that pleasing art, with a choice and valuable collection of odes, anthems, dirges and other favorite pieces of musick. Principally original American compositions. By Oliver Holden, author of the American Harmony.

As a work of this kind has never been attempted in this part of the Union, and as many have expressed a wish to see such a publication, it is presumed that it will be found exceedingly useful, and meet a very general acceptance with all those who wish to possess themselves of a valuable collection of tunes, which are not to be found in musick books calculated only for schools and publick worship. . . .

As the price is set so exceedingly low the editor flatters himself that little persuasion will be necessary to effect a speedy and extensive subscription; . . .

Coronation was first printed in Holden's *Union Harmony* (1793). His other sacred books included the *Charlestown Collection* (1803), and *Plain Psalmody* (1800).

At the time of Washington's death, Holden was one of the many composers who lent their talents to commemorating the father of the nation. According to the newspapers, the "tributary honors" to George Washington, announced at the Old South Meeting House in Boston in January, 1800, were to conclude with the singing of *From Vernon's Mount Behold the Hero Rise*, the music by Oliver Holden. In February of the same year the Mechanics' Association of Boston requested him to write a cantata on the subject of Washington. He provided a *Dirge, or Sepulchral Service*, in which the first "Solemn Recitative" began: "Lo! sorrow reigneth, and the nation mourns."

Aside from *Coronation*, Holden's most important work was done in association with Samuel Holyoke and Hans Gram. This was the editing and compiling of *The Massachusetts Compiler* (1795), which was in many ways the most progressive work on psalmody to appear in the United States before 1800. It contained the "theoretical and practical elements of sacred vocal music, together with a musical dictionary." In 1797, Isaiah Thomas, the publisher, engaged Holden as editor and reviser of the *Worcester Collection* which, he presumed, would be "pleasing to its patrons." Holden lived until 1844.

SAMUEL HOLYOKE (1762–1820), coeditor with Holden in *The Massachusetts Compiler*, was the son of a clergyman from Boxford, Massachusetts. A versatile musician, with perhaps less natural talent than some of his contemporaries, he was nevertheless active in musical affairs. Holyoke was an avowed opponent of the Billings school, and in his first publication *Harmonia Americana* (1791), he made the following statement:

Perhaps some may be disappointed that fuguing pieces are in general omitted. But the principal reason why few were inserted was the trifling effect produced by that sort of music; for the parts, falling in, one after another, each conveying a different idea, confound the sense, and render the performance a mere jargon of words.

He was active in promoting choral concerts in and around Boston, especially in Salem, and on the programs he included some of the best music of the times. His fame rests chiefly on the hymn-tune *Arnheim*. Others of his works were the following collections:

The Columbian repository of sacred harmony. Selected from European and American authors with many new tunes not before published. Including the whole of Dr. Watts' psalms and hymns, to each of which a tune is adapted and some additional tunes suited to the particular metres in Tate and Brady's, and Dr. Belknap's collection of psalms and hymns. (Date unknown, probably 1800 or 1802.)

The Christian harmonist; containing a set of tunes adapted to all the metres. . . . To which are added, hymns on particular subjects . . . two anthems, and a funeral dirge . . . designed for the use of the Baptist Churches of the U.S.A. (1804.)

Vocal Companion. . . . (1807.)

Instrumental Assistant. . . . (Date unknown.)

As with Holden, the death of Washington called Holyoke's musical pen into play. The library of Harvard University possesses a copy of *Hark from the tombs*, etc. and *Beneath the honors*, etc. Adapted from Dr. Watts, and set to music, by Samuel Holyoke, A.M. Performed at Newburyport, 2nd January, 1800. The day on which the citizens unitedly expressed their unbounded veneration for the memory of our beloved Washington. . . .

Holyoke had not waited for Washington's death to extol him in music, for in September, 1790 the *Massachusetts Magazine* had printed his song *Washington*. This journal issued a number of Holyoke's compositions, among them *The Pensive Shepherd* (words by J. Lathrop); *Sally, a Pastoral*; and *Terraminta*, words from *The Apollo*.

The third editor of the *Massachusetts Compiler* was a foreigner, HANS GRAM, who settled in Boston some time before 1790, where he acted as organist of the Brattle Square Church. Gram enjoys the distinction of being the composer of the first orchestral score published in the United States. The Bethlehem group left behind them works for orchestral combinations, but they were all in manuscript. Gram's work was scored for strings, two clarinets, and two E-flat horns. It was entitled *The Death Song of an Indian Chief*, and was printed on a flyleaf in the *Massachusetts Magazine* of March, 1791. It is from the contents of this magazine that we know what Gram composed. Among the songs was one that bore the title *A Shape Alone let others Prize*. There were also *A Hunting Song* and *Till Noah's Time*, "A favorite song. Translated from the Danish by Mr. Hans Gram. The air a Gothick composition." Gram was a good musician, and was no doubt principally responsible for the superiority of the harmonizations in the *Compiler*.

Among the lesser composers of the day, DANIEL READ (1757–1836) was author of several collections: *The American Singing Book; or a new and easy guide to the art of psalmody* (1785); and *The Columbian Harmonist* (1807). Read was by trade originally a comb maker. He was clumsy as a harmonist and fond of "fuguing pieces."

TIMOTHY SWAN (1757–1842) was a New Englander who composed some tunes that survived him by many years, some in use today: *China, Poland, Ocean,* and *Pownall*. One of his works, *The Songster's Assistant* (1800), has a novel decoration; a canon for two voices engraved on a staff in the form of a French horn.

JACOB KIMBALL (1761–1826) left the practice of law to become a musician, and died in the Almshouse at Topsfield, Massachusetts. He was one of the "fuge" writers. In 1793 he published his *Rural Harmony*, and was coeditor with Holyoke in compiling the *Essex Harmony* (1800).

JACOB FRENCH (1754– ?), produced the *New American Melody* (1789); *Psalmodist's Companion* (1793), and *Harmony of Harmony* (1802), the latter containing five parts: 1. The ground work or principles of music: by way of question and answer. 2. The gamut . . . with observations on music. 3. A complete set of psalm-tunes. 4. A number of pieces set to particular psalms and hymns, together with odes, fuguing and flying pieces. 5. A number of anthems.

Secular music, and the giving of concerts, was with a few exceptions largely in the hands of foreign residents. One of the exceptions was JOSIAH FLAGG (1738–1794), who has been mentioned in a previous chapter as a psalmodist, and compiler of *A Collection of the Best Psalm Tunes* (1764). Flagg was familiar with the best music of his time, and being an energetic person he was possessed of ambitions. As early as 1771 he promoted a concert of "vocal and instrumental musick accompanied by French horns, hautboys, etc. by the band of the 64th Regiment." The program included works of both Handel and Bach. Two years later he left Boston, and in the announcement of a final concert, in which there would be "upwards of 50 performers," he expressed the hope that the receipts would be sufficient to enable him to leave the Province "in an independant manner." Evidently the career of concert manager was precarious in those days! Where Flagg spent the following years until his death in 1794 is not known, but his widow was in Boston in the following year, for we learn that Mr. Stone, the flutist, organized a concert for her benefit. Evidently her want had been caused by the misdeeds of her "vile miscreant son," the surgeon dentist Josiah Flagg, junior. The proceeds of the concert were $102, which, when the *Columbian Centinel* "considered the disadvantages unavoidably attending the business, must be considered as handsome." Mrs. Flagg and her daughters publicly thanked their friends for their efforts in their behalf, and in their announcement took pains to say that they "carried on the business of riveting and mending China and glass, and needle work of all kinds."

Flagg's program of vocal and instrumental music in 1771 contained a *Hunting Song* by W. S. MORGAN, a musician from abroad who provided color if little else of importance to Boston's musical life immediately preceding the Revolution. Morgan was evidently a good musician, but also something of a rascal. He had come to Boston in 1770, and had advertised himself as a "pupil of Signior Giardini" who intended "instructing ladies and gentlemen on the harpsichord, violin, etc., on the easiest terms and by the most approv'd methods." A year later he appeared before the Boston public in one of the subscription concerts of William Turner, a concert manager and dancing teacher. Morgan soon became involved with the sheriff, and Turner befriended him, not only by paying the board bill which was the cause of the trouble, but also by supporting him for the next six months. Morgan then went to Newport to become the organist of Trinity Church, but he got into trouble again and Turner was obliged to find him a job, this time in Portsmouth, New Hampshire. Then the ungrateful Morgan notified Turner that if he did not help him further, he would ally himself with Turner's newly arrived concert rival David Propert. Whereupon the exasperated Mr. Turner sent an officer to Morgan's house with a writ in which he "requested my just due, and desir'd he would settle with me and pay the balance or at least give security for it." This caused a postponement of the Propert concert, but Turner, probably not wishing to appear in the capacity of legally hindering a rival's concert, withdrew his complaint, and the concert was held on April 26, 1773.

Morgan appears again as a composer, this time for orchestra, when a concert was announced in 1774 "to conclude with a grand Military Symphony accompanied by kettle drums, etc. compos'd by Mr. Morgan." The last we hear of him is when he announced a concert for his own benefit in 1775, "when will be performed a Concert of Vocal and Instrumental Music; between the parts of which will be delivered (gratis) several comic Lectures on various subjects."

Josiah Flagg introduced the London organist and composer WILLIAM SELBY (1738–1798), who was largely responsible for the rapid progress of music in Boston during the following years. Soon after his arrival (about 1771), Selby was appointed organist of King's Chapel, and the vestry ordered a public collection for his benefit. During the Revolution he found it necessary to turn to other activities for a livelihood, and in his shop near Broomfield's Lane he advertised himself as selling "Port, Teneriffe, Malaga Wines, Tea, Brown and Loaf sugar, logwood, English soap, etc."

In 1782, Selby advertised for subscriptions to a work which seems never to have been issued, a monthly publication of music under the title *The New Minstrel*, each number to consist of "at least one composition for the harpsichord, piano forte or spinnet, one for the guitar, and one for the German flute, also of one song in French, and two songs in the English language." The advertisement for subscriptions gives a picture of conditions at the time:

Mr. Selby conceives that he need not urge the literary and other benefits which might arise from a due encouragement of works of the above kind. At this age of general civilization, at this aera of the acquaintance with a nation far gone in politeness and fine arts—even the stern patriot and lover of his country's glory, might be addressed on the present subject with not less propriety than the man of elegance and taste.

The promptness of this young country in those sciences which were once thought peculiar only to riper age, has already brought upon her the eyes of the world.

She has pushed her researches deep into philosophy and her statesmen and generals equalled those of the Roman name.

And shall those arts which make her happy be less courted than those arts which have made her great? Why may she not be "In song unequall'd as unmatch'd in war?"

A cry has gone forth against all amusements which are but a step from Gothism. The raisers of such a cry being unacquainted with distinctions, and little considering that "indulgences are only vices when pursued at the expence of some virtue" and that where they intrench on *No* virtue, they are innocent, and have in every age been acknowledged by almost all moralists.

When he first came to Boston, Selby was concerned chiefly with instrumental music. In many of his concerts he appeared as composer. At his initial appearance with Flagg he performed his *Concerto on the Organ*, and he featured his Harpsichord Concerto (probably a transcription of the same piece) on two of Morgan's benefit programs. Gradually his interest seemed to center in choral music, and through his efforts in organizing choral concerts in Boston, he can well be considered an indirect founder of the *Handel and Haydn Society,* which has played such an important part in the musical life of New England from the early nineteenth century.

One of Selby's concerts, September 22, 1773, on the anniversary of George III's coronation, shows the type of music he presented. The instrumental pieces were furnished by the Sixty-fourth Regiment Band, conducted by Morgan, and the choral music was probably performed by the Choir of King's Chapel. Handel was represented with three works: an overture, the *Hallelujah* Chorus, and the *Grand Coronation Anthem in 22 Parts.* In addition to songs, an organ concerto, and a sinfonia by unnamed composers, there was a *Glee in three parts, composed in the year 1600.* Morgan contributed a solo on the violin. In appealing to his public for support, Selby advertised that

Mr. Selby having been at great pains and expence to have this concert performed elegantly, humbly hopes to be patronized by his friends and the public.

In the spring of 1782, when Selby was again acting as organist at King's Chapel (he held the position until his death in 1798), he announced a concert of *Musica Spiritualis,* for the benefit of the poor of Boston. In 1786 came the mammoth event which marked the peak of his career. A *Musical Society* in which Selby seems to have been the moving spirit, sponsored a festival concert from which the proceeds would be devoted to much-needed prison relief. The *Massachusetts Gazette* printed a long announcement containing a program that was in truth stupendous for those days. Works of Handel and Bach, and compositions by Selby himself were performed.

The success of this concert encouraged the musical society and Selby to attempt in the following year another "Spiritual Concert for the benefit of those who have seen better days." An equally mammoth program, however, failed to draw an equally large audience.

When Washington visited Boston during his inaugural tour in 1789, the concerts arranged in his honor featured Selby's compositions. Although his name gradually disappeared from concert programs after 1793, he lived until 1798 in Boston, where he died at the age of fifty-nine.

It is chiefly because of his compositions that this book is concerned with Selby, and while his works have not survived, and his chief value was the stimulation he afforded to the musical life of Boston, he was exceedingly active as a composer. The Sonneck-Upton *Bibliography of Early Secular American Music* gives the titles of the following works:

Apollo, and the Muse's musical compositions . . . consisting of anthems in four parts, with symphonies for the organ,—Voluntaries or fuges for the organ or harpsichord—Sonatas or lessons for the harpsichord or pianoforte—Songs set for the voice and harpsichord or pianoforte, also, transposed for the German flute and guittar—A piece with variations for the harpsichord or pianoforte, in concert with the violin and guittar. —A concerto for the organ or harpsichord, with instrumental parts— A sonata for two violins and violoncello.

The Lovely Lass, a song, words by Mr. Brown.
Ode for the New Year.
An Ode in honor of General Washington.
Ode on the Anniversary of Independence.
On Musick, a song.
Ptalæmon to Pastora, "a new air."
The Rural Retreat, a song.

In addition, there were numerous sacred compositions, the anthems *O be Joyful in the Lord*, *Jubilate Deo*, *Now the King Eternal*, and others.

Another colorful figure from abroad was the blind organist and pianist JOHN L. BERKENHEAD who arrived in 1795, and from 1796 to 1804 was organist at Trinity Church in Newport. When he first arrived in Boston a concert was announced for his benefit at the Universal Meeting House. The advertisement said that

> Tho' he mourns a prison'd sense
> [he] Has music in his soul.

At the concert for Josiah Flagg's widow the program featured Berkenhead's playing of his own piece *The Demolition of the Bastile for piano forte or harpsichord*. There are records of many performances of this work by the composer—its name changed to the *Abolition of the Bastile* on a later occasion. He composed songs and instrumental pieces, and it is known that he traveled among near-by New England towns giving concerts with his associates. The *Columbian Centinel* of February 21, 1798 gave a glimpse of his entertainments:

Dr. Berkenhead and Co. entertained the inhabitants of Salem with a "Concert" on Thursday evening. Washington Hall was well filled. Mrs. Berkenhead, though indisposed, sang with feeling and taste; Mrs. Spencer with emphasis and correctness; and Mr. Spencer was loudly applauded and repeatedly *encored* by the gallery boys! The Bastile by the Doctor, was admirably played on an elegant harpsichord, belonging to a respectable family in that town.

It seems that Mrs. Berkenhead, even when sick, was easier to listen to than Mrs. Spencer.

Evidently Dr. Berkenhead had one lamentable weakness that called upon him the wrath of the vestry of Trinity Church. On his way to the church the organist was in the habit of calling upon a friend who had some excellent Scotch whiskey. He became confused in the order of his program after one of these visits, and the clerk called out, "Mr. Berkenhead, you are playing the wrong tune!" Undaunted, the bibulous Mr. Berkenhead calmly pulled apart the curtains in front of him and called the clerk a liar. In his next contract the vestry specified that his tenure of office was to exist "during good behavior and punctual attendance."

At the close of the century, Boston definitely accepted the theatre as at least permissible, and attendance had become a matter of individual conscience rather than one of law. The eighteenth-century theatre is closely associated with music, for a large proportion of the repertoire of the early companies was devoted to the English type of ballad-opera; plays interspersed with music, generally compiled from miscellaneous sources.

The Boston anti-theatre law of 1750 was for a number of years rigidly observed, but gradually the more venturesome made sporadic attempts to lure patrons to their exhibitions. Various terms were used to get around the law: "readings," "moral lectures," were advertised, rather than plays. In 1769, the ballad-opera *Love in a Village* was "read," and in 1770 a Mr. Joan (probably James Juhan, a Frenchman) gave a "reading" of *The Beggar's Opera*.

In 1775, the year of Bunker Hill, theatrical entertainment was offered by a number of officers and ladies, the proceeds devoted to distressed soldiers, their widows and children. Obviously the newly established Massachusetts government, independent of the King, could do nothing about such entertainments, but when Washington compelled Howe to evacuate Boston in the spring of the following year, the Boston authorities were free to regulate their own diversions. Consequently, there are practically no records of dramatic entertainments in the Hub during the following twelve years.

In 1778 a systematic agitation for repeal of the law of 1750 began. Subterfuges were again employed to fool the authorities. A Mr. and Mrs. Smith gave some "Moral Lectures" at Concert Hall, one of them being a "dialogue on the horrid crime of murder, from Shakespeare's *Macbeth*." Then followed a series of petitions to the Legislature, which were refused in spite of the growing strength of those who wanted their drama called by its right name. At length defiance of the law became systematic. A "New Exhibition Room" was opened, offering "a Gallery of Portraits, songs, feats of tumbling and ballet pantomime," and "Lectures Moral and Entertaining."

This was unmolested for several months, but at last Governor Hancock felt the necessity for respect of the law, and started legal action against the offenders. Though he never closed the theatrical speak-easy, he curtailed its repertoire considerably. In the spring of 1793 the anti-theatre law was talked to death in the Legislature, and though the necessary two-thirds majority never actually voted for repeal, sentiment in favor of the theatre was too strong for the authorities to attempt further enforcement.

After this the New Federal Street Theatre was built, and later the Haymarket, where Bostonians were treated regularly each season to comedies, tragedies, and ballad-operas. During the ensuing seven years the repertoire of the Federal Street Theatre embraced over ninety ballad-operas, and the Haymarket more than sixty.

The history of the theatre in Boston is important because it played a large part in introducing several musicians who were to become leading influences in the city's musical development; men like Gottlieb Graupner and the Van Hagens, father and son.

And so the century closes with Puritan Boston still stern, but sometimes smiling.

2. POST-REVOLUTIONARY IMMIGRANTS IN NEW YORK AND PHILADELPHIA

During the Revolution, matters musical were almost negligible in Philadelphia, and those in New York were largely in the hands of the British. The British officers and their Tory friends, who refused to consider the rebellion as serious an affair as it finally proved to be, sought lighter diversions, and Howe's *Thespians*, and other groups composed principally of military persons, gave plays, and often concerts. When the British evacuated Philadelphia in 1778, a number of professional actors tried to attract the members of the Congress and the people of Philadelphia to plays at the Southwark Theatre, but Congress discouraged this attempt by another resolution to supplement that of 1774, and the local legislature followed suit with an anti-theatre law.

In New York, the gallant Major André was the moving spirit among the military players, and officiated as manager, actor, and scene painter—the latter a somewhat harrowing occupation when a number of years later, in a play based on the André episode, a back-drop painted by André himself was used to depict the scene of his execution. Officers of the Army and Navy, and colonial sympathizers to the British cause, were subscribers to several regular concert series which prospered from 1781 until the last British regulars left the city in 1783. No doubt the unfortunate war sufferers (generally British) had their troubles considerably lightened by the proceeds.

In 1783, when Washington proclaimed hostilities at an end and retired to Mount Vernon where he hoped to enjoy the peace and quiet he was soon to be denied, musical activities came to life and assumed fresh vigor. Philadelphia started immediately with a series of *City Concerts* inaugurated by John Bentley, which continued under changing managements almost regularly for ten years. Then interest in the theatre and the establishment of summer concerts proved competition too strong to surmount. Postwar subscription concerts in New York were established in 1785 by William Brown, and they continued under different managements until 1796, when conditions similar to those in Philadelphia proved too discouraging.

Immediately after the war theatrical affairs were largely in the hands of the reorganized American Company, which reopened the John Street Theatre in New York in 1785, and in 1798 erected the famous Park Theatre in Park Row. In Philadelphia the American Company encountered much opposition because of the Quakers' energy in urging enforcement of the antitheatre law of 1778. As a result, Philadelphia paralleled Boston in witnessing "Lectures, properly diversified with music, scenery and other decorations, spectaculum vitæ," and other subterfuges calculated to hide forbidden fruit. One play, *The Gamester*, was offered as a "serious and moral lecture in five parts, on the sin of gambling," and *Hamlet* was introduced between the parts of a concert as a "moral and instructive tale called *Filial Piety, Exemplified in the History of the Prince of Denmark*." It was not until 1789 that the theatre law was repealed, and the old Southwark Theatre reopened officially with plays called by their proper names. Thereafter, the city enjoyed regular visits of the American Company, until the opening in 1794 of the Chestnut Street Theatre by the newly formed Wignell and Reinagle Company. This became Philadelphia's own company, and was the center of its theatrical life.

During these years a factor that has always been predominant in American music became increasingly apparent. Before the war, America had enjoyed the presence of a number of foreign musicians, and from 1783 scores of them appeared in the newly established United States. From their arrival they took largely into their own hands the management and performance of our musical affairs. Of course, this immigration offered advantages as well as disadvantages to the cause of American music, and it is difficult, if not impossible, to weigh the gains and drawbacks, and determine intelligently whether our musical life was eventually the gainer or the loser. We shall see that similar events occurred in the middle of the following century. Would our Billingses, our Hopkinsons, and Lyons have sowed the seeds of a truly national school of music, which would have gained in background and in craftsmanship, if its growth had been uninterrupted by the coming of skilled, thoroughly trained musicians whose knowledge and talents paled the glories of our native composers? Or would the crude yet native spark of creative genius have become sterile on virgin soil, where there was not the opportunity for exchange of ideas in a cultured environment?

Whether it was to our advantage or not, the musicians came, and as nearly all of them were active as composers as well as performers, they were the principal source of our late eighteenth-century secular music. Their concerts form the catalogue of the bulk of the music written in this country from the close of the Revolution to the early eighteen hundreds.

PETER ALBRECHT VAN HAGEN was a Hollander of German descent. Born of a musical family, he had been active in the musical life of Rotterdam before he settled in Charleston, South Carolina, in 1774. Having offered the inhabitants of that city a "Grand Concert of Vocal and Instrumental Music," he advertised for pupils in organ, harpsichord, pianoforte, violin, violoncello, and viola, and proposed to teach "the manner of composition to any that are inclined to be instructed therein." This list of subjects was subsequently put to shame when the family moved to New York fifteen years later, and Mr. Van Hagen advertised that he sold instruments of all sorts, and taught at six dollars a month (twelve lessons) and a guinea entrance fee, any or all of the following:

> violin, harpsichord, tenor, violoncello, German flute,
> hautboy, clarinet, bassoon, and singing.

Van Hagen's New York debut occurred in October, 1789, when he introduced to the public his son Peter Junior, eight years of age. According to the program, the father played two concertos on the violin and one on the tenor, while the boy rendered a vocal selection and played a concerto on the pianoforte. Peter Senior showed his versatility by playing a "solo upon iron nails, called Violin Harmonika."

Mrs. Van Hagen was also a musician, and in addition to participating in the family's concerts, she taught pupils. Her advertisement (1792) described her abilities:

Mrs. Van Hagen, lately from Amsterdam, respectfully informs the ladies of this city that she intends to teach the theory and practice of music on the harpsichord and Piano Forte with thoroughbass, if desired: also, the principles of vocal music and singing according to the most approved method and present taste in Europe.

As she has been for several years organist in the churches at Namur, Middleburg, Vlissingen and Bergen op den zoom, she also teaches on that instrument, as well church music, as lessons, sonatas, concertos, etc.

Mrs. Van Hagen hopes from her theoretic knowledge and successful experience in the science of music, to be as fortunate in the progress of her pupils in this city, as she has been in some of the first families in Holland.

As motives of delicacy may induce parents to commit the tuition of young ladies in this branch of education to one of their own sex, and the female voice from its being in unison, is better adapted to teach them singing than that of the other sex, which is an octave below, she flatters herself that she shall be indulged with their approbation and the protection of a respectable public.

In the same year the entire family presented a concert at which Mother Van Hagen played a "Forte Piano Sonata" and a "Forte Piano Concerto," Papa Van Hagen rendered a Tenor Concerto, little Peter played a Violin Concerto, and his sister, "Miss Van Hagen, *about* 13 years old," sang a "Song Duetto" with her little brother, and a trio with her mother and Peter, Junior.

In 1792, Van Hagen, Senior, joined with Henri Capron and George Saliment in the management of the annual New York subscription concerts, and in the following fall, when Capron had gone to Philadelphia, he gave three subscription concerts on his own account, with the assistance of several amateurs from a St. Cecilia Society, organized a year earlier. Again the entire family joined forces to make the affairs a success. In succeeding years Van Hagen was active in the management of the so-called "City Concerts," until the family departed for Boston in 1796. Here, in partnership with his son, he opened a Musical Magazine and Warranted Piano Forte Warehouse at 62 Newbury Street. He became leader of the Haymarket Theatre orchestra, and organist of Stone Chapel. He ultimately withdrew from the firm, which had begun to publish music in 1799, and his son continued the business alone.

As a composer, Van Hagen the elder left behind him records of having written music principally for the theatre, arrangements for ballad-operas that were performed at the theatres in Boston. To *The Adopted Child, or The Baron of Milford Castle*, for which Thomas Atwood had composed the original score, Van Hagen wrote entirely new music. For *The Battle of Hexham; Columbus, or The Discovery of America;* and *Zorinski, or Freedom to the Slaves*, he merely supplied some incidental music, and fitted the orchestral accompaniments to the instrumentation

James Hewitt (from a Painting Made in England When He Was
Twenty-One, a Year Before He Came to America)

(See pages 81–90)

Benjamin Carr
(See pages 96–101)

Alexander Reinagle (from a Drawing by Joseph
Muller after a Painting in the Possession of the Family)
(See pages 75–81)

of the Boston theatres. Of his original compositions, the *Federal Overture* was advertised for performance at the Haymarket Theatre in 1797, and his *Funeral Dirge* on the death of General Washington was published in 1800.

PETER VAN HAGEN, JUNIOR (1781–1837) must have been born in this country, presumably in Charleston, and was therefore doubly entitled to consideration as an American composer. Some of his works are preserved in the library of Harvard University, all of them issued by the Van Hagen publishing firm. There is a patriotic song *Adams and Washington*, whose words expressed the national state of mind when a state of war existed with France in 1798:

> Columbia's brave friends with alertness advance
> Her rights to support in defiance of France.
> To volatile fribbles we never will yield
> While John's at the helm, and George rules the field.

Others of his published songs were *Anna, Gentle Zephyr, May Morning, Pride of our Plains*, and *To Arms, Columbia*. He also composed an *Overture* which was played at the Haymarket in Boston.

One of the most prolific composers of the late eighteenth century was ALEXANDER REINAGLE (1756–1809), a man not only active in musical affairs both in New York and Philadelphia, but one who exerted an influence that made for high standards. Born of Austrian parents in England (1756), Reinagle inherited his love of music from his father. His early musical education was received in Scotland, where he studied with Raynor Taylor who followed him to America in 1792, and of whom we shall hear more later. From his correspondence with Karl Philipp Emanuel Bach, it was apparent that Reinagle was one of the younger Bach's intimate friends. No doubt he was well acquainted with other prominent Europeans of the time.

His activities in this country, centered largely in Philadelphia, were concerned with giving concerts and composing; and with managing a theatrical company in conjunction with Thomas Wignell. He first landed in New York in 1786, where he announced that "Mr. Reinagle, member of the Society of Musicians in London, gives lessons on the pianoforte, harpsichord and violin." New Yorkers did not offer the encouragement and patronage he needed, and he soon departed for

Philadelphia. As early as the autumn of 1786 he was busy with concerts in the Pennsylvania city.

On September 21 he assisted in a concert for Henri Capron's benefit by contributing a song, and a sonata on the pianoforte. In October he announced a benefit concert of his own, and showed himself something of a modern by opening and closing the program with works of Haydn. He joined forces with Capron, William Brown, and Alexander Juhan in the management of the season's subscription concerts, and gave the musical public of Philadelphia an adequate idea of his musicianship and high ideals. In the following season he continued the subscription concert management with Brown.

After he had been in Philadelphia but a year, Reinagle was the first to introduce four-hand piano music to America. At a concert for Juhan's benefit, he played with Juhan a Piano Sonata for four hands by Haydn. No less a celebrity graced this concert than General Washington, soon to be elected President; and when Reinagle gave a concert of his own three weeks later, Washington was again in the audience. Reinagle was the harpsichord teacher of Washington's step-granddaughter Nelly Custis.

By this time Reinagle had become interested in the theatre. Although the antitheatre law had not yet been repealed in Philadelphia, the Old American Company had reopened the Southwark Theatre with its moral lectures, and Reinagle became associated with the troupe, probably as harpsichordist. It must have been this connection that caused his return to New York late in 1788, where he was no doubt associated with the company's brilliant season at the John Street Theatre in 1789. New York had become the capital of the new government. Washington, always fond of the theatre and other amusements, was in constant attendance.

In September, 1788, Reinagle joined Capron, who had also left Philadelphia, in reviving New York's subscription concerts, which had been dormant since the war, except for the only partially successful series by William Brown two years earlier. In the following season three more concerts were offered by Reinagle and Capron, in September and October. At the first of these a chorus by Reinagle was sung. This work has been the subject of an interesting controversy. The advertisement of the concert contained the following information:

After the first act will be performed a Chorus, to the words that were sung, as Gen. Washington passed the bridge at Trenton—the Music now composed by Mr. Reinagle.

In 1789 the piece was published under the following heading:

Chorus sung before Gen. Washington as he passed under the triumphal arch raised on the bridge at Trenton, April 21st, 1789. Set to music and dedicated by permission to Mrs. Washington by A. Reinagle. . . .

Superficially, it would appear that Reinagle had written the music that had been sung at the Trenton ceremonies as Washington passed on his way to his inauguration as our first president; and casual students have so interpreted it. The concert advertisement speaks of "music *now* composed by Mr. Reinagle," and in the scoring of the published version there are significant differences with contemporaneous accounts of how the piece was sung. This discredits the theory that Reinagle composed the original music for the welcome to Washington, and indicates that the music later used in the concert and subsequently published was a new setting of the words that had been sung at Trenton, beginning:

Welcome, mighty chief! Once more. . . .

After the second series of New York concerts, Reinagle returned to Philadelphia, perhaps because the Old American Company had gone there to celebrate the repeal of the antitheatre law by reopening the Southwark Theatre. He was active in subscription concerts, and from the music that was played it would appear that he had a hand in the management. There were works of Haydn and Gossec, as well as the inevitable Pleyel and Stamitz.

The Philadelphia City Concerts of 1791–92 were under the joint management of Reinagle and J. C. Moller. Capron joined them the following season, when eight concerts were given at intervals of several weeks from December to March. Sonneck, in *Early Concert Life in America*, made some comments on the character of the programs:

In view of programs like these, I believe, the customary good-natured or ill-natured smile worn by historians in stumbling accidentally across an isolated eighteenth century program in our country will have to be cancelled once for ever. Though several of the composers who figured on these programs have since passed into (perhaps unmerited) oblivion, they were prominent masters in those days, and names like Haydn, Grétry, Bach, and Mozart are still household names in every musical community. If the arrangement of the "Plans" seems a trifled checkered at times to us moderns who fail to find the same or worse faults in the programs of our own time, we should not forget that the City Concerts ran strictly on European lines and contained no oddities which could not easily be duplicated by quoting European programs.

Meanwhile, Reinagle had become increasingly interested in matters theatrical and operatic, and had formed a partnership with Thomas Wignell, a brilliant English actor and singer who had been connected with the Old American Company since 1785. In 1791, Reinagle and Wignell commenced carrying out their plans for building a new theatre of their own in Chestnut Street, which would be the home for a permanent company that Wignell had recruited from abroad. So great was the competition the Wignell and Reinagle company offered to later visits of the American Company, that the older organization left the field to the newcomers after a final season in 1794. Although the Chestnut Street Theatre was actually ready a year before it was officially opened, the yellow fever epidemic that raged in Philadelphia in the winter of 1793 caused postponement of any but necessary gatherings. Though the company was not yet assembled when the plague subsided, Reinagle felt that he should no longer deny the public a chance to see the new playhouse, and he opened its doors with a "grand concert of vocal and instrumental music" on the second of February, 1793. In February of the following year it commenced its career as a theatre with a performance of *The Castle of Andalusia*.

Although Reinagle was in charge of the music and the orchestral department, George Gillingham, an English violinist who had sat with Reinagle in the orchestra of the Handel Commemoration at Westminster Abbey in 1784, was brought from England as conductor of the orchestra. Durang's *History of the Stage in Philadelphia* has the following picture of Reinagle:

Who that once saw old manager Reinagle in his official capacity, could ever forget his dignified person. He presided at his piano forte, looking the very personification of the patriarch of music—investing the science of harmonious sounds, as well as the dramatic school, with a moral influence, reflecting and adorning its salutary uses with high respectability and polished manners. His appearance was of the reverent and impressive kind, which at once inspired the universal respect of the audience.

Such was Reinagle's imposing appearance, that it awed the disorderly of the galleries, or the fop of annoying propensities, and impertinent criticism of the box lobby into decorum.

It was inspiring to behold the polished Reinagle saluting from his seat (before the grand square piano forte in the orchestra) the highest respectability of the city, as it entered the boxes to take seats. It was a scene before the curtain that suggested a picture of the master of private ceremonies receiving his invited guests at the fashionable drawing room.

Mr. Reinagle was a gentleman and a musician. His compositions evinced decided cleverness and originality, and some of his accompaniments to the old opera music were much admired by good judges.

William McKoy, in an article written twenty years after Reinagle's death in Poulson's *Daily Advertiser*, tells of the musician's participation in the performances:

Mr. Reinagle, one of the Managers, and a Professor of Music, used to be seen, but only on particular occasions, seated at the Piano Forte, then standing against the stage, in the rear of the band for the mere purpose of touching a few notes solo, by way of accompaniment to the silvery tones of Mrs. Wignell. . . . Mr. Reinagle, while thus enjoying the effect of her inimitable chant, exhibited to the audience a head not unlike that of Louis the XIV but divested of the simplicity, bushy, powdered hair, large high forehead, and round full face, illuminated by silver mounted spectacle glasses, a perceptible smirk at all times about the mouth, and an extraordinary depth of dimple in his cheek, while sitting there and surveying the irritability of Mr. Gillingham, the Leader of the Band, on his being obliged to leave the music of Handel and Mozart, and strike off into the "President's March. . . ."

Wignell died in 1803, and his widow continued the management of the Chestnut Street Theatre with Reinagle. During his later years, Reinagle managed a theatre in Baltimore, where he died September 21, 1809. He was married and had two sons, Thomas and Hugh, the latter a scenic painter who was named for Reinagle's brother, an eminent cellist.

Reinagle composed much music, and some of it has been preserved. His more important works seem not to be in existence, and it is not altogether fair to judge his abilities by the scattered pieces which are now in libraries and in private collections. The Library of Congress has a collection of *Sonatas for the Pianoforte* by Reinagle, which are probably the best of his works now extant. These sonatas, in manuscript, are in the manner of Philipp Emanuel Bach and the early Haydn, and at the same time show that Reinagle had some individuality of style and unquestionable taste.

Like the other composers of the day who were associated with the theatre, Reinagle made many arrangements of music used in ballad-operas, pantomimes, and so on: *Auld Robin Gray* (1795); *Blue Beard* (1799); *Columbus* (1797); *La Foret Noire* (1794); *Harlequin Shipwreck'd* (1795); *Harlequin's Invasion* (1795); *The Italian Monk* (1797); *The Mountaineers* (1796); *The Naval Pillar* (1800); *Pierre de Provence* (1796); *The Purse* (1795); *Robin Hood* (1794); *Sicilian Romance* (1795); *Spanish Barber* (1794); *The Witches of the Rocks* (1796). Copies of these arrangements are now practically nonexistent, but their titles indicate what was probably one of Reinagle's most significant contributions to the music of his time.

The most important of Reinagle's original works were a *Miscellaneous Quartett*, played at several of the City Concerts in Philadelphia in 1791, and the *New Miscellaneous Quartett*, offered in the same season; a *Concerto on the Improved Pianoforte with Additional Keys* (1794); *Preludes in three classes, for the improvement of practitioners on the piano forte* (1794); songs for the play *Slaves in Algiers* (1794); music for the musical farce *Savoyard, or the Repentant Seducer* (1797); *Monody on the Death of the much lamented, the late Lieutenant-General of the Armies of the United States*, composed by Reinagle in association with Raynor Taylor (1799); *Collection of favorite songs, divided into two books; The basses rendered easy and natural for the pianoforte or harpsichord* (probably 1789); *Masonic Overture* (1800); music written with Taylor to Richard Brinsley Sheridan's adaptation of Kotzebue's *Pizarro; The Volunteers*, Reinagle's "comic opera in two acts (written by Mrs. Rowson)," performed in Philadelphia, January 21, 1795; the much admired song in *The Stranger* (I Have a Silent Sorrow), a song *Rosa;* and *America, Commerce and Freedom*, published in 1794, and supposedly sung by Mr. Darley, Junior, a famous singer of that time, in the ballet pantomime of *The Sailor's Landlady*. This became widely used as a patriotic song.

Reinagle's *Federal March* was performed in the "grand procession," in Philadelphia, July 4, 1788, which celebrated the signing of the Constitution by a sufficient number of states to make it effective.

JAMES HEWITT (1770–1827) was one of the most important of the late century immigrants. He had an interesting background, he was himself a prime factor in the musical life of New York and Boston, and he established a line of descendants who are still carrying on the family tradition of music. John Hill Hewitt, his eldest son, was a ballad composer whom we shall meet later.

In September of the year 1792 the New York *Daily Advertiser* gave to the citizens of Gotham the promising information that James Hewitt, Jean Gehot, B. Bergmann, William Young, and a gentleman named Phillips, "professors of music from the Opera house, Hanover-square and professional Concerts under the direction of Haydn, Pleyel, etc., London," had arrived in town, and that they would give a concert on the twenty-first of the month at Corre's Hotel, at which "they humbly hoped to experience the kind patronage of the ladies and gentlemen, and public in general."

Inasmuch as Hewitt, Gehot, and Bergmann were violinists, Phillips played the violoncello and Young the flute, they provided among themselves the nucleus of an orchestra that was no doubt amplified by assistant performers. The program is one of the most interesting that has been preserved from this period. It shows that the members of this little group were possessed of imagination, whatever else they may have offered. The standard works were an Overture by Haydn, a *Quartetto* by Pleyel, and a Symphony and Flute *Quartetto* by Stamitz. Mr. Phillips contributed a Violoncello Concerto of his own, and the remainder of the program was devoted to two works of major proportions by Hewitt and Gehot.

Of these, the first was Hewitt's *Overture in 9 movements, expressive of a battle*, which pictured successively: 1. *Introduction*, 2. *Grand March; the army in motion*, 3. *The Charge for the attack*, 4. *A National Air*, 5. *The Attack commences, in which the confusion of an engagement is heard*, 6. *The Enemy surrender*, 7. *The Grief of those who are made prisoners*, 8. *The Conqueror's quickmarch*, and 9. *The Finale*. It is probable that Hewitt composed this *Overture* before he left England, no doubt inspired by the vogue of Kotzwara's *Battle of*

Prague, an insipid though highly popular piece written as early as 1788. But the other new work on the Hewitt-Gehot-Bergmann program must have been written on American soil, and while Hewitt's *Overture* represented a series of incidents he probably never experienced himself, Gehot's *Overture* told the story of their journey to America, and was therefore not only programmatic, but autobiographical as well.

This was the *Overture in 12 movements, expressive of a voyage from England to America.* The titles of the several movements afford a miniature history, as follows: 1. *Introduction,* 2. *Meeting of the adventurers, consultation and their determination on departure,* 3. *March from London to Gravesend,* 4. *Affectionate separation from their friends,* 5. *Going on board, and pleasure at recollecting the encouragement they hope to meet with in a land where merit is sure to gain reward,* 6. *Preparation for sailing, carpenter's hammering, crowing of the cock, weighing anchor, etc.,* 7. *A Storm,* 8. *A Calm,* 9. *Dance on the deck by the passengers,* 10. *Universal joy on seeing land,* 11. *Thanksgiving for safe arrival,* 12. *Finale.*

Immediately following their benefit concert, Messrs. Hewitt, Gehot, Bergmann, and Young decided to enter the subscription concert field in New York, which at that time was controlled by the Van Hagens. Although they announced a promising program for October 4, and advertised for a series of twelve concerts, they soon learned that their terms were too high and their series too long for the spending habits of New Yorkers. Consequently, they announced a postponement with this reason for the delay:

to obtain the celebrated singers, Mrs. Pownall (late Mrs. Wrighten) and Mrs. Hodgkinson, both recently of England, and as they were determined to engage the first singers in America, they have spared no expence nor trouble (by separate journeys to Philadelphia, etc. etc.) to gratify the amateurs of music.

Meanwhile, the Van Hagens, stirred by the thought of competition, had given their three subscription concerts in the fall of 1792, and Gehot had left his comrades to go to Philadelphia where he participated in the City Concerts of 1792–93, then managed by Reinagle and Capron. Gehot probably settled definitely in Philadelphia and later became a violinist in the orchestra of Wignell and Reinagle's Company. Although he is probably identical with a Gehot who published over thirty-six quartets, trios, and similar numbers; a *Complete Instructor of Every Musical Instrument;* and other educational works in London prior to 1790, the only composition, other than the *Overture,* of which we know in this country was the Quartet played at the City Concert in Philadelphia, December 1, 1792, and a few songs. John R. Parker's musical Reminiscences in the *Euterpeiad* (1822) tell that he died in obscurity and poverty.

It was not until January, 1793 that Hewitt, with Bergmann and Phillips, finally launched the subscription concerts and gave a series of six at Corre's Hotel, lasting until April 6. Young, too, had dropped out and had accompanied or followed Gehot to Philadelphia, where a few years later he was sentenced to death for having killed a constable who came to arrest him for his debts. The programs of the 1793 concerts were interesting for a number of reasons. Not only did they offer, as promised, the vocal talents of Mrs. Pownall and Mrs. Hodgkinson —singers from the Old American Company—and several works by Phillips and Hewitt (including a repetition of the *Battle* Overture), together with the accustomed list of Pleyel and Stamitz; they also included works of Vanhall and Haydn played from manuscript. On the program of the fifth concert (March 25), America probably heard its first performance of what was termed Haydn's *Passion of our Saviour,* identical with the famous *Seven Words,* composed for the Cathedral of Cadiz in 1785, and later performed in London as the *Passione Instrumentale.*

In the following winter the competition in subscription concerts continued. Capron, returning from Philadelphia, joined forces with Hewitt in promoting three "City" Concerts at the City Tavern in December and January, while Phillips took charge of the ball at a series which the Van Hagens offered as the "Old City" Concerts in Corre's Hotel in January and February. Bergmann remained with Hewitt. While the Van Hagen series emphasized the virtuoso element, offering Mr. and Mrs. Hodgkinson and Mr. Prigmore as vocalists, and numerous solos by the infant prodigy *Master* Van Hagen, the Hewitt concerts were more devoted to instrumental music. The songs of Mrs. Pownall and Madame de Seze, plus an occasional duet with Capron, were the only vocal offerings. Haydn was well represented on each of the programs.

Hewitt probably effected a merger with his rivals in the following season, for the series of three concerts in 1795 were offered by Mr. and Mrs. Van Hagen, Hewitt, and Saliment. Then Hewitt withdrew from the City Concerts, and devoted himself largely to his duties as leader of the orchestra of the Old American Company. His activities were by no means exclusively confined to any single undertaking, for he appeared as conductor of a band at Joseph Delacroix's celebrated summer concerts, held in the house and garden of "the late alderman Bayard," and called "Vaux Hall Gardens," where the two shillings admission entitled the patron "to a glass of ice cream punch," and the privilege of witnessing the fireworks "made by the celebrated Mr. Ambrose." He also had conducted the orchestra when in 1793, Mrs. Melmoth "from the Theatres Royal of London and Dublin" presented "*Select Extracts*, from the most eminent authors, recited by particular request." Evidently Hewitt was called upon to organize and conduct orchestras for occasions of all sorts.

He was born in Dartmoor, England, June 4, 1770. His father was Captain John Hewitt of the British Navy, a generous and brave man, who later followed his son James to America, where he lived until he was killed by a fall from his chaise in 1804, at the age of one hundred and one years. James entered the navy when he was a lad, but resigned as a midshipman when he saw the cruel treatment of the sailors on board his man-of-war. He was musically talented and his father decided to give him a musical education. Family accounts say that he studied under Viotti, but according to Grove's Dictionary, Viotti did not come to London until 1792; so if Hewitt actually took lessons from him it could hardly have been in London, as Hewitt was in New York in September of that year.

His progress was rapid, for before he came to New York he was leader of the Court Orchestra during the reign of George III. He was intimate with the Prince of Wales, and the future George IV presented him with an Amati cello, valued at five hundred dollars.

In 1790, Hewitt married a Miss Lamb, but his wife and their infant child died a year later, and in 1792, Hewitt came to America. According to the directories, he lived in New York almost continuously until

1812. He was connected with the orchestra of the Old American Company, he was for a time organist of Trinity Church, he conducted the orchestras at various outdoor summer resorts in town—Delacroix' Vaux Hall, Columbia and Mount Vernon Gardens. From 1805 to 1809 he was director of all the military bands in the city and commanded the Third Company of artillery.

About 1798, Hewitt purchased the New York branch of Carr's Musical Repository, and established a publishing business which was carried on by his son until the middle of the next century. On December 10, 1795, Hewitt married a second time. His bride was Eliza King, and the ceremony was performed at Trinity Church by Bishop Moore. Eliza was the daughter of Sir John King of the Royal British Army, who had come to America to settle some estates that had been bequeathed to his wife. Had Hewitt attended properly to securing the property in his wife's behalf, his descendants would have been wealthy. But Hewitt was never a good business man.

His second wife was an accomplished woman. She had been educated in Paris, and was there during the French Revolution. At the time of the Reign of Terror she was confined for safety in the Bastille with her mother. She saw the guillotine in action and would often recount its gruesome work with a shudder. She knew Napoleon Bonaparte when he was first making a name for himself.

Hewitt and his wife had six children, whom we shall meet in later chapters. His wife survived him by many years, living until 1865, when she died at the home of her youngest son in Burlington, New Jersey.

In 1812 the Hewitt family moved to Boston, where Hewitt took charge of the music at the Federal Street Theatre. He was also organist of Boston's Trinity Church. His name appears in the Boston directories until 1816, and in 1818 it reappears in New York. He must have traveled somewhat during the next few years. He was in Boston for a year—about 1820. Parker's *Euterpeiad* refers to a grand oratorio he conducted in Augusta, Georgia, in 1821, and in biographical data regarding his son, there are references to Southern theatrical companies in which James Hewitt was interested. Under date of 1826 there is a note that he was succeeded by George Gillingham as musical director at the Park Theatre in New York. Presumably he resigned because of ill health, though there are references to a subsequent connection with the Chatham Theatre.

Hewitt died in 1827 in Boston. For a time he had been estranged from his wife, and while she lived in Boston with their son James L. Hewitt, he was boarding in New York. There is in existence a series of letters written to this son late in 1826 and in January, 1827, which show that he was very ill at the time they were written. These last letters are interesting. They speak of his work, his financial and personal affairs. Some references throw light on the surgery of the period.

Dec. 27, 1826—This day at 12 o'clock closes the 6 weeks since the operation was performed, and I am at present no better for it.

Jan. 26, 1827—In a conversation I've had with Dr. Mott, he acknowledged the Lachrymal duct was cut but not so as to destroy its usefulness—but that is not the complaint, my present sufferings are from some part of the Jaw being left which was injured at the finishing of the operation before he closed the wound (he had been cutting away part of my nose) I heard him say to his assistant that there appeared some small part yet but he thought it would be of no consequence and did not wish to continue my sufferings—therefore had the wounds closed. . . . My sufferings are great and my death slow, but certain. I hope my dear James you will be here to receive my last breath. I feel the want of home—tho every kind attention is paid me here—yet my heart longs once more to behold my family.

In an undated letter he refers to his manuscripts:

In the large Red Box my clothes. In the smaller Red Box all manuscripts which I think you had better be careful of, they may eventually be of value to you. Among those Mans Books you may find music worth your printing. A Box for the whole of the Theatrical music, should you wish to pack it, is in the cellar, but I believe they have burnt the lids.

He had neglected looking after his own father's property as well as that belonging to his wife:

I did mean, if it pleased God to have spared my life, to have made secret inquiries respecting my father's affairs. Is it to be supposed that he could live here thirty years without some means? there are persons to whom he has lent money which has never been paid. What has become of the acknowledgments, and previous to his death he was known to have plenty of money. On his deathbed . . . he had something of consequence to communicate! Be assured there is something wrong, which if it had pleased God, my dear

James to have suffered me to have lived, I should have endeavoured to have found out.

A number of Hewitt's works are preserved in libraries, and while they represent his less important efforts, they nevertheless show that he was important in the development of American music. Many of his songs were early forerunners of our modern sentimental ballads. While none of these descended to the mawkish depths that our popular songs were to achieve in the next century, they do show "heart" tendencies that are prophetic. *The Music of the Harp of Love, The Wounded Hussar, When the Shades of Night Pursuing* (these three in the New York Public Library), and *How Happy Was My Humble Lot*—a favorite ballad sung by Mrs. Oldmixon and Miss Broadhurst (preserved in the Library of Congress)—are illustrative of this trend.

A year after his arrival, and immediately following the first series of subscription concerts, Hewitt advertised for subscriptions to a book of songs which he had written and compiled in association with Mrs. Pownall. The announcement contained the following details:

Flatter'd by the unbounded applauses which the songs of the Primrose Girl, Jemmy of the Glen, etc. [the latter was by Mrs. Pownall], have met with in this city and Philadelphia, M. A. Pownall and J. Hewitt, are induced to publish them (with four others entirely new) arranged for the Harpsichord and Pianoforte. A work which they hope will do credit to themselves and give satisfaction to those Ladies and Gentlemen who will please to honor them by becoming subscribers.

The book was published a year later and was advertised to contain, in addition to the other songs, *Song of the Waving Willow* and the celebrated French national air *La Carmagnole*. It actually contained, however, along with the several songs by Mrs. Pownall, Hewitt's songs *A Rural Life* and *The Primrose Girl;* also his adaptation of *La Chasse* and a *Canzonet* by Jackson of Exeter. Apparently *The Waving Willow* and *La Carmagnole* dropped out.

In addition to the *Overture* "expressive of a battle," Hewitt composed another *Overture,* "to conclude with the representation of a Storm at Sea," and an *Overture de Demophon, Arrangé pour le fortipiano par Jacques Hewitt.* The latter may be found in the Boston Public Library and in the Hopkinson collection at Philadelphia.

The Library of Congress has recently acquired two interesting Hewitt items. One is a set of *Three Sonatas for the Pianoforte*, Opus 5, published probably in 1796, four years after he came to America. The other is *The 4th of July—A Grand Military Sonata for the Pianoforte*, published some time between 1801 and 1811. In the collection of Joseph Muller, at Closter, New Jersey, I found a setting by Hewitt of the *Star-Spangled Banner*. Purely manufactured music, technically sound, but awkward to sing. Hewitt, like others, no doubt deplored the singing of our anthem to an English drinking song, and tried to provide a setting composed on native soil.[1] Mr. Muller's collection contained also a sonata by Hewitt [2]—*The Battle of Trenton*, published anonymously in 1797 and dedicated to "General Washington." This is interesting because of its similarity to the Battle Overture Hewitt presented at his first concert in New York, both of them reflective of the vogue of Kotzwara's *The Battle of Prague*, which was known in England in 1788, and performed for the first time in America in 1794. *The Battle of Trenton* has an elaborate program:

Introduction—The Army in motion—General Orders—Acclamation of the Americans—Drums beat to Arms.

Attack—cannons—bomb. Defeat of the Hessians—Flight of the Hessians —Begging Quarter—The Fight Renewed—General Confusion—The Hessians surrender themselves prisoners of War—Articles of Capitulation Signed—Grief of Americans for the loss of their companions killed in the engagement.

Yankee Doodle—Drums and Fifes—Quick Step for the Band—Trumpets of Victory—General Rejoicing.

The most important work that Hewitt wrote for the theatre was his score for the opera *Tammany*, produced in New York in 1794 under the auspices of the Tammany Society, the ancestor of the present Tam-

---

[1] The Boston Public Library has had a copy of this rare piece for several years. In 1930 a third copy appeared in the possession of C. A. Strong and C. J. Nagy of Philadelphia. Muller's copy, however, is undoubtedly from the first edition, as it bears Hewitt's imprint as publisher. The Strong-Nagy and Boston Library copies were published by J. A. & W. Geib of New York, somewhere between 1818 and 1821. The first edition was probably published by Hewitt in 1816.

[2] The Muller copy is now in the Americana Music Collection of the New York Public Library; others are in the Huntington Library in California, the Library of Congress, and in the private collection of Malcolm N. Stone, West Englewood, New Jersey.

many Hall. The libretto was written by Mrs. Anne Julia Hatton, a sister of Mrs. Siddons, and wife of a musical instrument maker in New York. In those days feeling between the Federalists and anti-Federalists ran high, and Mrs. Hatton was an ardent supporter of the anti-Federalists, who at that time were favoring support of the French Revolution. The powerful Tammany Society was also anti-Federalist, so Mrs. Hatton based her opera plot on the legend of the society's patron, the Indian Chief Tammany.

Because its presentation was largely political it was but to be expected that it would arouse a storm of controversy. The anti-Federalists hailed it with fervor and the Federalists denounced it in hostile terms as a "wretched thing," and "literally a mélange of bombast." Although the complete libretto and the score were never published we may gain an idea of its underlying theme by reading the prologue, supplied by another poet, R. B. Davis:

> Secure the Indian roved his native soil,
> Secure enjoy'd the produce of his toil,
> Nor knew, nor feared a haughty master's pow'r
> To force his labors, or his gains devour.
> And when the slaves of Europe here unfurl'd
> The bloody standard of their servile world,
> When heaven, to curse them more, first deign'd to bless
> Their base attempts with undeserved success,
> He knew the sweets of liberty to prize,
> And lost on earth he sought her in the skies;
> Scorned life divested of its noblest good,
> And seal'd the cause of freedom with his blood.

One writer went so far as to accuse the promoters of *Tammany* of attracting an audience by circulating a rumor that a party had been gathered to hiss the performance, and evidently there was considerable disturbance.

It is not known whether any of Hewitt's music from *Tammany* was published, although there did appear proposals for printing the "Overture with the songs, chorus's, etc., etc., to Tammany as composed and adapted to the pianoforte by Mr. Hewitt." Others of the operas to which he composed music were as follows: *Columbus* (1799); *The Mysterious Marriage, or The Heirship of Rosselva* (1799); *The Pa-*

triot, or Liberty Asserted (1794), "founded on the well-known story of William Tell, the Swiss patriot, who shot an apple from his son's head at the command of Tyrant Grislor who first gave liberty to the cantons of Switzerland"; the New York production of *Pizarro, or The Spaniards in Peru* (1800), (it will be remembered that Reinagle composed music for this work); *Robin Hood, or Sherwood Forest* (1800) (also by Reinagle); *The Spanish Castle, or The Knight of the Guadalquivir* (1800); and *The Wild Goose Chase* (1800).

Of the remaining two "Professors of Music from Hanoversquare, London," Phillips, as far as he has been traced, remained in New York, where in addition to his work as a cellist, he handled the terpsichorean features of concerts and parties, for, as he announced at the first concert in America, he had been connected abroad (probably in London) with the Pantheon and City Balls, and was qualified to introduce new English dances which, "if the ladies and gentlemen request, will be performed by a concert band." Bergmann became a member of the theatre orchestra which Hewitt conducted, but remained in New York only until 1795, after which he appeared at various times in Charleston, South Carolina and Boston. That he went directly from New York to Charleston is evident by the fact that he arranged the orchestral accompaniments for the presentation at the City Theatre, April 26, 1796, of a *pasticcio, The Doctor and Apothecary.*

A prominent member of the group who led musical affairs of Philadelphia well into the following century was RAYNOR TAYLOR (1747–1825), an older man than his pupil Reinagle, yet one who outlived him by sixteen years. Taylor was born in England in 1747 and was educated as a child in the King's Singing School at the Chapel Royal. The choirboys attended Handel's funeral in a body in 1759, and young Raynor, leaning too close to the grave, accidentally let his hat fall, so that it was buried with the remains of the great composer. "Never mind," consoled a friend, "he left you some of his brains in return."

In 1765, Taylor became organist in a church at Chelmsford, near London, but his interest in theatrical matters procured him the position of music director at Sadler's Wells Theatre in London, the playhouse made famous to our generation by Pinero's play *Trelawney of the Wells*. He had also made an enviable reputation as a ballad composer by the time he followed his friends to America in 1792.

When he arrived in Baltimore he sought to establish himself as a "music professor, organist, and teacher of music in general," and he announced his debut as a performer, when for the evening of October 17 he proposed

to perform a musical entertainment on a new plan, the whole of which will be entirely original, and his own composition. In the course of it many songs will be sung by his pupil, Miss Huntley, late of the theatre Royal, Covent Garden, a young lady, whose performance has been highly approved both in London and America.

With this and similar entertainments Taylor proceeded to introduce to America a species of extravaganza, or musical olio, which bordered on our present vaudeville or revue skits.

Taylor then settled in Annapolis, where in October, 1792, he had been appointed organist of St. Anne's Church. The parishioners evidently had no objection to their organist's being an entertainer, and on January 24 and February 28, 1793, he again engaged Miss Huntley for two of his burlesque entertainments. The program for January 24 consisted of three parts, the first devoted to a selection of comic and pastoral songs. The second part presented a "Dramatic proverb (performed in London with great applause) being a burletta, in one act, called *The Gray Mare's Best Horse.*"

This sketch consisted of *A Breakfast scene a month after marriage*, a duet by Mr. Taylor and Miss Huntley. Next the *Mock wife in a violent passion*, a solo number by Miss Huntley. This was followed by *A Father's advice to his son-in-law*, *Giles the countryman's grief for the loss of a scolding wife*, and the *Happy Miller*, performed by Mr. Taylor; then, in order, *Dame Pliant's obedience to her husband*, by Miss Huntley; a duet, the *Obedient wife, determined to have her own way;* and finally, two more duets, *New married couple reconciled*, and *All parties happy.*

The third part of the show was a burlesque on Italian opera, called *Capocchio and Dorinna.* In this presentation Mr. Taylor and Miss Huntley appeared in costume, Taylor portraying *Signor Capocchio*, an Italian singer and director of the opera; Miss Huntley, *Signora Dorinna*, an Italian actress. There were recitatives, airs, and duets, probably parodies of the Italian style, which offered a contrast to the

English type of ballad-opera, in which the main action was carried by dialogue between songs. The entertainment was further lengthened by "a piece on the Grand Pianoforte, preceding each part, by Mr. Taylor."

Affairs at Annapolis did not progress smoothly for Taylor. Those who had offered to guarantee his salary as organist did not make good their promises with actual money, and the employment of a collector failed to bring forth what was due him. So by the end of May he publicly thanked the families who had employed him as a music teacher and departed for Philadelphia. Here he became organist of St. Peter's Church, and held that position for almost the rest of his life. He lived until 1825, and was one of the leading spirits in founding the Musical Fund Society of Philadelphia in 1820. His brilliant powers of improvisation helped him as an organist, and no doubt lent an added charm to his entertainments.

Shortly after he went to Philadelphia he presented, on January 18 and 28 (1794) two more of his entertainments: the first, *An Ode to the New Year*, "with a variety of other pieces, consisting of songs, duets and trios, pastoral, serious and comic, entirely original," and the second similar to his entertainments in Maryland, consisting of

The Poor female ballad singer, a pathetic song; Hunting song; Algerian captive; Sailor's song; Ding Dong Bell, or the Honeymoon expired, being the courtship and wedding of Ralph and Fan; Character of smart Dolly, a laughing song; Rustic courtship or the unsuccessful love of poor Thomas, a crying song with duet, trio, etc.

In 1796, Taylor offered for his own benefit a concert at Oeller's Hotel, April 21. The program consisted of music from the Handelian school, and works of his own which occupied the entire second half of the concert. The announcement afforded a full description of the orchestra that was to be used. Though it would be small in a modern symphony hall, it was large for the time. The *concertino*, or small band of soloists, was constituted as follows:

First violin and leader of the band .... Mr. Gillingham
Principal violoncellos .... Mr. Menel
Double bass .... Mr. Demarque
Principal hautboy .... Mr. Shaw
Tenor .... Mr. Berenger

Bassoon and trumpet .... Mr. Priest
Horns .... Messrs. Grey and Homman
Violins .... Messrs. Daugel, Bouchony, Stewart and Schetky

With the supplementary band, or *ripieno,* the orchestra assumed large proportions. Of Taylor's own works on the program, the most important were a *New Overture,* and a *Divertimento* for orchestra, and his Violin Concerto, played by George Gillingham. In addition, there were a number of vocal numbers, sung by Miss Huntley.

In 1814, when the Vauxhall Garden in Philadelphia was opened in May for concerts and other entertainments, Taylor was engaged as organist for the opening night, and Gillingham was conductor of the orchestra. This garden was a popular resort in the summer, and even though smoking was not permitted "in or near the temple," the music and the temple and garden, "brilliantly illuminated with variegated lamps," seemed amply to justify the dollar admission. One of the entertainments for Lafayette was held at the Vauxhall Garden, when he paid us his second visit in 1825.

In the New York Public Library there are three anthems by Taylor, written and published before he came to America. These were printed in the *Cathedral Magazine* in London: *Hear my crying, O God* (Psalm 61), for two voices; *Hear, O Lord, and Consider my Complaint* (Psalm 17); and, *I will give thanks unto the Lord.* In the same library there are several songs and the libretto of a melodrama *The Rose of Arragon, or The Vigil of St. Mark,* published in 1822, for which Taylor had written music.

In addition to the Violin Concerto and instrumental works, there is a *Sonata for the pianoforte, with an accompaniment for violin,* published in 1797, "price one dollar, to be had at the music stores," and a "new symphony," which was advertised for performance at the Federal Street Theatre in Boston during the same year. As we have seen from his entertainments, Taylor composed many songs, sentimental and humorous, most of them either lost or unpublished. The Hopkinson collection in Philadelphia possesses a manuscript piece for piano *The Bells;* and printed copies of *The Wounded Sailor* and *The Philadelphia Hymn.* The Yale library at New Haven has two songs published in Carr's *Musical Miscellany—The Merry piping lad,* "a ballad in the Scot's taste," and *The Wand'ring village maid.* The Boston Public Library has a copy of Taylor's arrangement for piano, four hands, of the famous *President's March*.

Capitalizing his experience at Sadler's Wells in London, Taylor did some writing for the theatre after he came to America. In 1795 his *La Petite Piedmontese, or The Travellers Preserved*, a "serious panto-mimical ballet," was produced in Philadelphia. Two years later he supplied the music for a production of Colman's play *The Iron Chest*, which was given in Baltimore. He wrote a "serious pantomime," *La Bonne Petite Fille or The Shipwrecked Mariner Preserved*, which was performed at Philadelphia, Baltimore, and Boston. He collaborated with Reinagle in music for the Philadelphia presentation of *Pizarro, or The Spaniards in Peru* (1800), as well as in the composition of the *Monody* on the death of Washington (1799). There is also record of an educational work by Taylor, published at Carr's Musical Repository in 1797: *Divertimenti, or familiar lessons for the pianoforte, to which is prefixed a Ground for the Improvement of Young Practitioners*.

VICTOR PELISSIER first appeared in Philadelphia in 1792. This accomplished French musician had been the first horn player at the theatre in Cape François, and though his participation in concerts was largely confined to playing the French horn, his association with the orchestra of the Old American Company (which he joined a year after his arrival) led him to compose many scores for its productions, and to act as arranger and adapter of foreign ballad-operas.

Pelissier has been described as short in stature, and so nearsighted that he was almost blind. It was said that he was always a cheery person, whose thoughts were as fully occupied by notes as any banker or broker in Wall Street. Some historians have claimed that his opera *Edwin and Angelina* (presented in New York, December 19, 1796) was the first work of its kind composed in America, but it is evident that such was not the case. It is probably true that Pelissier's score, a setting of lyrics to a libretto by Elihu Hubbard Smith, had been accepted several years before Carr's *Archers* was produced April 18, 1796, but neither is entitled to the distinction. Hewitt's *Tammany* was produced in 1794, and Hopkinson's "oratorial entertainment," *The Temple of Minerva* (1781), has as much right to be considered an opera as these later works. There is not at hand sufficient evidence to designate any of the early operas as the first written on American soil.

Smith, the librettist, adapted *Edwin and Angelina* from Goldsmith. Its deliciously romantic plot was highly illogical and offered the audience many surprises. It was designed for audiences who delighted in a sentimentality that overcame stage villainy. And it at least afforded the popular actors of the day ample opportunity to display their vocal gifts in the dozen or more lyrics. Whether the libretto or the music was at fault, the work did not meet with sufficient success to warrant a second performance.

Pelissier's next work was a "piece, in one act, never performed in America," called *Ariadne Abandoned by Theseus, in the Isle of Naxos*. This was a melodrama of unknown authorship. Of the music the advertisement said:

Between the different passages spoken by the actors, will be Full Orchestral Music, expressive of each situation and passion. The music composed and managed by Pelissier.

The New York production of *Ariadne Abandoned* occurred in 1797, and it was played in Boston soon after.

In the same year John Hodgkinson produced in Boston a patriotic spectacle *The Launch, or Huzza for the Constitution*, "the Musick selected from the best Composers, with new Orchestra parts by Pelissier." The advance bulletins told that

The whole will conclude with a striking Representation of Launching the New Frigate Constitution. Boats passing and repassing on the Water. View of the River of Charleston, and the neighboring country. . . .

Two years later (1799) Pelissier offered two more scores. The first was music for William Dunlap's *Sterne's Maria, or The Vintage*. Dunlap later wrote in his *History of the American Theatre*, that though "the piece pleased and was pleasing," it was "not sufficiently attractive to keep the stage after the original performers in it were removed by those fluctuations common in theatrical establishments." Three of Pelissier's songs from *Sterne's Maria* are still in existence. In his own collection of *Columbian Melodies* (published in 1811) appeared *I laugh, I sing; Hope, gentle hope;* and *Ah! why on Quebec's bloody plain*, all from the score of the opera.

Pelissier wrote music for the performance of a "splendid allegorical, musical drama, never exhibited," called *The Fourth of July; or Temple of American Independence*, presented in New York on July 4, 1799. It was thus described in the newspaper advertisement:

[there] will be displayed (among other scenery, professedly intended to exceed any exhibition yet presented by the Theatre) a view of the lower part of Broadway, Battery, Harbor, and Shipping taken on the spot.

After the shipping shall have been saluted, a military Procession in perspective will take place, consisting of all the uniform Companies of the City, Horse, Artillery and Infantry in their respective plans, according to the order of the March.

The whole to conclude with an inside view of the *Temple of Independence* as exhibited on the Birthday of Gen. Washington. Scenery and Machinery by Mr. Ciceri—Music by Mr. Pelessier.

In 1800, Pelissier supplied music and accompaniments for the *Castle of Otranto*, which had been altered from the *Sicilian Romance*. He also arranged orchestral accompaniments for many other performances in New York, and adapted the music of other composers to the requirements of the Old American Company orchestra. In fact, he did for New York what Reinagle was doing in Philadelphia. Among the works adapted or arranged by Pelissier were: *The Deserter* (1795), with Benjamin Carr; *The Flitch of Bacon* (1796); *La Foret Noire* (1795); *Harlequin Pastry Cook* (1794); *The Haunted Tower* (1795); *Inkle and Yarico* (1796); *The Jubilee* (1800); *Lock and Key* (1799); *Maid of the Mill* (1796); *The Mountaineers* (1796); *My Grandmother* (1796); *The Mysterious Monk* (1796); *Poor Vulcan* (1796); *Robinson Crusoe* (1796); *Rosina* (1796); *The Siege of Belgrade* (1796); *The Son-in-Law* (1798); *Sophia of Brabant* (1794); *The Virgin of the Sun* (1800); *The Waterman* (1796); *Zorinski* (1798).

The only purely instrumental works by Pelissier, of which there is record, are a *Quartet* and a few occasional pieces, including a *Waltz* contained in his *Columbian Melodies*, and reprinted in a modern arrangement in the present author's *A Program of Early American Piano Music*.[3]

Like Hewitt and Taylor, BENJAMIN CARR (1768–1831) was one of the musicians who bridged the turn of the century, arriving in this

[3] New York, J. Fischer & Bro., 1931.

country in the post-revolutionary days, when concert activities were re-awakening from their early beginnings. He lived to see musical affairs in a far more advanced stage than when he had come. Carr, who arrived in Philadelphia in 1793, achieved distinction as composer, opera and concert singer, choral conductor, organist, pianist, and music publisher and dealer. He was an Englishman of breeding and culture. Born in 1768, he had received his musical education from the foremost church musicians of England, and had participated in a number of concert ventures in London.

A full-length biography of Benjamin Carr would make good reading. The man was many sided, and in his sixty-two years of life he saw much, and gave to those around him many times the value of what he absorbed. When he came to Philadelphia his first venture was the establishment of Carr's Musical Repository, claimed to be the first music store in Philadelphia. It seems, however, that this honor must be shared with the firm of Moller and Capron who opened their Philadelphia store this same summer (1793)—in fact, probably a few months earlier than Carr. Carr's activities as music publisher were important to American music, for it was through his establishment that many of the works of contemporary composers were issued, both in Philadelphia and in New York. Carr's *Musical Miscellany*, and the *Musical Journal for the Pianoforte* (distributed from Baltimore by J. Carr) were to the early nineteenth century what our modern publishers' trade-marked editions are to us today. A year after its establishment in Philadelphia, a branch of the firm was started in New York. Later this was sold to James Hewitt.

Carr's participation in concerts commenced soon after his arrival. In the spring of 1794 he appeared with Reinagle, Gillingham, and Menel as one of the directors of a series of "Amateur and Professional Concerts" at Oeller's Hotel in Philadelphia. Tickets for the concerts were sold at the Repository. On each of the four programs Carr appeared only as a singer. In the following December he made his debut as an opera singer, appearing at New York in the Old American Company's production of Arne's *Love in a Village*. The *New York Magazine's* review of the performance had this to say of Carr:

Mr. Carr made on this occasion his first appearance on our stage; and we confess, to us a very prepossessing first appearance. Good sense and modesty, united to a perfect knowledge of his profession as a musician, and a pleasing and comprehensive voice are not the only qualifications which this young gentleman possesses for the stage; he speaks with propriety, and we doubt not but practice will make him a good actor, in addition to his being an excellent singer.

In February of the following year he was engaged by Hewitt and the Van Hagens, who had dropped their competition and formed a temporary merger, as a vocalist at the City Concerts in New York. In the following December he rendered a vocal solo, and appeared as an instrumentalist by playing a pianoforte sonata. During the ensuing years his name appears frequently on Philadelphia concert programs as a vocalist, and occasionally as an instrumentalist. In 1797 he was one of the principal singers at Mrs. Grattan's "Ladies' Concerts," which this feminine impresario presented because "necessity obliges her to make this effort for the maintenance of her infant family," and for which "any subscriber on paying his subscription, will have a right to demand tickets for the unmarried part of his family."

But in spite of his evident popularity, Carr was least important as a singer. His work as church organist and his interest in choral matters, as well as his activities as a pianist, kept him in the center of Philadelphia's musical life, and finally led to his part in founding the Musical Fund Society in 1820. This organization has been to Philadelphia what the Handel and Haydn Society has been to Boston. In 1816 a musician named Charles Hupfield, and several others, endeavored to establish a society to meet each week for regular practice. It was difficult to keep a large enough group of musicians together for concerted playing, and finally it was decided to give concerts for the relief of needy musicians; "decayed musicians" they were called in the articles of incorporation. The prime object of the society was to "reform the state of neglect into which the beautiful art of music had fallen."

The first concert of the Musical Fund Society, at which Carr was one of the choral conductors, was given April 24, 1821, and repeated May 8. In addition to a number of choral works, for which Carr arranged the orchestral accompaniments, the program marked what has been claimed for many years as the first American performance of Beethoven's First Symphony. It now seems probable that the first American performance of this symphony was that given at Lexington,

Kentucky, November 12, 1817, under the direction of Anton Philip Heinrich. (In each case possibly only the first movement, however.)

But it is as a composer that we are chiefly concerned with Carr, and fortunately many of his works are extant. His music, like that of Hewitt and others of his contemporaries, represents a tendency that is definitely apparent in our music of today. Students of the *sob-song* will find its beginnings in this eighteenth–nineteenth-century literature. Yet for all this, Carr did not always descend to sentimentality, and in his editing of standard works he showed himself a capable musician, with powers of discretion.

He has been known for the production of his opera *The Archers, or Mountaineers, of Switzerland,* erroneously termed "the first American opera." This work was produced by the Old American Company in New York, April 18, 1796, and belongs to the English ballad-opera type. Carr's score to this adaptation of Schiller's *Wilhelm Tell* antedates Rossini's setting by thirty-three years. The piece met with gratifying success and was repeated on numerous occasions. Of the music to this drama only a few pieces have been preserved, but so charming as to cause regret at the loss of the others. The *Rondo* from the Overture to *The Archers* was copyrighted in 1813 as No. 7 of the *Musical Miscellany,* and an extremely graceful song *Why, Huntress, Why* appeared in Carr's *Musical Journal.* There is also *A Fragment* (There liv'd in Altdorf City fair) to be found in the second book of *Elegant Extracts* for the German flute or violin (1796); and a *March in The Archers* occurs in *Military Amusement* (1796) which presumably comes from this opera.

Like many of his colleagues, Carr composed a piece in honor of Washington when the national hero died in 1799. The *Dead March and Monody* was first performed at the Lutheran Church in Philadelphia. When published it was advertised as "being part of the music selected for funeral honors to our late illustrious cheif [sic] General George Washington. Composed for the occasion and respectfully dedicated to the Senate of the United States by their obedt. humble servt. B. Carr. . . ."

Carr's songs and ballads have survived him in abundance, and the New York Public Library, and the private collection of Mr. Arthur Billings Hunt in Brooklyn, New York, are among those possessing many of these historically valuable pieces. Taken from their rather thin, tinkling setting in the accompaniment, and arranged in the manner of our modern ballad songs, these lyrics are in many cases quite as effective in their climaxes as the lyric ballads of today. Carr showed his experience on the concert platform. *Ellen, Arise* is singularly effective; sopranos must have won great applause with its high *A*. *The Soldier's Dream* is somewhat bombastic, but *Mary Will Smile* and the *Hymn of Eve* are Handelian in the chaste simplicity of their melodic line. *Noah's Dove* is altogether a charming song, with a compelling power in its sequential phrases. He wrote a song that has so far escaped the notice of those who sponsor toothpaste radio programs. *Thy Smiles are all Decaing* [sic], *Love*, is its charming title, and in its verses the hero swears that he will continue to love his lady, even though her smiles do actually decay, her "lip shed its sweetness," her "form lose its fleetness."

Mr. Muller's collection at Closter had a curious Carr item; a lengthy piece for the piano called *The History of England, from the close of the Saxon Heptarchy to the Declaration of American Independence, in familiar verse, adapted to music by B. Carr, Op. XI*. An explanatory note under the title reads as follows:

The following Poetical sketch of events, so intimately connected with our own History, being adapted to Music of the most familiar kind, has been consider'd by several, as a means of improvement for Juvenile Students in History and Music. A Publication of this nature has already appeared in England; but unfit for the purpose intended—the Poetry being mere doggerel, and the Music (tho good) extraneous in its modulation and too difficult of execution to be of service to young pupils, a literary friend has kindly supplied new Poetry—The idea being of using known airs of appropriate title and character for the vocal parts, as well as illustrative symphonies, is taken from T. Carr's Composition to, and arrangement of Roscoe's beautiful little Poem of the Butterfly's Ball.

N.B.—Should this humble effort to combine improvement in other branches of education with the practice of music be received with approbation, other matters of the same kind may be given in some future numbers.

To the biographer, the most interesting and helpful relics of Benjamin Carr are three manuscript books, in his own handwriting. One of these, devoted to sacred music, is in the New York Public Library;

the other two, chiefly secular, are in Mr. Hunt's possession. These books were evidently used by Carr not only for original composition, but also for editing the works of others for publication.

He also published instrumental pieces, a collection of Masses, Litanies, Hymns, Anthems, Psalms, and Motets, and did additional writing for the stage in Philadelphia and New York productions.

After his death in 1831, the Musical Fund Society erected a monument to his memory in St. Peter's Church, Philadelphia. The inscription is a testimonial to his achievements and to his character:

BENJAMIN CARR

a distinguished professor of music
died May 24, 1831, aged 62 years.

Charitable, without ostentation,
faithful and true in his friendship,
with the intelligence of a man
he united the simplicity of a child.

In testimony of the high esteem in which he
was held, this monument is erected by
his friends and associates of the
Musical Fund Society of Philadelphia.

There were many other early immigrants who played an active part in our musical life at this time, and who wrote music of which we have definite knowledge. One of these, H. B. VICTOR, dates back to the Revolution, for he arrived in Philadelphia in 1774. Announcing that he had been "musician to her late Royal Highness, the Princess of Wales, and organist at St. George in London," he offered to instruct the "musical gentry in general . . . on the harpsichord, forte piano, violin, German flute, etc. and in the thorough bass both in theory and practice." The versatile gentleman then sought to startle his public by advertising a concert at which he would play two instruments of his own invention: the one a "Tromba doppia con tympana," on which he was to play first and second trumpet and a pair of annexed kettledrums with the feet, all at once; the other, a "Cymbaline d'amour" which resembled "the musical glasses played by harpsichord keys, never subject to come out of tune."

But it is not as a freak that Victor is most interesting. In 1778 he advertised for publication a work which was a forerunner of our modern *courses* or *methods*. This was *A New Composition of Music, consisting of four separate books, viz.:*

The *Compleat Instructor* for the violin, flute, guitar and harpsichord. Containing the easiest and best method for learners to obtain a proficiency; with some useful directions, lessons, graces, etc. *By H. B. Victor.*

To which is added, A favourite collection of airs, marches, minuets, etc., now in vogue; with some useful pieces for two violins, etc. etc.

JOHN BENTLEY has already been mentioned as the manager of the Philadelphia City Concerts in 1783. In 1785 he became harpsichordist of the Old American Company, and "selected and composed" the music for several of their productions: *Genii of the Rock, The Cave of Enchantment*, and *The Touchstone*. He also figured in the Old American Company as an occasional pantomimist.

Through a controversy which was aired in the newspapers, and which is strikingly similar to the Turner-Morgan dispute in Boston, Bentley's name is associated with WILLIAM BROWN, the composer who published *Three Rondos for the Pianoforte or Harpsichord*, "composed and humbly dedicated to the Honorable Francis Hopkinson, Esqr."

This Brown, something of a trouble-maker, was the first of the musicians to appear in New York after the war, and in August, 1783, he gave New York the last concert it was to hear during the British regime. He then went to Philadelphia, where he offered two concerts at the City Tavern in October, "having been prevailed upon by several gentlemen to continue his stay in Philadelphia, and being inclined to gratify them." In addition to benefit concerts he seems to have participated in Bentley's Subscription Concerts, for in the *Pennsylvania Journal* of February 12, 1785, both Bentley and Henri Capron saw fit to tell the public their side of a dispute to which Brown had probably been treating his friends verbally. It seems that Brown had accused Bentley and Capron of declining to assist at his benefit concerts. Bentley addressed his "card" directly to *Mr. Brown:*

. . . And first, Sir, allow me to enquire, whether at any time, you desired my assistance at your concert; nay, whether by refusing the loan of the harpsichord usually lent, you did not give me room to suppose it was neither wished nor expected?

That you raised an opinion in the public that I occasioned the absence of two performers, is certain; but as truth is contrary to that opinion, I must request you to declare the grounds upon which so invidious an insinuation was founded? The gentlemen alluded to, for reasons which I have no right to control, objected to any further correspondence with Mr. Brown, on footing of favour.

. . . here let me recall to your remembrance your own conduct upon our first acquaintance. Did you not live free of every expence in my house for the whole of last winter, and some months after the concerts were closed? Did this induce you to perform without a premium . . . ? No, Sir, You were supported at my cost; your demand of three pounds for every night's performance was paid; and . . . you were ungrateful enough to traduce me in private, and to attempt my ruin with a most respectable character, whose friendship I had essentially experienced. . . .

Mr. Capron's card appeared above Mr. Bentley's in the same paper:

Mr. Capron being informed that the motives maliciously assigned for his absenting himself from Mr. Brown's benefit concert, may operate to his prejudice; and being solicitous on all occasions to evince the highest respect for the public, he begs leave to observe that he would chearfully have contributed his abilities to the entertainment of the evening, had Mr. Brown condescended to make the request.

. . . In truth Mr. Capron has acquitted himself of every obligation to Mr. Brown, and . . . he could never be again induced to enter into an intercourse of favours: . . . surely it is sufficient triumph . . . that every concert for the benefit of that Gentleman opens a scene of considerable profit, while the only opportunity which the public has had to assist Mr. Capron, scarcely supplied the means to defray his expenses.

If Brown was personally a troublesome character, his abilities as a flutist and musician must have been of a high order, for Capron soon again engaged him for concerts, and later Brown joined Reinagle and Capron in the management of the Subscription Concerts.

HENRI CAPRON was one of the most prominent of the French musicians who came to the United States. He first appeared in Philadelphia (1785), and soon became active in the management of subscription concerts both in Philadelphia and New York. As a cellist he was a

member of the Old American Company orchestra. Among his compositions were a *New Contredance*, a particularly attractive *Favorite Song*
(*Softly as the breezes blowing*) and a "new song" *Delia*. After spending the years 1788 to 1792 in New York he settled permanently in
Philadelphia in 1794, where he became the principal of a French boarding school. In 1793 he kept a music store in Philadelphia with JOHN
CHRISTOPHER MOLLER, a composer, organist, pianist, and editor, who
had appeared in New York as a harpsichordist in 1790.

Moller came to Philadelphia immediately after his concerts in New
York, and took part in the City Concerts both as manager and performer. On many of his programs he appeared with his daughter, a
musical prodigy. In addition to being organist of Zion Church in Philadelphia, he entered partnership with Capron in the music store, and
combined with it a music school. In 1796, Moller moved back to New
York and took Hewitt's place in the management of the City Concerts
with the Van Hagens. When Van Hagen left for Boston, Moller made
an unsuccessful attempt to continue the subscription series.

He was a talented musician, and his compositions had considerable
merit. The New York Library possesses the violin part of six *Sonatas
for the forte piano or harpsichord, with a violin or violoncello accompaniment*, which Moller composed and published in London before
coming to America. *Moller and Capron's Monthly Numbers*, a collection of music published in 1793, of which four issues are still extant,
contained several compositions of Moller, among them a graceful
though innocuous *Sinfonia* and a *Rondo*. He wrote also an *Overture*,
and a *Quartetto* for "harmonica [this was Benjamin Franklin's *ar-
monica*, or musical glasses], two tenors, and violoncello." In addition
there was a *Duetti*, for piano and clarinet, advertised for performance
at one of the 1792 City Concerts in Philadelphia.

ALEXANDER JUHAN (1765–1845) "junior, master of music," who
appeared in Philadelphia in 1783, was probably the son of a James
Juhan, who had come to Charleston as a music teacher in 1771, and
who had announced himself in 1786 at Philadelphia as the maker of
the "Great North American Forte Piano." Some authorities link Juhan
the elder with the Mr. *Joan* who gave the "reading" of *The Beggar's
Opera* in Boston in 1770. Alexander Juhan (believed to have been
born in Halifax and brought to Boston in 1768) was a violinist who

was for a time one of the managers of the City Concerts in Philadelphia, and as a composer he advertised in Charleston (where he lived for a year or two before his return to Philadelphia in 1792) for subscriptions to *A Set of Six Sonatas,* for the pianoforte or harpsichord, "three with an accompaniment for the flute or violin, and three with out"; and a book of twelve songs, with an accompaniment for the same instrument.

Juhan's career provides interest because of his part in another of the controversies that seemed often to trouble the peace of early American music. This time the dispute was based partly on artistic rather than on wholly personal grounds. The trouble came from Juhan's position as conductor of the orchestra at the concerts of ANDREW ADGATE (? –1793), a Philadelphian who founded in 1784 an *Institution for the Encouragement of Church Music,* and in the following year established a *Free School for Spreading the Knowledge of Vocal Music* —which developed into the *Uranian Academy* in 1787.

Adgate was to Philadelphia what Tuckey had been to New York, and what Selby was to Boston. The elaborate "plan" of the Uranian Society, published five days after the Constitutional Convention had first assembled, was the first document on record that urged the necessity and advantage of having music "form a part of every system of education." Philadelphia heard a number of Mr. Adgate's "Vocal Music Concerts" during 1784 and 1785, at which such musicians as Brown and Juhan furnished instrumental numbers. On May 4, 1786, the year of Selby's mammoth concert for prison relief in Boston (January 10), Adgate, no doubt spurred by the review of the Boston concert that had appeared in the *Pennsylvania Herald,* offered Philadelphians *A Grand Concert of Sacred Music,* for the benefit of the Pennsylvania Hospital, Philadelphia Dispensary, and the Poor, for whom there has, hitherto, been no regular provision made. There was a chorus of two hundred and thirty voices, and an orchestra of fifty pieces conducted by Mr. Juhan. Aside from Handel's *Hallelujah* Chorus, and an Anthem by A. Williams (probably Aaron Williams, an English psalmodist), the vocal numbers were principally devoted to American composers—Lyon, Billings, and Tuckey.

The *Pennsylvania Packet,* in its extended review of the concert, had this to say of the conducting:

To the skill and attention of Mr. Adgate, in training and instructing the voices, and of Mr. Juhan, in arranging and leading the instruments, may be attributed that forcible and uniform effect so manifestly produced throughout the exhibition.

Juhan evidently had a different opinion of Mr. Adgate's share in the proceedings, for in the following year, prior to the first concert of the new Uranian Society, he wrote to the *Pennsylvania Packet* (April 5, 1787):

. . . the subscriber thinks it his duty to state the reasons that have induced him to decline any part in the concert, intended to be performed . . . the 12th instant.

The applause of some . . . has certainly so far elevated the subscriber in his own opinion that he rates himself superior to the instruction of a person, who, with little knowledge in the theory, is confined in the practice of music to the humble province of Solfa. . . .

Another and very forcible reason for the subscriber's conduct upon this occasion, is the neglect of consulting the principal performers as to the pieces of music, and the arrangement of the band. . . . It would surely therefore have improved the general effect of the entertainment and could not have been considered as a very extraordinary indulgence, had those who were best able to determine upon the respective powers of the performers, been invited to select the music and to suggest what could be attempted with the greatest probability of success. . . .

Juhan's "card" closed with the statement that his work at Adgate's concerts had entailed great sacrifices, interfered with his teaching, and the necessary exertions had injured his health. Adgate's reply was printed in the same paper, two days later:

Before the Plan of the Uranian Academy was drawn . . . I mentioned to Mr. Juhan that I had it in view to establish an institution, at which the poor might be instructed in church music, free of expense; and, as the first measure, . . . to have a concert performed. . . . I introduced the subject that I might have the opportunity of consulting him thereon and engaging him as a principal in carrying the concert into effect. His answer to my proposition . . . was immediate and unequivocal! *"We have agreed not to play any more for the poor."* This peremptory declaration . . . foreclosed effectually all consultation. I believed Mr. Juhan, and, in consequence, took my measures, independently of him, as well as I was able . . . he had an

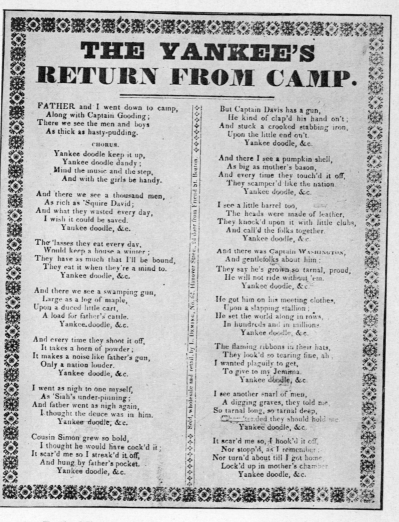

THE YANKEE'S RETURN FROM CAMP.

FATHER and I went down to camp,
  Along with Captain Gooding;
There we see the men and boys
  As thick as hasty-pudding.

CHORUS.

Yankee doodle keep it up,
  Yankee doodle dandy;
Mind the music and the step,
  And with the girls be handy.

And there we see a thousand men,
  As rich as 'Squire David;
And what they wasted every day,
  I wish it could be saved.
    Yankee doodle, &c.

The 'lasses they eat every day,
  Would keep a house a winter;
They have as much that I'll be bound,
  They eat it when they're a mind to.
    Yankee doodle, &c.

And there we see a swamping gun,
  Large as a log of maple,
Upon a duced little cart,
  A load for father's cattle.
    Yankee doodle, &c.

And every time they shoot it off,
  It takes a horn of powder;
It makes a noise like father's gun,
  Only a nation louder.
    Yankee doodle, &c.

I went as nigh to one myself,
  As 'Siah's under-pinning;
And father went as nigh again,
  I thought the deuce was in him.
    Yankee doodle, &c.

Cousin Simon grew so bold,
  I thought he would have cock'd it;
It scar'd me so I streak'd it off,
  And hung by father's pocket.
    Yankee doodle, &c.

But Captain Davis has a gun,
  He kind of clap'd his hand on't;
And stuck a crooked stabbing iron,
  Upon the little end on't.
    Yankee doodle, &c.

And there I see a pumpkin shell,
  As big as mother's bason,
And every time they touch'd it off,
  They scamper'd like the nation.
    Yankee doodle, &c.

I see a little barrel too,
  The heads were made of leather,
They knock'd upon it with little clubs,
  And call'd the folks together.
    Yankee doodle, &c.

And there was Captain WASHINGTON,
  And gentlefolks about him;
They say he's grown so tarnal, proud,
  He will not ride without 'em.
    Yankee doodle, &c.

He got him on his meeting clothes,
  Upon a slapping stallion;
He set the world along in rows,
  In hundreds and in millions.
    Yankee doodle, &c.

The flaming ribbons in their hats,
  They look'd so tearing fine, ah,
I wanted plaguily to get,
  To give to my Jemima.
    Yankee doodle, &c.

I see another snarl of men,
  A digging graves, they told me,
So tarnal long, so tarnal deep,
  They 'tended they should hold me.
    Yankee doodle, &c.

It scar'd me so, I hook'd it off,
  Nor stopp'd, as I remember,
Nor turn'd about till I got home,
  Lock'd up in mother's chamber.
    Yankee doodle, &c.

Sold, wholesale and retail, by L. DEMING, No. 62, Hanover Street, 2d door from Friend St. Boston.

An Early Nineteenth-Century Broadside of *Yankee Doodle*
(See pages 113–118)

The Bettmann Archive

Francis Scott Key
(See pages 122–124)

undoubted right to be the sole judge of what would contribute most essentially to his *interest* and *health*.

Consequently, the Uranian Concert, on April 12, was given without the assistance of either Mr. Juhan or Mr. Brown, who, known to be troublesome, may have been in league with Juhan in the dispute. The program again contained works of Tuckey, Lyon, and Billings, as well as those of Handel, Arne, and Arnold. Further Uranian concerts and "concerts of sacred music for benevolent purposes" may be traced through the following years. Adgate died in 1793 during the yellow fever epidemic, and left behind him several publications: *Lessons for the Uranian Society* and *Uranian Instructions* (1785–87); *Select Psalms and Hymns* (1787); *Rudiments of Music* (1788); *Selection of Sacred Harmony* (1788).

The violinist who took Juhan's place as soloist at the First Uranian Concert was PHILIP PHILE (? –1793), a composer who played a concerto of his own on the occasion. Phile had come to Philadelphia before 1784, when he appeared in a concert advertised for his benefit. Soon he was associated with the Old American Company orchestra, and until his death in 1793 he was to be found either in New York or Philadelphia, participating in concerts and in the orchestras of the theatres. Phile is important historically because of his authorship of the famous *President's March*, now known as the musical setting of *Hail Columbia*, the words by Joseph Hopkinson, son of Francis Hopkinson. Phile also wrote a piece called *Harmony Music*, which was announced for performance at Gray's Gardens, a Philadelphia summer retreat where the Concerts of "harmonial music" were rendered by two clarinets, two French horns, two bassoons, and one flute.

The name of PHILIP ROTH (? –1804) is linked with that of Phile, because Roth was formerly supposed by some to have been the composer of the *President's March*. Roth's residence in America dates back to 1771, when he appeared in a concert for the benefit of John M'Lean in Philadelphia. He was presented as "Master of the Band belonging to his Majesty's Royal Regiment of North British Fusiliers," and his contribution to the program was an *Overture*, composed for the occasion. From 1785 to 1804, the year of his death, he lived in Philadelphia as a music teacher. His advertisements showed that he was fully as versatile as any of his colleagues, for he taught all kinds of Instrumental Music in the shortest manner [short cuts to knowledge are not altogether a purely twentieth century demand], viz: Harpsichord or Piano Forte, Guitar, Flute, Hautboy, Clarinet, Bassoon, French Horn, Harp and Thorough-Bass, which is the Ground of Music. . . .

William McKoy described him as

of middle size and height. His face was truly German in expression; dark grey eyes and bushy eyebrows, round pointed nose, prominent lips, and parted chin. He took snuff immoderately, having his ruffles and vest usually sprinkled with grains of rappee. He was considered an eccentric and a kind of drole.

GEORGE SCHETKY (1776–1831) was a Scotch musician who, according to Madeira, was a nephew of Reinagle. Madeira said that he came to Philadelphia to live with his uncle in 1792. This date is incorrect, for Schetky appeared as a cellist on Philadelphia concert programs as early as 1787. About 1800 he was in partnership with Carr in the music publishing business, and later became one of the prominent founders of the Musical Fund Society. His name appears frequently on concert programs of this period as the author of the military band arrangement of Kotzwara's *Battle of Prague*.

MRS. MARY ANN POWNALL (1751–1796), who had been known in England as Mrs. Wrighten, was one of the most popular actresses and singers in the Old American Company. She first came to Boston in 1792, for the American Company was playing at the Federal Street Theatre that season. She had splendid dramatic and vocal gifts and was also prolific as a composer. She wrote both words and music of many songs that were featured in concerts and in operas and plays. Among them were *Advice to the Ladies of Boston*, and *Address to the Ladies of Charleston*; *Jemmy of the Glen* (copy in the Library of Congress); *Mrs. Pownal's Adres* (sic), in behalf of French musicians, "delivered on her benefit concert night to a very crowded audience: to which are added, Pastoral songs; written by herself at an early period of life," *On by the spur of valeur*; *Kiss me now or never*; *Poor Tom Bowling*; *Italian Song*; *My Poll and my partner Joe*; *A smile from the girl of my heart*; *'Bly the Colin* and *Cottage Boy*.

Mrs. Pownall also paid homage to the President with a song, *Wash-*

ington. The New York Library possesses a copy of *Primroses,* "a favorite song by Mrs. Pownall, with additions and alterations by a lady." She died in Charleston in 1796, following the shock she received when her daughter eloped with a pantomimist named Alexander Placide.

A violoncellist and composer named DEMARQUE may have been one of the musicians who fled with Pelissier from Cape François and arrived in America in 1793. At any rate, he first appeared in that year as a concert artist in Baltimore, and soon afterwards became a prominent member of the Wignell and Reinagle orchestra at the Chestnut Street Theatre in Philadelphia. He also played in the City Theatre Orchestra in Charleston. Demarque wrote several pieces for the cello, one of them a Concerto, and he also composed music for several pantomimes: *The Elopement, Harlequin Shipwreck'd,* the *Miraculous Mill,* and *Rural Revels.*

Nor may we forget JOHN HENRY SCHMIDT, the Dutch organist, composer, and music dealer, who first came to New York in 1793, and was later organist at St. Peter's in Philadelphia. Whether or not he was the same Mr. Smith who had offered lectures in Philadelphia in 1788, "interspersed with music and singing," he nevertheless composed a Sonata which he advertised with this comprehensive announcement:

His [Schmidt's] easy Sonata for beginners, consisting in a larghetto, minuet and trio, and Yankee Doodle, turned into a fashionable rondo, may be had of him at No. 50 Green street, where he has furnished rooms to let.

As the century closes, the flirtation and the courtship end. Euterpe enters the trials of early married life, for America has definitely taken her to its bosom and knows her charms. In the wilderness she will clear the forest.

Her way has not been easy. The early New Englanders would admit her only to their churches, and then only upon pledge of what they considered the utmost decorum. Philadelphians loved her, but the Quakers would have none of her themselves, and tried to interfere in her friendship with their broader-minded neighbors.

But youth will have its way, and even though it was necessary for new arrivals to point out Euterpe's perennial charms and beauty, Hopkinson the aristocrat, Lyon the clergyman, and Billings the tanner who awakened Boston, all contrived to keep the Goddess on native soil. And then Selby in Boston, Tuckey in New York, and Adgate in Philadelphia showed the joys of choral music. Reinagle, Carr, Hewitt, Taylor, and their fellows came from Europe to tell of Euterpe's doings abroad, and to show how her gifts might be used. These are names and faces we shall meet in later chapters, for their lives and influence do not end in this century, though it was in the eighteenth century that they were most important, for their coming hastened Euterpe's conquest of America.

PART TWO

1800–1860

EUTERPE CLEARS THE FOREST

CHAPTER FOUR

Our First National Airs

I. YANKEE DOODLE

OUR early national airs have survived in spite of the many unkind things that have been said about them. It is easy to pick flaws in any one of them, yet they are all so vital that they fire our emotions and force us to sing with the crowd. Relegate *Yankee Doodle* to the category of jingle, *Hail Columbia* to mere bombast, and cry against the impossibly wide vocal range of the *Star-Spangled Banner*, yet the songs persist. They were not intended as national anthems when they were written; no patriotic organizations commissioned their composers to write them, and none of their authors realized how far his influence would reach.

Many pretty stories are attached to our national ballads, some of them so fanciful that it is a pity to explode them. Yet tireless researchers have been at work, and it becomes a duty to consult them and to select between the true and the false, where possible. *Yankee Doodle* has caused more quarrels between historians and scholars than any of our songs, for this impertinent, jolly little tune has thumbed its nose at many a dignified sage, and grayed hundreds of hairs by hiding its origin.

The controversy has covered about everything a song can possess— its name, its words, and its tune, and as yet little has been settled. When O. G. Sonneck was chief of the Music Division of the Library of Congress, he was commissioned to examine all of the traditions regarding the origin of *Yankee Doodle*, as well as our other airs, and to decide which were right and which were wrong. As far as *Yankee Doodle* was concerned, he summed up his examination of all available evidence by writing: "The origin of *Yankee Doodle* remains as mysterious as ever, unless it be deemed a positive result to have eliminated almost every theory thus far advanced and thus by the process of elimination to have paved the way for an eventual solution of the 'puzzle.' " [1] Sonneck may not have been altogether pessimistic—he apparently expected further evidence to turn up. Unfortunately, the almost forty years that have passed since his report was published have produced nothing conclusive.

Today the term *Yankee* means a New Englander, a term of whimsical approval when used by his friends, and one of derision when uttered by his less enthusiastic countrymen from the South. Exactly where the word came from and what it meant is a mystery, though there are plenty to tell of their theories. Some would have it the Indians' corruption of the word "English," or if you prefer French, "Anglais." Even Washington Irving's satirical *Diedrich Knickerbocker's History of New York* has been taken seriously when it suggests that

the simple aborigines of the land . . . discovering that they [the settlers] were a lively, good-humoured race of men . . . gave them the name of *Yanokies,* which . . . signifies silent men—a waggish appellation, since shortened into the familiar epithet of *Yankees,* which they retain unto the present day.

Friends of the *Yankees* claim that back in 1713 the word was used as a superlative of excellence. A "Yankee" horse or a "Yankee" team denoted the last word in fine horse flesh. One etymologist has gone so far as to claim that the word *Yankee* was a corruption of "Yorkshire." But whether it meant good or evil, and from whatever source it may have been derived, it was a far from complimentary term when used by the British just before the Revolution. It was hurled at the colonists with the utmost scorn by the British commanding officer at the Boston Massacre.

Doodle is not quite so baffling, though the reader may still choose the theory that pleases him best, and have as good a chance at winning as his neighbor. The term may be traced in English dramatic literature as far back as 1629, when one of the characters in *The Lover's Melancholy* shouts, "Vanish, doodles, vanish!" Possibly the word is a corruption of *do little,* and means a simpleton or a silly. Another theory holds that it is derived from "tootle," which, in turn, springing from

[1] *Report on The Star-Spangled Banner, Hail Columbia, America, Yankee Doodle.* Washington, Library of Congress, 1909.

the "tooting" into German flutes that was such a popular occupation of eighteenth-century gentlemen, would indicate that *Yankee Doodle* was a purely instrumental tune at first, and that the many different sets of words were added later. In other words, the *Yankee Doodle* was the Yankee air that was "tootled" on the flute. This theory has some logic to support it. Most of the early printed versions had no words, and the very diversity of the later verses suggests that it was first known as an instrumental air.

Theories regarding the origin of the tune are more numerous than those pertaining to the title. Few have survived critical examination. The legend that it was sung in the time of Charles I and of Cromwell cannot be proved; the tunes from these times bear no relation to our *Yankee Doodle*. The lines

> Lucy Locket lost her locket
> Kitty Fisher found it

show an early nineteenth-century *use* of the tune, rather than its origin. It could hardly have been composed during the Revolution for it is one of the tunes mentioned in Andrew Barton's *The Disappointment*, in 1767. Suppositions that it is of Spanish, Dutch, Hungarian, and German origin are highly improbable. The burden of proof is on the claimants.

While there are contemporary references to *Yankee Doodle* as early as 1767, its first known appearance in print did not occur until 1782, when it appeared in James Aird's *Selection of Scotch, English, Irish and Foreign Airs, for the fife, violin or German flute*, published in Glasgow. The discovery of this first printed version was made by Mr. Frank Kidson, who believes that the tune may be of American origin, for the same volume contains several "Virginia" airs, a *Negro Jig*, and other tunes from America. It was probably first printed in America as part of Benjamin Carr's popular *Federal Overture*, composed in 1794 and published in 1795. The *Overture* was a potpourri of such airs as *Yankee Doodle, La Carmagnole, Caira*, the *Marseillaise Hymn, Oh, Dear, What Can the Matter Be*, and others.

Several stories center around the French-Indian War, principally with the army of General Amherst. An early account from *Farmer & Moore's Literary Journal* (1824) tells the following story:

. . . the British army lay encamped in the summer of 1755, on the eastern bank of the Hudson, a little south of the city of Albany. . . . In the early part of June the eastern troops (Colonial) began to pour in, company after company, and such a motley assemblage of men never before thronged together on such an occasion. It would . . . have relaxed the gravity of an anchorite to have seen the descendants of the Puritans making through the streets of our ancient city to take their station on the left of the British army, some with long coats, some with short coats, and some with no coats at all. . . . Their march, their accoutrements, and the whole arrangement of their troops furnished material of amusement to the wits of the British army. Among the club of wits that belonged to the British army there was a physician attached to the staff, by the name of *Doctor Schackburg*, who combined with the science of the surgeon the skill and talents of a musician. To please Brother Jonathan he composed a tune, and, with much gravity, recommended it to the officers as one of the most celebrated airs of martial musick. The joke took, to the no small amusement of the British Corps. Brother Jonathan exclaimed that it was a "nation fine," and in a few days nothing was heard in the Provincial camp but "Yankee Doodle"!

With characteristic thoroughness, Sonneck analyzed this theory in his report, tracing Dr. Shuckburg's (this is the proper spelling) probable whereabouts throughout this entire period. He found it extremely unlikely that Shuckburg was either in Albany in the summer of 1755, or attached to General Amherst's army. It is possible, however, that the Doctor was with General Abercrombie's division when it was encamped on the Van Rensselaer estate near Albany, in 1758, and it is plausible that he should have written humorous *Yankee Doodle* verses to an existing familiar tune. Which of the many sets of verses he wrote cannot be determined.

There is one fact in the history of *Yankee Doodle* that may be accepted without reservation. It was used by the British to make fun of the Yankees, and later adopted by the Yankees it taunted as their own song. One of the favorite pastimes of the British troops was to gather in front of the New England churches and sing *Yankee Doodle* as the congregations were singing their psalms. When Lord Percy's troops marched out of Boston on an April night in 1775, bound for Lexington to aid in the capture of John Hancock and Samuel Adams, they kept step to the strains of *Yankee Doodle*. When the colonials routed British troops at Concord, they immediately appropriated the song as their own, and since then it has been the exclusive property of Americans.

Tradition has it that when Cornwallis surrendered at Yorktown and the British band played *The World Turned Upside Down*, the American band replied with *Yankee Doodle*. Unfortunately, this incident is apparently mentioned only in later accounts, and its truth cannot be established by any contemporary evidence that has as yet come to light. As for the British playing *The World Turned Upside Down*, that story was widely circulated by John Fiske in *The American Revolution*, published in 1891, so it, too, is in the realm of legend. A poem with that title appeared in *The Gentleman's Magazine* in 1767 (vol. 36, page 140), stating that it was to be sung to the old English air *Derry Down*. Unfortunately, the verses do not fit satisfactorily any known version of that tune.

It is probable that the lines containing *Yankee* and *Doodle* did not appear in England until considerably after 1770, though they were fairly current in America by 1767. The verse that is best known today:

> Yankee Doodle came to town
>   Riding on a pony
> Stuck a feather in his cap
>   And called it macaroni

may have had an origin which had nothing to do with the *Yankee Doodle* of colonial America. Katharine Elwes Thomas, in *The Real Personages of Mother Goose*,[2] states that the original Yankee Doodle was Prince Rupert. Accordingly, if the Yankee Doodle of the Macaroni was actually from Mother Goose, then he had no connection with our tune until much later. And if "Yankee" used to be "Nanky," then the jingle is not even the origin of the title.

About 1775, when John Hancock was the bane of the British, this verse appeared:

> Yankee Doodle came to town
>   For to buy a firelock:
> We will tar and feather him
>   And so we will John Hancock.

An accompanying illustration shows a broadside of *Yankee Doodle* printed in Boston about 1835. For many years this was the current ver-

[2] New York: Lothrop, Lee & Shepard, 1930.

sion of *Yankee Doodle*, and some writers connect it with Dr. Shuckburg. It is not likely that this doggerel goes back as far as 1758, and
Sonneck inclined to the belief that it originated in the vicinity of the
"Provincial Camp" (near Cambridge) in 1775 and 1776. George
Washington's arrival at this camp July 2, 1775, after he had been appointed commander-in-chief of the American Army, would account for
the reference to *Captain* Washington.

But whatever the controversies, whatever words were sung at certain
times, and whatever the real origin of the tune, the description contained in one of the stanzas is indisputable:

> It suits for feasts, it suits for fun;
> And just as well for fighting.

2. HAIL COLUMBIA

While *Yankee Doodle* was associated principally with the Revolution, *Hail Columbia* had its origin in the war we almost had with
France in 1798. The French Revolution had broken out nine years
before, and in 1793, France was at war with England and Prussia. The
anti-Federalist party in America favored our supporting the French,
but President Washington kept us neutral. When John Adams was
inaugurated in 1797, matters had come to a crisis. The French government had so insulted our ministers and violated our rights, that by
1798 an actual state of war existed with France, though it was never
formally declared by Congress.

It was at this time that *Hail Columbia* came into being. The words
were written by JOSEPH HOPKINSON, a young man of twenty-eight, the
son of Francis Hopkinson, our first native composer. Hopkinson has
told the story of the song himself:

"Hail Columbia" was written in the summer of 1798, when war with
France was thought to be inevitable. Congress was then in session in Philadelphia, debating upon that important subject, and acts of hostility had
actually taken place. The contest between England and France was still
raging, and the people of the United States were divided into parties for the
one side or the other, some thinking that policy and duty required us to
espouse the cause of "republican France" as she was called, while others were

for connecting ourselves with England, under the belief that she was the great preservative power of good principles and safe government. The violation of our rights by both belligerents was forcing us from the wise and just policy of President Washington, which was to do equal justice to both but to part with neither, and to preserve an honest and strict neutrality between them. The prospect of a rupture with France was exceedingly offensive to the portion of the people who espoused her cause, and the violence of the spirit of party had never risen higher, I think not so high, in our country, as it did at that time upon that question.

The theatre was then open in our city [Philadelphia]. A young man belonging to it [Gilbert Fox], whose talent was high as a singer, was about to take a benefit. I had known him when he was at school. On this acquaintance he called on me one Saturday afternoon, his benefit being announced for the following Monday. His prospects were very disheartening; but he said that if he could get a patriotic song adapted to the "President's March" he did not doubt a full house; that the poets of the theatrical corps had been trying to accomplish it, but had not succeeded. I told him I would try what I could do for him. He came the next afternoon, and the song, such as it is, was ready for him. The object of the author was to get up an American spirit which should be independent of, and above the interests, passion and policy of both belligerents, and look and feel exclusively for our honor and rights. No allusion is made to France or England, or the quarrel between them, or to the question of which was most in fault in their treatment of us. Of course the song found favor with both parties, for both were American, at least neither could disown the sentiments and feelings it indicated. Such is the history of this song, which has endured infinitely beyond the expectation of the author, as it is beyond any merit it can boast of except that of being truly and exclusively patriotic in its sentiment and spirit.

The advertisements of the benefit were designed to arouse the curiosity of the public:

Mr. Fox's night. On Wednesday Evening, April 25. By Desire will be presented . . . a Play, interspersed with Songs in three Acts, called *The Italian Monk* . . . after which an entire *New Song* (written by a Citizen of Philadelphia) to the tune of the "President's March" will be sung by Mr. Fox; accompanied by the Full Band and the following *Grand Chorus:*

> Firm united let us be
> Rallying around our Liberty
> As a band of brothers join'd
> Peace and Safety we shall find!

Two days after the performance, Benjamin Carr, then a music publisher in Philadelphia, advertised publication of the song:

. . . the very New Federal Song, written to the tune of the President's March, by J. Hopkinson, Esq. And sung by M. Fox, at the New Theatre with great applause, ornamented with a very elegant portrait of the President.

For many years there was a lively controversy as to which of existing editions was the first, particularly since some of them were "ornamented with a very elegant portrait" of George Washington, and others with an eagle. In 1920 a copy was discovered bearing a portrait of John Adams, and since he was President in 1798, this is undoubtedly the first edition. In recent years several other first-edition copies have been discovered and are now deposited in the Library of Congress, the Historical Society of Pennsylvania, and in several private collections, including that of Mr. Arthur Billings Hunt of Brooklyn, New York, who was the first to discover the original edition.

There have been many controversies also on the origin of the *President's March*, but its date and authorship have been satisfactorily established. It is generally accepted that the *March* was composed in honor of George Washington's becoming President in 1789, and all authorities are agreed that it dates before 1793.

Its authorship is even clearer and more definite than the date of its origin, although there have been several claimants to the honor. For example, William McKoy in 1829 stated that the *March* was composed by a German teacher of music in Philadelphia, named Johannes Roat, or Roth, "the seat of the Federal Government . . . being removed to Philadelphia and in honour of the new President Washington, then residing at No. 190 High Street."

He undoubtedly referred to the Philip Roth we discussed in a previous chapter, but Roth lived until 1804, after the song was famous. According to present knowledge, he never claimed authorship of the piece. Moreover, Philadelphia did not become the seat of the Government until 1790 and, if a new march had been played in honor of General Washington when he was accorded "an elegant Entertainment of 250 covers at the City Tavern" in Philadelphia on April 20 (1789), some of the newspapers would certainly have mentioned the fact.

The other composer who appears to have a claim is Philip Phile, who died in Philadelphia in 1793. For many years the claim in Phile's behalf was as difficult to prove as that of Roth, but a number of years ago the collection of former Governor Pennypacker of Pennsylvania yielded an unnumbered page, torn from an engraved music collection, bearing two marches. One of these was the *President's March* by Phile, the other a *March* by Moller. This music-sheet was issued about 1793, and it seems to establish Phile's authorship of the *President's March* beyond reasonable doubt.

3. THE STAR-SPANGLED BANNER

Up to the time of the Spanish-American War, *Hail Columbia* shared honors with the *Star-Spangled Banner* as one of our national anthems, and it was not until Admiral Dewey officially designated the *Star-Spangled Banner* that *Hail Columbia* lost its place. From that time, the Army and Navy regulations have included a statement that when an occasion arose on which the national anthem of the United States was required, *The Star-Spangled Banner* should be played. These regulations, however, governed only the Armed Forces, not the civilian population, and the confusion continued until the Seventy-first Congress, during its Third Session, passed Public No. 823 which designated as our national anthem "the composition consisting of the words and music known as *The Star-Spangled Banner.*" This bill was signed by President Hoover on March 3, 1931, the day before he left office.

Our national anthem had a dramatic birth. During the War of 1812, one of the principal stratagems of the British had been to blockade Chesapeake Bay. Reinforcements arrived from England in August, 1814, intending that the major portion of the fleet would be moved around for the attack on New Orleans. Before departing, however, the British wished to teach the upstarts a lesson. Washington was attacked and easily taken, since nothing but untrained militia defended it. After burning many public buildings, including the Capitol, they returned to their boats in the bay.

On their way to Washington, Dr. Beanes, a leading physician of Upper Marlborough, Maryland, proved to be something of a "collaborationist," lavishly entertaining some British officers, who in return had his property protected from marauding soldiers. After the main body of troops had safely passed Upper Marlborough on their way back to their ships, Dr. Beanes turned his coat back again, and had three stragglers arrested. Unfortunately for him, he turned it a little too soon. The British learned of his "treachery" and sent a detachment back to release their men and take Dr. Beanes prisoner. Friends attempted to get him released, but he was unceremoniously loaded on the ships for a trip to Halifax.

Knowing that a young lawyer named FRANCIS SCOTT KEY (1779–1843) was an acquaintance of Dr. Beanes and that he had influential connections in Washington, the friends asked Key to intercede. He left Washington on September 2, armed with a letter to Colonel John S. Skinner, the cartel agent for the United States who was stationed in Baltimore. Boarding an unidentified sloop, the party reached the British fleet off the mouth of the Potomac on September 7. Encouraged by their easy success in Washington, the British had meanwhile decided to attack Baltimore. The city had been one of the most ardent proponents of the war in the first place and had served as one of the chief bases for privateers who had been taking the place of our practically nonexistent Navy.

Key and Skinner finally prevailed on the British to release Dr. Beanes, but all three, together with their crew of fourteen, were held on the British ships for fear they might reveal the plans for the new attack. The fleet started up the bay on the eighth, arriving off Baltimore harbor during Sunday church services on the eleventh. Troops were landed on North Point, and early the next morning they started along the northern shore of the harbor to attack Baltimore from the side. To support the land attack, a group of small bombing vessels were moved up the harbor to make a frontal attack on Fort McHenry.

Unfortunately for the British, their burning of the Capitol had so electrified all the large cities along the eastern coast that the citizens, from beggars to bankers, had pitched in to build fortifications and trenches surrounding their cities. Consequently, Key and his friends, who had been put aboard their own flag-of-truce ship under guard with orders not to attempt to land, had the thrill of watching a far more stubborn resistance than that which had been put up on the outskirts of Washington. Since Key had taken a conspicuous part in that engagement, he knew from personal experience what it was like to retreat before the British, and he also knew what would happen to Baltimore if the city was taken.

All during the night of the thirteenth he stayed on deck watching the rockets arching about the Fort and exploding in mid-air. He knew that some small boats were going to try to sneak past Fort McHenry under cover of darkness, and when the firing ceased around one o'clock on the fourteenth, he had no way of telling whether their mission had been successful. As time wore on, the tension became terrific, until as the dawn crept out of the East, he gradually saw the outlines of the fort through the drizzle and mist, and suddenly discovered that the flag was still flying. This was too much for his emotional nature. Inspired by his countrymen's triumph he took an envelope from his pocket and feverishly wrote the words of the *Star-Spangled Banner*, adapting them to one of the most popular songs of the period, *To Anacreon in Heaven*. The next day a printer struck off a handbill with the poem; it was sung that night in a tavern, a week later it was printed in a Baltimore newspaper, and since then its career has been history.

This story, in effect, has never been disputed; controversies have been confined to such details as to who the printer was, who first sang it and where, and what has become of the envelope on which Key wrote his first sketches. The manuscript preserved in the Walters Art Gallery in Baltimore is probably the first complete copy the author made from his first notes. It is obviously not the draft he made on the flag-of-truce ship.

Copies of the handbill, or broadside, are still in existence. It bore the title *Defence of Fort McHenry*, and following a brief description of the circumstances under which the poem was written, designates the tune to which it is sung—*To Anacreon in Heaven*. Recently, through the research of Virginia Larkin Redway, it has been established that the first sheet-music edition of the song was published by Joseph Carr of Baltimore, father of Benjamin Carr, and was arranged by a younger son Thomas. Probably this edition was issued not later than October 19, 1814, or about a month after the bombardment. According to the papers of the Carr family, now in the possession of descendants, Key called on Carr and requested him to arrange the song and adapt his words to the music. Presumably the title of the song was agreed upon at that meeting, for the Carr edition is entitled *The Star-Spangled Banner.*[1]

It has been claimed that Key had no music in mind, and that either the printer or some early singer discovered that its meter would match the tune, accent for accent. It is hard to see how these legends ever grew, since it is preposterous to suppose that anyone would just happen to write a verse in such a complicated verse structure. They have now been disproved quite definitely. Not only was the Anacreontic Song one of the three most parodied melodies of the period (nearly a hundred sets of verses, mostly patriotic, have been found in the songsters of that day, but Key had written another parody earlier and sung it himself at a dinner in honor of Stephen Decatur early in December, 1805. Key used several ideas from this earlier poem in *The Star-Spangled Banner,* and thus there can be no doubt that the tunes were intended to be the same.

The authorship of the tune has never been satisfactorily established, although a vast amount of research has been conducted over a period of more than half a century. For a time during the last century the music of *To Anacreon in Heaven* was widely credited to the English scholar and composer SAMUEL ARNOLD (1740–1803), presumably because he was the director of the symphony concerts which took up the first three hours of the meetings of the Anacreontic Society. In 1873, William Chappell advanced a theory, later adopted by other scholars —notably Oscar George Theodore Sonneck—that the composer was actually JOHN STAFFORD SMITH (1750–1836). The evidence is much too complex to present, let alone analyze, here, but it will be sufficient to state that for a time it was quite generally accepted. Closer examination of the evidence, however, reveals it to be extremely equivocal, and there are a growing number of people who suspect that the attribution was mistaken. It is entirely possible that the author of the words simply adapted them to an earlier melody whose source has not yet been located. Ralph Tomlinson, a lawyer of Lincoln's Inn and one of the presidents of the Anacreontic Society in London, is regularly given as the author of the words in all the early editions of the song, but no composer is ever mentioned. In itself, this would be a little startling in case the music had been specifically written for the song by men of the

[1] Joseph Muller, *The Star-Spangled Banner*, New York: G. A. Baker & Co., 1935.

standing of Arnold or Smith. Whatever the origin of the tune, Tomlinson made a very competent, if not exactly inspired, job of the words. They are addressed to Anacreon, the famous lyric poet of Greece around 500 B.C., whose verses became increasingly popular during the course of the eighteenth century. Inspired by love and wine, his poems sometimes advise continence—a practice he may have followed himself, since he lived to his eighty-fifth year, only to choke to death on a grape seed. The song begins:

> To Anacreon in Heaven, where he sat in full glee,
> A few sons of harmony sent a petition,
> That he their inspirer and patron would be; . . .

And each of its six stanzas end with an adaptation of the couplet:

> And, besides, I'll instruct ye, like me, to intwine
> The myrtle of Venus with Bacchus's vine.

Just when the song reached these shores cannot be definitely established, since the country depended largely on imported songbooks for its music. It was not included in any of the fifteen extant songsters which were printed here between 1786 and 1794, but one parody— "The genius of France from his star begem'd throne"—appeared in a New York newspaper in 1793. *To Anacreon* was included in two songsters published in 1795, and its popularity seems to have increased rapidly after that date. Whatever implications of conviviality the song may have had in England were soon combined with expressions of patriotism, and new parodies were constantly being written for Fourth of July banquets and for dinners in honor of military heroes. A few sample first lines are:

"Ye sons of Columbia, determined to keep"
"To Columbia, who gladly reclin'd at her ease"
"Ye sons of Columbia, unite in the cause"
"Brave sons of Columbia, your triumph behold."
"In years which are past, when America fought"
"Columbians, arise; let the cannon resound"
"When our sky was illuminated by freedom's bright dawn"
"Hark! the trumpet of war from the East sounds alarm."
"Of the victory won over tyranny's power"

In June, 1798, the Massachusetts Charitable Fire Society, at its ban-
quet in Boston, sang a song it had commissioned Robert Treat Paine
to write for the occasion. This was *Adams and Liberty*, to the tune *To
Anacreon in Heaven*. Paine is said to have received $750 for his copy-
right to the song. The author's name was originally Thomas, and he is
frequently confused with the early patriot and freethinker of the same
name. As a young man he was much struck with the stage and its gayer
ways. His father, Robert Treat Paine, a signer of the Declaration of
Independence, disapproved, and there was an estrangement. When an
older brother, who also bore the name Robert Treat, died, Thomas took
his brother's name in an effort to get back into the good graces of his
family. The reconciliation lasted only a few months, however, and
eventually he died in drunken destitution. It was not to be expected
that *Adams and Liberty* would have long life. No song with a title
referring to a single president could become a permanent national
anthem.

One more set of verses is worthy of comment—*The Battle of the
Wabash*. The battle was the famous engagement at Tippecanoe that
made William Henry Harrison famous (November 4, 1811). A music-
sheet containing this poem gives also the words and music of *To Anacreon in Heaven*, and facing the first page of music, the verses of the
Star-Spangled Banner are printed under the title *Fort McHenry, or
The Star-Spangled Banner*. This is the only known music-sheet on which
the words of both *To Anacreon in Heaven* and *The Star-Spangled
Banner* are printed.

4. AMERICA

The song *America* is unique among our early national airs; its origin
is associated with no war, and it voices no belligerent sentiments. In
this regard it is truly our national *hymn*. The complaint that its tune is
British in origin may be viewed from two sides. Before the Revolution
it belonged to our British colonial ancestors as fully as it did to their
brothers in the mother country. After we were independent of England,
our fathers kept the English language and their English customs. Why
should they have abandoned their English anthem, so long as it dropped
its allusion to their former monarch?

New verses were plenteous: *God Save America, God Save George Washington, God Save the Thirteen States, God Save the President*. A pioneer suffragette in 1795 went so far as to write a poem called *Rights of Woman*, which began

> God save each female's right
> Show to her ravish'd sight
> Woman is free.

Traditions about the origin of the tune are numerous. It has been claimed that it was taken from a Swiss hymn, written to celebrate the victory of ancient Geneva over the troops of the Duke of Savoy in the early seventeenth century, and was some years later arranged by DR. JOHN BULL (1563–1628), the English composer. Some say that early in the eighteenth century the French musician Lully made it into a French patriotic song in honor of Louis XIV, and that Handel arranged it as a song in praise of the Elector of Hanover who became George I of England. These are merely legends, but the fact remains that the tune is used in many countries.

It is probable that it was really written by HENRY CAREY (1685?– 1743), the English composer of *Sally in our Alley*. Carey sang the song, with the words "God Save Great George our King," at a tavern in Cornhill in 1740 on the occasion of a dinner party held to celebrate Admiral Vernon's capture of Porto Bello. He announced that the words and music were his own, and it is probable that they were, for he would have had a hard time escaping detection had he stolen so striking a melody.[1]

The words of *America* date from 1831, and were written by SAMUEL FRANCIS SMITH (1808–1895). Smith claimed that when he wrote his poem he did not realize the tune was that of the British national anthem. On several occasions he told of writing *America*:

The origin of my hymn, "My Country 'tis of Thee" is briefly told. In the year 1831, Mr. William C. Woodbridge returned from Europe, bringing a quantity of German music-books, which he passed over to Lowell Mason. Mr. Mason, with whom I was on terms of friendship, one day turned them over to me, knowing that I was in the habit of reading German works, say-

[1] In James Lyon's *Urania*, 1761, the melody appears as *Whitefield's* tune, set to the words *Come, Thou Almighty King.*

ing, "Here, I can't read these, but they contain good music, which I should be glad to use. Turn over the leaves, and if you find anything particularly good, give me a translation or imitation of it, or write a wholly original song, —anything, so I can use it."

Accordingly, one leisure afternoon, I was looking over the books, and fell in with the tune of "God Save the King," and at once took up my pen and wrote the piece in question. It was struck out at a sitting, without the slightest idea that it would ever attain the popularity it has since enjoyed. I think it was first written in the town of Andover, Mass., in February, 1832. The first time it was sung publicly was at a children's celebration of American independence, at the Park Street Church, Boston, I think, July 4, 1832. If I had anticipated the future of it, doubtless I would have taken more pains with it. Such as it is, I am glad to have contributed this mite to the cause of American freedom.

Smith recalled two of his dates incorrectly. Woodbridge returned from Europe in 1829, not in 1831, and the Independence Day celebration at which *America* was first sung occurred in 1831, not in 1832. The program of the event is in the collection of the American Antiquarian Society of Worcester, Massachusetts, and in the Chapin Library at Williams College. Furthermore, an account of the affair was printed in the *Christian Watchman* of July 8, 1831.

At any rate, *America* was written by a young clergyman who had no idea he was writing a national hymn, but whose sentiments proved so expressive of our ideals that they have been an inspiration to generations of peace-loving Americans.

CHAPTER FIVE

The Turn of the Century

I. FOREIGN AND NATIVE ARTISTS

IN many respects the beginning of the nineteenth century forms a dividing line in the history of our musical development, just as it marks a division in our political and economic history. The year that saw the downfall of the Federalist party and the election of Thomas Jefferson witnessed many changes in administrative policies. It was a year when the ambitions of Napoleon Bonaparte threatened the well-being of the young United States; it was only because his problems in Continental Europe were all he could handle that he made a treaty with us in 1801, one of the last acts of Adams's administration. Then followed the closing of the Mississippi's mouth by Spain, the final purchase of the Louisiana Territory from Napoleon (for $15,000,000), the Burr-Hamilton duel, the Lewis and Clark Expedition, and the constant disputes with England over the impressment of our seamen, which finally led to the War of 1812. Eventful years, forcing our new constitutional government to prove its stability at the very outset of its career.

The first years of the century still saw the foreigners who had migrated to our shores in control of our musical life, but with a difference. The Hewitts, the Carrs, Van Hagens, and Reinagles had become thoroughly naturalized—they, too, were American musicians. Young when they came, they had made their reputations principally in America; this was their home, and their foreign origin was in the background. Their descendants today may cite several generations of American ancestors.

Among the important foreigners was GOTTLIEB GRAUPNER (1767–1836), who came to America shortly after 1790, but whose life in Boston, where his influence was most felt, was chiefly in the nineteenth century. Graupner has been called the "Father of American Orchestral Music," and while there were others who did much to develop orchestra playing in this country, Graupner is most assuredly entitled to credit for true pioneer work.

His full name was Johann Christian Gottlieb Graupner; born in Hanover, October 6, 1767, the son of Johann Georg Graupner, oboist in the regiment of Colonel von Groten from Andreasberg. Gottlieb himself became an excellent oboist and played in a Hanoverian regiment when he was twenty years old. Receiving an honorable discharge in 1788, he went to London, and, like Hewitt, played in Haydn's orchestra when Salomon brought the great composer to London in 1791. After a few years in England, Graupner sought new fields. He went first to Prince Edward Island, and finally came to Charleston, South Carolina. Here he married, in 1796, a singer named Mrs. Catherine Comerford Hillier, known to the public as Mrs. Heelyer. It may be possible that Graupner had been in America prior to landing in Charleston, for a manuscript biography in the Boston Public Library written by a descendant, Mrs. George Whitefield Stone, speaks of his leaving London in June, 1792, and making an American debut in Boston, December 15, 1794. As the same document speaks of his returning to London *February* 4, 1794, and remaining until *August* 15, 1795, it is apparent that there is some confusion of dates. It was probably Mrs. Graupner who made the 1794 debut at the Boston Theatre.

The biography describes Graupner as a tall, somewhat austere man of precise speech and manner, who became white haired before he reached middle age. He had received a thorough musical education, and was able to perform on every known musical instrument, with the oboe and double bass as favorites. As a skilled oboist he was much in demand; good players on the oboe were rare in those days, though the tradition that Graupner was the only oboist in the country is hardly accurate.

There is record of a concert in Charleston in November, 1795, when Graupner played a concerto on the oboe between the performance of the drama and the farce that followed it. The summer of 1797 found Mrs. Graupner acting in Salem, Massachusetts, and in the autumn appearing with the Solee theatrical company in New York. In the spring of 1798 both Mr. and Mrs. Graupner were in Salem, and shortly afterwards the family settled in Boston, where Graupner was to play an active part in the city's musical life until his death in 1836.

Among his other activities, Graupner kept a music store and published considerable music of his own and others' composition. He advertised that he had "pianofortes for sale and to let, and that private instruments would be tuned in town and in country." An old newspaper clipping describes his place of business:

Gottlieb Graupner's music store, hall, and house, No. 6 Franklin Street, was four doors on the left from Washington Street. This was a place of great resort for young and old, teachers, pupils, and music lovers. Mr. Graupner's name was an honored one in the musical history of Boston. He was an eminent teacher of the piano-forte and of all orchestral instruments. He struck the first blow in the cause of true musical art, and continued the strife until a taste for good music, and a fair understanding of its intrinsic value was established in Boston.

Although it is known that Graupner composed music, there is little extant today. No doubt he wrote some of the oboe concertos that he performed at concerts, and *Columbia's Bold Eagle*, "a patriotic song, words by a gentleman of Salem—music by Mr. Graupner," was on the program of a concert in Salem in 1799. He was a pioneer in compiling educational works for the pianoforte, and in 1819 wrote and published his *Rudiments of the art of playing the pianoforte, containing the elements of music*, as well as "remarks on fingering, with examples, 30 fingered lessons, and a plain direction for tuning."

In 1810, Graupner started a small organization that was to be his greatest contribution to the future music of Boston. This was the Philharmonic Society, at first a social meeting where a number of musicians gathered regularly to practice Haydn's symphonies and other works for their own delight. Aside from nondescript theatre orchestras and the bands that gathered together for special concerts, there had been few organizations that met regularly for playing symphonic music. Graupner played the oboe. The first violinist was Louis Ostinelli, the Italian who married James Hewitt's daughter Sophia. Two clarinetists were members—Thomas Granger and Louis Schaffer, though Schaffer probably played the cello at the meetings. Francis Mallet, a vocalist, could play the contrabass, and he became a useful member. The professionals were assisted by amateurs of the city. The orchestra lived for at least fourteen years, for the last concert announcement did not appear until November 24, 1824. Parker's *Euterpeiad and Musical Intelligencer,* one of our early musical journals, spoke of the organization in 1821:

The Concerts of this Society are chiefly instrumental; the music is always heard with attention and oft times delight. The orchestra consists of nearly all the gentlemen of the profession in town, and its members are principally amateurs both vocal and instrumental; its support is derived from an annual assessment of ten dollars upon its members, who gain admission by ballot. The public Concerts are always fully attended by a large assemblage of ladies and gentlemen, introduced by members who possess certain privileges of admission on public nights.

Graupner became an American citizen in 1808. In 1821 he was saddened by the death of his wife, who was but forty-nine years old at the time. He later married again, for at the settlement of his will after his own death in 1836, his widow, Mary H. Graupner, inherited the estate of $975.

Aside from his more serious achievements it is possible that Graupner was also the originator of one of our lighter musical diversions—the minstrel songs that were so popular in the middle and later nineteenth century. A New York newspaper in 1889 offered the following information and surmises:

The Beginning of Negro Minstrelsy—the Banjo-Opera a Generation Ago.—In the current number of Harper's Magazine, Mr. Lawrence Hutton essays to trace the history of Negro minstrelsy in America, and succeeds in bringing together a large number of interesting facts in connection with early music and theatricals. In one respect the most surprising of these facts is the one stated on the authority of Mr. Charles White, an old Ethiopian comedian, which credits a Mr. Graupner with being the father of Negro song. This Graupner is said to have sung "The Gay Negro Boy," in character, accompanying himself on the banjo, at the end of the second act of "Oroonoko," on December 30th, 1799, at the Federal Street Theatre, Boston. This was Gottlieb Graupner, a hautboist. . . . In Boston, he led the orchestra of the old Federal Street Theatre, kept a music shop, played the oboe, the double-bass, and nearly every other instrument; gave lessons in music, organized the Philharmonic Society, and joined in the first call for the organization of the Handel & Haydn Society in March 1815. . . . Mr. Graupner's sojourn in Charleston suggests where he, a German, became acquainted with the banjo, and also offers evidence on the question mooted by Mr. Hutton, whether or not the banjo was common among slaves of the south.

Graupner, together with Thomas Smith Webb and Asa Peabody, signed the invitation that was issued in March, 1815, for a meeting to consider "the expediency of forming a society for cultivating and improving a correct taste in the performance of sacred music, and also to introduce into more general practice the works of Handel, Haydn and other eminent composers." Sixteen responded to the call and in April of the same year an organization was formed, with Webb as president, that became the *Handel and Haydn Society* of Boston, today one of the largest, and, with the exception of the Stoughton Musical Society, the oldest living musical organization in the United States. The first concert was held in the Stone Chapel on Christmas night in 1815, and one critic wrote that there was nothing to compare with it; that the Society was the wonder of the nation. The Handel and Haydn was not only influential in raising the standards of choral music in New England, but it led the way to the formation of similar organizations throughout the country.

One of the earliest organists of the Society was GEORGE K. JACKSON (1745-1823), a schoolmate of Raynor Taylor; born in Oxford, England. He came to America in 1796, landing at Norfolk, Virginia, and living in turn in Alexandria, Virginia; Baltimore; Philadelphia; Elizabeth, New Jersey; and New York, before he finally settled in Boston in 1812. He soon became active as a teacher, and at various times held the position of organist in several Boston churches—Brattle Square, King's Chapel, Trinity, and St. Paul's. Together with Mr. and Mrs. Graupner, Mallet, and other musicians, he organized performances of oratorios and concerts of choral music.

Before Dr. Jackson left England he had published *A treatise on practical thorough bass*. It was he who was largely responsible for Lowell Mason's start in music, for when he was organist of the Handel and Haydn Society, the manuscript of Mason's first collection of hymns and anthems was brought to his attention. Seeing its merits immediately, Jackson recommended that the Society publish it. Mason himself was anxious that his name should not appear, and Jackson was mentioned as the chief compiler. He had, moreover, added a number of his own compositions and arrangements to the collection.

Jackson had eleven children. He has been described as somewhat undemonstrative, though mentally keen. He was probably a ponderous person, for General Henry K. Oliver remembered him as "a very incarnation of obesity. . . . Like Falstaff he 'larded the lean earth as he walked along.' " When he died in 1823 he left an even smaller estate than Graupner was to leave thirteen years later. Metcalf, in his *American Writers and Compilers of Sacred Music*, says that the total inventory consisted of $98.86, including one hundred and twenty-nine volumes of old music books valued at six cents each.

BENJAMIN CROSS (1786–1857), one of the founders of the Philadelphia Musical Fund Society, was a contemporary of Benjamin Carr, and was active in Philadelphia as a teacher and singer. He was one of the conductors of the Society, and also appeared as a concert pianist, sometimes playing his own compositions. At some New York concerts in 1839 he played his pianoforte "Fantasia—Introducing two Irish airs"; a Potpourri, "introducing airs from *La Dame Blanche*, *Masaniello*, and *Fra Diavolo*"; and other pieces.

A New England musician whose importance has sometimes been overlooked was OLIVER SHAW (1779–1848), significant because he was prominent at a time when the country was commencing to reassert itself in music; when it had absorbed the foreigners and the new ideas they had brought with them, and was again turning its attention to its nativeborn music makers. Shaw was one of those who paved the road for Lowell Mason.

He was born March 13, 1779, in Middleboro, Massachusetts, the son of John Shaw and Hannah Heath. When he was a young lad he accidentally shoved the blade of a penknife into his right eye. Later the family moved to Taunton and the father went to sea. When Oliver was seventeen he attended the Bristol Academy at Taunton, and shortly after graduation he joined his father in his sea-faring enterprises. When he was twenty-one he was stricken with yellow fever. While not fully recovered he helped in taking nautical observations from the sun. This so affected his remaining eye, weakened from sickness, that the young man soon became totally blind.

It was this affliction that probably turned him to music, for otherwise he might have continued his maritime career. Wondering where to turn for a living, he came in touch with John L. Berkenhead, the blind organist of Newport, who gave him music lessons. Here was a profession he might follow in spite of his blindness. His progress was rapid, and he later went to Boston to study with Graupner. He also took clarinet lessons from Granger, and when he finally settled in Providence in 1807, he went there as a thoroughly trained musician.

Employing a little boy to lead him to the homes of his pupils he gave many music lessons, and he became the organist of the First Congregational Church. In 1809 he gathered a group of fellow musicians, among them Thomas Webb (who later moved to Boston), and founded the Psallonian Society, formed by its founders "for the purpose of improving themselves in the knowledge and practice of sacred music and inculcating a more correct taste in the choice and performance of it." The society lasted until 1832, and in its twenty-three years gave thirty-one concerts. In 1812, Shaw married Sarah Jencks and raised a family of two sons and five daughters.

As a composer he devoted himself almost entirely to sacred music. Among his hymn-tunes were *Taunton, Bristol, Weybosset*, and others. One of his most popular sacred songs was *Mary's Tears*, "a favorite song from Moore's sacred melodies; sung at the oratorio performed by the Handel & Haydn Society in Boston, July 5th, 1817, in presence of the President of the United States." (Monroe.) The program also contained his duet *All things bright and fair are thine*.

Others of his sacred melodies were: *Arrayed in clouds of golden light; The missionary angel; There is an hour of peace and rest; There's nothing true but heaven; To Jesus the crown of my hope*, and others which are significant because they show the trend of nonliturgical church music toward the ballad type of sentiment.

Shaw also compiled several collections of sacred music: *Melodia sacra*, "or Providence selection of sacred musick—from the latest European publications; with a number of original compositions"; and *The social sacred melodist* (1835). His secular compositions included the *Bangor March*, the *Bristol March*, and *Gov. Arnold's March*; the songs *Sweet Little Ann*, *Love's last words*, *The Blue Bird*, and the *Death of Commodore O. H. Perry*. In 1807, H. Mann of Dedham, published Shaw's

For the Gentlemen: A favourite selection of instrumental music . . . for schools and musical societies. Consisting principally of marches, airs, minuets, etc. Written chiefly in four parts, viz: two clarinets, flute and bassoon; or two violins, flute and violoncello.

These are the men who appeared at the opening of the century to join those who had bridged its turn. Some of them were of foreign birth and some were natives, but together they helped finish the foundation on which Lowell Mason, in one direction, and others in their own fields, cultivated the beginnings of a native art.

2. LOWELL MASON (1792–1872) AND THE RETURN OF THE NATIVE COMPOSER

Early in the nineteenth century there arose a group of native composers who carried on the tradition of New England's church music. After Billings, there had been a reaction against his "lively, fuguing pieces." Music for the church again assumed a more stately character. Singing schools had helped in developing singers who could sing at least correctly in church, and conditions were favorable to the development of a style of music in some respects individual in character. Immediately following the time of Tuckey, Selby, and Adgate, who gave American composers a place on their programs, the foreign immigration had diverted the attention of the musical public from native composers, and the music of Billings and his contemporaries was forced to the background. After two or three decades, this alien element was absorbed, and our church music, at least, fell to the hands of men better educated musically than the early New Englanders, men who had opportunity to study abroad, and were thoroughly grounded in considerably more than the rudiments of the art. From all this sprang the *hymnology* of the American Protestant church, which, though it has had its ignoble products, has formed a contribution to the sacred song of the entire world. Born chiefly in New England, it is nevertheless the expression of the American people at large. In some ways the hymn-tunes of Lowell Mason and his colleagues are as much folk songs as the melodies of Stephen Foster.

Lowell Mason appeared at a time when American *hymnology,* with its origin in the psalmody of the Puritans, was beginning to develop in two distinct directions. One branch was expressed in the dignified, stately type of hymn-tune which appears in the better collections today; the other found its outlet in the gospel song, used effectively in camp-meetings, revivalist campaigns, and in many Sunday Schools. Mason was identified with the better type.

We know Mason principally as the composer of *Bethany* (for *Nearer My God to Thee*); *Olivet* (for *My Faith Looks Up to Thee*); *Missionary Hymn* (for *From Greenland's Icy Mountains*); and of a great number of other hymn-tunes, most of which have now dropped out of use, but his influence has been felt in other directions, equally important. He was the pioneer in music teaching in the public schools, and the teachers' conventions that he organized have been the parents of our annual music festivals and our summer normal schools for teachers. They bridged the work of the old-fashioned traveling singing teacher and modern music schools. Mason was the chief factor in the third revival of singing in New England, and because of his abilities and personality, and because of greatly improved methods of communication, his influence spread far and wide across the country. Few single American musicians have ever exerted so wide an influence in the improvement of musical taste and standards as did Lowell Mason over a period of forty years.

Mason is one of the few pioneers who profited by his work. Royalties from the sale of his collections netted him a handsome fortune, and during his lifetime he was recognized and honored. For his services to education New York University awarded him the honorary degree of Doctor of Music in 1855, the first ever granted in America.

His American ancestry dated back seven generations. Robert Mason, born in England in 1590, had landed at Salem with John Winthrop in 1630. Lowell Mason was born in Medfield, Massachusetts, January 8, 1792, the son of Johnson Mason and Catharine Hartshorn. Although his parents did not want him to become a musician they encouraged the boy's early fondness for music, and saw to it that his talent was cultivated. When he was twenty he left home for Savannah, Georgia, for he had heard of a position in a bank that was open to him. In his spare hours he studied music, and found an instructor to help him—a man named F. L. Abel. He soon began to try his hand at composition, and wrote some hymn-tunes, and anthems. In the fourteen years in Savannah he led several church choirs, and acted as organist in the Independent Presbyterian Church.

During these years he worked at the compilation of a hymn collection. Some of the tunes he selected from William Gardner's *Sacred Melodies*, and others he wrote himself. He took the bulky manuscript and offered it to several publishers in Philadelphia and Boston, and was turned down by all of them. He was about to lay it aside when someone suggested that he submit it to George K. Jackson, at that time organist of the Handel and Haydn Society of Boston. Jackson saw its merits and recommended it highly, with the result that it was published as the *Boston Handel & Haydn Society's Collection of Sacred Music*. It became popular immediately, and its many editions totaled 50,000 copies during the following thirty-five years, netting Mason and the Society $30,000 apiece.

Mason still had no thought of making music his profession, and he was so afraid that being known as a musician might hurt his standing as a banker, that he did not allow his name to appear on the collection. Later editions acknowledged his work in the preface.

All this was in 1822. When he had arranged the details of publication he returned to Savannah, where he stayed for five more years. He had married Abigail Gregory in 1817, and had the responsibility of a growing family, a family that still has its impress on American musical life. Of the four sons, Daniel Gregory and Lowell, Junior founded the publishing business of Mason Brothers in New York, which continued until 1869. Lowell, with his younger brother Henry, then founded the firm of Mason & Hamlin, which first made organs and then pianos. The youngest son, William, became one of the most influential musicians in America during the last half of the nineteenth century.

When he was thirty-seven years old, Lowell Mason accepted an offer to return to Boston, and was guaranteed an income of $2,000 a year to lead the music in three churches, six months in each. He soon asked to be released from the contract and for a short time went back to

Lowell Mason
(See pages 136–141)

Characteristic Mid-Century Title Pages
(See pages 176–181, 163)

banking. But not for long. Music asserted itself as his chief interest, and he gave it his entire time, largely as a reformer. He was honored with the presidency of the Handel and Haydn Society for several years, beginning in 1827, but declined re-election in 1831 that he might give his whole attention to the establishment of music teaching in the public schools. Mason was among the first to preach the doctrine that every child has a right to receive elementary instruction in music at public expense. And he was the man who gained them that right.

At this time the public schools were first becoming recognized as an American institution, and the Boston schools were a fertile field for Mason to work in. Such a revolutionary doctrine was not welcomed immediately by the school board; Mason had to conduct many experiments to prove that his ideas were sound.

By 1829 he had studied the Pestalozzian methods of teaching which W. C. Woodbridge, author of school geographies, had brought back from Europe. Having learned what the system had accomplished in other subjects, he determined to apply its principles to music teaching. Accordingly, in conjunction with George J. Webb, Samuel A. Eliot, and others, he founded the Boston Academy of Music in 1832 to try his ideas. Sessions were held in the rooms of the Bowdoin Street Church and later at the Odeon. Children were taught free of charge, if they would promise to attend for the entire year. In the first year there were 1,500 pupils. Mason himself taught 400 of them, and Webb took care of 150.

In a few years the school board began to be impressed, and some of its members saw that they were wrong in fearing that music study would divert the pupils from their regular tasks. Those who studied music had an added zeal for other subjects. The board passed a resolution that "one school from each district be selected for the introduction of systematic instruction in vocal music." In 1836 the introduction of music into the schools was formally authorized, but the board forgot to appropriate any money. Even this failed to stop Mason. He taught without pay for an entire year, and bought music and materials for the pupils from his own pocket. A year of this was too much for the public conscience, and in 1838 the board went the whole way and appropriated the necessary funds.

It was while he was conducting the classes at the Academy of Music that Mason started his music conventions. If he was to spread his ideas, there must be teachers trained to do the work. The first was held in 1834. Twelve teachers came. By 1838 there were 134, coming from ten states, and in 1849 the attendance had grown to 1,000. The meetings generally lasted for two weeks. Those who came were taught to sing chiefly by rote, and then went home and became teachers. Meager instruction, but considerably more than they had ever had before. Moreover, the results were so successful that Mason spent much of his time traveling around the country in answer to the demand for "conventions" elsewhere. He would often go as far west as Rochester, New York, a real journey in the days of early railroading, to meet choruses of 500 voices, many of them teachers who had traveled a hundred miles to attend.

By 1850, Mason's pioneer work in Boston was finished. He had made the Hub a self-developing musical city, not largely dependent, like New York, on musical culture from abroad. The Academy passed out of existence in 1847 because its mission had been fulfilled. In 1850, Mason went to Europe for two years, and lectured in England on his application of the Pestalozzian method to music teaching. In 1853 he returned and established his headquarters in New York, where with George F. Root and William B. Bradbury he established the New York Normal Institute for training teachers. He bought a home on the side of the Orange Mountains in New Jersey which he named *Silver-spring*, and he continued his activities until his death at the age of eighty, August 11, 1872.

Mason had opposition in his lifetime, and even after his work had borne fruit in Boston the intelligentsia of the day said that he and his fellow writers of hymn-tunes were degrading and cheapening music. From certain standpoints this may be true; Mason was no Handel or Bach; his tunes incline to the sentimental and their appeal is to the emotions rather than the intellect. But compare what had been before him with what he left, and then decide whether he cheapened and degraded it. Mason was the first who preached music for the masses. The festivals that grew from his conventions may have been a sorry contrast to modern performances in both program and execution, but think of the thousands who participated in making music far better than anything they had ever heard before.

It has been estimated that over a million copies of Mason's books have been sold; one collection alone brought him $100,000. The best known were the *Boston Handel & Haydn Collection* (1822); *Juvenile Psalmodist* (1829); *Juvenile Lyre* (1830); *Sabbath School Songs* (1836); *Boston Academy Collection of Church Music* (1836); *Lyra Sacra* (1837); *Boston Anthem Book* (1839); *The Psaltery* (1845); *Cantica Laudis* (1850); *New Carmina Sacra* (1852); and *The Song Garden* (1866).

3. MASON'S CONTEMPORARIES

Among Mason's contemporaries and associates, THOMAS HASTINGS (1784–1872) deserves a prominent place. He was a few years older than Mason and like his colleague enjoyed long life. Between the two men there was one marked difference. With Mason, music was first, and he appreciated its power to make worship more beautiful. Hastings was a pious soul who believed that music should be used to exemplify the teachings of the gospel, occupying an entirely subordinate place. Moreover, Hastings was not the musician that Mason was.

Hastings was born in Washington, Connecticut, October 15, 1784. His father, Seth Hastings, combined the professions of country doctor and farmer. Thomas and his two brothers were complete albinos, with absolutely white hair from childhood. When Thomas was twelve the family moved to Clinton, New York, and the boy obtained all the education he ever had in the country schools. His experience was practical, however, for at eighteen he was leading a village choir. He started to compile hymn collections when he was about thirty years old, and in 1816 an editor named Solomon Warriner suggested that they merge his own *Springfield Collection* with Hastings's *Utica Collection*. The joint product was called *Musica Sacra*.

Hastings moved to Utica in 1828 and was active in a Handel and Haydn Society of that city. For several years he edited a weekly religious paper *The Western Recorder*, and expressed his views on church music in many of his editorials. He had already published an *Essay on Musical Taste*, in which his ideas were considered radical and advanced. The essay was widely read, and a new edition was printed in 1853.

In 1832, Hastings settled in New York, where he later became associated with Mason in the New York Normal Institute. For a number of years he was choirmaster of the Bleecker Street Presbyterian Church. His works were widely used, and his influence was second only to Mason's. In 1858, New York University paid him the same honor it had accorded Mason three years earlier, and conferred on him the degree of Doctor of Music.

Hastings is supposed to have written the words of six hundred hymns, and to have composed over a thousand tunes. He issued fifty volumes of music altogether. While modern hymnals contain many of his hymns, the best known is the famous tune *Toplady*, sung to Augustus Toplady's words, *Rock of Ages, cleft for me*. Many of his tunes appeared under nom de plumes, for Hastings was one of the first American composers to believe that a foreign name impressed the American public. He once wrote: "I have found that a foreigner's name went a great way, and that very ordinary tunes would be sung if 'Palestrina' or 'Pucitto' were over them, while a better tune by Hastings would go unnoticed." A number of his hymns were composed by "Kl—f," and there is reason to suppose that those signed "Zol—ffer" are from his pen. Hastings died in New York, May 15, 1872, eighty-eight years old. He was active until three years before his death.

It may be that the good die young, but if devotion to church music is any sign of virtue, Mason and Hastings disproved the theory by their eighty and eighty-eight years of life. To support the argument of his elders, their young associate, GEORGE JAMES WEBB (1803–1887), decided that the average was what he wanted, and lived for eighty-four years.

Webb was an Englishman who came to Boston in 1830. The son of a landowner with an estate near Salisbury, England, he was born June 24, 1803. His father was a singer, and his mother a cultured amateur musician. He received his first musical instruction from his mother before he was seven years old, and when he attended a boarding school near his home he studied music with Alexander Lucas. He became proficient in playing both the piano and violin, and by the time he was sixteen decided to make music his career.

To continue his education he went to Falmouth where he studied with an organist, and soon succeeded his teacher at the organ. After a few years in Falmouth he decided to try America, for many friends had told him of its opportunities. He had booked passage for New York, but the captain of a boat sailing for Boston persuaded young Webb to come with him. He went to the New England city and within a few weeks was engaged as the organist of the Old South Church and, what was most important, met Lowell Mason.

Mason needed a man like Webb, for he was beginning to formulate his plans for teaching children. Webb accordingly became one of the organizers of the Boston Academy of Music, and took charge of the secular music courses, while Mason devoted himself to the church music department. His talents as a choral conductor led to his becoming president of the Handel and Haydn Society for three years, and with Mason he was influential in promoting better choral music throughout the country.

Webb also cultivated instrumental music at the Academy, and organized an orchestra that gave regular concerts, following in the footsteps of Graupner's Philharmonic group. This orchestra existed for fourteen years, and when the Academy had served its purpose and ceased to exist in 1847, a Musical Fund Society was organized by Tom Comer, and Webb later became conductor of its orchestra. He held the position until 1852 when he resigned because of other duties, though he remained president of the society which continued until 1855. As an orchestral conductor he was an important link in Boston's musical life; he formed the bridge between Graupner's pioneer efforts and the future work of Zerrahn with the orchestra of the Harvard Musical Association.

In 1871, Webb followed Mason to New York and established his home in Orange, New Jersey. He taught vocal pupils in New York and in the summers conducted normal courses for teachers at Binghamton, New York. He died in Orange, October 7, 1887.

Only one of Webb's many compositions has survived to our day, the famous tune sung to the words, *Stand Up, Stand Up for Jesus.* This originally appeared as a secular song, then as a setting to *The Morning Light is Breaking,* a hymn by Samuel Francis Smith, author of *America.* At first the tune was called *Goodwin,* but it is known today by the name of its composer, *Webb.*

Webb wrote many sacred songs and cantatas, and compiled many collections of hymn-tunes, a number of them in association with Lowell

Mason. Among these were *The Massachusetts Collection of Psalmody*, published in 1840 by the Handel and Haydn Society, *Cantica Ecclesiastica*, consisting largely of English anthems (1859), and a number of collections for young singers—*The American Glee Book* and others. The connection with the Mason family was further strengthened when Lowell Mason's son William married Webb's daughter Mary.

He also wrote many secular songs, some published in 1830, the year of his arrival in America. *Art Thou Happy, Lovely Lady* was published in that year by C. Bradlee in Boston. An announcement at the end of the voice and piano copy stated that "the orchestral accompaniment may be had on application to the publisher." There were a number of songs in these early Boston years—*I'll Meet, Sweet Maid, with Thee; Homeward Bound; Oh, Go Not to the Field of War* ("as sung by Miss George with rapturous applause"); *When I Seek My Pillow*; and many others. There was also a *Boston Cotillons*, for piano, "composed and dedicated to the ladies of Boston." Between the graceful phrases of music are printed directions for the dancers. "Right and left four—balance and turn partners—half promenade—half right and left." And again, "First Lady balance to 2nd Gent; turn the next—balance to next, turn partners and come in the center—four Gent: hands around the Lady—turn partners."

Mr. Howard Van Sinderen, husband of Minna Mason Van Sinderen, daughter of William Mason and granddaughter of Lowell Mason and Webb, very kindly placed at my disposal some of Webb's manuscripts —a number of sacred and secular songs, showing careful workmanship. Most interesting is the *Ode to the 4th July, 1832*, for soli and chorus. Also the cantata *Song of Death*, to words selected from Burns. One of the manuscripts has on one side the outline of a song, with merely the start of an accompaniment; and on the other side a penciled canon, which may have been a sketch for a choral piece, or merely an exercise for his own routine.

Among the members of the Mason group was WILLIAM BATCHELDER BRADBURY (1816–1868), a younger man than Mason, but one who was imbued with his ideas and well equipped to help carry them out. Bradbury, like Mason, was successful in his work with children; he loved them and understood them and they responded readily to his teaching. His forte was music for Sunday Schools, and he was the author and compiler of books with colorful titles. There was the *Golden* series: *Bradbury's Golden Shower of Sunday School Melodies; Bradbury's Golden Chain of Sabbath School Melodies; The Golden Censer* (a musical offering to the Sabbath Schools of children's hosannas to the Son of David); as well as *Bright Jewels for the Sunday School* and *Musical Gems for School and Home.* The suggestion of gold and jewels had its point for the author, too, for the books made him a fortune. His handling of children would have won the approval of the most modern of psychologists. In his later years his home in Bloomfield, New Jersey, lay directly opposite the town school. Bradbury had fruit trees which he prized highly. Every year he protected his orchard from schoolboy raids by sending baskets of cherries, apples, and pears to the pupils.

He was born in York, Maine, October 6, 1816. His parents were musical and he had advantages of training in his youth. By the time he was fourteen he could play every instrument known to York. When he went to Boston he took lessons in harmony from Sumner Hill and became a pupil of Lowell Mason. In 1836, when he was twenty, Mason recommended him to the authorities in Machias, Maine, where he taught for a year and a half. After this, Bradbury went to St. John's, New Brunswick. Then he divided his time between Boston and northeastern points for a few years, and finally moved to New York in 1840, where he became the organist of the Baptist Tabernacle. As a disciple of Lowell Mason he started music conventions in New Jersey, the first held in Somerville in 1851. When Mason came to New York, Bradbury joined his former teacher in founding the New York Normal Institute. By this time he had added considerably to his musical background. He spent almost two years in Europe, after leaving the Baptist Tabernacle in 1847, and studied with Moscheles, Hauptmann, Wenzl, and Böhme.

In 1854 he formed a partnership with his brother for manufacturing pianos, and the firm that produced the Bradbury piano was highly successful. Bradbury was a natural money-maker, but overwork brought on an ailment of the lungs which caused his death at his New Jersey home, January 7, 1868. His best-known hymn-tunes were: *He Leadeth Me; Woodworth (Just as I am, without one plea)*; and *Bradbury (Saviour, like a shepherd lead me)*.

Church music and songs for Sunday Schools were in great demand in the early and middle nineteenth century, and many of the composers who wrote them made large sums of money. Most of these musicians are known to us by an occasional hymn-tune; their ambitious collections have been replaced by modern editions.

SILVANUS BILLINGS POND (1792–1871) was born in Worcester, Massachusetts, became a piano maker in Albany, New York, and moved to New York City in 1832, where he entered the publishing house of Firth & Hall. In 1848 the firm became Firth, Pond & Company and was one of the principal publishers of Stephen Foster's songs. In 1863, Pond left the Firth interests and established the business now known as William A. Pond & Company. He wrote many Sunday School songs, some secular songs, and compiled the *United States Psalmody*.

CHARLES ZEUNER (1795–1857) was a German who came to Boston in 1824. Baptized *Heinrich Christopher*, he changed his name to *Charles*, possibly to seem more like an American. He is best known today for his *Missionary Chant*, which is contained in many hymnbooks. For seven years he was organist of the Handel and Haydn Society. After thirty years in Boston he moved to Philadelphia, where he held the position of organist in several prominent churches. Unfortunate moodiness and eccentricities of temperament made it difficult for him to get along with others, and a mental ailment culminated in death by his own hand when he was sixty-two years old.

Zeuner's largest composition was an oratorio, *The Feast of Tabernacles*, which was published and performed in Boston. Tradition has it that Zeuner demanded $3,000 when he offered the manuscript to the Handel and Haydn Society. The Society felt this was too much. When the work was later given eight performances by the Boston Academy of Music at the Odeon, it resulted in complete failure financially. The hot-tempered Zeuner broke into the Academy one night and destroyed all copies of the work that he could find, including the manuscript.

Several years later a correspondent of *Dwight's Journal of Music* wrote as follows:

I doubt if Zeuner is appreciated. There is hardly a great composition for church or stage which one person at least would rather hear than Zeuner's "Feast of Tabernacles," the oratorio which after a few performances in Boston some years since he withdrew—there is too much reason to fear—forever!

For long life HENRY KEMBLE OLIVER (1800–1885) ranks with Mason, Hastings, and Webb. He lived to be eighty-five years old. He is known best as the composer of the hymn-tune *Federal Street*, sometimes sung to Oliver Wendell Holmes's *Lord of All Being, Throned Afar*, but originally written for Miss Steele's hymn *So fades the lovely blooming flower*.

Oliver was truly a man of parts, and a dominant factor in the business and cultural interests of nineteenth-century New England. Although he was a choirmaster and organist, music was his avocation. In middle life he was Adjutant-General of Massachusetts for four years, superintendent of the Atlantic Cotton Mills in Lawrence for ten years, mayor of Lawrence for a year, treasurer of Massachusetts during the Civil War, and for ten years chief of the state's Department of Labor. He was active in musical organizations, some of which he organized and managed himself. He was born in Beverly, Massachusetts, and died in Salem, where he had lived for many years.

He published several volumes of hymn-tunes: *Oliver's Collection of Hymn and Psalm Tunes*; and with Tuckerman and Bancroft *The National Lyre: a new collection of sacred music*.

BENJAMIN FRANKLIN BAKER (1811–1889) was Lowell Mason's successor as teacher of music in the Boston schools. He was a singer and director of church choirs in Salem and Boston, and participated in the work of the music conventions. From 1841 to 1847 he was vice-president of the Handel and Haydn Society. He founded a Boston Music School in 1851, acted as its principal and took charge of the vocal department. When the school went out of business in 1868, Baker retired from active work.

Although Baker was himself a composer, one of his most interesting works was the *Haydn Collection of Church Music*, in which the tunes were selected and arranged from the works of Haydn, Handel, Mozart, Beethoven, Weber, Rossini, Mendelssohn, Cherubini, and others. In like manner the *Classical Chorus Book* contained anthems, motets, and hymns arranged from the works of Mozart, Beethoven, and so on. He was the author of a treatise on *Thorough Bass and Harmony*, and wrote three cantatas: *The Storm King, The Burning Ship*, and *Camillus the Conqueror*.

Baker spent his whole life in New England. He was born in Wenham, Massachusetts, and died in Boston.

ISAAC BAKER WOODBURY (1819–1858), like General Oliver, was born in Beverly, Massachusetts. In his early life he was apprenticed to a blacksmith, and devoted his spare time to music. At thirteen he went to Boston for study, and when he was nineteen went to Europe and studied in Paris and London. When he came back to America he taught in Boston, and joined the Bay State Glee Club, which traveled through New England. In 1851 he went to New York and became editor of the *New York Musical Review*. Because of ill health he went again to Europe, and later decided to spend his winters in the South. The rigors of one of these trips proved too much for him, and he died in Columbia, South Carolina, in 1858, thirty-nine years of age.

In his lifetime, Woodbury's music was used in churches more than that of any of his contemporaries, and though little of it is heard today, a number of his tunes are still found in our hymnbooks. Certainly he had the benefit of a good advertising man, for in Dwight's staid *Journal of Music* this advertisement appeared in 1853:

125,000 Copies in Two Seasons!
Live Music Book!
The Dulcimer
A Collection of Sacred Music
by I. B. Woodbury

The "learn-music-at-home" idea had an early advocate in Woodbury, for one of his works was called *Woodbury's Self-Instructor in Musical Composition and Thorough Bass*. With B. F. Baker he compiled the *Boston Musical Education Society's Collection of Church Music* (1842) and *The Choral* (1845). One of his first songs was a ballad *He Doeth All Things Well, or My Sister*. He sold this for ten dollars to George P. Reed of Boston, who published it in 1844. Another of his songs which had wide use was *The Indian's Lament*, with its first line: "Let me go to my home in the far distant West."

Metcalf has given a sympathetic portrait of Woodbury: [1]

Gentleness was the characteristic of the man and his music. His compositions were for the church, the fireside and the social circle. He wrote with remarkable fluency and it was surprising how much he could accomplish in a short space of time. . . . He had a beautiful voice and sang various styles, but excelled in the ballad and descriptive music. For sport he was fond of hunting and duck-shooting. And in a letter to his paper he wrote that even in winter it was his daily custom to ride on horseback, or, when Old Boreas blew cold, in his carriage, among the leafless trees or the evergreen pines.

[1] From *American Writers and Compilers of Hymn Tunes;* copyright, 1925, by Frank J. Metcalf. Quoted by permission of the Abingdon Press.

CHAPTER SIX

Our Nineteenth-Century Background in Secular Music

I. CONCERT LIFE

CITY dwellers in the early nineteenth century had plenty of musical entertainment. Both foreign and native artists found it profitable to offer their services for public and private occasions. Sometimes the concerts were for the benefit of the artists themselves, and sometimes for charity. Old newspapers ran advertisements of such affairs as a "Vocal Concert for the benefit of the Respectable Aged and Indigent Female Assistance Society" (New York, 1839) and others to raise funds for equally worthy objects. In New York the concerts were held at the City Hotel, Niblo's Gardens, the Lyceum, the Apollo, or the Broadway Tabernacle. Even Davies' Hot Pie House was not without its musical affairs; the New York *Herald* of January 7, 1839, told its readers that

A musical party will meet this evening, at 8 o'clock, at Davies' Hot Pie House, No. 14 John Street. A professor will preside at the Piano Forte. Admission 12½ cents.

Some of the artists made impressive claims. Signor de Begnis, first buffo singer from the Italian Opera House in London, promised that at one of his concerts he would sing six hundred words and three hundred bars of music in the short space of four minutes. Many of the concerts assumed mammoth proportions. At a "Great Union Performance of Sacred Music," in the Broadway Tabernacle (New York, 1839) the New York Sacred Music Society was assisted by choirs from twenty surrounding towns, one thousand singers in all.

Each of the three leading cities had a group of serious musicians in whom the better musical life centered, and who cultivated a following and did much to raise standards. Benjamin Carr, Raynor Taylor, Hupfeld, Cross, and others in Philadelphia formed a group that culminated in the Musical Fund Society. In Boston, Graupner, Ostinelli, Mallet, Granger, and others founded a Philharmonic Society; Graupner, Peabody, and Thomas Webb the Handel and Haydn Society; and Mason and George Webb the Boston Academy of Music.

New York, too, had its musicians, and though they were forced to compromise with the public taste, they kept their own standards high and did much for the cultivation of good music. The eighteenth century had seen musical organizations in New York. James Hewitt with his English friends had formed a Philharmonic Society which flourished for a number of years; the Germans had founded the Concordia, and the Euterpean Society celebrated its forty-eighth anniversary in 1847. There was also a New York Sacred Music Society, directed by U. C. Hill, which presented *The Messiah* in 1831, and Mendelssohn's *St. Paul* in 1838. In 1839 a "Musical Solemnity" was held in the memory of Daniel Schlesinger, a thoroughly trained musician who had made his home in New York at the time of his death; and from this concert, largely orchestral in character, the idea of a permanent professional orchestra was born. With Hill as the motivating spirit, the Philharmonic Society of New York was founded in 1842, an orchestra which is today acknowledged one of the finest in the world. An account of the men who formed the Philharmonic is the history of New York's musical life in the first half of the century.

Ureli Corelli Hill (1802–1875) deserves credit, above all others, for forming the Society and for maintaining its existence in its first years. H. E. Krehbiel, in his monograph *The Philharmonic Society of New York,*[1] presents a brief sketch of Hill:

He was not a New Yorker, but a Connecticut Yankee, and the strangeness of his Christian name suggests the idea that some of his mental peculiarities were an inheritance. In all probability his father was fond of the violin. . . .

Yankee "push," energy, shrewdness, enthusiasm, industry, pluck, self-

[1] H. E. Krehbiel; *The Philharmonic Society of New York*, Novello, Ewer & Co.

reliance, and endurance were all present in the composition of Hill's character. It seems incontestable from the evidence that his natural gifts as a musician were not great. When he went to study with Spohr in 1835, he had already occupied a prominent position in the musical life of the city for some years. He could plan and could organize. Obstacles had no terror for him; he thought that patience and industry would surmount them. He did achieve wonderful things with the crude material at his disposal, but though he labored hard he never overcame the limitations which nature had set for him as an executant.

He remained over two years with Spohr, and when he returned he gave great vogue to that master's "School for the Violin," and became the most popular and successful violin teacher in the city. He was of the stuff that pioneers are made of, and filled with a restless energy. Despite his achievements as a conductor of amateur and professional bodies, he was continually looking for new fields to conquer. He had some of the spirit of the New England convention leader, and would have been supremely happy had he been able to count his performers by the hundreds or thousands, instead of scores. But with all his eagerness he inculcated a taste for good music, and his pupils bless his memory.

His fate was a melancholy one. Though he could earn money he could not keep it. He sought his fortunes out West, five years after the foundation of the Philharmonic, and was gone three or four years, only to find that the best field for his energies was New York. Once the Society helped him with a loan of practically all the money in the sinking fund, and had to wait long for its return.

He played in the orchestra until 1873, and was then retired because of old age, being seventy. For a while, he played as an extra at Wallack's Theatre, but was unable to maintain himself there. Some operations in New Jersey real estate had proved abortive. He tried to get up a concert for a daughter in Jersey City, and was shocked at the lack of interest in his enterprise displayed by the musical profession.

Then, the painful conviction was forced on him that he "lagged superfluous on the stage." At his home in Paterson, N.J., on September 2, 1875, he killed himself by taking morphine. In a letter of explanation and farewell he wrote these words:

"To live and be a beggar and a slave is a little too much for me, maugre I am an old man. Look at all of us! Is it not heartrending to contemplate? Ha, ha! the sooner I go the better. O, merciful father, take good care of my wife and family! Blessings on all they have done for me."

In the first five seasons of the Philharmonic, Hill conducted five of the concerts. The first program, presented at the Apollo Rooms, December 7, 1842, shows that the standards of the group were high though their performances may have been ragged. Hill conducted the orchestra in Beethoven's Fifth Symphony, Weber's Overture to *Oberon,* and an Overture in D by Kalliwoda. Five instrumentalists played the Hummel D Minor Quintette, and the vocal numbers, rendered by Madame Otto and C. E. Horn, consisted of selections from *Oberon,* Beethoven's *Fidelio,* Mozart's *Belmont and Constantia,* and a duet from Rossini's *Armida.* There is further discussion of the early Philharmonic performances in our chapter on Theodore Thomas.

The program of the first concert stated that "the vocal music will be directed by Mr. Timm." HENRY CHRISTIAN TIMM (1811–1892) was one of the first competent pianists who lived in New York. Born in Hamburg, Germany in 1811, he had settled in New York in 1835, and after giving a concert at the Park Theatre had immediately come into public favor. His debut was followed by an unsuccessful concert tour through New England, and to make a living he became second horn player in the Park Theatre Orchestra. Next he went South as conductor of an opera troupe that traveled for six months, and settled in Baltimore where he had a position as organist. He soon returned to New York, and became chorus master and trombone player for a company organized by C. E. Horn, who had leased the new National Opera House. When the theatre burned down, Timm became organist of St. Thomas's Church in New York, and later played at the Unitarian Church, where he remained for eighteen years. He lived until he was eighty-one years old, when he died in New York in 1892.

Timm was active in the formation of the Philharmonic, and was its president from 1847 to 1864. From contemporary accounts he was an excellent pianist. One legend has it that he could play scales with a full wine glass on the back of his hand without spilling a drop. The New York correspondent of Dwight's *Journal* in Boston described him as "the most elegant of our pianists," and in reviewing a concert in November, 1852, said:

The next instrumental piece was the first movement of Hummel's Concerto in B minor, the piano-forte by Mr. Timm. How finely that gentleman plays you need not be told. The deeply melancholy character of the music was admirably conveyed in the performance of both pianist and orchestra, and was doubly effective from its contrast to the Symphony (Beethoven's 8th).

Timm was also something of a composer. He wrote a grand Mass, part-songs, and made many transcriptions for two pianos, which he played in concerts with his colleagues.

DANIEL SCHLESINGER (1799–1839), whose memorial concert was largely responsible for forming the Philharmonic, was a German pianist who came to New York in 1836. He was an excellent musician, pupil of Ferdinand Ries and Moscheles, and if he had been spared he would undoubtedly have proved a powerful influence in this country.

Concert notices of the time tell something of Schlesinger's activities. On one occasion he played a Hummel concerto with orchestra; on another he joined his colleague Scharfenberg in playing the Rondo and Variations for two pianos by Henri Herz; and with Scharfenberg and another pianist, Czerny's "Grand Trio Concertante, for six hands on two pianos."

At the memorial concert after his death in 1839—"The Musical Tribute to the Memory of the late Daniel Schlesinger"—held at the Broadway Tabernacle in 1839, an orchestra of sixty performers, the Concordia (a chorus of forty amateurs of which he had been the director), and distinguished *virtuosi* played a program that included his *Grand Overture, Full Orchestra, Composed expressly for the London Philharmonic Society;* and the *Adagio and Finale of the celebrated Quatuor in C minor, for piano, tenor, violin and violoncello.*

WILLIAM SCHARFENBERG (1819–1895) was also a German. U. C. Hill met him when he went to Cassel to take lessons from Spohr. Hill painted an enthusiastic picture of the opportunities for young musicians in America, and finally persuaded the young German to come here. He arrived in New York in 1838 and made his debut as a pianist under Hill's auspices.

Scharfenberg at once took a leading position among the musicians of the city, for he had only one rival as a pianist, Daniel Schlesinger, and the latter died a few months after Scharfenberg came. Moreover, it was a rivalry, as Krehbiel wrote, that was "sweetened by a most unselfish and friendly interest on the part of the elder musician." Excerpts from Dwight's *Journal* afford descriptions of Scharfenberg and his colleagues. May 1, 1852:

The Philharmonic Orchestra is admirably drilled. The members are all inspired by the same sympathies,—mostly Germans, they believe in the German Composers, who would not regret to sit among the audience and hear their own immortality so assured. Mr. Timm . . . is President; Mr. Scharfenberg, whose delicate and polished style evinces the student of the best classics only, is vice-president. They assist in the orchestra, taking very humble parts. Mr. Scharfenberg, I think, played the cymbals. . . .

Mr. Scharfenberg played a Concerto of Mendelssohn's with the orchestra. I wish he were more impassioned. Yet his reverence for the master is very beautiful, and the quiet, uncompromising purity of his style is sure to secure your most judicious approval. Later in the evening he and Mr. Timm played a Grand Duo of Mendelssohn's upon the Bohemian march from "Preciosa." It was effective, but not striking. In fact, neither of the piano performances were strictly interesting. They were learned and skillful rather than inspired. But the audience made it a point of honor to listen silently, and recognized by their applause the admirable performance, although there was no great enthusiasm for the works.

And from Newport, Rhode Island, August 28, 1852:

The lover of music has great privileges here. Besides the many concerts, always of a high order, there is sometimes at the hotels, but constantly in private circles, a great variety of choice music. In Mr. Scharfenberg's little cozy parlor, Beethoven, Chopin and Mendelssohn, Spohr, and other worthy associates, are daily worshipped by a few of the true worshippers. . . .

Scharfenberg was active in the Philharmonic Society from the start. In its third season he was secretary; in the ninth, vice-president; and from 1863 to 1866, president. He also formed, in 1845, the music publishing firm Scharfenberg & Luis, whose store on Broadway was headquarters for the Philharmonic. The business lasted until 1866, when Scharfenberg left to live temporarily in Havana. On his return he became associated as reader and editor with the publisher who was to become one of the foremost in America, Gustave Schirmer. Although Scharfenberg was something of a composer on his own account, it was as editor that he made his great contribution, and hundreds of the volumes in the Schirmer *Library of Classics* were annotated and prepared by his careful pen. He enjoyed long life, and died in 1895 at the age of seventy-six in Quogue, Long Island.

CHARLES EDWARD HORN (1786–1849) belongs both in this chapter and the next. He was a serious musician, singer, pianist, and composer; as a ballad singer and composer he was influential in shaping a type of song popular to our own day. Unlike Scharfenberg and Timm, Horn had made a reputation abroad before he came here. He was the son of Karl Friedrich Horn, a German musician who came to London in 1782 and became the vogue as a teacher among the English nobility. The father was appointed music master in ordinary to Queen Charlotte and the princesses, and was organist at St. George's Chapel at Windsor from 1824 until his death in 1830.

The son Charles was born in St. Martin's-in-the-Fields, and received most of his musical training from his father. By the time he came to America in 1833, at the age of forty-seven, he had been one of the composers at the Vauxhall, director of music at the Olympia, and was highly popular as an opera singer (although his voice was poor, and useful principally because of its enormous range). He had composed and produced twenty-two operas, some, like his setting of Moore's *Lalla Rookh*, highly successful.

When Horn came to New York he first produced English operas at the Park Theatre, where he met with great success. During the following years he was active in theatrical affairs, concert appearances with his wife, who was also a singer, and he found time to write and produce an oratorio *The Remission of Sin*. When he directed this work in London some years later he presented it under the brief, but alluring, title *Satan*. In 1842 he was one of the founders of the Philharmonic and sang at its first concert. Shortly after this a severe illness cost him the use of his voice, and he was obliged to give up singing. With a man named Davis, he established a publishing house called Davis & Horn. His partner withdrew after a year, and Horn continued the business alone.

In 1843, Horn returned to England for four years, and acted as musical director at the Princess Theatre in London. When he came back to America in 1847 he settled in Boston, where he was elected conductor of the Handel and Haydn Society. In 1848 he went to England for a few months to produce another of his oratorios, *Daniel's Predic-*

tion, and when he went back to Boston in June of the same year he was re-elected conductor of the Handel and Haydn. He performed these duties for the ensuing season only, for he died in 1849.

In the year 1839, Horn made almost thirty concert and recital appearances in New York City. First, there were the six *Soirées Musicales* that were offered by Mr. and Mrs. Horn on the Thursday of each alternate week during February, March, and April. Then he appeared in a number of concerts for charity; at the affair for the benefit of "Indigent Females"; at the Schlesinger Memorial; at a "Grand Sacred Concert" at the Broadway Tabernacle; and at a benefit for his partner Davis. He participated in many recitals offered by his colleagues—Knight, Russell, Signor Rapetti, Signora Maroncelli, and others.

Many of the songs on the programs were composed by Horn, but he often presented works by Purcell, Beethoven, Rossini and like composers, as well as songs by his colleagues Joseph Knight and Henry Russell. At the first and second of the *Soirées Musicales,* half of the programs were devoted to Handel's *Acis and Galatea.* Horn appeared not only as a singer; many concert programs bore the line, "Mr. C. E. Horn will preside at the pianoforte." With Henry Russell, also a singer, he played the *Zampa* Overture of Herold as a piano duet, and on several occasions he played duets with Scharfenberg. At one of his *soirées* he conducted an orchestra that numbered Scharfenberg and U. C. Hill among its members. The same program presented a solo and chorus from his oratorio *The Remission of Sin*—"Oh, myriads of immortal spirits."

Horn paid many musical tributes to America in his music, and he made several attempts to adapt what seemed to him to be Americanisms. On many of his programs there were excerpts from his *National Melodies of America,* a song cycle set to poems of George P. Morris, at one time editor of the New York *Home Journal* in conjunction with N. P. Willis. In his settings, Horn used supposedly native melodies. The first, *Northern Refrain,* was based on the "carol of the sweeps of the city of New York"; *Meeta,* and *Near the Lake, Where Drooped the Willow* were made from Negro airs. One of Horn's most popular songs was *Cherry Ripe.* Many were tenderly sentimental—*All Things Love Thee, So Do I; Tell Her She Haunts Me Yet* ("the words by a young lady of Louisville"); *Do You Remember, Mary?; Dark Eyed One;*

Child of Earth with the Golden Hair, and others. In some of his songs
he caught the old English spirit of merriment—*Thru the Streets of
New York, Blithely and Gay; How Roses Came Red; If Maidens
Would Marry;* and a setting of *I Know a Bank Whereon the Wild
Thyme Grows.* The majority of his larger works were composed and
published in London, though a number had been reprinted in New
York before he came to this country.

2. EARLY SONG WRITERS

Sigmund Spaeth once wrote that the history of American manners,
morals, tastes, and absurdities is largely written in our songs. Famous
historical events have always been commemorated musically, but our
lighter ballads have gone further; in intimate fashion they tell of what
we were thinking, and how we were consoling ourselves at the time
they were written.

The last chapter discussed early nineteenth-century concerts, and
musical organizations of a fairly serious character. The popular concerts
and recitals of the day, bordering often on entertainments, were closely
associated with songs and ballads that have either survived to our time,
or have at least formed a definite link in the evolutionary chain of our
popular music.

Some of these concert programs were devoted exclusively to ballads,
some to operatic selections, and others to a mixture of light orchestral
pieces, instrumental solos, and contemporary ballads. The New York
Musical Review gave an account of an anniversary concert given by the
Euterpean Society at the City Hotel, January 30, 1839, in which the
"orchestra was superior to that we have heard in New York, in respect
to the amount of *talent* it contained." For this, it said, "much praise
is due to the Society, which consists of amateurs, and especially to Mr.
Quin, the leader, who is also an amateur, for the manner in which the
overtures were got up."

The orchestra consisted of amateurs, with the first desks occupied
by professionals. There were six first violins, five second violins, four
tenors (violas), three cellos, and two contrabasses. The wind section
consisted of two clarinets, two oboes, two bassoons, four horns, and two
trumpets. Drums, cymbals, and kettledrums formed the percussion

group. Mr. and Mrs. Horn were the vocalists, and U. C. Hill and William Scharfenberg were among the professional instrumentalists.

A compilation of New York newspaper references to music in the year 1839, made by Miss Kathleen Munro, shows that there were at least seventy concerts. Of these, ten were devoted to sacred music, some of them performances by the New York Sacred Music Society with the assistance of church choirs from surrounding towns. Ten offered operatic selections from the Italian repertoire, presented by the Seguins and such visiting artists as Madame Albini, Madame Vellani, and Signora Maroncelli. Six were chiefly instrumental recitals, one given by Baron Rudolph de Fleur, pianist of His Majesty the Emperor of Russia. Fourteen were a mixture of vocal and instrumental selections. The largest classification was that of the ballad concerts; there were at least thirty of them. The Horns were the most prominent of the recitalists, and not only offered their own ballad concerts, but participated in those given by others, and in concerts and recitals of various types.

Two of the most prominent singers of the time were visiting Englishmen who were also ballad composers. The name of Joseph Philip Knight will be immortal, among bassos particularly, for *Rocked in the Cradle of the Deep*, which he wrote when he visited America in 1839. Henry Russell can be forgiven much for his setting of Morris's *Woodman, Spare That Tree*.

JOSEPH PHILIP KNIGHT (1812–1887) was a prolific ballad composer and singer who became eventually a clergyman of the Church of England, and was ordained by the Bishop of Exeter to the charge of St. Agnes in the Scilly Isles. At the age of sixteen he had studied harmony under Crofe, at one time organist of Bristol Cathedral. The single year he spent in the United States, 1839, was one of the most productive of his career.

At the concert for the benefit of the Indigent Female Assistance Society it was announced that "Mr. J. P. Knight will make his first appearance in this country, and will sing four of his most popular songs." Two of these songs were written by himself: *Oh Lord, I Have Wandered*, and *The Veteran*. Three days later, March 1, he sang his setting of T. H. Bayly's *She Wore a Wreath of Roses*, in which the unfortunate heroine is introduced, first wearing roses, then orange blossoms, and finally a widow's somber cap.

Knight made nine appearances in New York in the first half of the year, and returned to the city in the fall for another series of concerts. For October 9, the newspapers announced a Grand Concert at which "Mr. Knight, in addition to his most popular songs, will introduce three of his latest compositions, which have never yet been heard in public." These were *Cupid, 'mid the Roses Playing, Twenty Years Ago*, and most important of all, *Rocked in the Cradle of the Deep*. His American visit also inspired *Oh, Fly to the Prairie*, and *The Old Year's Gone, and the New Year's Come*.

The song that did much to establish Knight's vogue as a song writer was *The Grecian Daughter*, to words by Thomas Haynes Bayly, composer and writer of *Long, Long Ago*. The verses were prophetic of the coming school of self-pity:

> Oh! never heed my mother dear,
> The silent tears I shed;
> Indeed I will be happy here,
> Then ask me not to wed.
> By day you shall not see me weep,
> Nor nightly murmur in my sleep;
> But ask me not to be a bride,
> For when my own dear Lara died,
> I kiss'd his brow, I breath'd a vow,
> Ah! bid me not to break it now.

HENRY RUSSELL (1812–1900) spent more time in America than Knight; he was here for nearly nine years—1833 to 1841. He had a keen sense of dramatic values and platform effectiveness. A master of hokum, he could draw cheers from his audiences at will. He was well educated musically, and at one time he had been a pupil of Rossini in Naples. Although of Jewish extraction, he came to America as organist of the First Presbyterian Church in Rochester, New York, and then traveled extensively as a concert singer.

Russell was very busy in New York during the year that Knight was in this country, and the two often appeared on the same programs. He must have been a drawing card, for his appearance was generally featured. On February 25, the Board of Managers of the New York Sacred Music Society had "the honor to state that they had prevailed on Mr. Russell to remain in town for this occasion, when he will perform his celebrated Sacred Songs of *The Skeptic's Lament, Wind of the Winter's Night, The Maniac, The Charter Oak,*" and others. The performance was "intended to surpass that of any other occasion." Three days later the committee of the concert for Indigent Females felt "happy to announce that Mr. H. Russell had kindly volunteered his services." His participation in Mr. Davis's benefit (March 1) was announced as "Mr. Henry Russell's Last Appearance in New York." Like many other farewell appearances it was followed by concerts March 5 and May 24.

After a number of Russell's concerts in the fall of 1839, Mrs. Horn, giving a concert of her own, advertised that she had "the pleasure of announcing the valuable services of Mr. H. Russell, who has politely postponed his departure for the South." Whether he lacked funds for traveling, or just decided he didn't want to go, the latter part of December found him still in New York, giving a series of concerts with the Seguins.

John Hill Hewitt gave an account of Russell in his book *Shadows on the Wall:*

He spent much of his time in Baltimore, though New York was his headquarters. In person he was rather stout, but not tall. His face was prepossessing, of the Hebrew cast, dark and heavy whiskers and curly hair. He was an expert at wheedling audiences out of applause, and adding to the effect of his songs by a brilliant pianoforte accompaniment. With much self-laudation he used often to describe the wonderful influence of his descriptive songs over audiences.

On one occasion he related an incident connected with "Woodman, Spare that Tree." He had finished the last verse. . . . The audience were spellbound for a moment, and then poured out a volume of applause that shook the building to its foundation. In the midst of this tremendous evidence of their boundless gratification, a snowy-headed gentleman, with great anxiety depicted in his venerable features, arose and demanded silence. He asked, with a tremulous voice: "Mr. Russell, in the name of Heaven, tell me, was the tree spared?" "It was, sir," replied the vocalist. "Thank God! Thank God! I breathe again!" and then he sat down, perfectly overcome by his emotions. This miserable bombast did not always prove a clap-trap; in many instances it drew forth hisses.

Russell's voice was a baritone of limited register; the few good notes he possessed he turned to advantage. His "Old Arm Chair," for instance, has but five notes in its melodic construction. . . .

Russell once called on me and asked me to write him a song on an "Old Family Clock" (he was remarkably fond of the prefix *old*; a wag of a poet once sent him some words addressed to an "Old Fine-tooth Comb"). I wrote the words. He then changed his mind, and employed me, promising good pay, to write a descriptive song on the "Drunkard," to stir up the temperance people. I pleased him much by beginning the song in this way: "The *old* lamp burned on the *old* oaken stool." He made a taking affair of it; and he made money on it too, but I never even got his promise to pay. . . .

The Old Arm Chair was published in 1840, and is one of our very early mother songs.

> I love it! I love it, and who shall dare
> To chide me for loving that old Arm chair.

> 'Tis bound by a thousand bands to my heart
> Not a tie will break, not a link will start,
> Would ye learn the spell, a mother sat there.

A few years later Russell decided that the idea was good for another song, especially if it drew a moral from the first. Accordingly, he published *Oh! Weep Not*, a companion to *The Old Arm Chair*, copies of which sold for six and a fourth cents.

> Oh! Weep not, oh! weep not, nor idly sigh
> Thy tears can recall not the days gone by.

> But neglect not the precepts, forget not the prayer
> Which thy mother taught thee from her old arm chair.

This custom of following a successful song with a companion, or sequel, was prevalent at the time. When Bayly had scored a success with *Oh, No, We Never Mention Her*, he may have decided that he had been a bit hard on the lady, and presented her side of the story to the public with *She Never Blamed Him, Never*, "answer to the admired ballad *Oh, No, We Never Mention Her*." Instead of "blaming him,"

> She sighed when he caressed her
> For she knew that they must part;
> She spoke not when he press'd her
> To his young and panting heart;

The banners waved around her
And she heard the bugles sound—
They pass'd—and strangers found her
Cold and lifeless on the ground.

In one respect times were changing. In the eighteenth century, songs were sung by certain artists with "unbounded" applause. As competition became keen they were announced as sung with "rapturous" applause—which must have proved emotionally wearing to the audience.

The songs that belong to Russell's American period were *The Brave Old Oak; The Charter Oak; The Old Bell; The Ivy Green; Our Way Across the Mountain, Ho; Woodman, Spare That Tree; The Wreck of the Mexico; A Life on the Ocean Wave; I Love the Man with a Generous heart; Those Locks, Those Ebon Locks*, and many others, including *The Old Sexton*, the gravedigger who sings, as he "gathers them in": "and their final rest is here, down here on the earth's dark breast."

Although he was a favorite with the public, Russell had his critics, for there were some who did not fall victim to his theatrical charms. One reviewer in Boston wrote that the only item Russell had omitted from his program was the "old boot jack." His methods were not designed for Americans alone, for when he returned to England, he continued the same kind of concerts, and the same ways of getting publicity. If he had his tongue in his cheek here, he at least failed to remove it when he went home. Dwight's *Journal* of April 16, 1853 contained the following item, under the heading "Miscellaneous."

A Life on the Ocean Wave! Ho, ho, etc. Mr. Henry Russell, a great charlatan, has put forth a scheme for ameliorating the condition of the poor, by advertising in the program of a week's entertainment, just concluded at the Strand Theatre, that he will each evening present a ticket to every person at entrance, which will entitle them to a chance of obtaining a free passage to America. The drawing will take place after his entertainment.

He lived to be eighty-eight years old. In 1889, *A Life on the Ocean Wave* was made the official march of the Royal marines, and *Cheer, Boys, Cheer* has for many years been the only air played by British regimental fife and drum corps when a regiment goes abroad. His sons achieved fame on their own account. One, Henry Russell, was an impresario, and the other, Landon Ronald, an eminent British composer.

And now for the rest of the Hewitt family, the sons and daughters of the James Hewitt who came to New York in 1792. Few of the songs of JOHN HILL HEWITT (1801–1890), his eldest son, are sung today, but they were once so popular that their composer became a decided influence in shaping the style of our lighter ballads. His life was so varied, and his exploits so colorful, that he occupies a unique position in both the musical and literary history of America. Any man who won a poetry contest against Edgar Allan Poe warrants mention as a curiosity, if for no other reason. Hewitt has been termed the "Father of the American ballad." Obviously, this is too great a claim, for English influences have been too pronounced for us to grant that title to any of our native composers.

In the letters of his father, written just before his death to his younger son James Lang Hewitt, the elder Hewitt expressed his concern over the ways of John, the rolling stone:

John I am still uneasy about. When you see him, or write, tell him his father in his latter moments did not forget him—left him his blessing, with the hope that he will turn his mind to one particular object, that he may get thro the World respected.

And a few weeks later:

In the *Weekly Mirror* and *Advertiser* of here [New York] I see the last two papers that have poetry of John's. Very pretty, but he ought to write to me.

In an undated document addressed to James L., in which the father disposes of his worldly goods, there is another reference to John:

. . . there is a reserve in my character which others have said was pride. No—it has been that I should not force myself into others' company. John unfortunately has this latter—it is right for a young man to be in some degree reserved—but in case of business that must in a great degree be laid aside, as it is necessary to have some degree of effrontery to get on in the world. This I am afraid will keep John, with all his talents, poor like myself. It is a fact that a man with independence, without talent, will make a fortune, while the modest man, let his talents be ever so great, will be kept in the background.

John, as we shall see, never let modesty deter him in later life.

This eldest son of James Hewitt was born in Maiden Lane, New York, July 11, 1801. When he was eleven the family moved to Boston, and the boy was placed in the public schools. Later he was apprenticed to a sign painter, but he disliked the work so much that he ran away. He then entered the employ of a commission firm named Lock and Andrews, and stayed with them until they failed a few years later. By this time the family had moved back to New York, and in 1818, John secured an appointment to West Point. Various legends have sprung up regarding his career at the military academy, one to the effect that he was breveted a second lieutenant after successfully completing three years of study. Another story tells that at the end of four years he was graduated, but resigned his commission immediately afterwards. Still another connects him with a plot of the Southern cadets to get control of the Academy and blow up the superintendent in 1820.

None of these accounts is accurate. The records of the War Department show that Hewitt was admitted to the academy from New York on September 21, 1818. When he was a member of the graduating class in 1822 he was turned back to the next line class because of deficiency in studies, and did not return the following year. There is no record of his participation in any disturbance.

At the time of his death in 1890, an obituary notice in the Baltimore *American* said that among his fellow cadets were Beauregard, Robert E. Lee, Polk, Johnson, and Jackson. While at the academy he had studied music with Willis, the leader of the West Point band, and when he left and went South, he turned to music teaching as the pleasantest way to earn a living. He also started his editorial work, and became associated with newspapers in the various cities in which he lived. Soon after leaving West Point he married his first wife Estelle Mangin, who bore him seven children.

Shortly after his marriage, Hewitt's father persuaded him to join a theatrical company he was organizing to tour the South. The venture ended in failure, and the company was burned out in a fire in Augusta, Georgia. He stayed in Augusta for a short while and then went to Columbia, South Carolina, where he taught music, composed, and commenced the study of law. From Columbia he went to Greenville, and established a newspaper called the *Republican*. Meeting with reverses he returned to Augusta.

It was about this time (1825) that he composed his first song *The Minstrel's Return from the War*. On the original manuscript of this song, now at the Library of Congress, the composer in later years penciled the following memorandum:

This song, as crude as it is, was one of my first musical efforts. It was composed in 1825 in the village of Greenville, S.C. now a city of 10,000 souls. When I returned to the North, I took this book with me to Boston. My brother James was a music publisher. I gave him a copy to publish—he did it very reluctantly—did not think it worthy of a copyright. It was eagerly taken up by the public, and established my reputation as a ballad composer. It was sung all over the world—and my brother, not securing the right, told me that he missed making at least $10,000.

He returned to the North because of his father's death in 1827. He remained for a short while in Boston, and worked on the staff of the *Massachusetts Journal*. He soon departed for the South again, intending to go back to Georgia, but a visit to Baltimore determined him to stay in that city, where he spent the greater part of his long life.

In Baltimore he immediately became active in newspaper work, music, and matters theatrical. He was also achieving some contemporary fame as both composer and poet. He became the editor of the *Visitor*, and when that paper sponsored a literary contest, he entered a poem under a nom de plume. He called it *The Song of the Wind*, and it was awarded the prize over Edgar Allan Poe's *The Coliseum*. In his book of memories, *Shadows on the Wall*, Hewitt told the story of the contest:

The proprietors of the journal . . . offered two premiums; one of $100 for the best story, another of $50 for the best poem. I was editor of the paper at the time. The committee on the awards . . . decided that Poe's weird tale entitled "A Manuscript Found in a Bottle" should receive first premium. There were two poems selected from the four-score offered, as worthy of the second award. They were "The Coliseum" by Poe, and "The Song of the Wind," by myself. The judges were brought to a stand, but, after some debate, agreed that the latter should receive the second prize, as the author of the former had already received the first. This decision did not please Poe, hence the "little unpleasantness" between us.

Poe received his money with many thanks; I preferred a silver goblet, which is now in my family.

The opening lines of Hewitt's poem were as follows:

> Whence come ye with your odor-laden wings,
>   Oh, unseen wanderer of the summer night?
> Why, sportive, kiss my lyre's trembling strings,
>   Fashioning wild music, which the light
> Of listening orbs doth seem in joy to drink?
>   Ye wanton 'round my form and fan my brow,
> While I hold converse with the stars that wink
>   And laugh upon the mirror stream below.

The "little unpleasantness" between Poe and Hewitt had had fuel to feed it several years before the contest. When a volume of Poe's poems, *Al Aaraaf, Tamerlane and Minor Poems*, had appeared three years earlier (1829), Hewitt, as reviewer for the *Minerva*, admiring "the richness and smoothness of Thomas Moore and the grandeur of Byron," took occasion to assail the uneven and irregular rhythm of the comparatively unknown poet, whom with all his "brain cudgelling," he could not compel himself to understand "line by line, or the sum total."

The result of the contest, added to previous insults, was a little too much for the moody Poe. The next time he met Hewitt on the street, he accused him of using underhand methods as editor of the *Visitor* to win the prize. Words resulted in blows, but they were separated before any serious damage was done. Hewitt never forgave Poe for achieving fame; they parted as friends outwardly, but in *Shadows on the Wall* he expressed his real opinion:

Poe was not the poet he was said to be; he added but little to the literary reputation of our country. His "Raven" to be sure, gained him vast renown (particularly after he had rested in the grave for nearly 26 years!); but the idea was not original—it was taken from the old English poets. The "Manuscript Found in a Bottle" a composition which won several prizes, was only a new version of the "Rhyme of an Ancient Mariner."

For many years tributes to Poe have called forth reminders of the contest from Hewitt's admirers. When the University of Virginia unveiled the Poe monument, a correspondent of the New York *Herald* asked if it "would not be well to recognize the talents of one who was contemporary with Poe, and whose poetic genius won the prize over the very poem, the 'Coliseum,' quoted in the editorial column of the New York *Herald* of October 2!" The underrated genius complex went to extremes among Hewitt's admirers; there was even a tradition that he had sold ten of his song manuscripts to Stephen Foster, one of them *Old Folks at Home*.

In 1840, Hewitt moved to Washington, where he established and edited a paper called the *Capitol*. Five years later he went to Norfolk, Virginia, and then returned to Baltimore in 1847. Shortly after this he was offered a position as music teacher at the Chesapeake Female College in Hampton, Virginia. He went there and stayed for nine years. In Hampton his wife died.

When John Brown's raid made it apparent that northern Virginia would be an active scene for future hostilities between North and South, Hewitt left Hampton for Chambersburg and later went to Richmond. When Virginia seceded from the Union, he offered his services to the Confederacy, but he was then over sixty and was not accepted for active military service. Because of his West Point training, Jefferson Davis appointed him to the thankless task of drill master of raw recruits.

In 1863 he went to Savannah, Georgia, and married a former pupil, Mary Alethea Smith. Four more children were subsequently added to the family.

After the war, Hewitt returned to Baltimore and remained there for the rest of his long life. He became one of the characters of the city, and when he died at the age of eighty-nine, Baltimore felt that it had lost one of its links with the past. He had seen Fulton's first steamboat on the Hudson, he was present when the first dispatch was sent over Morse's telegraph line between Baltimore and Washington, and he was a passenger on the first train of cars that had been pulled out of Baltimore by a locomotive.

Hewitt composed over three hundred songs. *The Minstrel's Return from the War* brought him a reputation early in life. This was followed by another song which his brother James published, and had the foresight (or was it hindsight?) to copyright. This song was *The Knight of the Raven Black Plume*, agreeable both in words and music. The opening phrase is akin to Mendelssohn's *On Wings of Song,* undoubtedly a mere coincidence, as Hewitt could hardly have been familiar with Mendelssohn's song at the time. *On Wings of Song* was probably written in 1834; Hewitt's song was published before 1835. Others of his songs were *The Mountain Bugle; Take Me Home; Our Native Land; All Quiet Along the Potomac; Rock Me to Sleep, Mother;* and *Where the Sweet Magnolia Blooms. Take Me Home to the Sunny South* expressed the Southern sentiment after the war.

Although his greatest success was in a narrative type of ballad, Hewitt's oratorio *Jephtha* was given successfully in Washington, Georgetown, Norfolk, and Baltimore. When it was presented at the Broadway Tabernacle in New York with a chorus of two hundred and an orchestra of fifty, it was roughly handled by the critics. The composer also published several cantatas: *Flora's Festival; The Fairy Bridal; The Revellers;* and *The Musical Enthusiast.* His operas were *Rip Van Winkle; The Vivandière; The Prisoner of Monterey;* and *The Artist's Wife.*

In 1838, N. Hickman of Baltimore published a volume of Hewitt's miscellaneous poems. Many of these possess true imagery, and show genuine talent. *Shadows on the Wall,* the book of memories published in 1877, contains many of his later poems. His connections with theatrical enterprises led him to write plays, several of which were produced: *Washington; The Scouts; The Jayhawker; The Marquis in Petticoats; The Log Hut;* and *Plains of Manassas.*

The musical tradition of the Hewitt family has survived to the present generation. HORATIO DAWES HEWITT, the eldest son of John Hill Hewitt, was a musician and composer as well as a music critic. Born in Baltimore, he spent much of his life there, though he lived at various times in New Orleans and St. Louis, owning music stores in both cities. He composed a comic opera and many songs that enjoyed success. He survived his father by only four years, and died in Baltimore in 1894.

Of the brothers of John Hill Hewitt, JAMES LANG HEWITT, born in 1807, devoted his life to the music publishing business which had originally been started by his father when the latter bought Benjamin Carr's New York branch of the Musical Repository in 1798. He first appeared as a publisher on his own account when he joined J. A. Dickson at 34 Market Street, Boston, in 1825. After his father's death he moved back to New York, and became one of the prominent dealers and publishers of the city until the late 1840's. He died in 1853.

The third son of James Hewitt, HORATIO NELSON HEWITT, continued the music business in Boston for a number of years and later moved to New York. The youngest son, GEORGE WASHINGTON HEWITT, was trained as a musician and after a disastrous publishing venture in Philadelphia, settled in Burlington, New Jersey. He was a prolific composer, and his salon pieces for piano were much in demand. His son HOBART DOANE HEWITT, born in 1852, lived for many years in Burlington as a teacher of violin and piano. He died there in 1932. At one time associated with the publishing firm of Theodore Presser in Philadelphia, he published many compositions.

Both of James Hewitt's daughters were musicians. SOPHIA HENRIETTE, the eldest, married Louis Ostinelli, the violinist, who was one of the group that formed the Philharmonic Society with Graupner in Boston. Her daughter ELIZA OSTINELLI became a well-known opera singer after studying at the Conservatory at Naples. At one time she was a prominent prima donna in Europe. She married the Italian Count Biscaccianti, a cellist.

Sophia was organist of the Handel and Haydn Society from 1820 to 1829. She had been brought before the public as a pianist when she was only seven years old, in New York. She also sang and appeared occasionally at the New York concerts of the Euterpean Society. Parker's *Euterpeiad* of May 11, 1822, gave the following estimate of her performances on the piano:

Her playing is plain, sensible and that of a gentlewoman; she neither takes by storm, nor by surprise, but she generally wins upon the understanding, while the ear, though it never fills the other senses with ecttacy [sic] drinks in full satisfaction.

Sophia died in Portland, Maine, in 1846. Her younger sister ELIZA never married, but was a music teacher, first in Boston, and then in Burlington where she lived with her brother.

There were many other song writers in the first half of the nineteenth century who contributed to our ballad literature. JOHN C. BAKER was perhaps best known for his song *Where can the soul find rest?* From this account, the soul has a long search. First the winds are consulted:

Stephen Collins Foster (from a Painting by Marie Goth in the Stephen Foster Conservatories, Carmel, Indiana)

(See pages 184–198)

The first column is the amt I have already rec'd on the Songs. The second column is the computed future value to me.

			$	c			
Oar Forks, music & arrangements			164	46	100	"
Kentucky Home.	do.	do.	137	06	100	"
Dog Tray	"	"	105	025	150	"
Massas in &c.	"	"	90	676	50	"
Nelly Bly	"	"	56	437	20	"
Farewell Lilly	"	"	55	112	50	"
Ellen Bayne	"	"	64	234	350	"
Oh boys	"	"	39	470	25	"
Willie we have missed	"	"	49	777	49 77	"
Maggie by my side	"	"	27	801	75	"
Hard Times	"	"	28	384	200	"
Eulalie	"	"	203	14	50	"
Jeanie with light &c.	"	"	217	80	350	"
Willie my brave	"	"	91	15	20	"
Old Memories	"	"	62	52	15	"
Some Folks			59	91	25	"
Come where my love lies dreaming			59	88	100	"
Little Ella			50	72	10	"
Come with thy sweet voice			54	33	25	"
Way down in Cairo			44	72	5	"
Ring de banjo			35	24	1	"
Village Maiden			36	05	15	"
Crystal Schottisch			44	06	20	"
Farewell old Cottage			30	53	5	"
Wilt thou be gone love			22	20	10	"
My hopes have departed			25	04	5	"
Gentle Annie			39	08	500	"
Jolly Times			21	46	1	"
Annie my own love			19	12	1	"
Lilly Ray			18	08	1	"
Voice of by gone days			17	54	1	"
Holiday Schottisch			17	37	5	"
I cannot sing tonight			16	98	1	"
The hour for thee and me			14	30	1	"
Mary loves the flowers			8	98	1	"
Once I loved thee Mary			8	00	1	"
Social Orchestra			150		$2786 77	
For arranging			10			

In the amts rec'd I have included
$15 on each of the two songs Old
Folks and "Farewell Lilly", from E. P. Christy,
also $10 on each of the songs Dog Tray,
Oh boys", Massas in & Ellen Bayne.

Foster's Own Account of His Income from
Royalties (1857)

(See page 195)

Tell me, ye winged winds, that round my pathway roar,
Do ye not know some spot, where mortals weep no more,
Some lone and pleasant dell, some valley in the West,
Where free from toil and pain, the weary soul may rest?

Chorus

The loud winds dwindled to a whisper low
And sighed for pity as it answered, No! No!

The second and third verses address the "mighty deep" and the "serenest moon," with no better results. Finally the bard goes to headquarters and finds the answer:

Tell me, my secret soul, oh! tell me hope and faith,
Is there no resting place from sorrow, sin, and death;
Is there no happy spot where mortals may be bless'd
Where grief may find a balm, and weariness a rest?

Chorus

Faith, Hope, and Love, best boons to mortals giv'n
Wav'd their bright wings and whispered, "Yes, in Heav'n."

THOMAS BRICHER was organist of the Bowdoin Street Church in Boston in the fifties. Among his contributions to balladry were *Oh! Home of My Boyhood, My Own Country Home;* and *Our Fathers' Old Halls,* "as sung at the concerts of the Boston Musical Institute."

To WILLIAM CLIFTON we owe one of the most complete examples of noble resignation—*The Last Link is Broken* (published about 1840):

The last link is broken that bound me to thee,
And the words I have spoken have rendered me free;
That bright glance misleading on others may shine,
Those eyes smil'd unheeding when tears burst from mine:
If my love was deem'd boldness that error is o'er,
I've witnessed thy coldness and prize thee no more.

Refrain

I have not lov'd lightly, I'll think on thee yet,
I'll pray for thee nightly till life's sun has set.

If FREDERICK WILLIAM NICHOLLS CROUCH (1808–1896) had postponed writing *Kathleen Mavourneen* for twelve years we might have been able to claim it as an American song. Crouch was an Englishman who came here in 1849 at the age of forty, and lived here until his death in 1896. An excellent cellist, he had been a member of the Drury Lane Theatre in London, and had taught singing. *Kathleen Mavourneen* was first published in 1839, and scored an immediate success.

The composer came to America as cellist in the Astor Place Theatre in New York. Later he went to Boston. Next to Portland, Maine, where he gave an excellent series of chamber music concerts; then to Philadelphia as conductor of a series of Saturday concerts, and afterwards to Washington, where he started an unsuccessful music school. At the time of the Civil War he was in Richmond, and joined the Confederate Army as a trumpeter. If Stonewall Jackson, on a forced march, had not ordered burned all superfluous baggage of officers and troops, Crouch would have published his manuscript notes as a history of the Civil War. After the war he settled in Baltimore as a singing teacher, and many years later died in Portland. Among the songs he wrote in America was *The Blind Piper*, published in Philadelphia in 1856. He was also the composer of two operas, *Sir Roger de Coverley* and *The Fifth of November*.

Many of the songs of the day were published anonymously, and it is difficult to determine which were of American origin, and which were reprinted by American publishers from British editions. A great variety of subjects were treated. Love predominates, of course, and sometimes such renunciation of worldly joys as was expressed in *I Will Be a Nun*:

> I've been long enough in mischief, 'tis sufficient I have done
> And my Mother's often told me that I must be a Nun.
>
> My Mother now is satisfied; and men must let me be,
> The Nuns will surely like to have a Novice mild as me.

Sometimes the songs dealt with more practical subjects, such as the *Multiplication Table*, published by John G. Klemm in Philadelphia, which covered all items up to twelve times twelve.

3. SINGING FAMILIES

An institution which had a profound effect on the song literature of the nineteenth century was that of the "singing family." These singing-family troupes traveled far and wide, and the songs they sang became the popular songs of the American people. They were at the height of their popularity from the early 1840's to the 1860's, and many of them offered instrumental as well as vocal music.

The best known of the troupes were the Alleghanians, Amphions, Bakers, Barkers, Bohannas, Browns, Burdetts, Cheneys, Foxes, Gibsons, Harmoneons, Hutchinsons, Moravians, Orpheans, the Peak and Berger Families of Bell Ringers, and Father Kemp's Old Folks. Each troupe usually consisted of four singers, including one or two women. They called themselves "families," and in such songs as *Our Home Is on the Mountain Brow* (Alleghanians) or *Will You Come to My Mountain Home* (Orphean Family), they tried to convey the atmosphere of the American outdoors. Some of them did come from the mountains—the Hutchinson and the Baker Families of New Hampshire, and the Cheney Family of Vermont. These groups did not sing what we would now call folk songs, but rather "ballads" of every description—sentimental, dramatic, comic, and realistic. They often wrote their own verses and sometimes even their own tunes. They gave their performances in whatever buildings were available—concert halls, churches, and even barns. In their style of singing they differed noticeably from that of Italian opera which then dominated American musical taste. They sang their songs in simple harmonizations, sometimes improvised, and with closely blended voices. They enunciated their words most clearly, though with utter informality.

The best known of the early troupes was the Hutchinson Family, whose members had a farm in Milford, New Hampshire. About 1842 they began to make concert tours, first as a trio, and soon as a quartet consisting of the brothers Judson, John, and Asa, and their sister Abby. For some time they accompanied their songs with two violins and a cello, and occasionally a guitar. Later, however, they sang without instrumental accompaniment. In early years they styled themselves "Aeolian Vocalists," a name which they soon replaced with that of "The Hutchinson Family."

Giving concerts was not the sole concern of the Hutchinsons. Their aim was to serve a progressive cause—that of abolitionism. Mincing no words on this explosive issue of their time, they made many friends and many enemies. Their reputation steadily increased. They counted among their admirers John Greenleaf Whittier, Henry W. Longfellow, William Lloyd Garrison, Frederick Douglas, and many others. Besides abolitionism, the Hutchinsons advocated temperance, religious socialism, revivalism, and even spiritualism. As their theme song they adopted a tune which was popular around 1840—*You Will See Your Lord a-Coming*—a hymn of the Second Adventists. The Hutchinsons wrote their own words for it:

> We have come from the mountains,
> Of the "Old Granite State."
> We're a band of brothers
> And we live among the hills.
>
> With a band of music,
> We are passing round the world.
> We have left our aged parents,
> In the "Old Granite State."
>
> We obtain'd their blessing,
> And we bless them in return.
> Good old-fashioned singers,
> They can make the air resound.
>
> Equal liberty is our motto
> In the "Old Granite State."
> We despise oppression,
> And we cannot be enslaved.

The songs the Hutchinsons sang ran into the dozens. One of their antislavery songs was called *Get Off the Track*, and it began:

> Ho, the car Emancipation
> Rides majestic through our nation.

Though the singing mountain families became an American institution, their roots were in Europe. In the 1830's, when interest in folk music was rampant in Europe, small ensembles of folk singers and instrumentalists from the Bavarian, Austrian, and Swiss Alps roamed the continent, yodling and fiddling their native music in beer gardens as well as in theatres and concert halls. One of the first of these ensembles —the first, at least, to gain wide recognition—was a vocal group, the brothers Felix, Anton, and Franz Rainer, and their sister Maria. They were originally cattle dealers at Fuegen in the Ziller Valley of the Tyrol. In 1824 they went on their first concert tour and met with instantaneous success. When they appeared in London during the season 1827–28, they became literally the rage of the town, and through the active support of the composer-pianist Ignace Moscheles, they entered the most exclusive circles of society.

A little more than ten years later, during the fall of 1839, another Rainer Family arrived in New York, consisting at first only of distant relatives of the older group. Soon, however, they were joined by Franz Rainer, and they stayed in the United States for four years, giving concerts with hardly an interruption in New York, in Southern cities, in the Northeast, and in Canada. During the season 1840–41 they made Boston their headquarters, and it did not take them long to arouse the enthusiasm of New England audiences. Local musicians, including Lowell Mason, praised them for the perfect blending of their voices and the unanimity and simplicity of their expression. They were held up as models by music educators who were working to stimulate the interest of the average American in the pleasures of choral singing.

The success of the Rainers encouraged Americans to form similar ensembles. Thus, the Hutchinsons were sometimes called the "New Hampshire Rainers," and they started out by imitating the Tyrolese mountain style of singing, and by having "Alpine" songs in their repertoire, such as *The Vulture of the Alps*, and *The Lament of the Alpine Shepherd Boy*. The Hutchinsons' song *We Are Happy and Free* was nothing but an adaptation of the *Grand March* of the Rainers. They were, however, keenly conscious of the competition of foreign troupes, and at the beginning of their career they printed the following lines on their programs:

> When foreigners approach your shores,
> You welcome them with open doors.
> Now we have come to seek our lot,
> Shall native talent be forgot?

4. MINSTREL SHOWS AND THEIR SONGS

Negro minstrelsy—the impersonation of Negroes in action and song by white men—was more characteristically American. It developed about the late 1820's and lasted approximately to the turn of the century, though it degenerated after the Civil War. At that time Negro minstrelsy began to lose its "Negroid" flavor and to develop in the direction of a sumptuous vaudeville show. It was then that the term "show business" originated.

American theatrical performances in the 1820's and 1830's generally offered a variety of features in one evening: short dramas and farces, dances, and songs. Black-face acts came to be included, and two types of Negro impersonators developed: one, in ragged clothes, fashioned after the Southern plantation hand; the other portraying the Northern Negro, the dandy, who, with ridiculous effect, tried to emulate the white man.

It has been claimed that Gottlieb Graupner may have been the first of the black-face singers, but the men who first popularized the type were Thomas Dartmouth ("Daddy") Rice, Bob Farrel, and George Washington Dixon. Rice is said to have started the idea more or less spontaneously by borrowing an old Negro's clothes, and imitating his singing of the *Jim Crow* song.

Rice literally whipped his audiences into a frenzy, in America and in England. He must have been an actor of great imagination. He sang the first part of *Jim Crow* in a more or less static pose:

> Come listen all you gals and boys,
> I'm just from Tuckyhoe;
> I'm going to sing a leetle song,
> My name's Jim Crow.

But in the refrain:

> Wheel about and turn about,
> And do jis so;
> Eb'ry time I wheel about,
> I jump Jim Crow

he used grotesque gestures and steps of a style which would delight the modern American painter Thomas Benton.

The other early type of impersonation was that of the "Broadway swell." He swaggered about the stage in his modish coat, his "long-tail blue," as he called it, his silk hat, his walking cane, his lorgnon, and told his audience how successful he was with the ladies. Either in the refrain or during the instrumental music between stanzas he did a few dance steps. The name of one of these dandies was *Zip Coon*, whose song— generally entitled *Turkey in the Straw*—is still sung. No Negro minstrel, or "Ethiopian Delineator," as he figured on playbills, forgot to make his quips about the political issues of his time.

In the late thirties, the solo black-face banjoist and the solo "Negro dancer" became popular. Joe Sweeny and Billy Whitlock were famous banjoists who tapped out the rhythm while they played and sang. John Diamond was one of the best-known dancers. His "Negro breakdowns" were a mixture of Irish and Scotch jigs with Negroid gestures and steps. These dances were popular among the Western boatmen and backwoodsmen long before they were performed on the stage. They were characterized by comic jumps and a heel-and-toe technique which anticipated modern tap dancing.

From the early forties on, small ensembles of "Negro" performers appeared in ever increasing numbers on the theatrical stage and in the circus ring. Some of the teams consisted of a banjoist and a dancer (such as Whitlock and Diamond), or two dancers who also sang and acted. Soon banjoists, fiddlers, singers, and dancers formed trios in various combinations.

Some comic scenes were included and were called "Negro extravaganzas." There were also Negro plays which were longer and had a larger cast, figuring as "Ethiopian Opera." They were the successors of the English ballad-opera and the forerunners of our modern musical comedies. They included spoken conversation and a great deal of music—songs with choral refrains, duets, and dances. Popular minstrel songs were mostly used, though occasionally vocal or instrumental excerpts were borrowed from real operas. T. D. Rice is credited with having written the two well-known "Ethiopian operas"—*O Hush, or The Virginny Cupids* and *Bone Squash*. Female roles were played by men who made a specialty of impersonating "Negro wenches."

At the beginning of 1843, the first minstrel band—an early "jazz band"—made its appearance, and along with it came the first real minstrel show. Many companies have claimed to have originated the idea, but the Virginia Minstrels were without doubt the first to make a success. "Old Dan Emmit" (later "Emmett," the composer of *Dixie*) was the "leader" of the band. He played the fiddle, Billy Whitlock the banjo, Frank Brower the bones (a kind of linked castanets), and Dick Pelham the tambourine. When they performed they sat in a semicircle with the bone and tambourine players at the ends. Their program consisted of songs and choral refrains, banjo solos, Negro dances, comic stump speeches, jokes, and comic repartee. Scraping, thumping, rattling, and jingling, they produced a merry and humorously incongruous sound. There was no body to the tone of the ensemble, since all instruments were fairly high pitched and the banjoist played no chords. Instead, he picked his tunes, as was the custom with minstrel music, and when he had warmed up, he would invent variants and variations by adding notes of the open strings, especially the highest one.

The first full-length show of the Virginia Minstrels was given March 7, 1843 at the Masonic Temple in Boston. This event may be considered the official beginning of the "minstrel show," even though many other bands appeared only a few weeks after the Virginia Minstrels had made their New York debut, probably on February 6, 1843, at the Bowery Amphitheatre. Some of these companies were the Columbia Minstrels, Kentucky Minstrels, Alabama Minstrels, Kentucky Rattlers, Missouri Minstrels, Ethiopian Serenaders, and the Congo Minstrels.

Most of these bands performed as "Northern Darkies" in the first part of their show and as "Southern Darkies" in the second. This division led in the fifties to the almost complete elimination of "Negroid" features in the first part and to the introduction of sentimental salon music.

The banjo, the fiddle, and the bones were used by the real plantation Negroes. Whether the tambourine was indigenous with them is uncertain, though they might have borrowed it from their white masters. In combination with the fiddle, it was well known to Western river boatmen; and these rivermen served the early minstrels as models just as much as the Negroes did. Some minstrel bands included the triangle, and another Negro instrument—the jawbone of an ass, ox, or horse, whose loose teeth rattled as the players struck it with a stick, or simply shook it.

The size of the minstrel band steadily increased during the 1840's, until towards the end of the fifties, it often numbered a dozen players. The old instruments, with the exception of the jawbone, were still in use, but regular orchestral instruments had been added. Among the prominent minstrel companies of the fifties were the Christy Minstrels, White's Serenaders, Bryant's Minstrels, and others. From the sixties on, a trend towards large ensembles set in and resulted in mammoth companies which had to be transported from town to town in special railroad cars. The imaginative primitiveness of early minstrelsy had disappeared forever.

For songs, the Negro minstrels laid their hands on anything they thought would serve their purposes. They borrowed from folk music, mainly that of the British Isles, and even from the popular Italian operas of their time, adapting their own Negro words to these tunes. But they also created a music of their own which after a few decades turned out to be more indigenously American than any compositions of more learned composers. In its October issue of 1845, the serious New York magazine *The Knickerbocker* suggested that the creators of Negro minstrel songs be considered "our only truly national poets."

Negro minstrel songs of the 1820's and 1830's are clearly indebted to foreign sources. Some show unmistakably the style of eighteenth-century opera buffa—*Bonja Song* and *Coal Black Rose*. *Jim Crow* is a characteristic variant of an English song from English eighteenth-century opera. *Zip Coon* cannot hide its Irish origin. One of the least derivative and perhaps the most original of minstrel songs of the 1830's is *Sich a Gitting Upstairs*. Its tune possesses a true folk vigor and jaunti-ness. Its first stanza reads:

> On a Suskehanna raft I come down de bay
> And I danc'd and I frolick'd, and fiddled all de way,
> Sich a gitting up stairs I never did see
> Sich a gitting up stairs I never did see.

In the late 1840's the production and publication of minstrel songs increased. A characteristic style now evolved. Scotch and Irish elements, plus features typical of banjo music, were blended into something that bore the flavor of the American scene. It possessed nonchalant humor, brevity, sturdiness, and the inflection of Negro dialect or everyday slang. How much the slaves contributed to this style is hard to say. If they stimulated the white composer at all, it was more in rhythm than in melody. But the short, recurrent phrases of minstrel tunes, characteristic of all primitive music, appealed so much to them that they took these tunes over enthusiastically and completely identified themselves with them. Many of these early minstrel songs are still sung today in the backwoods. Among the best are *Old Dan Tucker*, *Dandy Jim*, *'Twill Nebber Do to Gib It Up So*, *Ole Pee Dee*, *Jonny Boker*, *Old Gray Goose*, *I'm Gwine Ober de Mountains*, *O Lud Gals Gib Me Chaw Terbackur*, *Ole Bull and Old Dan Tucker*, and *De Boatmen's Dance*. A most characteristic song was *Ole Dad*, published in Boston in 1844. Its first two stanzas read:

> I'be sung so much ob Dandy Jim,
> Ob course you knows all about him;
> I'be heard it sed when I was a lad,
> 'Twas a wise child knew his own old dad.

(Refrain)

> Old Dad!
> Old Dad!
> Old Dad he took a swim all along,
> He dive like a fedder an he swim like a stone.

> One day my daddy took a swim,
> Him hung he clothes on a hick'ry limb,
> He could not swim an dibe berry bad,
> So dat was de last ob my old dad.

> Old Dad!

The refrain, along with its accompaniment, really anticipates jazz in its partly somber, partly sensual tone, its slangy, rhythmic shouts followed by brief, "hot" instrumental passages, and in its latent syncopations.

Many of these songs cannot be traced to any author or composer, though almost all Negro minstrels were capable of writing their own literary and musical material. Many of the texts and some of the tunes were composed by Dan Emmett. He is usually credited with *Old Dan Tucker*, but he wrote only its words. During the late 1840's, Stephen Foster composed his humorous, nonsentimental minstrel songs. Though skillful, they follow traditional patterns. *Oh, Susanna* is indebted to *Gwine Long Down* (published by Emmett in 1844, though not composed by him); *Nelly Bly* to *Clare de Kitchen* of the early 1830's; and *Camptown Races* to *Picayune Butler*.

Banjo jigs and variants of songs, full of tricky syncopations, were a part of the imaginative music of Negro minstrelsy. One of the best collections that covers the 1840's and 1850's is Phil Rice's *Correct Method for the Banjo*, Boston, 1858.

The most prominent minstrel song composers of the 1850's and 1860's were Stephen Foster and Dan Emmett. While Foster wrote his plaintive "plantation melodies" for the first part of the minstrel show (which was hardly "Negroid" in character), Emmett composed humorous walk-arounds for the "plantation festival" at the end of the show. Foster's songs were performed by soloists; Emmett's by the entire company.

The name DANIEL DECATUR EMMETT (1815–1904) was once on the lips of thousands of Americans, but for years it became almost forgotten. Little is generally known today of Emmett's activities as a musician, comedian, and composer, for *Dixie* is the only one of his numerous songs that has survived. If it were not for a recent movie, *Dixie* would hardly be associated with Emmett's name. Nevertheless, he actually composed some of the most popular songs of the forties, fifties, and sixties. In the forties it was *'Twill Nebber Do to Gib It Up So, I'm Gwine Ober de Mountains*, and *Old Dan Tucker*. In the fifties his *Root, Hog or Die* and *Jordan Is a Hard Road to Trabel* were great favorites; and in the late fifties and sixties his plantation "walk-arounds" were performed by practically all minstrel companies and were heard in towns and villages all over the United States. Some of the best-known "walk-arounds" were *Billy Patterson; Johnny Roach; What o' Dat; Black Brigade; High Daddy;* and *Dixie's Land*.

Many minstrel songs consist of two sections of about equal length, the second being the refrain, which was usually sung in chorus. The first section is not a mere introduction as it is in modern "popular" songs; it is just as expressive as the refrain itself. Emmett's songs frequently follow the same pattern. The first part of his "walk-arounds" is definitely Negroid in form; it consists of solo passages alternating with recurrent choral ejaculations. Yet if one looks for what we recognize today as Negroid features he is apt to be disappointed. It is true that Emmett asserted: "In the composition of a 'walk-around' (by this I mean the style of music and character of the words) I have always strictly confined myself to the habits and crude ideas of the slaves of the South," but the result was a white man's creation, flavored by not only the Negro's language, manners, and gait, but even more by banjo music and Irish and Scottish influences.

A few quotations may illustrate at least Emmett's literary ideas, his humor, and the form of his songs. The first example is taken from *De Wild Goose Nation,* published in 1844. Only the words of the song are by Emmett:

> Away down south in de wild goose nation,
> I first come to life mong de rest ob creation;
> Dar's where I used to hab de old times ober,
>
> I'd go to bed dead drunk and get up sober;
> I first begin to peep,
> And den I 'gin to creep;
> In de year ob our Lord eighteen hundred fast asleep.

The following stanza from *Jordan Is a Hard Road to Trabel,* published in 1853, is a sample of a later style:

> David and Goliath both had a fight
> A cullud man come behind 'em.
> He hit Goliath on de head wid a bar of soft soap
> And it sounded to de oder side ob Jordan.

(Refrain)
> So take off your coat, boys,
> And roll up your sleeves,
> For Jordan is a hard road to trabel.
> So take off your coat, boys,
> And roll up your sleeves,
> For Jordan is a hard road to trabel, I believe.

The third example is from the walk-around *Sandy Gibson's, or Chaw Roast Beef,* which abounds in nonsense rhymes.

(solo)	In eighteen hundred and forty-four
(chorus)	Oh, hurry up,
(solo)	We used to swim in close to shore;
(chorus)	Fare y'e well, ladies all
(solo)	But when we got beyond the reef,
(chorus)	Oh, hurry up,
(solo)	The boys all holler out "chaw roast beef!"
(chorus)	Fare y'e well, ladies all.

(Entire company)
Sandy, old Sandy, Sandy, old Sandy clam,
Makry, old Makry, Makry, old Makry ham,
Den jis before de break ob day
"Chaw roast beef!"
Dem boys dey stole our clothes away,
"Chaw roast beef!"
De Jack takes ten, an' de ten takes de nine
And we "chaw roast beef" for de rail-road line.

Dan Emmett (or Emmit, as he called himself in early years) spent his childhood in Mount Vernon, a little frontier town in Ohio. He was born there on October 29, 1815. In this struggling, hard-working community his education could hardly be more than elementary. He had his first jobs as a printer with local newspapers. Music was his pastime. He joined the Army at the age of eighteen, pretending to be twenty-one, and there received the only formal musical training he ever got in his life: instruction in reading music and in fifing and drumming. He was stationed in Kentucky, and later in Missouri. Since he showed talent, he was employed as fifer in the "Field Music." After fourteen months in the Army, he probably worked as printer in wintertime and traveled with circuses in summertime, playing in the band. In about 1838 or 1839 he wrote his first Negro lyrics, and in 1840 he learned the banjo. During the next season he appeared for the first time as a black-face singer and banjoist in the circus ring. He afterwards went to New York and performed there, successfully, in trios and duos in variety shows and circuses. As mentioned above, he established his reputation as a "Negro delineator" when he became the "leader" of the Virginia Minstrels, a troupe that made history in the American theatre.

After having traveled with his band through the British Isles, Emmett returned and carried on chiefly as a solo banjoist and singer, always appearing with prominent minstrel companies. In the early fifties he was a member of "White's Serenaders." In the late fall of 1858 he joined "Bryant's Minstrels," the finest troupe of their time, as a composer, black-face instrumentalist, vocalist, and comedian. During the eight years he stayed with them, he wrote his best songs, including *Dixie*. The story of that song is given in Chapter IX. In the middle fifties and the early sixties, Emmett appeared in Chicago, and made numerous tours. In Chicago, as well as in New York, he owned minstrel theatres, but he always gave them up after a while. He was not a good business man. When he left the Bryants, his career was practically at an end. The type of minstrelsy which he represented was fast becoming out of date. He moved to Chicago where the fire of 1871 ruined him completely, and in 1888 he retired with his wife to a little cottage just outside Mount Vernon, Ohio. A few years earlier and again in the nineties he traveled for a while with mammoth minstrel companies, but he was nothing more than a museum piece. In Mount Vernon he eked out a living by doing manual labor and occasionally selling a manuscript copy of *Dixie*. In the last years of his life he was supported by the Actors' Fund of New York. On June 28, 1904, he passed away. Many newspapers ran a notice of his death, but public interest in his person lasted hardly longer than a day.

5. STEPHEN COLLINS FOSTER (1826–1864)

I

Stephen Foster provided one of the summits of American music. To-day he could offer his work without apology or without reservation, for time has proved its worth. Foster was one of the greatest melodists we have yet produced, and some of his simplest songs are among the most beautiful that have ever been written, anywhere. He accomplished what many a better-trained musician has failed to do: he wrote melodies that can be understood by everybody—so poignant, so direct in their appeal that they grow in our affections the more we hear them.

Father Time has had the privilege of correcting John S. Dwight, who once wrote in his *Journal of Music* (1853):

We wish to say that such tunes [*Old Folks at Home*], although whistled and sung by everybody, are erroneously supposed to have taken a deep hold of the popular mind; that the charm is only *skin-deep;* that they are hummed and whistled *without musical emotion,* whistled "for lack of thought"; that they persevere and haunt the morbidly sensitive nerves of deeply musical persons, so that they too hum and whistle them involuntarily, hating them even while they hum them; that such melodies become catching, idle habits, and are not popular in the sense of musically inspiring, but that such and such a melody *breaks out* every now and then, like a morbid irritation of the skin.

A less musical writer in the *Albany State Register* (1852) was more tolerant:

We confess to a fondness for negro minstrelsy. There is something in the melodious "Uncle Ned" that goes directly to the heart, and makes Italian trills seem tame. . . . God bless that fine old colored gentleman, who we have been so often assured has

"Gone where the good niggers go."

Old Folks at Home the *last* negro melody, is on everybody's tongue, and consequently in everybody's mouth. Pianos and guitars groan with it, night and day; sentimental young ladies sing it; sentimental young gentlemen warble it in midnight serenades; volatile young "bucks" hum it in the midst of their business and their pleasures; boatmen roar it out stentorially at all times; all the bands play it; amateur flute players agonize over it at every spare moment; the street organs grind it out at every hour; the "singing stars" carol it on the theatrical boards, and at concerts; the chamber maid sweeps and dusts to the measured cadence of *Old Folks at Home;* the butcher's boy treats you to a strain or two of it as he hands in the steaks for dinner; the milk-man mixes it up strangely with the harsh ding-dong accompaniment of his tireless bell; there is not a "live darkey," young or old, but can whistle, sing, dance and play it, and throw in "Ben Bolt" for seasoning; indeed at every hour, at every turn, we are forcibly impressed with the interesting fact, that—

"Way down upon de Swanee Ribber
 Far, far away,
Dere's whar my heart is turnin' ebber
Dere's whar de old folks stay."

Old Folks at Home had been published less than a year when this was written.

In some respects, Foster was akin to Schubert. He had a natural gift of melody that shone because of its simplicity. Schubert with all his natural genius lacked the power of self-criticism and produced hundreds of works that are forgotten today. From a little over two hundred of Foster's published works only fifty or so are sung nowadays, but these fifty are so potent in their charm that they have long since earned their composer's immortality. His limitations were his power; the few chords he used made his songs direct and simple, and always natural. Had he been a trained musician, his charm might have vanished.

Many legends have grown around Stephen Foster, many of them untrue. Unfortunately, they are still being perpetuated by motion pictures, radio programs, and by magazine writers who do not take the trouble to learn facts. Up to a quarter century ago, this was understandable, and pardonable, for very little had been written about Foster which was based on contemporary documents. In 1920, Harold Vincent Milligan issued a biography of Foster which was more complete than any that had been issued before, not excepting the short biography Stephen's brother Morrison had written in 1896. Yet, while Milligan had the benefit of consultation with several members of the Foster family, only a small number of the Foster family letters and documents were available at that time.

It was not for another decade that a systematic attempt was made to gather together everything in existence pertaining to Stephen Foster. This task was undertaken with distinguished success by Josiah K. Lilly of Indianapolis, who had long been a lover of Foster's songs and who determined to collect and make available to posterity, all first editions (and later editions, too) of Foster's songs, and all the material regarding his life that could be found. Assisted by Fletcher Hodges, Junior, and an able staff, Mr. Lilly achieved his object on a scale that even he had not dreamed of when he began his collection. For several years the material was housed in a stone building in Indianapolis, which was appropriately named "Foster Hall." Then, when it had become truly comprehensive, and had been fully catalogued and indexed, it was given by Mr. Lilly to the Stephen Foster Memorial of the University of Pittsburgh, where it is now available to the public as the "Foster Hall Collection," and is still directed by Mr. Hodges as curator.

Foster Hall has issued a number of publications of its own, most notably a complete set of reproductions of the first editions of every known Foster composition. The collection has also been the main source of information for subsequent writings on Foster, including my own *Stephen Foster, America's Troubadour*, and it has sponsored the writing and publication of the most extensive work on the Foster family to date, *Chronicles of Stephen Foster's Family*, by Evelyn Foster Morneweck, a niece of the composer.

II

Foster's life was altogether tragic. It represented a disintegration that ended almost literally in the gutter. From a parentage of aristocrats on one side, and hardy pioneers on the other, a weakling who lacked the stamina to fight life's battles was produced. Stephen's family loved him, did all in their power to protect and shield him, and yet failed to understand him. Pioneer surroundings are rarely kind to artistic souls, and Stephen was probably born too soon, for it never occurred to the Fosters that the young man's indolence, and his dreaming ways, were in fact his very strength. In the family letters there were many references to the boy's "strange talent for music," but not once was there the thought that the talent should be cultivated. There were few music teachers near at hand, and such diversions were not for able-bodied men. It may be that the world would have been the loser if a musically trained Stephen Foster had not been satisfied to write songs of the utmost simplicity—but his own fate might have been less tragic.

He was born in Lawrenceville, Pennsylvania, near Pittsburgh, on July 4, 1826, the day John Adams and Thomas Jefferson died. He spent his boyhood around Pittsburgh and Allegheny, attended the local schools, and academies at Athens and Towanda, near his eldest brother's home at the time. At seventeen he wrote his first published song *Open thy Lattice, Love*. In 1846 he went to Cincinnati to act as bookkeeper for his brother Dunning, and there he met W. C. Peters, a music publisher his family had known in Pittsburgh. He virtually made Peters a present of *Old Uncle Ned, Oh! Susanna*, and two other songs, which were published as *Songs of the Sable Harmonists*. The publisher is said to have made ten thousand dollars from the songs. This determined Foster to give up the bookkeeping he disliked so heartily, and to make a business of song writing.

Orders began to come to him for songs, and he made a contract with Firth, Pond & Company of New York through which he received a royalty on every copy published. The common belief that Foster did not receive adequate payment for his works is not altogether true— from some he gained many hundreds of dollars. Later, when dissipation had reduced him to a vagabond, he was exploited by unscrupulous publishers. Because he needed money, he had to accept anything that was offered him, but in his better days he dealt chiefly with reputable firms who gave him the benefit of what his compositions earned.

In 1851, E. P. Christy, of Christy's Minstrels, asked Foster to write songs for him which he could sing before they were published. One of these was *Old Folks at Home*, and a clause in the agreement specified that the printed copies were to name Christy as the composer. Morrison Foster said that Christy paid five hundred dollars for this privilege, but this, as we shall find later, was greatly exaggerated. Foster reserved the publishing rights, and had the royalties on the sales.

Except for possible visits to Louisville and Bardstown, Kentucky, Stephen Foster had never been south of the Ohio River when *Old Folks at Home* was published. His idea of Negro singing had been gained from colored church services and from minstrel shows. The name of the *Swanee River* had been suggested by a brother who found the name on the map, and Foster used it because it sounded better than the "Pedee" he had used originally. In 1852 he did take a trip through the South, and observed many incidents of Southern life.

III

When Stephen was six his mother wrote:

. . . Stephen has a drum and marches about with a feather in his hat and a girdle round his waist, whistling "Auld Lang Syne." There still remains something perfectly original about him.

When he was ten he himself wrote to his father:

I wish you to send me a commic songster for you promised to. If I had my pensyl I could rule my paper or if I had the money to buy black ink but if I had my whistle I would be so taken with it I do not think I would write a tall. . . .

This same year he went on a shopping trip with his mother to the music store of Smith & Mellor in Pittsburgh. He picked a flageolet from the counter, and in a few minutes amazed clerks and customers by playing *Hail Columbia*.

Brother Morrison wrote, years later: [1]

Melodies appeared to dance through his head continually. Often at night he would get out of bed, light a candle and jot down some notes of melody on a piece of paper, then retire to bed and to sleep.

And yet to his adoring family these countless indications of talent never once suggested a solution for the boy's future. His musical inclinations troubled them. In 1840 his mother wrote, with apparent relief:

He is not so much devoted to music as he was; other studies seem to be elevated in his opinion; he reads a great deal and fools about none at all.

It is not hard to understand why Stephen's family did not take his love for music seriously. Colonel William Barclay Foster, his father, was a man of practical affairs. A love of pioneering, and disregard of its dangers, left little room for softer pleasures. He had settled in Pittsburgh when it was a border settlement, twenty days from Philadelphia by pack horse and wagon. Finding employment with Anthony Beelen and Ebenezer Denny, merchants "in dry goods, hardware, groceries, stationery, perfumery, china, glass and queensware," he made himself valuable by taking charge of the firm's shipments of furs, pelts, flour, salt, and other products of the neighboring country (including whiskey), and seeing that they reached New Orleans safely by way of the huge flatboats that navigated the rivers. Sometimes he would return overland, with frequent encounters with Indians. Often he would sail from New Orleans to New York, through the heart of the Spanish Main and its pirates. In New York and Philadelphia he bought goods for the Pittsburgh store, carrying them over the mountains on six-horse wagons.

[1] Morrison Foster, *Biography, Songs and Musical Compositions of Stephen Collins Foster*.

In Philadelphia he met Eliza Tomlinson, daughter of an aristocratic family from Wilmington. In 1807 they were married, and spent their honeymoon on the three-week horseback trip to Pittsburgh. William Foster became so valuable to his employers that they gave him a partnership. He became a substantial citizen, and acquired wealth which he placed at the disposal of his country when the national treasury was depleted in the War of 1812. In 1814 he bought a large tract of a hundred and seventy-one acres about two miles out of the city. This he named Lawrenceville. Part of the land he donated as a burial ground for soldiers; thirty acres were sold to the government for an arsenal, and on a spot overlooking the river he built the "White Cottage" that became the Foster homestead.

IV

With the exception of Stephen, the baby of the family, the Foster children were like their father, well equipped to fight frontier battles. The eldest son, William Barclay Foster, Junior, was about twenty years older than Stephen, and became a civil engineer who helped build the Pennsylvania Railroad by taking charge of the most difficult part of the work—the section that crossed the Allegheny Mountains. The other three sons, Henry, Dunning, and Morrison all became successful men of business, so where was there thought for a musician when Stephen came to manhood?

"Little Stephy" was loved and petted. Brother William was like a father, and when the boy was in his early teens he took him to live with him in Towanda, that he might go to the Academy at Athens. But Stephen found little anywhere to hold his interest for long. He was generous, he was loving, he had his longings, but while he was in the most important years of his life there was no one who understood, who could show him where to turn.

Only one of the many relatives seemed to have any conception of Stephen's temperament. Uncle John Struthers lived in a log house in Youngstown, Ohio. The visits to Uncle Struthers were glorious—the old man let the boy do as he pleased, and told him stories of Indians and hunting that fired his imagination. The uncle prophesied that Stephen would become "something famous." Pity he could not point out where that fame would lie!

The outward, self-created standards of business success and solid citizenship were all the Fosters knew, and inability to meet those standards was failure. All sorts of occupations were suggested, and some of them tried. When he dropped out of Jefferson College after a few dismal days, his father wrote to William:

I regret extremely that Stephen has not been able to appreciate properly your generous exertions in his behalf by availing himself of the advantages of a college education, which will cause him much regret before he arrives at my age and he will no doubt express these regrets in much sorrow to you, should you both live long after I shall be no more. He is at school now with Mr. Moody, a first rate teacher of mathematics in Pittsburgh, and it is a source of comfort to your mother and myself that he does not appear to have any evil propensities to indulge; he seeks no associates and his leisure hours are all devoted to musick, for which he possesses a strange talent.

It was not until the songs he had written as a diversion became popular beyond even the publisher's hopes, that Stephen, grown to manhood, realized that here was his occupation. Too late to learn how to write with the mind as well as the heart, he had nothing in him that would cultivate his gifts so that they would grow to something bigger. He could acquire no background that would withstand the ravages of early success. The "evil propensities" his father had feared became realities, and Stephen had nothing with which to fight them.

His marriage was not altogether a success, though he worshiped his wife and little daughter. Jane Denny McDowell was the daughter of one of Pittsburgh's physicians. She was an amateur singer and had been a member of the "Stephen Foster Quartet" which gathered for singing at the Foster home. For this group Foster wrote some of his earliest songs. Stephen and Jane were married July 22, 1850, and lived for several years with Stephen's parents.

There were apparently two separations. In 1853, for some reason not clear from the family correspondence on the subject, Stephen left Jane and lived alone in New York. The fact that there was some sort of estrangement is indicated by a letter written by Stephen's sister Henrietta, which expressed concern for "poor Stephy," who had "had trouble enough already." By the summer of 1854, however, the little family came together again, and for a few months they lived in a rented house in Hoboken, New Jersey. By October they were back in Allegheny. At this time Stephen was not the inveterate drinker he later became; so dissipation could not have been the cause of the first separation. His wife and little girl were with him part of the time he lived in New York from 1860 to 1864, but he lived alone at the time of his death. When news of his passing reached Pittsburgh his wife came to New York with Morrison to bring the body back home.

There were probably a number of reasons for partings. It is not unlikely that love for his parents, the "Old Folks at Home," was so uppermost in his heart that his wife felt a neglect that was not consciously intended. Stephen was not fitted for the harness of a marriage that demanded his whole being. He was a dreamer, thoroughly impractical, wholly improvident, and probably difficult at the breakfast table. How could he have been an ideal husband?

V

He was never business man enough to realize the full commercial value of his best songs. The gift to Peters was quite in keeping with his methods. Common law copyright was not established in those days, and many of the early songs of which Foster gave manuscript copies to minstrel performers were published by others. Sometimes they were copyrighted by those who had no right to them.

It was in 1849 that Foster made a contract with Firth, Pond & Company which protected his interests. The letter from the firm gives the details:

Your favor of the 8th instant is received and we hasten to reply.

We will accept the proposition therein made, viz., to allow you two cents upon every copy of your future publications issued by our house, after the expenses of publication are paid, and of course it is always our interest to push them as widely as possible. From your acquaintance with the proprietors or managers of different bands of "Minstrels," and from your known reputation, you can undoubtedly arrange with them to sing them and thus introduce them to the public in that way, but in order to secure the copyright exclusively for our house, it is safe to hand such persons printed copies only, of the pieces, for if manuscript copies are issued, particularly by the author, the market will be flooded with spurious issues in a short time.

The next paragraph contained advice that Foster would have done well to follow:

It is also advisable to compose only such pieces as are likely both in the sentiment and melody to take the public taste. Numerous instances can be cited of composers whose reputation has greatly depreciated from the fact of their music becoming too popular and as a natural consequence they write too much and too fast and in a short time others supersede them.

The minstrel troupes did indeed spread the popularity of Foster's songs. Some were well known to the public before they were published. For a number of years E. P. Christy had the official privilege of being the first to sing his works. Existing letters show what arrangements were made. On June 12, 1851, Foster wrote to the singer:

I have just received a letter from Messrs. Firth, Pond & Co. stating that they have copy-righted a new song of mine ("Oh! boys, carry me 'long") but will not be able to issue it for some little time yet, owing to other arrangements. This will give me time to send you the m.s. and allow you the privilege of singing it for at least two weeks, and probably a month before it is issued, or before any other band gets it (unless they catch it up from you). If you will send me 10 $ immediately for this privilege, I pledge myself, as a gentleman of the old school, to give you the m.s. I have written to F. P. & Co. not to publish till they hear from me again. This song is certain to become popular, as I have taken great pains with it. If you accept my proposition I will make it a point to notify you hereafter when I have a new song and send you the m.s. on the same terms, reserving to myself in all cases the exclusive privilege of publishing. Thus it will become notorious that your hand brings out all the new songs. You can state in the papers that the song was composed expressly for you. I make this proposition because I am sure of the song's popularity.

Eight days later Foster acknowledged receipt of the check and forwarded the manuscript with the following explanation:

I regret that it is too late to have the name of your band on the title page, but I will endeavor to place it (alone) on future songs, and will cheerfully do anything else in my humble way to advance your interest.

There are many references to arrangements with Christy. Some of these disprove Morrison Foster's statement that Stephen received $500 from Christy for *Old Folks at Home*. John Mahon published some reminiscences of Foster in the New York *Clipper* (1877). He tells of meeting him in 1861, "a short man, who was very neatly dressed in a blue swallow-tailed coat, high silk hat." At Mahon's home they talked of many things:

. . . my wife asked Stephen if he knew "The Old Folks at Home."

"I should think I ought to," he replied, "for I got $2,000 from Firth, Pond & Co. for it."

"Why," said I, "how could that be? Was not E. P. Christy the author and composer?"

"Oh, no," he replied, laughing, "Christy paid me $15 for allowing his name to appear as the author and composer. I did so on condition that after a certain time his name should be superseded by my own. One hundred thousand copies of the first edition were soon sold, for which I received a royalty of two cents a copy. . . ."

Foster had himself suggested to Christy that the minstrel's name be given as composer of *Old Folks at Home.* When he wrote it there was some public prejudice against Negro songs, and Foster preferred to remain in the background. In his biography of Foster,[2] Milligan publishes the following letter, written by Foster to Christy, May 25, 1852, less than six months after *Old Folks at Home* was first copyrighted:

As I once intimated to you, I had the intention of omitting my name on my Ethiopian songs, owing to the prejudice against them by some, which might injure my reputation as a writer of another style of music, but I find that by my efforts I have done a great deal to build up a taste for the Ethiopian songs among refined people by making the words suitable to their taste, instead of the trashy and really offensive words which belong to songs of that order. Therefore I have concluded to reinstate my name on my songs and to pursue the Ethiopian business without fear or shame and lend all my energies to making the business live, at the same time that I will wish to establish my name as the best Ethiopian song-writer. But I am not encouraged in undertaking this so long as "The Old Folks at Home" stares me in the face with another's name on it. As it was at my own solicitation that you allowed your name to be placed on the song, I hope that the above reasons will be sufficient explanation for my desire to place my own name on it as author and composer, while at the same time I wish to leave the name of your band on the title page. This is a little matter of pride in myself which it will certainly be to your interest to encourage. On the receipt of your free consent to this proposition, I will, if you wish, willingly refund the money which you paid me on that song, though it may have been sent me for other

---

[2] Harold V. Milligan, *Stephen Collins Foster,* G. Schirmer, Inc.

considerations than the one in question, and I promise in addition to write you an opening chorus, in my best style, free of charge, and in any other way in my power to advance your interests hereafter. I find I cannot write at all unless I write for public approbation and get credit for what I write. As we may probably have a good deal of business with each other in our lives, it is best to proceed on a sure basis of confidence and good understanding, therefore I hope you will appreciate an author's feelings in the case and deal with me with your usual fairness. Please answer immediately.

It is easy to sympathize with Stephen Foster in his making this request, but it must have placed Christy in an exceedingly embarrassing position. For eight months the minstrel had been receiving the applause of nightly audiences for a song he had claimed as his own, so it is not surprising that he apparently refused to acknowledge Foster's authorship. At any rate, it was not until 1879, when the first term of copyright expired, and fifteen years after Stephen's death, that his name appeared on printed copies of the song.

A royalty account in Foster's handwriting, dated January 27, 1857, gives some interesting data. A footnote at the bottom states:

In the amounts recd. I have included $15 on each of the two songs "Old folks" and "Farewell Lilly," from E. P. Christy, also $10 on each of the songs, "Dog Tray," "Oh boys," "Massa's in" & "Ellen Bayne."

There are two columns of figures: one the amount Foster had already received on the songs, the other what he thought they would bring him in the future. He used the latter estimate to determine the amount he would ask his publishers for his future rights to the songs. For those of the songs which were published by Firth, Pond & Company of New York he had received in a little over seven years, $9,-436.96. From another publisher, F. D. Benteen of Baltimore, he had received $461.85. These amounts, together with sums received for miscellaneous items, totaled over $10,000, and made his average income a little over $1,400 a year.

Old Folks at Home headed the estimate Foster made in 1857. In its five and a quarter years it had yielded $1,647.46; Foster considered it good for a hundred more. *My Old Kentucky Home*, only three and a half years old, had brought $1,372.06. This, too, should bring another hundred. *Old Dog Tray*, a youngster of two years, had over a thousand dollars to its credit, and promised another hundred and fifty.

The account shows that Foster's chief income came from a few of his songs—some of the oldest had brought as little as eight dollars altogether. *Willie, We Have Missed You* had earned almost $5,000, and Foster expected that its future would bring an equal amount. *Gentle Annie* was but an infant; her $39.08 should increase to over $500.

Altogether, over a period of eleven years, from the date of his first contract in 1849 with Firth, Pond & Company until he came to New York in 1860, Foster's earnings from songs totaled a little more than $15,000. Unfortunately, more than $3,600 of this amount represented the proceeds from outright sales of further rights in some of his best works, made necessary by the fact that his expenses were higher than his income from royalties.

VI

Soon after Foster sold out his royalty interests. The "profitable offer" that took him to New York in 1860 was possibly an arrangement with Firth, Pond & Company whereby they agreed to pay him $800 a year for twelve songs, and another, which came to little, for six songs at $400 per year from Lee & Walker.[3] Stephen did not have character enough in his last days to keep producing even under the promise of an assured income. He was constantly drawing ahead on his payments, and before he died he took anything he could get for his songs. He would write one in the morning, sell it for a pittance in the afternoon, and have the money spent by evening. He formed a sort of song-writing partnership with George Cooper, who afterwards had a long career as a writer of song lyrics.

Morrison Foster gave only a brief account of his brother's death:

In January, 1864, while at the American Hotel, he was taken with an ague and fever. After two or three days he arose, and while washing himself he fainted and fell across the wash basin, which broke and cut a gash in his neck and face. He lay there insensible and bleeding until discovered by the chambermaid who was bringing the towels he had asked for to the room. She called for assistance and he was placed in bed again. On recovering his senses he asked that he be sent to a hospital. He was so much weakened by

[3] For further discussion of these arrangements see *Stephen Foster, America's Troubadour* by John Tasker Howard.

fever and loss of blood that he did not rally. On the 13th of January he died peacefully and quietly.

The first indication the family had of Stephen's accident was a letter from Cooper to Morrison Foster, then in Cleveland:

January 12th, 1864

Your brother Stephen I am sorry to inform you is lying in Bellevue Hospital in this city very sick. He desires me to ask you to send him some pecuniary assistance as his means are very low. If possible, he would like to see you in person.

The letter had probably not been delivered when a telegram passed it:

STEPHEN IS DEAD. COME ON.
GEORGE COOPER.

Cooper gave Milligan a detailed and presumably accurate account of Foster's death: [4]

Early one winter morning I received a message saying that my friend had met with an accident; I dressed hurriedly and went to 15 Bowery, the lodging-house where Stephen lived, and found him lying on the floor with a bad bruise on his forehead. Steve never wore any night-clothes and he lay there on the floor, naked and suffering horribly. He had wonderful big brown eyes and they looked up at me with an appeal I can never forget. He whispered, "I'm done for," and begged for a drink, but before I could get it for him, the doctor who had been sent for arrived and forbade it. He started to sew up the gash in Steve's throat, and I was horrified to observe that he was using black thread. "Haven't you any white thread," I asked, and he said no, he had picked up the first thing he could find. I decided the doctor was not much good, and I went down stairs and got Steve a big drink of rum, which I gave him and which seemed to help him a lot. We put his clothes on him and took him to the hospital. In addition to the cut on his throat and the bruise on his forehead, he was suffering from a bad burn on his thigh, caused by the overturning of a spirit lamp used to boil water. This had happened several days before, and he had said nothing about it, nor done anything for it. All the time we were caring for him, he seemed terribly weak and his eyelids kept fluttering. I shall never forget it.

I went back to the hospital to see him, and he said nothing had been done

[4] Harold V. Milligan, *Stephen Collins Foster*, G. Schirmer, Inc.

for him, and he couldn't eat the food they brought him. When I went back again the next day they said "Your friend is dead."

So ended the life of a man who made the world a better place to live in. A man to whom home meant everything, and for whom home was impossible. This longing was the strongest emotion of his nature; and it is as a poet of homesickness that he was greatest. Many times he descended to the banal, but time has not preserved the things that were unworthy of him. When he tried his hand at sentimental love songs, a lesser Stephen Foster sang.

A few of his nonsense songs have survived along with the songs of home. *Oh! Susanna* is still the joyous thing it was when it was written. *De Camptown Races,* in which the "Camptown ladies" chant "doo-dah," is still popular with college boys, young and old. The melodies are vital.

Why try to analyze his tunes, so lovely in their simplicity? Classifying their intervals may well be left to scholars. Foster at his best was inevitable rather than obvious. He was good enough musician to harmonize his songs as they should be harmonized—quite simply. What more can we ask of a man who has touched our hearts?

In 1940 the tributes and memorials to Foster reached a climax in the greatest honor Americans can pay to their great men of the past. In that year Stephen Foster became the first musician to be elected to the Hall of Fame at New York University. In fact, in the election of that year, Foster was the only candidate on whom a majority of the one hundred electors could agree.

6. RAMPANT VIRTUOSI

By the middle of the nineteenth century each of the principal cities of the United States had its music-loving public—small indeed, but no doubt representing as high a percentage of the general population as that which fills our concert halls today. For these music lovers there were a few organizations that provided good music, played by those who loved it for its own sake. Nor was the man on the street neglected, for early in the 1800's bright stars of the musical firmament abroad scented our American dollars and came over here to gather them in abundance. The fact that people will pay any amount to *see* famous artists they have read about in the papers is as old as the hills. Modern press agents may learn much from their grandfathers.

It is not easy to believe that a New York hatter paid several hundreds of dollars for a pair of seats to Jenny Lind's first New York concert merely because he must hear some beautiful music. The hatter became a person, and he sold more hats. Under the leadership of P. T. Barnum advertising became an art, and music profited—in dollars anyway. Some of the artists were sincere, others were tricksters and showmen. The latter made the most money. They all had their share in making the musical history of America, and one should be cautious in making fun of our ancestors for their hero worship, for we are not one whit different today in our attitude towards music and in our box-office habits.

Few of the early *virtuosi* were Americans; most of them were periodical visitors from abroad, but they affected our musical life so deeply that they cannot be ignored. Most important of all was the effect on the newer communities in the West. While New York, Boston, and Philadelphia had resident organizations which attempted the best music of the day, some of the Western cities were too busy clearing land and building houses to give much thought to music; but they had money to spend, and the bright stars of the musical world went among them to get their share of it. The West acquired the listening habit before it learned to make music itself. The eccentricities of some of the *virtuosi*, and more especially their imitators, may have been responsible for a prevalent opinion regarding all musicians. An editorial in the Pittsburgh *Evening Chronicle* (1853) calls a spade a shovel:

A hobby of society at the present day is to be music-mad, and the adulation and toddyism lavished upon every Piano-Forte player of any talent is enough to disgust all sensible people with the instrument forever. From the language of the musical critiques of the Eastern press, one would suppose that there was nothing else worth living for in this life but music, and Piano Forte playing especially, and the musical world, following the key-note, look for the advent of each fresher greater Signor Pound-the-keys with a devotion and religious constancy unparalleled. He makes his advent and the whole town talks. . . . And Signor Pound-the-keys for having rattled and splurged and hammered and tinkled and growled through three or four musical compositions with long-line names, fills his pockets for one night's work with as many dollars as three-fourths of the community earn in a year, while the mustached gentleman who assists him by quavering, quivering and shouting through three or four songs in as many different European languages, which is all gibberish to all of the audience with perhaps the exception of some dozen, pockets one-half as much more.

We think music is an art which deserves fostering and cultivating as much as any other among our people, but we feel no ways backward in saying that from a common-sense point of view, the musical furore which pervades this country for wonderful piano playing and extraordinary effects of vocal powers in foreign languages, like what it is, is thorough humbug.

The Americans are a musical people, but we want to be educated up to the science and so long as nine-tenths of our people do not know even the A.B.C. of music, it is folly for them to listen to the most finished and eloquent combinations of it.

OLE BULL (1810–1880) was the most brilliant violinist of his time. He was a Norwegian who enjoyed international fame, and spent much of his time in America—five visits altogether. Huge audiences were always thrilled by the fire of his playing, but more sober critics called him a trickster. He could play on all four strings of his fiddle at once. His admirers said that his colossal strength enabled him to do it, while sceptics claimed he had a flat bridge. Vast crowds were awed by the way he ended his pieces with the softest of pianissimos. Some who stood in the wings said that at such times his bow never touched the strings at all. William Mason wrote that Ole Bull was a law unto himself. He burst into full blossom without first showing various degrees of growth.

Born in Bergen, Norway, in 1810, he first came to America in 1843. His first tour lasted over two years, and he gave over two hundred concerts in the Eastern states, and in Havana. His box office receipts were about $400,000. When he returned in 1852 he stayed for five years, and went all the way to California with a concert party that included the child prodigy ADELINA PATTI. Early in 1855 he tried his hand at managing an opera company, and took over the Academy of Music in New York. He really tried to make it an American institution, and offered a prize of $1,000 for the "best original grand opera by an American composer, upon a strictly *American subject*." Foreign adaptations would not be accepted. In his announcement he gave native composers a chance to declare their independence:

The national history of America is rich in themes both for the poet and the musician; and it is to be hoped that this offer will bring to light the musical talent now latent in the country, which only needs a favorable opportunity for its development.

But the Academy closed its doors in March, and none of our latent talents had a chance to show their manuscripts.

It was during his second visit that Ole Bull embarked upon his most ambitious scheme—establishing a colony in Pennsylvania called *Oleana,* where there would arise a New Norway "consecrated to freedom, baptized in independence, and protected by the mighty flag of the Union." He purchased a large tract of land, described in Dwight's *Journal of Music:*

Ole Bull's Norwegian Colony is situated in Potter County, Pa. . . . Ole Bull has built himself a beautiful Norwegian cottage for his summer residence. He proposes to establish a Polytechnic school for this colony for the advancement of the arts and sciences generally, to be conducted by the most scientific men of Europe. His plan is to make it a civil and a military school to be open to the youth of the Union. . . . An armory and a foundry are to be built for practical purposes. . . . The corps when graduated, to be received into the regular army as a new corps. The Government is to have the benefit of the result of all discoveries in the arts and sciences, in return for which he asks the preference in all contracts for cannons, arms, ammunition etc. . . . This idea of the Norwegian is certainly a good one. . . . West Point has become an exclusive and aristocratical institution, and we greatly want an institution as proposed by Ole Bull, for the people at large. . . . His knowledge of the sciences extends vastly beyond horse hair and fiddle strings.

But it was not to be. Bull had fallen victim to a group of frauds who had no title to the land; who sold him what was not theirs. Even the improvements he had already made were a trespass on the property of others, and long litigation followed that almost broke his health, as well as his heart. He returned to Bergen in 1857, and did not come back for ten years.

When he returned in 1867 he gave his first concert in Chicago, and a year later married an American, Sara Chapman Thorpe, in Wisconsin. He spent the summer of 1872 in Norway, and then came back here for his fourth visit, which lasted for a year. His last tour was in the season of 1879–80, with Emma Thursby. His failing health resulted in his death in Norway the following summer.

Bull's compositions are interesting because they represent a translation of everything into his own style. In a way, he was an intense nationalist, as much of a Norwegian as Grieg. The climate of his native country was in his veins—he had a wild, poetic, northern imagination that fired everything he did. He chose many American subjects for the works he played here, but they were probably no more American than Dvořák's *New World Symphony*. He described the Revolution by introducing *Yankee Doodle*, "piped and screamed" alternately with *God Save the King*, "amid discordant tremolos and battle storms of the whole orchestra."

His war horse was the *Polacca Guerriera*, a warlike piece which he played with orchestra with telling effect. Among his tributes to America was the *Grand March to the Memory of Washington*, published in 1845; *Niagara*; and *Solitude of the Prairie*. In his *Musical Memories*,[1] George P. Upton described Bull:

Ole Bull belonged to no school. Perhaps that was another secret of his success, for people neither know nor care about schools, but like a player to be himself. Ole Bull certainly was all that. He imitated certain of Paganini's eccentricities by attempting effects of a bizarre sort, but he was always Ole Bull. . . . He rarely attempted the classical, probably because it is so unyielding in construction that it does not admit of moods or humors, so his repertory was comparatively small. . . . It was impossible to resist the magic of his bow even when you suspected it of sleight-of-hand.

There has been nothing in American history to compare with the furore that JENNY LIND (1820–1887) created in the fifties. But if Americans made fools of themselves, they at least had the comfort of knowing that their English cousins had done so before them. Probably no more curious combination has ever existed than that of Barnum as manager and Jenny Lind as artist. Barnum the showman, who first showed how to work the press, and planted stories of his own as news in any paper he wished; and Lind, the plain little lady with angelic voice, deeply religious by nature, who abandoned opera and stage because it was too immoral. There can be no question of her consummate

---

[1] George P. Upton, *Musical Memories*, A. C. McClurg & Co.

artistry and her exquisite voice. The masses were not alone in worshiping her. Clara Schumann said: "What a great, heaven-inspired being she is! What a pure, true artist soul! Her songs will ever sound in my heart." And Mendelssohn: "She is as great an artist as ever lived and the greatest I have known," though he admitted on a later occasion, "She sings bad music the best."

Barnum had a double motive in bringing Jenny Lind to America. He was fairly certain that he would make money by it, even if he did have to guarantee her $1,000 each for a hundred and fifty concerts, pay all her expenses, and deposit $187,500 in cash with his London bankers as security for fulfilment of the contract. He confessed the other motive himself:

Inasmuch as my name has long been associated with "humbug," and the American public suspect that my capacities do not extend beyond the power to exhibit a stuffed Monkey-skin or a dead mermaid, I can afford to lose fifty thousand dollars in such an enterprise as bringing to this country, in the zenith of her life and celebrity, the greatest musical wonder in the world. . . .

And so the man who managed Tom Thumb, who had made a fortune by charging two shillings for a look at a horse with his tail where his head should be, sold Jenny Lind to the American public as extensively as he sold his circus years later.

She had fears of Barnum that she never quite overcame. A rival manager who bid for her American tour told her that Barnum would put her in a box and exhibit her about the United States at twenty-five cents admission. Because Barnum was sensitive about his reputation as a showman, Jenny capitalized his inferiority complex by altering the contract in her own favor on every possible occasion.

Her first concert in America was given at Castle Garden, New York on the eleventh of September, 1850. Its program was in many ways typical of the period. Singers or instrumentalists rarely gave recitals. The star of the occasion would make two or three appearances, and the rest of the evening was generally devoted to music of the orchestra, and of assisting artists. Despite her lavish contributions to charity, Jenny Lind made $100,000 from her two years in America. She toured both East and West, and conquered wherever she went. She did little to raise musical standards by presenting good music, but she did allow Americans to hear a voice and artistry that were very nearly perfect.

There were other famous singers. MARIA MALIBRAN, daughter of the Manuel García who gave New York its first taste of Italian opera, had been here with her father in 1825, and had stayed two years. HENRIETTE SONTAG, who had made a great success in opera and a sensation in concert, was in America when Jenny Lind was with us. Sontag went to Mexico City in 1854, where she died of cholera.

Among pianists, HENRI HERZ was largely responsible for the fondness of variations, fantasias, and florid runs and trills that permeated nineteenth-century piano music. Herz was a Viennese who spent most of his life in Paris. After several successful years as a pianist, writer, and teacher, he joined a piano maker in Paris, and lost a fortune. To repair his losses he came to America in 1845, and toured the United States (going all the way to California), Mexico, and the West Indies. He was here for six years. His brilliancy and bravura were immense, but he lacked solider qualities. He knew what the public wanted, and he was able to give it to them. He dazzled foreigners as well as Americans. He once wrote that Parisians could understand and appreciate nothing but variations.

Herz was known to Americans by his compositions long before he actually came. Schlesinger and Scharfenberg often played the *Rondo and Variations for Two Pianos*, as well as the *Bravura Variations on the Romance of Joseph*. There were also *Grand Variations* for the harp and piano, and other "grand duos." When he died in 1888, Herz had written eight piano concertos, and over two hundred piano pieces, all forgotten today.

SIGISMUND THALBERG, who came in 1856–57, was a pianist of more thorough musicianship than Herz, but he, too, won by display. Upton [2] remembers his playing as

almost entirely confined to his own operatic fantasies, like the "Moise" and "Lucia." . . . The melody of the aria stood out very clearly in the midst of a most dazzling display of scales, arpeggios, shakes, and coruscations of every sort, and the whole keyboard was none too big for the exhibition of his elegant and absolutely perfect technic. But there was no more soul in it than there is in the head of a kettledrum. It was simply marvellous mechanism.

[2] George P. Upton, *Musical Memories*, A. C. McClurg & Co.

. . . It was rather a pyrotechnic display, with the rockets left out, for Thalberg never soared. The real attraction of his work was its elegance and its clearness, even in the most intricate mazes with which he enclosed a melody. He had a host of imitators, and the Thalberg fantasies were all the rage for a time. Every little piano thumper tackled them. But Thalberg, his school of virtuosity, and his fantasies are now only memories. The fantasies to-day are empty as last year's birds' nests.

7. LOUIS MOREAU GOTTSCHALK (1829–1869)

Gottschalk was a native American, but he had spent so much time abroad, and had achieved such a substantial foreign reputation, that he was regarded as a foreigner by the great majority of Americans— and was accordingly most successful. He combined the attractions of pianist-composer and *beau ideal*. He was the first of our matinee idols.

He was born in New Orleans in 1829, the son of Edward Gottschalk, an English Jew who had studied medicine in Leipzig, and Aimée Marie de Braslé, a Creole. Because of his precocious talent, the little boy was given music lessons when he was three years old. When he was only six, he was able to substitute for the organist of one of the churches, and at eight he gave a public concert for the benefit of one of the violinists from the French opera in New Orleans.

When he was thirteen he went to Paris, and studied with Hallé, Stamaty, and Maledan. Through his aunt, La Comtesse de Lagrange, he was admitted to the exclusive social circles of Paris, and in many countries he became the favorite of royalty and the aristocracy. He started his career as composer in his early youth, and several of his most popular pieces, including the *Bananier* and *Bamboula*, were written when he was fifteen. He became a pupil of Berlioz, who said of him:

Gottschalk is one of the very small number who possess all the different elements of a consummate pianist—all the faculties which surround him with an irresistible prestige, and give him a sovereign power. He is an accomplished musician—he knows just how far fancy may be indulged in expression. He knows the limits beyond which any liberties taken with the rhythm produce only confusion and disorder, and upon these limits he never encroaches. There is an exquisite grace in his manner of phrasing sweet melodies and throwing light touches from the higher keys. The boldness, the brilliancy, and the originality of his playing at once dazzles and astonishes, and the infantile naïveté of his smiling caprices, and charming simplicity with which he renders simple things, seem to belong to another individuality distinct from that which marks his thundering energy—thus the success of M. Gottschalk before an audience of musical cultivation is assured.

Chopin predicted that he would become a "king of pianists." After concert tours through France and Spain, he returned to America, where he made his debut in Niblo's Garden, New York, February 10, 1853. The resulting sensation was almost comparable to Jenny Lind's reception a year and a half before. Perhaps the highest tribute was an offer from Barnum for $20,000 a year and all expenses. This Gottschalk refused, no doubt with scorn. He commenced his tours of other cities, and in the winter of 1855–56 gave eighty concerts in New York alone.

After this he spent six years in the West Indies. In 1862 he came back to the States, and for three more years toured his native America. In 1865 he went to South America, and lived there for his few remaining years. He died in Rio de Janeiro in 1869.

Some of Gottschalk's music is played today and much of it is still in print. *The Last Hope* may belong to the Victorian era, with its saccharine melody punctuated with runs that delighted many an aspiring pianist at pupils' recitals, but its restful phrases are still useful as movie music. *The Dying Poet* may have achieved its vogue because of its title, but it was effective, nevertheless. *Pasquinade* represented Gottschalk in a capricious mood, and in such he was at his best. There was true individuality in *The Banjo, Le Bananier, Bamboula, Dance Ossianique,* and others of their kind. Gottschalk in many ways was a forerunner of Ethelbert Nevin—at heart and by necessity a sentimentalist, he was a composer of *salon* music *par excellence.* And we must never forget that he was the first American composer and pianist to make a foreign reputation; he achieved an international rank that would satisfy the most ardent propagandists for American music today.

To know the man himself, it is a simple matter to piece together contemporary accounts. Gottschalk never married, but it is certain that his erotic nature led him into many love affairs. Women literally flung themselves at him. There are records of ladies of the audience rushing to the piano in a body, seizing his white gloves, tearing them to bits and fighting over the pieces for souvenirs. When he practiced on the second floor of a piano store in New Orleans, women fought for places on the stairs where they could listen, maybe catch a glimpse of him, and, if they were lucky, actually touch him. One of his biographies was written by Octavia Hensel. Her friendship with Gottschalk, which she presents in the third person, is described in terms of such fervor, and her opinions are offered with such bias and such scorn for adverse criticism of her hero, that one is tempted to suspect her own relations with him. She refers to slanders which were circulated when Gottschalk left for South America, never to return. He wrote that it was best to ignore them:

It is beneath my dignity as a man of honor to notice such slanders. Surely my friends can never credit them; and, if believed by those who are not my friends, I only pray kind heaven had given them better minds. A man whose nature allowed him to commit so dishonourable an act could also lie, and disown it! Let the story of my whole life be told, every act scrutinized; and, if you can find in it anything to prove me capable of such unmanly conduct, cast me from your regard, blot my name forever from your memory.

According to Mme. Hensel, Gottschalk died from natural causes. He was giving a monster festival in Rio de Janeiro. There were to be eight hundred performers, led by the composer. He had been appointed director-general of all the bands of the army, navy, and national guards. Several new works had been composed for the occasion. The festival started at the opera house, November 26, 1869. On the morning after the first program Gottschalk awoke too ill to get up, and had to be carried to the opera house in the evening. He collapsed before the first number, was taken to Tijuca, a neighboring village, and died there December 18.

Contradicting Hensel's account, many stories persist to the effect that Gottschalk was assassinated. If these are true, the assassin and his motive are today a mystery. The composer's body was brought back to New York, and he was buried in Greenwood Cemetery, Brooklyn, where a large monument marks his grave.

He was something of a *poseur*. He always wore white gloves to his concerts, and never took them off until he was on the platform facing his audience. Then, with perfect deliberation, and supreme indifference, he would remove them, one finger at a time, as he calmly surveyed his audience, and nodded to friends in the front rows. He once told George Upton that he did this to compose himself before playing.

Richard Hoffman wrote in his *Recollections:* [1]

I have often seen him arrive at a concert in no mood for playing, and declare that he would not appear; that an excuse might be made, but that he would not play. He cared no more for the public than if he had been in a private drawing-room where he could play or not as he pleased, but a little coaxing and a final *push* would drive him onto the stage, and after a few moments the fire would kindle and he would play with all the brilliancy which was so peculiarly his own.

There was a genial, friendly side of his nature that he showed to his friends. William Mason in his *Memories of a Musical Life* [2] published a note he once received from him:

If you have nothing to do, come and spend the evening with me on Sunday next. No formality. Smoking required, impropriety allowed, and complete liberty, with as little music as possible. I was going to mention that we will have a glass of wine and chicken salad.

Your friend,

GOTTSCHALK.

He had a sense of humor, and was delighted when an engraver printed the title page of a revised edition of *The Last Hope* as "The Latest Hops."

To know Gottschalk as a pianist it is best to read contemporary criticisms, and recollections by those who heard him. These indicate that he was really an excellent pianist, a sound musician, who could have played the best in music if he had wished, but who sensed what the vast public most wanted to hear, and gave it to them with a vengeance. No artistic conscience stood between him and material success. He craved applause, and used the surest means of gaining it. In Boston, the intolerant Dwight, who had fallen under the spell of Ole Bull's bow, perhaps unwillingly, steeled himself to Gottschalk's charms, and wrote what he thought of him, or possibly what he thought he ought to think of him:

[1] Richard Hoffman, *Some Musical Recollections of Fifty Years*, Charles Scribner's Sons.
[2] William Mason, *Memories of a Musical Life*, Century Co.

. . . It *was* great execution. But what is execution without some thought and meaning in the combinations to be executed? . . .

Skilful, graceful, brilliant, wonderful, we own his playing was. But players less wonderful have given us far deeper satisfaction . . . of what use were all these difficulties? . . . Why all that rapid tossing of handfuls of chords from the middle to the highest octaves, lifting the hand with such conscious appeal to our eyes? To what end all those rapid octave passages? since, in the intervals of easy execution, in the seemingly quiet impromptu passages, the music grew so monotonous and commonplace: the same little figure repeated and repeated, after listless pauses, in a way which conveyed no meaning, no sense of musical progress, but only the appearance of fastidiously critical scale-practising.

The New York papers, musical and unmusical, were loud in their praise. The *Tribune* even went so far as to make comparisons with Beethoven which were not altogether flattering to Beethoven; Gott-schalk, a young man, went beyond the old fogies of classical music. The *Home Journal* said that his playing had the effect of an orchestra, and quoted a lady of the audience who said that he had the dexterity of Jaell, the power of de Meyer, and the taste of Herz—all of which was intended as a compliment.

Richard Hoffman [3] wrote:

. . . Thalberg and Gottschalk joined forces and played some duets for two pianos at the Niblo concerts. One in particular, on themes from "Trovatore" composed by both of them . . . was wonderfully effective and created the most tremendous furore and excitement. A remarkable double shake which Thalberg played in the middle of the piano, while Gottschalk was playing all over the keyboard in the "Anvil Chorus," pro-duced the most prodigious volume of tone I have ever heard from the piano. . . . Possessed of the languid, emotional nature of the tropics, his music recalled the land of his birth and the traits of his people.

William Mason can be trusted for a sound opinion: [4]

I knew Gottschalk well, and was fascinated by his playing, which was full of brilliancy and bravura. His strong, rhythmic accent, his vigor and dash, were exciting and always aroused enthusiasm. He was the perfection of his

---

[3] Richard Hoffman, *Some Musical Recollections of Fifty Years*, Charles Scribner's Sons.
[4] William Mason, *Memories of a Musical Life*, Century Company.

school, and his effects had the effervescence and sparkle of champagne. He was far from being an interpreter of chamber or classical music, but notwithstanding this some of the best musicians of the strict style were frequently to be seen among his audience. . . . He first made his mark through his arrangement of Creole melodies. They were well defined rhythmically, and he played them with absolute rhythmic accuracy. . . . He did not care for the German school, and on one occasion, after hearing me play Schumann . . . he said, "Mason, I do not understand why you spend so much of your time over music like that; it is stiff and labored, lacks melody, spontaneity, and naïveté. It will eventually vitiate your musical taste and bring you into an abnormal state."

Although an enthusiastic admirer of Beethoven's symphonies and other orchestral works, he did not care for the pianoforte sonatas, which he said were not written in accordance with the nature of the instrument. It has been said that he could play all the sonatas by heart, but I am quite sure . . . that such was not the fact. . . .

George Upton [5] tells a different story:

Gottschalk was a great lover of Beethoven's music, especially the sonatas. How well I remember the last time I saw him! We spent an afternoon together in 1864, and he played for me in his dreamy way the so-called "Moonlight" sonata of Beethoven, some of Mendelssohn's "Midsummer Night's Dream" music, and his "Lieder ohne Worte," running from one piece to the other with hardly a pause except to light a fresh cigar or interview the Merry Widow Cliquot. I remember asking him why he didn't play that class of music in his concerts. He replied: "Because the dear public don't want to hear me play it. People would rather hear my 'Banjo' or 'Ojos Creollos,' or 'Last Hope.' Besides, there are plenty of pianists who can play that music as well or better than I can, but none of them can play my music half so well as I can. And what difference will it make a thousand years hence, anyway?"

If he had played any other sonata but the "Moonlight," it would be easier to credit his love for the Beethoven Sonatas.

[5] George P. Upton, *Musical Memories*, A. C. McClurg & Co.

CHAPTER SEVEN

The Foreign Invasion of 1848

THE middle of the nineteenth century saw hundreds of foreign musicians migrating to America. Many of them came in 1848 because they were reduced to poverty by the series of revolutions in Central Europe which had reached their climax in that year. It was natural that they should seek America, where gold had been discovered in California, the war with Mexico had just ended in victory for the United States, and the country was about to have one of its most prosperous periods.

It is difficult to determine precisely what the effect of this invasion has been. Some think that American composers were forced to give way to the Germans and Austrians, and that American music would be a more vital thing today if it had not been shoved aside by foreigners. In many ways the experience of the latter eighteenth century was repeated. This mid-century immigration was the second of the foreign invasions.

It is obvious that the immigrants did not kill American music. They may have increased our ancestors' love of a foreign label, and thus made it harder for Americans of average ability to earn a living. Yet Stephen Foster's career was just starting when they came, and Lowell Mason was at the height of his fame. Moreover, many of the newcomers were highly skilled musicians who helped to raise our musical standards.

It is not with foreign *virtuosi* that this chapter is concerned. The brilliant soloists who reaped a harvest at the box office were mostly visitors—the immigrants we are now discussing were musicians who came here to live, to play in our orchestras, to teach, and to take an active part in our everyday musical life. Living among us they exerted a far more powerful influence than those who merely dazzled us at occasional concerts.

The most important group of musicians who came from Europe was an orchestra of about twenty-five members called the Germania Society. There had been a few well-trained foreign orchestras who attempted concerts here from 1846, but none of them had been able to get a foothold. The Germania was the first orchestra in America whose members made it their principal business to play together, and rehearsed daily. The Philharmonic in New York, and the few orchestral societies in other cities gave only a few concerts a year, and the players were all engaged in other musical pursuits. The Germanians' playing was better than any that Americans had heard before. They did not achieve great financial success—Boston was the only city that gave adequate support to their concerts—but they did manage to hold together for six years, and in that time played in all our principal cities.

They brought to America some music we had never heard before— theirs was the first performance of Wagner's Overture to *Tannhäuser*. Native orchestras had tried Mendelssohn's *Midsummer Night's Dream* music, but none before the Germanians had played it with the necessary finesse and lightness. When the orchestra finally disbanded, its members settled in various of our cities, joined other organizations, and continued their activities separately.

When the little band first came to New York in 1848, it made a modest beginning. It was booked to appear as part of the bill at Niblo's Astor Place Theatre. In a small advertisement in the *Tribune* and other newspapers of October 5, William Niblo respectfully announced that the *Lady of Lyons* would be performed that evening,

after which the Grand Instrumental Concert by the Germanic Music Society, consisting of 25 performers, from Berlin, directed and conducted by Herr Lenschow.

The performance was to conclude with the farce *The Secret*.

In a few days the Germanians started their own concerts at the Broadway Tabernacle. The *Tribune* had a music critic who deplored concessions to public taste:

. . . the company seemed to excel particularly in the execution of light waltzes and polkas. . . . We should be glad to hear more of the old classical compositions of Beethoven, Mozart, and Weber, which they are capable of giving with such power and expression.

In the same issue the Germanians had a paid advertisement, which gave their own ideas of how their concerts should be reviewed:

. . . Selections from Donizetti, Strauss, Auber, Rossini and others were greeted by the audience with perfect enthusiasm. The march by Lenschow was a gem. . . . The prompt and efficient manner of the conductor presented [surely a careless compositor was responsible for this "s," instead of "v"] those too common vexatious delays, so that the concert was finished at an early hour. The modest and gentlemanly deportment of the whole band was the subject of general remark. An overwhelming house is expected at their next concert. . . .

The Germanians did make concessions to the apparent taste of the public, and for their early programs, at least, put together some potpourris to satisfy the demand for descriptive fantasias. Thomas Ryan, in his *Recollections of an Old Musician*,[1] describes *Up Broadway:*

It was supposed to be a graphic tone-picture of sights and sounds seen and heard from Castle Garden to Union Square, which was at that time the boundary of New York's bustling life.
This potpourri began with a musical picture of Castle Garden. . . . Moving up . . . you next came to Barnum's Museum, with "Barnum's Band" of six or eight brass instruments, which . . . played all day long on a high balcony outside his Museum on Broadway, nearly opposite the Astor House. It was side-splitting to hear the imitation of this brass band. . . .
. . . a fireman's parade with brass band came next. Naturally it was preceded by a violent ringing of firebells, and a rushing down a side street with the machine. When that noise died away, music from the open door of a dance hall was heard; with of course all its accompaniments—the rhythm of dancing feet, and the calling out of the figures. Then . . . we passed by a church whence came the sound of organ music and the chanting of a service by a number of voices. After that we heard in the distance a faint kind of Turkish patrol music; then a big *crescendo* and sudden *fortissimo* introduced us to Union Square and its life; and two brass bands in two different keys prepared our nerves for the usual collision and fight between two opposing fire companies. Finally, fireworks were touched off, the *Star-*

[1] Thomas Ryan, *Recollections of an Old Musician*, E. P. Dutton & Co.

Spangled Banner was played, and the potpourri ended, sending every one home in smiling good humor.

All of this, remember, was in America, around 1850. Surely there is nothing new.

CARL LENSCHOW resigned after a year or so of conducting the Germanians, and settled in Baltimore. He was succeeded in 1850 by CARL BERGMANN (1821–1876) who had joined the orchestra as cellist a few months before. Bergmann was a talented and capable musician, an inspired conductor, and something of a composer. It was he who arranged the *Broadway* potpourri. When the Germanians disbanded in 1854, he went to New York, and a year later became one of the conductors of the Philharmonic Society. For ten years he alternated with Theodor Eisfeld as director, and from 1866 to 1876 was the sole conductor of the orchestra. At his death in 1876 he was succeeded by Theodore Thomas.

Bergmann was responsible for one of the pinnacles of the Philharmonic's career; his methods of conducting and his interpretations are still a tradition. Toward the end of his life he went to pieces physically and morally, and the directors had to force his resignation. He died soon after.

Boston was the scene of most of the Germanians' triumphs, for Boston had a group of music lovers who enjoyed the classics. During several seasons the orchestra made the city its winter headquarters; in 1852–53 it gave a series of twenty subscription concerts there. In these concerts were played six symphonies by Beethoven, two by Mozart, one each by Haydn and Mendelssohn. Alfred Jaell played a number of piano concertos with the orchestra; Ole Bull engaged the band for his Boston concerts; it toured with Jenny Lind.

On November 27, 1852, the Germanians gave Boston, and America, its first hearing of *Tannhäuser* when they played its *Finale*. Dwight the critic, lover of the classics and champion of the romanticists Mendelssohn and Schumann, could never swallow Wagner, and he wrote:

. . . an arranged Finale from Richard Wagner's Tannhauser agreeably disappointed us in being less strange than the fame of this bold innovator had led us to expect. . . . The melody was beautiful, not particularly original, but rather *Spohr*-ish.

It later proved most important to New England that CARL ZER-
RAHN (1826–1909), flute player of the Germanians, decided to make
Boston his home when the orchestra disbanded. Until his death in 1909,
at the age of eighty-three, he was one of the most influential of Boston's
many musicians. From 1855 to 1863 he conducted one of the several
orchestras known in Boston by the name of Philharmonic. From 1865
to 1882 he led the concerts of the Harvard Musical Association. For
forty-two years (1854–1895), he was conductor of the Handel and
Haydn Society, and the other choral organizations which prospered
under his direction included the Worcester, Massachusetts, Music Festivals, which he conducted for thirty years.

There were others who settled here. THOMAS RYAN, an Irishman
who came in 1844 at the age of seventeen, lived in New England until
he died in 1903. In 1849 he became an early member of the Mendelssohn Quintette Club, one of our first chamber music organizations.
This club traveled through the country for fifty years. It was most
important in the middle of the century, for it was then that it acted
as musical missionary. Ryan played viola and clarinet. The first violinist was August Fries, a German who came to Boston in 1847. His
brother Wulf Fries was cellist. Wulf played with the club until 1870,
and from 1875 until his death in 1902 was one of New England's best-
known teachers. Francis Riha, the second violinist, had come to America in 1846 with the ill-fated Steyermark Orchestra. Edward Lehmann
played viola when Ryan played the clarinet, and flute when Ryan
played the viola.

The club jumped into immediate favor. William Schultze, who had
been first violinist of the Germanians, succeeded August Fries as first
violin of the Quintette Club in 1859. He was with it for almost twenty
years. In 1854 Carl Meisel took Riha's place as second violin. Ryan
and Wulf Fries were still with the club when it disbanded in 1895.

Dwight wrote of them in 1852:

Dear especially and justly to the lovers of good classic music is this fraternity of five young artists. . . . To them we owe our *sphere* of periodical
communion with the great German masters in their most select and genial
moods. . . . No society has ever given us such a series of good programs.
. . . Think how much of Haydn, Mozart, Beethoven, and Mendelssohn
—of the masters, who used to seem so far off, unapproachable to us novices

in music—they have this winter opened to us in their eight subscription concerts.

One more word, since now is the time for it. We earnestly trust that the Messrs. Fries, Riha, Ryan and Lehmann will not abandon the high ground they have taken, from any dismay at a momentary fluctuation in their outward success. Recent rehearsals, the programme of that last "extra" concert, together with paragraphs in newspapers congratulating us that the Club were henceforth to "play more miscellaneous music," have been ominous. There is but one ground on which such a Society can stand and outlive temporary discouragements, and that is the ground of almost strict adherence to classic chamber compositions, in their original forms. Mr. Ryan's *arrangements* of things like the "Invitation to the Dance," movements of pianoforte sonatas, &c. are certainly clever and creditable to him; but such things are never as satisfactory as the originals to hear, and they crowd out of the programme too many genuine works, which it seems due to our musical culture that we should have every chance to hear. Classic music is the peculiar field of this little Club; if they enter other fields, the weakness of a mere quintette enables them but poorly to compete with popular orchestras and bands.

THEODOR EISFELD (1816–1882) was in America for only eighteen years (1848–1866), but he did much for our musical life, especially in New York. When he arrived he had been director of the Court Theatre at Wiesbaden, and of the Concerts Viviennes in Paris. For fifteen years (until 1864), he was a conductor of the Philharmonic Society in New York, alternating with Bergmann in later years. In 1851 he commenced a series of chamber music concerts which, like the Mendelssohn Quintette Club, did real pioneer work. The first program offered Haydn's Quartet in B flat, Mendelssohn's D Minor Trio, and Beethoven's Quartet in F. In 1857, Eisfeld became the first conductor of the Brooklyn Philharmonic Society, and from 1864 shared the directorship with Theodore Thomas, until he returned to Wiesbaden in 1866. His health had suffered greatly from exposure and shock when he had been one of the few survivors of the burning of the ship *Austria*, in midocean in 1858.

Eisfeld was something of a composer. One of his works was played by the orchestra at a Jenny Lind concert. One newspaper critic became poetic in reviewing it:

Mr. Eisfeld's "Concert Polonaise" was a spirited, refreshing orchestral piece. It moved on with a triumphant and intoxicating wealth of harmony, worthy to clothe the noble rhythmic outline of the Polonaise form, like a young Bacchus crushing red grapes with every step.

OTTO DRESEL (1826–1890) was the pianist at the first of the Eisfeld *soirées*. He was one of the musicians who came in 1848. He had been a pupil of Hiller and Mendelssohn, and was an intimate friend of Robert Franz. Apthorp, in *Musicians and Music Lovers*,[2] coupled Franz and Dresel in a splendid tribute:

In both of these men was found in the highest perfection . . . the sense of musical beauty, the keenest sense for beauty of expression, beauty of form, proportion and color. They were staunch, life-long friends; their agreement on musical subjects was as complete as their friendship; they both worked together toward the same end; though they lived long apart, neither gave anything to the world without the ordeal of its passing through the other's criticism; they died within two years of each other.

In 1852, Dresel moved to Boston, where he lived until his death in Beverly, Massachusetts, in 1890. Forty-two of his sixty-four years were spent in America. He became the leading pianist of Boston, and gave chamber music concerts similar to Eisfeld's in New York. Under "Local Intelligence," Dwight's *Journal* announced his coming:

With great pleasure we announce the arrival of Mr. OTTO DRESEL, a pianist and composer of the highest order, who formerly in New York held rank with Timm, Rackeman and Scharfenberg. We have truly needed such an artist and such a teacher among us. Those who have read the papers upon Chopin in our columns, will rejoice in the opportunity of hearing his most delicate and deep music from the hands of an authentic, passionate interpreter. Mr. Dresel, too, is equally at home in the works of Bach, Beethoven, Mozart, Mendelssohn, Schumann, Robert Franz, &c., which as well as his own tone poems, he possesses in his mind and fingers. Mr. Dresel is a gentleman of superior culture and refinement. He is not a mere finger virtuoso, but one who makes the piano a means and not an end. His intention is to reside in Boston and give instruction; and to no one can we more confidently commend those who would become initiated into the genuine and enduring

[2] William F. Apthorp, *Musicians and Music Lovers*, Charles Scribner's Sons.

classics, old and new, that have been written for our common parlor instruments.

Dresel's works have not had the immortality of those of his friend Franz. He was a musician of the head rather than the heart, and of the two the heart is more often required. Maybe he was too severe a critic of his own work. His few piano pieces and songs were highly praised in their composer's day, and his unpublished *In Memoriam*, to words by Longfellow, had several performances in its original form as a ballad for soprano and orchestra. The Civil War inspired his *Army Hymn*, to a poem by Oliver Wendell Holmes, for soli, chorus, and orchestra. There were also a Piano Trio and a Quartet for piano and strings, often played at his chamber music concerts.

JULIUS EICHBERG (1824–1893) did not come to America until 1856, but when he went to Boston in 1859 he started a career as conductor and educator that lasted until 1893. For years he was supervisor of music in the Boston Public Schools, and his chamber music, and *études* and pieces for the violin were much used. We know Eichberg today as a composer of operettas. *The Doctor of Alcantara* is still a favorite, and the patriotic chorus *To Thee, O Country* is widely sung.

We have had references to Dwight's *Journal of Music*, and perhaps there is no more fitting place than this to introduce its founder and editor JOHN S. DWIGHT (1813–1893), who was at the height of his career during the foreign immigration. He was so much the friend of classic music that he was often assailed as a *Germanophile* by those who wanted American musicians to have a better chance. Dwight was needed just at the time he was most effective, though the cause of American music may have suffered at his pen. He was the foe of humbug, of charlatanism, and though he made some grave errors, he generally knew what he was talking about.

Dwight was born in Boston in 1813, and after being graduated from Harvard in 1832, he became a Unitarian minister. But his heart was in music and teaching, and after a few years in the ministry, he became a teacher of music and Latin at the Brook Farm community. In 1837, with a group of five contemporaries, he founded the *Harvard Musical Association*, for the purpose of raising the standard of musical taste at the University, preparing the way for a professorship of music, and collecting a library that would contain music and musical literature in all its branches. These aims were all realized, and the association's *soirées*, and later its orchestral concerts, were a regular part of the musical life of Boston. It is still in active existence.

It was the moral backing of the Harvard Musical Association that led Dwight to establish his *Journal of Music* in 1852. He was editor, publisher, and proprietor for six years. In 1858 the Oliver Ditson Company took it over, and retained Dwight as editor. In 1878 it was sold to other publishers and was discontinued in 1881. Dwight probably never had more than five or six hundred subscribers until he went with Ditson, but he was an influence, nevertheless. Musicians read his paper and courted his praises.

An account of Jullien's career in America may well belong in the chapter on *virtuosi*, for Jullien was certainly a prima donna conductor. Yet many of the men in his orchestra, such musicians as the Mollenhauer brothers, stayed here when Jullien returned. LOUIS ANTOINE JULLIEN (1812–1860) could almost have taught Barnum some tricks, and maybe he did, though he did not come here until three years after Jenny Lind. His father was a bandmaster, and the son was familiar with instruments and music from the cradle. As a youth he studied composition with Le Carpentier and Halévy at the Paris Conservatoire. In 1836, when he was twenty-four, he left the Conservatoire without graduating, and soon became a conductor of dance music. In 1840 he appeared in London as conductor of the *Concerts d'été* at the Drury Lane Theatre. He had an orchestra of ninety-eight and a chorus of twenty-four. Then came the *Concerts d'hiver*, and the *Concerts de société*, and Jullien began to be the fashion.

His aim was always to popularize music, and to do this he used the largest band, the best performers, and the most attractive pieces. When he had attained vogue, he played whole symphonies on a program, and sometimes two in an evening. Jullien would have made a fortune in our movie palaces. Almost eighty years ago he did what our movie conductors do today—presented music with showmanship. And if good music could be made theatrical it would and does appeal to the masses.

Jeweled baton, white gloves, both contributed to the effect. None of these details was assumed for the benefit of Americans alone—they were part of his stock in trade both here and abroad. When he came in 1853 he had considerable foreign reputation, and his advance agents did much to excite the curiosity of New Yorkers. One newspaper was playful:

Jullien's "monster" ophicleid is exhibited in Broadway, and there is much talk of his *Monster drum*, used in his concerts when great, *striking* effects are required, and played upon, it is said, by a drummer at each end. This has not yet arrived, it probably will take two ships to bring it. But Jullien has a bigger drum than that at his command; namely the great *press* drum, which stretches its sheep skin over the whole land, and is a wonderful *E pluribus unum* made up of a vast number of all sorts of drums, including *snare* drums, *side* drums, *bass* drums, humdrums and doldrums. This is the great drum suspended over Jullien's orchestra, one end of it in Europe, the other (now the loudest) in America; and Jullien is the king of the drummers thereupon.

Jullien was an apostle of the bigger and better idea. His preliminary advertisements occupied nearly an entire column on the front pages of the newspapers for an entire week:

CASTLE GARDEN
M. JULLIEN

has the honor to announce that his first series of

GRAND CONCERTS
VOCAL AND INSTRUMENTAL

In the United States of America
will commence on

MONDAY EVENING, Aug. 29, 1853,

and be continued

EVERY EVENING
For
ONE MONTH ONLY

.   .   .   .

Encouraged by his European success, M. JULLIEN has been induced to introduce his musical entertainments to the American public, well assured that such patronage as it may be considered they merit will be liberally awarded. With this view, he has engaged CASTLE GARDEN. When the improvements now in progress are completed, from both its natural and artificial advantages Castle Garden will form the most perfect

SALLE DE CONCERT
IN THE WORLD

M. JULLIEN'S Orchestra will be complete in every department and will include many of the most distinguished Professors, selected from the Royal Opera Houses of London, Paris, Vienna, Berlin, St. Petersburg, Brussels, etc.

.   .   .   .

The selections of music, in addition to those of a lighter character, will embrace the grander compositions of the great masters, the gradual introduction of which, with their complete and effective style of performance, cannot fail, it is believed, to contribute to the enhancement of musical taste.

GENERAL ARRANGEMENTS

The programme (which will be changed every evening) will be selected from a Repertoire of

TWELVE HUNDRED PIECES

and will include a Classical Overture and two Movements of a Symphony by one of the great masters, a grand Operatic Selection, together with Quadrilles, Waltzes, Mazurkas, Polkas, Schottisches, Tarantelles, Galops, etc.

.   .   .   .

In addition to the above general arrangements, M. JULLIEN will each evening, introduce one of his celebrated NATIONAL QUADRILLES, as the English, Irish, Scotch, French, Russian, Chinese, Indian, Hungarian, Polish, &c.: and at the beginning of the second week will be produced the

AMERICAN QUADRILLE

which will contain all the

NATIONAL AIRS

and embrace no less than

TWENTY SOLOS AND VARIATIONS,

for twenty of M. JULLIEN'S solo performers, and conclude with a

TRIUMPHAL FINALE

The American Quadrille has been composed by M. JULLIEN since his arrival in America, and is now in active preparation. Several other new Quadrilles, Waltzes, Polkas, &c. will also be introduced during the season.

And the amazing part was that it was all true. The audiences saw a good show, and they heard some good music along with the clap-trap, all played perfectly. Whatever Jullien's faults may have been, he was a musician and he knew how to conduct an orchestra. The New York *Courier and Enquirer* knew what it was talking about when it said:

Monsieur Jullien is a humbug; which may be news to our readers, but it is not news to M. Jullien. Let us not be misunderstood. M. Jullien is not a pitiful humbug, or a timorous humbug, or worse than all, an unsuccessful humbug; he is a splendid, bold, and dazzlingly successful humbug; one who merits his great success almost as much as if he had not employed the means by which he has achieved it. M. Jullien, having blazoned himself and his principal artists in infernal scarlet and black all over the town, for some months—having issued an infinite series of portraits of himself, and ruined the prospectus of the Art Union by establishing several free galleries of portraits of his colleagues,—having occupied (and handsomely paid for) a large portion of valuable space in our columns and those of our principal contemporaries by informing them of what they knew perfectly well before or did not want to know at all,—having brought over from England forty and odd orchestral performers, when we could hardly support those who were already here, and created a dearth in the musician market by recklessly buying up the services of sixty more . . . having done all this, he sends us a vast and ponderous card of admission printed in scarlet and gold. . . .

. . . Exactly in the middle of the vast orchestra was a crimson platform edged with gold, and upon this was a music stand, formed by a fantastic gilt figure supporting a desk, and behind the stand a carved arm chair decorated in white and gold, and tapestried with crimson velvet, a sort of throne for the musical monarch. He steps forward, and we see those ambrosial whiskers and moustaches which Punch has immortalized; we gaze upon that immaculate waistcoat, that transcendent shirt front, and that unutterable cravat which will be read about hereafter; the monarch graciously and gracefully accepts the tumultuous homage of the assembled thousands, grasps his sceptre, and the violins wail forth the first broken phrase of the overture to *Der Freyschutz*. The overture is splendidly performed.

. . . Other conductors use their batons to direct their orchestras. Not so with M. Jullien. His band is so well drilled at rehearsal that it conducts itself at performances, while he uses his baton to direct the audience. He does everything with that unhappy bit of wood, but put it to its legitimate purpose of beating time. . . . The music is magnificent, and so is the humbug, as M. Jullien caps its climax by subsiding into his crimson gilded throne, over-whelmed by his exertions, a used up man. . . .

. . . The discipline of his orchestra is marvellous. He obtains from fifty strings a pianissimo which is scarcely audible and he makes one hundred instruments stop in the midst of a fortissimo which seems to lift the roof, as if a hundred men dropped dead at the movement of his hand . . .

Jullien started a custom which modern jazz bands claim as their own. He arranged airs from *Masaniello*, and other works, so that the men in the orchestra sang as they played.

Even Dwight capitulated when Jullien went to Boston, though his New York correspondent had warned him that he was extravagant and foppish as compared to Bergmann, and that Anna Zerr, his soloist, "shame to say, had stooped to pick up one night and sang 'Old Folks at Home' for the b'hoys; one would as soon think of picking up an apple-core in the street." Probably Dwight forgave the quadrilles and galops for the way in which Jullien played the *Scherzo* from Mendelssohn's *Scotch* Symphony, or the *Allegretto* from Beethoven's A Major Symphony. He wrote:

Jullien *can* play the best kind of music . . . if he makes a colossal toy of the orchestra in his quadrilles and polkas, he has also his Beethoven, his Mendelssohn and Mozart nights, in which he proves his love and power of interpreting the finest works. . . . We were present last week at his Mendelssohn night, and never before have we so felt the power and beauty of the A minor or Scotch Symphony.

The climax of Jullien's American career came when he was playing at the Crystal Palace in New York. One night the program announced a piece called *Night, or The Firemen's Quadrille*. He had always gone after vivid effects. If his music pictured a battle he used everything but real cannon. Even Handel once said that he would introduce the dis-charge of artillery into his choruses if he could. Pat Gilmore, the band-master, did actually use heavy guns for the first beat of each measure in the national anthems at the Boston Peace Jubilee in 1869, but he had more room outside the hall than Jullien had in New York, and there were fewer horses to be frightened. Jullien had to content himself with his monster drum.

Before the *Firemen's Quadrille* commenced, the audience was warned that something unusual might happen. Jullien loved to spring a surprise, but a lot of fainting women might be too much of a good thing. Wiping his brow with his gorgeous silk handkerchief, he arose from his throne and faced his men. The piece started quietly, like a nocturne or lullaby. A hush through the house made the suspense more thrilling. Then the music picked up a bit, the violins fluttered as they told of the awesome mystery of darkness. You could almost see ghosts. Suddenly the clang of firebells was heard outside. Flames burst from the ceiling. Three companies of firemen rushed in, dragging their hoses behind them. Real water poured from the nozzles, glass was broken. Some of the women fainted, and the ushers were rushing here and there yelling that it was all part of the show. And all the while the orchestra was playing at a tremendous fortissimo.

When Jullien thought they had had enough, he signaled for the firemen to go, and in a glorious blare of triumph the orchestra burst into the *Doxology*. Those of the audience who were conscious joined in the singing.

Such was Monsieur Jullien. When he went back to Europe in 1854 he may have had some money in his pocket, but he didn't know how to keep it. When Covent Garden burned in 1856, the manuscripts of all his famous quadrilles were lost. In 1857 he sank between five and six thousand pounds in an opera venture. Then he toured the British provinces with a small orchestra.

His hard luck was too much for him; it got on his nerves, and he finally ended in a madhouse, where he died in 1860. Maybe he belonged there all the time, but he at least practiced insanity in the grand manner.

It is not because of his showmanship and his playing that we are chiefly concerned with Jullien, though they were highly important in cultivating American concertgoers. It is principally because Jullien was shrewd enough to play works by native American composers during his visit. He gave them a hearing and at the same time crystallized the beginning of a controversy that has not yet ended, and which will probably never end. At this time a few of our composers began to be conscious of their nationality, and to feel slighted over the recognition they were not receiving. And after all, this was probably the most important result of the foreign invasion of 1848. It made the American composer conscious of himself, and if at first he had to fight for his existence with poor equipment and meager talents, the very contrast afforded by his foreign rivals made an issue of his rights.

CHAPTER EIGHT

The Awakening of a National Consciousness

1. ANTON PHILIP HEINRICH (1781–1861)

WE are anxious today to make an important person of the American composer. He must have international standing and at the same time be a nationalist. He must appeal to music lovers throughout the world, and yet choose native subjects for his musical ideas. He must be both Wagner and Grieg. Whether he is here or not, we must make a place for him, and secure his recognition in advance. If he doesn't exist, we must create him by hothouse methods. We want bigger and better composers in this country. All of which sounds like a twentieth-century idea, a final awakening to the fact that our composers haven't had a fair chance. Seventy-five years have passed since Ole Bull hoped that his offer of a thousand dollars for an American opera "would bring to light the musical talent now latent in this country, which only needs a favorable opportunity for its development." And he was careful to specify that it be the work of an American composer, upon a strictly American subject.

Even Ole Bull, in 1855, was only repeating what had been said before, for there were a few brave apostles of the American composer from the beginning of the century. Strange to say, one of the first who felt he should be encouraged because he was an American composer was a foreigner, a Bohemian named Anton Philip Heinrich. He called himself Anthony when he came to America.

Histories of American music have quite neglected Father Heinrich, and if he is to be judged on the lasting merits of his work, he is hardly entitled to much of a place among our composers. Yet he is highly important, not alone as an eccentric, but because he was one of the first to seek for nationalism, and to capitalize his limitations. In his own

226

mind, these limitations were geographical, not flaws in his own powers of expression.

Heinrich was born to wealth, and subsequent reverses turned him to the music he loved as a source of livelihood. Had he only had talent equal to his ardor, his life story would have satisfied the most romantic of biographers; for there are scenes in garrets, interviews with royalty, and disappointments that sing the old, old song of genius starving for want of recognition. The only thing missing is the genius. His friends hailed him as the Beethoven of America, but the only similarity was that he may have written as many notes.

Some years ago the Library of Congress acquired a whole trunkful of Heinrich's manuscripts, his own copies of his published works, and his personal scrapbook. Sonneck catalogued these works with his accustomed thoroughness, and in his notes called attention to the various duplications of similar material in separate works. Through Heinrich's own data on his manuscripts it is possible to piece together the principal facts of his life.

He was born in Bohemia in 1781. As a young man he became an officer in a large banking house. His business called for traveling, and once when he was in Malta he bought a Cremona violin, which he learned to play. On a visit to this country he married an American in Boston, a lady "abundantly rich in beauty, accomplishments and qualities of a noble heart," who died in 1814. A few years later Heinrich came to America and settled in Philadelphia, where he was director of music at the Southwark Theatre. It was at about this time that news reached him that his banking house had failed, and he was reduced to poverty. He went to Kentucky, and for a while gave violin lessons in Louisville, and then lived among the Indians at Bardstown. Parker's *Euterpeiad* (April 13, 1822) tells of his reverses:

The author but a few years since was merely an amateur and a prosperous merchant whom sudden misfortune transformed into a professor, the only character in which he expected to gain honest livelihood . . . this transformation had not taken place until he was verging on forty.

It was in 1820 that he published his *Dawning of Music in Kentucky, or the Pleasures of Harmony in the Solitudes of Nature*. In his preface to this work he stated his position as an American composer:

In presenting this work to the world, the Author observes, that he has been actuated much less by any pecuniary interest, than zeal, in furnishing a Volume of various *Musical Compositions*, which, it is hoped, will prove both useful and entertaining.

The many and severe animadversions, so long and repeatedly cast on the talent for Music in this Country, has been one of the chief motives of the Author, in the exercise of his abilities, and should he be able, by this effort, to create but one single *Star* in the *West*, no one would ever be more proud than himself, to be called an *American Musician*.—He however is fully aware of the dangers which, at the present day, attend talent on the crowded and difficult road of eminence; but fears of just criticism, by *Competent Masters*, should never retard the enthusiasm of genius, when ambitious of producing works more lasting than the *Butterfly-effusions* of the present age. —He, therefore, relying on the candour of the public, will rest confident that justice will be done, by due comparisons with the works of other Authors (celebrated for their merit, especially as regards Instrumental *execution*) but who have never, like him, been thrown, as it were, by *discordant events*, far from the emporiums of musical science, into the isolated wilds of nature, where he invoked his Muse, tutored *only* by ALMA MATER.

So much for Heinrich's own opinion of himself and his work. Parker's *Euterpeiad* quite agreed with him. Under the head of *Criticism* appeared the following review:

In attending to other duties we fear we have too long neglected the pleasing task of recommending the above *American production* to the favorable notice of the public. . . . It is . . . with great satisfaction that we feel ourselves authorized to say, that whoever has the will and ability to overstep the fence and unveil the hidden treasure, will be no less surprised than delighted with his discovery. With what success the first attempt of this kind was made in Boston, and to whom the honor of it belongs, has already been stated in our former numbers; and we can only add now that the vigour of thought, variety of ideas, originality of conception, classical correctness, boldness and luxuriance of imagination, displayed throughout this volume, are . . . extraordinary. . . . His genius . . . triumphs over everything. —He may, therefore, justly be styled the *Beethoven* of America, and as such he is actually considered by the few who have taken the trouble to ascertain his merits. . . .

In another paragraph the writer holds that one of the melodies "is a strain that would do credit to the Beethoven of Europe."

In 1827, Heinrich went to London, presumably to study music. By 1832 he was back in America, this time in Boston as organist of the Old South Church. Another trip to Europe followed shortly, and penciled notes on his manuscripts tell of incidents during his travels and sojourns. In 1834 he was in London, playing in the orchestra of the Drury Lane Theatre for thirty-six shillings a week. There were frequent trips to the Continent, and in 1835 he suffered a severe illness. Notes on one of his manuscripts (*The Jager's Adieu*) are dated London, November 24, 1835:

Composed and arranged under severe bodily affliction, and at the time of finishing this work, I was under the painful necessity of becoming a patient in the London Hospital. . . . Later, during the above year, I was also laid up very sick, in the Hospital of the Merciful friars at Buda (Hungary) and at Vienna, "im Spital der Barmherzigen brüder."

When he was in Grätz in 1836 he had a performance of his symphony *The Combat of the Condor*. Things didn't go too well.

The gentlemen of the orchestra went this introductory movement twice very handsomely through, namely on the 25th of May, 1836. On the 7th of June another rehearsal took place, but having obtained only a few violin performers, and those mostly strangers to their parts, there was great deficiency in the effect. The actual concert took place on the 10th of June following, when this first movement met with public introduction; however, as there were by far too few violin performers and basses, and again some new gentlemen, not enlisted before, the author must confess that he suffered by it.

In 1837 he was in Bordeaux, where he suffered more misfortune:

After having been severely robbed in the Hotel de la Paix, Rue Chapeau rouge, kept by a Mr. Sansot, I retired for consolation to a solitary garret in the boarding house of Madamoiselle Jouano, Rue devise Ste. Catharine no. 7, and wrote this work [*The Columbiad, Grand American national chivalrous symphony*]. I finished at the same place "The Condor," and my instrumental phantasy "Pocahonta." The Muses had not favoured me with a pianoforte, in fact, since two years, I have been so situated, as constantly travelling about, that practical music is estranged to me, but I trust notwithstanding, that at some day or other, this work and those other productions alluded to will be found worthy of public patronage, especially in the United

States, and should I not live, to derive any benefit from these works may my daughter Antonia, the child of my sorrows, be benefitted by them or should she be in prosperity, may they then serve to some other charitable purpose. I have travelled so far through France without letters of introduction and without holding a special converse with any human being, that after my disaster in the "Hotel de la Paix," not to mention other disappointments and misfortunes on my journey, I found it necessary to seclude myself for a few weeks at Bordeaux and find diversion and comfort in these compositions. May the blessings of Heaven rest upon them, and on my daughter Antonia, who alas! is far distant from me, and whom my eyes, as yet, have never beheld.

When his wife died in 1814, he had left his infant daughter with a relative at Grund, near Rumburg. When he came to Europe she had disappeared. When he went back to America in 1837 he found that she had followed him, and they eventually discovered each other.

From this year until his death in 1861, Heinrich spent most of his time in and around New York. There were a couple of years abroad shortly before he died, but he devoted himself principally to the business of being an American musician. In 1840 he solicited subscriptions to his *Jubilee,* "a grand national song of triumph, composed and arranged for a full orchestra and a vocal chorus—in two parts, commemorative of events from the landing of the Pilgrim fathers to the consummation of American liberty." In publishing this work he asked for the support of "statesmen, legislators, and other distinguished citizens." He spent several years in lining up his patrons for the piece, and journeyed to Washington to get the names of high government officials. It may be that this is the work that he wished to dedicate to the President. He asked John Hill Hewitt to introduce him, and Hewitt described the incident in *Shadows on the Wall:*

The eccentric Anthony Philip Heinrich . . . visited Washington while I was in that city, with a grand musical work of his, illustrative of the greatness and glory of this republic, the splendor of its institutions and the indomitable bravery of its army and navy. This work Heinrich wanted to publish by subscription. He had many names on his list; but, as he wished to dedicate it to the President of the United States, and also to obtain the signatures of the Cabinet and other high officials, he thought it best to call personally and solicit their patronage.

He brought with him a number of letters of introduction, among them one to myself from my brother, a music-publisher in New York. . . . I tendered him the hospitalities of my house . . . promising him to go the rounds with him the following morning and introduce him to President Tyler.

Poor Heinrich! I shall never forget him. He imagined he was going to set the world on fire with his "Dawning of Music in America"; but alas! it met with the same fate as his "Castle in the Moon" and "Yankee Dood-liad."

Two or three hours of patient hearing did I give to the most complicated harmony I ever heard, even in my musical dreams. Wild and unearthly passages, the pianoforte absolutely groaning under them, and "the old man eloquent," with much self-satisfaction, arose from the tired instrument, and with a look of triumph, asked me if I had ever heard music like that before? I certainly had not.

At a proper hour we visited the President's mansion, and . . . were shown into the presence of Mr. Tyler, who received us with his usual urbanity. I introduced Mr. Heinrich as a professor of exalted talent and extraordinary genius. The President after learning the object of our visit, which he was glad to learn was not to solicit an office, readily consented to the dedication, and commended the undertaking. Heinrich was elated to the skies, and immediately proposed to play the grand conception. . . .

We were shown into the parlor. . . . The composer labored hard to give full effect to his weird production; his bald pate bobbed from side to side, and shone like a bubble on the surface of a calm lake. At times his shoulders would be raised to the line of his ears, and his knees went up to the key-board, while the perspiration rolled in large drops down his wrinkled cheeks. . . .

The composer labored on, occasionally explaining some incomprehensible passage, representing, as he said, the breaking up of the frozen river Niagara, the thaw of the ice, and the dash of the mass over the mighty falls. Peace and plenty were represented by soft strains of pastoral music, while the thunder of our naval war-dogs and the rattle of our army musketry told of our prowess on sea and land.

The inspired composer had got about half-way through his wonderful production, when Mr. Tyler arose from his chair, and placing his hand gently on Heinrich's shoulder, said:

"That may all be very fine, sir, but can't you play us a good old Virginia reel?"

Had a thunderbolt fallen at the feet of the musician, he could not have been more astounded. He arose from the piano, rolled up his manuscript, and taking his hat and cane, bolted toward the door, exclaiming:

"No, sir; I never plays dance music!"

I joined him in the vestibule . . . As we proceeded along Pennsylvania Avenue, Heinrich grasped my arm convulsively, and exclaimed:

"Mein Gott in himmel! de peebles vot made Yohn Tyler Bresident ought to be hung! He knows no more apout music than an oyshter!"

Heinrich was active among the New York musicians of the forties and fifties. He was the chairman of the first meeting of the Philharmonic Society, although there is no record of any further connection with the orchestra. On June 16, 1842, a "Grand Musical Festival" at the Broadway Tabernacle was devoted largely to his works. At this time he lived at 41 Liberty Street. A note on his *Warrior's March to the Battlefield* states that it was

Finished on the 1st of May 1845 at my lodgings, say: desolated garret in Liberty Street no. 41, where I had dwelt for many years *quasi* in solitude, wrote many things etc. etc. but which lodging I was obliged leaving, with much melancholy, the house góing to be pulled down, as Music had no charms for the proprietor of the building, but more the hammer's din, in order to destroy the composer's garret, to make room for cocklofts and commercial stores. I loved thee dearly cherished and sequestered attic, notwithstanding many sorrows and inconveniences which I experienced there, but where my imagination wandered free and independent.

William Mason, in his *Memories*,[1] gives a picture of Heinrich at about this time:

. . . there lived in New York an elderly German musician who had somehow gained the cognomen of Father Heinrich. During a visit which he made to Boston . . . I was presented to him as a youth of some musical promise. He immediately showed me one of his pianoforte pieces in manuscript, and said:

"Young man, I am going to test your musical talent and intelligence and see if you appreciate in any degree the importance of a proper observance of dynamics in musical interpretation."

He had placed the open pages of the Mss. on the pianoforte desk, and I was glancing over them in close scrutiny.

"I wish to tell you before you begin to play that I have submitted this piece

[1] William Mason, *Memories of a Musical Life*, The Century Co.

to one or two of the best musicians in New York and they have failed to bring out the intended effects in an important phrase. . . ."

About half way down the 2nd page I discovered a series of sforzando marks over several notes of the inner parts, and immediately determined to bring out these notes with all possible force. . . . On coming to the passage referred to I put a tremendous emphasis on the tones marked sforzando, playing all the other voices by contrast quite softly. To my boyish satisfaction I found I had hit the mark. The excitement and pleasure of Father Heinrich was excessive and amusing. "Bravo, bravo!" he cried; "you have great talent, and have done what none of our best musicians in New York have accomplished."

When Jenny Lind came in 1850, Heinrich tried to call her attention to his works. If he could only get the "nightingale" to sing some of his songs, his fortunes were made. He was ready when she arrived. One of the works could be played by her orchestra as a feature number— *Jenny Lind and the Septinarian,* "an artistic perplexity" (he wasn't quite seventy yet, but that made little difference). The first part was "Jenny Lind's Journey across the ocean, a grand divertissement for the orchestra"; the second was "Jenny Lind's maelstrom on the ship-wreck of a book, a phantasy for the pianoforte." Then there was *Barnum: invitation to Jenny Lind, the museum polka.*

He didn't get very far with Jenny Lind. After she married Gold-schmidt he tried to see her husband about his works. He sent him a whole volume of songs. Receiving no reply he wrote him a couple of letters, asking when he could see him. Goldschmidt returned the volume of music without comment, and enclosed a pair of tickets to one of Jenny Lind's concerts. Heinrich called this the greatest insult of his artistic career.

The Philharmonic also offended his dignity. He had enough works scored for orchestra to fill the Society's programs for an entire season. The committee was a little too slow in considering his music to please Heinrich, and when he was finally informed that they would give him a performance, he withdrew his application, and continued to enjoy the sweets of martyrdom.

In 1853 came a triumphant moment in Heinrich's career. He was given a Grand Valedictory Concert at Metropolitan Hall. Nearly all of the prominent musicians took part. The orchestra, "a numerous and powerful one," was under the direction of Theodor Eisfeld and Heinrich himself. Mme. Otto was the principal vocalist. H. C. Timm presided at the pianoforte. Advance information spread to Boston, where Dwight's *Journal* told its readers that the

enthusiastic veteran is to have a concert, for the production of those strange and elaborate works of his. He has gone on in his solitary attic, composing oratorios, operas, symphonies, and songs, merely composing, not publishing [this is not altogether accurate] till he has accumulated several large chests full of original compositions, his only wealth. May the devoted old servant of St. Cecilia be cheered by a full house, and may some of that inspiration, which has sustained his long labors appear in his works and be felt by his audience.

The program was lengthy, and of course the majority of the works were by Heinrich. The opening number was for orchestra—*The Wildwood Troubadour, a musical Auto-Biography*. This "festive ouverture" was in four movements, representing the "Genius of Harmony slumbering in the forest shades of America."

After songs by Wallace, Loder and Hobbs, there came another of Heinrich's orchestral works, *The New England Feast of Shells*, a "Divertimento Pastorale Oceanico." This opened with an *Andante* movement—"The home Adieus of the Nymphs and Swains departing to the Maritime Festival." Then an *Andantino*—"The fanciful curvetings of the Mermaids in the ocean surf" (Yes, in New England!). The *Finale Brillante*—told of "The romantic 'Love Feast,' resulting in the destruction of the 'bivalves' at the 'sacrifice of shells,' *vulgate* 'Clam Bake.'"

The second part of the concert commenced with a tribute to England —*National Memories*, a "Grand British Symphony, by gracious acceptance, dedicated to H.B.M. Queen Victoria." Then came arias by Mozart and Weber, and a Quintette from Heinrich's Oratorio *The Pilgrim Fathers*. The closing selection was intended as a climax—*The Tower of Babel, or Language Confounded*. This consisted of two parts —first, the *Sinfonia canonicale*, and then the *Coda fugato*, representing "The Dispersion, which will be characterized by a gradual cessation of melodies, and consecutive retirement of each individual performer." Heinrich may have had his doubts about the endurance of the audience,

Harvard Theatre Collection

Daniel Decatur Emmett

(See pages 181–184, 255–258)

From a Photograph, Copyright 1902, by J. E. Purdy, Boston

Julia Ward Howe

(See page 259)

Photo by Brown Bros.

Henry Clay Work
(See pages 266–268)

Photo by Brown Bros.

George F. Root
(See pages 264–266)

for the program adds: "If time permits, the whole Symphony will be given; if not, the *Dispersion* alone."

In 1857 he went to Europe again, and spent a season in Prague and in Dresden. A note on the manuscript of *Der Felsen von Plymouth* is dated Prague, April, 1859:

The foregoing musings were chiefly written during the winter season of 1858 & 1859 in a desolate, comfortless chamber, without any fire whatsoever, during great sufferings of cold, as without the aid and solace of a pianoforte. The wanderer leaves now his winter-quarter for more genial climes, on his musical experimental tour, under the banner: *Hope on, hope ever.*

He eventually came back to America, and lived to see his eightieth birthday in New York. He was very ill at the time and died two months later—May 3, 1861.

Detailed review of Heinrich's music from a critical standpoint is difficult. His works are marked by extravagance, repetition, and a constant striving for the grand manner. Yet, in spite of his eccentricities (musical and otherwise), there must have been something very appealing about the man himself and even something akin to native genius in his music. He might well take a real pride and pleasure in a letter he received from the well-known German composer Heinrich Marschner (May 10, 1849), which, in translation, read in part as follows:

Although you are sometimes tempted through your originality, to offer the performers too great difficulties, and to require of the human voice too extensive a compass: still the originality, and the deeply poetic ideas, which are developed in your compositions, repay the painstaking to master them; and are a splendid testimonial of German talent in the West. Remain assured of my most perfect esteem, and may you be gladdened long yet with the applause of every lover of the art. This wish is from my heart.

And another distinguished musician and critic of that day, Joseph Leopold Zvonar of Prague, in reviewing Heinrich's concert in that city (May 3, 1857) wrote of Heinrich's musical personality as "so absolutely untouched by any fundamental art culture such as is obtained through the study of theory and musical literature, but forced to rely solely upon its own exceedingly sensitive and innately expressive spirit. That the effect is often surprising and strange is easily understood,"

Zvonar continued, "yet it cannot be denied that on occasion we find not only true spiritual essence, but also its eminently worthy expression. Then, too, there are moments showing a well-disciplined, consistent, logically correct musical diction, and a carefully worked out and originally conceived instrumentation; all of which places the really artistic personality of our worthy countryman in a very advantageous light."

The statement in Dwight's *Journal* that Heinrich merely composed in his attic, and did not publish his works, is hardly accurate when the Library of Congress collection contains nearly two hundred printed pieces. Many of these are pianoforte editions of the manuscript orchestral works. There are a number of duplications under different titles; the composer had a habit of reworking his material.

His works were played in his time. Scharfenberg featured the *Pocahontas* Waltz at a number of his recitals and Mrs. Ostinelli (Sophia Hewitt) played *Paganini's Incantation* at a concert in Boston.

Heinrich's importance in a history of American music lies in his treatment of nationalistic material. Others had taken the Indian as a subject for musical description, but Heinrich was the first to use the red man as a theme for orchestral works on a large scale. In this he was truly a pioneer. The *Indian Carnival or The Indian's festival of dreams* was a "Sinfonia eratico fantachia" [sic] for orchestra, with a score of sixty-four pages. He used its theme for a *Toccata* for piano, published in 1849. His *Indian Fanfares* (published for piano, but recommended as quick-steps for military band) comprised *The Comanche revel, The Sioux galliarde,* and *The Manitou air dance. The Mastodon* was programmatic. The score of this "grand symphony in three parts" occupies three volumes. The movements are: *Black Thunder, the patriarch of the Fox tribe; The Elkhorn pyramid, or the Indians' offering to the spirit of the prairies;* and *Shenandoah, a celebrated Indian chief.*

Manitou mysteries, or the voice of the Great Spirit was described on the manuscript title page as a "Gran sinfonia misteriosa indiana." *Pushmataha, a venerable chief of a Western tribe of Indians,* was a fantasia for thirty-three instruments. A note at the end states that "the author composed this fantasia under peculiar circumstances which have given it great wildness. An arrangement from the score for the pianoforte will be found at the end. The composer begs, that no decision on its merits will be made, unless performed by a master."

In at least one of his works Heinrich claimed that he was transcrib-
ing authentic voices of nature. He explained this phenomenon in a note
on the manuscript score of *The wild wood spirits' chant, or Scintilla-
tions of Yankee doodle, forming a grand national heroic fantasia scored
for a powerful orchestra in forty-four parts, designed as introductory
to the second part of the oratorio of the Pilgrim fathers, entitled The
consummation of American liberty. Composed and inscribed as a legacy
to his adopted country, the land of Washington, by Anthony Philip
Heinrich.* The note was as follows:

There is no fact better authenticated than that poets, (who were grave
historians in ancient times), heard, or feigned to hear, the voices of spirits,
and the music of the spheres, and men have always believed that "myriads
of beings walk the earth unseen by mortal eyes."—But, whether that be fact
or fable, the author has himself heard the *genii of music*, (if any credence is
to be given to his imagination) in an American forest—and although strange
vicissitudes have chased him since, and as the storms of more than sixty
winters have left their chill upon him, yet, the impressions of that ethereal
music were so deep, and his recollections so vivid, that by the help of sketch-
ings *scored* upon that mystic ground in the State of Kentucky, then the abode
of Sylphs and Naiads, he has been able to *note* down that music on these
pages, as he heard it from an invisible hand.

When he dedicated a work to the Musical Fund Society of Philadelphia, he chose a subject appropriate to that city—*The treaty of William
Penn with the Indians—Concerto grosso—An American national dramatic divertisement, for a full orchestra, comprising 6 different characteristic movements, united in one.*

He considered it entirely appropriate to use foreign languages in
titles and programs of works on American subjects, and occasionally to
indulge in a confusion of tongues. Hence *Der Felsen von Plymouth,
oder die Landung der Pilgrim Väter in Neu-England*, and the published *Storia d'un violino of the premier violon to His Majesty Andrew
the 1st, King of the Yankee Doodles.* . . . "Composto dal General
Jackson's primo fiddler."

Heinrich liked to make gestures, especially magnanimous tributes to
such colleagues as Beethoven and Mendelssohn. *To the spirit of Beethoven* was a "monumental symphony for a grand orchestra—an echo
from America to the inauguration of Beethoven's monument at Bonn."

The tomb of genius was a "sinfonia sacra, for grande orchestra, to the memory of Mendelssohn-Bartholdy."

The account of Heinrich's music could continue for many pages, but lack of space forces us to leave that task to his biographer. We may laugh both at and with the dear old man, principally at him, I fear, and yet he had a real idea in his poor eccentric head, an idea that others more talented than he have failed to carry out. We must respect him for what he tried to do, and never forget that he was the first to make the attempt. That he failed to accomplish his ends was unfortunate, in many ways tragic, but the important fact is that Heinrich was the first to attempt American nationalism in the larger forms of musical composition.

2. WILLIAM HENRY FRY (1815[?]–1864)

William Henry Fry is important as the composer of the first publicly performed grand opera by a native American. He is equally important as one of the first who fought the battle of the American composer; not wisely perhaps, but bravely. A curious combination, this Fry, the son of the publisher of the *National Gazette*, well educated, and a discriminating critic who let his patriotism get the better of his judgment. Modern societies for the spread of American music might well take Fry as their patron saint.

Fry was educated principally along literary lines, but he had an overwhelming love for music. His older brother had piano lessons, and William taught himself to play by following the instructions he heard given to his brother. After he had composed an overture at fourteen years of age, he studied theory and composition with Leopold Meignen, the Philadelphia musician and publisher who had studied at the Paris Conservatoire. Before he was twenty, Fry had written three more overtures; one of them won him a gold medal, and a performance by a "Philharmonic Society" that existed in Philadelphia.

Grand opera was heard frequently in the principal American cities by the time Fry reached manhood. New Orleans had started its operatic career with Paisiello's *Barber of Seville* in 1810, and during following seasons enjoyed three or four operas a week. New York heard *Der Frieschütz*, in 1825. Soon after this, in the same year, Manuel García brought his family and troupe to New York, and gave seventy-nine performances in a year's time at the Park and Bowery Theatres. Other companies had followed. Rossini and Boïeldieu were favorites, even though their works were adapted to the capacities of resident and traveling companies. In 1832, Lorenzo da Ponte was living in New York— the Italian poet who had written the libretto to Mozart's *Don Giovanni*. He persuaded Montressor to bring his opera troupe to America.

Arthur Seguin and his wife Ann, distinguished opera singers from England, came to America in 1838 and soon formed their own company. They made extended visits to the cities of the United States and Canada. Filippo Trajetta, an Italian, had come to Boston as early as 1799, and after living in New York and Virginia, settled in Philadelphia as a singing teacher in 1822. He founded an "American Conservatorio," and was an earnest propagandist for Italian opera.

Fry had plenty of opportunity to know the works of Rossini, Bellini, Donizetti, and Auber, so he tried his hand at opera and wrote *Leonora*, a lyrical drama in three acts. The libretto was the work of Fry's brother, Joseph R. Fry, who adapted it from Bulwer's *The Lady of Lyons*. It was produced at the Chestnut Street Theatre, Philadelphia, June 4, 1845, by members of the Seguin troupe, and enjoyed a run of twelve nights. Eighty-four years later, in May of 1929, Dr. Otto Kinkeldey, then music chief at the New York Library, arranged a presentation of excerpts from *Leonora* in concert form. It was presented at a concert of the Pro Musica Society, following a number of works by American moderns. The critics were all present and offered their opinions. Chotzinoff, in the New York *World*, said:

When Mr. Kinkeldey . . . arrived at the music of Mr. Fry's opera the joke seemed to me to be on Pro Musica, for "Leonora," though outmoded, was found to contain tunes the absence of which was the main feature of the modern pieces which preceded the exposure of the operatic antiquity.

Oscar Thompson, in the *Post*, deplored the levity of the audience, and added:

. . . at least one tenor-soprano duet in mellifluous thirds would not have been laughed at, it is fair to assume, if it had been heard in a performance of "Norma," "Puritani" or "Somnambula" at the opera.

Henderson in the *Sun* said that Mr. Fry evidently lived in his time, and probably thought "Norma" the greatest opera ever written. Peyser in the *Telegram* made comparisons with the present:

. . . As much of the music as one heard last evening played the sedulous ape to Bellini, Donizetti, and Auber, besides faintly remembering the neo-Weberian ways of Reissiger tradition. Who shall say that, properly mounted and sung, Fry's ambitious opus would not, in its archaic way, furnish better diversion than "Egyptian Helen"?

The original production in Philadelphia was lavish; the composer paid for it himself. There was a chorus of eighty, and an orchestra of sixty; the settings were the finest that could be built. In true operatic style, the work presented recitatives and arias, ensemble numbers, choruses, coloratura cadenzas, and a climax that was indeed melodramatic.

The libretto was almost too well adapted to musical setting. The regularity of rhythm and meter prevented Fry from achieving much in the way of variety. The Philadelphia performances were given in English, for Fry was one of the first to cry for opera in the native tongue. The Grecian muse spoke Greek. "Shall our American muse chant in a foreign tongue? Forbid it, national sense, pride, ambition." But thirteen years later, when *Leonora* was revived and sung by an Italian company at the New York Academy of Music, practical considerations demanded that it be translated into Italian. Even Fry could compromise with necessity.

As music critic for the *Tribune* he failed to supply a precedent for Deems Taylor in reviewing his own work. He stepped aside and allowed his colleagues to fill his column for him. The *Express* was a bit patronizing:

Our impressions of "Leonora" are of a mixed character. The opera seems to us a study in the school of Bellini. It is full of delicious, sweet music, but constantly recalls the Somnambula and Norma. It is marked by skill in instrumentation, the secret of which the composer seems effectively to have probed. It has many flowing melodies, many pretty effects, much that should encourage its author to renewed efforts; but, like all early efforts, it is full of reminiscences. . . . The peculiarities which most strongly distinguish his production are sweetness of melody and lack of dramatic characterization.

All the characters sing the same sort of music—a love passage or a burst of stormy passion is treated much in the same style. . . . Were Mr. Fry now to write an opera, he would probably rely more on his own strength—he would know when he was composing, and when he was remembering. . . .

The *Times* attempted analysis:

"Leonora" is Mr. Fry's first operatic effort for the public, and like all first works, it contains much that is admirable, and much that might be better. Its principal characteristic is melody. The fertility of Mr. Fry's invention in this respect is remarkable, and it is the more remarkable from the fact that he does not seek his inspiration in the shady and sentimental groves of the minor scale, like most young composers, but in the broad and healthful uplands of the major mode. The best melodies of the opera, orchestral and vocal, are in the long-breathed, deep-chested major. The exceptions to this general rule are, we should suppose, intentional, as in the drinking song, "King Death," where sackcloth and ashes and a touch of brimstone are needed, and in the opening of the second act, where sentimentalism and an oboe are necessary, and elsewhere as occasion demanded. But the prevalent coloring of Mr. Fry's sentimentality is manly; it does not remind you of the greenhorn who trembles when he speaks to a lady, and sits down on his hat in a perspiring tremor. What the literature of the day (especially dramatic literature) lacks, this Opera supplies and illustrates—namely, *abandon.* . . .

A frank acknowledgment of the superabundant merit of one of the first essentials of opera leads us naturally to the contemplation of a fault which is sometimes unpleasantly apparent in Mr. Fry's work. There is a certain suggestiveness in the opening bars of some of the melodies which carries our memory to past pleasures afforded by other composers. . . . It happens, invariably, that the first works of any composer bear certain ear-marks of other hands. It is the case in Mr. Fry's first opera, and it was the case in Mr. Beethoven's first symphony.

The *Musical Review and Gazette* saw little of merit in *Leonora:*

. . . The inexperienced hand can be traced not only in the choruses and *ensemble*-pieces, but in the phrasing of most of the songs of the opera. Almost everything is poorly shaped and put together, and what is still worse, worked closely after the most common pattern. . . .

We have learnt to esteem Mr. Fry in his literary pursuits for the very opposite qualities he displays in his music. . . . Mr. Fry, as *homme de lettres* presents to us a strong-minded individuality, while the music to his opera has not a fathom of individuality whatever. . . . Mr. Fry knows his own language thoroughly, but he has no command over that of music. . . . The whole orchestration of *Leonora* is somewhat like a picture in which trees and houses are daubed in red, and the people make a very green appearance.

. . . it is not a very pleasant task to tell a man whose *literary* ideas we respect and have often made our delight, that he bores us with the poverty of his *musical* ones. . . . Mr. Fry can be passionate and inspired; he seems to be one of those men—of which our country seems to be richer than any other—who attempt everything grand and beautiful; but whether he has on the musical field, the power to finish his attempts successfully, can only be added when he favors us with another opera of more recent composition. *Leonora* makes us fear he has not.

Soon after the Philadelphia production of *Leonora*, Fry went abroad as foreign correspondent for the New York *Tribune*. He stayed in Europe for six years, and though he was unsuccessful in getting *Leonora* produced in Paris, he found much to enjoy. He made the acquaintance of Berlioz, and had the friendship of a number of leading European musicians.

When he returned to America in 1852, he was ready to take up the banner for the American composer. He had had some experiences in Paris which furnished him with ammunition; he had tasted some of the joys of martyrdom. He became music editor of the *Tribune*, and in the winter of 1852–53, he gave New York a series of lectures on music, which, except for the audience, rivaled our present educational series on the radio. Fry's own paper gave him its moral backing, and ran this announcement:

Wm. Henry Fry, Esq., proposes a course of lectures upon the Science and Art of Music, and upon the most colossal scale. Yet imposing as is his programme, it does not seem to us impossible, and of the very great benefit and actual necessity of such an undertaking there is no doubt. Mr. Fry's proposition is nothing less than to give a general, and, to a fair extent, adequate comprehension of the whole subject of musical composition, including its scientific relations, its history, its ethics and its æsthetics.

To accomplish this design, which implies extensive illustration, the following essentials are named: A corps of principal Italian vocalists; a grand chorus of one hundred singers; an orchestra of eighty performers; a military band of fifty performers.

Lectures of this sort are clearly not matters to be lightly undertaken or executed, and ample time is allowed for the preparation, because negotiations must be commenced with artists. Ten lectures are proposed, at five dollars for the course, and ten thousand dollars is the estimated whole expense. The proposal has a lordly air, and it promises such real advantages to the many who love music and yet know nothing about it, that we shall hope for its entire success.

The subscriptions were sold, and the series actually started in Metropolitan Hall, November 30, 1852, with a chorus and an orchestra of eighty.

Mr. Fry [said the *Tribune*] at first labored under considerable embarrassment, but it soon wore off. . . . He began with a glowingly poetic assertion of the universal presence of Music in Nature . . . then explained the elementary ideas and technical expressions and rules of music in a very succinct manner, the orchestra and chorus illustrating as he went along. As an illustration of the ordinary major chord the "Star Spangled Banner" was performed.

The second part of the lecture . . . opened with some specimens of Chinese music. . . . This was followed by the overture to Der Freyschutz which marked all the advance of Christian upon Pagan civilization.

The second lecture . . . indicated . . . a degree of curious learning in the music of China, Siam, India and Europe of the middle ages.

Following lectures covered the human voice, the ballad, the orchestra, church, oratorio, and chamber music, the nature and progress of musical ideas, the "difference between formal and inspired music," the lyrical drama, and the connection between literature and oratory and music.

It was in the last lecture that Fry cut loose and gave his American ideas about music. The *Musical World* reported his statements at length, and if there is a familiar sound in their phrases, kindly remember that they were uttered in 1852. He was reported as saying that there is no taste or love for, or appreciation of, true Art in this country. The public, as a public, know nothing about Art. We pay enormous sums to hear a single voice, or a single instrument, but we will pay nothing to hear a sublime work of Art performed. As a nation we have totally neglected Art. In this country politicians reap all the public applause and emoluments to the exclusion of their betters. Our colleges ignore Art.

Hitherto there has been too much servility on the part of American artists. The American composer should not allow the names of Beethoven, Handel, or Mozart to prove an eternal bugbear to him, nor should he pay them reverence. He should reverence only his Art, and strike out manfully and independently into untrodden realms, just as his nature and inspirations may incite him, else he can never achieve lasting renown.

Until this Declaration of Independence in Art shall be made—until American composers shall discard their foreign liveries and found an American school—and until the American public shall learn to support American artists, Art will not become indigenous to this country, but will only exist as a feeble exotic, and we shall continue to be provincial in Art.

We have some good musical societies, said Fry, and they should devote a portion of their rehearsals to American compositions, and perform the best of them in public. The American public decry native compositions, and sneer at native artists. We now have symphonies, operas, cantatas, and other American compositions which are as good and better than the *first* similar compositions by the much talked of "great masters," and we should listen to these first compositions of American composers with as much respect and as bright anticipations as the people of former days listened to the *first* symphonies of Handel, Beethoven, and Mozart.

An American composer cannot get his works brought out at home unless he has a fortune which will enable him to bear the expense himself. An American composer cannot get his works brought out in Europe at all—not even by paying for it. In Europe, an American artist is spit upon, and finally the whole world over, artists are not and never have been treated as they should be—especially at mealtime. Instead of being assigned seats of honor at the table with other guests they are too often consigned to the kitchen to take their chance with the servants.

When the *Musical World* printed these statements, Fry protested that he had been misquoted in a number of important places. It was not the public, but the *critics* who ignored the existence of American musical works. Nor had he said that an American artist was spit upon in Europe; merely that when he had tried to have an opera produced, he was spit upon because he was an American.

I took the best possible introductions, and offered to pay the expenses of a rehearsal, according to my invariable custom to expect nothing as a favor. I wished the music to be heard simply; given book in hand without dress or decoration, and so pronounced upon—a frightful hazard, but one which I was willing to abide by, in the same way that I had my works performed at my lectures in New York without the necessary aids of the opera house. . . . When I asked for this simple rehearsal—so easily accorded and so fairly required—the director of the opera in Paris said to me: "In Europe we look upon America as an industrial country—excellent for electric telegraphs, but not for art . . . they would think me crazy to produce an opera by an American."

It was when Jullien brought his orchestra to America in 1853 that Fry's symphonies were heard, for Jullien liked new music. He may also have realized that Fry was critic of the *Tribune*. There were four of these symphonies: *Childe Harold*, *A Day in the Country*, *The Breaking Heart*, and the *Santa Claus* Symphony. A colleague on the *Tribune* described *Santa* for the public:

We have seen it stated that the composer of Santa Claus intended it for an occasional piece—a sketch, etc. This is not so. He intended it—in regard to instrumentation—as the means of exposing the highest qualities in execution and expression of the greatest players in the world. As to spirit, he designed it in the introductory movement to represent the declamatory style in which he conceives oratorios ought to be written. Next, the verisimilitude which should mark music adapted to festivities from its rollicking traits and abandon. Then, he designed to show all the sexual peculiarities of the orchestra, *dramatically* treated. Likewise the accents of English speech as related to English music. He wished also, to prove as he believes, that the Lullaby, poetically handled, is as sublime as the Madonna and Child, if looked at artistically, and connected with it may be four separate counterpoints, all distinct and all painting different ideas and facts.

Next he wished to connect the music of nature with the tragedy of human life—the latter played by M. Bottesini—and the composer essayed, too, to paint the sublimest music in the world—that of the deity singing the monody of the passing world in the winter's wind. Next, he wished to individualize in music our only remaining fairy,—the character being grotesque, yet withal gentle and melodious, and with the sweetest mission that ever fairy performed. Next he desired to paint the songs of the stars—the fluttering ecstasies of hovering angels—on the purest harmonies of the violins, only to be achieved by artists who have given a life of labor and love and lyrical devotion to extract the transcendental element in their instruments.

Next, he designed to paint the change from starlight to sunlight by poetical analogies and mathematical facts. Then he sought to imitate the mother's cry to her little ones by rousing them on Christmas morning, and by the playing of Bo-peep, which as a little love story, admits of dramatic harmonies. The introduction of toys into the orchestra at this point, may be considered by the thoughtless as a burlesque, but not so did the composer consider it. The divine words, "Suffer little children to come unto me, for of such is the kingdom of Heaven," make the artistic painting of children and their toys, as much of a mission of art as the writing of a hallelujah chorus. The finale, too, of this symphony, where an orchestra of drums is introduced to represent the rolling of the spheres, is among the composer's ideas of the necessity of towering sonority to crown a long work designed to be of religious and romantic character.

With all these preparations for a heaven-storming work that would plunge its creator into immortality, Fry was naturally hurt when Richard Storrs Willis, brother of Nathaniel, dismissed *Santa Claus* with a few lines in the *Musical World* and termed it a composition hardly to be criticized as an earnest work of art. It was rather "a kind of extravaganza which moves the audience to laughter, entertaining them seasonably with imitated snow-storms, trotting horses, sleighbells, cracking whips, etc."

Fry rushed for his pen and wrote a twenty-five-page letter, which Willis published. He said that his piece was the longest "unified" instrumental composition that had ever been written on a single subject, and therefore entitled to an extended review. Any work which began in Heaven "and then swings down to Hell, returns to Heaven and thence to earth to depict the family joys of a Christmas party" was certainly worth more than passing notice.

He pleaded his Americanism:

I think that the American who writes for the mere dignity of musical art, as I understand it, without recompense deserves better treatment at the hands of his countrymen at least. This is more due from an American, as the Philharmonic Society of this city is an incubus on Art, never having asked for or performed a single American composition during the eleven years of its existence.

. . . As the chances for an American to put before the public any work of musical High Art depend, in this country, upon the accidental presence of such [conductors] as M. Jullien . . . there ought to be at least one technical journal in this city where technical criticism and extended analysis of works are habitually rendered.

In replying, Willis made the most of his opportunity:

. . . the length of a piece of music is novel ground, certainly, upon which to base its musical excellence, or its requirement for a very long criticism.

Dwight lent his voice from Boston:

Why . . . is not friend Fry willing practically to submit the merit of the American symphonies to what he himself maintains to be the only true test?—namely to time and the world's impression. . . . Of course the bulk of our public concerts and musical entertainments must consist of pieces of a guaranteed excellence, of works that the world *knows* to be good, sure to give pleasure, sure to inspire and reward attention. It will not do to invite the public to perpetual experimental feasts of possibilities; to assemble a concert audience, like a board of jurors, to listen to long lists of new works and award prizes . . . If a work have genius in it, it will sooner or later make its mark upon the world. . . .

It is of no use to tell us why we ought to like *Santa Claus*, the thing is to make us like it.

3. GEORGE F. BRISTOW (1825–1898)

Fry's reference to the Philharmonic Society drew another man into the controversy—George Frederick Bristow, a native composer who had been one of the first violins of the Philharmonic since the Society was founded in 1842. Bristow wrote to the *Musical World:*

As it is possible to miss a needle in a hay-stack, I am not surprised that Mr. Fry has missed the fact, that during the eleven years the Philharmonic Society has been in operation in this city, it played once, either by mistake or accident, one single American composition, an overture of mine. As one exception makes a rule stronger, so this single stray fact shows that the Philharmonic Society has been as anti-American as if it had been located in London during the Revolutionary War, and composed of native-born British tories. . . .

It appears the society's eleven years of promoting American art have embraced one whole performance of one whole American overture, one whole rehearsal of one whole American symphony, and the performance of an overture by an Englishman stopping here—Mr. Loder—(whom your beautiful correspondent would infer is an American) who, happening to be conductor here, had the influence to have it played. . . .

This drew an official statement from the Philharmonic, as well as Bristow's resignation. The Society had formulated a policy in regard to American compositions at the very beginning, and had included this clause in its constitution (April 23, 1842):

If any grand orchestral compositions such as overtures, or symphonies, shall be presented to the society, they being composed in this country, the society shall perform one every season, provided a committee of five appointed by the government shall have approved and recommended the composition.

H. C. Timm, as president, signed the answer to Bristow's letter, and it was printed in the *Musical World* two weeks after Bristow's challenge:

In your journal of the 4th inst. appears a letter from Mr. Geo. F. Bristow, in which he undertakes to censure the spirit and action of the New York Philharmonic Society in such a remarkable and unjustifiable manner that the Board of Directors feels it a duty to the public and their constituents to make a reply. . . .

Now the society had existed four years before any American composition was suggested to members for performance. . . . During the remaining seven years, several American compositions by either native or adopted citizens of this country were brought to the notice of the Society and performed, as follows:

Overture to Marmion, by George Loder (English), performed twice at concerts.

Overture by H. Saroni (German) performed at public rehearsal.

Overture by F. G. Hansen (German) performed at public rehearsal.

Overture by Theo. Eisfeld (German) performed at public rehearsal.

Overture by Geo. F. Bristow (American) performed at concert.

Indian March by F. E. Miguel (French) performed at public rehearsal.

Descriptive Battle Symphony, by Knaebel (German) at public rehearsal.

Symphony No. 1, by Geo. F. Bristow (American) performed twice at public rehearsal.

Duetto for two cornets, by Dodworth (American) performed at concert.
Serenade by William Mason (American) performed at concert.
Several songs by W. V. Wallace (Irish) performed at concert.
Application was also made by A. P. Heinrich (German) for the performance of several of his compositions, and when he was informed the society was ready, withdrew.

The same issue of the *World* contained this item:

At the regular meeting (March 11, 1854), Mr. Bristow's resignation as one of the Board of Directors and as performing member of the Society was accepted.

Forgiveness followed soon, and Bristow was not absent from the Society's roster for very long. He was connected with the orchestra for almost forty years from its founding. He had a long and honorable career. His father, William Richard Bristow, was an English musician who came to New York in 1824. The son George was born in New York in 1825, and at the age of eleven was playing the violin at the Olympic Theatre. In addition to his work with the Philharmonic, he was conductor of the Harmonic Society from 1851 to 1862. From 1854 until his death in 1898 he was a visiting teacher in the New York public schools.

As director of the Harmonic Society, Bristow did what he could to bring out the works of American composers. In 1852 the society performed *The Waldenses,* an oratorio by Asahel Abbot, who was described as "a phenomenon, . . . a sturdy self-made New Englander who has for some years taught music in New York; but, what is more, can boast himself the composer of an incredible number of oratorios and other scores in great forms."

Dwight had his doubts about Abbot:

He has instructed several of his pupils to be likewise composers of great oratorios. To hear him talk, you would suppose that great oratorios grew on every bush, where he resided. We know nothing of the merit of Mr. Abbot's music, and trust that it will have a fair chance. The "Waldenses," we understand, is one of a series which he designs to sketch in honor of the different races that have struggled for liberty through the last 1600 years.

W. J. Henderson has described Bristow as "a most earnest man, filled with real love for his art, and self sacrificing in labor for its benefit; one of the earliest of the long-suffering band of American composers, who will be remembered always as one who strove to push American music into artistic prominence."

Bristow may be coupled with Fry for another reason than being a pioneer fighter for the rights of the native composer. Fry wrote the first native grand opera to be produced; Bristow composed the second. And what is more, Bristow chose a native subject—Irving's legend of *Rip Van Winkle*. Bristow's opera was produced in New York in 1855, soon after the Fry-Willis controversy, and Bristow's differences with the Philharmonic. It was also the same year that Ole Bull had announced his prize for an American opera during his ill-fated management of the Academy of Music. Fry's *Leonora* had been produced in Philadelphia ten years before, and three years were to pass before it was to have its New York production. It must have been a bitter pill for Fry to see his colleague's work produced before his own. The *Musical World* hinted at a political situation:

Mr. Bristow's grand opera *Rip Van Winkle*, produced at Niblo's on Thursday evening, is the second one composed in this country by an American. As musical intelligence it is due to the reader that we should give the following historical facts. . . . The first opera by an American was *Leonora*, composed by Mr. W. H. Fry, and produced in Philadelphia by the Seguin troupe about ten years ago. . . . Mr. Fry composed several other operas, which have not yet been produced. The managers of all the theatres in New York, as is well known, are in utter fear of a journal whose editor has made war on Mr. Fry and all his productions from the moment *Leonora* appeared. The public is sufficiently acquainted with the causes of this hostility, but is hardly aware that its exercise up to this time, through the acknowledged subserviency of the managers of all the theatres, deprived Mr. Fry of a hearing in New York for any of his operas; though his symphonies through Mr. Jullien, who defied the wrath of the editor in question, have been frequently performed. . . .

This tends to contradict the belief that *Leonora* enjoyed its New York performances because its composer was music critic of the *Tribune*.

Willis, whom Fry had assailed as unfriendly to American composers, was one of the first to welcome *Rip Van Winkle:*

Sebastopol has fallen, and a new American opera has succeeded in New York! The clash of Russian steel with the bristling bayonets of the Allies has not been more fierce and uncompromising than the strife in lyric art between the stronghold of foreign prejudice and the steady and combined attacks of native musicians. It is true, the enemy has long since given evidence of his respect in other departments of art. But chiefly by a blind deference to the pompous pretensions of foreign interpreters of the art divine, has the real strength of our native musical genius been kept in abject abeyance, or suffered to linger in worse than aboriginal obscurity by our chilling reserve, if not studied neglect.

It is, however, neither good nor wise in us, to remain longer insensible to our own sources of power, or to the palpable weakness and misgivings of the enemy. This position may not be questioned, either in view of a proper respect for ourselves, or of a sincere regard to the welfare of the natives of other climes. Indeed, the truest policy for the foreign artist or artisan, is to labor long and largely for the development of the *creative* as well as the executive ability of the community in which he dwells, since hereby he most thoroughly exemplifies the workings of a truly benevolent heart, and most directly contributes to the permanent employment of a larger number of his brother artists.

Rip Van Winkle had a run of four weeks at Niblo's, following its première, September 27, 1855. Comparison of box-office receipts with those of other current attractions shows that it was third in popularity among the New York theatres. On the Monday of the week following its opening, *Rip Van Winkle* drew $700. The Metropolitan Theatre drew $4,500, and the Broadway $1,050. The Italian opera at the Academy of Music was next to *Rip Van Winkle* with $600. Wood's Minstrels and Buckley's Minstrels took in but $300 and $250 apiece.

J. R. Wainwright's libretto to the opera took a few liberties with Irving's story, though it followed the original in its essentials. The librettist introduced imaginary episodes from the Revolution, and conceived a love affair between Rip's daughter Alice and a British officer. This gave opportunity for love duets, as well as soldiers' choruses by both Continental and British troops. In the *Musical World*, Willis discussed the American elements of the score:

But if the subject be quite American, is the music of Mr. Bristow quite American?

Though agreeable and fluent it is somewhat devoid of character. It takes a long time before a nation has adapted art to its own nature. . . . If the English had a genuine form of opera, it is probable that it would serve as a model to composers of this country; as the English have not yet an opera of their own (sui generis), it would be unfair to demand of Mr. Bristow a school of an American stamp. It is from such a point of view that we must judge his work. It would be absurd to demand of one who writes for the stage for the first time a great creation or a masterpiece; for this requires, first of all, experience. If we find in Mr. Bristow's work an appropriate use of the forms of the existing musical drama he will be fully justified.

The opera of *Rip Van Winkle* exhibits an easy flow of melody. This melody is free from effort and spontaneous—an important quality in a dramatic composer. But in none of the arias of Mr. Bristow do we meet with large conception or rich development of ideas; none of them is shaped after a large pattern. The same remark will apply to the choruses. . . .

Mr. Bristow has produced before the public of this city several fragments of symphonies, which evidenced experience of the orchestra. We were rather disappointed, when hearing this opera, to find that the deficient part of his work was precisely the instrumentation. . . . The orchestra of *Rip Van Winkle* is in general inanimate and lifeless, and devoid of that brilliancy which we must meet with in modern opera.

Bristow outlived Fry by many years. Fry died of tuberculosis in the West Indies in 1864, the year his second opera *Notre Dame de Paris* was produced in Philadelphia. It was given later in New York under Thomas. Bristow lived until almost the close of the century. His *Rip Van Winkle* was revived in 1870, and by that time he had heard two more of his symphonies played—the second in 1856 and the third in 1859. In 1874 he presented his *Arcadian* Symphony. There were also two symphonies that were not performed, two string quartets, two oratorios, and two cantatas, some of them published. When he died in 1898 he was at work on another opera, *Columbus*.

It is not because they wrote great or fine music that Heinrich, Fry, and Bristow are important. Some of their writings may even seem ridiculous. Their consciousness of nationality is what is important to the cause of American music, for they were early prophets. In their controversies they went to extremes, and laid themselves open to refutation by those who thought and spoke more calmly. Yet they fired the first cannon in a fight that has never ended.

PART THREE

1860 TO THE PRESENT

EUTERPE BUILDS HER AMERICAN HOME

CHAPTER NINE

Songs of the Civil War

I. DIXIE AND THE BATTLE HYMN

WARS have always produced songs, and people keep on singing them long after thoughts of war have gone from their minds. Generally it is only the inspirational songs that survive, rather than those associated with the actual facts and episodes of the war that gave them birth. The Civil War produced hundreds of songs that could be arranged in proper sequence to form an actual history of the conflict; its events, its principal characters, and the ideals and principles of the opposing sides.

We all know *Dixie* and *The Battle Hymn of the Republic*—these are national songs now, and though they were put to partisan uses in the war days, they may be heard without resentment by descendants of either North or South today. Strangely enough, *Dixie* was written and composed by a *Northerner*, and the tune of *The Battle Hymn of the Republic* was claimed by a Southern composer of popular Sunday School songs—WILLIAM STEFFE.

There have been many myths concerning *Dixie*. At a time when copyrights were not always respected, various composers and authors claimed *Dixie* as their property. Even now there are many people who doubt Daniel Decatur Emmett's authorship.[1] To Southerners it may be an almost irreconcilable fact that *Dixie*, *their* song since the Civil War, was written by a Northerner. But there can be no doubt whatever that *Dixie* was composed by Emmett. His name is clearly stated on playbills of the earliest performances on the original edition of Firth, Pond & Company of 1860, which was copyrighted on June 21 of that year. His name also appears on the contract of February 11, 1861 which

---

[1] For an account of Emmett's career, see pp. 181–184.

transferred all of his rights to the publishers for only $300. Moreover, the style of the tune is Emmett's.

In order to minimize Emmett's contribution, some have asserted that his *Dixie* is heavily indebted to other songs. It is true that Irish and Scotch elements have gone into its making. But the result is not a weak, synthetic product, but a lively, original tune that holds its own. A melody, however unique, shows some relation to earlier or contemporary music. What may make it outstanding is the new meaning which has been given to existing material. This is true of *Dixie*.

There are some sources which Emmett, unconsciously, blended into a tune all his own. The opening measures are slightly related to a number of melodies of the British Isles. The refrain, too, might some day be traced back to earlier material, possibly to a Scotch song. It is similar to the refrain of another song by Emmett, *Billy Patterson*, written a few months later than *Dixie*.

Emmett wrote also the words of *Dixie*. Their accents and inflection are in perfect harmony with the melodic line. People who enjoy hunting for sources might be interested in the fact that the expressions "I wish I was in" [name of a Southern state or city] and "Away down South," appear in minstrel songs of the forties. The latter was a Stephen Foster song. The second stanza of *Dixie*, which contains the story of "Old Missus" and "Will de weaber," the "gay deceiber," was inspired by a stanza in *Gumbo Chaff*, a minstrel song of the thirties. It was the custom of minstrel-song writers—as indeed of the minstrels of the Middle Ages—to borrow from each other. Various explanations of the word "Dixie" have been given, but most of them are completely unsatisfactory. The most plausible seems to be the one which derives "Dixie" from "Mason and Dixon's Line." The word "Dixie" does not appear in print before 1860. Though it probably was used before that time, perhaps by the slaves and by white showmen, it was Emmett who established and popularized its meaning as the name of the place where Negroes could live in happiness. A few weeks before it appeared in *Dixie's Land*, it was used by Emmett in the last stanza of his song *Johnny Roach*:

> Gib me de place called "Dixie's Land" [or "Dixie Land"]
> Wid hoe and shubble in my hand;

> Whar fiddles ring and banjos play,
> I'd dance all night and work all day.

A few months earlier Emmett, in his song *I Ain't Got Time to Tarry*, spoke of the "land of freedom" as the home of the Negroes, without calling it "Dixie," however. This song received its first performance in November, 1858.

On April 4, 1859, *Dixie's Land* was presented for the first time anywhere by the Bryant's Minstrels at Mechanics' Hall on Broadway. It was performed as a Negro "walk-around"; that is, sung and danced by a few soloists in the foreground, and the rest of the company— about six or eight men—in the background of the stage. Appearing at a time when the Southern question was in everybody's mind, *Dixie* was an immediate success. It spread like wildfire all over the nation. Minstrel companies picked it up, and black-face comedians added their own words to the popular tune. From 1860 on, publishers in the North and South issued it in its original form or with its tune varied and its words changed, in piano arrangements and paraphrases—by no means always giving credit to Emmett. The list of *Dixie* editions is a long one. It was perhaps the greatest song success in America up to that time, but the composer realized very little money from it.

On February 18, 1861, *Dixie* was played in Montgomery, Alabama, at the inauguration of Jefferson Davis, and from then on became the symbol of the Confederacy. Its original tempo which was *Allegro* was undoubtedly changed to that of a fiery military quickstep. General Albert Pike wrote the following revolutionary words to the tune in 1861:

> Up, lest worse than death befall you!
> To arms! To arms! To arms in Dixie.
> Lo! all the beacon fires are lighted,
> Let all hearts be now united.
> To arms! [and so on]

At about the same time the North adapted anti-Southern words to *Dixie*. A stanza of a broadside reads:

> Away down south in the land of traitors,
> Rattlesnakes and alligators,
> Right away come away, right away come away.
> Where cotton's king and men are chattles,

> Union-Boys will win the battles.
>
> Right away [and so on]

The tune was used by the Union Army until 1862 and probably later, though it had never the exclusive popularity which it had in the Confederate Army.

Yet, in spite of its Southern associations, *Dixie* has come to be something more than a song of just one section of our country. There is something indefinably American about the tune; a jauntiness, an impertinence, a carefree spirit that seems to be one of our characteristics as a people. In some ways *Dixie* is one of the few pieces of music that can be said to be American; it represents a state of mind common to all parts of the nation.

The melody of *The Battle Hymn of the Republic* was first popular around Charleston, South Carolina, where it was sung as a hymn to the words:

> Say, brothers, will you meet us?
> Say, brothers, will you meet us?
> Say, brothers, will you meet us?
> On Canaan's happy shore?

and the refrain:

> Glory, glory, hallelujah,
> Glory, glory, hallelujah,
> Glory, glory, hallelujah,
> For ever, evermore!

The tune was rousing and easily remembered. It had a swing that made it a splendid marching song, and it was inevitable that it should spread like fire. The actual date of William Steffe's writing it has never been determined, but it dates back at least to 1856. It became popular in colored churches, with firemen, and especially in the army posts which were beginning to be more fully manned in the years that led up to the war.

In the summer of 1859, John Brown made himself famous and helped to precipitate the actual war by leading his little band in the misguided raid on Harpers Ferry. His hanging was hailed by Northern Abolitionists as martyrdom. About this time, the "Tigers," a battalion of Massachusetts Infantry, was stationed at Fort Warren in Boston Harbor. The men had formed a glee club, and one of their favorite songs was the Sunday School hymn from the South. Many new verses were improvised, some of them far from the accepted Sunday School idea. Rhymes were nonessential, for each line was repeated twice.

One of the men was a Scotchman named John Brown, who was the butt of many jokes, practical and otherwise. The John Brown incident in the South was a brilliant opportunity for the humorists, and a John Brown verse was accordingly improvised:

> John Brown's body lies a-mouldering in the grave,
> John Brown's body lies a-mouldering in the grave,
> John Brown's body lies a-mouldering in the grave,
> His soul is marching on.

then the "Glory hally, hallelujah" refrain.

Other verses were added:

> He's gone to be a soldier in the army of the Lord, *etc.*
> His pet lambs will meet him on the way, *etc.*

and then when the Confederacy was formed:

They will hang Jeff Davis to a tree (later extended to a "sour apple tree" for purposes of rhythm).

Other regiments took up the song, and to Colonel Fletcher Webster's Twelfth Massachusetts Regiment belongs the credit of spreading its fame on the march to the South. As the men passed through New York and other cities, they halted and sang it over and over again.

Edna Dean Proctor tried to save the tune from ribaldry by setting Abolitionist words to it, but with indifferent success. In December, 1861, JULIA WARD HOWE visited Washington. With her husband, Dr. Howe, she saw a skirmish a few miles from the city, and heard the troops go into battle singing *John Brown's Body*. The Reverend James Freeman Clark, a member of the party, asked her why she shouldn't write new words to the song. That night she wrote the lines beginning, "Mine eyes have seen the Glory of the coming of the Lord." Steffe's Sunday School hymn achieved respectability along with immortality as *The Battle Hymn of the Republic*.

2. OTHER WAR SONGS

Historically, the most interesting of the war songs are those which refer to actual episodes, even though their musical value is doubtful, and as songs most of them are forgotten today. In the early days of secession there were a number of doubtful states, especially those along the border. Maryland actually stayed in the Union, but she was a slave-holding state, and Southern sentiment was strong among her people. One of her native sons, JAMES RYDER RANDALL, was living in New Orleans when he heard that Massachusetts troops had been fired on as they passed through Baltimore. He hoped that this episode would swing his native state to the Southern cause, and in a moment of inspiration he wrote his appeal in verses that have ever since been sung to the old German song *O Tannenbaum:*

> Hark to thy wandering son's appeal,
> Maryland, my Maryland! *etc.*

and the second stanza:

> Thou wilt not cower in the dust,
> Maryland, my Maryland! *etc.*

The Northern bards were ready with an answer, and in addition to Maryland, they turned their thoughts to Missouri, another slave state loyal to the Union. To the same tune one of them wrote:

> Arise and join the patriot train,
> Belle Missouri, my Missouri!

The Southern poets also courted Missouri; one of them produced this lyric:

> Missouri! Missouri! bright land of the West
>
> .   .   .   .
>
> Awake to the notes of the bugle and drum!
> Awake from your peace, for thy tyrant hath come,
> And swear by your honor that your chains shall be riven,
> And add your bright star to our flag of eleven.

In some of the songs the wish was father to the thought; the *Song of the South* bore a caption on its title page—"Kentucky and Tennessee Join Hands." But of course this was not to be; Tennessee joined the Confederacy and Kentucky stayed with the Union.

One song, written before the outbreak of the war, proved to be a powerful propaganda weapon for the Abolitionist movement in the North. This was *Darling Nelly Gray*, composed in 1856 by BENJAMIN RUSSELL HANBY (1833–1867). Hanby's father was a minister whose Ohio home was a station of the underground railroad. One of the slaves whom he helped to escape had found that his own sweetheart had been sold, chained and taken to Georgia. Benjamin Hanby based his song on this episode, and it achieved a tremendous circulation. He composed over eighty songs altogether, but none of them gained the popularity of *Darling Nelly Gray*.

In 1862, when Lincoln issued a call for three hundred thousand more troops, James Sloan Gibbons, an Abolitionist writer, wrote a poem *We are Coming, Father Abraham, three hundred thousand more*. For many years these verses were attributed to William Cullen Bryant, who at one time issued a signed denial of the authorship. The swing of the words made them easily adapted to musical setting and many of the wartime song writers tried their hands at it. Among them was LUTHER ORLANDO EMERSON (1820–1915), a gospel-hymn composer who had already achieved something of a reputation with his *Golden Wreath* collection of songs for schools. Stephen Foster also made a setting of the Father Abraham song.

In the difficult days of the war, when the cause seemed lost to the North, and further financing of operations seemed impossible, one wag wrote a parody on *Father Abraham* which dealt with the new issue of paper currency:

> We're coming, Father Abram
> One hundred thousand more
> Five hundred presses printing us
> From morn till night is o'er;
> Like magic you will see us start
> And scatter thro' the land
> To pay the soldiers or release
> The border contraband.

Chorus

With our promise to pay
"How are you, Secretary Chase?"
Promise to pay,
Oh, dat's what's de matter.

Many of the Southern songs commemorated historic events. In the
first year of the war, General Beauregard ordered that all church and
plantation bells in Louisiana should be melted into cannon. This gave
birth to a song called *Melt the Bells,* published for the benefit of the
Southern Relief Association.

The Southern Girl told of the privations Southerners were willing
to endure:

My homespun dress is plain, I know,
My hat's palmetto, too,
But, then, it shows what Southern girls
For Southern rights will do!
We've sent the bravest of our land,
To battle with the foe,
And we will add a helping hand,
We love the South, you know.

The Star-Spangled Banner was used for the *Cross of the South:*

Oh, say, can you see, thro' the gloom and the storm,
More bright from the darkness, that pure constellation, *etc.*

The second verse had a fling at New England:

How peaceful and blest was America's soil,
'Til betrayed by the guile of the Puritan demon,
Which lurks under Virtue, and springs from its coil
To fasten its fangs in the lifeblood of freemen.

The tune of *The Marseillaise* was adapted by A. E. BLACKMAR, an
Ohioan who had engaged in music publishing in New Orleans, where
his business suffered when the city was captured by Federal troops:

Sons of the South, awake to glory,
A thousand voices bid you rise,
Your children, wives and grandsires hoary,
Gaze on you now with trusting eyes, *etc.*

Blackmar wrote a number of Southern war songs, among them *The Sword of Robert E. Lee;* and a tribute to Carolina:

> 'Mid her ruins proudly stands,
>   Our Carolina.
> Fetters are upon her hands,
>   Dear Carolina.
> Yet she feels no sense of shame,
> For upon the scroll of Fame,
> She hath writ a deathless name,
>   Brave Carolina.

Except for *Dixie*, the most popular Southern song was *The Bonnie Blue Flag*, written by HENRY McCARTHY. Its words told the story of secession:

> First gallant South Carolina nobly took the stand,
> Then came Alabama, who took her by the hand; *etc.*

with the refrain:

> Hurrah! Hurrah! for Southern rights, hurrah!
> Hurrah for the bonnie blue flag that bears a single star.

The North was ready with an answer. With words to the same tune it shouted:

> Hurrah! Hurrah! for *equal* rights, hurrah!
> Hurrah for the brave old flag that bears the Stripes and Stars!

Northerners celebrated their victories with songs: *Charleston is Ours* and *Richmond is Ours* were typical. Heroes were commemorated by both sides. Flora Byrne's *Jefferson Davis* shared popularity with *General Beauregard's Grand March*, by Mrs. V. G. Coudin. The North sang the praises of *Jenny Wade, the Heroine of Gettysburg*, in a song beginning "Raise high the monumental pile." The death of Ellsworth was mourned with JOSEPH PHILBRICK WEBSTER's *Brave Men, Behold Your Fallen Chief.*

One group of song writers was shrewd enough to sense the commercial value of sentimental songs that could be sung by both sides. There were hundreds of these lyrics, possibly the most famous of them, *Tenting on the Old Camp Ground*, written by WALTER KITTREDGE after he was drafted in 1862. Pacifists were squelched in Civil War days, as they have been in all times of war. One of the most sentimental ballads was Henry Tucker's *Weeping, Sad and Lonely, or When This Cruel War Is Over*. CHARLES CARROLL SAWYER was the author of the words. The effect of the song was so mournful that the generals of the Army of the Potomac had to forbid the troops to sing it—it lowered their morale. SEPTIMUS WINNER (1827–1902), another song writer who sometimes appeared under the pen name of Alice Hawthorne, soon answered the Sawyer-Tucker song with *Yes, I Would the Cruel War Were Over*, and then stated some conditions:

.   .   .   .

> Would the cruel work were done;
> With my country undivided
>   And the battle fought and won.
> Let the contest now before us,
>   Be decided by the sword,
> For the war cannot be ended
>   Till the Union is restored.

It was Winner, under the Hawthorne pseudonym, who wrote *Listen to the Mocking Bird* and *Whispering Hope*.

Sawyer reveled in sentimentalism, and his fellow poets often found it necessary to publish "answers" to his songs. In *Who Will Care for Mother Now?*, set to music by his publishing partner in Brooklyn, C. F. Thompson, he told the story of a dying soldier who wondered what would become of the mother he supported. From Ohio came the reply: *Do Not Grieve for Thy Dear Mother; answer to Who Will Take Care of Mother Now*. The idea was that Mother would be all right, for Heaven would look after her.

Stephen Foster wrote almost a dozen war songs, but they came from his last years, when his powers were spent and he was grinding out songs to order. None of them is representative of the real Foster. They included the *Father Abraham* setting; *Was My Brother in the Battle; Stand Up for the Flag; We've a Million in the Field; Willie Has Gone to the War; For the Dear Old Flag I Die;* and several others.

GEORGE FREDERICK ROOT (1820–1895) was one of the most famous of the composers of Northern war songs. Before the years of the war he had made a considerable reputation as a writer of gospel hymns and ballads, but his *Battle Cry of Freedom* and *Tramp, Tramp, Tramp,* were as popular as anything he wrote. Root's songs fell into three groups: sentimental songs, such as *Hazel Dell* and the ever lovely *There's Music in the Air;* war songs; and finally, sacred songs—*The Shining Shore* and others of the gospel-hymn type.

Root was born in Sheffield, Massachusetts, in 1820. When he was six the family moved to North Reading, a town rich in musical history, not far from Boston. From childhood his ambition was to be a musician, and he made the most of the few opportunities that came his way. As a youth he went to Boston, and through the help of his teacher, B. F. Baker, he soon began to have pupils of his own, and also taught a number of singing schools. He met Lowell Mason, and was asked to help with the music in the Boston public schools, and in the teachers' classes at the Boston Academy of Music.

About 1845 he went to New York, where he became the music teacher at Abbot's Institute for young ladies. He formed a vocal quartet which became popular and sometimes appeared at the concerts of the New York Philharmonic Society. He went to Europe in 1850 for further study, and in 1853, when Lowell Mason had come to New York, he helped to organize the New York Normal Institute.

The vogue of Stephen Foster's songs made Root want to try his hand at song writing, so he had a former pupil, the blind Fanny Crosby, write a few verses for him, and he wrote the music to *Hazel Dell, There's Music in the Air,* and *Rosalie, the Prairie Flower.* A friend in Boston, who had started a publishing business, asked Root for a few songs. Instead of a royalty, Root asked six hundred dollars for the six songs he selected. The publisher thought this figure too high, and sent Root a royalty contract instead. *Rosalie* alone paid $3,000 in royalties.

In 1859, Root went to Chicago. His brother had opened a music store there in partnership with C. M. Cady, under the name of Root & Cady. G. F. Root became associated with the business. The fire of 1871 ruined them temporarily, but the firm was soon restored. In 1872, Root was awarded the Doctor of Music degree by the University of Chicago, and he continued his active career until his death in 1895.

When the war broke out, Root, like many other song writers, tried to write war songs. *The First Gun Is Fired* was unsuccessful, but when Lincoln issued his second call for troops, Root read the proclamation and conceived the idea for his *Battle Cry of Freedom.* The song was written hurriedly at Root & Cady's store. Two popular singers of the day, Frank Lombard and his brother Jules, came to the store and asked for a song to sing at a rally to be held that day in the Court House Square. Root gave them his manuscript copy of the *Battle Cry*, and after the Lombards had sung it over they went directly to the meeting and not only sang it as a duet, but had thousands joining in the refrain before the last verse was ended. Then the Hutchinson Family, a traveling troupe of singers, took the song all over the country, and it was soon shouted in camps, on the march, and on the battlefield. *Tramp, Tramp, Tramp, the Boys Are Marching* enjoyed an almost equal success.

These, of course, were Northern songs, expressing Union thoughts, but some of Root's sentimental songs, such as *Just Before the Battle, Mother*, were sung by the people of both North and South. Another of this type was *The Vacant Chair*, to verses that Henry Washburn had written about the death of a lieutenant in the Fifteenth Massachusetts Infantry.

Root was definitely of the Lowell Mason, Webb, and Bradbury school, with strong evangelical tendencies, as far as his sacred music was concerned. Probably his most famous hymn was *The Shining Shore*, with its first line, "My days are gliding swiftly by." He wrote no great music, and nothing in the larger forms, except a few cantatas for mixed voices. George P. Upton described him as a courteous, refined gentleman of the old school, always wearing a genial smile, and the cheeriest of optimists.

It was through Root's persuasion that another song writer, HENRY CLAY WORK (1832–1884), lent his abilities to composing war songs. Work's name is still anathema to the South, for his most famous song, *Marching Through Georgia*, celebrates an event that the South has never condoned—Sherman's march from Atlanta to the sea in 1864. No matter what a person's heritage may be, he must admit that *Marching Through Georgia* glorifies episodes that admittedly had their darker sides. Moreover, it goes into details that cannot fail constantly to reopen old wounds.

And yet the seeming immortality of the song has had its humorous aspects. When the Democratic National Convention was held in New York in 1924, the band leader was told to play an appropriate song

Theodore Thomas
(See pages 280–289)

GOING TO THE PEACE JUBILEE.

Going to the Peace Jubilee (from a Contemporary Cartoon)

(See page 297)

for each state delegation. *Maryland, My Maryland* received almost hysterical applause; *My Old Kentucky Home* made everyone ecstatic, and then when the misguided leader, stronger on geography than history, swung into *Marching Through Georgia*, he was greeted by a silence that turned into hisses and boos noisier than the applause he had heard before.

Work's intense partisanship is understandable. He was born in Connecticut in 1832, and when he was a lad the family moved to Illinois, where the elder Work's antislavery views soon got him into trouble. He helped maintain one of the stations on the famous "underground railway" which helped runaway slaves to escape, and before long he was put in prison for his activities. When he was released in 1845 the family went back to Middletown, poverty stricken.

So young Henry was himself an ardent, fiery Abolitionist. As a boy he thought of little else but music, and when he was very young he sold his first song to Christy's Minstrels—*We're Coming, Sister Mary*. In 1855 he went to Chicago, where he later came to know George Root. He continued his trade as a printer, and often composed the words of his songs as he set up the actual type. There is also a tradition that when he had access to music type he composed his music directly with the type, without first writing out a manuscript copy. If this be true, Work was a good musician; and anyway, it makes a good story.

One of his first war songs was *Kingdom Coming*, which Root & Cady published in 1862. It became popular immediately, and the composer followed it with *Babylon Is Fallen* the next year. *Wake, Nicodemus* was published in 1864, and *Marching Through Georgia* in 1865.

Work was famous for temperance songs, for he was an ardent temperance advocate as well as an Abolitionist. The most famous was *Come Home, Father*, issued by Root & Cady in 1864. Even today we hear the immortal opening lines:

> Father, dear father, come home with me now,
> The clock in the belfry strikes one.

And then the rest of the story, with the other verses telling how the clock strikes *two*, and then *three*, when it is too late for father, dear father, to do any good. Others of his songs were *The Song of a Thousand Years, King Bibber's Army, The Lost Letter, The Ship That Never*

Returned, Phantom Footsteps, and *Grandfather's Clock.* Work lived until 1884, when he died suddenly of heart disease.

These are the principal writers and songs associated with the Civil War. They occupy a unique place in song literature, and in our national history. In many ways the songs are historical documents, for they afford a study of the contemporary state of mind of both sides in a conflict that was probably inevitable.

CHAPTER TEN

The Spread of Musical Culture

1. WESTWARD EXPANSION

ONE of the remarkable features of the development of music in America is the rapidity with which the inland cities have become music centers. Boston has been a center of culture from its earliest days, Philadelphia has had a nucleus of art and music lovers from its beginnings, and New York, as our principal seaport, has enjoyed a cosmopolitan population that would naturally have its percentage of art patrons. The early pioneers who joined the westward marches were hardy men, noted for their ability to endure hardships and for their dogged persistence in overcoming the terrific odds arrayed against them. Like the early settlers in New England and the South, they had little time for softer pleasures. Men who have spent a long day chopping logs for their cabins can hardly be expected to make immediate plans for the formation of a symphony orchestra. For these reasons, the seaboard cities had a long, running start on their Western cousins in musical matters.

Yet, since 1850, from the time when the Midwest pioneers have had a chance to enjoy themselves, they have more than made up for the time they lost. The history of music in the American provinces is yet to be written, but when the facts are gathered and the full truth is told, it will be something of a revelation. In our day, New York still holds its place as the American center of *world* music, for it is the port of entry; but there are other *American* centers. Chicago, Cincinnati, Detroit, St. Louis, Rochester, the Pacific coast towns; in fact, all of our large industrial cities are music centers as well. Some musicians still dread the local tag which may result from living in any city but New

York, or possibly Boston or Philadelphia, but the day is rapidly passing when they need be afraid of being known as merely Cincinnati, Milwaukee, or any other locality's musicians.

Before 1850 there was little music in the West. The Southwest, of course, could be proud of the opera at New Orleans, which dated from the beginning of the century, but this activity was the result of the French element in a city where conditions were far different from the settlements on the frontiers. There is record of a Haydn Society in Cincinnati, formed in 1819, and a Musical Fund Society in St. Louis in 1838. In 1849 a *Saengerfest* was held in Cincinnati, and a *Musikverein* was founded in Milwaukee during the same year. It is significant that these were towns with large German populations.

As a city, Chicago is well past its hundredth birthday, and also its musical centennial. In 1833, the few residents heard their first local musician when Mark Beaubien, public ferryman, played his fiddle for the dancing at his Saguenash Tavern. Moreover, he was accompanied by a piano which his brother had brought to Chicago on a schooner. A year later a Miss Wyeth opened a music school; and the Old Settler's Harmonic Society gave its first concert in the Presbyterian Church. In 1837, Dean and McKenzie opened a theatre where the nine-year-old Joseph Jefferson played in the company. By 1840 entertainments had multiplied. Barnum came with a minstrel troupe, and Henry Russell and other ballad singers made visits.

The short-lived Chicago Sacred Music Society was organized in 1842, and in 1847 a Mozart Society was formed by Frank Lumbard, who was appointed vocal teacher in the public schools in that same year. This, it is well to remember, was only eleven years after Lowell Mason's first experiments in the Boston schools, and but nine years after the Boston authorities had made music a regular part of the school routine. Soon after this came the debut of Richard Hoffman, the first piano virtuoso to visit Chicago, and then other great soloists, vocal and instrumental, included the city on their regular tours. But these beginnings were humble indeed, and the middle of the century found Chicago little advanced in musical culture.

The year 1850 marks two important events in Chicago. In July, theatregoers heard the first performance of a grand opera—*La Sonnambula*, at Rice's Theatre; and in October a Philharmonic Society, which had recently been organized, gave an orchestral concert. This group had been formed by Julius Dyhrenfurth, a German violinist who came to America in 1830, and after giving concerts in the Ohio Valley and in New Orleans and the South, had returned to Germany. He came back in 1847 and settled in Chicago. The orchestra grew from frequent gatherings of German musicians at Dyhrenfurth's home. After they had practiced and played together for a time, they decided to give a few concerts, and advertised for subscriptions to a series of eight programs, one a week. The first presented an orchestral potpourri, a song with vocal quartet accompaniment, a cello solo, a *Chicago Waltz* written by one of the players (Carlino Lenssen), a medley overture of Negro airs, and a chorus from Weber's *Preciosa*.

The Philharmonic under Dyhrenfurth lasted for two seasons, but its career was financially disastrous. Efforts were made to revive the society, and in 1853 it was decided that the band should be legally incorporated. The petition made something of a stir at Springfield, the state capital. Some of the farmer members of the legislature were a bit scornful of such trivialities as musical societies. Their feeling may account for the title of the bill when it was finally passed—"an act to encourage the science of fiddling." In these years two or three conductors tried unsuccessful hands at directing the orchestra, until Carl Bergmann came to Chicago in 1854. He thought of moving from New York permanently. When he was appointed conductor of the Philharmonic there was trouble among the men, and Bergmann hurriedly resigned and left town.

Then this Chicago Philharmonic fell to pieces. A teacher named C. W. Webster tried to bring it together in 1856 but with no good results. Then a trumpet player, Henry Ahner, from the old Germania orchestra came to Chicago and built up a really good orchestra of twenty-six players. He gave concerts for two seasons, which were popular for a time, but later failed to attract an audience. Another ex-Germanian followed Ahner—Julius Unger. He reorganized Ahner's orchestra and gave afternoon concerts. Competition then appeared; a musician with the musical name of J. M. Mozart organized a rival orchestra and drove Unger out of town. Then this Mozart found his own reward in bankruptcy.

Meanwhile, opera troupes were playing regularly at the theatres.

In December of 1859, two companies fought an opera war—an English troupe at McVicker's and an Italian company at Metropolitan Hall. The Englishmen won. In 1865 the Crosby Opera House was built by the enterprising Uranus H. Crosby. The magnificent structure was a combined opera house, art gallery, and studio building. For a year or so it housed lavish productions of opera with the finest singers of the day, but somehow the enterprise fell on evil ways, and before many years had passed it was given over to Humpty Dumpty shows, families of bell ringers, trained animals, acrobats, and pantomimes. In 1871 the opera house was restored to its original purpose and Max Maretzek brought a German troupe to its stage. During the summer and fall it was redecorated, and was about to be reopened when the great fire in October ruined the Crosby Opera House and almost everything else in Chicago. The fire marked the end and the beginning of two distinct epochs in Chicago's career—musical and otherwise.

The year 1860, like 1850, brought two important musical events to Chicago. One was the coming of HANS BALATKA from Milwaukee. Balatka was a Moravian who had been a choral conductor in Vienna. He came to Milwaukee in 1849, where he directed the newly formed *Musikverein*. In 1857 he led the annual Northwestern *Saengerfest* in Chicago, and made such a favorable impression that he was persuaded to live in Chicago. So in 1860 he left Milwaukee, and was soon appointed conductor of the once more reorganized Philharmonic. His first program was given in Bryant Hall, and it contained not only an entire symphony (Beethoven's Second, which the Germanians had played in Chicago on their visit some years before), but also the first performance of a Wagner composition in Chicago—the Chorus from *Tannhäuser*. The Balatka concerts became the fashion, and the conductor a popular idol. This vogue lasted for about six years, and in the seventh season the audiences grew thinner, and the trustees decided it was of no use to go further in debt. There was an attempt to revive the orchestra in 1868 and 1869, but on the twenty-ninth of November, 1869, the day following one of Balatka's concerts, a young conductor from the East, Theodore Thomas, gave a concert with his Central Park Garden Orchestra from New York. The finesse of this band, the new meanings it gave to the music, were something that Chicagoans had never heard before. Thomas's concert sounded the death of the Balatka orchestra, for this man Thomas was later to mean everything to music in Chicago.

Balatka, despite his inability to equal Thomas's success, had a long and honorable career in American music. He lived until 1899 and directed many organizations in Chicago and Milwaukee. He was also something of a composer, and wrote a cantata, many choruses, some songs, and orchestral fantasias. Chicago owes him a great debt—he was really the first to espouse the cause of higher music there. He introduced eight of Beethoven's symphonies; two by Mozart; one by Mendelssohn; and several by Haydn and Schubert.

The other musical event of 1860 created less of a stir than Balatka's coming, but it was significant. Henri DeClerque, a violinist, inaugurated a series of chamber music recitals known as the Briggs House Concerts. The personnel consisted of DeClerque, a second violin, a cello, and a piano. They gave Chicago its first hearing of the chamber music of the classicists and of the romanticists. Again Chicago was only a few years behind the East. The Mendelssohn Quintette Club had been organized in Boston in 1849, the Eisfeld Chamber Music Concerts in New York in 1851, and the Mason-Thomas recitals in New York (of which more in the next chapter) in 1855. Hans Balatka also organized chamber music concerts in 1863, which had the advantage of a complete string quartet, augmented by a piano. It is not to be supposed that these organizations prospered—chamber music has rarely proved a box-office attraction for the general public—but the mere fact that the concerts were given at all is testimony to the fact that there were worthy attempts at music of a high order in places other than the East, at a date not much later than they were first offered in the older centers.

The fact that intensive musical activity seemed to start from 1850 in the West is explained not alone by the theory that the Midwest settlers by this time had opportunity to turn their thoughts to leisure enjoyment, although this may have had much to do with it. The wholesale immigration from Central Europe, which commenced in the late forties, affected the West as well as the East—possibly to an even greater degree. The German musicians who came to this country in 1848, and during the following years, sought many fields, and many of them settled in cities to which their friends had preceded them. We have seen how some of the members of the Germanian Orchestra finally landed in Chicago. It was the same in other cities—Cincinnati, St. Louis, Louisville, Chicago, and Milwaukee.

The *Saengerfest* which was held in Cincinnati in 1849 was the first meeting of the several German singing societies of Midwest cities. From this the North American *Saengerbund* was formed, and its festivals soon grew to large proportions. In 1870 one of them was again held in Cincinnati. A large hall was built to accommodate the two thousand singers and the audience. Cincinnati liked the festival so much that in 1873 the first annual Cincinnati Festival was held under the direction of Theodore Thomas, who conducted the annual concerts for many years.

Of course, the traveling virtuosos and prima donnas, who visited every city of importance in the West, did their part in molding the public taste for music; but brilliant concert stars have always had a box-office value that sometimes has little to do with music. People like to see famous artists, even though they cannot understand or enjoy their music. It is always the resident musical activity that is the better indication of the real musical life of a city, and it is significant that from 1850, hundreds of musicians and teachers found that they could gain a respectable livelihood in various parts of the country.

2. WILLIAM MASON (1829–1908)

Among the musical missionaries who have had a part in developing music in this country, the name of William Mason should always be remembered. Like his father, Lowell Mason, he had the spirit of a pioneer. He distinguished himself in several directions, and in at least two of them he was an influence of prime importance. He sacrificed much to bring chamber music to the public, and to play it so often that people would grow to like it. As a piano teacher, he is in a large part responsible for the really excellent piano playing in this country today. He was among the first of the American teachers to evolve a method for acquiring touch, and the remarkable feature of his work is that Mason evolved by empirical methods certain principles of muscular control that have recently been discovered by scientists after years of patient research. Then, too, he was a prolific composer of piano pieces that had considerable vogue for many years.

William Mason was born in Boston, January 24, 1829. He showed a love for music when he was a little child, and of course his musician father gave him every opportunity to develop his talents. When he was small he had little instruction in piano playing, but he used to practice regularly, and his mother sat by him and helped him as much as she could. He really acquired a remarkable facility.

He became useful to his father as an accompanist, and went with him to many of the music conventions. He also became an organist, and held several church positions before he was out of his teens. He made his first public appearance as a pianist when he was seventeen, at one of the concerts of his father's Boston Academy of Music. In the same year he played the piano part in a series of six chamber music concerts, given by the Harvard Musical Association at the piano warerooms of Jonas Chickering.

He began studying with Henry Schmidt, a violinist who was a careful and able piano teacher as well. It was Schmidt who helped him evolve what has since been known as the Mason "elastic finger touch," accomplished by quietly drawing the finger tips inward toward the palm of the hand. Mason analyzed the playing of the various concert pianists who came to Boston. He learned much from DeMeyer's method of tone production, and spent hours at the piano imitating his manner and style, and striving to acquire the habit of devitalizing the upper arm muscles. He learned to play for hours without tiring, and at length arrived at the conclusion that the secrets of touch and technique lay not so much in the muscles of the fingers as in those of the arm.

Then came the years abroad, when Mason lived among the most celebrated of the world's musicians, and not only gained the finest instruction, but formed rich associations that colored the rest of his long and active life. Armed with introductions from Boston musicians, he sailed in 1849 on the side-wheel steamer *Herrman*. These were the years of the German revolutions, when foreign musicians found it profitable, and in some cases healthier, to come to America. Mason had intended to go directly to Leipzig to study with Moscheles, but his plans had to be postponed because of the insurrections. But the time was well spent, for he was invited to visit Julius Schuberth, the famous music publisher from Hamburg he had met on the steamer. Schuberth took a fancy to one of Mason's pieces, *Les Perles de Rosée*, and when he went to Weimar he showed it to Liszt, who was delighted with it and gladly accepted the young composer's dedication. Schuberth's report of this visit gave Mason courage to try immediately what he had intended to do later, to ask Liszt to take him for a pupil. Liszt replied with a vaguely worded letter, which Mason took for a polite refusal. Several years after, when Mason met him at Weimar, Liszt remarked that he never took pupils for regular lessons, but that those who lived in Weimar had frequent opportunity to hear him and to meet the artists who visited him. Liszt actually meant this as an invitation to study with him, but Mason was a bit too literal to take the remarks as they were intended. When he actually did go to Liszt for study in 1853, he was surprised to learn that Liszt had been wondering why he had not come before.

In the meantime he worked with Moscheles, and studied harmony and counterpoint with Hauptmann. Then he went to Dreyschock in Prague, where he had over one hundred lessons. In 1853 he received an invitation from Sir Julius Benedict in London to play at one of the concerts of the Harmonic Union in Exeter Hall. The praise of the critics was somewhat qualified. The *Times* reviewer wrote:

Mr. William Mason was somewhat foolishly, we think, announced as "the first American pianist who had ever performed before an English audience,"—as if the bare fact of nationality, independent of actual merit, was a matter of any importance. Happily Mr. Mason possesses talent; and although very young, already exhibits promise of excellence. He played the pianoforte part in Weber's Concert Stuck with a great deal of spirit; so well, indeed that we are confident he will play it still better when he has acquired a more perfect command of the instrument. It is in mechanism that Mr. Mason is deficient. This deficiency makes him nervous and uncertain, imparts unsteadiness to his accentuation, and robs his passages of clearness. He has, nevertheless, a light and elastic touch, and evidently understands his author.

The *Chronicle* was no more flattering:

A pianist from New York, Mr. William Mason, who appeared for the first time in London, selected somewhat boldly for his début the single concerto of Weber. His performance was smoothly correct, but tame and uniform. His touch is light, rapid, but it wants delicacy of expression, and there is also a lack of color and verve about his playing. Mr. Mason is, no doubt, an able and accomplished pianist; but more than that is demanded of those who would now-a-days take the place to which he aspires in his art.

It is significant that both accounts, contradictory in many points, should praise his touch.

After the London visit Mason decided to go directly to Liszt at Weimar. There might still be hope of being accepted as a pupil. When he arrived, Liszt remarked that Mason let people wait for him for a long time. Then he told him to go to Leipzig and select a piano; and that he could find pleasant rooms in the same house with Klindworth. So Mason stayed at Weimar for a year and three months, a member of the little group that studied under the wing of one of the greatest pianists of all time. There were only three of them—Karl Klindworth from Hanover, Dionys Bruckner from Munich, and Mason. Joachim Raff was there too, a former pupil, who acted as Liszt's private secretary.

There were no formal lessons. Mason wrote in his memoirs: [1]

His idea was that the pupils whom he accepted should all be far enough advanced to practice and prepare themselves without routine instruction, and he expected them to be ready whenever he gave them an opportunity to play. . . . We constituted, as it were a family, for while we had our own apartments in the city, we all enjoyed the freedom of Liszt's home, and were at liberty to come and go as we liked . . . We were always quite at ease in those lower rooms, but on ceremonial occasions we were invited up-stairs to the drawing room, where Liszt had his favorite Érard. . . . During the entire time I was with him I did not see him give a regular lesson in the pedagogical sense. He would notify us to come up to the Altenburg [Liszt's home]. . . . We would go there, and he would call on us to play. I remember very well the first time I played to him after I had been accepted as a pupil. . . . After I was well started he began to get excited. He made audible suggestions, inciting me to put more enthusiasm into my playing, and occasionally he would push me gently off the chair and sit down at the piano and play a phrase or two himself by way of illustration. He gradually got me worked up to such a pitch of enthusiasm that I put all the grit that was in me into my playing.

All kinds of musicians came to Weimar. The pupils met them all, heard them play, and in turn played for them. Berlioz, Joachim,

[1] William Mason, *Memories of a Musical Life*, Century Co.

Wieniawski, and Rubinstein were welcome visitors. One evening Liszt sent for the "boys" to come up to his house to meet a twenty-year-old composer who was said to be very talented. His name was Brahms, and he was making a concert tour with Rémenyi, the violinist. Brahms was so nervous that he was unable to play his music, so Liszt took the almost illegible manuscripts and played at sight the E-flat Minor Scherzo, and part of the first Sonata. Brahms was delighted. Then someone asked Liszt to play his own Sonata. After he had started, Brahms dozed in his chair, and Liszt rose from the piano and left the room. Soon after this, Brahms had his famous meeting with Schumann, who published an article that established Brahms's fame throughout Europe—to the utter amazement of the Liszt group at Weimar.

There were others whom Mason met, at Weimar and elsewhere. He called on Schumann in 1850. He was received by Wagner in 1852, long before the great composer had been recognized as a towering giant. With these associations, and a background that had been gained by few American musicians of his time, Mason came home in 1854 to take up his life work in his own country.

His first act on landing was to hurry to Boston, to see again the daughter of George James Webb, his father's associate. Mason had met the young lady years before and had never forgotten her. They became engaged, and were married a few years later.

His first musical enterprise was a concert tour, possibly the first of its kind ever undertaken by a pianist alone. Concerts had generally offered a variety of talent. He went as far as Chicago, stopping for recitals at Albany, Troy, Utica, and all the towns along the way. He had a versatile manager, Oliver Dyer, who had been associated with Mason's brothers, Daniel and Lowell, in their music publishing business. Dyer was a newspaper man who could write well, and he prepared a pamphlet about Mason which he distributed among the townsfolk before the concerts. Then he would go to the newspaper editors, and offer to do odd reporting jobs for them. They were so grateful that they would print any advance notices of Mason's concerts that Dyer might give them.

On the way to Chicago, Mason's audiences were none too large, and when they had played two concerts in Chicago, Dyer was all for a speedy return to New York while they still had their carfare. Mason had more courage; he insisted on playing again in each of the towns they had visited, to see if the people had liked his playing well enough to come again. The halls were filled on the return trip.

He always closed his program with improvisations on a theme suggested by the audience. This was a custom started by Ferdinand Hiller, and no doubt it did lighten the proceedings for many of the listeners. All sorts of tunes were suggested, but the climax came when someone suggested that he play *Old Hundred* with one hand, and *Yankee Doodle* with the other. He did it, but he had to mollify the religious element by announcing afterwards that he meant no disrespect to *Old Hundred*.

Mason soon decided that the career of piano virtuoso was not for him. It was for this that he had prepared himself in Europe, and his concert tour had been encouraging. Yet he disliked the constant repetition of the public's favorite pieces, and he had already commenced to take pupils. He found himself singularly well fitted to teach. The occasional engagements with the New York Philharmonic, and the chamber music recitals, would satisfy his desire for public performance.

Probably the immediate reason for starting the chamber music concerts was to introduce the Brahms Grand Trio in B Major, Opus 8. He had for some time wanted to give New York music lovers something of the flavor of Weimar. Every Sunday morning he had heard the Weimar String Quartet in the two lower rooms of Liszt's house, and to Mason this had meant *Go thou and do likewise*. So he gathered a quartet about him. Theodore Thomas was first violin; Joseph Mosenthal, second; George Matzka, viola; and Carl Bergmann, cello. When friction developed between Bergmann and Thomas, Bergmann resigned and Frederick Bergner took his place. Thomas became the leader, and the maker of the programs, a field in which he displayed true genius. The first program was given in Dodworth's Hall, next to Grace Church on Broadway. The major works were the Brahms Trio, and the Schubert D Minor Quartet. There were also solos, vocal and instrumental, but in a few years the concerts were devoted to chamber music exclusively.

The refusal to compromise with public taste represented a real sacrifice. Often there was little left in the cash box after the hall rent was paid; yet in spite of all discouragements, the valiant little group played on for thirteen years. Then Thomas had other interests; he had become an orchestral conductor, and anyway the real missionary work was done. The last concert was given April 11, 1868. Though they played mostly in New York, the Mason-Thomas ensemble went regularly to Farmington, Connecticut, where the music teacher of Miss Porter's School, Karl Klauser, had aroused a real interest in music. There were also frequent concerts in Brooklyn, and in Orange, New Jersey.

Mason's influence as a teacher was tremendous. Many of his pupils, such men as W. S. B. Mathews, William Sherwood, and others, studied with him, became his disciples, and passed his methods on to their own pupils, who in their turn became teachers. His technical works, *Touch and Technic*, and several others, are still available to teachers and students, and they are still being used.

His compositions are not played as much today as they used to be. They belonged to a period of music that has quite definitely passed, and as music they have not had enough vitality to survive their idiom. *Silver Spring*, named for his father's estate in Orange, was highly popular. *Amitié pour Amitié* was a favorite with Liszt, who often played it. The *Ballade* and *Capriccio Fantastico* were well contrived and graceful.

But it is not as a composer that William Mason will be known. His place as a musical missionary, as a champion of the highest standards, and as the foremost piano teacher of his day, seems permanently assured. His span of life turned the century; he lived until 1908, when he died in New York in his eightieth year. He had a life full of many fine things; advantages of his youth that he was able to use; years of activity; and full recognition, by friends and the public, of all he had accomplished.

3. THEODORE THOMAS (1835–1905)

I

Theodore Thomas is an epic figure in American history—one of our great heroes. Compare the state of musical culture at the time of the Civil War with conditions today, and then thank Theodore Thomas for the difference. It is through his efforts that this country is the home of the best in orchestral music, that almost all of our major cities have symphony orchestras of the first rank, and, what is more important, that in each of these cities there is a public that will listen to the finest symphonic works. As for our composers, they can thank Thomas for orchestras to play their music, and to provide an incentive for writing in the larger forms.

It is important that Thomas was a masterful conductor, that he trained his men to standards of performance that had been unknown in this country, but it was more important that his whole career was devoted to carrying out a plan of education shrewdly calculated to develop our taste for good music. Other conductors had been concerned with single programs. Thomas occupied himself with a lifelong *series* of programs, progressively planned to cultivate the public's liking for the best in music literature.

Jullien had tried this, and so had the Germanians, but with one essential difference from the methods of Thomas. Like the early programs that Thomas arranged, theirs offered lighter works to offset the bugbear of the symphonies that appeared on their lists. But their lighter music was generally trash, and Thomas never offered any piece that lacked musical merit, no matter how light it might be. Jullien relied on theatrical methods to draw the crowds—*Firemen's Quadrilles* with real firemen. The Germanians had even produced in classic Boston a *Railroad Gallop*, illustrated by a miniature locomotive that ran around in a circle, with a tuft of black wool fastened to its funnel in lieu of real smoke.

When Thomas made a program he selected lighter pieces—and they were often very light—chiefly for their relations to the heavier works they were paired with. He would play a symphony that was over the heads of all but a few of his listeners. Then he would offer a waltz or light overture in which the themes would have some relation to those of the symphony. He knew that if he could get people to recognize the themes of a symphony, they would grow eventually to like it. Almost all of his programs have been preserved in the second volume of his autobiography; those who plan courses in music appreciation will do well to study them.

There were orchestras before Thomas's time, but the only group that was in any degree permanent was the New York Philharmonic, a band whose members played together more for the love of it than from any artistic results they achieved, or for any notable support they had from the public. In the early days there were from three to five concerts a season, and the public was admitted to some of the rehearsals. If a player had a professional engagement that would bring him real money, he kept it instead of going to rehearsal. Hence, the orchestra was often incomplete, and clarinet or oboe parts would be played on a violin, or a cello would do service for a bassoon. The concerts were held in Apollo Hall. Rough wooden benches were dragged in for the audience, and the music was a pleasant background for conversation. Yet the orchestra played bravely ahead, and as one commentator remarked, the players generally finished their pieces at the same time. Such was the state of musical culture when Thomas began his notable career. Starting with nothing but an inner feeling that people would come to want good music if it was brought to them, he devoted his life to their education. He was our first prophet of good music for the masses, and to him the term "good music" meant *good music*.

The list of positions he held during his lifetime reads like a catalogue of all the organizations in our musical history. And he paid the price of his eminence. When any great man holds a number of offices, and stays in the public eye for many years, he eventually becomes the target for savage attacks from every direction. Thomas was no exception. If all the hostile criticisms were gathered together and printed without comment, we would learn that he was a villain of the deepest hue. Incompetent, arrogant—yes, even dishonest. But when the truth was learned, the hero emerged untarnished and triumphant, greater for the attacks he had ignored.

II

And now for the catalogue of his doings—a long, long list. He was brought to America in 1845 as a lad of ten. His father had been *Stadtpfeifer*, or town musician, in Esens, Germany. There were too many little brothers and sisters to support on the meager income the little town could offer, so America beckoned. When they came to New York things were not much better, so little Theodore had to tuck his violin under his arm and go out to play in all kinds of places—for dances, weddings, theatres, even in saloons where he passed the hat.

He never had much training, but his inordinate curiosity led him into all sorts of artistic adventures, and he had the ability to absorb knowledge for himself. He had the kind of youth that makes great men, or causes the downfall of weaklings.

When he was still in his teens he took a concert trip through the South, all on his own. When he came to a town he would tack up a few handwritten posters announcing a concert by "Master T. T.," the remarkable prodigy. Then he would stand at the door and take in the money until he decided that all who were coming had arrived, rush backstage to change his clothes, and then appear before the audience with his violin.

Among his friends in New York, the Dodworth family did more than anyone else to find him work. These Dodworths deserve a place by themselves in our musical annals. All of them did something musical. Harvey was a cornetist, Allen played the violin. C. Dodworth was a virtuoso on the trombone, and C. R. played the concertina. They had a hall in Broadway next to Grace Church. Here the Mason-Thomas Quintette later gave its matinees. The Dodworths had orchestras for dances, weddings, or banquets. They offered brass bands with uniforms. They kept a music store; all of them were composers. Polkas, quicksteps, marches, and quadrilles flowed easily from their pens. They were one of the mainstays of the early Philharmonic. Whenever young Theodore Thomas needed money, he could count on Harvey Dodworth to find something for him to do; often a half-dollar engagement to play all night for a dance.

When Jullien came in 1853, Thomas was chosen as a first violin. The antics of the conductor disgusted him, but he nevertheless had his first idea of the symphony from playing in this great orchestra. It gave him something to think about—thoughts that later shaped the whole work of his life. He was elected a member of the Philharmonic in 1854, and in the next year the Mason-Thomas chamber concerts began. He traveled with famous soloists—Thalberg and others as a solo violinist. He was appointed concertmaster of the opera house orchestra. In 1858 he was suddenly called to take Anschütz's place as conductor, and led a performance of Halévy's *Jewess*, a score he had never seen before. The retirement of Anschütz became permanent, and Thomas was made conductor.

Conducting was a revelation to him. He was doing well as a violinist, looking forward to the career of virtuoso. Yet there was more thrill in leading an orchestra; it could be played as an instrument with subtle changes of color. And what is more important, he could make his life work the development of America's taste for music. He organized an orchestra of his own, and gave his first concert in Irving Hall, New York, May 13, 1862. This was the beginning of new things for musical America.

He soon realized that only a permanent orchestra could give the best results; an orchestra in which the players devoted all of their time to its rehearsals and concerts; a group whose members were under the sole control of their conductor; whose players were not constantly lowering their standards and injuring their tone by playing for dances, and staying out late nights to keep other engagements.

Without a subsidy, he found that the only way to maintain such an orchestra was by having enough concerts each season to keep its members busy. This meant traveling, and thus the Thomas Highway was finally established. It reached from New England to the Pacific Coast. To all the principal cities of the country, playing in whatever halls the towns offered—churches or railroad stations, it made no difference. For each of these cities this greatest of all program makers adopted his idea of progressive programs—leading gradually from the familiar to the unfamiliar. Always having something on each program that was a little above the heads of most of the audience, but not too far beyond their liking. Then compensating them with something more obviously tuneful. All of this until his work was done, and he was at the end of his career in Chicago, with a subsidized orchestra, backed by the authority of his trustees to make no concessions to the public taste, but to reap the benefit of his missionary work by playing only that which belonged on a true symphony program.

III

It sounds as though it had all been an easy and pleasant path. It most decidedly was not. Anyone but a man of iron and steel would have quit after a few years of it. In fact, most of those who tried it were beaten before they began.

In 1862, Thomas was made alternate conductor with Theodore

Eisfeld of the Brooklyn Philharmonic Society. Four years later he became its sole conductor. He also had his own orchestra and concerts. In 1866 he started his summer concerts at Terrace Garden, where he offered light music interspersed with masterworks, and those who came to listen could bring or buy refreshments. Two years later these concerts were moved to the Central Park Garden. In two more years he had the training of his audiences well under way. He remarked in his notebook: "At last the summer programs show a respectable character and we are rid of the cornet! Occasionally a whole symphony is given."

By 1867 his orchestra was truly a permanent one, and on his own resources he was able to guarantee his men a full season's work. The first tour came in 1869, and he dropped his poorly attended New York concerts until a delegation of prominent citizens begged him to give them again. He had visited Chicago, and the Chicago Philharmonic died soon after the citizens had once heard the Thomas orchestra. When other summer organizations, principally bands, gave him competition for his Central Park Garden concerts in New York, he was invited to give them in the old Exposition Hall in Chicago.

In 1873 he was asked to organize and conduct the Cincinnati Festival. Under his direction it grew to be one of the finest musical events in the world. He had charge of the Philadelphia Centennial Concerts in 1876. Their failure was financial rather than artistic. The next year the New York Philharmonic insisted that he be its conductor. He had been offered the position before, but he would not give up his own orchestra. This time he consented, for he was allowed to keep his own band in addition to his new duties. He arranged that his own concerts would be lighter than the programs of the Philharmonic, so that there would be no competition.

In 1878 he was asked to come to Cincinnati to head the newly formed College of Music. He thought he saw a chance to found an institution that would fulfill his ideals and dreams for an educational center, but he endured the task for only a year. He resigned when he found that the backers of the school intended it as a commercial rather than an artistic enterprise. Thomas had no time to waste on purely commercial ventures.

New York, which had had a share in his persecution, welcomed him back, and he was again made conductor of the Philharmonic. The orchestra was in bad shape, its receipts had fallen to their lowest point, and the playing was far from good. Thomas brought it to heights far beyond its former achievements in his first season. More people came to the concerts, and the men made more money. In 1882 he was asked to organize mammoth festivals in New York and in Chicago.

He made a serious blunder in 1885. He was under the impression that America would welcome an American venture in opera producing. He was induced to become conductor of an enterprise presumably sponsored by the wealthiest men of the country. He was led to think that the backers of the newly formed American Opera Company would carry it along even though it might lose money. He was mistaken, for at the end of the first season the deficit frightened these backers away. It was generally agreed that opera had never been given so magnificently in this country, but the company was left to founder, and Thomas, who had been merely a salaried employee (for a long time without the salary), was attacked as a deadbeat who failed to make good his promises.

He had known financial troubles before. When he was invited to give the concerts at the Philadelphia Centennial, the invitation had been entirely honorary. Thomas was expected to give the concerts at his own risk, and take the chances of profit and loss. The people who came to the Exposition came to see, and not to listen. Affairs became so bad that one day the audience included the sheriff, who loved the music of the auction block more than that of the orchestra. Thomas could have evaded all his debts by voluntary bankruptcy, but he preferred an easy conscience, and he paid off every cent he owed, even though it took him twelve years to do it.

Then came more years of traveling with his orchestra. His work was having its effect. The Boston Symphony Orchestra was founded and supported by Major Higginson in 1881, directly as the result of the Thomas concerts in Boston. This took Boston from the Thomas itinerary, but Thomas bore the loss of territory with the knowledge that it was for this he was working. In later years his territory was continually cut by the establishment of permanent orchestras in cities where he had created the desire for them. Yet to his last, weary days, he was continually taking the Chicago Orchestra to towns that had none of their own.

IV

The years after the opera tragedy were bad ones for Thomas. New York seemed to think that he was tarnished with the blame, though his only sin had been to do a good job. There was keen rivalry among the orchestras in New York. Back in 1878 the Symphony Society of New York had been founded as a competitor of both the Philharmonic and Thomas's own orchestra. There were factions. The followers of Leopold and Walter Damrosch, and later of Seidl, taunted those of Thomas, and rivalry was fostered where none might have arisen had the artists been left to arrange things for themselves. When Chicago beckoned in 1891 it found Thomas in a receptive state of mind. He was weary of promises, and here was a group of fifty Chicago business men who had actually signed pledges to contribute a thousand dollars each to make up the deficit that might be incurred by the symphony orchestra they wanted for their city.

A chance to get together the men from his old orchestra, which he had been forced to disband—everything he had dreamed of—yes, he would leave even New York for that. The New York that had turned its back to him, but which was nevertheless his home. He signed the contract, and became Chicago's. New York suddenly awoke to his leaving, and rushed to give him everything Chicago had offered, and more. He had given his word to Chicago, and he went.

For fourteen years he directed the Chicago Orchestra. The splendid concerts of those fourteen seasons are models of program-making for any conductor, anywhere. Standard works and new experiments, both were represented. Always aiming a little beyond the public taste, he was constantly bringing it to a higher level. And yet the hostile press still hounded him. Why ask people to listen to Wagner when they would rather hear *Yankee Doodle?* Who is this Thomas person that disturbs our idea of what we ought to like? And the guarantors continued to pay their share of the deficit without a whimper. And Thomas turned down handsome offers from Boston and elsewhere, because his friends in Chicago had the courage to back him.

1893 brought another failure—one that almost finished his career, bringing torment that would have destroyed a weaker man. He was appointed director of music for the Chicago World's Fair. He immediately set about making plans for an all-summer festival that would show the world what America was doing in music, and America, the music of the world. He arranged for an orchestra of over a hundred, and for an exposition chorus. He invited the leading soloists of the world to appear in the concert hall; he asked the finest orchestras of America and Europe, and the foremost choruses to come and give concerts. It was a mammoth plan, conceived by a man of great vision.

When he accepted the post he had been careful to specify that the musical events of the fair were to be run separately from the exhibits of musical merchandise. This condition looked well on paper, but it was not to be taken seriously by the business men and politicians in charge of the exposition. It happened that Steinway & Sons, whose pianos were played by several of the soloists, was not one of the exhibitors. Those who had spent their good money for exhibit space could see no reason why a piano that was not exhibited should get the free advertising that came from the use of its piano in the concert hall. Thomas saw the justice of this, but the great artists had already been invited to play, and he had always been a firm believer in allowing musicians to choose their own instruments. So in defiance of the ruling against nonexhibited pianos, the proceedings commenced with a concert at which Paderewski played his Steinway.

The storm broke; the autocrat must be in the pay of instrument manufacturers. He was brought up on charges, hostile newspapers slung mud from the river bottom—Thomas was a crook. Even proof that he was innocent, incapable of being bribed, could not still the savage snarling of his enemies. Yet it was impossible to force his resignation, and the concerts proceeded according to the huge schedule. Finally the financial panic of 1893 nearly ruined the fair. People could no longer afford the trip to Chicago, and in August the foes of Theodore Thomas had their revenge by cutting his appropriation for music. Seeing no chance of continuing his plans he resigned, and went East to his summer home in Maine for a chance to cure his hurt. Times improved, people had more money, and the fair was again prosperous. Thomas was invited to come back, but he had had enough, and he felt he couldn't stand much more. He waited to join his friends until it was time for the third season of the Chicago Orchestra.

V

One of the significant features of his program at the Chicago Fair was the invitation to American composers to write works for performance. Those with established reputations—Paine, Chadwick, Foote, Mrs. Beach, Dudley Buck, and others—were definitely commissioned to compose something for the occasion. Other composers were invited to submit works to a committee of judges. Twenty-three were submitted, and seven were chosen.

Thomas was all for the American composer, but he always said that he would never play anything merely because it was American. It must be good music. Study of his programs reveals the fact that as the years progressed he found more and more American works that deserved performance, and he was always the first to welcome them when they came. And it was because of Theodore Thomas that there are orchestras today to play the works of Americans, or of any composers.

When Thomas died January 4, 1905, he had lived to see the last of his dreams fulfilled—the building of a permanent home for his permanent orchestra—and the concert which dedicated Orchestra Hall in Chicago was the greatest triumph of his career. He was still assailed by the press, chiefly because the orchestra did not sound as it had in the great Auditorium where it had been necessary to play much louder. But, though the sound of the orchestra was new to the ears of the public, Thomas went to his end knowing that it would not be long before its tone could be adjusted to the new and better acoustics. He also knew that the young assistant conductor he had selected some years before—Frederick Stock—was fully capable of doing the job, though he must have dearly wanted to do it himself, and thus vindicate his plans and his unfailing judgment.

4. OTHER TEACHERS AND COMPOSERS OF THE PERIOD

There were many others, contemporaries of Mason and Thomas, who did much to shape our musical culture. Some of them came from abroad and some were American born. They all had a hand in making us musical, and in training teachers who are still at work. Some of them wrote music representative of the period, important as a link in the development of our music.

RICHARD HOFFMAN (1831–1909) was an Englishman who came to America when he was sixteen years old. He was the well-trained son of an accomplished musician. He had studied with DeMeyer, Moscheles, Rubinstein and Liszt, and was a talented pianist by the time he arrived in America. He made his debut with the Philharmonic in New York, when he played a Mendelssohn concerto. He played at Jenny Lind's first concert at Castle Garden, and was engaged for her concert tour. In 1854 he introduced Chopin's Concerto in E Minor to the Philharmonic audiences, and was elected an honorary member of the Society. When the Philharmonic gave its fiftieth anniversary concert in 1892, Hoffman was a soloist. Then, when he celebrated the fiftieth anniversary of his own coming to America, his friends gave him a testimonial concert.

As a composer Hoffman was prolific; many of his works were effective transcriptions of popular orchestral works—the Scherzo from Mendelssohn's *Scotch* Symphony, airs from *Trovatore* and other operas. There were also many original works that were considerably used; a *Caprice de Concert; Impromptus; Tarantelles;* and an effective anthem for mixed quartet based on the 137th Psalm—*By the Waters of Babylon.* As a teacher Hoffman stood high in his profession. Though he could command his own terms he accepted many talented pupils for what they could pay. He lived to be honored at an old age, and died in Mount Kisco, New York.

SEBASTIAN BACH MILLS (1838–1898), another English pianist, like his colleague Hoffman, was influential as a teacher. He was always fond of getting showy effects from his pupils, but he was nevertheless careful to play good music on his own programs. For many years he had a reputation for introducing works new to New York. Among them were Chopin's *Fantasia* and F Minor Piano Concerto, Mozart's posthumous Concerto in C, Liszt's E-flat Concerto, and the Weber-Liszt *Polonaise.* He came to New York as a visiting pianist in 1856, and was so warmly received that he made his home in New York, though he made frequent concert trips to Europe. Among his many pupils was Homer Bartlett, of whom we shall hear more later.

He was a prolific composer for the piano, and if most of his pieces were frothy and trivial, that was what the public of the day wanted most from its recital favorites. *Recollections of Home,* the first *Tarantelle, Fairy Fingers,* the second *Barcarolle,* were ready favorites. There were also *The Murmuring Fountain,* and transcriptions of favorite melodies—*Home, Sweet Home,* and others.

FRÉDÉRIC LOUIS RITTER (1834–1891), an Alsatian music teacher, is known today principally as the author of the first complete history of music in this country, *Music in America,* written in 1883. This work was useful, because it was truly the first thorough study of the subject. Yet he was not in sympathy with our musical past, and some of his scathing remarks were uncalled for. Moreover, he was not always accurate, and not particularly careful to confirm his statements of fact.

Ritter came to America in 1856, when he went to Cincinnati to organize the Cecilia Choral Society, and a Philharmonic Orchestra. He came to New York in 1861, where he stayed as teacher and conductor of choral societies until he was appointed director of music at Vassar College in 1878. Eventually he returned to Europe, and died in Antwerp in 1891. In addition to his *Music in America,* he was the author of a two-volume *History of Music,* and a volume on *Music in England.* He was also active as a composer, and while he was in this country he published *8 Clavierstücke;* a set of six songs; some sacred songs; and a set of arrangements of Irish melodies. He wrote several treatises on harmony and musical dictation.

Among Ritter's pupils in New York was a youngster from Sandusky, Ohio, ALBERT ROSS PARSONS (1847–1933), a man who lived to be the dean of New York music teachers. When he went abroad in 1867, Parsons studied with Moscheles, Reinecke, and Tausig, and returned to his native country to become one of the leading musicians in New York. He was an organist at some of the principal churches, and head of the piano departments of several leading conservatories. He was an early American apostle of Wagner, and translated several of the great composer's literary efforts—the essay on *Beethoven* and others. He was also a composer of songs and piano pieces.

WILLIAM SMITH BABCOCK MATHEWS (1837–1912), born in New London, New Hampshire, was at one time a pupil of William Mason, and later a collaborator in several of Mason's technical works. All of his musical education was gained in this country, and when he was twenty-three he started his career of teaching, in Georgia and other places in the South. By the time he was thirty he landed in Chicago, and from then to the rest of his life he was a powerful influence in developing the musical life of the Middle West. Shortly before he died he moved to Denver and finished his days in editorial work.

It is principally as a writer on musical subjects that we know Mathews today, though in his time he was active as a musician and teacher. Six years after Ritter had published his *Music in America,* Mathews compiled a second volume on the subject—*One Hundred Years of Music in America.* As an American, it was to be expected that Mathews would have more sympathy with his subject than Ritter; but Mathews leaned too far in the other direction, he failed to keep his sense of values, and his overhasty production lost much of the worth it might easily have possessed.

Another pupil of Mason to distinguish himself as a pianist and teacher was WILLIAM HALL SHERWOOD (1854–1911), son of a clergyman who had founded a musical academy in Lyons, New York. Sherwood had been a boy wonder, and had taught at his father's school from the time he was twelve years old. In 1871 he went to Mason, then to Berlin where he studied with Kullak and others, and finally with Liszt at Weimar. After he had made some successful appearances as a pianist in Germany, he came back to America, and made a concert tour of our principal cities. Then he went as a teacher to the New England Conservatory in Boston, and after subsequent years in New York he went to Chicago in 1889, where eventually he founded the Sherwood Piano School. He was a brilliant pianist, and he was in demand with the orchestras as a soloist. He should always be remembered as one of the first pianists to make a regular practice of including a number of American compositions on each of his concert programs. He was also something of a composer himself, and in his published works for piano there are interesting ventures in chromatic harmonies.

In New England, BENJAMIN JAMES LANG (1837–1909) was an influence of prime importance. Known chiefly as an organist and choral director, he was nevertheless prominent as a teacher of piano, and had for his pupils many young musicians who were to become prominent in later life—Arthur Foote, Ethelbert Nevin, and his own talented daughter, Margaret Ruthven Lang. Lang was born in Salem, and in addition to lessons at home, he traveled abroad to study with Satter and Jaell, and finally with Liszt. He was organist and at one time conductor for the Handel and Haydn Society in Boston, and for years he directed the Apollo Club and the Cecilia Club. Although he wrote a great deal of music, he never published it nor often allowed it to be played, for he felt he would rather be known in other fields than that of composer.

CHAPTER ELEVEN

The Parents of Our Contemporaries

I. THE GRANDFATHERS

THE second half of the century saw our young musical talents flocking to Europe to study with the master teachers of the Continent. Most of them went to Germany, then the musical center of the world. The effect was inevitable; they came home thoroughly saturated with German ideas, and those who were composers wrote their music after the models of the Germans. Although this denied individuality to their own work, the foreign influence at least produced music that was workmanlike, and it led to standards of craftsmanship that American composition must follow in later years. The hymn-tune writers had gone abroad for their education early in the century; now those who had larger ambitions were doing likewise.

The files of Dwight's *Journal of Music* often contained news of the young Americans studying abroad. A correspondent wrote in the issue of June 11, 1853:

At Leipsic I called on Mr. C. C. Perkins, but did not find . . . him at home; but I was informed that he was still pursuing his studies with much diligence and has recently finished another Quartet for stringed instruments, which is considered above par.

In the fall of the same year, the London *Athenæum* announced:

We must take a fresh paragraph to announce the publication at Leipsic of a Quartet by Mr. C. C. Perkins . . . the first American who has devoted himself to classical instrumental composition. So far as we can judge of this Quartet by examining its single parts, the themes appear pleasing—the working of them neat—and the taste of the whole laudable, as eschewing the modern defects calling themselves romanticisms, against which there is reason to warn American musical imagination.

The June 11 issue of Dwight's *Journal* contained an item about another American:

Mr. Parker is still making rapid progress in playing, as well as in composition. It will interest his friends to know that he has also composed a Quartet for strings, which is pronounced very clever. A Quartet is one of the most difficult things to compose, requiring pure musical talent, as well as a thorough knowledge of the power and effects of the several instruments for which it is written. It costs genius and much study to write the parts so that they harmonize effectively and melodiously and are at the same time expressive; comparatively few are written that are worth playing through.

These two young men, CHARLES CALLAHAN PERKINS (1823–1886) and JAMES CUTLER DUNN PARKER (1828–1916), were fellow students in Germany. They were friends of William Mason, who met them on several occasions while he, too, was studying abroad. Perkins was slightly older than Parker. Born in Boston, he had been graduated from Harvard in 1843, and had already been in Italy and Paris to study painting. Music delighted him, and he added its study to his various pursuits. Then he came back to Boston in 1849, and for a year he was both president and director of the Handel and Haydn Society. Soon after this he went back to Europe for further study.

By this time his friend Parker, also a native of Boston and a graduate of Harvard, had decided to give up the career of lawyer for which he had been preparing himself, and he, too, went to Germany to learn to be a musician. He studied with Hauptmann, Richter, and Moscheles, and had a thorough training. One had to be serious minded to win the approval of the classic-minded John S. Dwight.

Perkins and Parker came back to Boston in 1854, to follow different paths. Perkins was never particularly active in music as a profession. He left a few published works: a Quartet, a Trio, and a few pieces for piano and violin, published in Germany. His most important work was as a patron of the fine arts and as a critic. He was one of the chief factors in building the Music Hall in Boston (1851), and his *History of the Handel and Haydn Society*, which he never lived to finish, is an important document for the student of American music history. When he died in 1886, the work was completed by John S. Dwight.

Parker came back from Germany for an active career as a musician, a career that lasted until his death in 1916, when he was eighty-eight years old. He taught piano and composition, and some of his pupils became our leading composers of the next generation. Arthur Whiting was among them, and they all attest to Parker's thorough methods. He was organist of Boston's Trinity Church for twenty-seven years; he played the organ for the Handel and Haydn Society. He was a teacher of piano, organ, and harmony at the New England Conservatory, and for a time at Boston University.

He wrote a great deal of music. Aside from a few instrumental works, and the String Quartet which Dwight's foreign correspondent had said "was pronounced very clever," most of his music was for chorus. For this he had something of a flair, though his sentimental nature led him into paths of sweetness that have kept his works from living. His most significant work was the *Redemption Hymn,* which the Handel and Haydn Society performed in 1877. For many years this cantata was in the standard repertoire of choral societies generally. *The Blind King* (1886) was a secular cantata, and there were other oratorios—*St. John,* and *The Life of Man* (1895). In many ways *The Life of Man* was a better work than the *Redemption Hymn.* Its canons and fugal imitations were well contrived, and lent themselves effectively to the voices of a choir. The seven churches of Asia were pictured by seven voices, each entering in canonic imitation. There were also a few piano pieces and a miscellaneous assortment of church music.

Then there was ELLSWORTH C. PHELPS (1827–1913), a native of Connecticut. From his nineteenth year he was an organist, first at New London, Connecticut, at Syracuse, New York, and from 1857 in Brooklyn, where he was also a teacher of music in the public schools. Phelps composed two symphonies, four symphonic poems, several overtures, two comic operas, and a number of cantatas. He often chose native subjects for his music; one of his symphonies was based on Longfellow's *Hiawatha.*

And there were foreigners, too. MATTHIAS KELLER (1813–1875) came from Germany in 1846. He was a violinist and bandmaster, and after living in Philadelphia and New York he finally landed in Boston.

He became an ardent patriot, and wrote an *American Hymn* for which he himself supplied the words of the text. This hymn, sung by full chorus, supported by grand orchestra, organ, and military band, was a feature of the first concert of Gilmore's Peace Festival in Boston in 1869. This festival and the one that followed it in 1872 deserve a volume by themselves. PATRICK SARSFIELD GILMORE was a bandmaster who had the bigger and better idea with a vengeance. He had conducted festivals in former years, but the affairs in classic Boston were the climax of his career. A coliseum to seat fifty thousand persons was erected. A chorus of ten thousand and an orchestra of one thousand were assembled. Railroads arranged special excursions from all over the country to see and hear "the grandest musical festival ever known in the history of the world." Barnum himself could not have staged the affair one bit more effectively. President Grant, with members of his cabinet, governors of states, army and navy officers, notables of every kind, came to Boston to be present at the Great National Peace Jubilee, "to be held in the city of Boston, to commemorate the restoration of peace throughout the land." Five days were devoted to programs of colossal dimensions. Besides Gilmore, conductors of genuine ability, Zerrahn and others, helped in leading the musical forces. It proved too much for John S. Dwight, who left town to spend the week at his summer home at Nahant, where he hoped he could not hear the cannon used to mark the rhythm of the national airs. But other musicians were not so particular; they helped Pat Gilmore make his party a huge success. Besides the cannon, which were fired by electric buttons on a table in front of the conductor, one hundred real firemen in red shirts helped in the proceedings by pounding real anvils in the Anvil Chorus from *Trovatore*.

Gilmore was only forty in 1869, and he found it hard to rest on his laurels so early in his career. He must have another festival. The idea of peace in America was somewhat old by then, but there had been a war in Europe, so why not an international music festival which he could call a World Peace Jubilee? To add to the international idea, Johann Strauss was brought from Europe to conduct the *Blue Danube*, Franz Abt came from Germany, and the soloists were all to be world famous. This time the size of the chorus would be doubled—twenty thousand would sing. It was here that Gilmore failed. Even Carl

Zerrahn could not keep such a vast body of singers together, and the results were almost calamitous.

But to return to the composers. MAX MARETZEK (1821–1897) was a Moravian who came to America in 1848. Fry had him brought to New York to conduct the opera at the Academy. He was a clever manager, too; successful with his companies in New York, Havana, and Mexico. He wrote two operas: *Hamlet*, and another based on Irving's legend *Sleepy Hollow*.

GEORGE MATZKA, the viola player of the Mason-Thomas chamber music concerts, came to New York in 1852. He was long a member of the Philharmonic, and for a short time in 1876 he acted as conductor. Matzka was a prolific composer; he wrote several overtures, two String Quartets, a Violin Sonata, and many choruses and songs.

ADOLF NEUENDORF (1843–1897) was born in Hamburg, but came to New York when he was twelve, where he studied the violin with Matzka. He was for years a violinist and conductor in theatre orchestras. In 1877 he conducted the first American performance of Wagner's *Die Walküre* at the Academy of Music in New York. When Theodore Thomas went to Cincinnati in 1878, Neuendorf succeeded him as conductor of the Philharmonic, but for one year only, for Thomas returned soon after his troubles with the directors of the college. Neuendorf composed two symphonies and several overtures, but he was best known by his comic operas, a field in which he had real talent. *The Rat Charmer of Hamelin* was a favorite for many years after it was first produced in 1880, and the works that followed it were successful, too: *Don Quixote* (1882), *Prince Woodruff* (1887), and *The Minstrel* (1892).

And so the path is cleared for the first native composer whose fame has endured as a writer in the larger forms, even though his works are seldom heard today. JOHN KNOWLES PAINE (1839–1906) lived to see himself the dean of American composers, and many of his younger brethren, some of them his pupils, making quite a name for themselves. Some say that American music starts with J. K. Paine, and in many ways they are right, for none of those who came before him had done much in the symphonic field. Certainly Fry and Bristow enjoyed but a short fame with their works, and the attention they attracted was based more on the fact that they were among the few Americans who

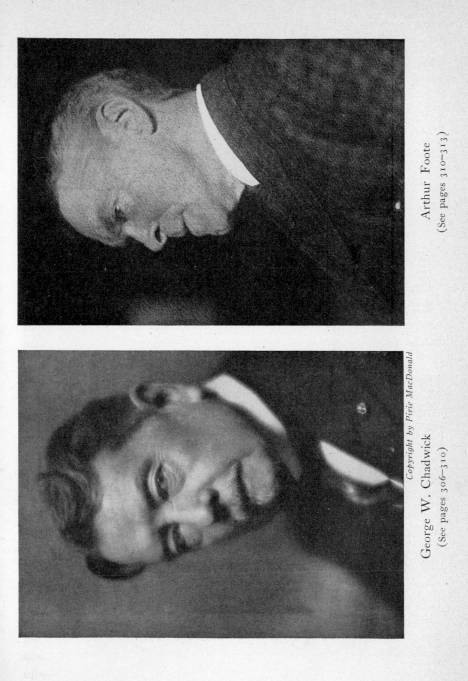

George W. Chadwick
(See pages 306–310)

Copyright by Pirie MacDonald

Arthur Foote
(See pages 310–313)

Horatio Parker

(See pages 313–319)

Mrs. H. H. A. Beach

(See pages 319–323)

wrote music. As such, they were curiosities who could win a following for the mere fact that they existed at a time when there were few others like them.

And as we grow further from the days of John K. Paine, the venerable father of our composers is relegated to a somewhat similar position. His music was infinitely superior to that of either Fry or Bristow, yet he holds his place in our music history because he stood alone at a time when we had few composers. Compared to his contemporaries, he was and still is a giant. Were he writing today the same music he wrote fifty years ago, he would be lost in the crowd, where hundreds of our present-day composers are writing far better music.

It is not to remove Paine from his pedestal that the critic of today makes reservations in praising his music. The fact that he was the first American composer to win serious consideration abroad is enough to deserve a monument. Yet it is but honest to admit that as a creative artist he was something of a pedant, wholly dominated by European composers of his time. As Daniel Gregory Mason has written,[1] "his *Island Fantasy* was supposed to be inspired by the Isles of Shoals, off Portsmouth, but artistically speaking it was within easy sailing distance of Mendelssohn's *Hebrides*."

Histories of American music written twenty-five and thirty years ago were too close to Paine to be entirely mature in their judgment of his work. Superlatives abound in their accounts of his music. Elson [2] speaks of the first symphony as an "epoch-making" work; to his mind the second symphony has a final movement that is a glorious outburst of thanksgiving almost comparable with the *finale* of the B-flat Symphony by Schumann. He also states that at the Philadelphia Exposition, Paine's *Centennial Hymn* was decidedly more of a success than Wagner's *Centennial March*. But he fails to add that the Wagner march, which had been commissioned by Theodore Thomas, was so unworthy of Wagner that Thomas never quite forgot the insult. Rupert Hughes,[3] writing in 1900, was ecstatic over the second symphony.

It seems wiser today to admit that Paine's music has not had im-

[1] D. G. Mason, *The Dilemma of American Music*. By permission of Macmillan Co., publishers.

[2] L. C. Elson, *The History of American Music*, Macmillan Co.

[3] Hughes & Elson, *American Composers*, L. C. Page & Co.

mortality for the good reason that it really did not deserve it. Concede that its freshness has somewhat wilted, and then proceed to do its composer the honor he merits as the first of our composers to have his works performed repeatedly for many years, and to have them published both here and abroad.

For they were performed often. By 1899 the Boston Symphony Orchestra had played his compositions more than eighteen times. Theodore Thomas gave the first symphony its initial performance in 1876 in Boston. He also commissioned Paine to write a *Centennial Hymn* for the Philadelphia Exposition in 1876, and the *Columbus March and Hymn* for the Chicago World's Fair. He performed his cantata *Song of Promise* at the Cincinnati Festival of 1888. When he was not yet thirty, Paine conducted his Mass at the *Sing Academie* in Berlin. In 1873 he directed the first performance of his oratorio *St. Peter* in his native town of Portland, Maine. A year later it was given by the Handel and Haydn Society in Boston. In 1881 his music for Sophocles's *Œdipus Tyrannus* was played at the Sander's Theatre in Cambridge, Massachusetts, and in 1904 this score won the gold medal at an international concert at the unveiling of the monument to Wagner in Berlin. His *Hymn to the West* was written for the St. Louis World's Fair in 1904, and the Handel and Haydn Society gave it a Boston performance the following year.

He was born in Portland, January 9, 1839. His first teacher was Hermann Kotzschmar, the German who came to America with the Saxonia Band in 1848, and settled in Portland in 1849 where he lived for the remaining sixty years of his life. Paine made his debut as an organist when he was eighteen, and then went to Berlin, where he studied organ, composition, and orchestration under Haupt and other teachers. He toured Germany as an organist, and acquired something of a reputation. Soon after his return to America he was appointed instructor of music at Harvard (1862), and thirteen years later he was honored with a full professorship. Harvard and the University of Pennsylvania ran a close race in creating the first professorships of music. Paine held his chair for thirty years, and then resigned to give all his time to composition. But not for long; he died April 25, 1906, while he was working to complete a symphonic poem based on the life of Abraham Lincoln.

The first symphony was published by Breitkopf and Haertel in Leipzig, but not until 1908, two years after the composer's death. The second symphony was issued by a Boston publisher, Arthur P. Schmidt, who deserves a monument for what he did to publish the larger orchestral works of our early composers. This second symphony is an attempt at program music. It bears the title *Spring*, and its first movement (like that of Raff's spring symphony, written one year before Paine's) is called *Nature's Awakening*. There are two motives, one "Winter" and the other "Awakening." The two conflict, and the strength of Winter fails. The second movement is *The May Night Fantasy*—the bassoon adds to the merriment. Then comes a Romance, *A Promise of Spring*, in rondo form; and the *finale* is a sort of hallelujah on *The Glory of Nature*.

Paine was much given to program music. At heart he was probably a romanticist, academic New Englander though he was. He wrote several symphonic poems inspired by Shakespeare. There was one to *The Tempest*, and an overture to *As You Like It*. The legend of *Poseidon and Aphrodite* inspired an "Ocean Fantasy." The *Island Fantasy* grew from his admiration for two paintings of the Isles of Shoals, New Hampshire, by J. Appleton Brown. The contrasting themes of the music suggest the dangers and the beauty of the sea.

Paine's opera *Azara* never reached dramatic performance, although it had a concert performance with piano accompaniment in 1903, and another in 1907 by the Cecilia Society of Boston, with orchestra, chorus, and soloists, conducted by B. J. Lang. It is said that there was a plan to produce *Azara* at the Metropolitan during Conried's regime, but the idea was abandoned because it was impossible to find a contralto or bass who could sing well enough in English to manage the leading roles.

Paine wrote his own libretto for *Azara*, a fact which may be responsible for its failure to gain performance. The dramatic action is a bit heavy and ponderous, and from a theatrical standpoint not particularly effective. As for the music, Paine knew how to write for voices; and the ballet music and the three Moorish dances from the score were frequently played on orchestral programs. There were traces of Wagner in the music, which show that Paine had changed his opinions of the great German. He was at first firm with the Boston clique that could see nothing of good in Wagner or his work, and his gradual awakening to his error did away with much of the pedantry of his own music.

As a professor, there are many traditions about Paine. Some of his pupils have told me that his teaching was as dry as the dust, and that they could find no inspiration in his classes. Others speak loyally of the grand old man, and what he did for them. Probably if he had not been academic, even to the point of dryness, he would never have been tolerated in a nineteenth-century university. If his courses had not been conducted according to the rigid classroom standards of the day, he might have failed in the same way that MacDowell failed to gain the support of the authorities some years later at Columbia.

List the names of his pupils in composition, and you cannot deny his influence, for good or for bad, on the native music of our day. The roster reads like a Who's Who of composers—Arthur Foote, Louis A. Coerne, Clayton Johns, Frederick S. Converse, John Alden Carpenter, Daniel Gregory Mason, *ad infinitum.*

It was Paine's own idea that he teach at Harvard. Shortly after his return from Europe he had been appointed organist and music director of the university, and he offered to give free of charge, a series of lectures on musical form. There was opposition, chiefly because it was a new idea, but he was finally allowed to lecture. No credit toward a degree was given for attendance, and few students came to hear him. Then Charles Eliot became president, and the lectures were started again in 1870. Paine also offered a course in harmony, which became popular, and then a course in counterpoint. For none of this early work did he receive any salary. In a very few years so many pupils were taking the courses that the work had to be recognized officially. Paine was made an assistant professor in 1873, and two years later he was given a full professorship, and his students were granted credit for their work in the music department.

This has led gradually to the Music School at Harvard, where there are courses in applied music, and in music as one of the arts. The Harvard curriculum has been a model for other universities to follow; and in the same way that Lowell Mason forced music into the public schools, John Knowles Paine was the pioneer in organized music courses in the American colleges. As a frontier composer when there were few of his kind, and as a prophet of music education, Paine's glory can never be dimmed merely because his music does not grip as it did thirty years ago.

There were other composers who came to the front in Paine's lifetime. Among them, WILLIAM WALLACE GILCHRIST (1846–1916), born in Jersey City. Gilchrist lived most of his life in Philadelphia. He had his training there at the hands of Hugh Clarke, the teacher who was appointed professor of music at the University of Pennsylvania in the same year Paine was awarded similar honors at Harvard (1875). Gilchrist was the organizer, and for forty years conductor, of the Philadelphia Mendelssohn Club. He led the old Philadelphia Symphony Orchestra which had been started by men from Gustav Hinrichs's Opera Company, and which was the ancestor of the present Philadelphia Orchestra. He was a vocal teacher and a choirmaster—an active career.

As a composer Gilchrist had an uncanny faculty for winning prizes. He was given a thousand dollars for his Psalm 46 at the 1882 Cincinnati Festival. The judges were Reinecke, Saint-Saëns, and Theodore Thomas. Before that, in 1878, the Abt Male Singing Society of Philadelphia had offered two prizes for choral works, and Gilchrist won both. Soon after this he won three more, awarded by the Mendelssohn Glee Club of New York.

· He wrote a Symphony that was played by the Philadelphia Orchestra in 1910 under the composer's direction. Unlike Paine, Gilchrist attempted no program in this work. It was absolute music, pure and simple. The man had a facile technique, and the chief attribute of this symphony was its scholarliness. His second Symphony showed more individuality. He wrote a number of works for small combinations—a Nonet for piano, strings, flute, clarinet, and horn. It was a graceful piece of writing, not without a certain distinction. There was a Quintet for piano and strings, as well as a String Quartet and a Trio. Despite his success in choral fields, Gilchrist was in happier vein when he wrote for instruments. He was less banal, and not led into temptation by the bombastic poems of Mrs. Hemans, and others.

FREDERICK GRANT GLEASON (1848–1903) was a native of New England. Born in Middletown, Connecticut, he was taken to live in Hartford while he was still a boy. His father was an amateur musician, but it was not until the son, at sixteen, had written a *Christmas Oratorio,* without any instruction in harmony or counterpoint, that he was allowed to prepare himself for the profession of musician. He was then put to work with Dudley Buck, and later he went abroad to study with Moscheles, Richter, and others. He came back to Hartford, but when he was thirty he moved west to Chicago, where he spent the rest of his life as one of the city's prominent organists and musicians.

Gleason was a prolific composer. Tinged with Wagnerisms, he yet had something to say for himself. He sometimes had arguments with proofreaders and copyists for his harmonic innovations. He generally knew what he was about, and when copyists wrote "Fifths!" in the margin of his scores, he could reply, "Certainly!" His works were often played by Theodore Thomas, and Thomas never put anything on his programs that did not in his opinion belong there.

Gleason wrote a work for the World's Fair concerts, a *Processional of the Holy Grail.* The connection with Wagner was not altogether confined to the title. There was a symphonic poem *Edris,* based on a novel by Marie Corelli. Thomas played this with the Chicago Orchestra in 1896. He made a setting of *The Culprit Fay,* for chorus. He wrote a Piano Concerto, and his *Auditorium Festival Ode* was performed at the dedication of the Auditorium in Chicago. Another orchestral tone poem *Song of Life* was presented by the Chicago Orchestra in 1900.

Gleason wrote a number of operas; some of them have never been known, for he left a clause in his will that their scores should not be examined until he had been dead for fifty years. One of his operas, *Otho Visconti,* was produced at the College Theatre, Chicago, in 1907. Excerpts from its score had been played before. The overture was performed in Leipzig in 1892, and Thomas presented it at the Chicago World's Fair. In *Montezuma,* another opera, Gleason used the Wagnerian system of leit-motifs. One of its soprano arias was sung in concert on several occasions, but the opera itself was never produced.

Probably Gleason's handicap was that his intellect was not properly balanced by his emotions. He was more of a harmonist than a melodist, and his harmonic combinations were the product of his mind rather than of his feelings. Yet the intellectuals command respect, and Gleason had his place in our music.

In some ways SILAS GAMALIEL PRATT (1846–1916) narrowly missed being another Father Heinrich. He certainly conceived ideas on a no less colossal scale than Heinrich had. But Pratt had a really thorough training, and though he did make himself ridiculous at times, there was something solid beneath all the bombast that he mistook for grandeur. Like others, Pratt wanted to be a nationalist, and turned to native subjects for his titles, if not for his mode of expressing them. The names of his symphonic works read like the chapter headings of a school history: *Paul Revere's Ride;* a *Fantasy* in which hostile themes depict the battles between North and South; *The Battle of Manila;* a *Lincoln* Symphony; and *A Tragedy of the Deep,* on the sinking of the steamship *Titanic.*

He wrote cantatas and operas—one of them *Zenobia, Queen of Palmyra,* first given in concert form in Chicago (1882), and a year later in full dramatic production in both New York and Chicago. *Antonio,* later called *Lucille,* was performed in Chicago in 1887. *The Triumph of Columbus* was intended to be his greatest work. It was written for the fourth centennial of the discovery of America, and produced in New York in 1892.

Pratt was a go-getter who would have warmed the heart of any sales manager. In youth his ambition to be a musician was thwarted by poverty, for as a boy he had to earn his living, and he worked in a music store in Chicago. He kept at his studies in music, and finally saved up enough money to go to Europe. When he was twenty-two he went to Germany and studied the piano under Bendel and Kullak, and composition with Kiel.

He came back to Chicago in 1872, but the effects of the fire were still apparent, and Pratt had to go back behind the counter of the music store. But not for long. He had some pupils, and after a while he gave some concerts, and then went back to Germany. To make up for lost time he practiced hours at a time, so frantically that he injured his wrists permanently. He went to Bayreuth in 1875, met Liszt, and gave a recital of his own pieces at Weimar.

He went to Berlin in 1876, and conducted a performance of his own *Centennial Overture.* Later he played it at the Crystal Palace in London while Grant, former President, was guest of honor. Home again for symphony concerts in Chicago, and the production of *Zenobia.*

Then back to Europe in 1885 for a performance of his *Prodigal Son* Symphony at the Crystal Palace.

For fourteen years after 1888 he lived and taught in New York. Then he moved to Pittsburgh, where he established in 1906 a musical institute. All of his training and all this imagination should have produced something far more lasting than Pratt was able to achieve. Maybe his ambition got the better of him, and he tried too much. If courage and industry were all that were required for immortality, Pratt would have been another Wagner. (In fact, he once generously proclaimed that the immortal Richard was the Silas G. Pratt of Europe.) Unfortunately, more was needed, and stability and the spark of genius were missing from the make-up of a man who had the initiative and the ability to make his work known and heard in high places.

2. THE BOSTON GROUP

John K. Paine lived to see a group of composers active in his native New England—a few men who are generally classed together because they have lived and worked side by side, and because they have something in common artistically. Yet the relationship is one of sympathy and background, rather than of any particular traits of style that mark their music. They were all the product of the same age—a time when the American composer was first having a respectful and interested hearing—and when all the musical world was under the spell of the German romanticists. These New Englanders are often called the Boston classicists, or the New England academics, yet neither term is quite accurate. None of them departed far from accepted paths, nor ventured into startling experiments of his own, yet to call a man an academic or a classicist is, after all, a rather arbitrary pigeonholing. It is safer to group these composers for their geographical kinship, and maybe for comradeship, and to let it go at that.

Paine's mantle as dean of our composers fell upon GEORGE W. CHADWICK (1854–1931). Arthur Foote was a year older, but Chadwick was the more significant. Historically, his importance lies in carrying on where Paine left off. Paine was one of the first to win respect, to write music that was practicable and playable. Chadwick added a spark of genuine inspiration; he had a sense of humor. He makes us chuckle, and he makes us think. And while we are thinking, he warms our emotions—even though he seldom thrills us. He had all of Paine's substance and more—in his scholarship he was indeed an academic— but he added life to the forms he used, and gave us something vital.

Tradition has it that Chadwick wistfully confided to his friends that he determined his career when he turned toward Munich and sought Rheinberger as a master, instead of going to César Franck in Paris. Maybe he had his regrets, for the Belgian was a great teacher, but it is hard to imagine Chadwick's Yankee thoughts robed in the mysticism of a Franck disciple. In many ways Chadwick was typically the American in his music—at any rate, a Yankee. Not from use of folk songs, or by choosing Niagara Falls or the life of George Washington for his subjects (which he didn't), but by something far subtler, something he could never have avoided even if he had tried very hard. Philip Hale described it as "a certain jaunty irreverence, a snapping of the fingers at Fate and the Universe," and it is no doubt this delicious impertinence that is genuinely American. None but a Yankee can say such things and get away with it.

In the spring of 1930 there were at least two festivals to mark Chadwick's fiftieth anniversary as a composer, dating his career from the time when he came back from Germany and his apprenticeship. The New England Conservatory in Boston, where he had been director for thirty-three years, and the Eastman School in Rochester, honored the deacon of our composers with festival concerts of his music. In Boston the final number was the *Rip Van Winkle* Overture which Chadwick had conducted at the May Festival of the Handel and Haydn Society in 1880. The 1930 audience found much of the charm left in a work that the Leipzig *Musikalisches Wochenblatt* had fifty years before found possessed of "interesting traits which reflect an emotional life of personal cast."

Chadwick was born in Lowell, Massachusetts, November 13, 1854. He was of New England stock on both sides of his family tree. Orthodox, devout Congregationalists. His mother died when she gave him birth, and he was placed in the care of relatives until he was three. Then his father married again, and had a wife who could take care of little George. The father was a good musician, and in his spare time taught a singing class and organized a chorus and an orchestra in the neighborhood. He prospered in his business; first a farmer, he had gone to Lowell to become a machinist; then moving down to Lawrence in 1860, when George was six, he started a life and fire insurance company. When Boston was devastated by fire in 1872, the citizens of Lawrence flocked to Chadwick for policies.

Music always held George Chadwick in its spell. The musical gatherings of his relatives were the high spots of his childhood. His older brother Fitz Henry had had piano lessons, so he taught George to play, and together they learned the four-hand arrangements of the Beethoven Symphonies. Then George played the organ in church, and when he was graduated from high school he was allowed to take regular trips to Boston for piano lessons. He went into his father's business, and worked there until he was twenty-one. He had some lessons at the New England Conservatory, and studied harmony with Stephen A. Emery.

In 1876 he decided to teach music himself, and had an appointment as music professor of Olivet College. From this he saved money to go abroad. Then came opposition from his God-fearing father. Teaching was one thing, especially in a college, but to have an out-and-out professional musician in the family was a quite different matter. Anyway, the insurance business was making money, and likely to make considerably more. But George had decided to go, and George went.

He arrived in Berlin in the fall of 1877, and tried studying with Karl August Haupt. But Haupt was not to Chadwick's liking, for he wanted teaching in orchestration, which Haupt confessed he could not give him. He went to Leipzig where he worked with Jadassohn. Others have called Jadassohn's classes a joke, but the teacher took a personal interest in Chadwick, and would often give him lessons at his house. He offered his pupil training in counterpoint that gave him the command of his choral style, a polyphonic freedom that makes voices of orchestral choirs. With Jadassohn for teacher he wrote the *Rip Van Winkle* Overture, and two String Quartets.

Chadwick was not quite satisfied after two years with Jadassohn. He felt there was something more to learn, somewhere, before he went back to Boston. He chose Rheinberger (instead of Franck), and in Munich he learned the power of self-criticism. Rheinberger knew how to build on what Chadwick had already learned, and he gave him what Carl Engel has termed "an orderly idea of strict composition." The straightforwardness of the German pedants was surely more suited to the expression of Yankee ideas than the subtleties of the Frenchmen.

He came back home in 1880, where he rented a studio and hung his sign on the door as teacher. Horatio Parker was one of his first pupils; Sidney Homer and Arthur Whiting soon joined his class. He conducted choral societies, and was a church organist for seventeen years. In 1882 he was made an instructor at the New England Conservatory, and fifteen years later he was asked to be its director. He held that position until his death, April 4, 1931.

Chadwick composed twenty major works for orchestra; eleven of them are published. Of his six chamber music compositions, three have been issued in printed form. This fifty per cent record does credit to the music, and says something in behalf of the American publisher. Orchestral works in Chadwick's prime were scarcely a commercial enterprise. The thirteen dollars he received in 1886 from the Boston Symphony Orchestra, for performance of a movement from his second symphony, established a new precedent.

Three of the orchestral works were symphonies and one was a sinfonietta. All but the first symphony, written in 1882, are published. The overture was a form that offered him a happy chance to express his notions. He composed six of them: *Rip Van Winkle* (1879); *Thalia* (1883); *The Miller's Daughter* (1884); *Melpomene* (1891); *Adonais* (1899); and *Euterpe* (1906). The works that show his jauntiness and carefree spirit most effectively are *A Vagrom Ballad* (No. 4 of his *Symphonic Sketches*, 1907), and the symphonic ballad *Tam o' Shanter* (1917). The *Suite Symphonique* won first prize in the 1911 competition of the National Federation of Music Clubs.

The chamber music list included five string quartets and a piano quintet. The Kneisels played some of these on a number of occasions. Engel [1] wrote of his treatment of the strings:

Chadwick does not lose himself in mere juggling with patterns when he writes for competing strings, nor is he preoccupied with questionable experi-

[1] Carl Engel, *George W. Chadwick* (*Musical Quarterly*, July, 1924).

ments in sonorities that go against the nature of the instrument. He loves a cantilena and is capable of endowing it with enough breath to let it sing its way calmly through all the registers from the E-string of the violin to the C-string of the 'cello.

Chadwick tried his hand at opera, yet his dramatic powers were more devoted to the narratives of his orchestral ballads. The lyric drama *Judith* was performed in concert form at the Worcester Festival in 1901. *Tabasco*, a comic opera, was first given professionally at the Boston Museum in 1894. There are also *The Padrone*, an opera, and *Love's Sacrifice*, an operetta, both to libretti of David Stevens, as well as incidental music to Walter Browne's morality play *Everywoman*.

Chadwick attained distinction as a composer of choral works. His *Dedication Ode* was written for the dedication of the Hollis Street Church in 1886. He made a setting of Harriet Monroe's *Ode* for the opening concert of the World's Fair in Chicago (1893); *Phœnix Expirans* (1892) was written for the Springfield (Massachusetts) Festival, of which he was the conductor for a number of years, as he was of the Worcester Festival also. *Ecce jam Noctis*, for men's voices, organ, and orchestra was written for the Yale commencement exercises in 1897; and the *Noël*, a pastoral for soli, chorus, and orchestra was first produced at the Norfolk (Connecticut) Festival in 1908.

He published over a hundred songs, and his setting of Sidney Lanier's *Ballad of Trees and the Master* ranks as a classic. It is in the folklike ballad that he was happiest as a song writer. Not the lyric ballad of the sentimentalists, but the true ballad that demands musical dramatization.

It is the fashion today to turn our backs to Chadwick and his colleagues, past and present. And it may be true that our recent composers make our earlier writers seem tame by comparison. Yet there is a steadiness in Chadwick's music that is always dependable, a freshness that is a matter of spirit rather than of style or idiom. After all, modernity is youth, and of youthfulness Chadwick had his full share. The man himself was far older than his music.

ARTHUR WILLIAM FOOTE (1853–1937) did not go abroad for study; in fact, it was not until he had been graduated from Harvard, when he was twenty-one, that he definitely made up his mind to be a musician. He had taken J. K. Paine's music courses in college, and had been conductor of the Harvard Glee Club. After he was graduated, he decided to pass a useful summer before going into business, so he had some organ lessons with B. J. Lang. Lang gave him so much encouragement that Foote decided then and there that music should be his profession. For two years more he studied organ and piano with Lang, and in 1876 he started on his own as a piano teacher. He was one of the prominent teachers of the Boston district for over sixty years.

He had shown little interest in music as a boy. He was born in Salem, and his Anglo-Saxon parents were not musically inclined. When he was fourteen, he was given some piano lessons as part of a general education. He soon found that he liked to play, and his curiosity led him to take a few harmony lessons with Stephen Emery before he entered Harvard. Then when he went to college, and found Paine conducting courses in music, he was one of the most eager of the students.

From 1878 until 1910, Foote was organist of the First Unitarian Church in Boston. He helped found the American Guild of Organists, and was at one time its president. Other than these, he held few regular positions, but was active as a free-lance teacher, pianist, and organist, giving many piano recitals and often playing chamber music with the Kneisel, and other quartets. He lived to be eighty-four years old, and only a few months before his death, April 9, 1937, he was present to acknowledge from the platform the applause that greeted the performance of his Suite in E for Strings, by the Boston Symphony.

Like the other composers of his early days, he reflected his likes and dislikes in music of the masters. The Brahmsian flavor of such pieces as his Quintet for piano and strings shows that in the nineties he was a progressive, interested in the thoughts of the post-romanticists. He called himself a conservative, but admiration of Brahms was by no means a conservative matter in the late Victorian era.

In his writing, Foote seems chiefly concerned with harmonic rather than with contrapuntal patterns. His scoring for male voices may owe its success to his glee club days at Harvard, when he acquired a fondness for chords in close formation, in the richness of the lower registers.

He wrote many works in the larger forms, eight for orchestra, five of which were published by Schmidt in Boston. *In the Mountains*, an overture, was first performed by the Boston Symphony under Gericke in 1887. It was repeated the following year. His *Serenade* in E, for strings, and his Suite in D, for string orchestra, had been played a year earlier. Foote took the episode of *Francesca da Rimini* from Dante for his symphonic prologue, probably his most distinguished work. Somewhat programmatic in its development, the music opens with an introduction that seems to be a long, deep sigh, followed by the shrieking and shuddering of the poor damned souls in inferno. The first theme, in its passion, seems to be Francesca's recital of her love story; the other themes and their development weave a dramatic and tragic tale of love and retribution.

Francesca was first performed in Boston in 1893. In the same year Theodore Thomas played the *Serenade* for strings at the World's Fair. Foote said that it was due to the interest of Thomas that his orchestral works were given a hearing. In 1894, Thomas conducted a performance of his Concerto for cello and orchestra (with Bruno Steindel as soloist) at one of the concerts of the Chicago Symphony Orchestra, then in its fourth season. After 1900 he composed only two works for orchestra: a Suite in E, for strings (1910), and *Four Character Pieces after Omar Khayyám* (1912).

Of his eight major works for chamber music combinations, only one is unpublished. Most of them had their first performances at concerts of the Kneisel Quartet; the G Minor Violin Sonata in 1890; the Piano Quartet, Opus 23 in the following year; the String Quartet in E, 1894; the Quintet in 1898, and the Piano Trio in B flat, 1909. In his Sonatas for violin and piano, and in the *Ballade*, Opus 69, Foote wrote in a broad style with an epic, narrative unfolding of theme and development.

There are a number of choral works with orchestra—*The Farewell of Hiawatha*, for men's voices (1886), and others for mixed voices—*The Wreck of the Hesperus* (1888), and *The Skeleton in Armor* (1893). He composed many works for chorus *a cappella* or with piano accompaniment, and a great deal of church music. In his many piano pieces and in his songs he wrote idiomatic music, playable and singable, of generally high taste, showing discretion and restraint in gaining intended effects. He was always sincere and genuine, and rarely if ever the sentimentalist when he was tender. He composed two suites for piano, three pieces for left hand alone, five poems after Omar Khayyám, and some thirty other piano pieces. There are almost one hundred and fifty songs, many from the English poets—Herrick, Marlowe, Shakespeare. Among the best known are *I'm Wearing Awa'*, *The Lake Isle of Innesfree*, *On the Way to Kew*, *It Was a Lover and his Lass*, *O Swallow, Flying South*, and *Irish Folk Song*. He published over thirty works for organ, most important being the Suite in D Major.

Foote followed in the paths of others from abroad greater than himself, but the modest, retiring gentleman nevertheless made a handsome contribution to American music. He was substantial, reliable, workmanlike, and, most important, agreeable. As a writer in *The Art of Music* puts it, "His music is the pure and perfectly formed expression of a nature at once refined and imaginative." He belonged to the Boston of the nineties, where most of the composers of that time worked and met each other for exchange of ideas—Chadwick, Parker, Whiting, MacDowell, Nevin, Mrs. Beach, Converse, Johns, and their artistic parent John K. Paine. He saw the musical idols of one period after another thrown down and broken. Why, in his later years, should he have become excited over Schoenberg or Stravinsky? As an early devotee of Brahms and Wagner, he had his fill of innovations in his youth. He at least had the satisfaction of knowing that confidence in his early Gods was well placed.

If HORATIO WILLIAM PARKER (1863–1919) had been as successful in his symphonic works as he was in his choral writings, he might in his time have been the greatest of our American composers. There are some who think he was, anyway. Certainly he produced outstanding works—the oratorio *Hora Novissima* may be mentioned in the same breath with Franck's *Beatitudes*, and the intelligentsia went so far as to class the opera *Mona* with *Salomé* and *Pelléas et Mélisande*. Parker was a composer who derived from a background of Puritan hymn singing, with a German training superimposed; yet the influences that shaped his style never prevented his being individual. His music was generally his own; even today, some of his passages have a modern sound.

Parker never achieved the popular fame of MacDowell, or some others of our American composers. He wrote few little tunes that may be taught to school children in music memory contests, or small piano pieces that are played by amateurs. His songs and smaller pieces are the least fortunate of his works, and the least distinctive. Besides, his operas are known today only to those who take the trouble to read the scores. That *Mona* was never repeated after four performances in its first season is a blot on the history of New York's Metropolitan Opera House. In many ways it is the finest music drama that has been written in this country.

He was primarily a composer for musicians, yet many of his passages can thrill layman and musician alike. His hatred of anything weak or sentimental made much of his music angular and austere, yet there is a fine emotional appeal in page after page of his scores.

Parker was born of a cultured family. His mother, Isabella Parker, the daughter of a Baptist minister, was a scholar and a musician, organist of the village church at Auburndale, Massachusetts, the town where Horatio was born September 15, 1863. His father, Charles Edward Parker, was an architect. Fine old English stock on both sides of the family, steeped in a New England heritage that had its Puritan phases. As a child Horatio went further than just not being musically inclined—he disliked anything connected with music. His mother often wondered how she could get him to take any interest in it. Suddenly, when he was fourteen, he seemed to wake from his musical sleep and wanted to know all about it, how it was played, and how it was made. He had piano lessons from his mother, and then with local teachers. He started to compose, and in two days set to music fifty poems of Kate Greenaway, later published as songs for school children. At sixteen he was made organist of a church in Dedham, and for its services he wrote hymn-tunes, anthems, and choir services.

About this time Chadwick returned from Europe, and Parker became one of his first pupils. Chadwick writes: [2]

As my pupil he was far from docile. In fact, he was impatient of the restrictions of musical form and rather rebellious of the discipline of counterpoint and fugues. But he was very industrious and did his work faithfully and well. His lessons usually ended with his swallowing his medicine, but with many a wry grimace.

[2] George W. Chadwick, *Horatio Parker*, Yale University Press.

In 1882 he went to Europe, to Rheinberger in Munich, where he studied organ playing and composition at the Royal School of Music. By placing himself wholly in Rheinberger's hands, he acquired a contrapuntal mastery that helped him later to reach the summits of choral writing.

When he came back to America he settled in New York. He was put in charge of the music teaching at the Cathedral School in Garden City; he was organist at St. Andrew's and later at Holy Trinity; and he taught at the National Conservatory of Music in New York, where Antonin Dvořák was director. Seven years later, in 1893, he had a chance to return to his native Boston as organist and choirmaster of Trinity Church, then famous for the sermons of Phillips Brooks. In the next year he was invited to head the Music Department of Yale University at New Haven; and he held that position until his death in 1919.

While at Yale, Parker organized the New Haven Symphony Orchestra, subsidized by the University. For a comparison of our educational facilities with those of England, it is illuminating to read what *The Musical Times* (London, September 1, 1902) had to say about the Music Department at Yale:

Professor Parker teaches counterpoint, composition and instrumentation. He gives lectures on the history of music, and conducts six orchestral concerts every season. An additional orchestral concert is devoted chiefly to the compositions of the students. No anxiety is felt in regard to the financial result of these concerts. The orchestra is supported by the University as a laboratory for the Department of Music, where, as in a chemical laboratory, the students may, by means of their compositions, blow themselves up. Courses in orchestration are offered by the University, and common sense requires that the means of practical exemplification of the results of studies in such courses should be available. Where have we in old England, or even in Auld Reekie, anything to approach such a boon and privilege as is enjoyed by the students in music at Yale?

The same article tells of Parker's relations with the University, concluding its account with this felicitation:

Professor Parker enjoys a vacation of four months every year, and one year in every seven is a Sabbatical Year—twelve months' complete rest from his ordinary vocations! Who will say that his lot is not a happy one?

Nobody! But the poor man must have needed all the summer rest he could get, for his weekly routine would have killed a weaker man far sooner than it eventually killed Horatio Parker. He always had a church position in some city other than New Haven—first, Trinity in Boston, and later, St. Nicholas's in New York. He conducted choral societies in several cities. David Stanley Smith, his assistant at Yale and later his successor, recounts a typical Parker schedule in the *Musical Quarterly*, April, 1930:

Late Saturday afternoon, choir rehearsal in New York; Sunday, service morning and evening; Monday afternoon and evening in Philadelphia for rehearsals of the Eurydice and Orpheus Clubs; night train to New York, thence to New Haven for two classes on Tuesday; Tuesday evening, by trolley to Derby for a rehearsal of the Derby Choral Club, arriving in New Haven at midnight; Wednesday, a lecture on the History of Music and a class in composition; Thursday, again two classes; Thursday evening, rehearsal of the New Haven Oratorio Society; Friday morning, rehearsal of the New Haven Symphony Orchestra; Saturday, off again for New York.

And then Smith adds: "It seems incredible, but through this period Parker composed incessantly. There was always a score in the making." He found some time for recreation. He loved to ride his bicycle, and he played some golf with his friends. Without some out-of-doors life, he could have stood but a few years of such a grind.

Parker was quite the man of the world. Fastidious, immaculate, he commanded a social standing often denied musicians of his time. He had for his friends artists, writers, and men from the several professions—seldom musicians. He was at ease in talking on any subject; he could hold his own in prolonged discussions on topics far removed from music. His friends were fascinated by him; those who were not his friends feared him. His brusque manner frightened the timid, and he despised those who were afraid of him. In this he was something of the bully; he would often wilfully confuse his pupils in class, and then scoff at their confusion. But for those who stood on their two feet and talked back to him he had the profoundest admiration. His manner was a challenge which he expected would be met in kind. The wags of New Haven say it was a pleasure to be insulted by Horatio Parker, he could apologize so handsomely.

His life at home with his wife and daughters was in many ways ideal. His wife had been a fellow pupil abroad—Anna Plössl, the daughter of a Munich banker. Though he later hated the Germans, Parker loved this wife of his. His life was her only interest. When they were first married she taught pupils herself, so that they could meet their daily bills.

These personal traits are apparent in his music. He was intolerant of anything that was too easy, of anything facile. His horror of the obvious made him avoid repeating a phrase whenever he could keep from doing it. If an idea must be repeated, let it be changed in some detail. True enough, he was often trivial, so trivial that we may wonder whether he was not trying to force himself to write in a popular vein against his better judgment. But he was never cheaply superficial; his lighter moments were doubtless more studied and conscious than his more serious, happier efforts.

He wrote over forty works for chorus, religious and secular; two operas; nine pieces for orchestra (one published: an Organ Concerto); four chamber compositions (one, a Suite for trio, published); seven groups of pieces for organ; four for piano; and twelve sets of songs. Added to these, he wrote incidental music for a masque, and for a Yale commencement, and he acted as editor-in-chief for a graded series of songbooks for schools. He felt that when school children sang, they had a right to the best in music.

Hora Novissima was written in 1891–92, his Opus 30. While he was composing it, he was grieving for the loss of a sister and some other members of his family. The work of these years has a background of absolute sincerity where pathos is concerned. For the text of *Hora Novissima* he used the Latin hymn of Barnard de Morlaix; his mother made the English translation. Here, as in so many of his choral works, Parker shows his instinct for massed effects, for fine choral texture, for full development of hymnlike themes. Masculine, vital music, with often the sweep of the inevitable. Fugal writing and chant, contrasted with stunning effect.

Parker submitted *Hora Novissima* and a cantata *The Dream King and His Love*, Opus 31, in a prize contest at the National Conservatory in 1892. He won the prize, but not for *Hora Novissima*—the judges, including Dvořák, liked the *Dream King* better. *Hora Novissima* had its first performance in 1893 by the Church Choral Society of New

York at the Church of Zion and St. Timothy. The next year it was
sung by the Handel and Haydn Society in Boston, and later at the
Cincinnati Festival. In 1899 it was performed at the Three Choirs
Festival at Worcester, England, and it made such an impression on
the English audience that Parker was commissioned to write a new
work for the Hereford Festival. This produced the *Wanderer's
Psalm;* and the *Star Song* was written for the Norwich Festival in
1902.

His fame in England was almost greater than in America. The
English have a warm place in their hearts for choral music, and Parker
had enough of the Englishman in his blood to write what they liked
best. *The Legend of St. Christopher,* sung at Bristol, completed all
that was needed for an award of the Doctor of Music degree by Cambridge University in 1902. Like *Hora Novissima, St. Christopher*
shows largeness of conception, breadth of structure; but it goes further,
for it shows Parker trying some experiments in religious drama. He
employs the leit-motif in Wagnerian fashion. It was possibly the
writing of *St. Christopher* that led him to try opera a few years
later.

Like many of his works, *Mona* was written for a definite purpose.
Parker was able to do this, generally without sacrificing quality. Commissions, or prize contests, never drew hack work from him. The
directors of the Metropolitan Opera House in New York offered a
prize of $10,000 for an opera by an American composer, with an Eng-
lish text. Parker heard of the offer and was tempted. His friend Brian
Hooker, professor of English at Yale, wrote the libretto—the tale of
Mona, princess of Britain in the days of the invasion, torn between
her love for the son of the Roman governor and her hatred of the
Roman conquerors.

The judges (and his teacher Chadwick was one of them) agreed
that no other decision was possible than to give the prize to *Mona.*
The opera was produced March 14, 1912. There had been American
operas at the Metropolitan before—Converse's *Pipe of Desire* in 1910
and Herbert's *Natoma* a year later (by the Philadelphia-Chicago
Company)—but neither had made as profound an impression as *Mona.*
The performance was inadequate, but the gravity and vitality of the
music, its lovely blending with the words of the text, were apparent

to all who heard it. Whatever the reasons, box office or politics, *Mona* was dropped after its first short season, and has never been heard again. Whether Gatti-Casazza and the directors of the opera house gave the work which they themselves had called into being a fair chance, is a question that seems almost to answer itself.

For *Mona* is truly a fine and a great work. Uneven, yes, but its unevenness is almost its charm. It is Parker's own music, rarely synthetic. While it is obviously written by a man who knows his choral writing best, its very churchliness often establishes precisely the right atmosphere. It has telling moments—Mona's narrative of her dream, the love duet, the prelude to the third act, the orchestral passage that follows Mona's killing of her lover. In *Mona*, Parker is Parker, and no one else.

A year or so later he wrote another opera; like *Mona* to a libretto by Hooker. Like *Mona*, it won a $10,000 prize. The work was *Fairyland*, and the prize was offered in 1913 by the National Federation of Music Clubs. The opera was performed six times in Los Angeles at the Federation Biennial in 1915. Lighter than *Mona*, *Fairyland* offers charming, unaffected music.

Of course, Parker was not primarily a composer for the stage, any more than he was a symphonist. His field was the oratorio and the choir loft. His orchestral conception seems often to be confused with his feeling for the tones and color combinations of the organ. His orchestra sometimes comes between his chorus and his hearers. Yet the music itself is large, healthy, alive, and probably enduring. Daniel Gregory Mason has described Parker's music as "so facile, and so voluminous, and on the whole so characterless." With this I cannot agree; at any rate in regard to those things by which we know him best. Undramatic, poor theatre, *Mona* may be; but never characterless. Parker's own character—strong willed, intolerant, individual—is stamped on every page of his major works.

I once asked Mrs. H. H. A. BEACH (1867–1944) if she ever resented being called an American composer. "No," she answered, "but I would rather be called a composer." I might have put it still stronger, and asked if she minded being known as an American woman composer. For whether we are to judge Mrs. Beach for her music alone, or for the added interest of her nationality and sex, the fact remains that she was the outstanding composer among American women, a highly talented and able creative musician.

Mrs. Beach was the youngest of the Boston group, the little sister who accomplished much on her own; who, as a youthful prodigy, caused the intolerant old John S. Dwight to scratch his head and to bow in admiration of her extraordinary gifts. She once fooled Dwight and his friend Otto Dresel. Neither of them could see much good in Brahms. One day the young pianist played them a *Capriccio* that had just come to America. They were enchanted; what was it? who wrote it? "Brahms," said the young Miss Cheney. Dwight and Dresel choked and muttered that it was the best thing he ever wrote.

When Theodore Thomas engaged her to play the Mendelssohn D Minor Concerto with his orchestra in Boston, she had to go to Worcester for rehearsal. Thomas was playing there the day before the Boston concert. She was seventeen at the time, and Thomas thought he would make things easy for her in the last movement. He started the orchestra at a leisurely tempo. At the entrance of the piano, the young artist started at her usual pace, and the startled Thomas had to follow.

Mrs. Beach was born September 5, 1867—Amy Marcy Cheney. Her birthplace was the little village of Henniker, New Hampshire, and her parents were New Englanders of colonial descent. She was musical from babyhood. She could sing songs when she was scarcely more than a year old, and her memory was so accurate that she always remembered a song exactly as she first heard it. She would rebel whenever she heard it sung differently. She was extremely sensitive to melody—anything sad or sentimental upset her. When she must be punished, her mother would play Gottschalk's *Last Hope*, instead of giving her a New England spanking.

Amy started to play the piano when she was four; two years later she had lessons. She insisted on having them from her mother, who was herself a singer and pianist. In a short time the child mastered *études* of Heller and Czerny, the Handel *Harmonious Blacksmith* Variations, several Beethoven Sonatas, some Chopin Waltzes, and Dresel's arrangements of Mendelssohn songs. And she had written some pieces of her own.

When she was eight the family moved to Boston, where instruction continued under various teachers—Ernst Perabo, Junius Hill, Carl Baermann. She had some harmony lessons with Hill when she was fourteen. Then she gave herself some training without outside help. She became so engrossed in her study of instrumentation that she made her own translation of treatises by Berlioz and Gavaert. At about this time her father and mother had to decide between Europe and America for their daughter's final education. They chose America.

She made her first public appearance in Boston when she was sixteen, and played the Moscheles G Minor Concerto with a symphony orchestra. The next year she was soloist with the Boston Symphony, and played the Chopin F Minor. Then she played Mendelssohn with Thomas. In 1885, when she was eighteen, she married Dr. Beach, a physician who achieved distinction as a surgeon and medical authority. Until his death in 1910, Mrs. Beach and her husband lived in Boston.

The year after Dr. Beach died, Mrs. Beach went to Europe to stay for almost four years, playing in concert and introducing her works in Germany. She played her own Piano Concerto with orchestras in Hamburg, Leipzig, and Berlin. Her *Gaelic* Symphony was heard in Hamburg and Leipzig, and she played the piano part of her Quintet, and the Sonata for violin and piano, in various cities. The years abroad were something of a triumph. Foreign critics were more than friendly —many of them reviewed her works with enthusiasm. She achieved an international standing.

Upon her return from abroad she busied herself with composing and playing in concert. She had an energy for work that seemed almost inexhaustible—and yet she was never hasty or feverish. She once wrote me that it seemed as if a century must separate the present from her earlier life, devoted mostly to composition in her own home, with only occasional concert appearances.

"I have literally lived the life of two people," she explained, "one a pianist, the other a writer. Anything more unlike than the state of mind demanded by these two professions I could not imagine! When I do one kind of work, I shut the other up in a closed room and lock the door, unless I happen to be composing for the piano, in which case there is a connecting link. One great advantage, however, in this kind of life, is that one never grows stale, but there is always a continual interest and freshness from the change back and forth.

"My outdoor summer life is another story, and a most delightful one. Life in the woods is my greatest joy, with my friends and all that they have meant to me in these past years."

Mrs. Beach is best known to the layman for her songs—*Ah, Love, but a Day, The Year's at the Spring,* and *Ecstasy.* She composed over a hundred and fifty songs, but these named are the most sung, and in many ways her best song writing, for they are direct, free from the fondness for overelaboration that she often indulged. Musicians know her by her instrumental works. She published the *Gaelic* Symphony, a Piano Concerto, a Violin and Piano Sonata, a Quintet for piano and strings, a Theme and Variations for flute and string quartet, and a Suite for two pianos, founded on old Irish melodies. In addition, there are suites and many individual pieces for piano.

She was fond of writing music for the church. Her first important work (Opus 5) was a Mass, for soli, chorus, orchestra, and organ, which was first performed by the Handel and Haydn Society under Zerrahn in 1892. There are a number of anthems, and a complete Episcopal service.

She was commissioned to write a work for the dedication of the Woman's Building at the Chicago World's Fair, and she composed a *Festival Jubilate* in six weeks. In 1898 she wrote a *Song of Welcome* for the Trans-Mississippi Exposition at Omaha, and in 1915 a *Panama Hymn* for the Panama-Pacific Exposition in San Francisco.

She used folk songs in many of her works—the *Gaelic* Symphony is made from Gaelic themes. Yet she never felt that she was writing nationalistic music when she used national songs. She merely adapted for her own purposes melodies she happened to like. With her, nationalism was something subtler than using Indian or other tunes found in America—Americanism was something that could not be acquired by thinking about it. She used bird calls, Eskimo songs, Balkan themes, anything that happened to appeal to her. But she was not an Eskimo, or a Balkan, and she knew she was not writing Eskimo or Balkan music.

This theory is typical of the common-sense attitude she had in regard to many things, notably her music. She wrote sincerely, according to her thoughts, and she had the technical equipment to express those thoughts fluently. She lived to be seventy-seven years old, and died in New York, December 27, 1944.

3. EDWARD MACDOWELL (1861–1908)

I

In *Lonely Americans*, Rollo Walter Brown calls MacDowell "A Listener to the Winds." An apt characterization, for MacDowell was at heart a romanticist, at his best as a poet of nature. He caught the moods of the forest, the fields, and the ocean. He could express those moods in a way that made us understand what he was talking about. He was the first of the Americans to speak consistently a musical speech that was definitely his own.

It is not an easy matter to appraise MacDowell fairly in his relation to American music, or to the music of the world. Whenever American music is mentioned, the name of MacDowell comes forward immediately as the foremost of our composers. Yet there are many doubters who ask embarrassing questions. Does he loom largest because he was the greatest in his own time, when there were fewer good composers in America? Perhaps he would be less significant in company with those who would be his colleagues if he were living today. And, as for the rest of the musical world, has he held his own with Grieg, with whom he can best be compared, musically and temperamentally?

These are questions on which there can be many opinions. Some think that much music has been written in America since MacDowell's time which is fully as distinctive as that of MacDowell—maybe more distinctive. Since there are hundreds of well-equipped, talented composers today, against the dozen or so of MacDowell's time, we do not hear as much of individuals as we did of MacDowell. And as for Grieg, many feel that the Norwegian's star is constantly rising, while MacDowell's is gradually setting.

MacDowell's reputation today is somewhat in the same situation as that of his lesser brother artist, Nevin. There is always a penalty to be paid for remaining long in the public esteem. When we produce a famous artist in this country he must be idealized by his disciples, and belittled by his opponents. Common-sense appraisal is all too rare in the case of public heroes. And so with MacDowell—he must be a world master in the eyes of some, an overrated Pigmy to others.

Shortly after MacDowell's death, Lawrence Gilman in his revised edition of the biography he had first written in 1905 stated that he knew of no piano sonatas since the death of Beethoven that could compare with the four of MacDowell for passion, dignity, and breadth of style.

Paul Rosenfeld, writing in 1929 on *American Music*, devotes an early chapter to MacDowell.[1] A few quotations will suffice:

Were it not for MacDowell's celtic descent, one might almost be tempted to attribute this group-wide weakness for the odors of sanctity to a racial strain, so many instances arising in which saxondom and snobbery . . . seem almost synonymous. . . . In music, this weakness took the form of sentimentality. The feelings entertained about life by him seem to have remained uncertain; and while fumbling for them he seems regularly to have succumbed to "nice" and "respectable" emotions, conventional, accepted by and welcome to, the best people. It is shocking to find how full of vague poesy he is. Where his great romantic brethren, Brahms, Wagner, and Debussy, are direct and sensitive, clearly and tellingly expressive, MacDowell minces and simpers, maidenly and ruffled. He is nothing if not a daughter of the American revolution. . . .

And still, MacDowell brought something into the world not hitherto present in it; not, at least, as music. Impure in style and weak in spirit though they are; indeed of anything but the first water, a group of his compositions, particularly the ballade-like Norse sonata, certain of the more vigorous Sea Pieces, and the atmospheric Legend and Dirge of the Indian Suite for Orchestra, *actually have musical value* [the italics are mine]. . . . They constitute a beginning. And nature does nothing by bounds.

Somewhere between these two views there must be middle ground. It is surely too much to term MacDowell the composer of the greatest piano sonatas since Beethoven, nor can he be dismissed lightly as a mere beginner, whom we may patronize and pat gently on the back. Moreover, he was far from musically polite to the best people—when he came back from Europe in the late eighties his playing and his compositions were the dismay of many correct Bostonians.

There are a few important points that may be disposed of at the start. MacDowell need never be put forward with the chauvinism he

[1] Paul Rosenfeld, *An Hour with American Music*, J. B. Lippincott & Co.

hated so heartily himself. He is probably the first of our creative musicians for whom we need make no allowances for lack of early training. None of his limitations was caused by his being an American. Whether he shall eventually be judged great or small, he may be considered simply as a composer, without our being kind to him because he was our countryman. And after we have put him under the magnifying glass, stripped him of the idealization that has been wrapped about him by admirers more zealous than wise, he will emerge with several of his banners still flying.

II

If there must be comparisons, and it is often necessary to have a place to hang our opinions, Grieg and MacDowell have enough in common to warrant our looking at them side by side. Their artistic statures are comparable. Each had a style that is easily recognized. Both had a feeling for melodic and harmonic combinations that were individual. Each has had a host of imitators—so many that the terms "MacDowellian" and "Grieg-like" have become generic.

There are, of course, essential differences. One is strong where the other is weak. MacDowell seeks a broader pattern than Grieg in his sonatas, but in seeking breadth he sometimes grows diffuse. Grieg can accomplish more with fewer means. MacDowell is more heroic in his conception; when Grieg grows dramatic he seldom achieves effects that are more than theatrical. In his F Major Violin Sonata, Grieg is compact, to the point, vital in every phrase. In the C Minor there is more abandon, but not the closeknit perfection of the lesser work. Grieg's single Piano Sonata cannot compare in breadth of conception with any of the four that MacDowell wrote, yet Grieg shows more control of his medium, a far more distinct utterance.

Both are best as miniaturists. In larger works they come to frequent climaxes, and then make a fresh start. They are short breathed. Their themes are episodic in their treatment and development. Intense individualists, each limited the scope of his appeal.

For MacDowell did indeed pay a high price for his individuality. Markedly original, he guarded his manner of speech jealously. In his latter years he often told his friends that he avoided hearing music, so that he would not be in danger of showing its influence. Possibly this explains the limitations of his own music, for all composers derive from some source. If they are great they add something of their own to the pattern of their predecessors; the fact that they were influenced does not in itself prevent them from saying something new.

It would be interesting to gather statistics that would show how kind the years have been to MacDowell and Grieg. Without them, and it would be impossible to make them accurate, comparison is mere guesswork. Surely the sparkling though shallow Piano Concerto of Grieg is more played today than either of those MacDowell wrote. Probably this may be explained by the fewer difficulties of Grieg's Concerto. MacDowell wrote nothing for orchestra that is heard as often as Grieg's *Peer Gynt* Suites, for the MacDowell orchestral works are not appearing on programs as often as they did twenty years ago. Yet in the field of the piano, MacDowell's pieces seem to be holding their own—especially the smaller ones. The sonatas, particularly the *Tragica*, are considerably played on recital programs, and amateur pianists and pupils still play the *Woodland Sketches*, a few of the virtuoso *études*, the *Sea Pieces*, and many others of a type in which MacDowell was altogether inimitable. Certainly his music today is more familiar to the music-loving public than that of any other American composer of serious music. Whether his works are as familiar as Grieg's is another matter, and not particularly important.

And then, the nationalist question. Was MacDowell an American composer in his idiom? Many say that he was more Celtic than American—his German training with Raff made him follow Teuton models. An obvious contradiction here, for it is apparent to anyone that German training (and he was educated in Paris before he went to Germany) did not kill the obvious Celtic traits in his music. What is an American, anyway? Aren't we all Scotch-Americans, Irish-Americans, English-Americans, German-Americans, Jewish-Americans, or whatever our ancestry may be? MacDowell's ancestry was Scotch—he himself was an American. If he showed Scotch tendencies in his music, was his work any the less American?

In his lectures at Columbia (some of these since published as *Critical and Historical Essays*),[2] MacDowell himself disposed of nationalism in music:

[2] Edward MacDowell, *Critical and Historical Essays*, Arthur P. Schmidt Co.

. . . nationalism, so-called, is merely an extraneous thing that has no part in pure art. For if we take any melody, even of the most pronounced national type, and merely eliminate the characteristic turns, affectations, or mannerisms, the theme becomes simply music, and retains no touch of nationality. We may even go further; for if we retain the characteristic mannerisms of dress, we may harmonize a folk song in such a manner that it will belie its origin, and by means of this powerful factor (an essentially modern invention) we may even transform a Scotch song, with all its "snap" and character, into a Chinese song, or give it an Arabian flavour.

Of course, he wrote an *Indian Suite* for orchestra, in which he used Indian themes, but I think he never seriously thought he was writing American music just because he used Indian melodies. He once said to Hamlin Garland: "I do not believe in 'lifting' a Navajo theme and furbishing it into some kind of a musical composition and calling it American music. Our problem is not so simple as all that."

Then again, in a lecture, he said: "What we must arrive at is the youthful optimistic vitality and the undaunted tenacity of spirit that characterizes the American man. That is what I hope to see echoed in American music."

As for the music MacDowell left us, Mr. Rosenfeld is correct in saying that it is not of the first water, if we mean by that the music of a Bach, a Beethoven, a Wagner, or a Brahms. But as one of the best of the lesser poets, MacDowell produced music of the first order, some of it charming, some of it stirring. Within its limitations, it is the work of a truly creative genius. Between the opus numbers 9 and 62, which include the bulk of his published work, there is much that will live for many years to come. Some of his music may have fallen by the wayside, but the best of it is still vital.

III

It is by his piano music that we know him best. There are four Sonatas: the *Tragica*, Opus 45 (1893); the *Eroica*, Opus 50 (1895); the *Norse*, Opus 57 (1900); and the *Keltic*, Opus 59 (1901). The last two were dedicated to Grieg, who acknowledged the dedication of the *Norse* Sonata with a charming attempt at English:

My Dear Sir:

Will you permit me in bad English to express my best thanks for your kind letter and for the simpathi you feel for my music. Of course it will be a great honor and pleasure for me to accept your dedication.

Some years ago I thought it possible to shake hands with you in your own country. But unfortunately my delicat health does not seem to agree. At all events, if we are not to meet, I am glad to read in the papers of your artistical success in Amerika.

MacDowell once said that if a composer's ideas do not imperatively demand treatment in the sonata form, if his first theme is not actually dependent upon his second and side themes for its poetic fulfillment, he has composed a potpourri rather than a sonata. Certainly Mac-Dowell has lived up to this principle in his own sonatas, for in each of them the themes are related and dependent on each other. There is always a nobility of conception, and an impatience with the limits of the piano that leads him to seek orchestral effects.

There was no definite program suggested in the *Tragica* Sonata, but the music itself is sufficiently vivid to enable the listener to understand what kind of thoughts the composer was thinking when he wrote it. MacDowell said that in the first three movements he aimed to express tragic details, and in the *Finale* a generalization—"to heighten the darkness of tragedy by making it follow closely on the heels of triumph." He probably wrote the third movement first—the *Largo*; for he played it in Boston at a recital in 1891, two years before the work as a whole was published. There is a beautiful dignity in this movement, a pathos which never sinks to bathos. He shows an artistic kinship with Rachmaninoff; there is a similar feeling for chordal effects between the younger Russian and the American.

The *Eroica* Sonata (dedicated to William Mason) bears the motto "*Flos regum Arthurus.*" Though admittedly program music, Mac-Dowell intended it to be less of an actual depiction of the subject than a commentary. He had in mind the Arthur legend. The first movement was the coming of Arthur. The *Scherzo* suggested a knight in the woods surrounded by elves. MacDowell's conception of Guinevere was the basis of the third movement, and the last was the passing of Arthur.

In the *Norse* Sonata MacDowell attempted to free himself further from the restrictions of form. In painting the barbaric feeling of the Norse sagas he extended the span of his phrases, his chord formations widened, and he achieved a still more epic breadth.

The fourth Sonata was the *Keltic*, to which he attached these lines:

> Who minds now Keltic tales of yore,
>   Dark Druid rhymes that thrall;
> Deirdré's song, and wizard lore
>   Of great Cuchullin's fall.

MacDowell wrote of this sonata:

Like the third, this fourth sonata is more of a "bardic" rhapsody on the subject than an attempt at actual presentation of it, although I have made use of all the suggestion of tone-painting in my power—just as the bard would have reinforced *his* speech with gesture and facial expression.

And it is true that MacDowell's music does heighten the meaning of the poem. He felt that a poem was far more valuable as a suggestion for instrumental music than as the text of a song, where syllables are generally distorted. As a text for an instrumental work, a poem of four words may contain enough suggestion for four pages of music.

Whether or not MacDowell sacrificed clarity and directness in reaching out so far for the nobler conception, the broader outline, is another matter. Surely he is never as tidy as Grieg—in the *Finale* of the *Tragica* he does not seem to proceed as directly to his goal as Grieg would have gone. Yet mere tidiness is not always inspiring, and Mac-Dowell showed a courage in his sonatas at which we well may wonder. If the sonatas do not thrill posterity, they are none the less the real expression of a truly poetic nature that sought epic forms for its outlet.

The *First Modern Suite*, Opus 10, was MacDowell's first published work. Since it was first issued in Germany in 1883 the composer made a number of revisions, and it still remains one of his well-known works. It has a number of characteristics that mark the later MacDowell, though the intense individualities are missing. The Prelude is probably played the most; its pianistic flow, not too difficult for many amateurs, makes it grateful to the player.

The two Piano Concertos (the first, A Minor, Opus 15, 1884; the second, D Minor, Opus 23, 1890) are both comparatively early works. As such they are brilliant, but they show the influences of his training—

marked fluency and ease, but not the imagination of his later works. It was really not until after 1890 that he showed his true colors— though some of the pieces written before that date have shown healthy life: *The Scotch Poem*, *The Eagle*, and the song *Menie* rank with his best work. But the *Twelve Virtuoso Studies* in 1894 began to show the real MacDowell as a composer for the piano. The *Novelette*, the *Improvisation*, and the *Polonaise* are among the finest work he has done. The *Woodland Sketches* were first published in 1896. *To a Wild Rose*, and *To a Water Lily* may have haunted him with their popu- larity, but they are exquisite. The *Sea Pieces* were issued two years later. Here is MacDowell at the height of his powers, lyric and dra- matic. He keeps within the limits that prevent his losing his breath, and within a smaller frame he writes pieces that are small only in their length; large in their ideas. The last two opus numbers on his list were the *Fireside Tales* and the *New England Idyls*. The next to the last of the idyls was *From a Log Cabin:*

> A house of dreams untold,
> It looks out over the whispering tree-tops
> And faces the setting sun.

Prophetic lines when we know how near he was to his own tragedy when he wrote them. Maybe he knew it, too, and gave us one of the sincerest bits of contemplation in the literature of music.

MacDowell wrote several major works for orchestra, but it was not his best medium. He liked best to write for piano. He felt that the modern pianoforte had developed to a degree where it would not be likely to change in the future, and whatever he wrote for it would be played the same both in the present and tomorrow. As for the orchestra, a friend, T. P. Currier, in an article in the *Musical Quarterly* (Jan- uary, 1915), reported him as saying:

> It's one thing to write works for the orchestra, and another to get them performed. There isn't much satisfaction in having a thing played once in two or three years. If I write large works for the piano I can play them my- self as often as I like.

Nevertheless, his orchestral works were often performed, even though we do not hear them as much as we would like today. His first purely orchestral piece was a symphonic poem *Hamlet and Ophelia*,

Edward MacDowell
(See pages 323–344)

Original Manuscript of MacDowell's *Told at Sunset*, No. 10 of His
Woodland Sketches

(See page 330)

Opus 22 (1885). Three years later he published another, *Lancelot and Elaine*, Opus 25. *Lamia*, after Keats, was written in 1888–89 but not published until after MacDowell's death. *The Saracens* and *The Lovely Alda*, two fragments after the Song of Roland, were numbered Opus 30 and published in 1891. According to Gilman, MacDowell originally intended these two pieces as movements of a Roland symphony. Four movements of the first Suite for orchestra, Opus 42, were published in 1891; the third piece (*In October*), although written at the same time as the others, was issued as a "supplement" to the Suite in 1893.

After the second (*Indian*) Suite, Opus 48, MacDowell wrote no more for orchestra. It was a fitting climax to his list in this field, for it is a fine work. The *Dirge*, like the *Largo* of the *Tragica* Sonata, has a nobility that makes grandeur in anguish. In explanation of his sources, the composer wrote:

The thematic material of this work has been suggested for the most part by melodies of the North American Indians. Their occasional similarity to northern European themes seems to the author a direct testimony in corroboration of Thorfinnkarlsefin's Saga.

The opening theme of No. 3 [*In War-time*], for instance, is very similar to the (presumably Russian) one made use of by Rimsky-Korsakow in the 3rd movement of his symphony "Antar."

MacDowell also said of the different movements: "If separate titles . . . are desired, they should be arranged as follows: I. Legend. II. Love song. III. In War-time. IV. Dirge. V. Village festival."

The Suite was first performed by Emil Paur and the Boston Symphony Orchestra (to whom it was dedicated) in New York City, January 23, 1896. MacDowell's own views on nationalism in music show clearly that he did not intend to write American music by using Indian themes, nor did he think that such material could be harmonized in a manner that would make it sound like the originals from which it was taken. He may, of course, have been experimenting; but he was no doubt content to catch the spirit of his theme, the joys and sorrows of a vanishing race. This he did most eloquently; the *Dirge* can rank with the funeral marches of the masters.

Although he was never satisfied with music's ability to match the syllables and inflection of a poem, MacDowell's songs show a rare ability to interpret the spirit and mood of the verses he chose for setting. Something of a poet himself, he was often happiest when he wrote his own poems for his songs, for then he had the music in mind as he fashioned his text. Aside from his choruses, he published over forty songs, some of them masterpieces. Writing in 1900, Henry T. Finck thought that Grieg and MacDowell were the greatest living song writers. But there was Strauss to be reckoned with, and we must remember that Finck never liked Brahms. Yet *Menie* (1889), *Thy Beaming Eyes* (1890), the poignantly emotional setting of Howell's *The Sea* (1893), and the tender treatment of his own poem *The Swan Bent Low to the Lily* (1898), are exquisite songs, created by a man who knew what a good song should be, without compromises with what singers like to sing.

IV

To understand MacDowell fully, to grasp his powers and to appreciate his limitations, it is necessary to know of his life and his personality. With all true geniuses, their character and environment shine through their writings. That is, if their work is sincere; and with MacDowell, whatever he wrote was himself. He cannot be separated from his music.

He had advantages that have not been given to many Americans—either before or after him. His talents were recognized by his parents at the start, and everything was done to foster and train his gifts. While he was still in his formative years he entered the Paris Conservatoire, where two years of rigid training gave him a groundwork that was the basis of everything he accomplished technically. Other Americans had studied abroad, but generally for polishing touches to finish what they had acquired at home. MacDowell had the best, the strictest training from almost the very beginning. Mrs. MacDowell once told me what this training had meant to him:

One of the most fortunate things that ever came to him was that period with Marmontel at the Paris Conservatory, where he had to learn rapidity and facility in writing notes, although at that time there was no idea of his ever being a composer. But it was part of the routine. They turned out a musician, whether he played the violin, piano, or sang, enormously equipped with a musical education. But the work was terrific.

It meant at eighteen when he went into Raff's composition class, although still the piano was his principal goal, that he outstripped all the other students, most of them men ten or fifteen years older than he. Outstripped them, I mean, in actual mechanical facility. Complicated fugue he could scratch off on the blackboard just as I might write a sentence in a letter. I don't have to think how to spell words, although sometimes I don't spell them correctly, nor did he have to think of the possible combinations that were allowed.

He was born December 18, 1861, in New York City, at 220 Clinton Street. He was the third son of Thomas MacDowell and his wife, Frances Knapp. The father was of Scotch ancestry, the mother Irish. There was a Quaker background, and probably the fact that he himself had not been allowed to become a painter, made his father sympathetic with his boy's extraordinary talents for music. Edward had his first piano lessons when he was eight—principally from a South American, Juan Buitrago. Buitrago was a great friend of Teresa Carreño, and on one of her trips to New York she became interested in the talented boy and gave him some lessons herself. It was a friendship that lasted for many years.

When Edward was fifteen it was decided that he should go abroad for study, and his mother took him to Paris. For a year he worked privately with Marmontel, and then his teacher urged him to enter the competition for a scholarship at the Conservatoire. He won it, and became a regular pupil in 1877. One of his fellow students was a lad with queer ideas—named Debussy. It was about this time that he had to decide between music and painting for his career. So that he could better understand the lectures at the Conservatoire, he attended a class in French given by a teacher who had a nose like Cyrano de Bergerac. It was too great a temptation for young Edward's facile pencil. Behind his textbook he sketched the teacher. The master saw that he was inattentive and demanded to see what he was doing. The drawing was tremblingly produced, and the teacher was overcome by the striking likeness. He took it to a friend, one of the famous French artists, who immediately offered to give the boy free lessons, and to pay for his support while he was teaching him.

Music or painting? It was not an easy choice. Here was a painter saying that he had a great career ahead of him, and Marmontel insisting that he should stick at his music. Yet they had come to Paris for music, he had worked hard and done well, so the family council agreed with Edward that he had better keep to his idea of becoming a pianist.

In the summer of 1878 he decided he had had enough of the Paris Conservatoire. After hearing Nicholas Rubinstein in a concert, he told his mother that he could never learn to play like that if he stayed in Paris. So to Germany to the Stuttgart Conservatory, where things were no more to his liking than they had been in Paris. He would have to forget all he had learned in Paris, and then start over again. A friend suggested Heymann in Frankfort, so to Frankfort they went, and after a few lessons during the summer with Ehlert in Wiesbaden, he entered Heymann's class at the Frankfort Conservatory in the fall. Here MacDowell was eminently happy, for he began to study composition seriously with Joachim Raff. Raff saw the possibilities of his gifts, and it was through his influence that MacDowell eventually decided to become a composer. He also formed a friendship with his teacher that was to be one of his fondest memories.

By 1880 he was a thoroughly trained musician, a finished artist. When Heymann retired from the conservatory in that year, he thought so highly of MacDowell's gifts as a pianist that he recommended him as his successor. But the youth of the young American, and politics, kept him from getting the appointment. He continued his studies with Heymann privately, and began to take pupils himself. Some of them were of the German nobility, who bored him excessively. He was also beginning to compose. The *First Modern Suite* was written between lessons, as a response to a sort of challenge on Raff's part. Raff had been disgusted with his mechanical exercises in composition, and told him to try something real. The Suite was Edward's answer. He wrote the *Second Modern Suite* on the train rides he had to take to visit his pupils.

His first Piano Concerto was also composed to show Raff what he could do. Raff paid him an unexpected call one evening, and abruptly asked him what he had been working on. "A concerto," fibbed MacDowell. "Bring it to the next lesson," said Raff. Fortunately, the next lesson was postponed several weeks, but MacDowell had to sit up late to have it ready when Raff was able to see him.

In 1882, when MacDowell was twenty-one, Raff urged him to call on Liszt at Weimar. Liszt received him cordially. D'Albert was there at the time, and he played the orchestral part of the concerto on a second piano. Liszt told D'Albert that he would have to bestir himself if he did not want to be outdone by the young American. MacDowell left some other manuscripts, and soon had a letter from Liszt telling him that he had recommended the *First Modern Suite* to the General Society of German Musicians. MacDowell was invited to play it at the society's meetings, July 11, 1882. Through Liszt's recommendations the Suite and the first Concerto were published by Breitkopf & Haertel.

But just before this Raff died, and MacDowell was heartbroken. He had grown to love his teacher, who had told him that his music would be played long after his own was forgotten. Raff could not see his pupil's triumph before the august body of German musicians, and it took much of the joy from the great event.

With Liszt's encouragement MacDowell began to give almost all of his time to composition. Conductors of the *kur-orchester*, the little bands at the health resorts, tried his new works at rehearsals, and he was able to gain firsthand experience. In 1884 he returned to America for a visit, and for a more important matter; he was to be married in Waterford, Connecticut, to an American girl who had been his pupil in Germany—Marian Nevins. The wedding took place in July, and the young couple went back to Europe, living first in Frankfort, where MacDowell began his second Concerto. In 1885 they moved to Wiesbaden, where in another year they bought a small cottage near the edge of a wood. He had already finished the second Concerto, and before that he had composed *Hamlet* and *Ophelia*. In the cottage he wrote *Lancelot and Elaine*, *Lamia*, *The Saracens*, *The Lovely Alda*, and a number of piano pieces. Moreover, his friend Carreño was telling America of its young music maker, by playing his works at home.

v

Liszt's death in 1886 was a sad blow. After Raff, it removed a friend who had already done much for him, and could and would do still more. It may have been one of the factors that determined him to return permanently to America in 1888, although he probably wanted to come back to his native country anyway. Rollo Brown claims that he wanted to prove that there is a place for the serious musician in the United States.

He first thought of living in New York, but B. J. Lang helped to persuade him that he would be better off in Boston. So for eight years, from 1888, he lived in the Hub as a composer, teacher, and concert pianist. He was not too anxious to be a pianist, for he had let himself get out of practice, but he was told that he would have to make his works known by playing them, and that if he wanted pupils he would have to establish his reputation as a concert pianist. It meant taking time from his composing, but he did it in spite of the work.

On the whole, the eight years in Boston were happy ones, although it was not until his third season there that he tasted financial success, and his studio was a mecca for pupils. Also, he was not altogether temperamentally fitted for the type of comradeship and social contacts that Americans demand of their famous artists. Delightful to his friends, he was in a shell when he met mere acquaintances. Shy to the extreme, he really suffered among people he did not know well. A brilliant conversationalist when at ease, he was awkward when he did not feel at home. Though he was blessed with a sharp sense of humor, he could never enjoy the back-slapping methods of the heavy-handed.

It is an easy matter to construct what should prove an accurate picture of MacDowell from the many printed memories written by those who knew him. T. P. Currier's recollections in the January, 1915, *Musical Quarterly*, Rollo Brown's chapter in *Lonely Americans*, several passages from Hamlin Garland, and some articles by W. H. Humiston afford intimate portraits of this sensitive, charming aristocrat. Brown calls him "the handsomest thoroughbred that ever stepped up to address a golf-ball." Currier writes of the Boston years:

Gradually the figure of "MacDowell the composer" became a familiar one on the Common's walks and the near-by streets. It is interesting to recall the change in his personal appearance that came about after several months' residence in Boston. For some time he had clung, innocently enough, as it afterward proved, to the high, full-crowned felt hat, the rather fiercely curled moustache, and the goatee. . . . Then suddenly he appeared in a derby hat, which became him extremely well; and shortly afterward the goatee vanished. Commenting one day on these changes as gratifying, to my eye at least, he replied in genuinely injured tones, "Why didn't you say so, long ago?"

And in another place in the article:

He looked strong. And his strength was practically evinced by his surprisingly vital hand-grasp. . . . MacDowell, had he not had an innate aversion to exercise for the mere sake of physical well-being, might easily have had a body to match his uncommonly strong and active brain.

Garland tells of his first meeting with him,[3] in 1894:

MacDowell, who had retreated behind the piano, now came forward to meet me, shyly, boyishly, one hand sliding along the edge of the piano as a child runs a hand along a banister to relieve his embarrassment. He was a glorious young figure. His scintillant, laughing blue eyes, his abundant brown hair and, beyond all, his smile and his jocund voice, delighted me.

The years in Boston were punctuated with concert tours, since his playing, especially of his own music, was much in demand. He enjoyed his independence, and was loath to tie himself down to a regular routine position when he was invited by President Seth Low, and the trustees of Columbia University, to come to New York and take charge of the new department of music, in 1896. Yet there were several reasons that were worth considering. A guaranteed income, a chance to put into effect some of his ideas for the education of American youth, and an opportunity to give musical training of the first order to some who could not afford to pay for it elsewhere. And so he notified the trustees of his acceptance, and from the fall of 1896 he occupied the Robert Center chair of music at Columbia, endowed with a fund of a hundred thousand dollars by its benefactors. Maybe he had his own doubts of the outcome, but few of his friends realized the fatal mistake he was making.

For it really was a fatal mistake. He was not temperamentally fitted for an organization job. He was an individualist, he did not understand university procedure. As Finck remarked after his resignation, it is never wise to harness Pegasus. Though he was a brilliant teacher for brilliant pupils, lecturing and teaching the less intelligent was for him hopeless drudgery.

[3] "Roadside Meetings of a Literary Nomad," by Hamlin Garland: *The Bookman*, March, 1930.

The first years at Columbia went well enough. Seth Low wanted him because he was an individualist, and it was to the glory of the University to have him there. MacDowell worked like a slave—lecturing on the history and aesthetics of music, and teaching classes in harmony and composition—correcting exercises with meticulous care, consulting with students, and attending to matters of routine. For a season or so he conducted New York's Mendelssohn Glee Club. In a year he had an assistant—Leonard McWhood, who had been his pupil. In 1899, Gustav Hinrichs was engaged to conduct the student orchestra and chorus. And all the while MacDowell was planning and dreaming of what a university music department should be, especially in its relation to teaching other branches of the fine arts.

VI

Exactly what happened to puncture this state of affairs, I do not know. Probably there were a number of factors that led to the final disaster. There are, of course, printed records of the controversy, newspaper accounts, letters, and records of trustee meetings. But most of the discussions that led up to the break were held verbally between President Butler and MacDowell, and the really inside story may never be known. Maybe there is no inside story. Possibly the printed records are, after all, complete.

I have consulted all the documents in the case, read the contemporary newspaper reports and comments, and talked to his assistants and a number of his associates and pupils. Probably there is something to be said on both sides of the controversy, though partisans have held that MacDowell was shamefully treated. The two points of view are briefly expressed by Butler's statement that MacDowell had resigned because he wanted more time to compose, and MacDowell's retort that he was leaving because he felt his work had been futile, and that he could see no chance for conducting the kind of department with which he would care to be associated at Columbia.

When Seth Low became the first mayor of Greater New York, Nicholas Murray Butler succeeded him as president of the University in 1902. From then on, MacDowell was never comfortable. Low had understood him and sympathized with his plans, but MacDowell felt that the new administration had ideas of its own. He had visualized a department of fine arts at Columbia that would embrace not only Belles Lettres and music, but architecture, painting, and sculpture, too. No doubt Butler wanted this, but MacDowell claimed he had dismissed his ideas as impractical. When he was absent on his sabbatical year in the season of 1902–3, Butler started a reorganization according to his own ideas. Possibly either MacDowell's or Butler's plan would have achieved the same goal in the end, but each had his own way of doing things. And as Currier wrote of MacDowell in the *Musical Quarterly:*

He was not fitted by nature to cope with situations where change, or interference with plans he had set his heart on, might have seemed advisable. He could not argue. Either he must do what he wanted to do in his own way, or not at all.

When he resumed his work at Columbia in the fall of 1903, MacDowell was highly nervous; the strain of work and worry was telling on his health. Maybe his perspective was clouded. After Christmas holidays at his summer retreat in Peterboro, New Hampshire, and after much discussion with his wife, he concluded to resign, and he so informed President Butler early in January. I think he had no hard feelings. He was merely discouraged, he felt he could not do the job he had planned, and therefore decided to quit. His assistant McWhood testifies that when MacDowell told him he was resigning, he pledged McWhood to absolute secrecy. He knew that his resignation would attract attention, and he wanted to give Butler a chance to choose a successor before the president's office was swamped with the applications that would be sure to pour in.

Yet MacDowell was in a state of mind that needed only a spark to send it into flame. Somehow the news of his resignation leaked out, and two student reporters called on him. At first he wouldn't talk. But then they chided him for being a quitter, and that was too much. He had to let off steam, and evidently he did, with a fury. When he had finished, he made the naïve request that nothing of the interview be printed—but who could expect youthful reporters to miss such a scoop? They made for the office of the *Evening Post* as fast as they could get there.

The afternoon of February 3, 1904, was fateful, for on the front page of the *Post* appeared this headline:

MACDOWELL TO RESIGN

Unable to Obtain the Reorganization of Work Which He Thinks Necessary

Then followed some details of his criticism. The next morning the papers had more of the MacDowell affair. The *Times* said that he called college graduates "barbarians." "During the time of his service, he had had only three pupils with whom he was entirely satisfied." The *World* had this headline:

COLLEGE MEN BOORS, SAYS PROFESSOR

No Idealism Left in Columbia, and MacDowell Will Give Up Department of Music

And so the lid was off. If it had not been for this interview, and its publicity, the affair might never have become public, and Mac-Dowell might have retired quietly to recover from the hurt he had sustained. Anyway, there would never have been the recriminations that followed.

VII

Butler answered MacDowell a few days later, in the *Times*. In a lengthy statement, he printed a letter he had received from Mac-Dowell, stating that the interviews were incorrect and unauthorized. He had forbidden the student reporters to give one word of his conversation to the press. (There was, however, no denial that the interview had taken place.) Butler then went on to explain that MacDowell's resignation had been wholly unexpected, that it was prompted by the composer's wish to have all his time and strength for composition. That MacDowell had been a delightful colleague, and the University was losing him with the greatest regret. Moreover, the trustees had offered him a research professorship which would carry with it no duties, and MacDowell was now considering this offer. In addition, the School of Fine Arts was under consideration. Professor MacDowell was now at work upon a paper outlining the status of music in universities in general, and from this paper the University hoped to obtain valuable suggestions. MacDowell's answer came two days later, in the *Post* of February 10.

President Butler has evidently misunderstood my interview with him when he affirms that my sole object in resigning from Columbia was to have more time to write: he failed to explain the circumstances which led to my resignation. . . . There is certainly individual idealism in all universities, but the general tendency of modern education is toward materialism.

Then followed a copy of the report he was sending to the trustees.

It is with some chagrin that I have to report the small results my efforts have brought to the development of art at Columbia. The reason for this is obvious. Few colleges in the United States consider the fine arts (except "Belles Lettres" and architecture) worthy of serious consideration.

. . . .

I have tried to impress the "powers that be" with the necessity of allowing no student to enter the university without some knowledge of the fine arts. Such knowledge may be very general, and not technical. This would force upon the preparatory school the admission of fine arts to its curriculum. . . .

In order to bring to a focus the art elements existing in Columbia I proposed that music be taken out of the faculty of philosophy and architecture out of the School of Mines, and with Belles Lettres form a faculty of fine arts, to complete which, painting and sculpture would be indispensable.

Owing to my inability to persuade rich men of New York into endowing a chair of painting and sculpture, the scheme, though approved by the "powers that be," was not realized. . . . The outcome of all this was the establishment of a division in fine arts during my absence last year. In this Division of Fine Arts the inclusion of Belles Lettres and Music, including kindergarten, etc., at Teachers College, seemed ill-advised. To me, expansion in this direction, before a focus be attained, means a swamping of Columbia's individuality. The Division of Fine Arts thus acquires somewhat the nature of a co-educational department store, and tends toward materialism rather than idealism.

The research professorship offered me by the president, consisted of my lending to Columbia the use of my name, with no duties, and no salary. I immediately refused it as I was unwilling to associate my name with a policy I could not approve of.

. . . .

For seven years I have put all my energy and enthusiasm in the cause of art at Columbia, and now at last, recognizing the futility of my efforts, I have resigned the chair of music in order to resume my own belated vocation.

More fuel for the flames. The authorities at the College were out-raged. A professor whose resignation had not yet taken effect had given an official report to the press. At their next meeting the trustees accepted the resignation, and put on record an official reprimand. They regarded "Professor MacDowell's act in making public an official re-port, as an offense against propriety, a discourtesy to the Board, and a breach of that confidence which the Board always seeks to repose in every officer of the University."

MacDowell wrote a letter which he sent to each of the trustees individually. He said in part:

My letter to the trustees was a condensed repetition of a long conversa-tion I had with President Butler. My aims and ideas he dismissed as being impossible and revolutionary. He, knowing all this, prints a plausible letter calculated to make the public think that my own work was my sole reason for leaving the University. My only means of righting this was an immediate protest. . . . As to my "breach of confidence which the Board always seeks to repose in every officer of the University," I beg to say that the officers seek to repose this same trust in members of the Board; and Mr. Butler's misleading communication to the press was a far graver breach of this confidence than my using the only means in my power to correct this statement.

Nor did the matter rest here. Some time later in the spring Presi-dent Butler announced McWhood's advancement to an adjunct pro-fessorship, stating that the promotion was well earned, as McWhood had for some time borne the burden of the teaching in the department. Maybe Butler meant merely to explain that McWhood was qualified to assume greater responsibilities, but it was an unfortunate way of putting it. MacDowell himself had tried to secure promotion for his assistant some time before, and there had been no funds to provide for it. In view of this, Butler's announcement stung MacDowell deeply. To his mind he was being called a shirker, and a shirker he never was. He sent the trustees a comparative schedule, showing ex-actly how many classes both he and McWhood had conducted each week. He felt that McWhood had been disloyal to him, and he told him so in no uncertain terms. McWhood has explained his part of the affair in a paper read before the Music Teachers' National Association in 1923. Butler's statement, he said, was wholly a surprise to him. It certainly did put him in an uncomfortable position, for MacDowell was in a frame of mind to think the worst of him.

June came, and after commencement it was all over. But not for MacDowell. He was not the kind who could shrug his shoulders, and turn placidly to his job of composing. He brooded and brooded. They had said he neglected his duties; all sorts of interpretations were being put on the entire affair. To make things worse, he was knocked down by a cab on the streets and injured. He lay awake nights—thinking restless thoughts.

VIII

For a year he did some private teaching, but in the spring of 1905 the end came, as far as he was concerned. His mind refused to do any more thinking, and he gradually sank into a state where he looked vacantly out of the window, staring blankly, comprehending nothing. For over two years his was a body without a mind, until he quietly passed away at the Westminster Hotel in New York, January 23, 1908.

The Columbia affair is almost forgotten today. The University is proud of the fact that MacDowell was its first professor of music, and recently the position he occupied has been named the Edward Mac-Dowell Chair of Music. Nor is it my purpose to recount these details of a past controversy merely to make interesting reading. To my mind, the events at Columbia were prompted by a nature that is clearly reflected in MacDowell's music. Impulsive, hasty, yet generous and sensitive, he sometimes lost his sense of perspective. His music reaches out for great heights. It often achieves them, yet it frequently stops for breath on the way to the summit. There was no compromise either in his music or in MacDowell. He must be himself. He was at a loss in adapting his ideas to the ways of others, even though both were after the same object. They must take the same road, or one of them must stay at home.

And finally a brighter side. A dream of MacDowell's that has been realized through the efforts of his wife, who knew it would please him if she built what he had vaguely planned. The listener to the winds had found a place where he could hear the sounds of nature more distinctly than anywhere else; where he had the quiet to write them down in his music. With his wife he had discovered Peterboro, in the lower New Hampshire hills, and there they had bought an eighty-acre farm soon after he had gone to Columbia. He built a log cabin, his "house of dreams untold," where he went early in the summer mornings to write his *Fireside Tales,* his *New England Idyls.* He often thought of having other artists share his retreat, and he talked of the artist colony they would some day found at Peterboro.

Mrs. MacDowell has made the fulfillment of this idea her life work. Her concert tours, playing her husband's music, have been undertaken for the distinct purpose of raising funds to maintain the colony at Peterboro. Today it is the summer refuge of artists, composers, poets, and writers who come to do their work in the spot where MacDowell wrote his last two Sonatas, his *Sea Pieces,* and his later miniatures.

4. LINKS WITH THE PAST

GEORGE TEMPLETON STRONG (1856——), a close friend of Mac-Dowell, was one of the first of our composers who decided to live permanently in Europe. When MacDowell came home he tried to persuade Strong to live here, too, but after trying Boston for a year as a teacher at the New England Conservatory (1891–92), Strong was so discouraged by the failure of American composers to find recognition in their own country that he went back to Europe for good.

He was born in New York, May 26, 1856, of musical parents. His father was president of the New York Philharmonic for four years, and an amateur organist. Strong went to Leipzig in 1879, and studied with Jadassohn. He became a Liszt disciple, and often visited the great musician at Weimar. Then he went to Wiesbaden, where he saw much of the young MacDowell, and finally settled in Vevey, Switzerland.

He wrote three symphonies, each with a title: *In the Mountains, Sintram,* and *An der See.* He composed two *American Sketches* for violin and orchestra, and a symphonic poem *Undine.* The Suite for orchestra, *Die Nacht,* is in four movements: *At Sunset; Peasants' Battle March;* the shadowy, atmospheric *In Deep Woods;* and the spooky *Awakening of the Forest-Spirits.* Most important are his two works for soli, male chorus, and orchestra: *Wie ein fahrender Hornist sich ein Land erblies*, and *Die verlassene Mühle*. Later orchestral works are a symphonic poem *Le Roi Arthur*, a somber, gloomy, tragic piece of rich and heavy texture, and an *Elegie* for cello and orchestra.

In 1935, the Philadelphia Orchestra played Strong's *Chorale on a Theme by Hassler*, beautifully textured music, exquisitely scored for strings. On October 21, 1939, the composer, at the age of eighty-three, had the pleasure of sitting by the radio in Geneva, Switzerland, and hearing his *Die Nacht* played by the National Broadcasting Symphony Orchestra under Toscanini.

Strong composed much piano music, running from the style of Debussy and Ravel to the outdoor spirit of America, as expressed in the Suite *Au pays des Peaux-Rouges*, with its *Le Cow-boy humoriste* and *Chant de guerre*. His songs are effective, a number of them written to cynical texts of his own.

ARTHUR BIRD (1856–1923) was another who preferred to live abroad. He was born in Cambridge, Massachusetts, July 23, 1856, and died in Berlin, December 22, 1923. His last visit to America was in 1886, and after that he lived in Germany for the rest of his life. He studied composition with Urban and spent a year with Liszt at Weimar. He wrote a Symphony which he called *Karnevalszene*; three Suites for orchestra; two *Decimettes* for wind instruments, which won the Paderewski prize in 1901; some ballet music, and a comic opera; and numerous piano pieces and songs.

EDGAR STILLMAN KELLEY (1857–1944) really belonged to the Chadwick, Foote, and Parker group, for he dated from the time when the American composer had to work hard to make himself heard. He also reflected the German models of his student days abroad. Yet he showed a venturesome nature, and his experiments in tone color led him to discoveries interesting to his listeners, as well as to himself. One of his early works was his Chinese orchestral suite—*Aladdin*. He listened to native music in San Francisco's Chinatown, and he used oboes, muted trumpets, and mandolins to imitate the Chinese instruments. When he wrote his *New England* Symphony he based his themes on bird notes, Indian songs, and Puritan psalm tunes. For incidental music to the New York production of *Ben Hur*, in 1899, he used Greek modes.

His best-known work is his oratorio *The Pilgrim's Progress*, with text by Elizabeth Hodgkinson, based on Bunyan's allegory. It was first performed at the Cincinnati Festival of 1918, and has since been given by the New York Oratorio Society, at the Worcester Festival, and at choral festivals in England, as well as many others in America. His symphonic poem *The Pit and the Pendulum* was first heard at the Cincinnati Festival of 1925, and was shortly afterwards repeated in Portland, Oregon, where it was awarded the prize in the annual contest of the National Federation of Music Clubs. *Alice in Wonderland*, a symphonic suite, was composed for the Norfolk (Connecticut) Festival of 1919.

Kelley was born in Sparta, Wisconsin, April 14, 1857. He studied first in Chicago with Clarence Eddy, and then went to Stuttgart to work at the Conservatory. He came back to America and settled first in San Francisco, where he was organist, teacher, and music critic on one of the papers. He went east in 1890 to conduct a comic opera company. In 1892 he produced an operetta of his own—*Puritania*. It ran over one hundred nights at the Tremont Theatre in Boston. In the season of 1901–2 he was acting professor at Yale University while Horatio Parker was absent on his sabbatical year; then for eight years he was in Berlin, teaching piano and composition.

In 1910 he was awarded a Fellowship in Musical Composition by the Western College at Oxford, Ohio, and he was invited to make his home and do his work on its campus.

Kelley's eightieth birthday, in 1937, was the occasion of a widely observed celebration, and during the following months his works were given many performances throughout the country. An Edgar Stillman Kelley Society was formed to underwrite publication of works by younger American composers. Among the "younger" composers whose pieces were selected was Dr. Kelley himself, and a work of his was chosen which had lain unfinished for many years—his First Symphony. This was a programmatic composition which he called *Gulliver*. The first movement had been completed years before, and the other movements had been sketched, but it was not until his seventy-eighth year that the composer finished the work and scored it.

The first movement of *Gulliver* tells of the voyage and shipwreck. In the second movement "Gulliver Sleeps and Dreams," and in the third the Lilliputians appear playing their national anthem. This becomes a double fugue when they enmesh the "Man Mountain" with their ropes. The *finale* is a hornpipe which celebrates Gulliver's rescue and his homeward journey. The première of the Symphony was given by the NBC Symphony Orchestra conducted by Walter Damrosch over a large network of radio stations, April 15, 1937.

Kelley's music has always been widely played. The *Ben Hur* score was performed five thousand times in English-speaking countries. His Piano Quintet and the String Quartet, Opus 25, are known in both Europe and America, and the *New England Symphony* is a standard item in the repertoire of our symphony societies.

Kelley lived to the venerable age of eighty-seven years, and up to the time of his death, November 12, 1944, was active in spite of failing health. Every winter he could be seen in New York where he and his wife, who was long active in Music Club Federation circles, would receive their friends at their hotel.

He had definite ideas on nationalism, and he tried to carry them out in his music. He once expressed his views in the following words:

The American composer should apply the universal principles of his art to the local and special elements of the subject-matter as they appeal to him, and then, consciously or unconsciously, manifest his individuality, which will involve the expression of mental traits and moral tendencies peculiar to his European ancestry, as we find them modified by the new American environment.

FRANK VAN DER STUCKEN (1858–1929) was said to be the first orchestral conductor to present all-American programs. He did this first in New York in the eighties, and then he gave one in Paris at the 1889 exposition. Van der Stucken was a prolific composer and an able conductor. He was in much demand for festivals.

He was born in Texas, October 15, 1858, of German and Belgian parents. Educated chiefly in Europe, his music teachers included Reinecke and Grieg. He came to New York in 1884 and made his debut in Steinway Hall. Then he was made conductor of a male choral society, the Arion, and he directed orchestral concerts. In 1895 he went to Cincinnati, to become the director of the College of Music and the conductor of the new symphony orchestra. When Thomas died in 1905, Van der Stucken succeeded him as conductor of the Cincinnati Festival, and he held the position regularly until 1912. He conducted many festivals abroad, for after 1908 he lived mostly in Europe, and died in Hamburg, August 18, 1929.

Some of Van der Stucken's early music was performed first in Europe, when he was a young man of hardly twenty-five. Liszt presented his prologue to Heine's tragedy *William Ratcliff* at Weimar, and his incidental music to Shakespeare's *Tempest* was played at Breslau. He had a fine talent for orchestration; his scores sparkle with subtle effects. He composed a Symphonic Prologue *Pax Triumphans*, in which peace is indeed triumphant, though noisy; a Festival March *Louisiana*; other shorter pieces for orchestra; and a *Festival Hymn* for men's voices and orchestra. He also wrote a number of songs and piano pieces.

CHARLES MARTIN LOEFFLER (1861–1935) was one of the picturesque figures in American music. There are many who denied his Americanism; not because he was born in Alsace, but because his music is so akin to the Frenchmen of Debussy's time that it is really not American at all. Yet to some all things are American; and if Loeffler, in his musical journeys around the world, picked something from France, a bit from Russia, and maybe a blossom or two from the banks of the Rhine, who shall say that he was any the less American for sampling whatever he found? Especially since he wrought it all with such exquisite perfection, and turned everything he touched to jewels and gold.

Loeffler lived the life of a recluse at Medfield, Massachusetts, twenty miles from Boston. Paul Rosenfeld believed that his many years in Boston had made his work sterile; that the brilliant musician succumbed to the correct manners and inhibitions of New England. Rosenfeld even went so far as to compare his music to the dead Queen of Castile, whose remains were swathed in royal robes, and hung with gold and precious stones.[1] But there are others who were dazzled by the jewels, and who felt the pulse within. The musical refinement and the brilliance of Loeffler were not any too common among the American composers of past decades.

[1] In *An Hour with American Music*. Philadelphia: J. B. Lippincott Company, 1929.

Loeffler first came to America in the summer of 1881. He had an unusual background. He was born in Alsace, January 30, 1861, had lived in Russia and had been one of Joachim's favorite violin pupils. He studied in Paris with Massart, pupil of Kreutzer, and played in Pasdeloup's orchestra. He was engaged for the private orchestra of Baron Paul von Derweis, who spent his summers at his castle near Lake Lugano and his winters at Nice. Whenever the court moved from summer to winter quarters, three special trains were needed to carry the family, the guests, the tutors for the children, the servants and the horses, the orchestra of seventy, and the mixed choir of forty-eight singers. Loeffler was a favorite with the Baron, and he was often asked to help in the performance of chamber music by members of the family.

Loeffler was in New York for about a year, playing in Damrosch's orchestra, and sometimes with Theodore Thomas. Then Major Higginson asked him to come to Boston to play in the Boston Symphony, which had just finished its first season. He shared the first desk with Listemann, the concertmaster. When Franz Kneisel succeeded Listemann, Loeffler played side by side with Kneisel until 1903. Then he resigned, gave up playing his violin in public, and decided to devote the rest of his life to composition, and to his farm at Medfield where he lived until his death, May 20, 1935.

Spiritually, Loeffler was a mystic, a deep student of medieval culture and thought. He was an authority on Gregorian plain song; the church modes of the Middle Ages. Living in the twentieth century, he seemed a wanderer searching for a place where pious mystics would speak his language. Not finding it, he lived in his dreams. There he polished his music until it was refined to a purity that would satisfy his sense of the exquisite. Even though Rosenfeld found him sterile, and his style chosen from many sources, he was frank to admit the skill with which he fashioned his music.

Loeffler published practically nothing until he had finished his career as a violinist. Many of his works had been performed, but he had kept them all in manuscript. In 1891 the Boston Symphony played his Suite for violin and orchestra, *Les Veillées de l'Ukraine* (after Gogol); in 1894 his *Fantastic Concerto* for cello and orchestra; and in

1895 his *Divertimento* for violin and orchestra. He had also written a number of songs and chamber music works which were performed by the Kneisels and others.

His first published orchestral works were the dramatic poem *La Morte de Tintagiles* (after Maeterlinck), and a symphonic fantasy based on a poem by Rollinat, *La Villanelle du Diable*. They were issued in 1905, though *La Morte de Tintagiles* had been written first in 1897 and revised in 1900, and *La Villanelle* in 1901.

Loeffler's most frequently played work is the *Pagan Poem*. It is based on the eighth Eclogue of Virgil, in which a Thessalian girl tries to become sorceress, to draw her truant lover home. The piece was first written in 1901, as chamber music for piano, two flutes, oboe, clarinet, English horn, two horns, three trumpets, viola, and double bass. Loeffler arranged the score for two pianos and three trumpets, and it was played in 1903 at the home of the famous Mrs. Jack Gardner. Then Loeffler remodeled the work and expanded it to symphonic proportions, for piano and large orchestra. It was first played by the Boston Symphony in 1907 and published in 1909.

The three trumpets are treated *obbligati*—they suggest the refrain of the sorceress: *Ducite ab urbe domum, mea carmina, ducite Daphnim* (Draw from the city, my songs, draw Daphnis home). First they are heard offstage, then nearer and nearer until they finally come onto the stage, and the orchestra voices the triumph of the sorceress in an outburst of exultant passion. Loeffler's dark, brooding music brings the odor of strange incense, the magic incantations. It paints a vivid picture of the lovesick sorceress, chanting her desirous songs.

The plain chant, Gregorian influence is most apparent in the *Music for Four String Instruments* (published in 1923); and in the Symphony *Hora Mystica*, written for the Norfolk (Connecticut) Festival of 1916, and still in manuscript. Loeffler supplied explanatory notes for the symphony:

The mood is one of religious meditation and adoration of nature. A lonely pilgrim winds his way through a land of ever-changing enchantments, a land where clouds move like a procession of nuns over the hills or descend upon a lake, changing it into a mysterious gray sea—a land where shepherds still pipe to their flocks. From far away comes a curious tolling of church-bells. At last the wanderer stands before the cathedral of a Benedictine monastery, contemplating its beauty—even the grotesque beauty of the gargoyles, placed on the house of worship to ward off evil spirits. In the church, with its rose-window still aglow with the last evening light, the office of compline—known to the Benedictine monks as Hora Mystica—is tendered to God, and peace descends into the soul of the pilgrim.

The Library of Congress, under the provisions of the Elizabeth Sprague Coolidge Foundation, commissioned and published Loeffler's *Canticum Fratris Solis*, a remarkable setting for solo voice and chamber orchestra of the "Canticle of the Sun" by St. Francis. It was first performed in Washington at the first chamber music festival at the Library of Congress in 1925. Again Loeffler used old church modes, and sometimes definite liturgical motives. It is rare music, a truly distinguished work.

Another commission from Mrs. Coolidge produced a *Partita* for flute, violin, and piano. For the Cleveland Orchestra Loeffler composed an *Evocation*, for orchestra, women's chorus, and speaking voice. This was first performed in Cleveland, February 5, 1931, and was published in the same year by the Juilliard Foundation. After a subsequent performance of this work by the Boston Symphony, a reviewer in *Musical America* (April 10, 1933) wrote that "its luminous clarity, delicate coloring, and fine workmanship are a constant delight."

Besides his songs (to poems of Verlaine, Baudelaire, Rossetti, Poe, Yeats), Loeffler composed and published two rhapsodies for oboe, viola, and piano (*L'étang* and *La Cornemuse*); a chorus for women's voices *By the Rivers of Babylon;* an eight-part chorus for mixed voices *a cappella, For One who Fell in Battle;* a *Poem* for orchestra; and an orchestral poem *Memories of my Childhood* ("Life in a Russian Village").

Much has been written about Loeffler's work, but there are few portraits of the man himself. Carl Engel provided as intimate an account of him as probably can be found, in the *Musical Quarterly* of July, 1925. He treated his subject with sympathy and understanding.

When this volume was first published, in 1931, WALTER DAM-ROSCH (1862——) frankly stated that he had abandoned all ambitions as a composer, that his other activities as conductor and musical ambassador and missionary were enough, and that a rival conductor was probably right in calling his first opera *The Scarlet Letter* the "Nibelungen of New England." After Dr. Damrosch's retirement from the conductorship of the New York Symphony Society, and when his Friday afternoon broadcasts for school children had become more or less a routine matter, he apparently changed his mind, for the list of works he has recently composed and produced would do credit to the industriousness of a far younger man.

First there was the *Abraham Lincoln Song*, for baritone solo, chorus, and orchestra which was performed at the Metropolitan Opera House, April 3, 1936, and broadcast over an NBC network. The following year brought an opera *The Man Without a Country*, to a libretto which Arthur Guiterman had adapted from Edward Everett Hale's story. This was produced by the Metropolitan Opera Company during its 1937 spring season. Then he rewrote his earlier opera *Cyrano de Bergerac*, which originally had been produced at the Metropolitan in 1913. In its revised form the opera was produced in Carnegie Hall, New York, by the Philharmonic-Symphony Society, with soloists and the Oratorio Society Chorus, under the composer's direction, February 21, 1941.

Next came another opera, a fantasy in one-act entitled *The Opera Cloak*, produced by the New Opera Company at the Broadway Theatre, New York, November 4, 1942. Virgil Thomson called the work "literate music, clear music, but rather dull music" which "would have made a pleasant eight-minute skit for the International Ladies' Garment Workers." [2] Most recently, in 1943, Damrosch made a setting of Robert Nathan's poem *Dunkirk*, for baritone solo, male chorus, and small orchestra. This work was first performed by the National Broadcasting Symphony, May 2, 1943, with Thomas L. Thomas as soloist.

Damrosch has had a long and honored career in America. Born in Breslau, Germany, January 30, 1862, he came to New York with his family when he was nine years old. His father, Leopold Damrosch, had come to America, first to conduct the New York Männergesang-verein Arion, a male chorus. In 1874 he organized the New York Oratorio Society, and in 1878, after a season with the Philharmonic, he was made conductor of the newly founded Symphony Society of New York. The elder Damrosch became a bitter rival of Theodore Thomas,

[2] New York *Herald Tribune*, November 4, 1942.

and the orchestra war of the late seventies and eighties added spice to table conversation and to the columns of the musical journals. And bitterness, too.

When his father died in 1885, Walter succeeded him as conductor of the Oratorio Society and the New York Symphony. He had been his father's assistant as conductor of German opera at the Metropolitan, and in 1894 he organized his own company, which gave German operas in New York and in other cities for five years. For two years after 1900 he was conductor of German operas at the Metropolitan. For the season of 1902–3 he conducted the Philharmonic, and when the Symphony Society was reorganized the following year he again assumed its leadership. In 1928 the orchestra was merged with the Philharmonic, and for a season Damrosch was one of the conductors of the combined orchestras. In 1929 he resigned to devote all of his time to radio broadcasting, giving weekly orchestral concerts in the evening, and a children's series, with explanatory remarks, in school hours.

During his conductorship of the Symphony Society, Damrosch introduced many new works which have since proved to be masterpieces —among them Tschaikowsky's Fifth and Sixth Symphonies, and Brahms's Fourth. He also directed the first American performances of several operas: Saint-Saëns' *Samson and Delilah*, Tschaikowsky's *Eugen Onegin*, and Wagner's *Parsifal*. He was a pioneer in welcoming the works of American composers to his programs, and it was he who commissioned George Gershwin to compose his Piano Concerto.

The Scarlet Letter, based on Hawthorne's novel, was Damrosch's first opera, and he produced it with his own company in Boston in 1896. It was thoroughly Wagnerian in conception, with leit-motives and everything else that goes with a post-romantic German music drama.

Cyrano, the opera after Rostand's play, was originally produced at the Metropolitan Opera House in New York in 1913. A comic opera *The Dove of Peace*, to a libretto by Wallace Irwin, was produced in 1912 in New York and Philadelphia. Damrosch also wrote incidental music to the Greek dramas *Iphigenia in Aulis, Medea,* and *Electra,* for performances in California in 1915. His Sonata for violin and piano bears the title *At Fox Meadow.* In his songs he achieved more individuality and better success than in his work in larger forms—particularly in setting ballads of the dramatic type: Kipling's *Danny Deever*, and others.

Yet, as I have remarked elsewhere: "Walter Damrosch does not need the role of composer for immortality, and it is not necessary that one admire him as a creative artist in order to do him high honor. His name will go on the roll with that of Theodore Thomas, as belonging to one who has done more than his share in helping to make America musical." [3]

HENRY FRANKLIN BELKNAP GILBERT (1868–1928) possessed a genuine talent which created music with a spontaneity and a raciness that makes it sparkle. Gilbert was not recognized for many years, and his association with Arthur Farwell and others of the composers who thought in nationalistic terms was no doubt one of the reasons that he was heard at all. Although his setting of Stevenson's *Pirate Song* ("Fifteen Men on a Dead Man's Chest") had been made popular by David Bispham, and his work for soprano and orchestra, *Salammbô's Invocation to Tanith*, had had a single performance by the Russian Symphony Orchestra in New York, it was not until 1911, when Gilbert was forty-two years old, that he was really brought to the attention of the musical public. In April of that year the Boston Symphony played his *Comedy Overture on Negro Themes*. It may have disturbed the audience, but those who heard it knew that it was something new. As Olin Downes remarked, "There were some who thought that the opening was undignified, and stopped thinking at that place."

The *Overture* had originally been intended as a prelude to an operetta based on the *Uncle Remus* tales of Joel Chandler Harris. Gilbert actually completed his sketches of the operetta and then found that the exclusive stage rights had been granted to another composer. So he could use only the overture, which he rescored for a larger orchestra. The first theme was a Negro melody from the Bahamas; the second a tune sung by the roustabouts of the Mississippi steamboats—*I'se G'wine to Alabammy, Oh*; and the middle section was a witty, rollicking fugue on the *Old Ship of Zion*. The genuine treatment of this material caused Gilbert to be talked about, and two years later he

---

[3] In *Our Contemporary Composers*.

was invited to write an orchestral work for the Litchfield County Festival in Norfolk, Connecticut.

For this occasion he wrote his *Negro Rhapsody*, which pictures first a Negro "Shout," alternating a savage dance tune and a spiritual; then a glorification of the spiritual in which the barbaric is supposed to fall away and the nobler elements take its place. It is interesting to contrast this final triumph of the spiritual with the reversion to paganism depicted in John Powell's rhapsody, discussed elsewhere in this volume.

Five songs of the Louisiana Creole Negroes were the basis of Gilbert's *Dance in the Place Congo*. First written as an orchestral piece, the composer later composed a ballet scenario, and the work was finally performed at the Metropolitan in New York, March 23, 1918. It is one of the best of Gilbert's works. The tropical grace of the Creole tunes is subtly emphasized, but the gloomy, tragic note of the slave dances in the old Place Congo of New Orleans forms a weird and fantastic background. First comes the Bamboula, then some light moments rising to frenzy, interrupted at last by the booming of the great bell that summoned the slaves back to their quarters. Then a pause and a cry of despair.

When Gilbert first hit upon the idea of using native themes is not known. Possibly he talked with Farwell about the example set for American composers by Dvořák, and by MacDowell with his *Indian Suite*. At any rate, Gilbert turned to the Negroes while others looked to the Indians and produced his *Americanesque*, an orchestral work based on three minstrel tunes—*Zip Coon* ("Turkey in the Straw"), *Dearest May*, and *Don't Be Foolish, Joe* (1903).

Gilbert was born in Somerville, Massachusetts, September 26, 1868. He studied first at the New England Conservatory, and then became MacDowell's first American pupil. During his student years, from 1889 to 1892, he earned his living playing the violin for dances and in theatres. This hack work disgusted him, and he determined to keep his music apart from the routine of getting money to feed himself. Olin Downes, in the *Musical Quarterly* of January, 1918, has told how he first became real estate agent, then a foreman in a factory, a raiser of silkworms, and finally a bread and pie cutter in a restaurant at the Chicago World's Fair. There he met a Russian prince who had been a friend of Rimsky-Korsakoff, and who, when he recovered from "the unconventional advances of the bread and pie cutter, was able to impart interesting information about this composer and other members of the 'Neo-Russian' school."

Gilbert was always interested in composers who used folk songs in their music, and his journeys after 1895, when he inherited a small sum of money, took him wherever he could find material and kindred spirits. He was so stirred when he heard of the première of Charpentier's *Louise* in Paris, knowing that it tended toward the use of popular themes, that he worked his way to Europe on a cattle boat to hear the first performance.

He left some works not based on American folk songs. In his *Symphonic Prelude* to Synge's drama *Riders to the Sea*, he makes use of a fragment of an old Irish melody. This was first written for small orchestra, to be played at some performances of the drama by the Twentieth Century Club of Boston in 1904. Later he expanded the work, scoring it for full orchestra, and it was performed at the music festival of the MacDowell Memorial Association in Peterboro, September, 1914. He also composed a one-act opera that has not yet been performed—*Fantasy in Delft*, with the scene laid in the Dutch town of Delft in the seventeenth century. Gilbert died in Cambridge, Massachusetts, May 19, 1928.

ARTHUR BATELLE WHITING (1861–1936) made his home and headquarters in New York from 1895 until the time of his death, July 20, 1936, but through his place of birth and early training and associations, he belonged to the Boston Group. He was born in Cambridge, Massachusetts, June 20, 1861, the nephew of George E. Whiting (1842–1923), composer and organist. He had his first instruction at the New England Conservatory—piano with Sherwood, and harmony, counterpoint, and composition with Maas and Chadwick. From 1883 to 1885 he was abroad, studying with Rheinberger in Munich. Then back to Boston for ten years, where he lived and worked among his New England colleagues. In 1895 he moved to New York, and after 1907 was active in giving chamber music concerts in our universities—Harvard, Yale, Princeton, Columbia.

As a composer, Whiting wrote little compared to his Boston contemporaries, but in spite of his small output he showed a genuine talent, which had its native characteristics. He was either a severe self-critic, or he wrote only when he felt that he had something definite to say. His principal works were a Concert Overture, a Suite for horns and strings, a Concerto, and a Fantasy for piano and orchestra. In his later years he wrote a String Quartet (1929), and he published a Dance Pageant *The Golden Cage,* with the music scored for small orchestra. The libretto was adapted from the poems of William Blake by C. C. Smith. He composed a number of small works, anthems, songs, and piano pieces, and made some transcriptions for piano of the toccatas and suites of Bach and Handel.

All his life Whiting was a man of wit and humor, the coiner of epigrams that have become traditions among musicians. He spared no one at whom he might level a gibe—Hale described him as "a man with a very pretty knack at sarcasm." It may be that this keen, acrid sense of humor kept him from taking anything too seriously, including himself, and that it was responsible for his comparatively small list of compositions.

The *Indian Dances* of CHARLES SANFORD SKILTON (1868–1941) have been played all over the country in their scoring for large orchestra, and in arrangements for smaller combinations in theatres, on phonograph records, and over the radio. Skilton wisely avoided over-elaboration and development. He used the resources of the modern orchestra to emphasize primitive effects, and wherever it was required, he employed the monotonous insistence of the percussion to sharpen the constant recurrence of drum rhythms.

Skilton was a New Englander by birth—he was born in Northampton, Massachusetts, August 16, 1868. He graduated from Yale University, and then after teaching in a school at Newburgh, New York, he went abroad to study music at the Berlin Hochschule. When he returned to America he studied further with Harry Rowe Shelley and Dudley Buck, and held several teaching positions, until he went to Kansas in 1903 to take charge of music at the state university. He held that position until his death, March 12, 1941.

Skilton first became interested in Indian music in 1915, when an Indian pupil offered to trade tribal songs, which he would sing to Skilton, for lessons in harmony. After that Skilton paid many visits to the near-by Indian school—Haskell Institute. His first works on

Indian themes were the *Deer Dance* and the *War Dance*, originally written for string quartet, and later expanded to orchestral form. These comprised the first part of his *Suite Primeval*. The second part was published four years later, consisting of four movements, all based on primitive songs: *Sunrise Song* (Winnebago); *Gambling Song* (Rogue River); *Flute Serenade* (Sioux); and *Moccasin Game* (Winnebago).

Skilton composed Indian operas. One, the three-act *Kalopin*, is based on the New Madrid Earthquake of 1811 and the legendary causes attributed to it by the Chickasaw and Choctaw Indians. The Indians believed that the disaster was the punishment sent by the great spirit because Kalopin, the young Chickasaw chief, went to another tribe for his bride. Skilton treated this as an allegory, representing the overwhelming of the Indians by the white race, just as the Indian village was overwhelmed by earthquake and flood.

Kalopin has not yet had a public performance, but a one-act opera by Skilton, *The Sun Bride*, was given a radio production over a network of the National Broadcasting Company in the spring of 1930. The plot is based on the sun-worshiping beliefs of the Pueblo Indians of Arizona. The composer used as one of the motives the Winnebago Sunrise Song found in the *Suite Primeval*. He also used a Chippewa melody. Exotic rhythms help to bring out the Indian locale and story, and in spite of a conventional melodiousness, the Indian atmosphere is effectively suggested.

Skilton composed other music than that founded on Indian sources. One of his first scores was the incidental music and choral odes for a performance of Sophocles's *Electra* given at Smith College, Northampton. His oratorio *The Guardian Angel* was performed under the auspices of the Kansas Federation of Music Clubs, which provided for its publication. His orchestral works include a *Legend*, first performed by the Minneapolis Orchestra in 1927, an Overture, *Mount Oread*, and an Overture in E which was performed at the American Composers' Concerts in Rochester, March 28, 1934.

CARL BUSCH (1862–1943) gained distinction for carrying into his music the spirit of the Western prairies, and for incorporating Indian material into his compositions. He was born in Bjerre, Denmark, March 29, 1862, and his early training was in the country of his birth, at the University of Copenhagen, and with Hartmann and Gade. In 1886 he went to Paris to study with Godard, and in the following year he came to America. He settled in Kansas City and was active there until the time of his death, December 19, 1943, as a composer, teacher, and conductor of various choral and orchestral organizations, many of which he himself founded.

Busch generally chose American subjects for his works. A piece for military band is entitled *Chant from the Great Plains; Ozarka* is a Suite for orchestra; *Minnehaha's Vision* is based on an episode from Longfellow's *Hiawatha*. He made many settings of actual Indian melodies, for voice, for piano, and for orchestra; for example, the *Four Indian Tribal Melodies*. He also composed two Symphonies; a symphonic prologue *The Passing of Arthur;* an *Elegy* for string orchestra; a String Quartet; and many cantatas, anthems, songs, and small pieces. In 1912 he was knighted by the Danish government.

HENRY HOLDEN HUSS (1862——) is a composer of the elder contemporary group who has written music of considerable charm in the romantic mold, even though he seems to lack enough of the power of self-criticism to give his works endurance. His Sonata for violin and piano is spirited and playable; in turn, rhythmically full of life, lyrical, and capricious. His Quartet for strings, Opus 31, has been performed by the Kneisel and Berkshire Quartets, and is published by the Society for the Publication of American Music.

Huss was a pupil of Rheinberger. Born in Newark, New Jersey, June 21, 1862, a descendant of the Bohemian patriot and martyr John Huss, he studied first with his father and later under Boise and Rheinberger abroad. Most of his life has been spent in New York, teaching and giving joint recitals with his wife, the former Hildegard Hoffmann, a soprano.

He has written two works for piano and orchestra—a Rhapsody and a Concerto in B Major. He has played them with orchestras abroad and at home. There are several Quartets, a Trio, the Violin Sonata, and a Sonata for cello and piano, as well as a number of piano pieces and about thirty published songs. He has written several works for chorus, one of them a *Festival Sanctus* for chorus, orchestra, and organ.

ROSSETTER GLEASON COLE (1866——) was a pupil of Max Bruch in Germany and of Middelschulte at home. He was born in Michigan,

February 5, 1866, and for many years he has lived in Chicago as a teacher, composer, organist, and lecturer. As a composer he has published over ninety works. His style has possibly been influenced more by the music of César Franck than by that of any other composer; but he has nevertheless succeeded in evolving something of a personal idiom. He feels that American music must grow on individual rather than on nationalistic lines.

His *Symphonic Prelude* for orchestra was first performed by the Chicago Symphony under Stock in 1916, and repeated in 1918. An overture, *Pioneer*, was written in commemoration of the Illinois State Centennial (1918), and dedicated to the memory of Abraham Lincoln. It was first performed in 1919, the composer conducting. A *Heroic Piece* for orchestra and organ was first played at a special concert of the Chicago Symphony in 1924.

Cole has written three choral works—*The Passing of Summer; The Broken Troth*, a cantata for women's voices; and *The Rock of Liberty*, a Pilgrim ode, composed for the tercentenary of the landing of the Pilgrims. His Sonata for violin and piano was first performed in Germany in 1892, and then in America by Theodore Spiering in 1897. It is an early work, conventional and long, though melodic and musical. The *Ballade* for cello and orchestra was introduced in Minneapolis in 1909.

Like David Stanley Smith, Cole composed an opera on the *Merrymount* theme several years before Howard Hanson's opera was produced in 1934. Cole accordingly changed the name of his opera to *The Maypole Lovers*. Although the opera has not been produced in its original form, an orchestral suite from its score was performed by the Chicago Symphony Orchestra, January 9 and 10, 1936.

Louis Victor Saar (1868–1937) was a Hollander who came to America in 1894 as an accompanist at the Metropolitan Opera House. He was born in Rotterdam, December 10, 1868. His family had been distantly related to Schubert. While he was in New York he taught at the National Conservatory and at the Institute of Musical Art. From 1906 to 1917 he was head of the theory and composition courses at the College of Music in Cincinnati; from 1917 to 1933 he held a similar position at the Chicago Musical College; and at the time of his death, November 23, 1937, he headed the theory department at the St. Louis Institute of Music. His orchestral works include a *Rococo*

Suite (1915); a Suite *From the Mountain Kingdom of the Great North West* (1922); and *Along the Columbia River* (1924).

* * *

At this point it is necessary, as it is in the succeeding chapters, to reduce our presentation of composers to little more than a listing. This is regrettable, but it is necessary to compress information about dozens of worthy composers into the limits of space practicable in a single volume. The following are presented in alphabetical order:

JOHANN HEINRICH BECK
> Born, Cleveland, 1856; died, 1924.
> Orchestral conductor and composer.
> Overtures and pieces for orchestra; Sextet for strings; String Quartet.

MAX BENDIX
> Born, Detroit, 1866.
> Violinist and composer, concertmaster and assistant conductor for Theodore Thomas.
> Violin Concerto; Theme and Variations for cello and orchestra; music for the play *Experience* and for Jane Cowl's production of *Romeo and Juliet;* music for the ballet by Fokine in the play *Johannes Kreisler; Pavlowa,* Valse-Caprice for orchestra; *The Sisters,* ballad for soprano with orchestra; songs.

JOHN A. VON BROEKHOVEN
> Born, Holland, 1852; died, United States, 1930.
> Composer; teacher at Cincinnati College of Music.
> *Creole Suite* for small orchestra.

BENJAMIN CUTTER
> Born, Woburn, Massachusetts, 1857; died, Boston, 1910.
> Chamber music, cantatas, and church music.

ELEANOR EVEREST FREER
> Born, Philadelphia, 1864; died, Chicago, 1943.
> Ardent supporter of American composers; founder of the American Opera Society of Chicago.
> Ten operas, including *The Court Jester* (1926) and *The Legend of the Piper* (1928); vocal quartets and trios; a song cycle; about 150 songs; many piano pieces.

PAOLO GALLICO

Born, Trieste, 1868.

Oratorio *The Apocalypse*, which won the $500 prize of the National Federation of Music Clubs in 1921. Orchestral works: *Euphorion, Rhapsodie Mondial, Rhapsodie Montereyan*. Chamber music, a Sextet, and an opera *Harlequin*. Songs and piano pieces.

WILLIAM EDWIN HAESCHE

Born, Connecticut, 1867; died, Virginia, 1929.

Symphony; Sinfonietta; tone poem *In the South;* two Overtures; *Forest-Idylle* for orchestra; chamber music; songs and choruses; violin pieces.

BRUNO OSCAR KLEIN

Born, Germany, 1858; came to America in 1878; died, New York, 1911.

An Overture; incidental pieces for orchestra; Sonata for violin and piano; Quintet for soprano, violin, cello, horn, and piano; church music; piano pieces; three volumes of songs, with eighty published separately.

ABRAHAM WOLF LILIENTHAL

Born, New York, 1859; died, New York, 1928.

Violin Sonata; Trio; two Quartets; a Quintet; a Sextet; songs; Sonata for cello and piano.

LOUIS KOEMMENICH

Born, Germany, 1866; came to the United States in 1890; died, 1922.

Choral conductor and composer of choruses and songs.

WILLIAM J. McCOY

Born, Ohio, 1848; died, 1926.

An opera, *Egypt;* a Symphony in F; Overture *Yosemite; The Najads Idyl;* Prelude; *Introduction and Valse Concertante*, for flute and orchestra; chamber music; music for plays of the San Francisco Bohemian Club, choral works; and many songs.

PAUL FRIEDRICH THEODORE MIERSCH

Born, Germany, 1868; came to America in 1892.

Cello Concerto; Violin Concerto; *Indian Rhapsody* for orches-

Walter Damrosch
(See pages 351–354)

Edgar Stillman Kelley
(See pages 345–347)

Photo by Pirie MacDonald

John Alden Carpenter
(See pages 368–372)

Henry K. Hadley
(See pages 372–374)

tra; String Quartet; Variations for string quartet; songs and pieces for violin and for cello.

WILLIAM HENRY POMMER

Born, 1851; died, Columbia, Missouri, 1937.

Director of music at University of Missouri from 1907.

Sonata for violin and piano, Quintet for strings.

HARRY NEWTON REDMAN

Born, Illinois, 1869.

Two Sonatas for violin and piano; two String Quartets; songs and piano pieces.

CLARA KATHLEEN ROGERS

Born, England, 1844; came to the United States in 1871; died, 1931.

Operatic soprano and composer of a Violin Sonata, songs, and piano pieces.

EDWARD BENJAMIN SCHEVE

Born, Germany, 1865; came to America in 1888; died, 1924.

One Symphony; Piano Concerto; Violin Concerto; Violin Sonata; Organ Sonata; oratorios and choral works; songs, anthems, and piano pieces.

HENRY SCHOENEFELD

Born, Milwaukee, 1857; died, Los Angeles, 1936.

An Indian opera; two Symphonies; two Overtures; two *American Rhapsodies* for orchestra; Concertos for piano, violin, and cello; Sonata for violin and piano; piano pieces, songs, choruses.

EDMUND SEVERN

Born, England, 1862; brought to America 1866; died, 1942.

Violinist, conductor, and composer.

Festival Overture; orchestral tone poems—*Lancelot and Elaine, Héloïse and Abélard;* Suite for orchestra, *From Old New England;* orchestral Fantasy on *The Tempest;* Concerto for violin; three String Quartets; a Trio; Sonata for violin and piano; many violin pieces.

HERMAN SPIELTER

Born, Germany, 1860; in the United States from 1880; died, 1925.

Cantatas and choruses; Sonata for cello and piano.

HUMPHREY JOHN STEWART

Born, London, 1856; came to the United States in 1886; died, 1932.

Prominent organist on Pacific Coast.

Grand opera; two comic operas; music for three plays of San Francisco Bohemian Club; two orchestral Suites—*Montezuma* and *Scenes in California;* choral works; church music; songs and instrumental pieces.

GUSTAV STRUBE

Born, Germany, 1867; came to America in 1890.

Founder and conductor of Baltimore Symphony Orchestra until 1930.

Three Symphonies; four Symphonic Poems; three Overtures; two Rhapsodies and four Preludes for orchestra; two Violin Concertos; symphonic music for chamber orchestra; Quintet for woodwind and horn; Trio; String Quartet; Sonatas for cello, for viola, and for violin; an opera *The Captive;* smaller pieces for violin.

ALFRED DUDLEY TURNER

Born, Vermont, 1854; died there, 1888.

Sonata for cello and piano, other chamber music, and piano pieces.

CARL VENTH

Born, Germany, 1860; in America from 1880; died, San Antonio, Texas, February 2, 1938.

Two operas; several orchestral works; chamber music; choruses and songs.

MAX WILHELM KARL VOGRICH

Born, Austria, 1852; in America from 1878; died, New York, 1916.

Three operas produced abroad; two Symphonies; a Violin Concerto; cantatas and choruses; church music; songs and instrumental pieces.

ARNOLD VOLPE

Born, Russia, 1869; came to America in 1898; died, Miami, Florida, 1940.

Composer and conductor; founder of the Lewisohn Stadium Concerts in New York.

String Quartet; songs, violin pieces; *Mazurka* for violin and orchestra.

ADOLF WEIDIG

Born, Germany, 1867; came to the United States in 1892; died, 1931.

Symphony; Symphonic Suite; Tone Poem *Semiramis;* three Overtures; Suite for string orchestra; three String Quartets; a String Quintet; a Trio; and several Suites for violin and piano; songs and choruses.

SAMUEL BRENTON WHITNEY

Born, Vermont, 1842; died, Vermont, 1914.

Pupil of John K. Paine.

Composed church music and chamber music.

CHAPTER TWELVE

Contemporary Composers

1. COMPOSERS BORN IN THE 1870'S

THERE are hundreds of composers today, where there were a few dozen fifty years ago, and the majority of them are excellently equipped technically, and able to express themselves fluently. Less than a half century ago, the majority of the American scores submitted to conductors of orchestras were so faulty in their instrumental writing that they must be either returned to their composers with thanks, and no performance, or else edited and extensively revised if they were to sound at all as their composers hoped. Nowadays an adequate technique is assumed, and is rarely even mentioned in discussing a contemporary American work.

The American composer works in a field far different from that of a half-century—or even a quarter-century—ago. He does not have to go abroad for training; the leading teachers of Europe are in this country, and our own American teachers are more than adequately equipped to give rigorous and sound training to young composers. It is not possible, of course, for our major orchestras to play all the American works that should be played, and there is still cause for complaint in the number of American works that appear on the programs of the leading symphony societies. But the augmented number of orchestras, and the increasing desire of their conductors to present American works, plus the existence of hundreds of lesser professional, semiprofessional, and amateur groups, have given American composers a broader opportunity, not only to achieve a greater public, but to gain experience by hearing their major works capably played. These matters are discussed more fully in the concluding chapter; it is sufficient to call attention to the fact that this chapter, devoted to contemporary composers, is by far the largest in the book, and that it is also very much larger than it was in the original edition, first published fifteen years ago.

At that time contemporary composers were presented under the headings—"Our Senior Contemporaries," "The Younger Group," and "The Modernists." These, perhaps, were satisfactory classifications in 1931, but some of the "seniors" have either passed on or have virtually retired from active creative work. A number of them have become what we have termed in the preceding pages "Links with the Past." In regard to "The Younger Group," it must be confessed that for this distinction an arbitrary maximum age was selected, which, strangely enough, was exactly that of the author. Anyone not as old as himself was put among the younger composers.

Obviously, such a compliment for these men and women does not hold good any more, nor will any other similar classifications of still younger musicians be valid a few years from now. Likewise, such terms as "modernists," "radicals," and others used to describe composers who are freer with innovations than are their more conservative colleagues, are dated almost before the ink is dry on the pages of any book. It has therefore seemed wiser to arrange the discussion of contemporary composers in an order which would remain logical permanently. One thing will always be true about a creative artist—the date of his birth. So in this edition of *Our American Music*, the contemporary composers are grouped in decades, according to the years in which they were born. The arrangement is not altogether chronological, however, for within each decade-group the sequence is arranged according to relative prominence, and according to recognizably kindred traits among certain composers. Thus, the outright experimentalists are placed with other innovators who are within ten years of their own age. This, admittedly, is an arbitrary system, but it is surprising how much the majority of the composers in each chapter have in common. And why wouldn't they? They have come from the same era, have undergone the same attitudes towards American music, and have erected, especially the older ones, the same defenses against the discrimination from which the American composer has suffered, and from the public apathy towards his work. These afflictions have lessened considerably in the last twenty-five years, so we find the younger composers far less subject to their effects. Perhaps in another twenty-five or fifty years, an American composer will be entirely free from inferiority complex.

At the end of each chapter we shall follow, with regret, the practice inaugurated in the preceding chapter of grouping in a list containing a minimum of information, many composers for whom there is not space for fuller discussion. It is necessary that this be done if the book is to be a comprehensive survey of the composers who should rightfully be included.

We begin, then, with JOHN ALDEN CARPENTER (1876——), whom Walter Damrosch once called the most American of our composers. In his ballet *Skyscrapers* Carpenter sought to portray our age of rivets and mechanism, and in *Krazy Kat* the exaggerated humor and slapstick caricature of the comic strip in the newspapers. Yet there are others who deny Carpenter his Americanism because of the French derivation of his style, or because he seems to feel so keenly, and so subjectively, the moods of nature. The rank and file of Americans are apt to think of the out-of-doors in objective terms—as a baseball game or an automobile ride.

For many years, Carpenter was entitled to amateur standing as a musician. Until his retirement in 1936 he was a business man; vice-president of George B. Carpenter & Company, Chicago merchants in mill, railway and vessel supplies. Yet for all his business interests, he found enough time for music to become one of the most important of our contemporary composers. He was born in Park Ridge, Illinois, February 28, 1876. His mother was a talented amateur singer who gave him his first lessons. He went to Harvard where he studied with John K. Paine, and took all the music courses the college offered. Then he studied for a short time with Edward Elgar, the English composer, and later with Bernhard Ziehn in Chicago.

His first important work for orchestra was the Suite *Adventures in a Perambulator*. It was written in 1914 and published a year later. It has been performed by all the important orchestras in America, and in London, Paris, Rome, Berlin, and Stockholm. Carpenter describes the sensations of a baby wheeled along the sidewalks by his nurse. He sees *The Policeman, The Hurdy-Gurdy, The Lake,* and the *Dogs.* It is witty, sparkling music, and the composer is skillful in gaining his effects—the street organ, dogs barking.

The *Concertino* for piano and orchestra, written a year later, suggests a lighthearted conversation between the piano and the orchestra —two friends who have traveled different paths and have become a little garrulous over their separate experiences. As Carpenter pointed out:

The rules of polite talk, as always between friends, are not strictly observed—often, in animated moments they talk both at once, each hearing only what he says himself. . . . Presently the moment comes, as always between friends, when no conversation is necessary—a relaxed moment, when friendship itself takes them in hand, and they have nothing to say. But the reaction is quick and strong—there is still so much that presses to be said —on a pleasant night—with youth in the air—beween friends.

The *Concertino* was published in 1917, and has had performances in many cities.

An early Symphony was written in 1916 for the 1917 festival at Norfolk, Connecticut. The other purely orchestral pieces are a *Pilgrim Vision* and *Jazz Orchestra Pieces*. He has written no opera, but he has achieved distinction with his ballets. *The Birthday of the Infanta* was first produced by the Chicago Civic Opera Company in 1919, and revived in 1921. In 1930 the Chicago Symphony played an orchestral suite based on the music. *Krazy Kat* was written in 1921, and was produced first in Chicago. It was an interesting experiment in transferring the jazz idiom to respectable company. The scenario and action were based on the George Herriman cartoons, which still gambol through the newspapers of the country. Krazy Kat's happy psychology ran through the score; the whines and the laughter helped the buffoonery.

Skyscrapers attracted much attention when it was first presented at the Metropolitan, in 1926. It was Carpenter's most radical score, and it dealt with modern phases of our American life. It was thoroughly impressionistic, and there was no attempt to spare the cacophony of our city streets. In 1928 it was produced at the *Staatoper* in Munich, and in a condensed version for orchestra alone it has been played by the principal American orchestras, and by Koussevitzky in Paris.

The condensed scenario score describes the action:

Skyscrapers is a ballet which seeks to reflect some of the many rhythmic movements and sounds of modern American life. It has no story, in the usually accepted sense, but proceeds on the simple fact that American life reduces itself to violent alternations of work and play, each with its own peculiar and distinctive character. The action of the ballet is merely a series of moving decorations reflecting some of the obvious external features of this life.

In 1928, Carpenter's String Quartet was performed at the Library of Congress Festival in Washington. It proved to be an interesting mixture of charm and whimsicality with moments of uncompromising severity. A few years later, in 1931, the United States George Washington Bicentennial Commission asked Carpenter to compose an ode for the forthcoming celebration in 1932. The composer responded with his *Song of Faith*, for chorus and orchestra, based on a text of his own.

Patterns, first performed by the Boston Symphony Orchestra in the autumn of 1932, was scored for orchestra and piano obbligato, and composed in one movement. Some of its passages proved to be distinctly sentimental, and at other times the atmosphere alternates between a Spanish flavor and jazz. Several of the critics at the première felt that the work lacked continuity, but they admitted that the composer may have anticipated such a criticism by his title.

A year after *Patterns*, Carpenter produced *Sea Drift*, inspired (like Delius's work of the same title and the *Sea Symphony* of Vaughan Williams) by the sea poems of Walt Whitman. This was first performed in November of 1934 by the New York Philharmonic-Symphony under Werner Janssen. Carpenter's Quintet for piano and strings was first performed at the Coolidge Festival at the Library of Congress, Washington, in April, 1935. It was natural and sincere music, and the use of the piano for percussive effects was altogether contemporary in feeling. The refinement of its idiom lent distinction to the work's rich chromaticism.

Danza, introduced by the Boston Symphony in January, 1936, is, perhaps, a less important piece than others of Carpenter's works, but it is charming and suggestive of the Spanish influence that appears every once in a while in his music. A year later, in 1937, Zlato Balakovic played Carpenter's Concerto for violin and orchestra with the Chicago Symphony.

In 1940, Carpenter composed a *Symphony in One Movement* for the fiftieth anniversary of the Chicago Symphony. This work was based on the principal theme of the 1917 Symphony, and was described by Francis Perkins of the New York *Herald Tribune* (November 23, 1940) as "sincere and appealing music, generous in melodic content, well knit and concise in form, ably wrought in its scoring and in the employment of its ideas."

Carpenter's Symphony No. 2 had its première October 22, 1942, by the New York Philharmonic-Symphony under Bruno Walter. Virgil Thomson called it "rich man's music, gentleman's composition." "Mr. Carpenter," he continued, "has been to Harvard and Paris. . . . His mind is cultivated and adult. He writes with force and some charm. This work is well woven, contrapuntally alive; it has no empty spots in it. . . . The whole is opulent and comfortable, intelligent, well organized, cultured and firm without being either ostentatious or unduly modest." (New York *Herald Tribune*, October 23, 1942.)

Carpenter's list of works includes a Sonata for violin and piano, and a number of pieces for piano alone, notably the *Polonaise Américaine*. Aside from his works for orchestra and his ballets, he is also well known as a song writer. In that field he has attained rare distinction. It is in his songs that he shows his leanings toward the French school of impressionists. Nor is such a comparison necessarily a denial of individuality, for Carpenter's refinement and aristocratic elegance are often his own. He is especially happy with the texts of Rabindranath Tagore, whose spirit he seems to catch more faithfully than any other composer. He has been penetrating in drawing from the poems the Oriental warmth of color, the sensitiveness to mood. From *Gitanjali* he selected: *When I bring you colour'd toys; On the day when death will knock at thy door; The sleep that flits on baby's eyes; I am like a remnant of a cloud of autumn; On the seashore of endless worlds;* and *Light, my light.*

He has called his settings of four Chinese poems *Water Colors,* and they are well named, for they deal in tints rather than in solid colors. He suggests the Chinese lute in the accompaniment, and he has been subtle in bringing out the drollery that lurks in the verses. In quite different spirit, similar in type to the *Perambulator* Suite, his *Improving Songs for Anxious Children* show real live children in every mood.

Sometimes they are good little boys and girls, other times not so good; but always little boys and girls, as liable to human failings as their parents.

HENRY KIMBALL HADLEY (1871–1937) became a real leader among American composers. Not only were his own works consistently performed, but his efforts and skill at organization advanced materially the well-being of his fellow composers. He was as much interested in having the works of his colleagues played as he was in gaining performances of his own music. During his three seasons as conductor of the Manhattan Symphony in New York, in the early 1930's, he presented thirty-six American works, only eight of which were his own. During his last years he founded the National Association for American Composers and Conductors, which has functioned since his death as a practical instrument for advancing the cause of American music, and which sponsors the Henry Hadley Memorial Library of works by contemporary Americans, deposited in the New York Public Library.

Hadley's facility made him one of the most prolific of our composers. The published catalogue of his works is a sizable pamphlet, and though he may have paid the penalty for writing so much, his music is so playable and so agreeable that its youthfulness and vigor atone for whatever it may lack in philosophical contemplation and deep reflection.

He was born in Somerville, Massachusetts, December 20, 1871. His father had charge of the public school music in that suburb of Boston. He gave his son lessons in piano and violin, and helped him to compose little pieces. Then Henry went to the New England Conservatory and studied composition with Emery and Chadwick. When he was twenty his Overture *Hector and Andromache* was performed by the Manuscript Society of New York, with Walter Damrosch conducting. When he was twenty-two he was made conductor of the Laura Schirmer–Mapleson Opera Company, and toured the country. Then he went abroad to study composition with Mandyczewski at Vienna. When he came back he was music director of St. Paul's School at Garden City on Long Island. From 1904 to 1909 he was abroad again, composing and conducting, the last year at the Stadt Theatre of Mayence, where he produced his one-act opera *Safie*.

In 1909 he went to the far West, to be conductor of the Seattle Symphony Orchestra. For five seasons from 1911 he conducted the San Francisco Orchestra. In 1920 he was made associate conductor of the New York Philharmonic, and in 1929 he organized the Manhattan Symphony Orchestra in New York which he conducted for three seasons.

He composed in all the forms, and for every combination, vocal and instrumental, seemingly with equal success in each. Five of his major works were symphonies. The first, *Youth and Life*, was first heard in 1897 in New York. The second, *The Four Seasons* won the Paderewski prize in 1901, and another from the New England Conservatory. The third Symphony was first played in Berlin in 1907, and in 1908 by the Boston Symphony. The fourth, *North, East, South, West*, was written for the Norfolk Festival in 1911, and was later played by the Boston Symphony and at Queen's Hall, London.

The fifth Symphony was composed in 1935. It was a programmatic work entitled *Connecticut-Tercentenary*, and was commissioned by Mrs. Carl Stoeckel for performance in the Music Shed at Norfolk, Connecticut. The three movements are labeled: 1635, 1735, and 1935. The first, depicting the perils and hardships of the early settlers, is interspersed with Indian themes. The second movement shows a rural contentment, and the last gives an impression of present-day life in Connecticut.

Hadley's operas have been performed by our leading companies. After *Safie*, the next was *Azora;* although *The Atonement of Pan*, the masque he wrote for the 1912 "High Jinks" of the California Bohemian Club, was virtually an opera. *Azora's* full title was *Azora, Daughter of Montezuma*, and its libretto by David Stevens dealt with the Aztecs of Mexico in the fifteenth century. It was presented in 1917 and 1918 by the Chicago Opera Company, in both Chicago and New York.

Bianca won the thousand-dollar prize, and the production offered by the Society of American Singers in 1918. Grant Stewart adapted the libretto from Goldoni's comedy *The Mistress of the Inn*. The first performance was at the Park Theatre in New York. *Cleopatra's Night* is probably Hadley's best opera. When it was produced at the Metropolitan in 1920, many critics hailed it as the most colorful

American opera that had yet been written. It was given a superb production, and its score was rich in its atmospheric treatment. It lasted for two seasons at the Metropolitan. Hadley's last operatic work was *A Night in Old Paris*, a one-act affair produced over the radio by the National Broadcasting Company, February 22, 1933.

In Bohemia was the first of his concert overtures to be published. It was first played in 1902, in Pittsburgh. Hadley himself felt that his tone poem *Salome* was the best of his orchestral works. It was introduced in Boston in 1907. In 1909 the rhapsody for orchestra, *The Culprit Fay*, was awarded the thousand-dollar prize offered by the National Federation of Music Clubs. Another tone poem *Lucifer* was written for the 1915 Norfolk Festival.

In 1935 Hadley produced his *Scherzo Diabolique*, which attempted the portrayal of "the hazards of fast driving, the onrushing myriad headlights of approaching autos, the whirring and whizzing of cars as they pass." It is perhaps an American counterpart of Dukas's *Sorcerer's Apprentice*; the listener expects to hear the car dashed to pieces on its wild midnight ride, and he joins the bassoon in its delicious sigh of relief at the safe ending of the journey.

Others of Hadley's orchestral works are a *Symphonic Fantasia*; an *Othello* Overture; a tone poem *The Ocean*; an Oriental Suite *The Streets of Pekin* which was performed by seventeen orchestras during the season 1930–31; three ballet suites; a Cello Concerto; and a Concertino for piano and orchestra.

Hadley was always successful in writing for chorus. His *Ode to Music*, from Henry van Dyke's poem, was the feature of the Worcester Festival in 1917. A secular oratorio *Resurgam* was performed in Europe as well as in America. Another choral work, *Mirtil in Arcadia*, was one of Hadley's favorites among his own compositions. A cantata *Belshazzar* received its first performance at the Robin Hood Dell, Philadelphia, in 1932. In 1933 he composed *The Legend of Hani* for the annual midsummer festival of the Bohemian Club in San Francisco. Fifteen years earlier, in 1912, he wrote *The Atonement of Pan* for the same organization.

In the field of chamber music Hadley composed a Quintet, a Quartet, and a Sonata for violin and piano. And as if all these were not enough, he published about one hundred and fifty songs. At the time of his death, September 6, 1937, he was a member of the American Academy of Arts and Letters.

DANIEL GREGORY MASON (1873——) is a composer who experimented with folk songs, but who came to the conclusion that American music is necessarily eclectic and cosmopolitan. That its distinctiveness must be individual, rather than national. Hence, in his own music he has followed his own taste. Taking little spontaneous pleasure in the impressionism of Debussy, Ravel, Scriabin, or in the primitivism of Stravinsky, he turns to the classic-romantic type of beauty worked out by Beethoven, Schumann, Brahms, and Franck. He is willing to risk the reactionary label. Yet he has the satisfaction of seeing a number of his fellow composers swing over to the standards he has been following.

Mason is a member of the famous Mason family. He is a grandson of Lowell Mason, and a nephew of William. His father was the Henry Mason who was one of the founders of the piano house of Mason and Hamlin. He was born November 20, 1873 in Brookline, Massachusetts. When he was a student at Harvard he attended the music classes of John K. Paine, but he found Paine so uninspiring that he virtually dropped his music while he was in college, except for writing the music for the Hasty Pudding Club shows. When he was graduated from Harvard he studied with Chadwick in Boston, and Goetschius in New York. Then he went to Paris to work with d'Indy. From 1900 he was active as lecturer and teacher. In 1910 he joined the music faculty of Columbia University, and in 1929 he was made the MacDowell Professor of Music. In 1940 he retired from the chairmanship of the Music Department at Columbia, and was succeeded by Douglas Moore.

Starting with Mason's early works, Opus 5 is a Sonata for violin and piano; Opus 7, a Quartet for piano and strings, played by Gabrilowitsch with the Kneisel Quartet. His *Country Pictures* for piano, Opus 9, have been played by Josef Hofmann, John Powell, and Percy Grainger. His first work for orchestra was the Symphony No. 1, published abroad, and played by Stokowski and the Philadelphia Orchestra. It has had later performances by the Detroit, New York Philharmonic, Chicago, and Boston Orchestras.

Mason's Sonata for clarinet (or violin) and piano was one of the first works selected by the Society for the Publication of American Music. His song cycle *Russians*, for baritone and orchestra, has been featured by Reinald Werrenrath with several symphony orchestras. His *String Quartet on Negro Themes* was first printed privately, but later withdrawn, revised, and issued in its new form by the Society for the Publication of American Music. Other works for string quartet are Variations on a theme by his friend John Powell, and a Folk Song Fantasy on the English theme of *Fanny Blair*.

Mason's orchestral works include a Symphony No. 2, in A Major, and a *Festival Overture* which was published by the Juilliard Foundation. In 1931 a *Chanticleer* overture was introduced by Nikolai Sokoloff and the Cleveland Orchestra and since that time the piece has had more than fifty performances. From these years also came the *Prelude and Fugue*, Opus 20, for piano and orchestra. This work is dedicated to John Powell, who introduced it in concerts with the Chicago, Boston, Philadelphia, and New York Philharmonic-Symphony orchestras.

In 1937 the New York Philharmonic-Symphony introduced Mason's *Lincoln Symphony*. The first movement of this Symphony is "The Candidate from Springfield," and is based largely on an actual tune from the 1860 period, the *Quaboag Quickstep*. The second part is called "Massa Linkum," the slaves' view of their friend, in which the English horn voices their grief in a quasi-spiritual. Then comes "Old Abe's Yarns," and the listener is asked to "sense . . . the relief he found in his grotesque, irresponsible, half-demoniac humor." The *finale* is "1865"; Lincoln "lies dead. . . . The quickstep we once marched with him in triumph has turned to a funeral march in our tragic hearts."

Mason's recent works include a *Divertimento* for symphonic band; *Sentimental Sketches* for violin, cello, and piano; *Serenade* for string quartet; and a *Free and Easy Five-Step* for small orchestra. He is known also as a writer on music. In the latter field he shows scholarliness and clear thinking. His critical-historical series—*Beethoven and His Forerunners, The Romantic Composers, From Grieg to Brahms*, and *Contemporary Composers*—is comprehensive, accurate, and, most important, interesting. *Tune In, America* is a searching analysis of music conditions in America. *The Orchestral Instruments and What They Do* is a guidebook that has been a boon to many concertgoers.

FREDERICK SHEPHERD CONVERSE (1871–1940) had the distinction of being the first composer to have an opera produced at the Metropolitan Opera House in New York. This was his one-act opera *The Pipe of Desire*, which was presented by the company March 18, 1910. It was a tragic little fairy tale, vividly portrayed by the music. Converse was a New Englander, born January 5, 1871 at Newton, Massachusetts. He was a student at Harvard and attended the classes of John K. Paine. Then he went into business for six months; left it for good, and studied with Chadwick. Then to Germany and Rheinberger. His Symphony in D Minor was played when he was graduated from the Royal Academy in Munich in 1898. When he came back to Boston in 1899 he taught harmony at the New England Conservatory, and two years later went to Harvard as a teacher of composition and later as assistant professor. He resigned in 1907 to devote himself to composition, but later went back to the Conservatory as professor of theory and composition. In 1931 he was appointed Dean of the Faculty, and held that position for seven years. He died two years after his retirement, June 8, 1940.

In 1927, Converse achieved fame for a masterful bit of musical humor, which he wrote chiefly to amuse himself. When Honegger sought to immortalize a mountain locomotive of the Pacific type, Converse thought of the Ford. If anything is American, surely it is the flivver. So Converse took his music paper, had a few rides in a Ford, and wrote *Flivver Ten Million*.

The work opens with *Dawn in Detroit*. The toilers march to work, and make their din as they build their machines. Then the *Birth of the Hero*, as he emerges from the welter, full fledged, ready for service. He tries his mettle, and wanders forth into the great world in search of adventure. "America's Romance" is a *May Night by the Roadside*. "America's Frolic" brings *The Joy Riders;* "America's Tragedy" *The Collision*. Then a reminiscence of the building theme, and in *Phoenix Americanus* the hero, righted and shaken, proceeds on his way with redoubled energy, "typical of the indomitable American spirit." For all this the composer requires the modern orchestra in all its glory of wind and percussion, plus muted Ford horn, a wind machine, a factory whistle, and an anvil. Koussevitzky gave it its first performance with the Boston Symphony in the spring of 1927.

Converse had a fluent technique, he wrote easily and with assurance. Chadwick was wise to send him to Rheinberger, for he acquired the contrapuntal facility common to Rheinberger's pupils. He had a long list of works. For orchestra, two concert overtures, *Youth* and *Euphrosyne*; a *Festival March*; two symphonic poems, *Ormazd* and *Ave atque Vale*; three Symphonies; two poems, *Night* and *Day*, for piano and orchestra.

Another opera, *The Sacrifice*, was given by the Boston Opera Company in 1911. Converse wrote an overture, entr'actes, and incidental music for the Philadelphia production of Mackaye's *Jeanne d'Arc* in 1906. His dramatic poem *Job* was first performed at the Worcester Festival of 1907, and a year later in Hamburg. On the same occasion Schumann-Heink sang his *Hagar in the Desert*, a dramatic narrative for low voice and orchestra.

In 1928, the year following the production of *Flivver Ten Million*, Converse was ready with another tone poem picturing America, this time *California*; and in 1929 he composed a Suite *American Sketches* which was given its first performance six years later by the Boston Symphony, February 8, 1935. The four movements of the *Sketches* were called "Manhattan," "The Father of Waters," "Chicken Reel," and "Bright Angel Trail."

After he had written the *American Sketches* Converse turned from American subjects to a more general field. He composed a tone poem for soprano and orchestra called *Prophecy*, founded on a text from Isaiah. This work was first performed by the Boston Symphony, December 16, 1932.

In his later years Converse produced also a String Quartet in E Minor and a Concertino for piano and orchestra. One of the high honors of his career came to him in 1937, when he and Albert Spalding were elected to fill the vacancies in the American Academy of Arts and Letters, caused by the passing of William J. Henderson and Henry K. Hadley.

RUBIN GOLDMARK (1872–1936) was the nephew of Carl Goldmark, the Austrian composer of *Sakuntula*. When Dvořák heard young

Rubin's Trio at one of the concerts at the National Conservatory in New York, he exclaimed: "There are now two Goldmarks!" And there were, for the nephew did very nicely in carrying on the family reputation. He was born in New York, August 15, 1872. He had his academic education at the College of the City of New York and the University of Vienna. He studied music at the Vienna Conservatory. After he returned to New York he studied piano with Joseffy, and composition with Dvořák at the National Conservatory.

Later he became a teacher of piano and theory at the Conservatory. Then his health failed, and he went to Colorado. That was in 1894, and when he was better he founded the Colorado College Conservatory. By 1902 he was able to come back to New York, where he became established as a composer, and as one of our leading teachers of composers. He headed the composition department at the Juilliard Graduate School from 1924 until his death, March 6, 1936. His pupils included such widely divergent types as Frederick Jacobi, Aaron Copland, Nicolai Berezowsky, Bernard Wagenaar, Vittorio Giannini, Paul Nordoff, and George Gershwin.

Goldmark's best known work was the *Requiem* for orchestra, suggested by Lincoln's Gettysburg address. It has an austere grandeur that is faithful to its subject, a directness of purpose that wastes no musical words, but proceeds in a straight line to its goal. His *Hiawatha* Overture was an earlier work, introduced in 1900 by the Boston Symphony. James Gibbons Huneker wrote of this performance:

At the first cantilena on the strings I nearly jumped out of my seat. It was bewilderingly luscious and Goldmarkian—a young Goldmark come to judgment. The family gifts are color and rhythm. This youth has them, and he also has brains. Original invention is yet to come, but I have hopes. The overture, which is not Indian, is full of good things, withal too lengthy in the free fantasia. There is life, and while there's life there's rhythm, and a nice variety there is. The allegro has one stout tune, and the rush and dynamic glow lasts. He lasts, does Rubin Goldmark, and I could have heard the piece through twice. The young American composer has not been idle lately.

The tone poem *Samson* was first played in Boston in 1914. The *Requiem* had its première with the New York Philharmonic in 1919. Goldmark tried Negro material in his *Negro Rhapsody*, published in

Vienna, and he caught the American locale in *The Call of the Plains*, for orchestra. He composed a String Quartet, a Piano Trio, a Sonata for violin and piano, and many smaller pieces and songs.

DAVID STANLEY SMITH (1877———) was Horatio Parker's successor as dean of the Yale University School of Music at New Haven. He had been Parker's assistant for many years. Born in Toledo, Ohio, July 6, 1877, he was the son of a self-taught organist and composer, a business man who played the organ in Toledo churches as an avocation. David's mother was a singer. He went to Yale, though not with the idea of studying music; but he came under Parker's influence from his freshman year, and then attended his classes. He began to play the organ, and while he was a student he had positions in various New Haven churches. When he was graduated, Parker urged him to go to Europe for a year; and he went, not for definite instruction, but to hear music and to broaden his horizon. When he returned after a year and a half, Parker put him on the music faculty at Yale, and in 1920 he succeeded his teacher as dean and professor, and as conductor of the New Haven Symphony Orchestra. He held the position at Yale for twenty years, and after his retirement as dean in 1940, continued his classes in composition.

As a composer, Smith likes to feel that music is an art worthy of the time of a man of serious purpose and intellectual attainments, and not, as he says, "a joke or a vehicle for proclaiming some 'ism.'" As for modernism, he holds that dissonance must be defended on the ground of logic, never used for mere caprice. All music must have architectural and technical interest as well as melodic intention and feeling. He has no sympathy for sentimentality, but he tries to avoid the extreme of harshness or cruelty in reacting against it. This creed is carried into his music. It is always obviously well thought out and planned. Whatever it may lack in spontaneity it supplies in its intellectual background.

Smith's First Symphony was played by Stock and the Chicago Orchestra in 1912; the Second was first heard at the Norfolk Festival in 1918; a Third dates from 1928; and a Fourth was written in 1937, and first performed by the Boston Orchestra on April 14, 1939. He has written also a *Prince Hal* Overture; a suite of *Impressions* (1916); a *Fête Galante* (1920), for flute and orchestra, played several times by

Georges Barrère; a *Cathedral Prelude* (1926), for organ and orchestra; an *Epic Poem* (1926); and a *Rondo Appassionato* for violin and orchestra. His *1929—A Satire* forms a pair with the Overture *Tomorrow*. Both pieces were written in 1932 and 1933.

For chamber orchestra, Smith has written a suite of four pieces entitled *Flowers* (1924); a Sinfonietta for string orchestra (1931); and a Sonatina for junior string orchestra (1932). He has composed also two large choral pieces: the *Rhapsody of St. Bernard* (1915), and the *Vision of Isaiah* (1927). An unproduced opera *Merrymount* was composed many years before Howard Hanson's work bearing the same title.

Smith has a most imposing catalogue of chamber music works. Two Sonatas, one for oboe and piano (1918) and one for violin and piano (1921), and two String Quartets, both in C Major (1921 and 1934), are published by the Society for the Publication of American Music. Thus Smith shares with Mason the honor, accorded no one else, of having had four works published by the Society for the Publication of American Music. He has written eight String Quartets in all. The eighth was heard at the Coolidge Festival in the Library of Congress on April 14, 1940.

Since his retirement as dean of the Yale School of Music, Smith has composed *Credo*, a poem for orchestra, played by the New York Philharmonic-Symphony in November of 1941; a *Requiem*, which was introduced by the New Haven Symphony Orchestra in 1942; and *Daybreak*, a choral work which opened the Centenary Celebration at the Temple Emanu-El, New York, February 25, 1945.

ARTHUR FARWELL (1872——) was one of the pioneers in nationalism. He keenly resented the fact that commercial publishers turned their backs to American composers whenever these musicians wrote anything not in the conventional mold. He had tried experiments with Indian music himself, and he felt a kinship with a group of younger composers who had ideas of their own about American music. He founded the Wa-Wan Press, a publishing organization with the avowed intention of issuing unsalable works by American composers; all progressive and individual work, whatever its tendencies and artistic affiliations, with a special welcome to any music that developed in interesting fashion any folk music to be found on American soil. This was in 1901, and for eleven years Farwell helped to support the Wa-Wan Press, and raised the money to pay its deficits by lecturing and writing. Through it he helped launch a number of his fellow composers: Henry F. Gilbert, Edgar Stillman Kelley, Harvey Worthington Loomis, and many others. At the end of eleven years he felt that his work was done, and he handed over the catalogue of compositions to the firm of G. Schirmer, in New York.

Farwell did not decide to become a musician until he was graduated from the Massachusetts Institute of Technology at the age of twenty-one. He was born in St. Paul, Minnesota, April 23, 1872, and though he had violin lessons from the time he was nine years old, there was no musical life in the St. Paul of his early years that would give him any idea of taking music seriously. It was when he went to Boston, just before he entered the Massachusetts Institute of Technology, that he heard a symphony orchestra for the first time (Nikisch with the Boston Symphony), and after that his principal reason for staying at the engineering school was that it kept him in Boston, where he could hear the concerts every week. The day he was graduated he had an interview with George Chadwick, and later he met MacDowell. He had been studying harmony in the summers, and he decided to become a composer.

Then he studied composition in Boston, and four years later went abroad to study with Humperdinck and Pfitzner in Germany, and with Guilmant in Paris. When he came back to America in 1899 he became lecturer on the history of music at Cornell University, and began his first experiments with Indian music. He founded the Wa-Wan Press at Newton Center, Massachusetts, in 1901. In the following years he made frequent journeys to the Far West, lecturing, and studying the songs of the Indians in the Southwest, and the folk songs of the Spanish Californians.

For six years from 1909 he was on the staff of *Musical America* in New York, and when Gaynor was elected mayor in 1910, Farwell was appointed to the newly created position of Supervisor of Municipal Music. He supplanted several of the park bands with orchestras, and he carried into effect some of his ideas regarding pageants. He wrote incidental music for Louis Parker's *Pageant Play*, and for *Joseph and*

His Brethren. He wrote and conducted the music for the presentation of Percy MacKaye's *Caliban,* which was given in New York's Lewisohn Stadium in 1916.

In 1915 he succeeded David Mannes as director of the Music School Settlement in New York, and in 1916 he organized the New York Community Chorus, together with Harry Barnhart. For nine years after 1918 he was in California teaching at the University of California in Los Angeles, and in Berkeley, organizing choruses and composing music for pageants. Often directing them, for this form of Community Drama has been one of his hobbies. In 1927 he went to East Lansing, Michigan, where he conducted the theoretical courses and lectures on music history at the Michigan State College until his retirement in 1939.

Farwell once said that his interest in folk music came from the fact that as a spiritual descendant of the tribe of Tom Sawyer and Huck Finn, he got "a great kick out of a rip-snorting development of a good old American tune," such as he used in his recent *Sourwood Mountain,* for piano. He made no flat break with tradition in his music, although in his later works he used Oriental scales instead of the major and minor modes. He felt that a new music can be evolved by applying the harmonies of the West to the scales of the East.

The first of his Indian compositions for orchestra was *Dawn,* played for the first time at the St. Louis Exposition in 1904. This was published in a piano arrangement by the Wa-Wan Press. His next large Indian score was called *The Domain of Hurakan*—the wind god of the Central American Indians. For piano, he has written a group of *American Indian Melodies;* a *Nuvajo War Dance; Impressions of the Wa-Wan Ceremony* (from the Omaha tribe); *Pawnee Horses;* and a *Fugue Fantasia.* He has also made settings of some Negro melodies, and cowboy and prairie songs.

These folk song developments are only a small part of Farwell's creative work. The opus numbers of his compositions run to one hundred and three. He has in his time tried innovations, one of them with a form that has an analogy to the choral-prelude of the Reformation. This appeared in his *Mountain Song,* which he termed a symphonic song-suite—with movements based on the themes of choral songs, the audience singing the songs whenever the form of the piece demands it. This technique was also used in the *Symphonic Hymn on March! March!* and in the *Symphonic Song on Old Black Joe.*

Among Farwell's later works, the most important is perhaps the orchestral suite *Gods of the Mountain,* after the play by Dunsany. This had its première in Minneapolis in 1929, and has had frequent performances elsewhere. He has composed also a *Rudolph Gott* Symphony, which is based on a fragment of something over a hundred bars by an ill-fated friend who was one of the composer's greatest inspirations.

Although he is well past seventy, Farwell is by no means through with innovations and experiments. They are too much a part of his nature for him ever to abandon them. He may be less aggressively nationalistic than he was thirty years ago, but he still feels that a creative artist is lost if he does not keep close to his own land and people, and in some degree reflect them. But he should not be thought of simply as a "folk" composer, for whatever he has done in that field (and he is happy to have done it) is far outweighed by his freely created work.

EDWARD BURLINGAME HILL (1872——) is of New England parentage and of the Harvard tradition. His grandfather was president of the university, and his father a chemistry professor. He was born in Cambridge, September 9, 1872, and lives there today. When he was graduated from Harvard he had highest honors in music (under John K. Paine). He later studied with Widor in Paris, and Chadwick in Boston. In 1908 he became a teacher at Harvard—first as an instructor, then a professor, and from 1928 to 1934 as chairman of the Division of Music. He continued as James E. Ditson Professor of Music until his retirement in 1941.

For many years Hill was known most widely for programmatic works, particularly for his two *Stevensoniana* Suites for orchestra. The second of these has been the most frequently performed. Its four movements are based on poems from Robert Louis Stevenson's *Child's Garden of Verses.* The scoring is rich and colorful, with a leaning toward the French impressionists; but also with a tenderness and simplicity that is altogether personal. Other of Hill's descriptive pieces are *Lilacs*, inspired by Amy Lowell's poem, and a symphonic poem based on Poe's *The Fall of the House of Usher*.

In more recent years Hill has preferred to compose absolute music, and he believes that his music has become more personal and more the product of his environment. He is willing to be labeled a conservative, for even though he has shown an occasional tendency towards mild polytonality, he realizes that radical devices are not for him.

He has composed three symphonies, the third of them introduced for the first time by the Boston Symphony, December 3, 1937. In a statement quoted in the program notes of the concert, Hill announced that the work had "no descriptive background," and that it aimed "merely to present and develop musical ideas according to traditional forms." One reviewer remarked that although the work did not sound especially modern, it bowed to modern devices, and that it had a type of humor that George W. Chadwick might have used had he lived long enough to have absorbed the newer devices.[1]

In 1931, Hill composed a Concertino for piano and orchestra which was first performed by Jesús María Sanromá with the Boston Symphony, April 25, 1932. In this work the composer made his bow to jazz, as he had done some years earlier in his four *Jazz Studies* for two pianos. The piece is a short work in three connected movements, the first and last employing lively, vigorous material which offsets the charming sentimentality of the middle section.

In the summer of 1932, Hill composed a Sinfonietta, Opus 57, which the Boston Orchestra performed in Cambridge, March 9, 1933, and then in Boston. Again animated rhythms characterized the work, which proved to be altogether stimulating, and skillfully written.

Professor Hill has another Sinfonietta on his list, numbered Opus 40A, and representing an orchestral arrangement of his String Quartet, Opus 40. The Quartet was composed in 1935, presented in Boston in February of 1936, and featured at the Harvard Tercentenary concerts the following September. As a Sinfonietta the work was introduced by the Boston Symphony during the season of 1935–36. It is conservative without suggesting a conscious harking back to the past. It has indi-

[1] *Musical America*, December 10, 1937.

viduality and the personal quality Hill aims to achieve, as well as lyric charm.

In addition to the Quartet, Opus 40, Hill has to his credit several chamber music works. An earlier Sonata for clarinet (or violin) and piano was published in 1926–27 by the Society for the Publication of American Music. A Sextet for wind instruments and piano, Opus 39, was commissioned by Elizabeth Sprague Coolidge and performed at the Coolidge Festival in Pittsfield, Massachusetts, September 20, 1934, and later published by the same society.

A more recent Quartet for piano and strings, Opus 42, had its first performance, by Sanromá and the Boston String Quartet in Boston, January 11, 1938. There is also a Concerto for violin and orchestra, composed in 1933–34, and its first movement revised in October, 1937, which was first played by Ruth Posselt and the Boston Orchestra in November, 1938; and a Concertino for string orchestra, Opus 46, introduced by Koussevitzky in Boston on April 19, 1940.

ERNEST SCHELLING (1876–1939) had a brilliant career. He was one of our leading concert pianists, pupil of Moszkowski and Paderewski; he had a number of vital compositions to his credit; and in his later years became one of the leading exponents of orchestral concerts for children, conducting Saturday morning concerts with the New York Philharmonic in New York and neighboring districts. He was born in Belvidere, New Jersey, July 26, 1876, and was a musical prodigy from childhood. When he was only four years old he made a public appearance as pianist at the Academy of Music in Philadelphia. When he was six he was taken to the Paris Conservatoire to study with Mathias. Later he worked with Moszkowski, Pruckner, Leschetizky, Huber, Barth, and finally for four years with Paderewski at his villa in Switzerland. He achieved international rank as a pianist, and has played in recital and with orchestras throughout America and in Europe.

When the first World War broke out, Schelling was made a captain, and later a major. In 1918 he went to Poland with his friend Paderewski, at the time when the great Pole became premier of his native country. In the summer of 1919 he was injured in an automobile accident in Switzerland, and it was necessary for him to give up most of his work as a pianist. He became active chiefly as a composer and orchestral conductor. His children's concerts with the New York Philharmonic Symphony achieved great success. Their object was primarily to explain the various instruments of the orchestra. Schelling collected illustrations of instruments from all over the world, and during his concerts he had them thrown on a screen by stereopticon projection. Schelling continued these concerts until the time of his death, December 8, 1939.

Schelling's most important works are the *Impressions from an Artist's Life* and *A Victory Ball*. The first is a set of variations for piano and orchestra. Each variation depicts one of the composer's artist friends. It was first played by the Boston Symphony under Muck, in 1916, and published in Leipzig. *A Victory Ball* takes its program from the poem by Alfred Noyes. The gayety of the dancers is halted by the sounds of war, by the spirits of the fallen, the roll of the drum, and taps. It is vivid music, uncompromising in its reminder of the horrors of war. It was first introduced in Philadelphia under Stokowski in 1923, and has had repeated performances since its première.

Schelling composed also a *Legende Symphonique,* played by the Berlin Philharmonic in 1906; a Symphony in C Minor; a *Suite Fantastique,* introduced by Mengleberg in Amsterdam (1905); a Violin Concerto, played by Fritz Kreisler with the Boston Symphony in 1917; a tone poem *Morocco,* played in 1927 by the New York Philharmonic with the composer conducting; and a number of piano pieces and some chamber music.

MORTIMER WILSON (1876–1932) was technically one of the best-equipped composers in this country. A disciple and pupil of Max Reger, he was definitely of the Reger tradition, and could toss complicated counterpoint from his pen as easily as he could talk to his friends. He was always to the point in his music. If he wished to develop a theme, he could write a symphony on the simplest of ideas. If he chose not to develop a melody, he stated it simply and stopped. He hated to be obvious; if he thought that another composer would have extended a theme if he had been writing his piece, Wilson snatched the tune away and told the listener he could have no more of it. A bit perverse sometimes; for Wilson liked to laugh at his audience.

He left an imposing list of published works. A Suite for trio, *From*

My Youth, later scored for full orchestra and played by the New York Philharmonic; two Sonatas for violin and piano; three Suites for piano (one of them, *In Georgia,* has been orchestrated by the composer); a Trio; an *Overture "1849";* a scenic fantasy for orchestra, *My Country;* and many shorter pieces. In manuscript there were five Symphonies; a *Country Wedding* Suite for orchestra; and an Organ Sonata.

Wilson was born in the Middle West, at Chariton, Iowa, August 6, 1876. He studied in Chicago with Jacobsohn, Gleason, and Middelschulte. Then he taught theory for six years (1901–7) at the University School of Music at Lincoln, Nebraska, and after that spent three years in Leipzig, studying with Hans Sitt and Max Reger, and teaching pupils of his own. When he returned in 1911 he went South, taught at the Atlanta Conservatory in Georgia, and conducted the Atlanta Symphony Orchestra. He went to New York in 1918, and made his headquarters there until he died, January 27, 1932.

He made some experiments that antedate the modern synchronized scores of our sound pictures. Before the day of the talkies, Douglas Fairbanks engaged him to write original scores to accompany his motion pictures, to be played by theatre orchestras during the presentation of the pictures. The idea was highly successful in the major cities, where the orchestras were adequate and had time to rehearse the timing of the music with the film. But in smaller cities and towns the results were not so happy. In the most ambitious of the scores, the one he composed for *The Thief of Bagdad,* Wilson wrote music on broad lines, with leit-motives for every character, and for underlying emotions.

So many years have passed since HOWARD BROCKWAY (1870——) has published any compositions that we may well use the past tense in writing of his work. And it is indeed a pity, for he possessed a genuine talent—a gift for melody and a harmonic gift that brought a luster to all he wrote.

Brockway was born in Brooklyn, New York, November 22, 1870. When he was a little boy he was taken regularly to the Theodore Thomas concerts, and to string quartet recitals. He sat by the hour while his teacher played him Bach, Mozart, Haydn, Beethoven, Schumann, Chopin. When he was nineteen he went abroad to study with

Barth, and composition with O. B. Boise. In 1895 the Berlin Philharmonic gave a program entirely composed of his works. He had written a number of pieces which were published in Berlin—a Sonata for violin and piano, a *Ballade* for piano, and a number of shorter works.

He came back to America in 1895 and settled in New York. He was active as a pianist and teacher, and in 1903 he joined the faculty of the Peabody Institute in Baltimore, where he stayed for six years. Then he returned to New York, and has been active principally as a teacher —privately, and at the Institute of Musical Art and the Mannes School.

Brockway's works for orchestra are a Symphony, a *Ballade*, a symphonic *Scherzo*, and a *Sylvan* Suite, which was published in 1900. The Suite was first performed by the Boston Symphony under Gericke in 1901. The Symphony was not heard until 1907, when the Boston Orchestra, then conducted by Muck, gave it a performance. He composed a number of works for chorus, and we have already spoken of his exquisite arrangements of songs from the Kentucky Mountains.

Brockway was at heart a conservative, enough to believe that melody is the basis of musical composition. He sensed the value of the astounding experiments that others have made in harmonic freedom, through polytonality and atonal structure. But he was wise enough to know that the ultimate use of these devices must be subjective, if they are to accomplish anything for music as an art.

ARTHUR NEVIN (1871–1943) was a younger brother of Ethelbert Nevin, and though his music covered many forms of musical composition, his principal work was based on his experiences with the Blackfeet Indians. He spent the summers of 1903 and 1904 on the Blackfeet Reservation in Montana, and there heard the story of *Poia*, which Randolph Hartley put into a libretto for the opera that Nevin composed. President Roosevelt invited the composer to give an illustrated talk on his work at the White House in 1907, but in spite of this indorsement and interest, the opera was performed, not in an American opera house, but in Germany, where it had four performances at the Royal Opera in Berlin during the summer of 1909. Humperdinck, then at work on *Königskinder*, assisted in the German translation of *Poia's* libretto. Humperdinck asked Nevin to stay in

Germany to assist him in preparing the orchestral score of *Königs-kinder*, but Nevin had to return to America.

Nevin wrote another opera in 1911—*Twilight*, in one act. This, it is said, was actually accepted for performance by the Metropolitan, but through a misunderstanding with the management it never came to performance there. Under the name of *A Daughter of the Forest* it was produced in Chicago in 1918.

Nevin was born in Sewickley, Pennsylvania, April 27, 1871, the youngest son of a family that boasted another distinguished musician, Ethelbert Nevin, composer of *The Rosary*. Arthur Nevin was educated at the New England Conservatory in Boston, and abroad with Klindworth, O. B. Boise, and Humperdinck. For five years he was professor of music in the University of Kansas, and for another five years director of municipal music in Memphis, Tennessee. In his later years he lived mostly in the East, and died July 10, 1943.

Nevin's instrumental works include five major orchestral pieces: *Lorna Doone Suite* (1897); *Miniature Suite* (1902); *Springs of Saratoga* (1911); a Symphonic Poem (1930), and *Arizona* (1935); as well as a String Quartet in D Minor (1929).

SIGISMOND STOJOWSKI (1870——) is a Pole, born April 18, 1870, who came to America in 1905. Except for visits abroad he has been with us ever since. He was a pupil of Delibes at the Paris Conservatoire, and had the guidance of Paderewski in his piano studies. He has been active in America as a pianist and a teacher of pianists. He has written a Symphony and a Suite for orchestra; two Concertos and a Rhapsody for piano and orchestra; a Violin Concerto and a Cello Sonata; a quantity of chamber music and many piano pieces. His *Prayer for Poland* is scored for chorus, organ, and orchestra.

FRANK PATTERSON (1871——) is the composer of two operas that have been produced. *The Echo* was presented in 1925 at the Biennial Conference of the National Federation of Music Clubs, in Portland, Oregon in 1925. *Beggar's Love* was performed in 1929 by the Matinée Musicale of New York. This was an earlier work than *The Echo*, for it had been written and performed some ten years before in Los Angeles, under its original title *A Little Girl at Play* (*A Tragedy of the Slums*). Later, in 1931, the overture to another opera, *Mountain*

Blood, was produced at the American Composers' Concerts in Rochester.

Patterson was born in Philadelphia, January 5, 1871. He studied music with Hugh Clarke at the University of Pennsylvania, and then with Rheinberger and Thuille in Munich. He has a reputation as a theorist, and he has delved deeply into the subject of tone relationships. For a number of years he was a member of the editorial staff of the *Musical Courier.* Then he lived for a time in Paris, but returned to America before the outbreak of World War II. He is the author of *Practical Instrumentation; How to Write a Good Tune;* and *The Perfect Modernist.* As a composer he is at heart a conservative; for he says that he loves melody and tries to write it. Yet he has an intense sympathy with his modernist colleagues; he helped organize the United States Section of the International Society for Contemporary Music, and for several years was the chairman of its music committee.

Although FREDERICK AYRES (1876–1926) did not use actual Indian melodies in his works, he nevertheless caught the spirit of the West—the breadth of the mountains, the vastness of the plains. Born Frederick Ayres Johnson in Binghamton, New York, March 17, 1876, he had an academic education at Cornell University, and then studied composition with Edgar Stillman Kelley and Arthur Foote. For a number of years he lived at Colorado Springs, and became a musical spokesman for the Rocky Mountain section, where he died November 23, 1926. He composed an Overture *From the Plains;* a String Quartet; two Trios; a Sonata for violin and piano, and one for cello and piano. His song cycle *The Seeonee Wolves* is vivid and startling.

HENRY EICHHEIM (1870–1942) won his spurs principally for his study of Oriental music and for his faithful settings of its melodies. He was born in Chicago, January 3, 1870, and was educated at the Chicago Musical College. For a year he was a member of the Theodore Thomas Orchestra, and from 1890 to 1912 was one of the first violins of the Boston Symphony. Then he resigned to give himself to composing and recital work. He died in Santa Barbara, August 22, 1942.

His *Oriental Impressions* for orchestra (published in 1927 by the Society for the Publication of American Music) was an enlargement of a series of *Oriental Sketches* composed for the Pittsfield (Massachusetts) Chamber Music Festival of 1921. He had journeyed several times to the Far East—Korea, Japan, China, India, Java, Burma. He studied various types of Oriental music, and returned from each trip with copious notes and a large collection of instruments. Of the *Impressions*, Carl Engel wrote in the *Chesterian:*

They are vivid, graphic and abound in unusual sonorities which pleasantly impinge upon the ear. Mr. Eichheim stops at no half measures; he does not hesitate to introduce all the "offensive" din and metallic racket dear to the pig-tailed music lover. To the untraveled, these brief sketches suggest a knowledge of the East as sensitively sympathetic as that of Paul Claudel, tempered as it is—in both cases—with Gallic thought and taste. To anyone enriched with recollections, they may conjure up the harmonious disorder of Yeddo and Peking.

Following his orchestral Suite *Burma* (1927), and his *Java* (1929), he composed *Bali* (1933), a series of Variations based on Balinese music which he heard in a temple court at Denpassar. When the composition was first performed by the Philadelphia Orchestra, Lawrence Gilman, in the New York *Herald Tribune* (December 6, 1933) pronounced it "a fascinating web of tone, cunningly wrought, perturbing, not easily to be forgotten." In addition to his earlier works, Eichheim's later compositions include a *Japanese Nocturne*, commissioned by Mrs. Elizabeth Sprague Coolidge in 1930; a *Korean Sketch* for orchestra; and a Sonata for violin and piano, performed at the Pittsfield (Massachusetts) Festival in 1934.

ARNE OLDBERG (1874———) has written many orchestral works and considerable chamber music: four Symphonies; two Overtures—*Paola and Francesca,* and *Festival;* an orchestral fantasy *At Night;* a *Rhapsody;* a symphonic poem *The Sea;* a set of twelve *Variations* for organ and orchestra; a Concerto for horn; a Concerto for organ; two Concertos for piano and orchestra; a String Quartet; two Quintets for piano and strings; a Quintet for piano and woodwind quartet; a Piano Sonata, and many smaller works.

Oldberg was born in Youngstown, Ohio, July 12, 1874, the son of an authority on pharmacy. He had his early training in Chicago, and then studied abroad under Leschetizky (piano), and Rheinberger (composition). Since 1899 he has been the head of the piano department at Northwestern University in Evanston, Illinois. His works have been brought out at the North Shore Festivals, and by the Chicago, Philadelphia, Minneapolis, and other orchestras.

His second Piano Concerto was awarded a first prize of $1,000 in the 1931 Hollywood Bowl competition. This work had its première in the Bowl under Frederick Stock in the summer of 1932, and subsequent hearings in Chicago on November 3 and 4 of the same year. Both in Hollywood and in Chicago the soloist was Oldberg's daughter-in-law Hilda Edwards.

Oldberg's symphonic poem *The Sea* was first performed by the Chicago Symphony, March 11 and 12, 1937. The reviewer for *Musical America* (March 25, 1937) found it "sound music, romantic in outlook and substance, and flawlessly expert in setting forth its picture." A little less than six years later, December 31, 1942, Oldberg's Fourth Symphony was introduced by the Chicago Symphony.

LOUIS CAMPBELL-TIPTON (1877–1921) had been a theory teacher at the Chicago Musical College up to the time he settled in Paris in 1901. Before he died he wrote that the prospect of getting a production for American works was not as hopeless as it had been, but that he had never been fond enough of work to be ready to sacrifice time and energy for writing a large composition, when he saw no hope of its ever being made known. Nevertheless, he had in manuscript two operas and a number of orchestral works.

His best works were his *Sonata Heroic* for piano and his songs. His style was principally of the German romantic stamp. He was born in Chicago, November 21, 1877, and died in Paris, May 1, 1921.

RUDOLPH GANZ (1877——) is best known to the public as a concert pianist, and as president of the Chicago Musical College and successor to Ernest Schelling as conductor of the Young People's Concerts of the New York Philharmonic-Symphony. He is also an accomplished composer, and has to his credit a Symphony; a *Konzertstück* for piano and orchestra; a Suite for orchestra on American scenes; a series of *Animal Pictures;* a Piano Concerto which the composer performed with the Chicago Symphony February 20 and 21, 1941; and numerous piano pieces and choral works. Ganz was born in Zurich, Switzerland, February 24, 1877.

BLAIR FAIRCHILD (1877–1933) was another expatriate. He was

born in Belmont, Massachusetts, January 23, 1877, and studied at Harvard, and with Buonamici in Florence. He went abroad as an attaché in the diplomatic service, at Constantinople and later at Teheran, and in 1903 settled in Paris as a music teacher. There he remained until his death, April 23, 1933. In 1938 a distinguished group presented a memorial concert of Fairchild's works at New York's Town Hall, with a program which included his Sonata for violin and piano, his Trio, a group of solo songs, and his four Psalms for soli and chorus, sung by the Schola Cantorum.

Others of Fairchild's works are Three Symphonic Tableaux for orchestra, *East and West;* three Symphonic Poems; a ballet *Dame Libellule,* which is in the repertory of the Paris Opéra Comique; considerable chamber music; and a number of choral works, songs, and smaller pieces.

LIONEL BARRYMORE (1878———), long distinguished as an actor on stage and screen, has been able partially to realize his ambition as a composer; his *Preludium and Fugue* received its première with the Indianapolis Symphony Orchestra in 1944. Barrymore has written also a symphonic poem *Beyond the Horizon;* an orchestral piece *The Woodman and the Elves;* an *Elegie,* for oboe and orchestra; *Farewell Symphony,* a one-act opera; *Russian Dances* and *Ballet Viennoise* for orchestra; two songs, *Johnnie Dear* and *Our Prayer;* and four piano pieces.

The *Southern Rhapsody* of LUCIUS HOSMER (1870–1935) has been a standard item in radio programs and in popular orchestral programs. Hosmer composed also a *Northern Rhapsody,* which is not played as often, and an *Ethiopian Rhapsody.* These pieces are somewhat in the nature of potpourris of familiar, appropriate melodies, but they are woven together in an integrated form, and are truly concert overtures. Hosmer was born in South Acton, Massachusetts, August 14, 1870, and died in the same city, May 11, 1935. He was a pupil of George W. Chadwick, and his works include a romantic comedy-opera *The Rose of the Alhambra;* a comic opera *The Walking Delegate;* and numerous orchestral pieces, piano music, and songs.

MABEL WHEELER DANIELS (1879———) has an honored place among our women composers. She was born in Swampscott, Massachusetts, November 27, 1879, the daughter of George F. Daniels, at

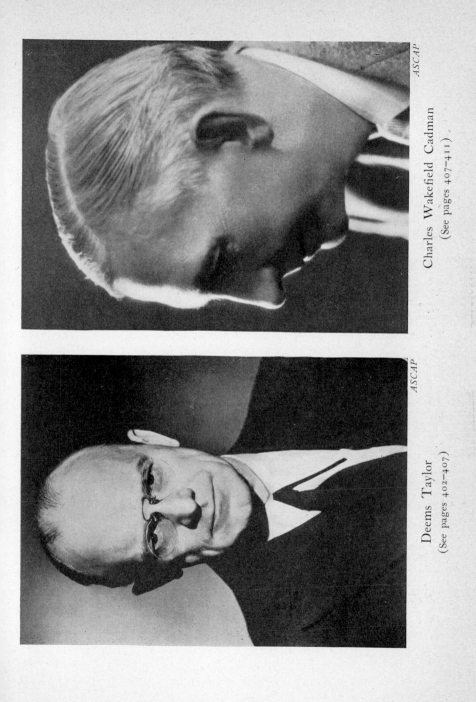

Deems Taylor
(See pages 402–407)

Charles Wakefield Cadman
(See pages 407–411)

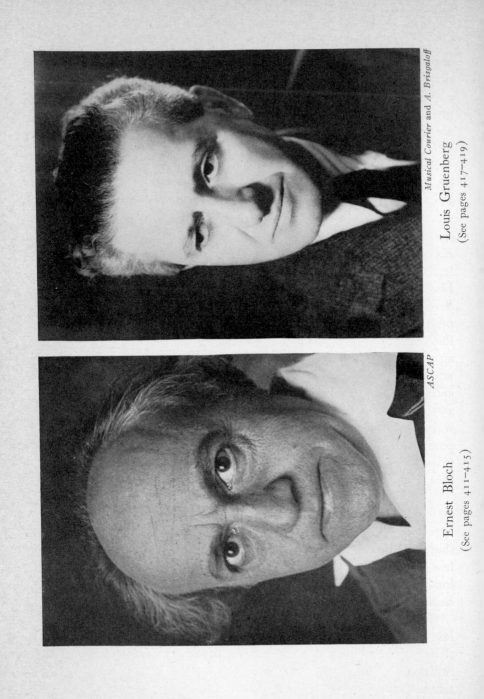

Louis Gruenberg
(See pages 417–419)

Musical Courier and A. Brisgaloff

Ernest Bloch
(See pages 411–415)

ASCAP

one time president of the Handel and Haydn Society. After graduation from college, she studied composition with George W. Chadwick,
and later with Ludwig Thuille in Munich. In 1911 she received two
prizes offered by the National Federation of Music Clubs, one for the
song *Villa of Dreams,* and the other for the two three-part songs
Voice of My Beloved, and *Eastern Song.*

Among her best-known works are *The Desolate City,* poem for
baritone and orchestra, first performed at the MacDowell Festival in
Peterboro, New Hampshire, 1913; *Peace with a Sword,* for mixed
voices and orchestra, first performed by the Handel and Haydn Society of Boston, 1917; *Songs of Elfland,* 1924; *The Holy Star,* 1928;
Exultate Deo, composed for the fiftieth anniversary of Radcliffe College in 1929, and presented by the Radcliffe Choral Society and the
Harvard Glee Club with the Boston Symphony Orchestra in 1932.
Song of Jael, a cantata for soli, mixed voices, and orchestra, was first
performed at the Worcester Festival in 1940. A *Pastoral Ode,* for
flute and strings, was first heard at the Boston Flute Players' Club, and
again with the National Broadcasting Orchestra. *Deep Forest,* a prelude for little symphony, had its première in 1932, and was rescored
and introduced in larger form by the Boston Symphony Orchestra in
1937. *Pirates' Island, In the Greenwood,* and *Fairy Scherzo,* orchestral
works, have appeared on programs of several orchestras. She has composed also many songs, including *Glory and Endless Years, The
Waterfall, Lady of Dreams, Daybreak,* and *Beyond;* a part-song *June
Rhapsody;* a number of choruses; and a Violin Sonata.

* * *

Several of our elder composers are radical experimenters, showing
that youth is not the only age in which musicians are daring and heed-
less of convention. And a number of these senior radicals became such
long before it was the fashion to disregard the traditions of romanticism.

CHARLES E. IVES (1874——) is a fascinating enigma. But his reckless courage in experimenting with polyharmonies and polyrhythms,
strong dissonances, atonality, and rhythmic intricacies, long before
Stravinsky, Schoenberg, and similarly famous Europeans had for-
saken conventional idioms, has become more and more widely recog-

nized. In recent years he has had numerous performances and broadcasts both in the United States and abroad.

Ives believes that the "old" and "new" are either parts of the same substance or they are nonexistent. That the apostles of each are usually taken up with abusing each other or getting in their own way. And he points out, truly enough, that while each examines and appreciates the other to some extent, the radicals fight in a bigger way than their opponents. They generally pay homage to the "old"; while many of the conservatives ignore the "new" and deride it. And as for the manner of speech, he writes:

If idioms are more to be born than to be selected, then the things of life and human nature that a man has grown up with—(not that one man's experience is better than another's, but that it is *his*)—may give him something better in his substance and manner than an overlong period of superimposed idiomatic education which quite likely doesn't fit his constitution. My father used to say, "If a poet knows more about a horse than he does about heaven, he might better stick to the horse, and some day the horse may carry him into heaven."

Ives was born in Danbury, Connecticut, October 20, 1874. His father was a musician, teacher of the violin, piano, and theory, who played in the town brass band at Danbury, led the village choir, the music at camp meetings and the local choral society. He also was a student of acoustics, and made many experiments in the character of musical instruments, tonal combinations, and tone divisions. The son was his pupil, and after his father's death he studied with Dudley Buck and Harry Rowe Shelley, and Horatio Parker at Yale.

For a time Charles Ives was an organist at Danbury, New Haven, and in New York; but in 1898 he entered business, and kept his music as an avocation until his retirement in 1930. His modernism developed while he was still in Yale, and in spite of the frowns he probably had from Parker, he tried his experiments on the orchestra of a local theatre at rehearsal time. His first work to be published, in 1919, was his second Sonata *Concord, Massachusetts, 1840–60*, with its four movements named *Emerson, Hawthorne, The Alcotts*, and *Thoreau*. It was accompanied by an essay, printed in a separate volume. The composer said that his Sonata was an attempt "to present one person's impression of the spirit of transcendentalism that is associated with the minds of Concord over half a century ago. This is undertaken in impressionistic pictures of Emerson and Thoreau, a sketch of the Alcotts, and a scherzo supposed to reflect a lighter quality often found in the fantastic side of Hawthorne."

When the sonata was first distributed most musicians were astonished by its appalling technical difficulties, bizarre beyond serious consideration. Part of it was played at the 1928 Salzburg Festival, but it was not publicly performed in this country until Ralph Kirkpatrick presented it in Town Hall, New York, January 20, 1939. The next day, Lawrence Gilman wrote in the New York *Herald Tribune:*

This sonata is exceptionally great music—it is, indeed, the greatest music composed by an American, and the most deeply and essentially American in impulse and implication. It is wide-ranging and capacious. It has passion, tenderness, humor, simplicity, homeliness. It has imaginative and spiritual vastness. It has wisdom and beauty, and profundity, and a sense of the encompassing terror and splendor of human life and human destiny—a sense of those mysteries that are both human and divine.

Not all members of the audience agreed with Gilman's extraordinary praise. Many felt that the work lacked organization, and that it was not sufficiently articulate. But almost everyone present felt that he had heard something moving and vital.

Ives's works include also four Violin Sonatas; another Piano Sonata; two cantatas; two overtures; a String Quartet; three Symphonies, of which the first two are in strict conventional form; three orchestral Suites, the first consisting of a group of three *New England Scenes:* "Boston Common," "Putnam's Camp (Redding, Connecticut)," and "The Housatonic at Stockbridge"; some quarter-tone music for two pianos; many pieces for small chamber groups, and a volume of a hundred and fourteen songs, privately printed in 1922.

JOHN PARSONS BEACH (1877——) is one of the older of the present-day "modernists"—one of the first to branch into radical paths. He was born in Gloversville, New York, October 11, 1877; trained at the New England Conservatory in Boston. Then for five years he taught piano in the Northwestern Conservatory at Minneapolis, and theoretical subjects at the University of Minnesota. After that he lived

for a time in New Orleans. Then he spent seven years in Paris, studying fugue and composition with Gédalge. He later returned to New
York, and since 1939 has divided his time between that city and Pasadena, California.

His orchestral works include *Asolani,* a series of three pieces; *New
Orleans Street Cries;* and the ballets *Phantom Satyr* and *Mardi Gras.*
For chamber music combinations he has written *Naïve Landscapes,*
for flute, oboe, clarinet, and piano; a *Poem* for string quartet; *Angelo's
Letter,* for tenor or baritone and chamber orchestra; and a *Concert
for Six Instruments,* flute, oboe, clarinet, violin, viola, and cello. He
has published a number of piano pieces and songs, and has written two
short works for the stage—*Pippa's Holiday,* a theatre scene for soprano
and orchestra, from the Introduction to Browning's *Pippa Passes;* and
Jornida and Jornidel, a short opera in two scenes from Grimm's fairy
tale.

Lawrence Gilman once called CARL RUGGLES (1876——) "the first
unicorn to enter American music," and added that he was "the master
of a strange, torrential, and disturbing discourse." Ruggles is a composer who chafes under the restrictions imposed upon him by the
capabilities of the instruments in the orchestra. Their limitations of
range prevent his themes from extending themselves as far as the
composer would like, and many added instruments are needed to
achieve the massive sonorities he desires.

Ruggles has composed a relatively small number of works, and
these have not been widely played. *Men and Mountains* and *Portals*
have been performed by a number of our symphony orchestras, and
Sun Treader was featured by the International Society for Contemporary Music at the Barcelona Festival.

The composer was born in Marion, Massachusetts, March 11, 1876.
He was educated at Harvard, and then settled for a time in Winona,
Minnesota. For many years he has lived in Arlington, Vermont, where
he has his home in a made-over schoolhouse. Those who are not
Ruggles enthusiasts claim that he composes by "formulae" which
bring reminders of the twelve-tone system of Schoenberg. But Ruggles
countered this view in an interview which appeared in the New York
Herald Tribune, February 10, 1943. "All real composers," he said,
"create their own formulas—I know I have created formulas of my
own and some moderns have said 'Ah, too bad, he goes by formula, if

he wouldn't do that he would be a good composer,' but I make the point that a real composer should be able to break the formula, to bust it all to hell when he felt it necessary to bust it; otherwise you are the victim of your own formula, you have created only a Frankenstein monster."

ARTHUR FICKENSCHER (1871———) is an avowed experimenter. He divides the octaves into no less than sixty subdivisions, and has invented an instrument called the "Polytone" which will sound these tones in accurate intonation. Fickenscher was born in Aurora, Illinois, March 9, 1871, studied in Munich, and after graduation from the Conservatory there toured as assisting pianist with famous singers, including David Bispham and Schumann-Heink. At present he is head of the Music Department of the University of Virginia. His orchestral works include the following: *Willowwave and Wellaway; Day of Judgment; Out of the Gay Nineties;* and *Variations on a Theme in Medieval Style.* He has composed also chamber music and choral works.

* * *

The following composers, whom we can mention only briefly, also were born in the 1870's:

FRANZ CARL BORNSCHEIN
> Born, Baltimore, 1879.
> Violin Concerto; String Quartet; Quintet; Sextet for flute and strings; *Three Persian Poems* for orchestra; symphonic scherzo *The Sea God's Daughter;* orchestral Suite *The Phantom Canoe;* symphonic ballad *Louisiana;* the symphonic poems —*The Rime of the Ancient Mariner, A Hero's Espousal, Leif Ericson* (1936), *Southern Nights* (1936), *The Mission Road* (1937), and *Ode to the Brave* (1944); many prize-winning choral works; songs and instrumental pieces.

JOSEPH CARL BREIL
> Born, Pittsburgh, Pennsylvania, 1870; died, Los Angeles, 1926.
> Several operas; *The Legend* produced at Metropolitan, New York, 1919.

ADOLF GERHARD BRUNE
> Born, Germany, 1870; came to the United States, 1889; died, 1935.

Three Symphonies; two Symphonic Poems; four Overtures; two Piano Concertos; five String Quartets; two String Quintets; one Piano Quartet; one Trio; cantatas, organ works, and miscellaneous pieces.

CLIFFORD DEMAREST

Born, New Jersey, 1874.

Anthems, songs, and part-songs; two cantatas *The Cross Victorious* and *The Shepherds of Bethlehem*. Organ works: Pastoral Suite in F, *Rip Van Winkle,* Prelude on *Materna, Rustic Song, Festival Postlude;* for organ and piano: *Fantaisie* in C Minor, *Grand Aria, Rhapsody.*

HENRY LAWRENCE FREEMAN

Born, Cleveland, 1875.

Negro composer.

Fourteen operas, including *Zuluki, The Prophecy, The Martyr, Valdo, The Octoroon;* the ballet *Zulu King* (1934); *The Slave,* a symphonic poem; many songs. Winner of the Harmon Award in 1930.

WILLIAM CLIFFORD HEILMAN

Born, Pennsylvania, 1877.

Orchestral tone poem *By the Porta Catania;* Suite for orchestra; Trio; Suite of dances for cello and piano; Suite for flute and piano; songs and piano pieces. Choral works: *Night Song, Knew Not the Sun, Among the Garden Ways.*

JOHN ADAM HUGO

Born, Connecticut, 1873.

Three operas—*The Temple Dancer* produced Metropolitan, New York, 1919, Chicago, 1922; Symphony; two Piano Concertos; Piano Trio; many songs and instrumental pieces.

ERNEST HUTCHESON

Born, Australia, 1871; came to America, 1900.

Prominent concert pianist and teacher.

Symphonic Poem; orchestral Suite; Piano Concerto; Violin Concerto; Concerto for two pianos; piano pieces.

WASSILI LEPS

Born, Russia, 1870; came to America, 1894; died, Toronto, Canada, 1943.

Several operas—*Hoshi-San* produced in Philadelphia, 1909.

HENIOT LEVY

Born, Poland, 1879; came to America in 1905.

Concert Overture; musical setting to Tennyson's *Guinevere*; Piano Concerto; Concerto for two pianos with string orchestra; String Quintet; String Sextet; two Piano Quintets; four String Quartets; two Piano Trios; Violin Sonata; pieces for piano and for violin.

MARY CARR MOORE

Born, Memphis, Tennessee, 1873.

Operas: *The Oracle* (1894); *Narcissa* (1912); *The Leper* (1912); *Los Rubios* (1931); *Davide Rizzio* (1932). Choruses, songs, and instrumental works.

COURTLANDT PALMER

Born, New York City, 1872.

Orchestral and chamber music; songs, piano pieces; Piano Concerto; *Berceuse* for violin and piano; *Elegie* for violoncello.

WALTER HENRY ROTHWELL

Born, England, 1872; came to America, 1904; died, 1927.

Orchestral conductor and composer.

Piano Concerto; two Piano Sonatas; incidental music for plays; songs.

BERTRAM SHAPLEIGH

Born, Boston, 1871; died, Washington, D.C., 1940.

Specialist in Oriental music.

Orchestral Suites *Ramayana* and *Gur Amir*; tone poem *Mirage*, for chorus and orchestra; *The Raven* (Poe), for chorus and orchestra; other choral works; two Symphonies; Symphonic Prelude; Poem for cello and orchestra; String Quartet; Piano Trio; five one-act operas; two grand operas; church music; over one hundred songs, many using Oriental themes.

FREDERICK STOCK (Friedrich Wilhelm August)

Born, Germany, 1872; came to America, 1895; died, 1942.

From 1905 conductor Chicago Symphony Orchestra (successor to Theodore Thomas).

Two Symphonies; Symphonic Variations; symphonic poem *Life* (in memory of Theodore Thomas); three Overtures; Violin

Concerto (played by Zimbalist at 1915 Norfolk Festival); *A Psalmodic Rhapsody* for tenor solo, chorus, orchestra, and organ. String Quartet; Quintet for strings; Sextet for strings; songs, instrumental pieces, and many orchestral arrangements.

FRANK EDWIN WARD

Born, Pennsylvania, 1872.

Symphony; *Ocean Rhapsody;* a Scherzo *Peter Pan,* for orchestra; two String Quartets (one awarded National Federation Music Clubs prize, 1917); Trio; two Sonatas for violin and piano; two Organ Sonatas; cantatas, anthems, songs, and instrumental pieces.

HERMAN HANS WETZLER

Born, Germany, 1870; died, 1943.

Orchestral works: Overture to *As You Like It; Symphonic Fantasy; Visions*—Six Symphonic Movements; *Symphonic Dance in Basque Style; Symphonie Concertante,* for violin and orchestra; and the legend *St. Francis of Assisi.* Choral work *Magnificat;* a String Quartet; and works for stage and films.

2. FROM THE 1880'S

It is now almost thirty years since DEEMS TAYLOR (1885——) composed his Suite *Through the Looking Glass,* and it remains today one of the most widely played American orchestral works. Without doubt it remains also Taylor's best work, for in his more ambitious scores, among them his operas, he has never surpassed the charm and grace with which he matched Lewis Carroll's wit, half tender, half mocking. From the lovely *Dedication* and *The Garden of Live Flowers,* on through the gallant struggle in *Jabberwocky,* in which the hideous creature is slain with a fugue for the woodwinds, through the shimmering *Looking Glass Insects,* to the droll and affectionate picture of *The White Knight,* who falls forward when his horse stops, and backward when it goes on again, the whole series is presented with brilliance and sparkling humor.

Taylor's career is a contradiction of the old adage about a jack-of-all-trades being master of none. He has been a successful newspaper man, a music critic, translator of verse and prose, a poet, radio commentator, a skilled and imaginative artist with brush and pen, and if he should ever decide to leave the field of arts and letters he could make a good living as a carpenter. In addition, he is a keen wit and man-about-town; and you may be sure that any gathering he attends will cease to be boring upon his arrival.

Taylor's music has been criticized for having too many reminders of other composers, particularly of Wagner and Puccini. This, to my mind, is not a supreme indictment in Taylor's case. All composers derive to some degree from earlier sources, and some are more successful than others in concealing their derivations by the magic of their own individualities. Whatever may be said about Taylor's music— that it is like old wine in bottles that are none too new, or that it shows its ancestry in too obvious a manner—it is marked by warmth and richness, and it is fashioned with expert craftsmanship. It is invariably satisfying, and very often it is compelling and gripping.

Sometimes I suspect that much of the criticism leveled at Deems Taylor, particularly by composers, is slightly tinged with envy. He has broken all the rules and traditions of an artist's life by becoming highly successful, and by doing altogether well for himself. Many composers have honors heaped upon them; Taylor has been awarded both honors and the jobs that bring material returns. Yet even the envious will have to admit that the reason he gets these jobs is that he generally does them excellently, by providing something that millions of people enjoy hearing—in his music, as radio commentator, or as master of ceremonies for Walt Disney.

Taylor was born in New York, December 22, 1885. After attending the Ethical Culture School, he entered New York University, where he wrote the music for four comic operas as part of his undergraduate activities. In 1910, four years after his graduation, Charles Dillingham produced one of these musical comedies, *The Echo*, as a starring vehicle for Bessie McCoy.

From 1908 until 1911, Taylor studied harmony and counterpoint with an obscure musician named Oscar Coon. He apparently learned much from Coon, who was his only teacher, but beyond these lessons the composer of *The King's Henchman* and *Peter Ibbetson* is entirely self-taught.

In the years immediately following graduation from college Taylor was a member of the editorial staffs of encyclopedias, *Nelson's* and the *Britannica*. From 1912 to 1916 he was assistant editor of an industrial house organ *Western Electric News*. The following year he was assistant Sunday editor of the New York *Tribune*, and in 1916–17, the *Tribune* correspondent in France. From 1917 to 1919 he was associate editor of *Collier's Weekly*. By this time he had won such recognition as a composer, largely because of the *Looking Glass* Suite, that he was appointed music critic of the New York *World*, a position he held until 1925. In that year the Metropolitan Opera Company gave him a commission for an opera, and he resigned from the *World* so that he could devote all his time to writing it. After the production of *The King's Henchman*, he was editor of *Musical America* from 1927 to 1929. Then followed the composition and production by the Metropolitan Opera Company of *Peter Ibbetson*, in 1931.

With his second opera produced, Taylor turned once more to other activities. For a time he was music critic of the New York *American*, he delivered a series of radio lectures on the history of opera, and in 1933 began the first of many series of radio programs under commercial sponsorship. In the fall of 1936 he was appointed consultant on music for the Columbia Broadcasting System, and began at that time his Sunday afternoon intermission talks on the broadcasts of the New York Philharmonic-Symphony. These continued for more than five years, and Taylor achieved a high mark in comments on music for the layman. He assumed that the listener was interested and intelligent, and then in direct, but never patronizing, manner he discussed the composer of a work being played at the time, or perhaps some related subject. These talks were subsequently published in two books: *Of Men and Music* (1937) and *The Well-Tempered Listener* (1940).

The movies as well as the radio have claimed Taylor's services. In 1940 he acted as commentator and master of ceremonies for Walt Disney's *Fantasia*. He has been a director of the American Society of Composers, Authors and Publishers for many years, and in 1942 he was made president of the society. He has been awarded the honorary degrees of Doctor of Music by New York University (1927) and Doctor of Letters by Juniata College (1931), and in 1935 was elected a member of the American Academy of Arts and Letters. He is a trustee of the American Academy in Rome.

Taylor's early works include an orchestral score *The Siren Song*, which won first prize in the National Federation of Music Clubs competition in 1913; *The Chambered Nautilus*, a cantata for mixed chorus and orchestra; and *The Highwayman*, a cantata for women's voices, composed for the MacDowell Festival at Peterboro in 1914.

Through the Looking Glass was first composed in the years 1917 to 1919 as a work for chamber orchestra, and was introduced by Carolyn Beebe and the New York Chamber Music Society. Then Taylor rescored it for full orchestra, and since 1922 it has been given repeated performances by almost every orchestra in America, and by many in Europe. The orchestral piece *The Portrait of a Lady* was composed shortly after *Through the Looking Glass* and revised in 1924, though it was not published until late in the 1930's.

The King's Henchman stayed in the Metropolitan repertoire for three seasons, at that time a record of performances for an American opera. When Taylor was commissioned by the board of directors in the winter of 1925 to write an opera for which they promised a production, he asked Edna St. Vincent Millay for a libretto. She responded with the story of Aethelwold, sent by King Aedgar of England to fetch Aelfrida for his queen. The subject of *Tristan*, doubtless, but of John Alden and Priscilla, too.

The première on February 17, 1927, was a gala event. It had been heralded by tremendous advance publicity. All of New York that could buy tickets at a premium turned out to hear the opera with which the Metropolitan, by commissioning an American composer to write it, had broken tradition. It met with stirring success, and the critics were as enthusiastic as the public. Lawrence Gilman was one of the leaders in bestowing laurels. In the *Herald Tribune* he called *The King's Henchman* "the best American opera we have ever heard." He wrote of the music as "richly textured, mellifluous," and praised its "grace and movement and flexibility." "It is," he remarked, "the writing of an expert craftsman, an artist of sensibility and warm responsiveness."

The success of *The King's Henchman* led the directors of the Metropolitan to commission another Taylor opera. This resulted in *Peter Ibbetson*, which was first produced February 7, 1931, with a cast including Edward Johnson, Lawrence Tibbett, and Lucrezia Bori.

For his libretto Taylor himself worked with Constance Collier on the play she had made from Du Maurier's novel, which had been produced some years before with herself and the Barrymore brothers in the leading roles. It is an appealing dream story, which spins a fancy all men would like to believe: that our dreams are more real than our bodily existence, and that if we "dream true" we can take ourselves wherever we wish to be. Taylor accomplished a thoroughly musicianly job in this opera. The music, even when it seemed derived from Wagner, Debussy, or Puccini, was always appropriate. The orchestration was rich and resourceful. The score was consistent and, in the symphonic interludes between scenes, eloquent. As incidental music to the drama it would have been almost perfect. The folklike songs of the chorus which accompany the dream scenes breathed a fanciful fragrance and mysticism. In a number of scenes, however, the music held up the action, and made the gestures of the singers stilted and stagey. — It may be that the critical fraternity felt that a composer might be forgiven for his derivations in his first opera, but that in his second he must stand on his own feet. At any rate, *Peter Ibbetson* did not meet with the almost unanimous acclaim from music critics that greeted its predecessor. With the public, however, it became more popular than even *The King's Henchman* had been, and in its third season at the Metropolitan it was accorded the honor of performance on the opening night. It remained in the repertoire for still another season, and in the summer of 1931 it was produced at Ravinia.

Taylor's third opera *Ramuntcho* dates from the spring of 1934, when the composer started his first sketches. It was finished three years later, and the orchestration completed in the summer of 1938. Taylor wrote his own libretto for *Ramuntcho*, adapting it from a novel by Pierre Loti. The scenes are laid in the Basque village of Etchézar, in the early part of the present century.

For this drama, Taylor composed a purely lyric opera. In contrast to the style of *The King's Henchman* and *Peter Ibbetson*, the voice is used melodically, not as a mere instrument of the orchestral whole. There are no leit-motives, except, possibly, the identifying theme of *Ramuntcho*. The score contains arias, duets, drinking songs, soldiers' songs, and a limited use of Basque folk songs.

Ramuntcho was produced not by the Metropolitan, but by the Philadelphia Opera Company in its home city, February 10, 1942. Reviewing the performance for the New York *Herald Tribune* (February 11, 1942), Francis Perkins wrote: "With some exceptions, the melodious score is integrated in style. There are some variously reminiscent moments, but the prevailing idiom is characteristic of its composer."

Taylor's purely orchestral works include *Jurgen,* a symphonic poem originally commissioned by Walter Damrosch for the New York Symphony Society; *Circus Days,* composed originally for jazz orchestra and then rescored for symphony orchestra with added saxophones (published in 1934); and, more recently, *Processional,* introduced by the Baltimore Symphony in 1941; *Marco Takes a Walk* (New York Philharmonic-Symphony, 1942); *A Christmas Overture* (New York Philharmonic-Symphony, 1944); and a *Fanfare for the People of Russia* (New York City Symphony, 1944). In 1945 he was asked to provide an adaptation of *Through the Looking Glass* for the "Alice in Wonderland" episode in The Ringling Brothers and Barnum and Bailey Circus.

Taylor has been much in demand for providing incidental music for the theatre. Two scores were for New York Theatre Guild productions—*Liliom* and *The Adding Machine.* Others have been for *Beggar on Horseback, Will Shakespeare, Humoresque, Rita Coventry,* Gilbert Miller's production of *Casanova,* and Katherine Cornell's appearance in *Lucrece.* Out of the music for the last two Taylor subsequently fashioned concert suites: the *Casanova* Ballet Music for orchestra, and the *Lucrece* Suite for string quartet.

CHARLES WAKEFIELD CADMAN (1881——) is one of the most widely known of our composers today, and, although he dislikes the specialist label, he was for many years famous as a composer who utilized Indian material. This is not strange, for his little song *The Land of the Sky Blue Water,* admittedly an Indian melody, ranks with Nevin's *Rosary* in popularity. Cadman is one of the very few composers who has been able to make his living principally through writing music. Aside from brief concert tours, he has been able to devote himself entirely to composition, and to make his work pay him well. The song *At Dawning* has reached a circulation well over a million copies, and has been translated into four languages.

Cadman has written two Indian operas: *Shanewis,* produced at the Metropolitan Opera House in 1918, and subsequently in various cities of the country; and *The Sunset Trail,* first heard in Denver in 1925 and later presented in 1926 at Rochester, by the troupe that afterwards became the American Opera Company. It was included in the company's repertoire on subsequent tours. Cadman qualified *Shanewis* as an Indian opera by calling it a phase of present-day American life, with the Indian in transition. Nelle Richmond Eberhart's libretto tells the story of Shanewis, an Indian maiden who goes to New York for musical training and falls in love with a white man. The second act shows the Indian Reservation, to which the hero has followed Shanewis. Her foster brother shoots her lover through the heart with a poisoned arrow.

A number of Indian melodies appear in the score. The *Spring Song of the Robin Woman* is based on a Cheyenne melody recorded by Natalie Curtis. The *Intermezzo* uses an Omaha song from Alice Fletcher's collection. There is an Osage ceremonial song, collected by Francis La Flesche, in the pow-wow scene near the close of the opera, and the first-act *finale* and two of the narratives of Shanewis were suggested by scenes described in Frederick Burton's book *American Primitive Music.*

The Sunset Trail is less in the style of grand opera than is *Shanewis.* In fact, its music seems better suited to an operetta. It tells of an Indian tribe gathered about the camp fire, debating the problem of submitting to the white man, or trying further to repulse him. The old men are for giving in, but the young braves decide to fight some more. They return defeated and wounded, and at the end the whole tribe takes the Sunset Trail and bows to the will of destiny.

Cadman's *Thunderbird Suite* for piano represents part of the music he wrote for the production of the drama by Norman Bel Geddes. In its original form the score first presented Omaha themes in unaltered form, sung with Indian vocables by the actors during the action of the play. Between the acts the melodies were heard in idealized form, harmonized and developed.

Although Cadman has for years pointed to Indian melodies as a source of native material for American composers, and in 1915 (*Musical Quarterly* for July) pleaded the cause of nationalism in our music, he does not care today to be identified with any group of composers who claim to write American music simply because they have used the songs of the Negro or Indian. He feels now that Americanism represents an attitude, a fundamental nationalistic temperament.

Cadman has passed through a number of distinct phases in his career as composer. In his early days he concerned himself principally with comic operas and operettas. Then he turned his attention largely to writing songs and part-songs. Next came his interest in Indian music. He had already made some settings of Indian themes, and in 1909, when he was twenty-seven years old, he went to the Omaha Reservation with Francis La Flesche, and spent the summer recording on the phonograph some of the tribal songs and flute music. For sixteen years, until 1925, he continued his interest in the subject, and gave many lecture-recitals on Indian customs and music. In later years he has been interested in composing operas and symphonic works of a more general nature.

He was born in Johnstown, Pennsylvania, December 24, 1881, the son of a metallurgist employed by the Carnegie Steel Corporation. Even though the Cadman home had no piano until Charles was thirteen, the boy was musical from earliest childhood. His teachers were Leo Oehmler of Pittsburgh and Luigi von Kunitz. When he started to compose, he had extreme difficulty in placing his first works with publishers, and in having them performed. For almost two years he walked the sidewalks of New York trying to interest theatrical agents and managers in an early comic opera. When he was twenty-three he had some song manuscripts accepted by a publisher, but these did not find a ready sale and the copies reposed peacefully, undisturbed, on the publisher's shelves. For a while the same fate was accorded a song published a few years later, in 1906. This was *At Dawning*, which remained practically unknown until John McCormack featured it in his concerts some years afterwards. Then it became a tremendous success, and eventually enjoyed a sale of over a million copies. The publishers showed their fairness by voluntarily offering Cadman a royalty contract, even though they had originally purchased his copyright for a small cash payment.

It is on this song and *From the Land of the Sky Blue Water* that Cadman's fame among the general public rests, but music lovers know him for many major works in the larger forms. He has composed the two Indian operas: *Shanewis* and *The Sunset Trail,* as well as *The Witch of Salem* which is probably Cadman's most successful attempt at grand opera. In this, Cadman explicitly states, there is but one Indian character. First performed by the Chicago Civic Opera Company in 1926, it deals with the witch-burning days of the Massachusetts colony. It is more unified in its structure than *Shanewis,* and shows a better sense of dramatic values. There was also an earlier opera, written in 1916, which did not have its first performance until 1925, at Carnegie Hall, New York. It was called *The Garden of Mystery,* and was based on Hawthorne's story of *Rappaccini's Daughter.*

Cadman has written a great deal of instrumental music. Among his earlier works are a Trio in D Major; a Piano Sonata; the *Thunderbird Suite* for piano; an *Oriental Rhapsody* for orchestra; and a Quintet *To a Vanishing Race.* All of these works seem to embody the composer's out-of-doors spirit, his love of the desert. The Piano Sonata derived its inspiration from Miller's *From Sea to Sea* and *The Ship of the Desert.*

The feeling for the desert is apparent also in the later Sonata in G Major for violin and piano. As might be expected, Cadman has not in this work composed music which is self-consciously modern, seeking dissonance for its own sake. He has tried to make the music vital by remaining himself and reacting honestly to his own musical moods. For this reason the Sonata is a quite individual and unified whole.

In July of 1932 the New York Orchestra, at that time conducted by Modest Altschuler, presented Cadman's *Hollywood Suite,* a work consisting of four contrasting tonal sketches: *Mary Pickford, Charlie Chaplin, To My Mother,* and *Hollywood Bowl.* Dating from the same period is another orchestral work, of a different type and marked by unusual rhythms, *Dance of the Scarlet Sister Mary.*

When the New York Philharmonic-Symphony under Barbirolli performed Cadman's *Dark Dancers of the Mardi Gras* (December 4 and 5, 1937), it accorded the work its fourteenth performance in America. Its première had occurred four and a half years earlier in the Hollywood Bowl. The work is scored for orchestra and piano obbligato and in most of the performances the composer himself has played the piano part. In spite of several limitations, the piece is effective in reflecting the grotesque, fantastic, and exuberant spirit of the carnival.

Simultaneously with the Sunday afternoon performance of *Dark Dancers* in Carnegie Hall by the Philharmonic-Symphony Orchestra (December 5), the Mozart Sinfonietta played Cadman's *American Suite* for string orchestra in the same building in the Carnegie Chamber Music Hall. This had already been played the preceding September at the Saratoga Spa festival under F. Charles Adler.

Cadman's later orchestral works include a Symphony in E Minor; and a tone poem for piano and orchestra, *Aurora Borealis*. In recent years he has added also to his long list of vocal works. Among them are the song cycle *White Enchantment*; a cantata *The Far Horizon*; and a twenty-five-minute opera *The Willow Tree*, written chiefly for radio and concert performances, with a libretto which sets forth a dramatic situation rather than a full-length plot. The author of this libretto was Nelle Richmond Eberhart, who supplied the texts for all but one of Cadman's operas, and for many of his songs and choral works. The work was first performed on the radio over a National Broadcasting network, October 3, 1932.

There is much discussion as to whether ERNEST BLOCH (1880——) should be considered an American composer. Born in Switzerland, he did not come to America until he was thirty-six years of age. Though he has lived here ever since, become a naturalized citizen, and sought to interpret our nation in his epic rhapsody *America*, so much of his important music was written before he came here that our claim to him as an American composer is open to question. His case is not that of Loeffler, who did most of his composing in this country. Yet Bloch did not make a reputation abroad; he achieved no signal recognition there. It was America that first acknowledged his genius, and an American publisher, Schirmer, who first published his orchestral works. Moreover, he is a musician whose gifts rank him with the outstanding contemporary composers of the entire world; and he has made America his home. If for no other motive than hospitality, we may place him here at the end of this chapter, separate from our other composers, and the reader may choose whether or not he will call him an American.

Bloch is a master of his medium, he can handle his instruments with skill, he can make his orchestra do his bidding. But one rarely thinks of the means he has used to achieve his effects; it is the music itself, the sum total of effect that carries its message and causes the listener to feel the primal urge that inspired it. Bloch is akin to Moussorgsky in this respect; his music drama *Macbeth* is like *Boris* in the power of its delineation of character. At one stage of his career, Bloch was the Hebrew prophet in his music. Not the modern Jew, the intellectual, but rather one of the sons of ancient Judea, moved by what he himself has termed "the vigor and ingenuousness of the Patriarchs, the violence that finds expression in the books of the prophets, the burning love of justice, the desperation of the preachers of Jerusalem, the sorrow and grandeur of the Book of Job, the sensuality of the Song of Songs."

This Jewish spirit was not apparent in his earliest works—the Symphony; the music drama *Macbeth;* or the symphonic poem *Hiver-Printemps* (1904). And it has somehow been tempered in his later music, written in this country. Bloch the Hebrew is met in the *Trois Poèmes Juifs* (1913); the three Psalms for single voice and orchestra; in *Schelomo* (Solomon) (1916), a Rhapsody for cello and orchestra; and in the Symphony *Israel* (1916). For when Bloch emerged from his first period, he became possessed of the gift to express himself faithfully and vividly. He has been profoundly moved by his own sufferings and exaltations; he has been given the power to put them into his music. Imbued with the Hebrew tradition, he awoke to find himself able to express it, and he is perhaps the only really Jewish musician in the history of music.

He was born in Geneva, July 24, 1880. None of his family was musical. He started to study the violin, and at the age of eleven solemnly vowed that he would devote his life to composing music. He studied in Brussels, Frankfort, Munich, and Paris, and finally returned to Geneva when he was twenty-four. He had little encouragement from orchestra leaders or others who could play his music. His father's business declined, and Bloch spent some time traveling in Germany taking orders for the cuckoo clocks his father made. Then in 1910 his opera *Macbeth* was produced in Paris, at the Opéra Comique. Publicly it was a success, but the critics did not like it, and politics commanded that it be dropped.

He conducted some concerts at Lausanne and Neufchâtel, he was professor of composition and aesthetics at the Conservatory of Geneva, until he was once more the victim of intrigue. Then he went back to his composing, and finally landed in America in 1916, unheralded and unknown, as conductor of an orchestra that played for Maud Allan, the dancer. When the tour closed in Ohio he came to New York penniless, without backing or friends. In 1917 he joined the staff of the David Mannes School, as teacher of composition. About this time the Flonzaley Quartet introduced his B Minor String Quartet, which made a deep impression, and Dr. Karl Muck invited him to conduct his *Trois Poèmes Juifs* with the Boston Symphony Orchestra. In May, 1917, the Friends of Music in New York, under Artur Bodanzky, presented an entire program of Bloch's compositions. In 1919 his Suite for viola and piano won the Coolidge prize at the Berkshire Festival. In 1920 he was appointed to direct the newly founded Cleveland Institute of Music. After six years there, he went to California where he headed the San Francisco Conservatory. Then in 1930 a wealthy music patron asked him to give all his time to composing, and arranged for an income for ten years, so that the business of making a living would not interfere with his creative work. In 1930 he was one of the four prize winners in the Victor Company's symphonic contest.

Bloch lived in Switzerland during almost the whole period from 1930 to 1939, making frequent visits to America. During this time his fame increased greatly abroad, especially in England, where an Ernest Bloch Society was formed to promote performances and recordings of his works, and in Italy where, until the inauguration of an official anti-Semitic policy, he received many performances and widespread appreciation among musicians, critics, and public. His official biography, by Mary Tibaldi-Chiesa, was published in Italy, and in 1938 his opera *Macbeth* was performed there, for the first time since its original production in Paris in 1910. During the 1930's not much new music by Bloch reached the public. In 1932 the *Sacred Service* for the synagogue was published, and in 1936 the *Voice in the Wilderness* for cello and orchestra, both in America. In the latter year, an Italian publisher brought out Bloch's Piano Sonata. A symphonic suite *Evocations* had its première in San Francisco in March of 1938, and the violinist Joseph Szigeti introduced Bloch's Violin Concerto in December of the same year with the Cleveland Orchestra.

After his intensely Jewish period, Bloch came into a new era. He achieved a universality of speech that goes beyond racial limits. In his String Quartet (1916), the Suite for Viola and Piano (since scored for viola and orchestra, 1919), in the Violin Sonata (1920), and in the Quintet (1923), the Hebrew spirit is only one of the elements that has gone into the mixture. As Paul Rosenfeld has said, he combines the East and the West, the Orient and the traditions of European music. In the *Concerto Grosso* (1924) he based his modernisms on the classics. And in *America* he tried to paint the ideals of our country, "the future credo of all mankind," . . . "the common purpose of widely diversified races ultimately to become one race, strong and great." Whether or not Bloch achieved an American speech in his score (and that is doubtful), it is his own declaration of allegiance, and his understanding of what America means to civilization.

America has not had many performances since it won the *Musical America* prize of $3,000 in the 1927–28 season and was then played simultaneously by a number of our major orchestras. The Boston Symphony played it again in 1933 and in 1942 it was revived by the Brooklyn Symphony, but there have been few performances beyond these.

When the work was first introduced it had a mixed reception, least friendly in the most "advanced" circles. For Bloch had frankly sought to reach a mass audience—had written an anthem quite in the "community sing" tradition, and based a whole programmatic work upon it. It seems likely that if and when conductors generally decide to revive *America,* they will find both public and critics in a more favorable mood to recognize its noble spirit and high craftsmanship, while not blinking the fact that it meets the man in the street rather more than halfway.

America ends with the anthem as sung by a chorus and the audience, with the orchestra, but the whole symphony is built upon its theme. From the first bars it appears, in root, dimly, slowly taking shape, "rising, falling, developing, and finally asserting itself" in the last bars of the final movement. There are three parts. First, *1620. The Soil—The Indians—(England)—The Mayflower—The Land-*

ing of the Pilgrims. Indian themes, the trumpet "Call of America," *Old Hundred,* a sea chanty, all combine to tell of the country before and after the Pilgrims landed in Plymouth. The second movement is *1861–1865—Hours of Joy—Hours of Sorrow.* The drama of the North and South; happiness, war, distress and agony. Negro songs; a bit from Stephen Foster; *Pop Goes the Weasel;* then war songs— *John Brown's Body, The Battle Cry of Freedom, Tramp, Tramp, Tramp.* Intensity paints the strife, yet the America call is heard above the din, and even though it shows a "bleeding America," it is still there. The *finale* is *1926—The Present—The Future.* Speed, noise, jazz, the pomp of material prosperity. An inevitable collapse, and a gradual rebuilding that comes at last to the anthem—the promise that our ideals will save us.

It may be argued that we have no more claim to Bloch's *America* than we have to Dvořák's *New World.* But this is hardly logical, for Dvořák never sought to become an American himself, and Bloch has established himself here, to all intents permanently. The music he has written in this country is the work of a man who wants to be an American.

Likewise, it seems altogether logical to claim PERCY ALDRIDGE GRAINGER (1882——) as an American composer, even though he was born in Australia and first came to us in 1915 with an assured reputation as a composer-pianist. For he has truly become an American; not only as a citizen, but in his associations, his sympathies and his understanding. His music is also American, in its idealism and in the verve with which it translates the Anglo-Saxon, Old English traits of our heritage. He is altogether an individualist—as a pianist and as a composer. Modern in feeling, with a bit of seasoning in his harmonies, he nevertheless clothes everything he writes with a sumptuous sonority that is warm and rich. He is individual as a contrapuntist, too. Never academic, he nevertheless weaves his instrumental or human voices so that they have a continuous polyphonic overlapping that keeps things constantly moving. A number of years ago (1937), Grainger favored the author of this volume with a statement of his views on modern music and on nationalism. He wrote, in part:

I find no "modern" or "futuristic" music modern enough. All the new music I hear (in which I am vitally interested) sounds to me amazingly old fashioned. Ever since I was about ten or eleven years old (in Australia) I have heard in my imagination what I call "free music"—music that is not tied down to the slavery of scales, intervals, rhythm, harmony, but in which the tones dart, glide, curve like a bird in the air, a fish in the sea, and in which changes of pitch and changes of tone-strength can occur with the smooth gradualness we see in nature. . . . I feel that all music (primitive music, folk-music, art-music in Asia and Europe) probably had a common origin, certainly should have a common appeal. I feel at home in music of all races, all periods, all styles. And I feel that every serious musician should know as wide a range of musics as we all know in the other arts (literature, sculpture, painting, architecture, etc.)

But in spite of this universalist feeling for music, outlook upon music, I also feel that music should have local roots—should express the feelings of its country, race, nationality just as it also expresses the individual, personal feelings of its composer. . . . I think I can express my view on universality and nationalism in music as follows: "local sowing, universal harvest."

I do not think my music, or my musical outlook has changed (essentially) since I was 10, in Australia. My life (as a composer and musician) has been an attempt to carry out the ideals and intentions I had formed at that age—ideals formed mainly upon Bach in music, the Icelandic Sagas, and Anglo-Saxon poetry in literature.

Grainger was born in Melbourne, Australia, July 8, 1882, and did not come to this country until he was thirty-three years old. Although his early studies were in Germany with Kwast and Busoni, his fundamental musical kinships were with his fellow students, the Dane—Sandby, and the Englishman—Cyril Scott. He was a friend and disciple of Edvard Grieg and has been active in propagating his music.

At the age of eighteen he went to London, where he became immensely popular as a pianist, and he has actively carried on a concert career ever since. In 1917 he interrupted it to enlist in the American Army, where he became a bandsman, playing the oboe and the saxophone, and taught in the Army music school. Soon afterwards he took out American citizenship papers, and has made his home in this country ever since, with frequent journeys to other parts of the globe—to Scandinavia, where he has done a good deal of folk song collecting; to the Orient; and to Australia and New Zealand, where he is a prophet far from being without honor in his own country. For a short time he was head of the Music Department in New York University.

He is best known for his brief settings of folk tunes of the British Isles: *Country Gardens, Irish Tune from County Derry, Mock Morris, Molly on the Shore, Shepherd's Hey,* and many others. His orchestral works include *To a Nordic Princess,* a bridal song for orchestra, written to commemorate his own marriage to a Norwegian, in California, and his *Tribute to Foster,* for five solo voices, solo piano, mixed chorus, orchestra, and musical glasses (a characteristically unorthodox scoring).

Much of the credit for the increased interest in folk music in this country belongs to Percy Grainger, both through the popularity of his transcriptions of similar English material and because of his yeoman service on the concert platform to transcriptions of such American folk classics as Guion's *Turkey in the Straw* and *Arkansas Traveler.*

LOUIS GRUENBERG (1884——) achieved his greatest distinction with his opera *Emperor Jones,* composed to Eugene O'Neill's play of the same name, and first produced at the Metropolitan Opera House, New York, January 7, 1933. On the occasion of its première Olin Downes called it "the first American opera by a composer whose dramatic instinct and intuition for the theatre seem unfailing, and whose musical technique is characterized by a very complete modern knowledge and a reckless mastery of his means" (*New York Times,* January 8, 1933).

In seeking to make an opera of Eugene O'Neill's play about the Pullman porter who made himself "Emperor" of an island in the West Indies, Gruenberg set himself a tremendously difficult task. His music for the play was at all times appropriate. The interludial outcries of the chorus, the orchestral comments on the drama, with rhythms not unlike the *Sacre du Printemps* of Stravinsky, and the dramatic fervor of the spiritual *Standin' in the Need of Prayer,* were all in keeping with the intensity of the drama. It is doubtful, however, that these elements added a new dimension.

It may be that O'Neill himself had originally provided all the music that was necessary for the effectiveness of his play. In the original version, the beat of a drum started offstage toward the end of the first scene, accelerating slowly and terrifyingly throughout the action, gradually pounding its way into the listener's consciousness. Gruenberg incorporated this drum beat into his score, but its elaborations were superfluous. It was far more effective in its naked simplicity.

Nevertheless, in spite of the fact that music may be uncalled for in a drama that can stand so eloquently on its own feet, Gruenberg's savage music, with its explosive detonations, its howls and outcries, did provide the most finished and theatrically effective American opera that the Metropolitan had yet produced.

Gruenberg was born in Russia, August 3, 1884. He was brought to America when he was two years old, and received most of his education in this country. At one time he was a pupil of Busoni. He has lived in Brooklyn, and at present makes his home in California, where he has been composing scores for sound pictures.

Gruenberg first came into prominence when his symphonic poem, *Hill of Dreams*, won the Flagler prize and a resultant performance by the New York Symphony Orchestra. In 1929 another symphonic poem, *The Enchanted Isle*, was selected by the Juilliard Foundation as its annual American work for publication. He won another prize in 1930—$5,000 for his Symphony, No. 1, from the Victor Company.

His style has undergone a number of changes, and he has gradually worked out for himself definite convictions which, he says, have taken the place of former vague conjectures. At one time he was concerned with the symphonic treatment of jazz; seeking to develop its medium so that its rigidity might be overcome, and that it would become something more than mere entertainment. So we had his *Jazzettes* for violin and piano; the *Four Indiscretions* for string quartet; *The Daniel Jazz*, for high voice and eight solo instruments; *The Creation*, a Negro sermon for high voice and eight solo instruments; and a *Jazz Suite* for orchestra. When the *Jazz Suite* was played in New York by the Boston Symphony in 1930, Lawrence Gilman wrote in the *Tribune:*

. . . The thrice familiar patterns are filled with an ingenuity and richness of fancy, are ordered by a civilized musical consciousness, which makes the issue engaging and profitable for other than merely primitive minds.

Yet perhaps Mr. Gruenberg is, after all, an incurable romanticist, for one caught him in the act of glancing a bit longingly over his shoulder at the love-making of Pelléas and Mélisande and the gallantries of the Rosenkavalier as he went through the motions of his Boston Waltz and his Slow Drag and One Step.

Gruenberg's first opera was a musical setting of John Erskine's *Jack and the Beanstalk*, which was presented by the Juilliard School of Music, November 19, 1931. It was a work which its authors subtitled, "A Fairy Opera for the Childlike." Erskine's libretto put its own interpretation on the age-old fairy story, and made of the cow a philosopher who comments on the situations, and on human nature in general.

For all this satiric fun-making, Gruenberg supplied a score that was singularly appropriate, marked by a flow of melody which had been carefully concealed in earlier works.

The League of Composers commissioned Gruenberg to write an orchestral work in 1934. He responded with a *Serenade to a Beauteous Lady*, which was first performed by the Chicago Symphony, April 4, 1935. It consisted of five movements in dance rhythms.

Gruenberg's most recent opera was composed especially for radio performance, on commission from the Columbia Broadcasting System, and first produced over its network September 17, 1937. In this work the composer attempted to fit his subject to his medium, and to make tone take the place of color and action. Thus, trees, clouds, a waterfall, birds, snakes, monkeys, must be heard as they cannot be seen. The libretto was drawn from a novel *Green Mansions*, by W. H. Hudson, and although the subject offered ample opportunities for the treatment the composer attempted to give it, the opera did not altogether accomplish its purpose.

Gruenberg's works include also a Quintet which won a $1000 prize in the Lake Placid Club chamber music contest in 1937; two String Quartets, and *Five Variations on Popular Themes* for string quartet; a Second Symphony; two Piano Concerti; and a Violin Concerto which was introduced by Jascha Heifetz with the Philadelphia Orchestra December 1 and 2, 1944.

The death of CHARLES TOMLINSON GRIFFES (1884–1920) was a sad loss to American music, for it took away one of our most promising talents when he was only thirty-six years old and had written a mere handful of works. But that handful was enough to give him a permanent place among our composers. His works fall into three distinct periods. First the student period, when he was definitely under the influence of his German teachers—Rüfer and Humperdinck. In his second style he leaned toward the Frenchmen, and also showed his fondness for the Russian Orientalism that was to appear as the mysticism of his later works. *The Lake at Evening,* from the *Three Tone Pictures* for piano, shows him in this period, and it also proves his power of musical description. The third period shows his modern trend; a grasping for something less rigid than the tempered scale, a medium to sound the overtones he wanted us to hear. Then he wrote his Piano Sonata and his orchestral works.

The Sonata has the intellectual consistency of a Schoenberg, a pursuit of tonal logic without the sacrifice of poetic conception. The themes are well defined, but it is their development that is interesting rather than the themes themselves. *The Pleasure Dome of Kubla Khan,* a tone poem, was his most important work for orchestra. It was first performed under circumstances that were indeed pathetic, as far as Griffes was concerned, for the labor of its composition was partly responsible for the illness that caused his death. When he knew it would have a performance by the Boston Symphony he set himself to copy out the parts, as all composers must do with a manuscript work unless they can afford to hire a coypist. He was tired and busy with his regular work of teaching music at a boys' school, and when he had finished he fell ill with an attack of pneumonia. Word of his great success was brought to him just before he died.

He took his inspiration from Coleridge's poem: the lines that describe the "stately pleasure dome," the "sunny pleasure dome with caves of ice, the miracle of strange device." In writing his music Griffes gave his own imagination free rein in his description of the palace, and of the revelry that might take place there. The vague, foggy beginning suggests the sacred river, which ran "through caverns measureless to man down to a sunless sea." Then the outlines of the palace gradually rise, "with walls and towers girdled round." Sounds of revelry and dancing rise to a wild climax and then suddenly break off. The original mood returns, and we hear again the sacred river, and the "caves of ice."

It is colorful music, and so is his *Poem* for flute and orchestra, which was first played by Georges Barrère with unforgettable mastery. In the orchestration of the *Poem,* Griffes surpassed his work in the *Pleas-*

ure Dome. It is the most mature of his works. Starting in a gray mood it merges into a dance movement of strange tonality, with a suggestion of Oriental rhythm and color.

In his works for the piano Griffes is best known for his *Roman Sketches.* First comes "The White Peacock," who makes his bow with a languorous chromatic theme. "Nightfall" brings the strange sounds of the early evening, an almost oppressive quiet. "The Fountain of the Acqua Paola" shows the rise and fall of the water, the shimmering lights of the foam. "Clouds" starts with a lofty chordal passage, suggesting the high and massive cloudbanks.

Griffes was born in Elmira, New York, in 1884. He was talented in other fields than music. He could draw well with pen and ink; he made excellent water color landscapes, and later in life he worked in etchings on copper. When he was in high school he decided to be a musician, and he went to Berlin to learn to be a concert pianist. It was not until he studied theory with Humperdinck that he decided to be a composer. Then he came back to America in 1908, and took the position of music teacher at the Hackley School in Tarrytown, New York, which he held until his death in 1920.

Griffes's songs are much used on recital programs, from the early settings of German poems, through those to texts by Fiona MacLeod, to the later songs. In these he showed that he was finding himself— *An Old Song Resung,* the *Sorrow of Mydah,* and others of their kind.

Whether Griffes would have gone further if he had lived, it is hard to say. Probably his ideals were high enough to have saved him from being spoiled by success. His equipment was so complete that he could have taken a high place in our music. The few works he left have made him important.

JOHN POWELL (1882———) probably achieved his greatest distinction with his *Rhapsodie Nègre* for piano and orchestra, first performed in 1919, but in later years he has become the leader of the group which believes in the fundamental importance to the cultural life of the nation of American folk music derived from Anglo-Saxon sources. Creator of the Virginia State Choral Festival, he has been a moving spirit in the annual White Top Mountain Folk Music Festival, and a friend to all who are interested in our Appalachian tunes and ballads.

Powell's Virginian antecedents and environment have given him a sense of profound nearness to the forerunners and founders of the nation. He believes intensely in the value of those ethnic and cultural forces which actuated the molders of our past, and he would preserve them in their integrity for the benefit of contemporary and future times and to ensure the persistence of those impulses and ideals which the world has come to regard as typically American. This conviction is reflected in the way he preserves the modal nature of his folk material and strives to induce his style from the innate character of the material itself, avoiding incongruous progressions and cadences or extraneous chromaticisms.

He was born in Richmond, Virginia, September 6, 1882, the son of John Henry Powell, headmaster of a girls' school in Richmond. His mother was a descendant of Nicholas Lanier, who had been court musician to Charles I in England, and was an ancestor of Sidney Lanier, musical poet. Powell grew up in an atmosphere of culture and intellectual activity, and from the time he could talk he showed musical leanings and interested himself in the musical activities at his father's school. He had music lessons with F. C. Hahr, and then went to Vienna to study with Leschetizky and Navrátil.

The *Rhapsodie Nègre* which first established Powell's reputation, became one of the most widely played of the larger works by American composers. In 1929 alone, it had more than fifty performances in New York City, with the composer often playing the piano part. In Europe it was heard from Rome to Amsterdam, and was chosen as the representative American work to be performed with soloist on the New York Symphony Society's European tour, under Walter Damrosch. Henry Hadley conducted it with the New York Philharmonic on the occasion of the twenty-fifth anniversary of the American Society of Arts and Letters.

Powell was careful to point out that in the *Rhapsodie* he was seeking to interpret the Negro as a race; he was not voicing America. The work begins and ends on a primal note, pagan, orgiastic; the idealization that creeps in during the middle section cannot maintain itself against the primitive instinct. The work is intense in a fervor that rises to fury, and was composed with the consummate craftsmanship that marks all of Powell's works.

The sociological aspects of the *Rhapsodie* were discussed by the late Donald Francis Tovey, who once wrote:

Mr. Powell has the profoundest respect for the Negro as artist and human being. But profound sympathy is very different from the facile sentimentality that refuses to recognize the dangers that threaten two races of widely different stages of evolution that try to live together. The "Rhapsodie Nègre" is music, not political propaganda; but it will be soonest understood by those who, whether from personal knowledge of the composer or from the capacity to recognize emotional values in music, manage to understand from the outset that this is not only an eminently romantic, but also a thoroughly tragic piece.

Powell composed two Sonatas for violin and piano, one of them the *Sonata Virginianesque* (1919), which presents certain of the more amiable aspects of plantation life in Virginia before the days of the Civil War. The first movement *In the Quarters* shows the Negro making merry with his own kind, free (to quote the composer) "from the self-consciousness imposed by the patronizing or repressing presence of the whites." Unrestrained gayety and salty humor lilt through the racy themes based on Negro dance songs—"Done pawn my wife, done pawn my chile, done pawn my di'mon' ring," and others. The second movement is more lyric. Called *In the Woods*, it presents the young Negro gallant alone in the forest on his way to a rendezvous with his dusky lady love. The theme is a Negro song of a type rare among the Negroes, for love is often more a matter of action than of contemplation—"Lulu my Darlin', why don't you come here." The final movement shows the Negro *At the Big House*, making music for the dancing of his masters and enjoying their gayety. The form is a rondo, and the themes are based on Virginia reel tunes derived from old English country dances.

Others of Powell's earlier works include an Overture *In Old Virginia* (1921); a *Sonata Noble*, for piano; a Suite for piano (also arranged for small orchestra) entitled *At the Fair*; another Suite *In the South*; a set of *Variations and Double Fugue*; and a Concerto for violin and orchestra.

One of Powell's most widely played orchestral pieces, *Natchez on the Hill*, was performed for the first time at the Worcester (Massachusetts) Festival in 1931. Since that time it has received many hearings by major orchestras and on the radio. The tune from which the piece takes its name is a close relative of *Turkey in the Straw*, and the two other country dances which appear in the score are typical country-fiddler tunes. The three folk tunes are attached to each other in a novel pattern, somewhat akin to rondo form, but with a third theme taking the place of a recurrence of the first theme. It is a form that the composer has used also in "Snowbird on the Ashbank," in which the succession of themes may be represented by the letter-symbols *A-B-C-B-A*.

More recent is *A Set of Three*, an orchestral Suite using Virginia tunes. The first of its three parts is entitled "Snowbird on the Ashbank," the name of one of the tunes on which the movement is based. The second part, "Green Willow," derives from a song the composer heard in Giles County, while the *finale* "Haste to the Wedding" utilizes several traditional folk-dance tunes. In his settings, Powell has adhered closely to the modes of the original melodies: Mixolydian, Dorian, and Ionian.

Although separate movements of the work had been given previous performances, the Suite as a whole had its initial presentation by the New York Philharmonic-Symphony Orchestra in February of 1940. Those who heard it on that occasion were impressed by the composer's skillful and effective instrumentation, and by the manner in which the essential flavor of the songs was preserved.

ARTHUR SHEPHERD (1880——) has an interesting background. He was born February 19, 1880, in Idaho, educated in music at the New England Conservatory, and then went to Salt Lake City, where he conducted a theatre orchestra as well as a symphony orchestra. In 1908 he went back to Boston to become a teacher at the New England Conservatory. A number of years later he went to Cleveland, where he inaugurated children's concerts, as assistant conductor of the Cleveland Symphony. In 1927 he became professor of music and chairman of the Music Division of Western Reserve University, and in 1929 he became music critic for the Cleveland *Press*.

As a composer, Shepherd won prizes with his early works: The Paderewski prize for his *Ouverture Joyeuse* (1902), and in 1909 two from the National Federation of Music Clubs—one for his Piano Sonata and the other for a song *The Lost Child*. These works were followed by two more Overtures, *The Festival of Youth* and *The Nuptials of Attila;* an orchestral Suite; and a *Humoreske* for piano and orchestra. *Song of the Sea Wind* was scored for women's voices and orchestra, and *The City of the Sea* was for baritone, chorus, and orchestra. Some of his early piano pieces were issued by the Wa-Wan Press—a *Mazurka,* a *Prelude,* and a *Theme and Variations.*

His *Triptych,* for soprano and string quartet, to poems by Tagore, was published in 1927 by the Society for the Publication of American Music. Soon afterwards he composed an *Overture to a Drama,* and *Horizons,* the latter published under the provisions of the Juilliard Foundation. *Horizons* is interesting because it is based partly on original material and partly on frontier ballads: *The Dying Cowboy, The Old Chisholm Trail,* and the *Dogie Song.* The Suite is full of the raciness, the adventure, the spacious life of the plains.

Other works are two Piano Sonatas, two String Quartets, the first published by the Society for the Publication of American Music and the second commissioned by the League of Composers (1936); a *Triptych* for voice and string quartet; two cantatas—*City in the Sea* and *The Song of the Pilgrims;* and, for orchestra, a series of *Dance Episodes on an Exotic Theme.* The *Dance Episodes* had their première in Cleveland by the Cleveland Symphony in October, 1931. They proved distinctly original in thematic material and in development, and were clothed in truly brilliant orchestral dress.

In 1940 (March 7 and 9), Shepherd himself conducted the Cleveland Symphony in the première of his Symphony No. 2. In the following November the Boston Symphony played the work, with the composer again conducting. A Piano Quintet was finished in 1940 and first performed by the Cleveland Chamber of Music Society, with the composer at the piano, January 31, 1941. On December 27, 1942, Shepherd's *Praeludium Salutorium,* for strings and wind instruments, was performed in New York at a concert of the League of Composers.

While Shepherd himself is concerned only with the communicative power of his music and avoids self-conscious attempts at modernism, there are those who detect racial traits in his music, chiefly Anglo-Celtic, resulting perhaps from his English parentage.

WERNER JOSTEN (1888——) has been a professor of music at Smith College since 1923, two years after his coming to America. He was born at Elberfeld, Germany, June 12, 1888, and studied with Rudolf Siegel in Munich. He then went to Paris, but returned to Germany at the outbreak of the first World War and became assistant conductor at the Munich Opera House. Since coming to this country he has become an American citizen.

Among his most important works for orchestra is the *Concerto Sacro*, completed in 1927, which, like his more recent music for the ballet *Joseph and His Brethren* (produced by the Juilliard School of Music in March, 1936), unquestionably shows the influence of the severe religious atmosphere of his childhood home. The two parts of the *Concerto Sacro* were introduced separately by major orchestras (No. 2 by Koussevitzky and the Boston Symphony in 1929, and No. 1 by Stokowski and the Philadelphians in 1933), but they form a single work, inspired by a triptych painted for the Isenheim altar at Colmar in Alsace, by the sixteenth-century Rhenish master Mathias Grünewald.

The first Concerto depicts "The Annunciation" and "The Miracle," while the second comprises a "Lament" (that of Mary after the Crucifixion), and a final division called "Sepulchre and Resurrection," which the composer describes as an "instrumental motet." Behind his music Josten has placed a background of plain song, with suggestions of the spirit and methods of the pre-Bach German composers.

Josten has written also two Symphonies (one for strings alone); two further ballets—*Batouala* and *Endymion; a Serenade* for orchestra; *Jungle,* a symphonic movement; Sonatas for violin, for piano, and for cello; a String Quartet; and several large-scale choral works.

Josten is distinctly modern in his viewpoint and his expression. Yet, though he seems at times affected subconsciously by the style of the later Stravinsky, he achieves a subtle blending of the old and the new by tempering his dissonance with long-breathed, sustained melodic lines, and with imaginative harmonic and contrapuntal structure.

EMERSON WHITHORNE (1884———) uses polytonality at times, and never hesitates to employ acrid disonance to gain his effects. Yet he often seems more of the romanticist than the realist; his impressionism is calculated to produce atmosphere rather than to speak for itself alone. In this he is a wise and practical person; he remains intelligible to the average concertgoer, and his music is welcome in the concert halls.

He was born in Cleveland, September 6, 1884, and studied there with James H. Rogers, and later with Leschetizky and with Robert Fuchs in Vienna. He lived in London for eight years, from 1907 to 1915, composing, teaching piano and theory, and writing musical criticisms for the *Pall Mall Gazette*. After his return to America he was music editor for publishing houses, until in 1922 he retired so that he might give all of his time to composition.

He wrote his first serious music in London: piano music, songs, and song cycles, and the String Quartet *Greek Impressions*. *New York Days and Nights* were composed later, in America. These pieces form a Suite for piano, and were later scored for orchestra and performed by symphony societies, in movie houses, and in special arrangements for jazz band. In 1923 the Suite was chosen to represent America at the Salzburg Chamber Music Festival.

The set consists of four pieces. *On the Ferry*, with its moaning horns, shrieking whistles, rhythmic chugging of paddle wheels and mendicant musicians; *Pell Street* shows Chinatown; *A Greenwich Village Tragedy* tells of the district where an episode becomes an epic, from trysting comes tragedy; *Times Square* paints flashing colors, swirling crowds, ribaldry and mirth, snatches of popular tunes through the nightly revels.

Whithorne's *Poem* for piano and orchestra had its first performance in 1927. Walter Gieseking was the soloist with the Chicago Symphony Orchestra. Later in the same year Gieseking played it again, with the New York Symphony under Fritz Busch. It is striking music, severe and granitic, with a determined shattering of its melodic line and persistently syncopated rhythms. *Fata Morgana*, a symphonic poem, was played by the New York Philharmonic in 1928. Again there is constant recurrence of patterns interrupted by unusual changes of rhythm.

Sooner and Later was a ballet composed in 1925 for the Neighborhood Playhouse in New York. The scenario, by Irene Lewisohn, dealt fantastically with three states of existence: a primitive tribal life, a mechanized city routine, and a resultant crystallized era where there are no primal passions; feeding was conducted by scientific apparatus, and relaxation was provided by a synthetic mood, or instrumental, vocal, and color prelude. Whithorne wrote incidental music for the New York Theatre Guild production of *Marco Millions*. He used authentic Chinese themes, and attempted to imitate native instruments with woodwinds, a violin with wire strings, a cello, guitar, mandolin, celesta, muted trumpet, gongs, tam-tams, and drums.

Saturday's Child, a setting of assembled poems by Countee Cullen, the Negro poet, was scored for tenor and soprano with chamber orchestra. The verses show the Negro somewhat on the defensive, yet with pride in his race. In his music Whithorne painted racial traditions, the love of the dance, the intense rhythmic instinct. *The Grim Troubadour*, for medium voice and string quartet, is a setting of three more Cullen poems. In this, more than in *Saturday's Child*, the composer showed that he had not abandoned melody, and that he still was practicing what he once preached in an article in *Modern Music* (November–December, 1926):

During the last decade we have so glorified the machine that it has almost enslaved us. Now we should cease to be its puppet and become its master. . . . There has been a sort of fetish worship of ugliness *per se*. It would be wise to neglect this idol somewhat and make obeisance to more propitious gods. There remains melody, whose crown was forfeited in the maelstrom. Why should our allegiance be withheld from one so radiant?

Moon Trail, a tone poem, was introduced by the Boston Symphony Orchestra, December 15, 1933. In this the expertly scored music, vivid and aptly descriptive, paints four scenes: "Death Valley," "The Devil's Kitchen," "Palos Verdes," and "Surf at Malibu."

When Whithorne's symphonic poem *The Dream Pedlar* was played in New York by the Philadelphia Orchestra, February 18, 1936, Lawrence Gilman remarked in the *Herald Tribune* the next day:

The music which Mr. Whithorne has woven about his dream of the little pedlar and the mysterious article of merchandise is luminous . . . full of pleasant sounds and fairy evocations; and if it sometimes suggests that what the Little Pedlar was really selling was a second-hand score of "Pelléas et Mélisande," why, there is no harm in that. Mr. Whithorne is a man of taste.

The Dream Pedlar shows Whithorne as a romanticist. The score shimmers with the delicate tones of the harp and of strings *divisi*, and the pleasant sounds of the celesta. Whithorne himself told of the incident which inspired his work:

A number of years ago I was strolling . . . along the left bank of the Seine in Paris. . . . I came upon a small crowd gathered about a little pedlar, who, for a few sous, was apparently selling some article of merchandise. . . . Suddenly there was an altercation in the centre of the crowd . . . all were voicing their anger at the little pedlar. Then in tones of strident self-defense he cried: "I am only selling you blind ones a glorious sunset; look at it and be grateful that you have bought beauty at so small a price."

When the piece had its première by the Los Angeles Symphony, January 13, 1931, the critic of the Los Angeles *Examiner* called it a work that was "descended from the past and nurtured on the present."

Whithorne's orchestral works include also three symphonies, two of them given their first performances by the Cincinnati Symphony Orchestra under Eugene Goossens—the first, January 12, 1934, and the second, March 19, 1937. Of the first, Whithorne remarked that he intended it to "mirror certain human experiences which are expressed in a forthright manner." The second is reflective, and somewhat somber in mood. It was the 1939 choice for the Juilliard Publication Award. A *Fandango* was played by Sir Thomas Beecham in 1932, and *Sierra Morena* was performed in May, 1939 by the National Broadcasting Symphony Orchestra under Monteux.

In the field of chamber music Whithorne followed his early *Greek Impressions* with a Piano Quintet, which was performed first at a League of Composers concert in New York, and in the following year (1929) at the Coolidge Festival in Washington; and with a String Quartet, composed in 1930. There are also a Violin Sonata and numerous works for piano.

ERIC DELAMARTER (1880———) is one of the leading organists of Chicago; since 1914 he has played at the Fourth Presbyterian Church, and his organ recitals have become famous. He is an orchestral conductor, and when Frederick Stock was absent during the season of 1918–19, Delamarter took his place as director of the Chicago Symphony. For a number of years he was assistant conductor of the orchestra. He has been a music critic for the Chicago *Record-Herald*, and for the *Tribune*. He was born February 18, 1880, in Lansing, Michigan, and studied with Middelschulte in Chicago, and Guilmant and Widor in Paris. As a composer he has written for orchestra an Overture *The Faun*, and a Suite from his incidental music to *The Betrothal*. His Sonata in E flat for violin and piano is a work of considerable originality with an interesting slow movement, and an individual *finale*. He has written many songs, piano music, organ pieces, and incidental music for plays.

LAZARE SAMINSKY (1882——) has become one of the leaders in Jewish musical circles, both as director of music at New York's Temple Emanu-El and as a composer who believes in the freshness of the racial element in art. He thinks that when this is allied with a sensitiveness to modern life and thought, it provides the highest type of creative stimulus.

Saminsky was born near Odessa, Russia, October 27, 1882. Though he was musical from childhood, he was first trained in languages, higher mathematics, and political economy. He did not start to study music seriously until he was fifteen. When he was twenty, his family met financial ruin, and he became a private tutor in mathematics and Latin. Then he received a scholarship at the Moscow Conservatory, but was expelled in 1906 for joining a revolutionary group and taking part in political demonstrations. He moved to the Conservatory at Petrograd and continued his studies. He began to compose, and gradually acquired a reputation as his pieces were performed. After the armistice he left Russia, went to Paris and then to London, and finally came to America in 1920.

Before he came to this country he had composed two symphonies, a number of separate orchestral works, some chamber music, a four-act opera, and some ballet music. Since he has been in America he has added three symphonies to his list, an opera-ballet based on Poe's *Mask of the Red Death* and entitled *Gagliarda of the Merry Plague* (first produced in New York, February 22, 1925); several large choral works; and for orchestra, a Suite *Ausonia*; a group of "poems" *Stilled Pageant; Three Shadows; Pueblo—A Moon Rhapsody; To a Young World;* and a Rhapsody, *Dunlap's Creek* for chamber orchestra.

Although Saminsky has lived in America only since 1920, he feels very definitely that America has had a greater influence on his creative work than anything he had known before he came here; that it has eaten so deeply into his creative being that American influences and images have crystallized within him almost without his being aware of the process. Thus, he feels, America has contributed to his musical emotion and thought the directness, the rhythm, the Western clarity which every artist of Oriental extraction needs.

In addition to his composing, Saminsky has contributed articles on music to current magazines, and is the author of two published books: *Music of Our Day,* and *Music of the Ghetto and the Bible.*

R. NATHANIEL DETT (1882–1943) was a Negro composer who emphasized the native character of his racial music. His *Juba Dance,* for piano, is one of the raciest bits of Negro-like music that has ever been published, and not too exotic for conservative ears. He was particularly successful in his settings of spirituals for chorus.

Dett was born at Drummondsville, Quebec, October 11, 1882. In 1903 he went to Oberlin, Ohio, to study music. After appearing as a concert pianist, and holding a number of positions as director of music in colored institutes, he was put in charge of music at Hampton Institute, Virginia, where he remained for eighteen years (1913–1931). From 1931 to 1937 he taught privately in Rochester, New York, and at the time of his death, October 2, 1943, he was in Battle Creek, Michigan, where he had organized a Negro WAC chorus, and was directing music activities at a USO clubhouse.

Dett's larger works include *Chariot Jubilee* for orchestra, and *The Ordering of Moses* for soloists, chorus, and orchestra. The latter work was performed at the Cincinnati Festival of 1937, the Worcester Festival of 1938, and by the Oratorio Society in New York, March, 1939. In 1938, Dett was one of the composers commissioned by the Columbia Broadcasting Company to write a work for radio.

CARL EPPERT (1882——) won third prize in the National Broadcasting Company contest of 1932 with his orchestral piece *Traffic.* This work is actually the opening movement of *A Symphony of the City* which has had numerous performances, both in its entirety and in separate movements. Eppert has since won a prize from the Chicago Symphony Orchestra for his *Symphonic Impressions*, first performed by that organization February 13 and 14, 1941.

He was born in Carbon, Clay County, Indiana, November 5, 1882, and studied in Chicago and in Germany. At present he is a resident of Milwaukee, where he organized, and for four seasons conducted, the Civic and Symphony Orchestras. He has been associated with several conservatories, and also has been active as a conductor and teacher in Terre Haute, Indiana, in Seattle, and in Berlin. Others of his orchestral works include a fantasy *The Argonauts;* a tone poem *The Pioneer; A Little Symphony;* a Symphony in C Minor; a satirical portrait *Escapade;* a Suite *Vitamins;* and a Concert Waltz Suite. He also has composed music for symphonic band, a number of choral works, and considerable chamber music.

SETH BINGHAM (1882——) is known to his fellow Yale alumni as the composer of the stirring Yale song *Mother of Men.* He was born in Bloomfield, New Jersey, April 16, 1882. At Yale he studied with Horatio Parker and in the years 1906–7 he worked with Widor, d'Indy, and Guilmant in Paris. As an organist he has held several church positions, and is now organist of the Madison Avenue Presbyterian Church in New York City. He is also professor of organ and composition at Columbia University. His organ works include *Harmonies of Florence, Pioneer America* and a Suite. He has an opera *La Charelzenn* (1917) in manuscript. Among his numerous choral works is the folk cantata *Wilderness Stone,* which has been performed by the Schola Cantorum of New York, and broadcast over both National Broadcasting networks. The piece is based on a love episode from Stephen Vincent Benét's epic poem of the Civil War, *John Brown's Body,* and consists of thirty-nine short numbers, set for narrator, soprano, tenor, bass, chorus, and orchestra. Bingham has written *Tame Animal Tunes* for chamber orchestra; a Suite for wind instruments; a *Wall Street Fantasy* (1912) for symphony orchestra; a Passacaglia (1918); two Suites *Memories of France* and *The Breton Cadence;* and an orchestral version of *Pioneer America.*

W. FRANKE HARLING (1887——) won high praise from the critics and bursts of enthusiasm from the audience when his opera *A Light from St. Agnes* was produced by the Chicago Civic Opera Company in 1925. The prima donna Rosa Raisa started things by kissing the composer before the curtain. That looked good to the audience, and the shy Mr. Harling had troubles in the lobby which have become history in the music and osculatory annals of the country. And yet in spite of its ovation, the opera had only one performance. One of the singers, Forrest Lamont, was taken ill, and no one was chosen to sing in his place for future performances. Nevertheless, Harling was awarded the David Bispham Memorial Medal of the American Opera Society of Chicago.

The score was a setting of a lyric tragedy by Mrs. Minnie Maddern Fiske, the actress. The locale was a village near New Orleans. The composer made of it a jazz opera, modernizing his orchestra with saxophones, banjo, and xylophone. All this was intended not as an effect in itself, but to gain realism.

He tried jazz effects again in *Deep River*, disqualified by purists as grand opera because the action is carried by spoken conversation. New Orleans was again the scene, the time 1830. Voodoo meetings and quadroon balls lent color to the melodrama. The work was performed by a special company of singers and actors—first for a run in Philadelphia and then in New York in the autumn of 1926.

Harling was born in London, January 18, 1887, but was brought to America before he was a year old. He was educated first in Boston, and then went to London and Brussels for music study. He was active for a number of years as a church organist and as a conductor, but since the early 1930's he has been in Hollywood as composer and arranger for sound pictures. Others of his works are a *Jazz Concerto*, a *Venetian Fantasy*, and *Chansons Populaires*, first performed in 1932 and based on themes by Berlin, Kern, and Gershwin. He has written some incidental music for plays, a number of songs, and works for chorus. *The Miracle of Time* is a symphonic ballad for chorus and orchestra. It was the prize composition at the Newark (New Jersey) Festival in 1916.

When ALBERTO BIMBONI (1882——) was conducting an opera season in Washington, and had in his portfolio the score of his own opera *Winona*, President Harding did all he could to further its interests and to see that influence was used to have it performed. Bimboni is an Italian who was born in Florence, August 24, 1882. He came to America in 1911, and was immediately engaged by Henry Savage to prepare his company for its tour with Puccini's *Girl of the Golden West*. After this, Bimboni was an opera conductor in various parts of the country.

The opera *Winona*, first performed in Portland, Oregon, in 1926, is founded on a Sioux-Dakota legend. The music is based on hunting songs, war songs, moccasin songs, a Chippewa lullaby, Indian flute calls, and Chippewa and Sioux serenades. Bimboni was careful not to violate Indian tradition. All of the choruses are presented in unison; there is no part-singing.

MARY HOWE (1882——) is a native of Richmond, Virginia, born there April 4, 1882. She studied in America with Ernest Hutcheson, Harold Randolph, and Gustav Strube, and in Germany with Richard Burmeister. Practically all of her life has been lived in Washington, where she is vice-president of the Friends of Music in the Library of Congress, and has directed two choral societies.

Her orchestral works include *Sand; Poema;* a *Dirge;* a *Spring Pastoral; Stars; Whimsy; Coulennes; American Piece;* and *Castellana,* for two pianos and orchestra. Her list of chamber music numbers a Sonata for violin and piano; a String Quartet performed at Yaddo, September, 1940; a Suite for string quartet and piano; and a Fugue for string quartet. For mixed chorus and orchestra she has composed a *Chain Gang Song* which was performed at the Worcester (Massachusetts) Festival in 1925.

MABEL WOOD-HILL (1889——) was known principally as a song writer until she became interested in the larger forms. She was born in Brooklyn, educated at Smith College and Columbia University, and did much of her studying with Walter Rothwell and Cornelius Rybner. Her first score for orchestra was an introduction to Lady Gregory's play *Grania*. Then she wrote a tone poem after Yeats's play *The Land of Heart's Desire*, and a Suite *The Wind in the Willows*. Her ballet-pantomime *The Adventures of Pinocchio* (1931) has been performed throughout the United States. She has scored several of Bach's works for string orchestra and has arranged for full orchestra Bach's chorale *By the Waters of Babylon*. She has orchestrated two Preludes and Fugues from the *Well-Tempered Clavichord* and some trios by Couperin (*Louis XIV Suite*). One of her newer works, the *Out-of-Doors Suite*, was broadcast by the Roth String Quartet in 1943.

ALOIS REISER (1884——) won second prize in the National Broadcasting Company Music Guild Contest of 1936 with his Second String Quartet. He was born in Prague, April 6, 1887, studied with Dvořák at the Conservatory there, and then came to New York in 1905 where for eleven years he was conductor at the Strand Theatre. In recent years he has been in Hollywood, conducting in motion picture studios.

In 1931, Reiser's Cello Concerto won second prize in the Hollywood Bowl Competition. He has composed also an opera *Gobi* (1912); several tone poems: *A Summer Evening* (1907), *From Mount Rainier* (1926), and *Erewhon* (1931); a *Slavic Rhapsody* for orchestra (1927); two String Quartets (1916 and 1930); two Trios (1910 and 1931); and a Sonata for violin and piano.

EDWARD BALLANTINE (1886——) is one of those composers who has written in the terms of post-romanticists, but who has been checked in his efforts by the bewildering growth of ultramodernism. He had to pause to discover whether he was old fashioned or the advanced brethren crazy. He had already shown his wit in the variations for piano on *Mary Had a Little Lamb*, in the style of ten composers. He has published a number of songs and piano pieces, and his orchestral pieces have been played by the Boston Symphony, and in Chicago, New York, St. Louis, Cincinnati, and elsewhere. *Prelude to the Delectable Forest* was introduced in 1914; *The Eve of St. Agnes* in 1917; the Suite *From the Garden of Hellas* in 1923; other orchestral works are a tone poem *The Awakening of the Woods*, and an *Overture to the Piper*.

Ballantine joined the music faculty at Harvard in 1912, and became an assistant professor in 1927. He was born in Oberlin, Ohio, August 8, 1886, educated in Springfield, Massachusetts; at Harvard (where he took highest honors in music); and in Berlin with Schnabel, Ganz, and Rüfer.

MARION BAUER (1887——) has had a keen sympathy with and an understanding of modern composers, and has helped to further their cause with the concertgoing public. In her own music, she was considered somewhat radical in the 1920's, but today her impressionism is accepted as almost conservative, and in comparison with her experimentalist colleagues, she has become decidedly "middle-of-the-road."

Her works include the early *Fantasia Quasi una Sonata* for violin and piano; a Viola Sonata; a *Dance Sonata* for piano; *Sun Splendor* for orchestra; a String Quartet; incidental music to *Prometheus Bound; Indian Pipes* for orchestra; and *Tryste Noël.*

Miss Bauer was born in Walla Walla, Washington, August 15, 1887. She studied music with her sister, Emilie Frances Bauer, and in New York with Henry Holden Huss, Eugene Heffley, and Walter Henry Rothwell. In Paris she worked with Raoul Pugno, Nadia Boulanger, Campbell-Tipton, and André Gédalge. In addition to composing she is active as a teacher and journalist: she holds the positions of associate professor of music at New York University, and New York editor and critic of the *Musical Leader.* As an author she has continued the series she started in *How Music Grew* (written in collaboration with Ethel R. Peyser) by writing another book with Miss Peyser, *Music Through the Ages,* and with a clear treatise on present-day composers and their idioms, *Twentieth Century Music.*

Being a clarinetist himself, BURNET CORWIN TUTHILL (1888——) has devoted himself largely to writing music for wind instrument combinations. His Opus 1 consisted of a *Scherzo* for three clarinets, and an *Intermezzo* for two clarinets and basset horn. His Variations on *When Johnny Comes Marching Home* are scored for five wind instruments and piano, and for band he has composed a march *Dr. Joe* (in honor of Joseph Maddy, founder of the National Music Camp), and a Symphonic Overture.

Tuthill was born in New York City, November 16, 1888. After a number of years in business he became manager of the Cincinnati Conservatory of Music. In 1935 he settled in Memphis, Tennessee, where he has become the director of the Memphis College of Music. With his father he founded the Society for the Publication of American Music. Others of Tuthill's works are a Pastorale for orchestra, *Bethlehem* (1934); *Come Seven,* a Rhapsody (1935); a Symphonic Poem *Laurentia* (1936); *Big River,* for orchestra (1943); a Quintet for clarinet and strings (1936); a Sextet for strings (1937); and a Sonata for violin and piano (1937).

PHILIP GREELEY CLAPP (1888——) grew up in what professional

biographers would call a musical atmosphere. His father was an amateur musician who sang in choruses and played in orchestras; his
mother a singer and pianist. From boyhood he made little tunes of his
own. He was born in Boston, August 4, 1888, put under the best music
teachers in town, and then sent to Harvard. Aside from music, he
gained three academic degrees from Harvard—Bachelor of Arts in
1908, Master of Arts in 1909, and Doctor of Philosophy in 1911. He
was awarded the Frederick Sheldon fellowship, and went abroad to
study composition with Max von Schillings.

He has held many positions. Director of music at Dartmouth Col-
lege, band leader in the American Expeditionary Forces, and since
1919 professor and director of music at the State University of Iowa.
During leaves of absence he has been director of extension for the
Juilliard Foundation; guest conductor of the American Orchestral
Society in New York, and at concerts of the Cincinnati Orchestra in
Birmingham, Alabama, and in Knoxville, Tennessee.

Clapp's works have had important performances. He has written
six symphonies; four symphonic poems; a Piano Concerto; a symphonic work for the Saxe-Alloo seven-valve independent trombone; a
String Quartet; a Piano Sonata; and several choral works. His earliest
symphonic poem *Norge* was first performed by the Pierian Sodality of
Harvard in 1908, then by the Boston Symphony in 1909; later by the
St. Louis, Chicago, and Minneapolis Orchestras. His first two symphonies were performed in 1914 and 1917 by the Boston Symphony,
with the composer conducting. An orchestral prelude *In Summer* has
been played in St. Louis, Minneapolis, and Chicago.

CLARENCE LOOMIS (1889——) was born in Sioux Falls, South
Dakota, December 13, 1889. He was musically educated in Chicago
and in Vienna. He became a teacher at the American Conservatory in
Chicago, and later at the Arthur Jordan Conservatory in Indianapolis.
He has written a Piano Concerto, and several operas. One of these,
Yolanda of Cyprus, was produced in Chicago and New York, and on
tour by the American Opera Company in the season of 1929–30. In
this work Loomis made an obvious attempt to subordinate the music
to the text. The voices had little to do musically, and whatever musical delineation there is was given to the orchestra. An interesting
experiment; and the future will decide whether this is to be the proper

balance for modern opera. In *Yolanda* the music is too obviously de-rived—from *Pelléas,* and some of it from Wagner, Puccini, and Moussorgsky. As Lawrence Gilman wrote of the New York perform-ances in the *Tribune,* "There was much applause. . . . Almost every-one concerned received his due—except Debussy."

In recent years Loomis has composed two further operas, one of them from Poe's *The Fall of the House of Usher,* and the other a work based on melodies by Stephen Foster—*Susannah, Don't You Cry.* Both works employ librettos by Ethel Ferguson, and the Foster opera was commissioned by Josiah K. Lilly, founder of Foster Hall in Indianapolis. It was produced in New York in the spring of 1939 by the American Lyric Theater. Three scenes from *The Fall of the House of Usher* were presented in Indianapolis, January 11, 1941.

ETHEL GLENN HIER (1889——) was one of the two women awarded Guggenheim Fellowships in music for the season of 1930-31. The other was Ruth Crawford. Born in Cincinnati, she was a pupil of Stillman Kelley, Percy Goetschius, and Ernest Bloch. In addition to numerous shorter works for voice and for piano including her Suite *A Day in the Peterboro Woods,* she has written several Quartets for voice, violin, cello, and piano; a Suite for string quartet; a Sextet for flute, oboe, violin, viola, cello, and piano; a setting of *America the Beautiful* for chorus and orchestra; and a ballet for orchestra—*Chorèographe.*

* * *

EDGAR VARÈSE (1885——) is the logical man to head the experi-mentalists from this decade-group, for he is one of the most radical of our composers in his approach to the musical language, and he has frankly expressed himself in sonority and rhythmic complexity at the expense, and sometimes to the exclusion, of all melody and harmony. His *Ionisation,* for example, is written for two groups of percussion players, thirteen in all, using only sounds of indeterminate pitch. Yet it is said (by Nicolai Slonimsky in his *Music Since 1900*) to be "written in a sonata form," with exposition, development, abridged recapitula-tion, and coda. Varèse was one of the pioneers in presenting music of radical tendencies to American audiences, having organized in 1926 the Pan-American Society, and, with Salzedo, the International Composers' Guild in 1921. His orchestral and chamber music has been widely performed abroad as well as in this country. His works include *Metal,* a poem for soprano and orchestra; *Espace, Amériques, Arcana, Intégrales, Hyperprism, Octandres;* and *Offrandes* for orchestra; a *Symphony with Chorus; Density 21.5* for flute solo; and *Equatorial,* for organ, percussion, brass, theremin instrument, and bass-baritone voice. Cowell has written of him: ". . . if stirring auditors to an almost unendurable irritation be taken into account, then the music can be said to be highly emotional. . . ."

Varèse was born in Paris, December 22, 1885, where he studied music with Widor, d'Indy, and Roussel. He came to the United States in 1915 and founded in New York the New Symphony Orchestra for the performance of modern music.

CARLOS SALZEDO (1885——) was graduated from the Paris Conservatory with honors in harp and piano, and is known as a brilliant harpist and an apostle of advanced musical tendencies, in his own music and in that of other men. He was born in Archanon, France, April 6, 1885. He eventually settled in this country and became an American citizen in 1924. He collaborated with Varèse in the founding, in 1921, of the International Composers' Guild, and he is a member of the Board of the United States Section of the International Society for Contemporary Music. He founded the harp department at the Curtis Institute, and teaches also at the Juilliard School. He has written numerous works for harp solo, harp and orchestra, and various combinations of instruments and voices including one or more harps. He has enriched the composer's orchestral vocabulary by demonstrating numerous hitherto unexploited sounds and colors of which the harp is capable. His music has been heard in many performances and broadcasts. It includes *The Enchanted Isle,* for harp and orchestra; an untitled work for harp, brasses, and strings; a Concerto and a *Préambule et Jeux* for harp with several other instruments; and a Sonata for harp and piano, published by the Society for the Publication of American Music.

WALLINGFORD RIEGGER (1885——) was rather conventional in his early pieces but in later years he has indulged in complete atonality. He believes that for composers of today still to use the idiom of Brahms or Wagner is to ignore the lessons of history and to imply a condemnation of such innovators as Bach, Beethoven, Chopin, Debussy, and others who violated tradition when it hampered the full expression of a musical idea. His *Study in Sonority* for ten violins "or any multiple thereof" shows that he is indeed an atonalist. Viewed on paper, with its constant minor seconds and close-lying intervals, it splits the ears. Yet with the strings its dissonance is not so harsh as it would be if percussion instruments were producing the noise. The work has had several performances: first, in 1928, in Rochester under Howard Hanson; then in New York by Leopold Stokowski and forty violins of the Philadelphia Orchestra; and the third at a *Pro Musica* concert in New York in 1930.

Riegger was born in Georgia in 1885. He was brought up in Indianapolis, and he had a thorough music education. Later he studied with Goetschius in New York, in Berlin with Edgar Stillman Kelley and Anton Hekking. Beside the *Study in Sonority* his works include a Trio in B Minor; a String Quartet; an *American Polonaise* for orchestra; *La Belle Dame sans Merci*, for eight instruments and four singers; a Rhapsody for orchestra; a Suite for flute alone; and Four Canons for woodwinds; a *Fantasy and Fugue* for organ and orchestra and a *Lyric Suite*; and for chamber music combinations: *Dichotomy, Scherzo, Divertissement* for harp, flute, and cello; a Suite for flute solo, the last movement of which contains "a series of thirty-six non-repeated notes," and a String Quartet. He has composed much music for the modern dance, written for Martha Graham, Charles Weidman, Doris Humphrey, Tamiris, and others. He was music director of the Dance Division of the Federal Theatre Project in New York, and a member of the executive boards of the Pan-American Association of Composers and the American Composers' Alliance. In recent years he has been editor for a publishing house. His Canon and Fugue for orchestra had its première with the National Orchestral Association February 14, 1944.

JOHN J. BECKER (1886——) is a champion of musical radicalism, in his own works and those of his colleagues. He was born in Henderson, Kentucky, January 22, 1886, was educated in the Middle West, and has stayed there (in Minneapolis and St. Paul) carrying on more or less singlehanded a strenuous battle for nonconformist music. He has been director of music at Notre Dame University; professor of fine arts at the College of St. Scholastica, conductor of two orchestras and the St. Cloud (Minnesota) Civic Choir, and state director of the Federal Music Project for Minnesota. He has written three Symphonies, of which the second was performed at the Frankfurt Music Festival in Germany in 1932; various Concerti with orchestra—for piano, for two flutes, for horn, and for viola; several *Soundpieces* for string combinations; choral and chamber music; and several stage works, including *Dance Figure* and *Obongo, Dance Primitive*. He has also experimented with new combinations of music and dancing and dramatic action in *A Marriage with Space*, and in *The Life of Man*, based on Andreiev.

* * *

The decade of the 1880's produced also:

JOSEPH ACHRON
Born, Lithuania, 1886; came to America, 1925; died, Los Angeles, 1943.
Three Violin Concerti; Two Sonatas for violin and piano; *Children's Suite* for piano, clarinet, and string quartet; *Golem Suite* for chamber orchestra; numerous orchestral and chamber music works.

PAUL HASTINGS ALLEN
Born, Massachusetts, 1882.
Seven operas, including *O Munasterio* (Florence, 1911), *Il Filtro* (Genoa, 1912), *Milda* (Venice, 1913), *The Last of the Mohicans* (*L'ultimo dei Moicane*, Florence, 1916), *Cleopatra* (1921), and *La piccola Figaro* (1931); two Symphonies, in D and in E; *Serenade* (1928) and *Ex Hocte* (1930) for orchestra; for chamber orchestra—Suite (1928), *Dans la nuit* (1928), and *Three Pieces* (1928); chamber music—four String Quartets; Quartet for two clarinets, basset-horn, and bass clarinet (1929); Trio for oboe, clarinet, and bassoon (1929); choral works—Three Women's Choruses (1929), Seven Madrigals (1930), and *Left But the Power* (1932); fifty Sonatas; and many songs and piano pieces.

EUGENE BONNER

Born, Washington, North Carolina, 1889.

Composer, critic.

White Nights for orchestra; *Whispers of Heavenly Death* for soprano and orchestra; four operas—*Barbara Frietchie, Celui qui epousa une femme muette, The Venetian Glass Nephew,* and *The Gods of the Mountain;* chamber music.

GEORGE FREDERICK BOYLE

Born, Australia, 1886; came to America, 1910.

Symphonic Fantasie for orchestra; *Slumber Song* and *Aubade* for orchestra; Concerto for piano and orchestra; Concerto for cello and orchestra; Sonata for piano; *The Pied Piper of Hamelin,* cantata; Concertino for piano and orchestra (1935); Suite for two pianos (1932); Sonata for piano and cello; Violin Sonata (1934); Cello Sonata (1928); Viola Sonata (1918); Trio for piano, violin, and cello (1934); about fifty songs and one hundred piano pieces.

CHALMERS CLIFTON

Born, Mississippi, 1889.

Conductor and composer.

Adagio for orchestra; *The Poppy* for baritone and orchestra; two Piano Sonatas; two pieces for clarinet and piano, Violin Sonata; Suite for trumpet and orchestra.

FRANCESCO BARTHOLOMEO DE LEONE

Born, Ohio, 1887.

Opera *Alglala* produced Akron and Cleveland, Ohio, 1924 (awarded David Bispham Memorial Medal, and Medal of the National Federation of Music Clubs); operettas; cantatas; light opera in Italian—*A Millionaire Caprice;* operettas—*Cave Man Stuff* and *Princess Ting-Ah-Ling;* four sacred music dramas—*Ruth, The Prodigal Son, The Golden Calf,* and *David;* oratorio—*The Triumph of Joseph;* orchestral works— Six *Italian Dances, Italian Rhapsody, Gibraltar Suite;* more than four hundred songs; many piano pieces.

JAMES PHILIP DUNN

Born, New York City, 1884; died Jersey City, New Jersey, 1936.

Composer, organist.

We, symphonic poem based on Lindbergh's flight to Paris (1927); *Overture on Negro Themes* for orchestra (1925); *Passacaglia and Fugue* for orchestra; two String Quartets; Piano Quintet; Violin Sonata; numerous songs.

ALBERT I. ELKUS

Born, Sacramento, California, 1884.

Teacher, composer; since 1935, professor of music, University of California.

GEORGE FOOTE

Born, Cannes, France, 1886.

Variations on a Pious Theme, for orchestra (American Composers' Concerts, Eastman School, 1931; Boston Symphony, 1935).

EDWIN GRASSE

Born, New York, 1884.

Blind violinist and composer.

Two Symphonies, in G and D; Suite in C for orchestra; *American Fantasie* for violin and orchestra; Violin Concerto in E Minor; three Piano Trios; seven Violin Sonatas; Sonata in D and *Pastorale,* for violin and organ; Sonata for violoncello; about twenty-five songs; and pieces for organ, for piano, and for violin.

VICTOR KOLAR

Born, Budapest, 1888; came to America, 1904.

Symphonic Suite, *Americana;* two symphonic poems *Hiawatha* and *A Fairy Tale;* one Symphony; *Lyric Suite* for orchestra; Slovakian Rhapsody for orchestra; two String Quartets; three *Humoresques* for violin and piano; seven Marches; and many songs.

CHRISTIAAN KRIENS

Born of Dutch parents in Germany, 1881; came to America in 1906; died, 1934.

Conductor and composer.

Two Symphonies; two orchestral Suites *In Holland* and *In Brittany;* Symphonic Poem; String Quartet; two Sonatas for violin and piano; songs and instrumental pieces.

EDWARD KURTZ

Born, New Castle, Pennsylvania, 1881.

Composer, teacher; head of Music Department, Iowa State Teachers College.

Three Symphonies (1927, 1937, 1941); *La Charmante* for orchestra (1914); March in D for orchestra (1919); *Parthenope*, tone poem for violin and orchestra (1922); *The Daemon Lover*, tone poem for orchestra (1933); Scherzo for orchestra (American Composers' Concerts, Eastman School, 1932); chamber music; instrumental pieces; songs.

RALPH LYFORD

Born, Massachusetts, 1882; died, Ohio, 1927.

Composer, teacher, conductor. Assistant conductor, Leipzig opera, 1907; assistant conductor, Boston Opera Company, 1916; faculty member, Cincinnati Conservatory of Music, 1925–27.

Concerto for piano and orchestra (first prize from National Federation of Music Clubs, 1927); opera *Castle Agrazant* produced 1926, Cincinnati (awarded David Bispham Memorial Medal).

HUGH MacCOLL

Born, Pawtucket, Rhode Island, 1885.

Romantic Suite in Form of Variations (Rochester Symposium, 1936).

EDWARD ROYCE

Born, Cambridge, Massachusetts, 1886.

Composer, teacher. Graduate of Harvard University (with honors) of Stern Conservatory, Berlin, 1913; founder and head of music department, Middlebury College, Vermont; head of theory department, Ithaca Conservatory of Music, 1916–21; since 1923 head of composition department, Eastman Conservatory of Music.

The Firebringers (1926), *Far Ocean* (1929) for orchestra; Piano Variations; piano pieces, songs.

FREDERICK PRESTON SEARCH

Born, Pueblo, Colorado, 1889.

Cellist, conductor, composer. Member Leipzig Gewandhaus Orchestra, 1910–12; first cellist, American Symphony Orchestra,

Chicago, 1915–16; assistant editor, *The Violinist,* 1915–16; Navy bandmaster, 1918.

The Bridge Builders, for soloists, chorus, and orchestra; Symphonic Poem *The Dream of McCorkle; Rhapsody,* for orchestra; *Exhilaration,* for orchestra; *Festival Overture;* eight String Quartets; two Cello Sonatas; Cello Concerto; Piano Quintet; Piano Septet; Sextet in F, published by the Society for Publication of American Music.

GUSTAVE SODERLUND

Born, Göteburg, Sweden, 1881.

Composer, teacher; faculty member, Eastman School of Music.

Symphonic Interlude (American Composers' Concerts, Eastman School, 1935); Symphony (same, 1941); *Festival Fanfare* (same, 1942).

CESARE SODERO

Born, Italy, 1886; came to America, 1906.

Conductor of various opera companies; in 1924 conductor of operas for National Broadcasting Company. Since 1936 with Mutual Broadcasting System; conductor at Metropolitan, 1942–44.

Two grand operas—one, *Ombre russe* (*Russian Shadows*) given first over the radio, then at Malibran Theatre, Florence, Italy; three Symphonic Poems; two orchestral Suites; two *Intermezzos* for orchestra; *Prelude Appassionata* for violin and orchestra; string quartet; also choral works, chamber music, and songs.

ALBERT SPALDING

Born, Chicago, 1888.

Noted violinist.

Two Violin Concertos; Sonata for violin and piano; Theme and Variations for orchestra; Suite for violin and piano; shorter pieces.

THEODORE STEARNS

Born, Ohio, 1881; died, 1935.

Several operas—*The Snowbird* produced at the Chicago Opera, 1923; symphonic works, and songs. Author of *The Story of Music* (1931).

MAX WALD

Born, Litchfield, Illinois, 1889.

Composer, teacher; chairman, theory department, Chicago Musical College.

The Dancer Dead, for orchestra (winner of second prize, National Broadcasting Company contest, 1932); *Comedy Overture, Sentimental Promenades, Retrospectives*, for orchestra; opera *Mirandolina*; chamber music.

EFREM ZIMBALIST

Born, Russia, 1889; in America since 1911.

Noted violinist.

Sonata for violin and piano; *Slavonic Dances* for violin and orchestra; Suite *In Old Style* for violin and piano; String Quartet; Phantasy on *Le Coq d'Or* for violin; and songs.

3. FROM THE 1890's

The music of GEORGE GERSHWIN (1898–1937) has been discussed more widely, and has been the subject for more debate, than that of any other American composer. As a man, he has become a legend. Those who knew him well have written hundreds of pages of anecdotes about him; the most complete collection, perhaps, is found in a chapter of Oscar Levant's book *A Smattering of Ignorance*,[1] entitled: "My Life, or the Story of George Gershwin." As a composer, Gershwin has become a symbol of the merging of American popular music and the music of the concert hall and opera house. The debates about him center largely on the success of the merger. Some say that he was most significant as a composer of gay tunes for musical comedies, and that his symphonic works were merely extensions of something that was better adapted to the dance hall and operetta stage; while others have held that he is truly the most important of any American composer that has yet lived, regardless of the origin of his inspiration.

The controversy still continues, but one fact stands out as incontrovertible. It is now more than twenty years since the *Rhapsody in Blue* was first performed at Paul Whiteman's concert in Aeolian Hall, and it has become the most widely and often played orchestral work by an American. And *Porgy and Bess*, first produced in 1935, revived

---

[1] New York, Doubleday, Doran & Co., 1940.

for a record-breaking Broadway run in 1942, and taken through the nation for an extended tour, has been heard and seen by more people than any other American opera, or, very likely, than any opera by any composer that has been produced in this country.

In the first edition of this book, published in 1931, and again in this author's *Our Contemporary Composers* (1941), Gershwin was discussed in the chapters devoted to popular music and jazz. In this revision it is time to change the emphasis on Gershwin's twofold output, and to present him in the gallery of serious composers. Certainly he is the best known of any of them to the greatest number of people, and he has had a more far-reaching influence on his colleagues and successors than any other American musician. It might have been logical to have discussed his concert works here, and his popular songs in a later chapter along with the other Broadway song writers; but Gershwin's lighter works are so much the germ and source of his larger compositions, that they cannot be considered separately.

Gershwin was born in Brooklyn, New York, September 26, 1898. He had some musical training with Charles Hambitzer and Edward Kelenyi from the time he was thirteen, and at sixteen he became a song-plugger for J. H. Remick & Company in New York.

He began to write songs of his own, songs with a spontaneity, an unexpected twist of rhythm, tune, or harmony that attracted immediate attention and soon had everybody whistling. His first song was *When You Want 'Em, You Can't Get 'Em; When You Got 'Em, You Don't Want 'Em.* His first success was *I Was So Young, You Were So Beautiful*, interpolated in a musical comedy called *Good Morning, Judge!*, produced in 1919. His first show was produced that year— *La, La, Lucille.*

Swanee was the song that first brought Gershwin real fame, after it was interpolated by Al Jolson in *Sinbad*. Then came the succession of musical comedies which contained songs that have become almost American folk songs: *George White's Scandals* (1920–24); *Lady Be Good* (1924); *Oh, Kay* (1925); *Strike Up the Band* (1927); *Funny Face* (1927); *Girl Crazy* (1930); and the political satires, *Of Thee I Sing* (1931), and *Let 'Em Eat Cake* (1933). From them came tunes which have not been surpassed in Tin-Pan Alley: *That Certain Feeling; Fascinating Rhythm; Do, Do, Do; Fidgety Feet; Maybe; Sweet and Lowdown; The Man I Love; 's Wonderful; My One and*

Only; Embraceable You; and many others, generally with words by George's brother Ira.

Gershwin had ambitions as a composer of serious music early in his career, and at one time he studied orchestration with Rubin Goldmark. But it was in 1924 that his opportunity came, when Paul Whiteman asked him to compose an original piece for his "Experiment in Modern Music" concert in Aeolian Hall, February 12.

Whiteman was faced with a difficult problem in planning this concert. It was all right to ask music critics to come around and listen to his arrangements of pretty little tunes and his jazzing of the classics, but there had to be some *pièce de résistance* to use as a climax, and as a reason for the band's being in the concert hall at all—something new, written especially for the party. So he turned to George Gershwin, who had always been obliging, and had shown on many occasions that he could write to order. George hit upon the idea of writing a piano piece which he himself could play with the orchestra, a sort of concerto. In ten days he completed the *Rhapsody in Blue,* and the trusty arranger Ferde Grofé, confronted with a task for which there was no precedent in musical history, orchestrated the piece for Whiteman's band, and thereby taught a few things to musical theorists in the way of tone coloring.

I remember the dress rehearsal of the concert. It was held in the Palais Royal; mid-afternoon when the heavy drapes looked gloomy and the tables bare. There was quite an audience, standing around or sitting here and there in groups on the scattered chairs. Victor Herbert was there to conduct the *Serenades* he had written for the program. Carl Van Vechten and Gilbert Seldes drifted in to see what it was all about. The music critics came for an advance hearing, and of course many Broadway friends of the composer. Things were interesting right along through the afternoon, but the climax came when Ross Gorman's clarinet started to laugh in the opening bars of the *Rhapsody.* And how it did chuckle. Here was something new; the conventional and not so conventional syncopations of the jazz artists given development and symphonic treatment. Real Broadwaylike tunes, blues and all, woven together. Then the middle section, with a more Tschaikowskian theme; warm and compelling.

The success of the piece was immediate and it established Gershwin's fame overnight. And it did as much for Whiteman as it did for Gershwin, for as Henry O. Osgood remarked in his book, *So This Is Jazz*, the *Rhapsody in Blue* was the first work "that allowed jazz to stick its head outside the cabaret door." [2]

In 1925, Walter Damrosch commissioned Gershwin to compose a Piano Concerto for performance with the New York Symphony Society. This time Gershwin decided to make his own orchestration, and he sought the counsel of Rubin Goldmark. The piece, of course, was to be for symphony orchestra, not the jazz band instrumentation of which Grofé was a master. So when he had finished his score, to make sure that it would sound as he had written it, Gershwin hired the Globe Theatre and an orchestra of sixty musicians to play the piece over for a few hours to see what it sounded like. Then when he had made a few changes in the string parts, he took the score to Damrosch.

Dr. Damrosch presented Gershwin and the Concerto with these remarks:

Various composers have been walking around jazz like a cat around a plate of hot soup, waiting for it to cool off, so that they could enjoy it without burning their tongues, hitherto accustomed only to the more tepid liquid distilled by cooks of the classical school. Lady Jazz, adorned with her intriguing rhythms, has danced her way around the world, even as far as the Eskimos of the North and the Polynesians of the South Sea Isles. But for all her travels and her sweeping popularity, she has encountered no knight who could lift her to a level that would enable her to be received as a respectable member in musical circles.

George Gershwin seems to have accomplished this miracle. He has done it boldly by dressing this extremely independent and up-to-date young lady in the classic garb of a concerto. Yet he has not detracted one whit from her fascinating personality. He is the Prince who has taken Cinderella by the hand and openly proclaimed her a princess to the astonished world, no doubt to the fury of her envious sisters.

After that George played his best, which is a very good best; but nevertheless the piece was not another *Rhapsody in Blue*. Technically it was better, but there were repressions that seemed to have gotten hold of him when he knew he had been invited to play in the best of music society. Perhaps Gershwin was a little too mindful of his musical

[2] Boston, Little, Brown & Co., 1926.

manners; his desire to hold his knife and fork correctly may have taken away much of the natural charm that had been found in his previous *Rhapsody in Blue,* where he had been less polite but more effective.

Nevertheless, there are many who think the Concerto in F is Gershwin's finest work. One of its admirers is the English-Russian conductor Albert Coates, who, when asked in 1930 to make a list of the fifty best musical compositions of all time, chose Gershwin's Concerto in F as the only work by an American to take a place with the other forty-nine world masterpieces. In announcing his choice, Mr. Coates was careful to add that his list had an unavoidable personal bias, for there is no such thing, he said, as absolute objectivity or complete detachment in art. His selection of fifty works was based on their universal appeal, their survival of the test of time, or, in the case of modern pieces, on their significance as an expression of the present day.

Gershwin's next symphonic piece was *An American in Paris,* which was also composed for Damrosch, and was first performed in 1928 on the same program that offered the première of Bloch's *America.* In this musical picture Gershwin found a subject perfectly suited to his style, and he created a charming and relaxed bit of writing. It had humor and gaiety, two of the things jazz could handle best. And its program—the adventures of an American (recognizably the composer himself) three thousand miles from home, opened the door to a "blue" mood and a blues theme that is one of Gershwin's happiest inspirations.

Four years later Gershwin offered a Second Rhapsody, for piano and orchestra, which he introduced as pianist with the Boston Symphony under Koussevitzky, February 5, 1932. This work was an expansion of a five-minute sequence which Gershwin had composed for a motion picture *Delicious.* Olin Downes described the piece in the *New York Times* (February 6, 1932): "This rhapsody has more orchestration and more development than the *Rhapsody in Blue.* Its main motive is reasonably suggestive of rivets and racket in the streets of the metropolis; also, if you like, of the liveliness and bonhomie of its inhabitants. There is a second theme, built into a contrasting section. Thus jazz dance rhythm and sentimental song are opposed and juxtaposed in this score. The conception is wholly orchestral." Downes then concluded his review with this opinion: "But with all its immaturities, the *Rhapsody in Blue* is more individual and originative than the piece heard last night . . . we have had better things from Mr. Gershwin, and we expect better in time to come."

This was a sound verdict, for the Second Rhapsody has not been often performed.

It was about this time (1931) that the satirical musical comedy *Of Thee I Sing* was produced. This work, which won the Pulitzer Prize for the best play of the season, poked fun at government official-dom, and its opening song *Wintergreen for President* has become a classic. The sequel to *Of Thee I Sing*, *Let 'Em Eat Cake*, was not a success.

It was perhaps inevitable that Gershwin should turn to the grand opera stage, and he did so with great distinction, even though there was much discussion as to whether *Porgy and Bess* was a high-class musical comedy, or a low-class grand opera. As a matter of fact, it was neither. It was nearest, perhaps, to a folk opera, but however classified, it is, to date, the most individual American opera that has been suc-cessfully produced, and it may very well be a pioneer in establishing a native school of American opera.

Porgy and Bess was based on the play *Porgy*, by Du Bose and Dorothy Heyward, and it was first produced at the Alvin Theatre, New York, by the Theatre Guild, in the fall of 1935. To gather ma-terial on the Negroes around Charleston, South Carolina, and to study the "Gullah" dialect, Gershwin spent considerable time in the South. There is no doubt that he produced something highly authentic, for the Negro-like music he composed made the audience feel that they were actually sitting in Catfish Row, rather than in a theatre.

Opinion was divided at the time of the original production as to whether Gershwin had produced a unified score for the entire dra-matic work, or whether he had supplied merely a succession of appro-priate song-hits—*Summertime*, *I Got Plenty of Nuthin'*, *It Ain't Necessarily So*, *Bess, You Is My Woman Now*, and the others. Brooks Atkinson remarked in *The New York Times* (October 11, 1935) that "Mr. Gershwin is still easiest in mind when he is writing songs with choruses."

In 1942 the opera was revived in a production sponsored by Cheryl Crawford. This time a number of cuts were made in the score and in the action, and the result was a far more unified whole, and one of the most touching creations in the theatre. The songs were still there, and they charmed the audience just as they did in the original production. But this time the action and the accompanying score had been tightened; they did not have a chance to wander from their main course, and as a consequence the song-hits became an integrated part of the drama.

The year 1937 found Gershwin in the prime of his career. His musical comedy songs were counted in the hundreds, and dozens of them showed enduring vitality. In the recital field his *Three Preludes* for piano were coming into the standard repertoire of pianists. His symphonic works were relatively few in number, and he had composed only one grand opera, but these were being performed so often that he was the most frequently heard of his colleagues. His works in lighter fields had brought him a large fortune, and he was adding to it each season. In the summer of that year he was in Hollywood working on the score of *The Goldwyn Follies*. He collapsed one day at the film studios, and two weeks later, July 11, 1937, he died of a brain tumor which was discovered too late for the attempted operation to be successful.

The following August 9 a memorial concert was given in the Lewisohn Stadium, New York, and since that time an all-Gershwin program during the Stadium season of the New York Philharmonic-Symphony has become an annual event which surpasses all other concerts in attendance records. In 1945, Warner Brothers produced a motion picture based on Gershwin's life and music, appropriately entitled *Rhapsody in Blue*.

In the original edition of this volume, issued in 1931, HOWARD HANSON (1896——) was presented as one of the most talented of the "younger group." The last fifteen years have upheld the estimate of his talent, but it is hardly accurate to refer to a man who is now in his forty-ninth year as a promising youngster, even though both Hanson and his music will always be youthful in spirit.

In my book on *Our Contemporary Composers* [3] I included the following paragraphs on Hanson's attitude towards nationalism in music:

[3] New York, Thomas Y. Crowell Co., 1941.

In spite of his devoted interest in the development of American music, Hanson is no chauvinist; he is not an advocate of a "nationalist" school. To him American music means music written by Americans. It makes no difference what their backgrounds may be, whether they are descendants of the settlers of Plymouth, Jamestown, or Wilmington, or whether they are sons of immigrants newly arrived. His sole interest is that America contribute its gift of music to the world, that a rich creative musical life may flourish in this country, that some of the glorious ideals that are American may be transmuted into living tone.

Similarly, he is not particularly concerned with conservatism versus radicalism. The radical of today may be the conservative of tomorrow, and the degree of his conservatism or radicalism is apt to have very little to do with the quality of his music.

Hanson also believes that every composer must constantly grow, both technically and creatively, must continually search himself to test the basic qualities of his own aesthetic philosophy, must constantly seek for new beauties, and must turn the microscope of his own analytical mind on each new approach evolved either by himself or by others, for the purpose of finding in that new approach the spirit of life which is the basis of all art. As for his own work, he believes that his Third Symphony comes closer to the realization of the ideals he has set for himself than any other work he has written.

But Hanson's importance to American music does not rest on any single work, nor, indeed, on any one phase of his activity. If he has a particular artistic creed, it is a belief in the necessity for absolute freedom of creative expression, each composer writing out of the depths of his own soul that which seems to him to be good. When such a creed is generally held by composers, critics, and music lovers, academic questions concerning degrees of newness will give way, he says, to the more essential problem of assaying each new work for the precious metal of vital beauty, without which no work can live.

Hanson was born in Wahoo, Nebraska, October 28, 1896. His parents were Swedish, and Howard was educated at Luther College, Nebraska, at Northwestern University, and at the Institute of Musical Art in New York. At the age of twenty he was appointed professor of theory at the Music Conservatory of the College of the Pacific, and in 1919 he became its dean. In 1921 he was awarded a Fellowship in the American Academy at Rome, and upon his return to America in 1924 he accepted the directorship of the Eastman School of Music at Rochester. He has held that position ever since, and besides carrying on his administrative work, and teaching, he inaugurated the American Composers' Concerts which are now in their twenty-first season. Through these concerts and the annual Festival of American Music at Rochester, Hanson has done more to encourage his fellow composers and to give new talent a hearing than any other individual or group in the country.

Hanson's works include four Symphonies (*Nordic*, 1922; *Romantic*, 1930; the Third, 1937; and the Fourth, 1943); five Symphonic Poems (*Before the Dawn*, 1920; *Exaltation*, 1920; *North and West*, 1923; *Lux Aeterna*, 1923; and *Pan and the Priest*, 1926); a Symphonic Prelude, 1916; a Symphonic Legend, 1917; a Symphonic Rhapsody, 1919; a Concerto for organ and orchestra, based on themes of *North and West*, 1926; an opera *Merry Mount*, produced at the Metropolitan in New York, 1934; a Quintet in F Minor, for piano and strings, 1916; a *Concerto da Camera*, for piano and string quartet, 1917; a String Quartet, 1923; *The Lament for Beowulf*, a choral work, 1925; a *Heroic Elegy* for chorus, 1927; and *Three Poems from Walt Whitman* (Songs from *Drum Taps*), for mixed chorus and orchestra, 1925.

The most widely performed of the orchestral works have been the *Nordic* and *Romantic* Symphonies, the latter commissioned by Serge Koussevitzky for the fiftieth anniversary of the Boston Symphony Orchestra, and two of the symphonic poems, *Lux Aeterna* and *Pan and the Priest*. The Third Symphony was commissioned by the Columbia Broadcasting System, and had its first performance on the radio September 19, 1937. On this occasion the work consisted of only three movements, and the composer announced his intention of adding a fourth at some future date. This seemed essential upon first hearing, for the third movement is a brief Scherzo which by no means brings the symphony to a satisfactory conclusion. As a whole, this Third Symphony is more polyphonic than Hanson's earlier symphonies, and purer harmonically.

The Fourth Symphony was first performed by the Boston Symphony, with the composer conducting, December 3, 1943. On the following January 2 it was broadcast by the National Broadcasting

Symphony under Stokowski. In the same month (January 28, 1944) it was played by the Philadelphia Orchestra, and a few days later, February 3, by the Rochester Philharmonic. The following April it won for its composer the Pulitzer Prize for musical composition.

The work is dedicated to the memory of the composer's father, and consists of four separate movements which follow the plan of the Requiem Mass: *Kyrie; Requiescat; Dies Irae;* and *Lux Aeterna.* There is no direct liturgical connotation in these titles; they serve rather to establish the mood. The symphony as a whole shows a significant departure from the romanticism of Hanson's early works, and in its structure and idiom it is the most compact and direct of his compositions.

The opera *Merry Mount* was produced by the Metropolitan Opera Company, New York, February 10, 1934, and given nine performances during that season. The work had been heard in concert form at the Ann Arbor Festival the preceding May 20.

Several years before the actual production of the opera, the libretto which Richard L. Stokes provided the composer was published as a poem in book form. On that occasion Lewis Gannett reviewed the text for the book column of the New York *Herald Tribune* (January 16, 1932), and thereby provided a highly readable and terse summary of the plot:

Thomas Morton set up a maypole at Merrymount, in Massachusetts, in 1625, to the scandal of his Puritan neighbors, danced, made merry, and sold liquor to the Indians. The Puritans cut down his maypole and shipped Morton back to England. And ever since that day Thomas Morton of Merrymount, of whom so little is known, has been a glamorous figure to historians seeking new light on old New England. . . .

A Puritan pastor, stirred by the beauty of women in his dreams, but not at all by the little Puritan girl to whom he becomes engaged, is Mr. Stokes' central character. When Marigold, one of the Mount's company of gay cavaliers, steps into the Puritan settlement, Pastor Bradford loses his head completely. He stops her marriage to a fellow cavalier; he provokes his fellow Puritans to rout the wedding festivities, killing her fiancé; he wrestles for the soul of Marigold, and loses his own. In the night he dreams of selling his soul for Marigold's body, bringing death and destruction upon the young Puritan colony as a penalty; and when he awakes to find drunken Indians sacking the Puritan village, it seems but confirmation of his demented imaginings. He seizes Marigold and marches with her into the flames, while the returning Puritans chant the Lord's Prayer.

At the concert performance in Ann Arbor the leading roles of the opera were sung by John Charles Thomas, Frederick Jagel, Leonora Corona, and Rose Bampton, under the baton of the composer. At the Metropolitan, Tullio Serafin conducted, and the singers included Lawrence Tibbett, Edward Johnson, Gladys Swarthout, and Goeta Ljungberg.

The Metropolitan première was a tremendously successful affair, and according to reporters the applause of the audience resulted in fifty curtain calls for composer, librettist, and performers. But in spite of the public acclaim, the critics were somewhat reserved in their praise. Olin Downes wrote in *The New York Times* (February 11, 1934): "The music is at times conventional and noisily effective. Otherwise, it displays neither originality nor any special aptitude for the theatre."

Lawrence Gilman, in the New York *Herald Tribune* (February 11, 1934) thought the choruses in the opera its most memorable artistic achievement. "As a whole," he wrote, "Mr. Hanson's score is impressive in its security and ease of workmanship, its resourcefulness and maturity of technique. It is unequal in musical value. But at its best, as in the more puissant choruses, it is moving and individual and expressive."

Now that ROY HARRIS (1898——) has produced his Sixth Symphony, it is time for writers on American music to face the issue, and to stop saying that time alone will decide whether or not he is a creative genius. In the first edition of this book (1931), I called Harris the "white hope of the nationalists," and in another volume, *Our Contemporary Composers* (1941), I remarked that "when we have absorbed his idiom, then we shall see if he reaches our emotions, and if he does, he is a great composer."

We have now had plenty of time to absorb Harris's idiom, which is highly individual, but we still have on our hands a curious contradiction. Hundreds of music lovers recognize a vital force in Harris's work, a primal, roughhewn vitality, but many of them frankly confess that they do not enjoy hearing the bulk of his music. To many his melodic line is distorted and unnatural; it seems as if the composer had gone to such extremes in avoiding the obvious that his themes rarely give the impression of being inevitable. At the same time these people feel that something important is being uttered, something natively American, even though they actively dislike what they are hearing.

There are several works which entitle Harris to a high place among American composers; perhaps they are enough to justify the recognition he has won. First comes the early Piano Sonata which he composed in Paris in 1928. Here, particularly in the racy Scherzo, was the Southwest that Harris grew up in. As Paul Rosenfeld remarked in his book *An Hour with American Music:* [4] "Its gaunt, homely forms seem charged with the feeling of many struggling, patient, tragical existences in this continent; in the farms, in the homes, long ago, here now."

Four years later, in 1932, came the "American Overture" *When Johnny Comes Marching Home*, which was commissioned especially for recording by the RCA-Victor Company. Here again was the "real McCoy," an American folk tune germinating its own treatment and development—a compact, to-the-point commentary on American ways of looking at things.

The work which has remained most consistently in the repertoire of major orchestras is the Third Symphony, first introduced by the Boston Symphony in 1939. When Toscanini and the National Broadcasting Symphony played this work a year later, Francis Perkins, in the New York *Herald Tribune* (March 18, 1940), called it "one of the most significant contributions of the last few years to the native orchestral repertoire, in breadth and scope, consequentiality of ideas and emotional force." The last five years have upheld this estimate.

Yet, while Harris can attain such enviable heights in some of his works, his facility for mass production has led him into many pitfalls. He may with justice pride himself on the fact that his vogue has not been achieved by concessions to the public; he has punished its ears cruelly upon occasion and it comes back for more, but a careful review of the "repeat" performances of Harris's works shows that his actual hold on the public and on the makers of programs rests on relatively few of his compositions.

[4] Philadelphia, J. B. Lippincott Company, 1929.

He was born in Oklahoma, February 12, 1898, of pioneer parents who staked a claim and tilled a farm. Malaria drove the family to California where they continued farming in the Gabriel Valley. Here Roy spent his youth and early manhood and had his grammar and high school education. When he was eighteen he started a farm of his own, and spent his leisure time studying Greek philosophy.

When America entered the first World War, Harris served as a private in the army. After a year he returned to Southern California, and gave himself largely to study. He entered the Southern Branch of the University of California, began to study harmony, and delved into Hindu theology. In the daytime he drove a truck, and in the evenings attended classes.

During his boyhood he had played a little on the piano, the clarinet, and the organ, but it was not until after the war that his real interest in music grew. It was while he was studying harmony and theory that he approached Arthur Farwell, still in California, and asked to become his pupil. Farwell taught him for two years, and later remarked, "I was convinced that he would one day challenge the world."

While Harris was working with Farwell he composed a Suite for string quartet, and an *Andante* for orchestra which was chosen from a mass of submitted manuscripts for performance by the New York Philharmonic-Symphony at the Stadium Concerts in the summer of 1926. Shortly after this he went abroad to study in Paris with Nadia Boulanger. During his first year there (1927) he composed his Concerto for string quartet, piano, and clarinet, and the next year his Piano Sonata. These works represented a tremendous advance over the somewhat groping *Andante* and were instrumental in winning for him a Guggenheim Fellowship.

In 1929 he suffered an accident which fractured his spine. He partially recovered in a Paris hospital, and then returned to New York for an operation. During his six months' convalescence he composed a String Quartet, and he believes that it was the enforced absence from a piano which freed him from the restrictions of the piano keyboard and rendered his technique more fluent.

Harris's vogue dates from these years and the early American performances of the Concerto and the Piano Sonata. With performances came recognition from other quarters, in addition to commissions for

new works. In 1931 the Pasadena Music and Arts Association awarded
him a fellowship which would provide him with leisure for creative
work. There were no conditions attached to the award except that he
produce according to his capacity and ability. Later, in 1933, Harris
moved to Princeton to become teacher of theory and composition at
the Westminster Choir School, where he remained until 1938. From
1941 to 1943 he was composer-in-residence at Cornell University and
in 1944 he was appointed to a similar post at Colorado College. In
1945 he obtained a leave of absence to become chief of the Office of
War Information Music Section's Radio Program Bureau.

Harris's orchestral works, in order of production, include an early
Andante, performed at the Eastman Festival of 1926; a *Toccata*
(1931); *Andantino* (1931); *Concert Piece* (1932); *Symphony, 1933,*
introduced by the Boston Symphony in 1934; *Chorale* for string orchestra (1933); *When Johnny Comes Marching Home* (1934);
Farewell to Pioneers (1935); *Second Symphony* (1935); *Prelude
and Fugue for Strings* (1936); *Time Suite,* commissioned by the
Columbia Broadcasting System (1937); Violin Concerto (1938);
Three Symphonic Essays (1938); Third Symphony (1939); *Prelude
and Fugue* for four trumpets and strings (1939); *Folk Song Symphony* (1940); *Challenge* (1940); *American Creed* (1941); *Ballad
of a Railroad Man* (1941); Three Pieces for orchestra (1941); Fifth
Symphony (1943); *March in Time of War* (1943); and Sixth Symphony (1945).

There are a number of choral works, of which the best known are
Song for Occupations (1934), and the *Symphony for Voices* (1935).
Both compositions are settings of texts by Walt Whitman, composed
for eight-part *a cappella* chorus. The Symphony is in three movements,
the first and second taken from Whitman's *Sea Drift,* and the third
from *Inscriptions.* The work makes cruel demands of the singers, and
in the last movement the triple fugue is harshly unvocal.

For chamber music combinations Harris has composed a Suite for
string quartet (1925); a Concerto for piano, clarinet, and string
quartet (1927); three String Quartets (1929, 1933, and 1938); a
Sextet for flute, oboe, clarinet, bassoon, horn, and piano (1932); a
Quintet for piano, flute, oboe, horn, and bassoon (1932); a String
Sextet (1932); a Trio (1934); a *Poem* for violin and piano (1935);

a Piano Quintet (1937); a String Quintet, and several others. Of these the outstanding works are the Sextet, the *Poem*, and the String Quintet. The *Poem* is marked by long, unbroken melodic lines, and the String Quintet has melodic beauty, and texture and color.

The Second Symphony of RANDALL THOMPSON (1899——) is one of the high marks of American music. First performed at the American Composers' Concerts in Rochester, March 24, 1932, it has come into the standard repertoire of our major orchestras, and continues to satisfy the audiences that hear it. For, although Thompson does not scorn the past, he is by no means a thorough conservative. His idiom is personal and forward looking, and even though he may not din our ears with dissonance, his medium is nevertheless thoroughly contemporary.

The Second Symphony offers an excellent illustration of this point. The work is highly rhythmic, but Thompson has not used the obvious percussion devices in producing and emphasizing his rhythms. The music itself is intrinsically rhythmic, and rather than utilizing a modern battery of percussion, the score contents itself with cymbals and kettledrums. As Lawrence Gilman once wrote of this symphony in the New York *Herald Tribune* (November 3, 1933): "He [Thompson] has not hesitated at times to be obvious; he has not strained, he has not constricted his fancy and his feeling; he has not been afraid to sound quite different from Schoenberg. His music has humor, and warmth and pleasantness; many will find it agreeable and solacing."

Thompson was born April 21, 1899, in New York City. He was graduated from Harvard in 1920 and received a Master's degree two years later. He studied music under Spalding and Hill at Harvard, and later worked with Ernest Bloch. From 1922 to 1925 he was a Fellow of the American Academy in Rome, and in 1929 and 1930 he was granted a Guggenheim Fellowship. He has been an assistant professor of music at Wellesley College and a lecturer at Harvard, and was for two years professor of music and director of the University Chorus at the University of California. From 1939 to 1941 he was director of the Curtis Institute in Philadelphia. He is the author of a survey *College Music*, made under the auspices of the Carnegie Foundation.

In addition to the Second Symphony, Thompson's orchestral works include two tone poems *Pierrot and Cothurnus* (1922) and *The Piper at the Gates of Dawn* (1924); a First Symphony, introduced in Rochester in 1931; and a *Jazz Poem* for piano and orchestra, introduced at a radio concert in the Brooklyn (New York) Academy of Music, February 21, 1941. Other instrumental works include a Suite for clarinet, oboe, and viola, and a String Quartet.

In addition to these works he has composed considerable choral music. The most extended piece in this form is *The Peaceable Kingdom*, commissioned by the League of Composers and first performed by the Harvard Glee Club and the Radcliffe Choral Society, March 29, 1936, in New York.This is a work for mixed voices, *a cappella*, subtitled "A Sequence of Sacred Choruses—Text from Isaiah."

The words are drawn verbatim from the Bible, and given modern treatment in the music. The opposed choirs of the double chorus are used to carry out the dual idea which was suggested to the composer by a painting entitled *The Peaceable Kingdom*, by Edward Hicks, an American painter of the eighteenth century. The picture shows on one side William Penn making peace with the Indians, and on the other, Daniel in the midst of a group of lions. As the composer remarked, "The lions in this part look as though they were trying to make peace with Daniel; they appear to be succeeding."

Satire is often the basis for Thompson's choral music, sometimes gentle and occasionally slapstick, as in *Americana*, which uses as a text excerpts from Henry L. Mencken's department in the old *American Mercury*. Here burlesque oratorio music matches the inanities of the items Mencken chose from the newspapers of the nation. In *Rosemary*, for women's voices, the four divisions are entitled "Chemical Analysis," "A Sad Song," "A Nonsense Song," and "To Rosemary, on the methods by which she might become an angel."

The Testament of Freedom, for men's chorus, was composed in 1943 in honor of the two hundredth anniversary of Thomas Jefferson's birth, and had its first New York performance December 19, 1943, by the Mendelssohn Glee Club. In April of 1945 it was performed by the Harvard Glee Club with the Boston Symphony Orchestra. The text of the work is drawn from Jefferson's writings.

In 1942 (March 29) the Columbia Broadcasting System gave over a national network the première of an opera it had commissioned from

Thompson in association with the League of Composers. This was *Solomon and Balkis*, which used a libretto adapted by the composer from Kipling's story "The Butterfly that Stamped," from *Just So Stories*. The radio performance was repeated the following October 4, and stage productions before audiences were given at Harvard University and at the Juilliard School in New York.

In 1941, Thompson was one of three composers awarded the Coolidge Medal for distinguished services to chamber music. The other composers honored were Benjamin Britten and Alexander Tansman.

WALTER PISTON (1894————) is easier to characterize than most contemporary composers because he is so distinctly a neo-classicist. In commenting on Piston's Second Symphony, which won the New York Music Critics' Circle Award in 1945, Virgil Thomson called it "impeccably tailored . . . straightforwardly expressive." And although he found it "a little thin of substance," Thomson felt that the thinness came from the composer's academic method of composition, "in which formalities about workmanship, rather than the immediacies of personal feeling, are the main preoccupation." [5]

Piston first gained prominence when Koussevitzky conducted his *Symphonic Piece* with the Boston Symphony, March 23, 1928. A Suite for orchestra was composed in 1929, and had its first performance several years later, April 1, 1932, by the Philadelphia Orchestra under Stokowski. Then came a Concerto for orchestra, introduced by the Boston Symphony, March 29, 1934; a *Prelude and Fugue* for orchestra (1934); and a Concertino for piano and chamber orchestra, commissioned by the Columbia Broadcasting System and first performed June 20, 1937. Piston's First Symphony was commissioned by the League of Composers in 1936 and completed the following year. It was first performed by the Boston Symphony, April 8 and 9, 1938.

After these works came music for a ballet *The Incredible Flutist*, which did much to enhance Piston's reputation. It was created in the spring of 1938 for the Boston "Pops" Orchestra, and was subsequently performed in November of the same year by the Hans Wiener Ballet with the Providence (Rhode Island) Symphony Orchestra. It has been subsequently performed in its entirety at the Eastman Festivals

[5] New York *Herald Tribune*, June 3, 1945.

the trade of arranging and orchestrating and practiced it for W. C. Handy, Paul Whiteman, Don Voorhees, and for such musical shows as *Earl Carroll's Vanities, Rain or Shine,* and the unforgettable *Shuffle Along.* Since then he has established himself as a serious composer who utilizes the Negroid elements of jazz, and has become by far the most widely recognized Negro composer today. He has been the recipient of the Harmon Award, the Rosenwald Fellowship, a Guggenheim Fellowship (three times), and commissions from the Columbia Broadcasting System, from Paul Whiteman, and from the New York World's Fair of 1939.

Still was born in Woodville, Mississippi, May 11, 1895, and studied at Oberlin and later with Chadwick and Varèse. It is characteristic of him that when he has outgrown a piece or a style he turns his back on it, or preserves what he can use and discards the rest. Thus he now considers his *From the Journal of a Wanderer,* first performed in 1926 at the North Shore Festival in Evanston, Illinois, with Frederick Stock conducting, a "lesson in what not to do!" And his *Darker America* (1924), published by the Eastman School of Music, he criticizes as fragmentary, containing too much material not sufficiently well organized.

About 1925, Still decided definitely to devote himself to the development of the Negro idiom and the treatment of Negro subjects in his programmatic works. Three of his larger works form a trilogy: *Africa,* the *Afro-American* Symphony, and the Symphony in G Minor. *Africa* has been revised no less than five times. The first version appeared in 1930; the sixth in 1935. It is in three movements: "Land of Peace," "Land of Romance," "Land of Superstition." The *Afro-American* Symphony also dates from 1930. Both works have been widely played, here and abroad. The Symphony in G Minor was introduced by Stokowski and the Philadelphia Orchestra in December, 1937. *Kaintuck,* for piano and orchestra, commissioned by the League of Composers, had its first performance in 1935 in Los Angeles, and *Lenox Avenue,* commissioned by the Columbia Broadcasting System, was first heard over the air in May, 1937.

Still has written also several stage works: *La Guiablesse* and *Sahdji,* ballets; *Blue Steel,* an opera; *Troubled Island,* another opera to a libretto by Langston Hughes; and considerable film music. His cantata *And They Lynched Him on a Tree*, with text by Katherine Garrison Chapin, wife of former Attorney-General Biddle, was first performed under the baton of Artur Rodzinski at the Stadium concerts of the New York Philharmonic-Symphony Orchestra in June, 1940. It is scored for two choruses, contralto solo, and orchestra. Howard Taubman wrote in *The New York Times* (June 26, 1940):

Mr. Still has written with utter simplicity and with deep feeling. . . . A few harsh, cruel chords evoke the brutal crowd. The music achieves its greatest eloquence in the pages devoted to the Negro men and women and especially to the solo sung by the boy's mother. Using themes that are akin to spirituals, he gives her poignant, searching music.

Mr. Still and Miss Chapin throw light on the tragedy of a lynching as poets should. And they end with the plea:

> "O trust your brother and reach out your hand!
> And clear the shadow, the long dark shadow,
> And clear the shadow that falls across the land."

In 1941 (October 23) the New York Philharmonic-Symphony under John Barbirolli gave the première of Still's *Plain Chant for America*. This work, for baritone and orchestra, is a setting of another poem by Katherine Garrison Chapin, and at its first performance it impressed the audience as an effective, dramatic, and worthily patriotic piece. Virgil Thomson, in the New York *Herald Tribune* (October 24, 1941), considered the melodic style "broad but not vulgar," the instrumentation "sure-handed and not unpleasantly brash," and the English declamation "of the first water." Wilbur Evans sang the solo part at the première, and James Pease was the soloist when the Philadelphia Orchestra presented the work in March of 1943.

In Memoriam, an orchestral work in honor "of the colored soldiers who died for Democracy," was introduced by the New York Philharmonic-Symphony January 5, 1944, and the same orchestra gave the first New York performance of Still's *Old California* on November 4 of the same year. The latter work was written in commemoration of the one hundred and sixtieth anniversary of the city of Los Angeles, and is frankly program music. First come the Indians, and then the Spaniards. After that the Americans arrive and the three groups merge. According to a reviewer in *Musical America*, "It is as simple as that, and we admire Mr. Still for admitting it. Needless to say, it is put together with a deft hand, and is richly orchestrated."

On December 7, 1944 the Cleveland Orchestra, under Rudolph Ringwall, gave the first performance of Still's *Poem for Orchestra.* This work was written on commission of the Fynette H. Kulas American Composers' Fund, and was based on a poem by Verna Arvey, which depicts man undergoing toil and tribulation, but overcoming evil and redeeming himself and the world through an understanding of God.

For many years VIRGIL THOMSON (1896——) was a resident of Paris, and our knowledge of him came principally from other American composers who had studied there. We heard from them of this young American who had come under the influence of Satie and Cocteau, and had made a setting of Gertrude Stein's *Capitals Capitals.* He had, it was said, a long list of unpublished compositions which included a *Sonata da Chiesa* for four wind instruments and viola, two Piano Sonatas, and a Symphony on a Hymn Tune, as well as a three-act opera on a text adapted from Gertrude Stein, entitled *Four Saints in Three Acts.* In recent years this legendary figure has returned to America and has become one of the most powerful figures of our music life—as composer and critic.

It was *Four Saints in Three Acts* which established him. In spite of the fact that the words meant absolutely nothing to anyone in the audience, people flocked to a Broadway theatre to sit for two and a quarter hours and hear the all-Negro cast sing such sentences as: "Pigeons on the grass alas. Pigeons on the grass alas. Short longer grass short longer shorter yellow grass," set to music which Lawrence Gilman in the New York *Herald Tribune* (February 21, 1934) called "deceptively simple, a little self-consciously candid and naïve, actually very wily and deft and slick, often subtly and wittily elusive, distinguished in its artful banality."

And so this work which had been produced largely as an experiment by the Friends and Enemies of Modern Music in Hartford, Connecticut (February, 1934), was brought to New York later in the same month where it enjoyed a run of several weeks at the Forty-fourth Street Theatre and, according to William J. Henderson, in the *New York Sun* (February 24, 1934), "created an illusion of serious opera."

"You cannot help believing it is about something," Henderson continued, "although you cannot find out from the text just what it is."

Gilman's phrase, "artful banality," describes what is perhaps one of the pleasantest features of Thomson's music. He is a professed romanticist, and he never hesitates to introduce familiar and often sentimental American tunes in such works as the ballet *Filling Station*, and the *Symphony on a Hymn Tune*. An early set of Variations and Fugues for organ used the hymn-tunes: *Come Ye Disconsolate*, *There's Not a Friend Like the Lowly Jesus*, *Will There Be Any Stars in My Crown?* and *Shall We Gather at the River?*

Thomson was born in Kansas City, Missouri, November 25, 1896. He was graduated from Harvard in 1922, and studied music there with Hill, Davison, Gebhard, and Goodrich. While in college he supported himself by accompanying singers, playing the piano in theatres, and becoming a church organist. For a time he played in King's Chapel, Boston. Meanwhile, he had interrupted his studies at Harvard for a year in Paris, studying organ and composition with Nadia Boulanger. From 1920 to 1925 he was an assistant instructor at Harvard; then he returned to Paris where he stayed for eight years. He came to New York again and saw the American production of *Four Saints in Three Acts*, but once more returned to Paris where he remained until the outbreak of the war.

In 1940 he was appointed to succeed the late Lawrence Gilman as music critic of the New York *Herald Tribune*. Thus began the second phase of his career, which has attracted even more attention than his work as a composer. His criticisms and comments are the most discussed of those of any of our reviewers. Generally informal and direct, they exasperate some and gratify others. He does not mind being opinionated in the extreme, and upon occasion the terseness of his comments are devastating for what they leave unsaid. To date, he is the author of two books: *The State of Music* (1939) and *The Musical Scene* (1945).

In addition to the works already mentioned, Thomson has composed two Symphonies; two String Quartets; a Suite for orchestra; a set of *Mayor La Guardia Waltzes* (commissioned by André Kostelanetz and introduced by him with the Cincinnati Symphony, May 14, 1942); an orchestral piece called *The Changing Frontier*; a *Stabat*

Mater for soprano and string quartet; and scores for two documentary films which subsequently have been made into concert pieces: *The River* and *The Plough that Broke the Plains*.

LEO SOWERBY (1895——) used to call himself a musical Dr. Jekyll and Mr. Hyde, for he had written church music and works derived from churchly inspiration; and then had toyed with "classical" jazz and written pieces for Paul Whiteman's noted band. He has the distinction of being the first composer to hold a fellowship in the American Academy at Rome. Most of his education was gained in Chicago, for he was born in Grand Rapids, Michigan May 1, 1895, and has lived principally in Chicago. Since his return from Italy he has been organist at St. James's (Episcopal) Cathedral, and teacher of composition at Chicago's American Conservatory of Music.

He has been prolific, and his works are marked by freshness and vigor. His setting of *The Irish Washerwoman* for piano is delightful in its whimsy and rollicking good spirits. His works had a number of major performances before he went to Rome in 1921. The orchestral Suite *A Set of Four* was played by the Chicago Orchestra in 1918; the Overture *Comes Autumn Time*, in the same year by the New York Symphony. The *Serenade* for string quartet was written as a birthday gift for Mrs. Elizabeth Sprague Coolidge, and played first by the Berkshire Quartet in 1918. The next year his Trio for flute, viola, and piano was played at the Berkshire Festival, and in 1921 his Suite for violin and piano was performed. Carolyn Beebe and her New York Chamber Music Society played his Quintet for wind instruments in 1920. He played his first Piano Concerto in 1920, and his first Symphony was introduced in Chicago in 1922.

While he was abroad his *Ballad* for two pianos and orchestra, and his first String Quartet were introduced in Rome. When he came back to America he presented his Sonata for violoncello and piano at the 1924 Berkshire Festival, and his cantata *The Vision of Sir Launfal* was sung in 1926. One of his most important works is the *Medieval Poem*, for organ and orchestra. It is dedicated to his fellow pupil in Rome, Howard Hanson, and is based on a hymn from the liturgy of St. James.

A number of his works are for organ: a Symphony in G and *Pageant of Autumn* for organ solo, the *Medieval Poem* for organ and orchestra, and a Concerto for organ and orchestra which E. Power Biggs played with the Boston Symphony Orchestra in April, 1938. There are also a Second Piano Concerto, composed in 1932 and first performed by the Boston Symphony in 1936; a *Passacaglia, Interlude and Fugue* which had its première with the Chicago Symphony in 1934; three further String Quartets, and a Sinfonietta for string orchestra. An earlier Suite for orchestra, *From the Northland,* is still heard in symphony concerts.

Sowerby's Symphony No. 3 was composed for the Golden Jubilee season of the Chicago Symphony Orchestra and first presented by that organization under Frederick Stock, March 6, 1941. A *Concert Overture* for orchestra was published in 1941, and a Sonata for clarinet (or viola) and piano in 1944 (by the Society for the Publication of American Music). In April of 1943, Jacques Gordon played Sowerby's Violin Concerto with the Eastman-Rochester Symphony at the Eastman Festival.

Sowerby does not believe in tags or labels for characterizing composers in groups or "schools"; he tries merely to be himself, and as he expresses it, "not thinking about my style, or idiom, trying constantly to improve my technic, so that when I shall have something to say, I shall be able to say it clearly and directly, and—God willing—simply."

DOUGLAS MOORE (1893——) was born at Cutchogue, Long Island, August 10, 1893. He was educated at Hotchkiss School and at Yale University where he studied music with Horatio Parker and David Stanley Smith. After service in the Navy during the first World War, he worked in Paris with d'Indy, in Cleveland with Ernest Bloch, and again in Paris, with Nadia Boulanger.

When he went to Cleveland in 1921, he was appointed assistant music curator of the Art Museum, becoming curator in 1922. He held this position until 1925, when he was awarded a Pulitzer Fellowship for study abroad. After his work with Boulanger, he returned to America and joined the music faculty of Columbia University. In 1928 he was appointed an associate professor. Six years later he received a Guggenheim Fellowship, which he enjoyed during a sabbatical year. He then returned to Columbia, where in 1940 he succeeded Daniel Gregory Mason as head of the Music Department.

Moore's first work of importance was a set of *Four Museum Pieces*, originally written for organ, and later scored for orchestra. The first movement is *Fifteenth Century Armor*, a knightly joust of bygone days. The second, *A Madonna of Botticini*, where a suggestion of plain-chant paints the clear-eyed serenity of the Madonna. *The Chinese Lion and the Unhappy Flutist* shows a flutist who awakens a sleeping lion, and is forever silenced with a horrendous roar; an amiable scherzo indeed. The last piece is *A Statue by Rodin*. A theme emerges from chaos; it becomes clearer, and the stark figure of the man of the bronze age wakes to the consciousness of his superb strength and power.

The *Museum Pieces* had their first performance in Cleveland in 1923. The following year the Cleveland Orchestra introduced the work by Moore which up to the present time has achieved the widest vogue, *The Pageant of P. T. Barnum*. This embodies a series of scenes dear to the hearts of all Americans. Here is music that comes from the dance halls, not of today, but of the era of the country fiddle and brass bands, when people were not afraid to be sentimental. To Moore's mind, we Americans come by our sentiment naturally, and this, together with our high spirits, is our greatest hope for the future. There are five episodes in the Barnum suite. First, *Boyhood at Bethel*—country fiddles, bands, early Connecticut hymnology, the sort of musical environment that probably influenced the youthful Barnum. Next comes *Joice Heth*, the one-hundred-and-sixty-one-year-old Negress who was Barnum's first exhibit, supposedly the first person to put clothes on George Washington. Here we have a Negro spiritual, the less familiar version of *Nobody Knows the Trouble I've Seen*. The third movement shows *General and Mrs. Tom Thumb*, the midgets. First a flourish in the drums, the report of a cap pistol, and then the flutes and oboes in a military theme with syncopated rhythm. *Jenny Lind* is the fourth to appear. After the arpeggios on the harp, and a melody in the flute, the woodwinds give a suggestion of coloratura—mid-century sentiment that brings back memories. The *finale* tells of Barnum's greatest and most permanent triumph, his circus. *Circus Parade* brings animals, wagon wheels, calliope, and the great Barnum himself. The only thing missing is the peanuts.

In 1928, Moore produced a symphonic poem *Moby Dick*, and in

1930 a Violin and Piano Sonata which was presented at a concert by the League of Composers. A year later, April 2, 1931, his *Symphony of Autumn* was played for the first time at the American Composers' Concerts in Rochester. This is a short, three-movement work which follows classic outlines. The first movement is in sonata form, and aims to portray the "majestic and mellow sadness of an Autumn afternoon." The second movement was suggested by the "triumphant song of the katydid." In the words of the composer, "Autumn may be theoretically a sad season, but to listen to the chorus of katydids against an ostinato of tree toads, with very white, cold stars overhead and a steamy earth beneath, is to distrust the idea." The last movement of the Symphony suggests the "irresponsible gayety of an autumn day at noon when the light on the water is silver and there is always a breeze to offer water surfaces to the light."

Moore's next important work was an *Overture on an American Tune*, which was originally named after the source of its inspiration—*Babbitt*. This, as the name implied, attempted a tonal portrait of Sinclair Lewis's hero, the sentimental, good-natured "go-getter." The work was introduced by David Mannes and the Manhattan Symphony, December 25, 1932.

A Quartet for Strings was first played by the Roth Quartet in 1936, and later, in 1938, by the Gordon Quartet at one of the Coolidge Foundation concerts at Columbia University. This is a short work in four movements. The first is pleasantly lyrical, with a rocking triple rhythm as its basis. The second movement is jaunty, with a brief suggestion of Scotch bagpipes. The third section, *andante cantabile*, places a thoughtful, meditative, melodic line over a rich contrapuntal texture; and the *finale* is a jolly *allegro*.

Moore feels that American composers should devote attention to the needs of amateur and school groups, and as an experiment in this direction he composed an operetta, *The Headless Horseman*, which had its first production in 1937 by the children of the Bronxville, New York, public schools.

In the spring of 1939, Moore's "folk opera" *The Devil and Daniel Webster* was produced by the American Lyric Theatre, an institution founded with the aims of stimulating the production and composition of opera in English and presenting works at prices within the reach of the general public. The American Lyric Theatre unfortunately did not survive its first season, but that was no fault of *The Devil and Daniel Webster*, which was generally conceded to be excellent entertainment. The libretto was by the distinguished poet Stephen Vincent Benét, and tells the story of a New Hampshire farmer who has sold his soul to the Devil for the material prosperity he needs in order to marry. The Devil, disguised as a Boston attorney, breaks in upon the wedding festivities to claim the bridegroom's soul, but he is thwarted by the legal skill and eloquence of Webster, who wins a verdict in favor of the farmer in a remarkable plea to a jury composed of famous traitors and scoundrels summoned from the infernal regions by the Devil. This plea, incidentally, is based on a speech actually delivered by Webster.

Moore provided the music for the documentary films *Youth Gets a Break*, and *Power and the Land*. In 1942 he published another work designed especially for school groups—*Village Music*, for small orchestra. This is a suite of four dances, using some of the music from the previously composed film scores. On December 27, 1942 a Quintet for Winds was played at a League of Composers' Concert in New York, and on April 27, 1944, an orchestral work *In Memoriam* was given its première at the Eastman Festival in Rochester.

FREDERICK JACOBI (1891——) achieved distinction as a young man of twenty-three with his *String Quartet on Indian Themes* (1924), and shortly afterwards with his *Indian Dances* for orchestra (1927-28). These were so widely played that they attached to him the label of a composer of American Indian music, but the diverse nature of his later works shows that this was but a passing phase of his creative career.

Jacobi does not believe strongly in nationalism in music, particularly a nationalism which is consciously sought. The composer, he feels, is too busy trying to create an expressive line, a satisfactory whole, to occupy himself, while composing, with matters other than those which are purely musical. If he does his job carefully and well, and if he has talent, the question of expressing his race, his nationality, his time, and even his emotions, will take care of itself. For, Jacobi remarks, these elements tap the subconscious and operate best when left to themselves.

While he is thoroughly modern and contemporary, Jacobi believes primarily in "line"—melody, which is at once an idea and its development. He is no atonalist, for he feels that tonality offers a pivot, a focal point, a base on which an architecture may be constructed; and architectural planning is the essence of music.

He was born in California, May 4, 1891, and educated largely in New York, where he attended the Ethical Culture School and studied music with Paolo Gallico and Rubin Goldmark. Then he studied in Berlin with Paul Juon at the Hochschule für Musik. When he returned to America, he became assistant conductor at the Metropolitan Opera House, from 1914 to 1917, and then went West to study the life and music of the Pueblo Indians in New Mexico and Arizona.

After the first World War—in which he served as a saxophone player in the Army bands—he made his home in New England, at Northampton, Massachusetts; and since 1936 he has been a teacher of composition at the Juilliard School in New York.

Jacobi's second String Quartet (published, like the first, by the Society for the Publication of American Music), is a far more mature work than its predecessor, and shows a more flexible technique and a more personal idiom. The opening movement may be a bit enigmatic in its introduction, but it soon comes to melodic patterns which are clear, and which appeal in spite of biting dissonances. The slow movement has warmth and genuine beauty, while the *finale* is humorous and brilliant. The work was first played by the Pro Arte Quartet at a concert of the League of Composers in New York, February 18, 1935.

Jacobi's early orchestral works include *The Pied Piper; The Eve of St. Agnes;* a Symphony; *Two Assyrian Prayers*, for voice and orchestra; and *The Poet in the Desert*, first performed by the Friends of Music, in New York. Aside from smaller pieces, his other important works are the Concerto for cello and orchestra; a Piano Concerto; and the *Sabbath Evening Service* which was commissioned by the Temple Emanu-El in New York.

The Jewish Service (1930–31) established Jacobi as one of the important Hebrew composers of the country. With melodies patterned after ancient Hebrew hymns, it offers moments of irresistible poignancy, of a passion that never sacrifices dignity.

The Cello Concerto was given its première in Paris at the Ecole Normale, May 30, 1933, and was subsequently published abroad. The first movement provides suspense and animation through a syncopated rhythmic pattern, and the entire work shows originality and an authentic racial quality. The Piano Concerto was composed in 1934–35, and in 1936 was given several performances in New York and Brooklyn, and at the American Composers' Concerts in Rochester, with the composer's wife, Irene Jacobi, playing the solo part. This work shows its American character in "Charleston" jazz effects, and in an Indian flavor which harks back to Jacobi's earlier period. A Violin Concerto was first performed by Albert Spalding with the Chicago Symphony Orchestra in March, 1939, and again with the New York Philharmonic in October of the same year in the festival of the American Society of Composers, Authors, and Publishers. In April, 1940, Jacobi's *Ave Rota* (Three Pieces in Multiple Style for small orchestra) figured on the programs of the tenth annual Festival of American Music in Rochester.

Jacobi's Piano Quintet *Hagiographa* was first performed at the Berkshire Festival in 1938. In 1941 it was issued on records by RCA-Victor. In 1943 (May 1) the Boston Symphony introduced Jacobi's *Ode for Orchestra.*

PHILIP JAMES (1890——), known equally as a composer, conductor, and music educator, has had notable success as a prize winner in numerous contests. In 1932 his *Station WGZBX,* for orchestra, won the first prize of five thousand dollars in a contest sponsored by the National Broadcasting Company; in 1936 his Overture *Bret Harte* was awarded honorable mention in a contest conducted by the Philharmonic-Symphony Society of New York, for which no one was given the cash prize; in 1937 his Suite for string orchestra was chosen for publication by the Juilliard School in New York; and in 1938 his orchestral *Song of the Night* won the $500 prize in a contest fostered by the New York Women's Symphony. In 1939 he received one of the Columbia Broadcasting System's commissions.

Station WGZBX shows James to be something of a modernist in spirit and idiom, as he depicts the mad hurly-burly of the radio offices and studios, static and interference on the air, with the honey-sweet voice of a crooner entering the chaos at odd moments. His *Kammer-*

symphonie, too, is modern in feeling, its Scherzo providing a tricky combination of multiple rhythms.

The overture *Bret Harte* was the composer's attempt to catch "the romance, the boisterousness, the animation, and the many other abstract qualities of the people of Bret Harte and the West," a people and a section of our country, James adds, "whose glamour has been bedimmed through the eyes of Hollywood as well as by the mawkishness of the radio hillbilly singer." The work was performed by the New York Philharmonic-Symphony Orchestra, December 20, 1936.

James has composed much choral music. Most notable is his setting of Vachel Lindsay's *General William Booth Enters Heaven,* first performed by the Downtown Glee Club of New York, under Channing Lefebvre, May 3, 1933. When this piece was published, the reviewer of *Musical America* (April 25, 1933) found that it possessed "a rhythmic variety and freedom that are arresting, all finely integrated in setting forth the poet's words."

James's other compositions are in various forms, his chamber music including a String Quartet and a Piano Quintet. His earlier works include the frequently performed *Overture on French Noëls;* a *Sea Symphony;* and an orchestral tone poem *Judith;* a Suite for chamber orchestra; numerous choral pieces; several works for organ; and many secular and sacred songs.

He was born in Jersey City, May 17, 1890. During the first World War he served for two years in the infantry, and after the armistice he became commanding officer of the A.E.F. General Headquarters Band, commonly known as General Pershing's Band. At various times he has been an organist in churches in and around New York, conductor for the theatrical productions of Winthrop Ames and for Victor Herbert operettas, conductor of the New Jersey Orchestra, which he helped to found, and of the Brooklyn Symphony Orchestra. From 1929 to 1936 he conducted the Bamberger Little Symphony on radio station WOR, New York, and he has appeared as guest conductor with several of the country's major orchestras, among them the Philadelphia and the National Symphony of Washington. Since 1927 he has been associated with the Music Department at New York University. In 1933 he became its chairman.

BERNARD WAGENAAR (1894——) first came to this country in 1921, when his fellow-Hollander, Willem Mengelberg, was conducting the New York Philharmonic. He joined the orchestra as violinist and also as harpsichordist, pianist, organist, and, upon occasion, as player of the celesta. Two years later he started his teaching career in New York—first at the Master Institute of the Roerich Museum, then at the Institute of Musical Art (1926–1927), and since 1927 at The Juilliard Graduate School. He was born in Arnheim, Holland, July 18, 1894, and he became an American citizen in 1927.

Two of Wagenaar's symphonies were introduced by the Philharmonic-Symphony Society of New York. The first was played by Mengelberg in 1928, while the second enjoyed the distinction of being one of the few American works performed by the orchestra while Toscanini was its conductor. The work was given three performances in November, 1932. The Third Symphony was introduced by the orchestra of the Juilliard School, with the composer conducting, January 23, 1937. In the following summer it was played at Chautauqua, under Albert Stoessel, and on March 8, 1941, it was performed by the New York Philharmonic-Symphony. On December 20 of the same year it was again played in New York, by the National Orchestral Association.

When Wagenaar's Triple Concerto for flute, harp, cello, and orchestra was first played by the Philadelphia Orchestra (Philadelphia, March 18 and 19; New York, March 22, 1938) the critics were somewhat divided in their opinions. Lawrence Gilman (New York *Herald Tribune*, March 23, 1938) felt that the composer was "amusing himself with experiments, or even spoofing Euterpe. . . . The work," he wrote, "lacks aesthetic tact." A few days later (*New York Times*, March 27) Olin Downes defended the composer. "Mr. Wagenaar," he claimed, "was writing for the public. . . . He appeared to be writing a concerto that aimed, in a modern and artistic way, to please. . . . He did not sacrifice his standards in so doing. . . . Some of Mr. Wagenaar's contemporaries could afford to take a leaf from this book. If they will look upon composition as a direct means of communication with their fellow-man they will find themselves in good company."

Wagenaar again attempted to write music to please the public in an "operatic comedy" entitled *Pieces of Eight*, which was presented by

the Columbia Theatre associates and the Music Department of Columbia University, May 10, 1944, at the Brander Matthews Theatre
of the University. The libretto of this opera was written by Edward
Eager, and it concerned itself with the attempt of a pirate to find hidden treasure of Captain Kidd on Long Island. The work was frankly
experimental, and not at all successful in its combination of Gilbert
and Sullivan traditions, with artificial, disjointed sophistication.

Aside from these two works in lighter vein, Wagenaar has been
altogether serious in his music; his three symphonies are marked by
various experiments in atonality and other twentieth-century devices.
For small orchestra he has composed a *Sinfonietta,* introduced by the
Philharmonic under Mengelberg in 1930. This was the only American work chosen in that year by the International Society for Contemporary Music for performance at the Liége Festival. A *Divertimento* for orchestra, which received an Eastman School Publications
Award, was first performed in 1929 by the Detroit Symphony under
Gabrilowitsch, and has subsequently received a number of performances by major orchestras. His Concertino for strings and wind instruments was played at a concert of the League of Composers in New
York, December 27, 1942.

In the field of chamber music, Wagenaar has written three String
Quartets, a Sonata for violin and piano, and a Sonatina for cello and
piano. The Sonata and the third String Quartet are published by the
Society for the Publication of American Music.

HARL MCDONALD (1899——) has been prominent not only as a
composer but as an educator, and as the manager of the Philadelphia
Orchestra. In spite of these time-consuming activities he has found the
energy to continue as one of the most prolific and frequently performed of our composers.

Born July 27, 1899, on his father's cattle ranch in the high Rockies
above Boulder, Colorado, McDonald grew up in Southern California.
He started to compose at the age of seven, and some of his earliest
pieces were published. As a young man he toured as accompanist with
several well-known concert artists, and in 1921 played his first Piano
Concerto with the San Francisco Symphony. After this he studied in
Germany, and his symphonic fantasy *Mojave* was performed by the
Berlin Philharmonic, and by Coates in London in 1922. In the same

year he taught at the Académie Tournefort in Paris, and then returned to the United States, at first teaching privately and appearing in recital. During the 1925–26 season he taught at the Philadelphia Academy of Music, and in 1927 was appointed to the faculty of the University of Pennsylvania. This connection he maintained until he became manager of the Philadelphia Orchestra in 1939.

McDonald's orchestral works include four Symphonies. The first bears the title *Santa Fe Trail,* and was played first by the Philadelphia Orchestra, November, 1934. The second was a *Rhumba Symphony,* introduced in October of 1935 by the Philadelphia Orchestra. Its scherzo movement, *Rhumba,* has been performed separately many times, and has proved popular on phonograph records. The third Symphony requires for performance a chorus and a soprano soloist. It bears the subtitle *Lamentations of Fu Hsuan,* and is based on a series of Chinese poems. The first performance of the work was given in January, 1936, by the Philadelphia Orchestra, the University of Pennsylvania Chorus, and Vera Resnikoff, soprano. The Fourth Symphony had no title, and disclosed no programmatic intention. Its chief novelty was the use of a cake-walk in the *Scherzo* movement. This work was also introduced by the Philadelphia Orchestra, April, 1938.

Following the evacuation of the Philippines by American forces in 1942, McDonald composed a symphonic poem *Bataan,* which was played first by the Philadelphians in October of that year, and by the New York Philharmonic-Symphony the following December. There arc also an orchestral Suite *Festival of the Workers;* a Concerto for two pianos and orchestra; a *Tragic Cycle,* for orchestra; the choral *Songs of Conquest,* first performed by the Mendelssohn Club in Philadelphia, 1937, and later at the Worcester (Massachusetts) Festival in the fall of 1939; a *Suite from Childhood* for harp and orchestra (1941); Orchestral Variations (1941); *Chameleon Variations* (1942); a Violin Concerto (1943); two String Quartets; two Trios; and other works, which include two evening pictures—*San Juan Capistrano,* and a rather curious *Lament for the Stolen,* a tonal elegy on the Lindbergh kidnaping, presented by the Philadelphia Orchestra and a chorus in December, 1938.

BERNARD ROGERS (1893——), since 1929 a teacher of composition at the Eastman School of Music, was awarded the Pulitzer Traveling

Scholarship in 1918, and the Guggenheim Fellowship in 1927–29. For nine years he was on the staff of *Musical America*.

Rogers thinks that whatever national idiom we may develop in America can never be conscious. It must be based on the hope that is in us. If we develop deep and strong personalities, our music will be deep and strong; universal, as all fine art always is.

Rogers was born in New York, February 4, 1893. He studied in America with Ernest Bloch and Percy Goetschius, and abroad with Frank Bridge and Nadia Boulanger. His first orchestral work was a tone poem *To the Fallen*, composed in memory of those who died in the first World War, and first played by the New York Philharmonic. *The Faithful* was written next, and then *Fuji in the Sunset Glow*. His *Soliloquy* is for flute and string quartet, and his *Pastorale* for eleven instruments. His symphony *Adonais* has been played by the Rochester Philharmonic, and at Chautauqua, New York. His String Quartet was introduced at one of the concerts of the League of Composers in New York, and his *Prelude to Hamlet* by the Rochester Philharmonic.

More recent are a Second and a Third Symphony; a second *Soliloquy*, this time for bassoon and strings; an opera *The Marriage of Aude*, produced at the Eastman Festival, May 22, 1931; a cantata *The Raising of Lazarus*, presented under the same auspices the following year; and a number of miscellaneous orchestral works which include *Two American Frescoes*, *The Supper at Emmaus*, and *Five Fairy Tales* ("Once Upon a Time"). The last was played at the Eastman Festival, April 4, 1935, by the New York Philharmonic-Symphony, February 27, 1936, and by the Chicago Symphony in 1937. It was this work that was accepted by the Juilliard Foundation as the 1936 orchestral work for publication. The subjects of these *Fairy Tales* are drawn from Andrew Lang, and the work proved to be faithful to the moods of its program and wrought with considerable imagination, skillfully orchestrated, and possessed of a liberal supply of melody in a more or less conservative treatment. At the tenth Festival of American Music in Rochester in 1940, the programs included a new *Dance of Salome* by Rogers, as well as a ballet piece *The Colors of War*.

The Dance of Salome was performed by the New York Philharmonic-Symphony, March 7, 1942. It is a work which uses Oriental sonorities and timbres. Percussion instruments play a predominant part in the ingenious orchestration, and the effect is most arresting. At the Eastman Festival in 1942 (April 28), scenes from Rogers's *The Passion* were presented. This is a choral setting of text adapted from St. Matthew and other New Testament sources by Charles Rodda. The six parts of the work are entitled: "The Entry into Jerusalem," "The Temple," "Gethsemane," "Pilate," "Calvary," and "The Triumph." In the following year (April 15, 1943) Rogers's *Hymn to a Free France* received its première at the Eastman Festival.

WERNER JANSSEN (1899——) is the son of August Janssen, proprietor of the famous Hofbrau Haus in New York, and originator of the slogan "Janssen wants to see you." The son was born in New York, June 1, 1899, and was educated at Phillips Exeter Academy and Dartmouth College. He was forced to obtain his musical education more or less in secret, for the father was violently opposed to his son's becoming a musician. After graduation from college, the young man went off on his own, became a writer of popular songs, played the piano in a variety of places, and used every moment possible to study symphonic scores. In 1930 he became a Fellow of the American Academy in Rome. Later, when Dartmouth conferred upon Werner Janssen the honorary degree of Doctor of Music, his father showed his forgiveness and acceptance of a musician-son by sitting on the platform during the ceremonies.

While the young Janssen was in Italy, the Rome String Quartet played his *Miniature Fantasy on American Popular Melodies* (1932). Then came several years of veritable triumphs. Conductorial successes abroad, and the pronouncement by Sibelius that Janssen was the greatest interpreter of his (Sibelius's) music, led to Janssen's appointment as one of the regular conductors of the New York Philharmonic-Symphony during the season of 1934–35. Unfortunately, the talented young man became the victim of his friends and his admirers. No living creature could have lived up to the advance accounts of his prowess as a conductor. The publicity was tremendous. It even included a two-installment "Profile" by Alva Johnston in *The New Yorker*.

The pity of the whole affair was that Janssen did well with the Philharmonic-Symphony; his performances and interpretations were sensitive and musicianly. Yet he was not the combination of all musical virtues that had been pictured, and people were inevitably disappointed. As a result he lasted for his first season's engagement, and then departed for other fields. He has been conducting and composing in Hollywood, has had profitable radio engagements, and for the 1937–38 season he was called to Baltimore to lead the symphony orchestra in the absence of Ernest Schelling. In March, 1938, he was named regular conductor of the organization, but after one more season he felt that in the three months of the year that the orchestra played together an adequate ensemble could not be developed, and he offered his resignation. Since 1940 he has been the composer of musical scores for Paramount Pictures in Hollywood.

Janssen's music has a truly American flavor. *New Year's Eve in New York* is vivid program music in its tonal description of revelry, and altogether contemporary in its inclusion of the musical sounds and rhythms of Broadway and Times Square; yet it is considerably more than mere picture music. It contrasts the elements of merrymaking and idealism with subtlety and telling effectiveness. The "Dixie Fugue" from the *Louisiana Suite* develops itself through intricate rhythms to a stunning *finale*, where the theme appears in augmentation.

Janssen has composed two String Quartets, the second having been performed at the 1935 Chamber Music Festival at the Library of Congress, Washington, D.C. One of the most notable of his film scores is his music for *The General Died at Dawn*.

The sudden death of ALBERT STOESSEL (1894–1943) brought to a close one of the most brilliant careers in the history of American music. Stoessel was born in St. Louis, Missouri, October 11, 1894, and had his musical training from local teachers and at the Royal *Hochschule* in Berlin. He made his debut in Berlin as a violinist, playing three concertos with orchestra. When he came back to America in 1915, he appeared as soloist with the St. Louis Orchestra, and toured the country as assisting artist with Enrico Caruso. In 1923 he was appointed head of the music department of New York University, but resigned in 1930 to become director of the orchestra and opera departments of the Juilliard Graduate School. These positions brought activities and duties enough to satisfy almost any musician, but in addition, he had been conductor of the Oratorio Society of New York since 1922, he had conducted the Worcester Festival since 1925, and since 1922 he had been musical director of the Chautauqua Institution. All of these duties proved too much for his strength, for he fell dead of a heart attack while conducting a performance of Walter Damrosch's *Dunkirk* at the American Academy of Arts and Letters, May 12, 1943.

Stoessel was important also as a composer. One of his early works was his *Suite Antique,* which was more or less conventional in style, and was frequently played. In his later *Concerto Grosso* for strings he became a neo-classicist, using traditional forms and patterns in the spirit and musical speech of the twentieth century. This piece had its first performance at the Juilliard School, January 17, 1936. The composer conducted and Ernest Hutcheson was the piano soloist.

In the fall of 1936, Stoessel completed an opera in which he collaborated with Robert A. Simon, the librettist. This was *Garrick,* which was produced by the Opera Department of the Juilliard School of Music, February 24, 1937. The following June it was performed at Chautauqua, New York, and in October at the Worcester Festival in Massachusetts.

Garrick proved to be a thoroughly pleasant affair, and showed that opera in English may not be as impossible of achievement as some people think, particularly when it is unpretentious and avoids the pompous and the grandiose. The plot deals with a supposed episode in the life of David Garrick, one in which the actor pretends to be a cad and a leering boor in order to discourage the love of a young lady who should have been otherwise engaged. At the end Garrick returns to Peg Woffington, although he is madly in love with the young girl.

Simon gave the composer lines which could be set to music expressively, and Stoessel did not fail to make the most of them. When necessary for dramatic action or emphasis, he left them entirely alone, allowing them to be spoken. Hence the drama is never halted or interrupted by musical gesturing or operatics for their own sake.

Stoessel's earlier works include a symphonic portrait *Cyrano de Bergerac,* and a *Hispania Suite* for orchestra (*Seguidilla, La Media Noche, In Old Castile, Jota*). He published a Sonata for violin and piano, numerous pieces and songs, and a number of choruses.

HAROLD MORRIS (1890——) received a Bachelor of Arts degree at the University of Texas, and then studied at the Cincinnati Conservatory of Music from which he was graduated with highest honors. He has been a lecturer at the Rice Institute in Houston, Texas, and in 1921 became a member of the faculty of the Juilliard School of Music in New York. In 1939 he was made a Doctor of Music by the Cincinnati Conservatory. He was born in San Antonio, Texas, March 17, 1890.

Morris's best-known work is his Piano Concerto. When he first played it with Koussevitzky and the Boston Symphony, October 23 and 24, 1931, H. T. Parker remarked in the *Boston Evening Transcript* (October 24): "No thin blood runs in Mr. Morris; none of the hesitating, refuge-seeking temperament that too often dulls American music-making. He speaks out. Yesterday his audience could not choose but hear. Some of us made bold to fancy we were 'sitting in' at an event."

In 1932 the Juilliard Foundation selected this Concerto as its work for publication the following season. Before it added to his reputation, Morris had achieved distinction with his first Piano Sonata, which in its published form is now in its third edition. He has also three other Piano Sonatas; a Violin and Piano Sonata which was chosen by the Curtis Institute as a representative American work for performance at the American Embassy in London; a Quintet for strings and piano; two String Quartets; a Quartet for piano, violin, cello, and flute; two Trios; a Symphonic Poem for orchestra after Tagore's *Gitanjali;* a Symphony after Browning's *Prospice;* and a Violin Concerto which won the award of the National Federation of Music Clubs for the best score submitted by an American composer. This latter work had its first performance in May, 1939, at the hands of Philip Frank and the National Broadcasting Symphony Orchestra under Dr. Frank Black.

QUINCY PORTER (1897——) has specialized in string quartets. He has composed seven—the first in 1923 and the seventh twenty years later. Two of them, the third and the sixth, were published by the Society for the Publication of American Music. Porter was born in New Haven, Connecticut, February 7, 1897, the son of a professor at the Yale Divinity School. He was graduated from Yale in 1919, and two years later from the Yale School of Music, where he was a pupil of Horatio Parker and David Stanley Smith. Later he went to Paris to study with d'Indy, and then returned to America for further work with Ernest Bloch.

For six years he taught at the Cleveland Institute of Music, and then in 1928 went to Paris on a Guggenheim Fellowship. He came back to Cleveland three years later, and after another year at the Institute accepted an invitation to Vassar College, where he was for several years professor of music. In 1938 he was appointed dean of the faculty at the New England Conservatory of Music in Boston, and in 1942 he was made director, to succeed Wallace Goodrich.

Porter has composed several major works for orchestra. The earliest, for strings, was the *Ukrainian Suite*, composed in 1925. Next came a Suite in C Minor, 1926; then a *Poem and Dance*, 1932; a First Symphony, composed in 1934 and awarded honorable mention in the New York Philharmonic-Symphony Society's prize competition in 1937, which had its first performance by the Society, with the composer conducting, April 2, 1938; a *Dance in Three-Time*, commissioned by the St. Louis Chamber Orchestra, 1937; and an orchestral work commissioned by the Columbia Broadcasting System—*Two Dances for Radio*, 1938. More recent is *Music for Strings*, a work in three short movements for five-part string choir, published in 1942.

Anyone who wants to become closely acquainted with the consummate technique and the exquisite taste of ROBERT RUSSELL BENNETT (1894——) need only to listen repeatedly to the phonograph records of the operetta *Oklahoma*. Bennett is the most sought after of all orchestral arrangers for musical comedies, and the audiences who attend these shows hear not only the sparkling melodies of Jerome Kern, Richard Rodgers, Harold Arlen, and the rest, but also the masterful counterpoint and the rich, luxurious instrumentation of a truly great craftsman.

Bennett was born June 15, 1894, in Kansas City, Missouri, the son of musical parents. His mother taught him to play the piano; from his father, who led a band and an orchestra, he learned to play many of the orchestral instruments, some through actual instruction, and more through having to "pick them up" when players were missing from the ensemble. When he was fifteen he began formal musical study in harmony with Carl Busch. During the years just before the first World War, Bennett was in New York as copyist and arranger. For a year he served in the Army, and then he was back, this time on Broadway, where he began his very successful career as an orchestrator of musical comedy scores.

A few years later he went to Paris to study with Nadia Boulanger; this was the beginning of Bennett's serious work as a composer. While he was there, in 1927, he won a Guggenheim Fellowship, which was renewed the following year, and during this period he turned out a considerable list of works, including a Symphony which won honorable mention in the *Musical America* contest that produced Bloch's *America*. He composed *Paysage,* for orchestra; a one-act opera *An Hour of Delusion; Endymion,* "an operetta-ballet à l'antique"; and numerous songs, choruses, and pieces of chamber music. There were also *Sights and Sounds,* "an orchestral entertainment," and *Abraham Lincoln, A Likeness in Symphonic Form,* composed in Berlin in 1929—pieces which won two of the five prizes into which the judges of the Victor contest of 1929–30 split the $25,000 award. Since 1930, Bennett has been in Hollywood, composing, arranging, and conducting music for the films, and in New York, making orchestral arrangements for musical comedies.

Bennett had an opportunity to use his theatrical experience in an original work when the Juilliard School presented his opera *Maria Malibran,* with a libretto by Robert A. Simon, music critic of *The New Yorker,* in April, 1935. The story of the opera concerns the famous singer, daughter of Manuel García, during the two-year visit she paid to American shores.

Bennett's purely instrumental works include a *Charleston Rhapsody* and an *Adagio Eroico* for orchestra; a *Concerto Grosso* using a small dance band as the concertino; a *March* for two pianos and orchestra; and several pieces of chamber music. The Philadelphia Orchestra presented his *Eight Etudes for Orchestra* in Philadelphia, January 10, and 11, 1942, and in New York, January 6. Bennett's intention in writing these *Etudes* was to give the orchestra and the conductor specific problems to overcome, in the same way that *études* for solo instruments present technical difficulties to the performer or student. Each of Russell's *Etudes* bore a dedication: to Walter Damrosch, Aldous Huxley, Noel Coward, "King" Carl Hubbell (a baseball pitcher), "to all Dictators," to the Grand Lama, to Eugene Speicher, the painter, and "to the Ladies."

The four paintings by Norman Rockwell were the inspiration for Bennett's symphony *The Four Freedoms,* which was played first by the National Broadcasting Symphony under Frank Black, September 26, 1943, and by the Philadelphia Orchestra the following December. The movements of the symphony followed the titles of the paintings: "Freedom of Speech" pictured musically a street orator; "Freedom of Worship" brought the atmosphere of a religious ceremony; "Freedom from Want" suggested gay dancing and merrymaking; and "Freedom from Fear" started with a lullaby and ended with a march symbolizing the United Nations advancing to victory. Unfortunately, the epic nature of the subject was not altogether realized by the music, which combined impressionism with graphic realism.

Bennett's *Hexapoda,* Five Studies in "Jitteroptera," for violin and piano, has been played frequently in recital, by Louis Kaufman and by Jascha Heifetz. In this work the composer has been successful in writing music that is tremendously effective for the violin, and which, while it is not itself swing music, depicts the reaction of varied listeners to swing music. The individual pieces of the set are entitled: *Gut-Bucket Gus; Jane Shakes Her Hair; Betty and Harold Close Their Eyes; Jim Jives;* and *Till Dawn Sunday.*

Louis Kaufman was also the violinist who gave Bennett's Concerto for Violin and Orchestra its first performance, with the National Orchestral Association in New York, February 14, 1944. Like *Hexapoda* this was an entertaining work, but its more ambitious form made some of its material seem trivial.

Like Bennett, FERDE GROFÉ (1892———) had a distinguished career as an arranger and as a master of specialized instrumentation. He did more than any other musician, perhaps, to develop the "sweet type" of jazz for which Paul Whiteman became famous.

Grofé was almost born a musician; in New York, March 27, 1892. His mother's father Bernhardt Bierlich was a cellist who shared first desk with Victor Herbert at the Metropolitan, and after that was solo cellist of the Los Angeles Symphony. His son, Ferde's uncle, was concertmaster of the Los Angeles Orchestra. When he was old enough Ferde himself played viola in the same band. His father had been a singer with the original Bostonians. So it was agreed that young Ferde should *not* be a professional musician. But the jobs he tried as bank clerk, bookbinder, printer, were not so interesting, and he drifted back to music; to playing for dances—the violin, viola, or piano; traveling with a patent medicine vendor; playing in a saloon at a mining camp. Finally he got back to Los Angeles and eventually landed a job in Whiteman's band at the Hotel Alexandria, in 1920. Whiteman was interested in developing new instrumental effects, and Grofé was interested, too. So they talked things over, and started to make their own arrangements. Before that, dance orchestras had borrowed the huddle system idea from football games, and had everything and everybody playing all the time. Just like the advertiser who hired a band for his radio program and came around to rehearsal. He noticed that in one passage the trombone player sat holding his instrument in his lap. "Why isn't that man playing?" he demanded. "There is no part for him here," said the leader; "he is supposed to rest during the second chorus." "Then write a part for him!" thundered the man who was paying the bills, "I'll have no loafers in my orchestra."

Grofé conceived the idea of instrumental contrast, especially the "harmony chorus," where some solo instrument, often a saxophone, croons the melody softly and the brass gives it a subdued chord accompaniment. This was one of the first departures from noisy jazz. After a while Grofé retired as pianist of the orchestra, and devoted himself principally to making arrangements. It was with the *Rhapsody in Blue* of Gershwin that Grofé made his reputation—and Gershwin's, too, for that matter. For if the scoring had not been right, the piece itself would have fallen flat and Gershwin might not have had his day as a serious composer.

In recent years Grofé has been heard more as composer than merely as an arranger of other men's music. His *Grand Canyon Suite*, particularly its *On the Trail* movement (part of it heard several times each week as theme song of the Philip Morris program), is played on the radio as often as many popular songs. Others of his major works are a *Mississippi Suite; Knute Rockne; Three Shades of Blue; Ode to the Star-Spangled Banner; Symphony in Steel; Wheels* ("a Transportation Suite"); and a *Hollywood Suite.* Grofé conducted concerts of his own compositions in Carnegie Hall, New York, in 1937, and during the 1940–41 season.

ARCADY DUBENSKY (1890——) has been a member of the New York Philharmonic-Symphony Society's orchestra since 1922. His wide orchestral experience has given him a highly developed technique in instrumentation. His *Stephen Foster Theme, Variations and Finale*, is one of the few really successful and satisfying symphonic treatments of Foster songs, for the brilliance and color of its orchestration never obscure the inherent simplicity of the songs themselves. This work was first played in Indianapolis (the home city of Josiah K. Lilly, founder of Foster Hall) by the Indianapolis Symphony during the 1940–41 season. It had its first New York performance by the Philharmonic-Symphony, March 21, 1942.

Dubensky was born in Viatka, Russia, October 3, 1890. At the age of eight he started singing in the cathedral choir there, and at thirteen he played the violin in a theatre orchestra. In 1904 he went to Moscow where he graduated from the Conservatory in 1909, after studying violin with Hřimaly and counterpoint with Iljinsky. In 1911 he became a member of the Moscow Imperial Opera Orchestra, where he remained until 1919. Since 1921 he has lived in New York.

In addition to *Stephen Foster*, Dubensky's works include a *Fugue for Eighteen Violins*, first performed by The Philadelphia Orchestra, April, 1932; an opera-miniature *Romance with Double Bass*, produced in 1916 at the Imperial Opera in Moscow; a symphonic poem *Russian Bells*; two Suites for orchestra; a *Fantasy* for tuba and orchestra; a "melodeclamation" *The Raven*, based on Poe's poem, and performed by Benjamin de Loache and the Philadelphia Orchestra in 1932; a *Tom Sawyer Overture*, composed for the Mark Twain anniversary in 1935, and first performed by Stokowski and the Philadelphia Orchestra; and a *Suite Anno 1600*, first played by the Philadelphia String Sinfonietta in 1937, and later by the New York Philharmonic-Symphony in April, 1939.

QUINTO MAGANINI (1897——) combines in his activities the roles of composer, conductor, educator, and music patron. As a composer he has written in almost every form: four operas, for which he himself supplied the libretti; a ballet; a number of large choral works; more than a dozen major orchestral works; several symphonic scores for band; and over a hundred compositions for solo wind instruments and for wind ensembles.

As a conductor, he has made guest appearances with leading orchestras in New York and Paris, and with the San Francisco Symphony. For a number of seasons he conducted the New York Sinfonietta, and in 1932 he founded the Maganini Chamber Symphony Orchestra, with which he made several nation-wide tours. In the summer of 1938 he alternated with Eugene Ormandy and José Iturbi as conductor of the New York Philharmonic-Symphony in a series of concerts at Silvermine, Connecticut. In recent years he has been the regular conductor of symphony concerts in Norwalk and Stamford, Connecticut, of the Danbury (Connecticut) Festival, and of children's concerts in Greenwich, Connecticut, and Scarsdale, New York.

As a music educator, Maganini has taught counterpoint and orchestration at Columbia University, and in the role of music patron he has given his fellow-composers the most practical form of assistance— playing their works at his concerts, and publishing their music in the Edition Musicus, a publishing firm which he himself founded, and which he directs and administers.

Maganini was born in Fairfield, California, November 30, 1897. He started his professional career as a flutist in the San Francisco Orchestra in 1917. Two years later he became a member of the New York Symphony Orchestra under Walter Damrosch, and remained with that organization until it was merged with the Philharmonic Society in 1928. In 1927 he was awarded the Pulitzer Scholarship in music, and in 1928 and 1929 a Guggenheim Fellowship.

His most extended work is one which deals with California history: *The Argonauts,* an opera cycle on which he worked for fourteen years, and which has been published but not yet performed in its entirety. It was awarded the Bispham Medal. California is also the subject of *Tuolumne,* a Rhapsody for orchestra which was first played by the New York Philharmonic in 1924 and the New York Symphony in 1925. *South Wind,* for orchestra, is described by the composer as "decorative music," unconcerned with facts, and seeking merely to picture a sunrise over the Mediterranean. It was originally entitled *Night on an Island of Fantasy.*

Some of Maganini's best work has been written for small orchestra:

George Gershwin
(See pages 446-452)

Howard Hanson
(See pages 452-456)

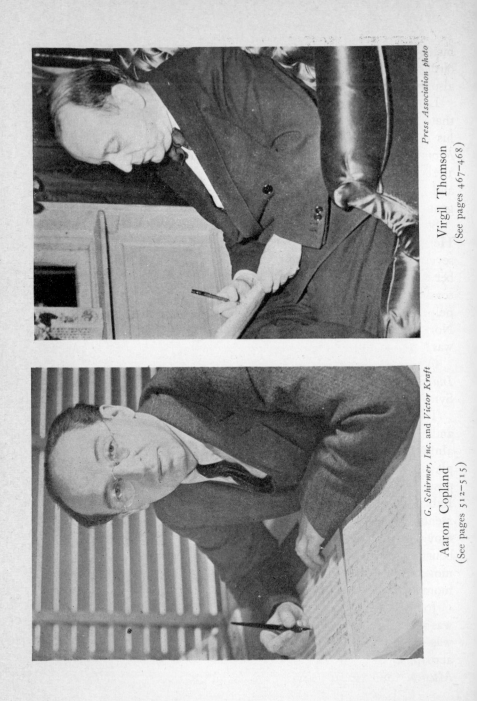

Press Association photo

Virgil Thomson
(See pages 467–468)

G. Schirmer, Inc. and Victor Kraft

Aaron Copland
(See pages 512–515)

his *Ornithological Suite* (with cuckoos, hummingbirds, and mocking-birds), the *Sylvan Symphony, Cuban Rhapsody,* and others. He has also made arrangements of early American music.

LAMAR STRINGFIELD (1897——) is one of the group who believes that the Anglo-American folk music heritage is the logical basis for his music. Following this line he has composed an orchestral Suite *From the Southern Mountains* (which received a Pulitzer Award in 1928); *Moods of a Moonshiner; Mountain Dew; Cripple Creek;* and a number of other orchestral works with an Appalachian background.

Stringfield was born in Raleigh, North Carolina, October 10, 1897. He studied at the Institute of Musical Art in New York, and for several years after graduation played the flute in orchestra and chamber music ensembles in New York. Returning to the South, he became conductor of the North Carolina Symphony Orchestra, and in 1930 helped to organize the Institute of Folk Music at the University of North Carolina. In 1938 he came again to New York, and for a time was a staff conductor at the Radio City Music Hall.

Others of Stringfield's orchestral works are a Symphonic Poem *Indian Legend, Negro Parade,* and *The Legend of John Henry,* a Symphonic Ballad.

Two orchestral works by HORACE JOHNSON (1893——), *Imagery* and *Streets of Florence,* have been so widely performed that they have almost achieved a record. During the season of 1937–38, *Imagery* was played twenty-six times by various orchestras. This work was composed in 1924–25 and was first performed in 1926. Quotations from Rabindranath Tagore provide programs for the three separate movements. The first is "Procession to Indra," which depicts the slow-moving caravan and the incantations, with woodwinds, brass, tambourine, and tam-tam establishing an Oriental background. The second movement is a dance "Aspara," as is the *finale,* "Urbasi" which grows more and more intense and impassioned.

Johnson was born in Waltham, Massachusetts, October 5, 1893 and was a pupil of Bainbridge Crist in Boston. For a number of years he was a music journalist in New York, and then spent several years abroad. Upon his return in 1931, he became managing editor of the *Musical Courier.* In May, 1939, he was appointed New York City

Director of the WPA Federal Music Project, succeeding Chalmers Clifton, and held that position until the Project was discontinued several years later.

Johnson's orchestral works include the previously mentioned *Streets of Florence; Astarte,* a tone poem; and *Joyance,* for strings. He is well known also for his songs, among them: *The Pirate, When Pierrot Sings, The Three Cherry Trees,* and *Thy Dark Hair.*

PAUL WHITE (1895——) is known best for his work for orchestra and chorus *The Voyage of the Mayflower,* and his orchestral Suite *Five Miniatures.* Both of these works were introduced at the American Composers' Concerts of the Eastman School, the first in 1935 and the second a year earlier, and both have been performed elsewhere— *The Voyage of the Mayflower* by the Philadelphia Orchestra, November 15, 1939, and the *Miniatures* at the Worcester (Massachusetts) Festival in 1936.

White was born in Bangor, Maine, August 22, 1895, and is a graduate of the New England Conservatory in Boston. For a number of years he played first violin in the Cincinnati Symphony, and then became a teacher at the Eastman School in Rochester. Others of his works include a Symphony in E Minor; *A Pagan Festival* Overture, *Feuilles Symphoniques, Sea Chanty,* and *To Youth,* for orchestra; a Sonata for violin and piano; and a Sinfonietta for string orchestra or string quartet.

EDWIN JOHN STRINGHAM (1890——) came to New York from the Midwest in 1930 to teach composition at Union Theological Seminary and to join the music faculty of Teachers College. He also taught acoustics at the Institute of Musical Art. From 1930 to 1933 he was music editor for Carl Fischer, Inc., and since 1933 has been general music editor of the American Book Company. In 1936 he went to Germany on a Cromwell Traveling Fellowship, and in 1938 was appointed chairman of the Music Department at Queens College.

Stringham was born in Kenosha, Wisconsin, July 11, 1890. Before coming to New York he was dean of the Denver College of Music (1920–28). His early compositions include three Symphonic Poems; a Symphony; a set of *Three Pastels;* a Concert Overture; and various pieces and songs. Because of the pressure of editorial and teaching duties, his more recent works are confined to a *Nocturne* for orchestra, played by the Philharmonic-Symphony, January 20, 1935; a *Notturno* for winds and harp; a Quartet for strings; and some choral music. Stringham is a firm believer in rhythmic counterpoint. He is fond of masses of orchestral color, and he frequently uses jazz rhythms.

CARL HUGO GRIMM (1890————) was awarded $1,000 by the National Federation of Music Clubs in 1927 for his *Erotic Poem*, and another of similar size for a choral work *The Song of Songs* by the MacDowell Club of New York in 1930. He was born in Zanesville, Ohio, October 31, 1890, educated in Cincinnati, and is living there today as organist, teacher, and composer. He had his music training from his father (author of several treatises on harmony), and from Van der Stucken, but in orchestration he is largely self-taught.

Grimm has composed a long list of works: four Symphonic Poems; a Suite for orchestra; a Suite for chamber orchestra; a String Quartet; a Fantasia for two clarinets, cello, and piano; a Serenade for wind instruments; many works for chorus; and numerous songs. His *Abraham Lincoln* was first performed at the American Composers' Concerts in Rochester in 1931. Idiomatically, Grimm uses the harmonic combinations which grow out of exotic scale forms, many of them Oriental.

THOMAS GRISELLE (1891————) was winner of the Victor Talking Machine Company's first prize of $10,000 in 1928 with his *Two American Sketches*. His orchestral compositions include *Cubist*, a "classical-jazz" work which was played in the Cohan Revue of 1918; *Two Pieces from the Olden Times* (1921); *Program Music*, a satirical sketch (1937); two tone poems; a *Dance Suite*; and two Sinfoniettas. He has also composed considerable chamber music, and a *Keyboard Symphony* for six pianos.

Griselle was one of the first to realize the artistic possibilities of jazz. He was born at Upper Sandusky, Ohio, January 10, 1891; studied first at the Cincinnati College of Music, and then with Nadia Boulanger in Paris. He has been associated with radio as conductor and arranger, and since 1939 has been in Hollywood.

SAMUEL GARDNER (1891————), a violinist-composer, was born in Russia, August 25, 1891, and was brought to this country when he was six years old. He studied with Franz Kneisel and Percy Goetschius, and then started his career as a concert violinist. He was a member of the Kneisel Quartet during the season 1914–15; the following year a member of the Chicago Symphony; and in 1916–17 of the Elshuco Trio.

As a composer, Gardner feels that music is a personal rather than a national expression. He became widely known to the concert public for a racy little violin piece *From the Canebrake,* but he has composed several works of larger dimensions. His *Broadway* was first played by the Boston Symphony in its 1929–30 season, and before that Gardner himself had played his Violin Concerto with the New York Philharmonic under Mengelberg. His String Quartet won the Pulitzer Scholarship, and a symphonic poem *New Russia* was awarded the Loeb Prize, both in 1918. He also has composed a Quintet *To the Fallen;* a Prelude and Fugue for string quartet; and a set of Variations for string quartet.

For many years the prolonged foreign residence of TIMOTHY MATHER SPELMAN (1891———) prevented his countrymen from hearing very many of his works. He was born in Brooklyn, New York, January 21, 1891; studied with Harry Rowe Shelley, and at Harvard with W. R. Spalding and Edward Burlingame Hill, and later at the Munich Conservatory with Courvoisier. From 1920 he lived for a decade and a half in Italy, returning to this country after the Fascists came into power.

Before he went abroad Spelman had two works produced in his native Brooklyn—a setting of Turgeniev's prose poem *How Fair, How Fresh Were the Roses,* and a four-act pantomime *Snowdrop.* His prelude for string orchestra *In the Princess' Garden* was performed in Cambridge and Boston, and a wordless fantasy in one act *The Romance of the Rose* was given in Boston, and later in St. Paul, Minnesota. He has written two one-act operas: *La Magnifica,* to a libretto by his wife Leolyn Louise Everett, and one to his own libretto *The Sunken City,* as well as a three-act opera *The Sea Rovers.* Two of his works have had performances at the American Composers' Concerts in Rochester: *Pervigilium Veneris* for soli, chorus, and orchestra in 1934, and the Symphony in G Minor in 1936.

FRANCES McCOLLIN (1892———) has achieved distinction in spite of the handicap of blindness. Her works have won a number of prizes from various organizations. She was born in Philadelphia, October 24,

1892, and studied with William Wallace Gilchrist and H. Alexander Matthews. Her father, an amateur singer and organist, was president of the Orpheus Club and of the Musical Fund Society.

Miss McCollin is active as a teacher and lecturer, and follows traditional rather than the contemporary styles. She has been most successful in her writing of part-songs and choral works, but has written instrumental music as well. Her Scherzo for strings *Heavenly Children at Play* was performed by the Philadelphia Orchestra in 1940. She has published a String Quartet; a Piano Quintet; an *Adagio* for string orchestra; a Trio for organ (or piano), violin, and cello; and many part-songs and choral works.

Music is an avocation to JAMES G. HELLER (1892———), for he is rabbi of the Plum Street Temple in Cincinnati. He writes the program notes of the Cincinnati Orchestra and composes for his own pleasure. Although he has written several works, he made no attempt to publish anything until the Society for the Publication of American Music selected his *Three Aquatints* for string quartet in 1929. Others of his works include *Four Sketches* for orchestra, performed by the Cincinnati Symphony, February 7, 1936; a Sonata for violin and piano; an *Elegy and Pastorale*, for voice and string quartet; a Trio; Four Solo Services for Friday Evening; and an oratorio *Watchman, What of the Night?*

He was born in New Orleans January 4, 1892. When he went to Cincinnati to study theology he learned orchestration from Edgar Stillman Kelley, and had some lessons with other Cincinnati music teachers.

ELIOT GRIFFIS (1893———) attracted attention in 1919 with the publication of an atmospheric Piano Sonata which enjoyed a number of performances. He was born in Boston, January 28, 1893 and studied under Horatio Parker at Yale and Stuart Mason at the New England Conservatory in Boston. He has written a Symphony and two other symphonic works—*A Persian Fable* and *Colossus*; a set of Variations for strings; three String Quartets, one of which won him a Pulitzer Scholarship; a Trio *To the Sun*, and a Suite for trio; an operetta; a Sonata for violin and piano; and numerous piano pieces and songs.

HERBERT ELWELL (1898———) was a Fellow at the American Academy in Rome (1926) and a pupil of Ernest Bloch and Nadia

Boulanger. He is best known for *The Happy Hypocrite*, originally music for a ballet and subsequently arranged as a Suite for orchestra. In the latter form it won the Eastman Publication Award. Elwell was born in Minneapolis, Minnesota, May 10, 1898. For a number of years he has been music critic for the *Cleveland Plain Dealer* and program annotator for the Cleveland Symphony. In 1935 he was appointed assistant director of the Cleveland Institute of Music, where he heads the theory and composition departments. His works include a String Quartet; a Quintet; a Piano Sonata; and a Sonata for violin and piano. His *Introduction and Allegro* won the Juilliard Publication Award in 1943.

MARK WESSEL (1894———), a pupil of Arnold Schoenberg, was twice awarded a Guggenheim Fellowship and was also the recipient of a Pulitzer Scholarship. He has composed a Symphony; a *Symphony Concertante*, for piano and horn with orchestra; *Holiday*, and *Song and Dance* for orchestra; a Concertino for flute and chamber orchestra; a Sextet for woodwind and piano; a String Quartet; a Quintet; *The King of Babylon*, a Symphonic Poem for orchestra, chorus, and mimers which won honorable mention in the 1938 contest of the New York Philharmonic-Symphony Orchestra; and other works.

He was born in Coldwater, Michigan, March 26, 1894, and was graduated from Northwestern School of Music. He has taught piano and theory at Northwestern, and more recently has been professor of piano and composition at the University of Colorado.

ABRAHAM WOLFE BINDER (1895———) draws on Jewish sources for his compositions for orchestra, piano, and voice. Born in New York, January 13, 1895, he studied at the New York College of Music, and received his Bachelor of Music degree in 1926 at Columbia University. Since 1917 he has directed the music of the Young Men's Hebrew Association, and in 1923 became the choirmaster of the Free Synagogue, New York. He was appointed professor of liturgical music at the Jewish Institute of Religion, New York, in 1937. In 1931 he was guest conductor of the Palestine Symphonic Ensemble in Palestine, and of the Manhattan Symphony Orchestra in New York. In this same year he edited the third edition of the *Union Hymnal*.

His compositions for orchestra are an Overture *Ha Chalutsim* (The Pioneers), 1931; *Holy Land Impressions*, 1933; *Symphonic Fantasy*

(The Valley of Dry Bones), 1936. Also a *Sabbath Eve Service;* a children's oratorio *Judas Maccabäus.* He has published songs, part-songs, anthems, and folk songs; violin and piano pieces; and a *New Palestinian Songbook* in two volumes. He has written many articles on Jewish music.

CARL McKINLEY (1895——) is best known for his *Masquerade,* an American Rhapsody for orchestra, introduced in 1930 by the Phila-delphia Orchestra under Gabrilowitsch. Following its première, the piece had more than fifty performances by major orchestras. It sug-gests the Mardi Gras of New Orleans, with waltz tunes of Spanish and French flavor. McKinley's first orchestral piece was the *Indian Summer Idyl,* played by the New York Philharmonic in 1919. He has written a number of works for organ that have been widely used. Probably the most popular is his charming *Cantilena.* He has pub-lished a number of works for chorus, for piano, and several songs.

McKinley was born in Yarmouth, Maine, October 9, 1895. Upon graduating from Harvard he won a Naumburg Fellowship which made it possible for him to study in New York during the winter of 1917–18 under Goldmark, Déthier, and Rothwell. For some years he was a church organist in Hartford, Connecticut, and later played the organ at the Capitol Theatre, in New York. The years 1927–29 he spent abroad on a Guggenheim Fellowship and on his return he was appointed to the faculty of the New England Conservatory of Music.

The works of CARL ERNEST BRICKEN (1898——) include a Suite, a Symphony and a Prelude for orchestra, and considerable chamber music. He received a Guggenheim Fellowship in 1930–31. Born in Shelbyville, Kentucky, December 28, 1898, Bricken studied at Yale University, and with Rosario Scalero. From 1925 to 1928 he was a faculty member of the Mannes School in New York, and then a teacher of theory at the Institute of Musical Art. In 1931 he became professor of music and chairman of the music department at the Uni-versity of Chicago, and in the summer of 1934 was guest conductor of the Chicago Symphony. In 1931 he became professor of music at the University of Wisconsin, and in 1944 moved to Seattle, where he had been appointed conductor of the Seattle Symphony.

AURELIO GIORNI (1895–1938) was widely known as the pianist of the Elshuco Trio. His Sonata for cello and piano was one of the early works chosen for publication by the Society for the Publication of American Music (1924). He had also composed a symphonic poem *Orlando Furioso* (1926); a Symphony in D (1936); a *Sinfonia Concertante* for piano with orchestra; a String Quartet (1936); a Piano Quintet (1926); a Piano Quartet (1927); a Piano Trio (1934); Sonatas for flute and piano (1932), violin and piano (1924), clarinet and piano (1933); and numerous other works. He was born in Perugia, Italy, September 15, 1895, came to the United States in 1915, and at the time of his death, September 23, 1938, was teaching composition at Smith College.

Although SAMUEL L. M. BARLOW (1892——) has participated in leftist political activities, his music is by no means extreme. He himself has characterized his work by saying: "My method of orchestration is as modern as I can make it, but tunes which wouldn't shock Papa Brahms keep sticking their necks out."

Barlow was born in New York City, June 1, 1892. He studied music at Harvard, and later studied piano with Isidor Philipp in Paris. He also studied theory with Franklin Robinson in New York, and orchestration with Respighi in Rome. His musical and political activities have been varied: lecturer for the New York Board of Education; First Chairman, New York Community Chorus; Lieutenant, United States Army in France; Director of the American Merchant Marine Insurance Company; teacher in various settlement schools; orchestral conductor for the New York Theatre Guild (during the season 1937–38 he composed and conducted the music for the Guild production of *Amphitryon*); newspaper critic; piano soloist with symphony orchestras; executive, National Committee for Defense of Political Prisoners; treasurer, American Guild for German Political Freedom; speaker for Musicians' Emergency Fund.

His works include a one-act opera *Mon ami Pierrot,* which was the first work by an American composer to be produced at the Opéra-Comique in Paris (January 11, 1935); two further operas, *Eugénie* and *Amanda;* a Symphonic Poem *Alba,* played by the Cincinnati Orchestra (1928); a symphonic work *Babar,* performed by the Philadelphia Orchestra (1935); a Piano Concerto, played by the composer with the Rochester Philharmonic (January 23, 1931) and later in

Europe; a set of *Biedermeier Waltzes* (the Augusteo, Rome, 1935); and *For Strings* (Monte Carlo Quartet, 1935).

CHARLES HAUBIEL (1894——) came into prominence when his symphonic work *Karma* won the first prize in the Schubert Centennial Contest, and consequently became one of the few American symphonic works recorded on the phonograph. He was born in Delta, Ohio, January 30, 1894, and studied music in New York—composition with Rosario Scalero, and piano with Rudolph Ganz and the Lhévinnes. For eight years he was a piano teacher at the Institute of Musical Art in New York, and later joined the music faculty at New York University.

In 1935 his *Ritratti* (Portraits) was awarded second prize in the symphonic contest sponsored by Swift and Company, and was performed by the Chicago Symphony Orchestra, December 12 and 13, 1935. Three years later (February, 1938) his *Passacaglia* in A Minor ("The Plane Beyond") shared with the *Little Symphony* in G by Robert L. Sanders the prize awarded by the New York Philharmonic-Symphony Orchestra, and was played by that organization under the composer's own direction on December 18, 1938.

Haubiel is a middle-of-the-roader in his music. His style is a synthesis of romantic-classic-impressionist elements, a sort of combination of Brahms and Debussy. Others of his compositions include the symphonic works: *Pastoral, Mars Ascending, Vox Cathedralis, Suite Passecaille*, and *Solari;* some chamber music; and many shorter pieces.

ERNST BACON (1898——) studied first in America, at the University of Chicago and at Northwestern, and then went abroad, where he continued his studies in Germany and Austria. He has been also a composition pupil of Ernest Bloch.

He was born in Chicago, May 26, 1898. His activities have covered a wide field. He founded and conducted the Carmel (California) Bach Festival; he was supervisor of the Federal Music Project and conductor of the Federal Symphony Orchestra in San Francisco; for a time he was acting professor of music at Hamilton College; and in recent years he has been in charge of the Music School of Converse College, Spartanburg, South Carolina. In 1932 he was awarded a Pulitzer Scholarship, and in 1939 a Guggenheim Fellowship.

Bacon's orchestral works include two Symphonies and two extended

Suites—*Ford's Theatre* (portraying in twelve successive movements the events leading up to Lincoln's assassination), and *From These States*. He has composed the score for an "American Music-Play" *A Tree on the Plains,* and incidental music for Shakespeare's *The Tempest.* Several of his works are for soloists with orchestra: *The Postponeless Creature,* for baritone or contralto, on poems by Whitman and Emily Dickinson; *Whispers of Heavenly Death* (Whitman), for baritone or contralto; *Midnight Special,* for mezzo-soprano; *Black and White Songs,* for baritone; *My River,* for mezzo-soprano, again on poems by Emily Dickinson. He has also written numerous songs; a *Suite to the Children,* for two pianos; and several pieces for the latter medium in lighter vein: *Wastin' Time, Kankakee River,* and, with Luening, *Coal Scuttle Blues.*

In 1941, OTTO CESANA (1899——) conducted a concert by an ensemble of seventeen musicians in New York's Town Hall, which presented no less than nineteen of his own compositions. The principal items on the program were a Piano Concerto and a *Symphony in Swing.*

Cesana, born in Brescia, Italy, July 7, 1899, came to this country as a child. He has been engaged in arranging music for dance orchestras and radio programs, and in consequence has brought to his serious music the flavor of Broadway and Hollywood. His formula for American music is frank and disarming: "Take material such as is used in current popular songs, refine it, and that is your subject matter. Orchestration should be symphonic type as represented on various outstanding radio hours. The form—Beethoven is O.K. Put it all together, shake well, and you have American music—maybe. Anyway, that's my story!"

Others of Cesana's works include two *American Symphonies;* an Overture; a Symphonic Poem *Negro Heaven;* a Concerto for two pianos and orchestra and a Concerto for three pianos and orchestra; *Three Moods* (played by the New York Philharmonic-Symphony Orchestra under John Barbirolli in April, 1939); a ballet-opera *Ali Baba and the Forty Thieves;* and a *Swing Sextet.*

WILLIAM LEVI DAWSON (1899——) was born in Anniston, Alabama, September 26, 1899, and studied at Tuskegee Institute in Kansas City under Busch, and with Weidig and Otterstrom in Chicago.

For a time he was first trombonist in the Chicago Civic Orchestra and he has been director of the School of Music and of the Choir at Tuskegee since 1931. In 1930 and 1931 he won the Rodman Wanamaker contest for composition. His *Negro Folk Symphony, No. 1* has been played several times by the Philadelphia Orchestra, and broadcast over the Columbia network. He has also written a Scherzo for orchestra, several choral works, a Trio for violin, cello, and piano, and a *Sonata* for violin and piano.

WESLEY LA VIOLETTE (1894——) heads the theory department at the De Paul University School of Music in Chicago, and is president of the Chicago section of the International Society for Contemporary Music. He was born in St. James, Minnesota, January 4, 1894, and was educated at Northwestern University and at the Chicago College of Music. His orchestral works include a *Requiem* (1925); *Penetrella*, for eighteen-part string orchestra (1928); *Osiris* (1929); *Dedications*, a Violin Concerto (1929); Nocturne (1932); *Collegiana* (1936); a Symphony (1936); a Chorale (1936); a Piano Concerto, and a Concerto for string quartet and orchestra (both 1937). There is also an opera *Shylock*, which won the Bispham medal in 1930. His chamber music includes several String Quartets; a Piano Quintet; an Octet; two Violin Sonatas; and other works.

From 1929 until the time of his death, ROBERT BRAINE (1896–1940) was a staff pianist at the National Broadcasting Company. He was born in Springfield, Ohio, May 27, 1896, and educated at the Cincinnati College of Music. His works included three operas and a number of orchestral works which have been heard on the radio: *S.O.S.*; *The Song of Hiawatha*; a *Concerto in Jazz* (also performed at a Paul Whiteman concert); *The House of Usher*; a Rhapsody in E flat; *Harlequin and Columbine*; and *City of Dreams*, for jazz orchestra.

Braine's *Choreographic Impressions* were performed in part at the October, 1939, Symposium of American Orchestral Music in Rochester, and his *Theater Sheet* figured in the ballet program at the tenth annual Festival of American Music in Rochester in April, 1940, with Howard Hanson conducting. Braine died August 23, 1940.

RICHARD HAMMOND (1896——) is the musical son of the noted mining engineer John Hays Hammond, and brother of the inventor

John Hays Hammond, Junior. He was born in England, August 26, 1896, when his parents were living there, was educated at Yale University, and after service in the Navy during the war, had further musical training with Emerson Whithorne, Mortimer Wilson, and Nadia Boulanger. His works include *Six Chinese Fairy Tales* for orchestra (1921); *Voyage to the East,* for voice and orchestra (1926); a ballad *Fiesta; Son of Heaven,* for orchestra (1929); *West Indian Dances,* for orchestra (1930); orchestral Suite *After Reading "The Woman of Andros"* (1930); *Sinfonietta* (1931); two orchestral Suites of *Dance Music* (1933 and 1937); an orchestral Suite *Excursion;* a Sonata for oboe and piano (1924); several works for chamber orchestra and for chorus; and three ballets.

LEOPOLD DAMROSCH MANNES (1899——) has a distinguished musical ancestry. His mother, a talented pianist, is the daughter of Leopold Damrosch. His father is David Mannes, the noted violinist and teacher. He was born in New York, December 26, 1899, studied with Goetschius and Rosario Scalero, and won several scholarships: one from the Walter Scott Foundation in 1924, which enabled him to study in Paris with Alfred Cortot; the Pulitzer prize for composition in 1925; and the Guggenheim Fellowship to study abroad in 1926. He became a teacher of composition at the David Mannes School and the Institute of Musical Art in New York, but later abandoned music as a profession to enter the research laboratory of the Eastman Kodak Company. With Leopold Godowsky (son of the pianist) he became co-inventor of the Kodachrome process of color-photography.

Mannes's compositions include a set of Variations for piano (1920); a Suite for two pianos (1922), played by Bauer and Gabrilowitsch, and by Cortot and the composer; a Suite for orchestra (1924); a String Quartet (1927), played by the Flonzaley and Lenox Quartets; incidental music for Shakespeare's *Tempest;* and a number of songs and choral works.

ARTHUR LOURIE (1892——) has a varied background. Born in Leningrad, May 14, 1892, he is now living in the United States. Following his education at the University and Conservatory of Leningrad, he accepted a government post as Music Commissar. He turned Communist during this period. After an unpleasant incident in Russia, he went to Paris in 1923. For three years he lived and studied there in semiseclusion. He grew interested in the ritual music of the early churches, and his style gradually changed from that of the "radical composer" in St. Petersburg to something more religious in character. This was first evidenced in his *Concerto Spirituale* in 1930.

He has written for orchestra, piano, and strings. His works include *Sinfonia Dialectica* (1933); Symphony No. 2, *Kormtchaia* (1941); *Sonate Liturgique* for voice and instruments; a chorale setting of the 42nd Psalm; *Feast During the Plague,* a Symphonic Suite in six movements (from an opera-ballet) which had its première with the Boston Orchestra in 1945; and a number of piano pieces.

CARLTON COOLEY (1898———) specializes in viola compositions because of their scarcity. He was born in New Jersey and had his early training at the Philadelphia Musical Academy, studying violin with Frederick Hahn and composition with Camille Zeckwer. He continued composition with Goetschius at the Institute of Musical Art, New York. He has been a member of both the Philadelphia and Cleveland Orchestras. With the latter he was violinist, then concertmaster, and finally head of the viola section. Among his works are *Eastbourne Sketches, Song and Dance* for viola and orchestra, a Sonata for piano and violin, a Quartet in A, *Promenade* for string orchestra, and an epic poem *Caponsacchi,* performed by the NBC Symphony in 1942 and by the Philadelphia Orchestra in 1943.

*　　*　　*

JOSEPH SCHILLINGER (1895–1943) achieved a limited reputation as a composer of somewhat experimental music—an *Airphonic Suite* played by the Cleveland Orchestra, and a *Symphonic Rhapsody* commissioned by the Soviet government to commemorate the twelfth anniversary of the Revolution (while Schillinger still lived in Russia)— but it was as a teacher of composers, with a unique system of instruction, that he was best known. He devised a method whereby scientific formulae were applied not only to harmonic and contrapuntal patterns, but also to the construction of melodies. His pupils included popular song writers—Mark Warnow, Hal Kemp, Oscar Levant, Benny Goodman, Tommy Dorsey—and a number of serious composers as well. George Gershwin is said to have written the entire score of *Porgy and Bess* under his supervision. In 1933, Schillinger published a book called *The Mathematical Basis of the Arts*. This did not achieve general circulation, but after his death a more detailed book *The Schillinger System of Musical Composition* was widely publicized.

Schillinger was born in Kharkow, Russia, August 31, 1895. He studied at the Petersburg Conservatory and the State University of Petrograd. From 1922 to 1926 he was music consultant to the Soviet Union's Board of Education. In November 1928 he came to New York as a lecturer, and in 1930 settled here permanently, becoming a citizen in 1930. He taught at Teachers College, Columbia University; New York University; and the New School of Social Research. He died in New York, March 23, 1943.

During the early years of the first World War, LEO ORNSTEIN (1895——) astonished the concert world as the bad boy of American music; as an impish youngster who was out to punish our ears as much as we would let him. Clusters of notes took the place of single tones, and in printing his music the engraver had to invent new stems at crazy angles to show what notes should be struck together. Today he has plenty of company, but he stood almost alone when he started to write in his advanced style.

He was born in southwest Russia, December 11, 1895. A musical prodigy, he had an excellent education that finally led to work with Alexander Glazounov at the Petrograd Conservatory. Then there were revolutions and counter pogroms of the terrorists. Russia was unsafe for Jews, and the Ornstein family fled to America in 1907. They lived on New York's lower East Side, and Leo went to the Institute of Musical Art and became a favorite pupil of Mrs. Thomas Tapper. Then there were some years in Europe, and finally he made his New York debut as a concert pianist in 1911.

He had already done some composing. First he had written some pieces in conventional mold, harmless and undistinguished. Then of a sudden he burst forth as a radical who had thrown aside all formalism and restraint, who had turned his back on every convention. The principle of emotional logic was to be his only law, the supreme and only reason for resolving certain chords into others. His note clusters were to represent a logical anticipation of overtones; he would have a language of his own.

He remained, however, a curious contradiction, for there were two distinct sides to his nature: one the barbaric urge of his own *Wild Men's Dance*—the steely, stony feeling for the strings of the piano, and the other an extreme sentimentalism, most often shown when as a pianist he played Chopin or Liszt. When he performed the Chopin Nocturnes or Liszt's *Liebestraum*, the syrup almost dripped from them.

In late years Ornstein has almost dropped from view. He has ceased to be the revolutionary, perhaps because so many of his successors and colleagues have been far more advanced than he ever thought of being. At any rate, he has achieved a highly respected place as a piano teacher in Philadelphia, where he has taught at the Philadelphia Musical Academy, and since 1940 has been director and head of the piano department of the Ornstein School of Music.

The Wild Men's Dance and *A la Chinoise* were Ornstein's piano pieces which attracted the most attention on his recital programs, but he also has a lengthy list of orchestral works, including a Piano Concerto (1923); a Quintet (1929); a Quartet (1929); two Sonatas for violin and piano; a Cello Sonata, and a Piano Sonata. In 1935 he was commissioned by the League of Composers to write an orchestral work: this was the *Nocturne and Dance of the Fates*, first performed by Vladimir Golschmann and the St. Louis Orchestra in February, 1937. In 1930 he won first prize in a contest for a national hymn, conducted by the National Anthem Society.

HENRY DIXON COWELL (1897——) has been one of the most ardent champions and propagators of modern American music of the nonconformist variety. He edited the symposium *American Composers on American Music*, and wrote many of its chapters; he later published *The Nature of Melody;* he founded the quarterly *New Music*, in which music of American and European innovators has been published; he organized many activities of the Pan-American Association of Composers, in Europe and in America; he developed in conjunction with Professor Leon Theremin the "rhythmicon"—a device for producing difficult rhythmic combinations; he has lectured on music in various colleges and universities and at the New School for Social Research in New York. In short, he is indefatigable, and his activities have been immensely varied on behalf of all composers of radical tendencies. He received a Guggenheim Fellowship in 1931 and went to Berlin to study comparative musicology. He has also cultivated an interest in exotic music.

He was born in California, March 11, 1897. When he was five he studied the violin, but when he was eight he gave his instrument away. Then he decided to become a composer, and deliberately developed his mind, and practiced on it, as he says, to acquire more perfect mental hearing. He claims that he did not break the rules of music, for he didn't know them; he rather composed without reference to them. He used simple concords to express simple thoughts; and dissonance to tell of anger or the passions of modern life. Then he studied music at the University of California and later in New York, and was shocked to find that the rules of music played favorites, and were partial to concords.

Cowell is often regarded as the inventor of the so-called "tone-clusters," or the striking, or sounding, of groups of tones simultaneously. Leo Ornstein introduced "note-clusters" as early as 1915, and Charles Ives, whom we discussed in a previous chapter, has employed chords in piano music that must be played with a board or ruler. Cowell, however, actually experimented with his clusters before Ornstein had made them famous, even though he did not have opportunity to publicize them until ten or a dozen years later.

In 1919, Cowell set forth his theories in a book *New Musical Resources* which was published in revised form in 1930. In this work he explained that the ear actually hears the natural overtones when a single tone is sounded, therefore, the composer is following acoustic principles when he has these overtones actually played in conjunction with the basic tone.

In experimental vein Cowell has composed a Symphony and three tone poems—*Vestiges; Some Music and Some More Music;* and *Communication;* a Concerto for orchestra and piano; and a Concerto "for piano strings." For chamber orchestra he has written a *Symphonietta;* a *Polyphonica;* a chamber ballet *Atlantis;* and for string quartet: the *Quartet Pedantic; Movement; Quartet Romantic;* and *Quartet Euphometric. The Building of Banba* is a two-act opera.

The titles of some of his experimental piano pieces are illuminating: *Six Ings—Floating, Frisking, Fleeting, Scooting, Wafting,* and *Seeth-*

ing; Advertisement; Amiable Conversation; Antimony; Dynamic Motion; Fabric; What's This; Sinister Resonance; and *Four Casual Developments.*

Aside from his purely experimental works, Cowell has developed another phase of his creative nature, a leaning toward the Celtic tradition, a love of the weird and of colorful whimsicality. This is most apparent in his *Celtic Set* for piano, his *Tales of a Countryside* for orchestra, and in his *Schoontree* for band. Another work for band is his *Sleep Music.* He has also delved into an American background for his *Old American Country Set,* and for his *Hymn and Fuguing Tune,* both for orchestra.

ADOLPH WEISS (1891——), an atonalist disciple of Arnold Schoenberg, has worked along lines similar to those laid down by the Viennese atonalists, although Schoenberg is said to consider Weiss too independent a personality to be called his pupil. But like Schoenberg, Weiss works with twelve-tone "rows"; he builds up an entire work on the basis of one or two intervals.

He was born September 12, 1891, in Baltimore, Maryland. His father had been a piano pupil of Busoni, and the son learned to play the bassoon, which he has done professionally in the New York Philharmonic-Symphony Orchestra, in Hollywood, and elsewhere. Weiss studied composition with Weidig in Chicago, Lilienthal and Rybner in New York, and Schoenberg in Vienna. In 1932 he won a Guggenheim Fellowship.

His works include a *Ballade;* a Scherzo *American Life;* a *Kammersymphonie;* and *Five Pieces*—all for orchestra; four String Quartets; a Quintet for wind instruments; *Chamber Music* for woodwinds; a Trio for clarinet, flute, and bassoon; a Violin Sonata; and a Piano Sonata. He has also completed the first act of an opera—*David.*

RICHARD F. DONOVAN (1891——) is one of the Yale group. He studied at the Yale School of Music, and for many years has been a member of its faculty. When David Stanley Smith retired as dean, Donovan was appointed acting dean, in 1940. He was born in New Haven, Connecticut, November 29, 1891, and in addition to his studies at Yale he attended the Institute of Musical Art in New York, and then studied for a short time with Widor in Paris. He has taught at the Institute of Musical Art, at the Taft School in Connecticut, and at

Smith College. In New Haven he conducts the Bach Cantata Club and is organist and choirmaster at Christ Church.

In his own music, Donovan is advanced in his idiom. He has been active in the Yaddo Festivals and many of his works have been performed on these programs. His works include a *Serenade* for flute, violin, and cello; a Symphonic Poem *Smoke and Steel,* for orchestra (1932); *Wood-Notes* (1926) and a Symphony, for chamber orchestra (1937); many choral works, both sacred and secular; a Sextet for wind instruments and piano (1932); Four Songs for soprano and string quartet (1933); a Trio for violin, cello, and piano (1937); and a Suite for piano (1933), published by *New Music.*

DANE RUDHYAR (1895——) belongs with the experimentalists. He is very much of an atonalist, and rejects what he calls our subservience to European tone systems. He was born in Paris, France (Daniel Chennevière-Rudyard), March 23, 1895, studied at the Sorbonne and the Paris Conservatoire, and came to America in 1916 for the performance of his *Poèmes Ironiques* and *Vision Végétale* at a dance recital at the Metropolitan Opera House (1917). He remained in this country and later became a citizen. His orchestral works include *The Surge of Fire* (1921); *To the Real* (1923); *Ouranos* (1924); a Symphony (1928); *Hero Chants* (1930); and a *Sinfonietta* (1931). In 1934 he completed the piano score of a symphonic poem with recitation *Paean to the Great Thunder,* the first member of a trilogy called *Cosmophony.*

NICOLAS SLONIMSKY (1894——) has lived in Boston since 1925, where he has been active as a conductor in promoting ultramodern music. He was born in St. Petersburg, Russia, April 27, 1894, and came to the United States in 1923. For two years he was an instructor at the Eastman School in Rochester. He became an American citizen in 1931. As a composer he has written *A Study in Black and White, Four Russian Melodies* for clarinet and piano, and several other works. The *Black and White* Study uses atonal and polytonal effects, but is based on counterpoint in consonant intervals. He is also the author of an encyclopedic work *Music Since 1900,* which lists in chronological sequence all important music events from the beginning of the century to 1937. In recent years he has spent considerable time traveling and visiting in Central and South America, and has prepared a comprehensive book on Latin-American music.

* * *

And for brief mention, we have the following, born in the 1890's:

ISIDOR ACHRON

Born, Warsaw, 1892; came to America after Russian Revolution. Concerto for piano and orchestra; *Suite Grotesque,* for orchestra; *Nocturne Fantasia,* for violin and piano.

HANS BARTH

Born, Leipzig, Germany, 1897. Came to America as a child. Pianist, teacher, composer. Experimenter with quarter tones. Two Piano Concerti; two Piano Sonatas; *Pantomime Symphony;* opera *Miragia;* numerous piano pieces; and in quarter tones— Suite for strings, brass, and kettledrums; Concerto for piano and strings.

MORTIMER BROWNING

Born, Baltimore, Maryland, 1891. Sonatina for piano, violin, and cello; *Mary Poppins Suite* for orchestra; Concerto in F for theremin and orchestra; Piano Suite in D; Incidental music for plays—*Gala Night* and *Paging Danger;* numerous concert songs and piano pieces.

THEODORE CELLA

Born, Philadelphia, 1897. Harpist, composer. Orchestral works: *On a Transatlantic Liner; Through the Pyrenees; Alpine Impressions; Carnival;* and *The Lido.*

LOUIS CHESLOCK

Born, London, 1899. Came to America in 1901. Violinist, teacher, composer. Symphony; Violin Concerto; Horn Concerto; String Quartet; Violin Sonata; several tone poems for orchestra; choral music.

AVERY CLAFLIN

Born, Keene, New Hampshire, 1898. Opera *Hester Prynne;* Symphony; *Moby Dick Suite* for orchestra; one-act opera *The Fall of Usher;* chamber music.

ROBERT DOELLNER

Born, Manchester, Connecticut, 1899.

Teacher of composition in Hartford, Connecticut.

String Quartet won $1,000 prize (RCA) for best quartet by an American composer in 1945. *Poem* (from Shelley), Rochester Symposium, 1936.

JOHN DUKE

Born, Cumberland, Maryland, 1899.

Pianist, teacher, composer. Faculty member of Smith College since 1923.

Overture in D Minor for string orchestra (1928); Suite for unaccompanied cello (1934); Fantasie in A Minor for violin and piano (1937); Trio for violin, viola, and cello (1937); and numerous songs.

HAROLD GLEASON

Born, Jefferson, Ohio, 1892.

Prelude on a Gregorian Theme, for organ and orchestra (American Composers' Concerts, Eastman School, 1931).

FREDERIC HART

Born, Aberdeen, Washington, 1898.

Composer, teacher; faculty member, Sarah Lawrence College.

One-act opera *Romance of a Robot*, produced by Federal Music Theatre, New York, 1937; three-act opera *The Wheel of Fortune*; String Quartet; Suite for string trio; Concert Overture for orchestra.

WALTER HELFER

Born, Lawrence, Massachusetts, 1896.

Composer, teacher; Fellow American Academy in Rome, 1925; faculty member Hunter College, New York.

Symphony on Canadian Airs; Concert Overture in D Major; Overture *In Modo Giocoso*; *Water Idyl* and Prelude—Intermezzo—Fugue, for orchestra; choral works, chamber music.

A. C. KROEGER

Born, Hamburg, Germany, 1890.

Symphony in E flat (American Composers' Concerts, Eastman School, 1931).

ALLEN LINCOLN LANGLEY
Born, Newport, Rhode Island, 1892.
Violinist, composer.
Two Symphonies; *Pastorale* for orchestra.

ERIK LEIDZEN
Born, Stockholm, Sweden, 1894.
Fugue with Chorale (Rochester Symposium, 1936); *Scottish Rhapsody* for band.

MARJORIE T. MACKOWN
Born, London, 1896.
Theme and Variations for cello and orchestra (American Composers' Concerts, Eastman School, 1934); Quartet for piano and strings (same, 1936).

GEORGE McKAY
Born, Harrington, Washington, 1899.
Composer, teacher; associate professor, University of Washington.
Fantasy on a Western Folk Song (1933); *Harbor Narrative;* American Dance Symphony *Epoch; Symphonic Prelude in American Idiom; Machine Age Blues;* three Sinfoniettas; *Retrospective Poem.*

BERYL RUBINSTEIN
Born, Athens, Georgia, 1898.
Composer, pianist, teacher; director, Cleveland Institute of Music.
Two Piano Concerti; Opera *The Sleeping Beauty,* produced by Juilliard Graduate School, 1938; *Scherzo* and *Suite* for orchestra; *Passepied* for string quartet; instrumental pieces, mostly for piano.

DONALD TWEEDY
Born, Danbury, Connecticut, 1890.
Composer, teacher.
L'Allegro, Symphonic Study; Three *Dances* for orchestra, from an unnamed ballet; incidental music for Sidney Howard's *Swords;* a Ballet *Alice in Wonderland;* chamber music.

CHARLES VARDELL
Born, Salisbury, North Carolina, 1893.

Joe Clark Steps Out, for orchestra (American Composers' Concerts, Eastman School, 1937, 1939, 1942); Symphony No. 1 *Folk Symphony from the Carolina Hills* (same, 1938). *Shelf Behind the Door* (same, 1942).

LAZAR WEINER

Born, 1897, Kiev, Russia.

Prelude, Dance, Little Story (American Composers' Concerts, Eastman School, 1934).

4. FROM THE 1900'S

AARON COPLAND (1900———) first won recognition as a talented composer who might someday conquer the jazz idiom and become its master rather than its servant. This phase of the composer's career culminated in two works which he composed in his middle twenties: *Music for the Theatre* (1925) and a Piano Concerto (1926). After the Piano Concerto, Copland cut the direct tie of his music to jazz, and became concerned with writing music for the new media opened to composers by the radio, the motion pictures, and the phonograph. His works in these fields, and his scores for ballets, render him truly a composer of *Gebrauchsmusik*—music for use, or, if you wish, music for a specific purpose.

Copland was born in Brooklyn, November 14, 1900, of Russian-Jewish parents. The family name was originally Kaplan, but his father, on landing in England in 1876, was supplied by immigration officials with an impromptu spelling of his name as it sounded when he pronounced it. So Copland it has been ever since.

After his graduation from the Boys' High School in Brooklyn, Copland started the study of harmony and composition with Rubin Goldmark in 1917. After four years he went to Paris to the American school at Fontainebleau, and finally studied with Nadia Boulanger. He came home in 1924, and has since been active in New York as a composer and as a lecturer. He was the first composer to receive a Guggenheim Fellowship (1925–27); he has been a lecturer at the New School for Social Research, New York; and he has been an active worker in helping to advance the interests of his fellow composers. With Roger Sessions he inaugurated and maintained for several years the Copland-

Sessions Concerts which presented programs largely devoted to the works of young and as yet unrecognized American composers. He was also the founder of the American Festivals of Contemporary Music which are held at Yaddo in Saratoga Springs, New York. He is a member of the faculty of the Tanglewood School in Lenox, Massachusetts.

His first work of distinction had its initial performance at Fontainebleau—a Scherzo-Humoristique for piano, *The Cat and the Mouse*. While he was abroad he wrote a one-act ballet named *Grohg* which was never performed in its original form, but which later formed the basis of another work. Howard Hanson conducted in 1925 an excerpt from *Grohg* entitled Cortège Macabre, but aside from that performance the entire work seemed laid aside and forgotten. When the RCA-Victor Company announced a $25,000 prize for a symphonic work in 1929, Copland immediately set to work on a *Symphonic Ode*, but about a month before the competition was to close he realized that he could not finish the *Ode* in so short a time. As a last resort he took *Grohg* from his shelves, extracted a set of three dances from it, called them a *Dance Symphony* and mailed it to the judges. The work was one of five which won the $5,000 each. The other awards went one each to Ernest Bloch and Louis Gruenberg, and two to Robert Russell Bennett. *Dance Symphony* was first performed by the Philadelphia Orchestra under Stokowski in April of 1931, and had its first New York hearing April 10, 1937 at a Philharmonic-Symphony concert under Rodzinski.

Copland's First Symphony, originally performed by Walter Damrosch and the New York Symphony in 1925, was a Symphony for organ and orchestra. Later it was extensively revised by the composer and played in Berlin (1932), by the Chicago Symphony (1934), and by the Boston Symphony in Boston and New York (1935).

The Suite *Music for the Theatre,* for small orchestra, was composed at the Peterboro Colony in the summer of 1925 and had its first performance in November of the same year by Koussevitzky and the Boston Symphony. In December it was performed at one of the League of Composers concerts in New York. It is an extremely effective piece, and is still heard occasionally.

The Piano Concerto was written in 1926 and the composer played it the following year with the Boston Symphony Orchestra. In this work Copland took jazz formulae and developed them so that they were formulae no longer. Some complained that the work had no spiritual value, only animal excitement.

In 1937, when Copland was commissioned by the Columbia Broadcasting System to compose an orchestral piece he responded with a work which he called merely *Music for Radio*. He felt that he was unable to give it a more specific title. The broadcasters accordingly asked members of the radio audience to suggest names. From over a thousand replies, *Saga of the Prairie* was selected. Copland's only description of the piece was that "it lasts about ten minutes, starting allegro vivace, forte, and ending quietly."

In the same year (1937) Copland produced an operetta for school children, *The Second Hurricane*. This was characteristic of his interest in *Gebrauchsmusik*; he felt that American composers have obstacles to overcome in addressing their music exclusively to concert audiences, and that the youth of the country provide a more open-minded and unbiased audience.

Continuing his interest in music for specific purposes, Copland has provided scores for the ballets *Hear Ye! Hear Ye!* (1934), *Billy the Kid* (1938), *Rodeo* (1943), and *Appalachian Spring* (1945) which was given a citation by the New York Music Critics' Circle. The music from *Billy the Kid* has been played in concert form by many of our major orchestras. For the sound pictures Copland has written the music for *Of Mice and Men, Our Town*, and the documentary film *The City* which is frequently heard as a concert piece under the title *Quiet City*.

The orchestral works of recent years include a *Symphonic Ode*, introduced by the Boston Symphony in 1932; *Statements*, commissioned by the League of Composers in 1935–36; *El Salón México* (1937) which has become a highly popular piece in orchestral concerts and on phonograph records; *An Outdoor Overture* (1938); *A Lincoln Portrait* (1942), for orchestra and narrator, commissioned by André Kostelanetz and first presented with the Cincinnati Symphony, May 14, 1942; a *Short Symphony* (1943); and a *Fanfare for the Common Man* (1944). The list of instrumental compositions includes also a set of Piano Variations; a Piano Sonata; a Trio; two pieces for string quartet; a Violin Sonata; and a Cello Sonata.

Copland is today one of the most performed of American composers, and he is undoubtedly one of the most important of them. His work is notable for its economy of means, for its ability to make its point directly and without overelaboration. At times he is highly dissonant, but his music is seldom forbidding or oversevere in its angularity. His film scores are a model of restraint, and mark a notable and refreshing departure from the Hollywood habit of using bombast and fanfares to underline the "stupendous" nature of its "bigger and better" feature films.

Copland's talents have shown a steady growth. He has passed through several periods in his development and he has come now to a command of his media and his materials and has ceased to grope for the expression he was seeking. In addition to his composing, Copland is the author of two widely used books: *What to Listen For in Music* (1939), and *Our New Music* (1941).

At the close of the 1941–42 season, the First Symphony of PAUL CRESTON (1906———) was voted the award of the Music Critics' Circle of New York as the best American orchestral composition played for the first time during the season. The work was first performed by the Symphony Orchestra of the National Youth Administration in New York, February 22, 1941, and has had subsequent performances by the Philadelphia Orchestra (1943) and the St. Louis Symphony (1944).

Creston was born *Joseph Guttoveggio* in New York City, October 10, 1906. His childhood nickname Cress later developed into the Paul Creston which is his official name today. He studied various branches of music with Randegger, Déthier, and Pietro Yon, but was self-taught in theory and composition. In 1938 and 1939 he was awarded Guggenheim Fellowships, in 1943 a $1,000 award from the American Academy of Arts and Letters, and in 1945 another $1,000 from the Alice M. Ditson fund. For a number of years he has been organist at St. Malachy's Church in New York. He also composes and conducts for radio programs.

The works of Creston's which, to date, have been heard the most are the two *Choric Dances* which were introduced by the National Symphony Orchestra under Hans Kindler, March 3, 1940. The second of them has had important repeat performances by the NBC Symphony Orchestra under Toscanini (1942) and by the New York Phil-harmonic-Symphony (1943). A *Pastorale and Tarantella* for or-chestra was played by the NBC Symphony, March 28, 1942, and by the National Orchestral Association in New York the following March 28.

Creston's interests are varied, and range from acoustics and aes-thetics to musicotherapy. He is not an experimentalist in his composi-tions, however, for although his harmonies are often advanced, the form and construction of his work move along conservative lines. In addition to a Second Symphony, performed for the first time by the New York Philharmonic-Symphony, February 15, 16, and 18, 1945, Creston's other works include a *Prelude and Dance* for orchestra; *Three Chorales from Tagore*, for orchestra; a *Threnody* which was played by the Cincinnati Symphony in January, 1941; a *Fanfare for Paratroopers; a Chant of 1942;* a Concerto for saxophone and orches-tra introduced by the Philadelphia Orchestra, January, 1944; a Partita for flute, violin, and strings; a Concertino for marimba and orchestra; a *Fantasy* for piano and orchestra; and a long list of chamber music works.

Since 1934, OTTO LUENING (1900——), known to music lovers as both composer and conductor, has been head of the Music Depart-ment at Bennington College, in Vermont. He was born in Milwaukee, June 15, 1900. From 1914 to 1917 he studied in Munich, and from 1917 to 1920 in Zürich, with Jarnach and Busoni, among others. Dur-ing these years he was active as a flutist and as a conductor of opera and light opera. From 1925 to 1928 he was coach and executive director of the opera department at the Eastman School in Rochester, also assistant conductor, and later conductor, of the Rochester American Opera Company. From 1930 to 1932 he worked on a Guggenheim Fellowship, and for the following two years was associate professor at the University of Arizona.

He has a long list of works. For orchestra there are two Symphonic Poems; a *Divertimento;* two Symphonic Interludes; a *Serenade;* a *Dirge;* a Symphony; a Suite for strings; and a work entitled *Amer-icana.* For chamber orchestra the list includes a Symphonietta; *Prelude to a Hymn-Tune;* and a Concertino; while the chamber music works add up to more than twenty—among them three Quartets; two Sonatas for violin and piano; a Sextet; and a Piano Sonata. Luening has written also an opera *Evangeline,* in four acts. With Ernst Bacon he composed a *Coal Scuttle Blues* for two pianos.

Luening holds extremely practical ideas about the problems of the American composer. He has been (and says he still is) called in turn "conservative, ultramodern, a stylist, vulgar, imposing, a melodist, folksy, insane," mostly by critics or audiences familiar with one or two of his works. He believes that a composer should write for all types of mediums, should do some experimenting, compose for any occasion for which he is called upon to supply music, expand all forms after having mastered them, create new forms, and generally interest himself and make himself useful whenever he can. Then, Luening points out, his immortality will be decided by audiences, critics, colleagues, and time—which may mean the next two hundred years, so he need not worry about it.

Before coming to the United States in 1922, NICOLAI BEREZOWSKY (1900——) was first violinist at the Bolshoi Theatre in Moscow, and music director of the School for Modern Art. He was born in St. Petersburg, May 17, 1900. For five years after his arrival in this country he was a first violinist of the New York Philharmonic-Symphony. He has been a member of the Coolidge String Quartet, and is now a violinist in the symphony orchestra of the Columbia Broadcasting System.

His works include four Symphonies, composed respectively in 1925, 1929, 1936, and 1943; two String Quartets; *Toccata, Variations and Finale* for a string quartet with orchestra; a Violin Concerto; a *Concerto Lirico* for cello; a Viola Concerto; a Harp Concerto; two Woodwind Quintets; a String Sextet; a Piano Sonata; a *Fantasia* for two pianos; a *Sinfonietta;* a *Hebrew Suite* for orchestra; and a *Christmas Festival Overture.*

The *Sinfonietta* was awarded fifth prize in the 1932 competition of the National Broadcasting Company. Berezowsky was the winner also of a $1,000 award granted to each of fifteen creative artists of the American Academy of Arts and Letters in 1944.

VITTORIO GIANNINI (1903——) was preceded on the road to prominence by his sister Dusolina Giannini, operatic soprano. Born October 19, 1903, in Philadelphia, Giannini studied first with his mother, then for a short time in Milan, and finally at the Juilliard School. In 1932 he was given a Fellowship at the American Academy in Rome.

His list of works includes a Suite for orchestra (1931); a *Symphony in Memoriam Theodore Roosevelt,* commissioned by the New York State Theodore Roosevelt Committee (1935); Concerto for piano and orchestra (1935), and Concerto for organ and orchestra, commissioned by the Vienna *Gesellschaft der Musikfreunde* (1937); four produced operas—*Lucedia* (Munich, 1934), *The Scarlet Letter* (Hamburg, 1938), *Beauty and the Beast* (commissioned by the Columbia Broadcasting System and given a radio performance November, 1938), and *Blennerhassett* (radio performance, Columbia Broadcasting System, November, 1939); a *Requiem* for double chorus, soli, and orchestra produced in Vienna, May, 1937; and for chamber music combinations: Sonatas for violin and piano (1936) and Sonatas for piano solo (1934); a Trio (1934); a String Quartet (1930); a Piano Quintet (published by the Society for the Publication of American Music, 1933); a Quintet for woodwinds (1934); a Madrigal for four voices and string quartet (1939); and a *Triptych* for voice and string orchestra (1937). His Concerto for two pianos was performed by Luboschutz and Nemenoff in January of 1940, and his *Prelude, Chorale and Fugue* by the New York City Symphony, March 1, 1942.

DANTE FIORILLO (1905——) has a remarkable ability to escape attention. A most prolific composer, whose work is known and highly respected by a few musicians, he has had few conspicuous performances, and his name does not appear in any of the reference books, though they list composers of far less striking attainments. He was born July 4, 1905, in New York City, studied the cello at the Greenwich House Music School, and is self-taught in composition. He received a Guggenheim Fellowship in composition in 1935 which was renewed for three further successive seasons. In 1939 he won a Pulitzer Prize of $1,500 "on the basis of eight of the twelve symphonies he had composed." His *Music for Chamber Orchestra* was performed by Hans Lange and the Philharmonic-Symphony Chamber Orchestra; his Concerto for harpsichord and strings by Ralph Kirkpatrick with the Durieux Ensemble; his Concerto for oboe, horn, piano, strings, and timpani at a concert of the Society of Professional Musicians. The list of his works is incredibly long, particularly in an age when writing music does not "come easy" to many composers. In addition to the twelve symphonies there are eleven string quartets; several partitas for orchestra; several concerti for various instruments with orchestra; a number of string quartets; several piano quintets and trios; numerous sonatas for piano and for other instruments; a horn quintet; and other pieces for orchestra and for organ, as well as songs and choruses.

DAVID VAN VACTOR (1906——) is a flutist in the Chicago Symphony Orchestra, and a teacher at the Northwestern University School of Music. He was born in Plymouth, Indiana, May 8, 1906, and studied at Northwestern and later abroad—in Paris with Paul Dukas and in Vienna with Niedermayr. In 1938 his Symphony in D was awarded first prize in the New York Philharmonic-Symphony contest, and was performed by that organization in January of 1939. It was later played by the Chicago and Cleveland Symphony Orchestras.

His orchestral works include a symphonic prelude *Masque of the Red Death* (1932) which won honorable mention in the Swift Competition; a *Chaconne* for strings (1928); an Overture *Cristobal Colón* (1930); a *Passacaglia and Fugue* in D Minor (1933); an *Overture to a Comedy* (1935); a Concerto Grosso (1935); the prize-winning Symphony (1937); a Concerto for viola and orchestra (1941); a *Credo* (1942); *Gothic Impressions* (1942); *Variations Solennelles* (1942); and *Music for Marines*, played by the Indianapolis Symphony, March 27 and 28, 1943, and by the Chicago Symphony the following April 15. He has also for smaller combinations a Concerto for flute and twenty-one instruments (1931); a Suite for two flutes (1940); a *Divertimento* for chamber orchestra; a *Bagatelle* for string orchestra; and a Quintet for flute and strings which was published by the Society for the Publication of American Music in 1942.

NORMAND LOCKWOOD (1906——) is most widely known as a composer of major choral works—for his *Drum Taps* (1930); *Requiem* (1931); *The Hound of Heaven* (1937); and for *Out of the Cradle Endlessly Rocking*, which was dedicated to the New York World's Fair, and won a $500 prize awarded by G. Schirmer, Inc. In 1945 the Experimental Theatre of Columbia University produced an opera Lockwood had composed to Percy MacKaye's play *The Scarecrow*, which had had a successful stage career in 1908.

Lockwood was born in New York City, March 19, 1906, and studied at the University of Michigan School of Music, and in Europe with Boulanger and Respighi. He was awarded a fellowship at the American Academy in Rome in 1930, and in 1932 became a faculty member of the Oberlin Conservatory of Music. In 1938 he was made an associate professor of music. In 1943, and again in 1944, he was awarded a Juilliard Fellowship.

His instrumental works include a work which won the Swift Award of $1,000 in 1935, *A Year's Chronicle;* a Symphony, performed in 1935 by the Chicago Symphony, and a Quintet for piano and strings.

ANIS FULEIHAN (1900——) was a piano pupil of Alberto Jonas, but was principally self-taught as a composer. He was born on the Island of Cyprus, April 2, 1900, and came to the United States in 1915.

Eugene Goossens was the first to introduce one of Fuleihan's major orchestral works—*Mediterranean,* a Suite for orchestra. That was in 1935 and the piece has since been performed by several other major orchestras. Concerto No. 1, for piano and string orchestra, was played by the composer with the National Orchestral Association; Concerto No. 2, for piano and full orchestra, by Eugene List with the New York Philharmonic in December, 1938. Both the earlier works have been performed in England, in concert and for broadcasting.

In 1936, Fuleihan's *Preface to a Child's Storybook* was played by the National Orchestral Association, and on New Year's Eve, 1936, the Philharmonic-Symphony Society, under Barbirolli, gave the première of his First Symphony. His further works include a *Symphonic Episode;* a Suite for chamber orchestra; a symphonic poem *Calypso; Fiesta,* for orchestra; a *Symphony Concertante* for string quartet and orchestra, performed by the New York Philharmonic-Symphony in April, 1940; a Concerto for two pianos and orchestra; a Violin Concerto (1943); a Concerto for theremin (1945); a Sonata for piano; a set of Preludes for string quartet; and a number of shorter pieces, including songs and choruses.

Fuleihan disclaims all nationalistic aims, as well as any attempt at "Germanic profundity." His music does not go in for heroics; it is simple and transparent in texture, and brilliantly scored. In 1939 he received a Guggenheim Fellowship.

ROSS LEE FINNEY (1906——), associate professor of music at Smith College, was awarded a Guggenheim Fellowship in 1937, and in the same year won a Pulitzer Traveling Scholarship. He was born in Wells, Minnesota, December 23, 1906, and studied with Roger Sessions, Donald Ferguson, and Edward B. Hill. In Europe he worked with Malipiero, Alban Berg, and Nadia Boulanger.

His orchestral works include a Piano Concerto (1934); a Violin Concerto (1936); and a *Prelude for a Drama* (1937). A choral work *John Brown* was composed in 1939, and the dance drama *Masse Mensch* (1936) was given nine performances at Smith College. His chamber music list numbers a Trio (1931); two Piano Sonatas (1932 and 1933); a Sonata for violin and piano (1934); two String Quartets (1935 and 1937), and a Sonata for two cellos (1942). In September, 1940, at Yaddo, he sang his own *Bletheris, a Monody, from the Hamlet of Archibald MacLeish*, with chamber orchestra accompaniment.

PAUL NORDOFF (1909———) is a graduate of the Juilliard School, and since 1938 has been head of the composition department at the Philadelphia Conservatory of Music. He was born in Philadelphia, June 4, 1909. In 1933, and again in 1935, he was awarded a Guggenheim Fellowship; in 1933 his *Prelude and Variations* for piano won him the Bearns Prize from Columbia University; and in 1940 he received a Pulitzer Scholarship.

While he was in Europe in 1934, Nordoff played his Piano Concerto with the Groningen Orchestra in Holland. In 1934 his *Triptych*, three songs with Dryden texts, was sung at the Juilliard School. His *Prelude and Three Fugues* for orchestra were played in their original version for two pianos at a League of Composers concert in New York, March, 1933, and one of the *Fugues* was performed in its orchestral form by Stokowski and the Philadelphia Orchestra in April, 1937. A Concerto for two pianos and orchestra was performed by the composer and Allison Drake with the Federal Symphony Orchestra of New York, May, 1939.

In addition to these works, Nordoff has composed a *Secular Mass* (1935); two String Quartets (1932 and 1935); a Piano Quintet (1936); a Sonata for violin and piano (1932); Incidental Music to *Romeo and Juliet* and to *St. John* (for Katharine Cornell); an opera *The Masterpiece* (1941); a Sonata for cello and piano (1941); and numerous songs and piano pieces. Among the latter are several modernized piano settings of Stephen Foster songs.

BURRILL PHILLIPS (1907——), a graduate of the Eastman School, has associated himself with American backgrounds in two orchestral works which have been widely played. The first is *Selections from McGuffey's Readers,* which was first performed at the American Composers' Concerts in Rochester, 1934, and later by major orchestras in various cities. Three American poems form its basis, and are presented in the simple manner of the McGuffey Readers—*The One Hoss Shay, The Courtship of Miles Standish,* and *The Midnight Ride of Paul Revere.* The other work, *Courthouse Square,* was first performed at the American Composers' Concerts in 1935, and was played by the Philadelphia Orchestra in 1937 (April 9 and 10). In 1937 it was presented as a ballet at the Eastman Festival in Rochester. It portrays various phases of small town life.

Phillips was born in Omaha, Nebraska, November 9, 1907, and was graduated from the Eastman School in 1932. He then took his Master's degree at Eastman, and was appointed a faculty member. In 1944 he was given a $1,000 award by the American Academy of Arts and Letters, and in the same year received a commission from the Koussevitzky Foundation. Others of his works include a *Grotesque Dance from a Projected Ballet* (1932); two other ballets, *Princess and Puppet* (1935) and *Play Ball* (1938); a *Symphony Concertante* (1933); a Piano Concerto (1937), first performed at the Eastman Festival in 1943; a *Concert Piece* for bassoon and strings (1940); a *Dance* for orchestra (1940); a String Quartet (1940); and *Three Satirical Fragments* for orchestra (1941).

VLADIMIR DUKELSKY (1903——) may belong more appropriately in the chapter on "Our Lighter Musical Moments," for under the pen name of VERNON DUKE he has composed some of our most popular Broadway and Hollywood songs. Yet, under his own name, and as a symphonic composer, he has attracted considerable attention. Many of his larger works have been performed by leading organizations.

Dukelsky was born in Pskoff, Russia, October 10, 1903. He studied with Glière, and following the Revolution he lived for a time in Paris and London. Then he came to America in 1929 and later became a naturalized citizen. His compositions include two Symphonies; two Piano Concerti; *Dédicaces* for piano and orchestra; a Violin Concerto

Paul Creston
(See pages 515–516)

William Schuman
(See pages 539–540)

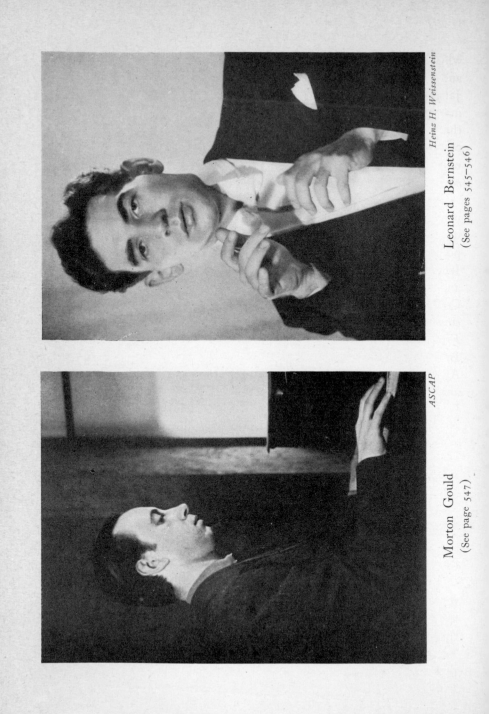

Heinz H. Weissenstein

ASCAP

Leonard Bernstein
(See pages 545-546)

Morton Gould
(See page 547)

which Ruth Posselt played with the Boston Symphony, March 19 and 20, 1943, and with the Philharmonic-Symphony in New York, January 5, 1944; an oratorio *The End of St. Petersburg*, performed in 1938 by the New York Schola Cantorum; some chamber music; three ballets; and a two-act opera *Demoiselle Paysanne*. He has also composed many suites of piano pieces, both under his own name and under that of Vernon Duke: among them, *Homage to Boston*, *Surrealist Suite*, *Barrel Organ Barcarolle*, and *Brooklyn Barcarolle*.

THEODORE WARD CHANLER (1902———) is known as a critic, having served both *Modern Music* and *The Boston Herald* in that capacity, but to a few people and by a very few works he is known as a composer of genuine talent and taste. He was born in Newport, Rhode Island, April 29, 1902, and studied with Shepherd, Goetschius, Bloch, and Boulanger. His Sonata for violin and piano was heard at the Copland-Sessions concerts in New York, and in Paris. He has also composed a Mass for two women's voices; a Suite for piano entitled *Five Short Colloquies*; and two series of *Epitaphs*, for voice and piano. In April, 1940, Chanler was commissioned under the terms of the Award in Composition offered jointly by Town Hall (New York) and the League of Composers to write a work for Dorothy Maynor, Negro soprano, to sing in the next season's Town Hall Endowment Series. In 1944 he was granted a Guggenheim Fellowship.

ISRAEL CITKOWITZ (1909———) was born in Russia, and was a pupil of Copland, Sessions, and Boulanger. His compositions are chiefly in the field of chamber music, with and without voices. His sensitive setting of William Blake's poem *The Lamb* has been performed by the Dessoff Choirs. His *String Quartet* was performed at the first Yaddo Festival; his *Sonatine* for piano was played by the Vienna section, and his *Song Cycle to Words of Joyce* by the London section, of the International Society for Contemporary Music.

The music of FREDERICK WOLTMANN (1908———) has been well represented on the programs of the American Composers' Concerts at the Eastman School in Rochester: by a Rhapsody for horn and orchestra (1935 and 1942); a Symphony, *Songs for Autumn* (1937); and *Variations on an Old English Folk Tune* (1939). He has also composed a Piano Concerto (1937); a tone poem *The Pool of Pegasus* (1937); a *Scherzo* (1937), and a *Poem* (1933), each for eight instruments; as well as numerous shorter works. His "The Coliseum at Night" from *Two Impressions of Rome* was performed by the New York Philharmonic Symphony under Mitropoulos during December of 1940.

Woltmann was born in Flushing, New York. As a child he sang for a season in the boys' chorus of the Metropolitan Opera House. He entered Columbia University and then received a scholarship at the Eastman School where he received his Bachelor of Music degree in 1937. In the same year he received a fellowship at the American Academy in Rome.

ELIE SIEGMEISTER (1909——) has identified himself with American folk music and early musical Americana in general. Coeditor with Olin Downes of *A Treasury of American Song,* and compiler of several collections of early American songs and ballads, he has done much to preserve our musical heritage and to make it available to the modern public. He has also been active as conductor of the American Ballad Singers and as a composer. He has written a Violin Sonata and several orchestral works—*A Walt Whitman Overture, Strange Funeral in Braddock,* and *Ozark Set;* numerous songs, including the war-inspired *Ballad of Douglas MacArthur, Freedom Train,* and *Great Guns.* Siegmeister was born in New York City, January 15, 1909, and studied at the Juilliard School. On numerous occasions he has lent his talents to political causes with his *May Day, Hip-Hip Hooray for the NRA,* and other songs. He is also the author and compiler of the widely circulated *A Music Lover's Handbook.*

BORIS KOUTZEN (1901——), before coming to America in 1923, was a member of the Moscow Symphony Orchestra under Koussevitzky. He was born in Uman, Southern Russia, April 1, 1901, and studied with Glière. Upon his arrival in this country he became a violinist in the Philadelphia Orchestra. Later he joined the NBC Symphony Orchestra in New York. He has also been head of the violin department of the Philadelphia Conservatory since 1930.

His orchestral works include a poem-nocturne *Solitude* (1927); a Symphonic Movement for violin and orchestra (1929); a symphonic poem *Valley Forge* (1931), presented by the National Orchestral Association, and by the NBC Symphony Orchestra, in 1940; a Symphony (1937); and a Concerto for five solo instruments (1934), which has been played by the National Orchestral Association and, in February, 1940, by the Boston Symphony Orchestra. He has also two String Quartets (1922 and 1936), one of them published by the Society for the Publication of American Music; a Sonata for violin and piano (1928); a Trio for flute, cello, and harp (1936); and numerous smaller works.

OSCAR LEVANT (1906——) became one of our most widely known musicians through his participation in the *Information Please* radio program. Here he displayed an amazing fund of facts about music and about other matters too. He was born in Pittsburgh, Pennsylvania, December 27, 1906. He studied piano with Stojowski and composition with Schoenberg and Joseph Schillinger. Before establishing himself as a serious composer he wrote successful popular songs and was a pianist in jazz bands. His major works include a Piano Concerto (1936) which he has played with many orchestras, including the NBC Symphony and the Philadelphia Orchestra; an *Overture 1912* and a *Dirge,* introduced by the Boston Symphony in March, 1942; a Sonatina for piano; a String Quartet (1937); a *Nocturne* for orchestra (1936); and a Sinfonietta (1934). He has also composed music for sound films, and is the author of a book which was on the best-seller lists of 1940—*A Smattering of Ignorance.*

ABRAM CHASINS (1903——) came to the attention of the public when Josef Hofmann, Benno Moiseivitch, Josef Lhévinne, and a half dozen other pianists played his little Chinese pieces. Then he wrote twenty-four Preludes for piano, and finally a Piano Concerto which he played with the Philadelphia Symphony Orchestra in 1930.

He was born in New York, August 17, 1903. Musical from babyhood, as a little boy he was put to work with Mrs. Thomas Tapper, the friend of all true talent and who first discovered Leo Ornstein. Then he was discovered by Ernest Hutcheson. Josef Hofmann took him to Europe, and Rubin Goldmark gave him lessons in composition. For several years he taught composition at the Curtis Institute in Philadelphia, but he resigned in 1933 to devote his time to composing, to concert tours, and to radio broadcasting. In the latter field he performs in the dual role of commentator and pianist.

In his music Chasins has a modern concept of tone relationships, but he pays homage to his musical idols: Bach, Brahms, Wagner, Chopin, and Rimsky-Korsakoff. He dislikes all that seems affected in modern music, and he is such a skillful workman himself that he has little patience with badly made music, where technique is missing.

Chasins has a Second Piano Concerto which he first played with the Philadelphia Orchestra under Stokowski, March 3 and 4, 1933. In this work he made a conscious attempt to deviate completely from accepted conventions of structure. In utilizing the idea of a solo instrument with orchestra, he brought into consolidation several of the smaller forms—waltz, fugue, and others. The drawback to this plan was, of course, its tendency to the episodic and fragmentary, but Chasins managed to overcome this difficulty to a partial degree with his melodic inventiveness. After the première performances he rewrote the Concerto completely; in its revised form he played it in the spring of 1938 with the New York Philharmonic-Symphony Orchestra under Barbirolli.

Although RUDOLF FORST (1900——) studied with Daniel Gregory Mason at Columbia, he is largely self-educated in music. He was born in New York, October 20, 1900, and at one time was a violinist in the orchestra at the Music Hall, Radio City, New York, and a violin instructor at the New York College of Music. At present he is associated with Quinto Maganini as music editor of Edition Musicus, a publishing firm, and is employed as a sound equipment expert by the Radio City Music Hall. His works include two String Quartets, of which the first won third prize in the NBC chamber music contest of 1937; a Symphonic Rhapsody (based on two Ozark folk tunes) (1937); a Symphony (1937); a *Symphonietta* for strings (1936); a *Sonata da Camera* (1937); and a Sonata for cello and piano (1932).

ALEXANDER LANG STEINERT (1900——), a pupil of Loeffler, d'Indy, Gédalge, and Koechlin, spent three years at the American Academy in Rome. His orchestral works number *Southern Night* (1926); *Leggenda Sinfonica* (1931); *Three Poems by Shelley*, with soprano solo (1932); and a *Concerto Sinfonico* with piano solo (1934); he has also a Sonata for violin and piano (1925); a Trio (1927); and a Sonata for piano solo (1929). He was born in Boston, September 21, 1900. Since 1940 he has been in Hollywood, composing and conducting music for motion pictures.

JOSEPH WAGNER (1900——) was for more than twenty years (from 1923) assistant director of music in the Boston Public Schools, and was the founder, and for nineteen years the conductor, of the Boston Civic Symphony Orchestra. He was born in Springfield, Massachusetts, January 9, 1900, and studied at the New England Conservatory. He had further lessons in composition with Nadia Boulanger, and in conducting with Weingartner and Monteux. His compositions include a Symphony (1934); a Piano Concerto (1929); a *Rhapsody* for piano, clarinet, and strings (1928); a *Dance Divertissement*; a ballet *The Birthday of the Infanta* (1935); and other works.

IRVINE McHOSE (1902——), a member of the composition faculty at the Eastman School, has composed a number of works, including a Concerto for oboe and orchestra, which was first performed at the Eastman Festival in 1932, and repeated ten years later. He was born in Lancaster, Pennsylvania, May 14, 1902, and was educated at the Eastman School.

ARTHUR KREUTZ (1906——) was a violin pupil of Cecil Burleigh and John Meganck, and studied composition with Edward Stringham, Roy Harris, and Sigfrid Prager. Since 1940 he has been instrumental director and conductor of the orchestra at the Georgia State College for Women.

His first Quartet, Opus 2, was published in 1935. A Symphony in three movements entitled *Music for Symphony Orchestra* (radio première, 1940), and his *Paul Bunyan* Suite were awarded the *Prix de Rome* in 1940. A *Study in Jazz* (*To a Jitterbug*) was produced in 1943, and in the same year he won a Guggenheim Fellowship. He was born in La Crosse, Wisconsin.

ZOLTAN KURTHY (1902——) is a first violinist of the New York Philharmonic-Symphony. His principal works are a *Passacaglia* for organ; a String Quartet on American Indian Themes; a symphonic rhapsody *Puszta*, 1940; a six-minute *Overture* scored for two of every woodwind, played by the CBS Symphony Orchestra in 1940, and by the New York Philharmonic-Symphony in 1941; and a *Scherzo* for orchestra, 1941. Born in Hungary, Kurthy had his first lessons with his father, Sandor Kurthy. At nine he entered the Royal Academy of Music at Budapest where he studied violin with Mambriny, Memeny, and Hubay; organ with d'Antalffy; and conducting with Weiner and

Kodály. In 1923 he came to New York and joined the Philharmonic Orchestra.

ROBERT MILLS DELANEY (1903———) was a Guggenheim Fellow in 1929–30, and in 1933 winner of a Pulitzer Prize for his setting of Benét's *John Brown's Body*. He was born in Baltimore, Maryland, July 24, 1903, and studied both at home and abroad. In the United States he worked at the University of Southern California, and in Paris he was a student of Nadia Boulanger at the *Ecole Normale de Musique* and a private violin pupil of Capet. On completion of his training he became a theory instructor at the School of Music in Concord, Massachusetts, and later was music director at the Santa Barbara School in California. His list of works includes a *Don Quixote Symphony* (1930); a Symphonic Piece No. 1 (1935) and a Symphonic Piece No. 2 (1937); many choral works in addition to *John Brown's Song* (1931); several string quartets; and an early Violin Sonata (1927). His *Work 22* was performed by the New York City Symphony Orchestra, a unit of the WPA Federal Music Project, in March, 1940.

HERBERT INCH (1904———) was a Fellow of the American Academy in Rome (1931), and a graduate of the Eastman School of Music. He was born in Missoula, Montana, November 25, 1904, and since 1931 has taught at Hunter College, New York. For orchestra he has composed a Symphony (1932); a Piano Concerto (1937); *To Silvanus* (1933); an earlier *Variations on a Modal Theme* (1927), as well as a Suite for small orchestra (1929); and a *Serenade* for woodwinds and strings (1936). His chamber music list includes a Quintet (1930); *Mediterranean Sketches* for string quartet (1933); a Sonata for piano and cello (1934); a *Divertimento* for brass instruments (1934); a Piano Sonata (1935); and a String Quartet (1936). His *Answers to a Questionnaire* was performed at the Eastman Festival in Rochester, April 25, 1944.

ULRIC COLE (1905———) has had two works published by the Society for the Publication of American Music—a Sonata for violin and piano, and a Quintet for piano and strings. One of the more widely played of her works is the *Divertimento* for string orchestra and piano, which she herself introduced as soloist with the Cincinnati Symphony, March 31, 1939.

She was born in New York and studied in Los Angeles, then in New York with Goetschius, Lhévinne, and Goldmark, and in Paris with Nadia Boulanger. Her works include two Sonatas for violin and piano, one of them published by the Society for the Publication of American Music; a Concerto for piano and orchestra; a Suite for orchestra; a String Quartet; a Piano Quintet; a Suite for trio; and a Fantasy Sonata for piano.

ROBERT L. SANDERS (1906———) is dean of the School of Music at Indiana University. Prior to holding that position he had been a faculty member of the University of Chicago and the Chicago Conservatory of Music, and also conductor of the Chicago Civic Orchestra. He was born in Chicago, July 2, 1906. He studied in that city at the Bush Conservatory, and then in Europe with Respighi, Bustini, and Dobici. From 1925 to 1929 he was a Fellow at the American Academy in Rome. He gained prominence in 1938 when his *Little Symphony in G* was a co-winner of the New York Philharmonic-Symphony's contest for a short symphonic work.

Several years before winning the Philharmonic-Symphony prize, Sanders had heard another of his works performed by the same organization, when *Saturday Night,* a "barn dance," was played in February, 1934. This piece, subsequently published, is built on four original melodies, and adheres closely to traditional form. Other works include a Violin Concerto (1935); a Suite for Large Orchestra (1928); the symphonic *Scenes of Poverty and Toil* (1935); a Trio (1926); a Violin and Piano Sonata (1929); a Cello and Piano Sonata (1932); a String Quartet (1929); and several choral works.

ISADORE FREED (1900———) studied at the Philadelphia Conservatory of Music and the University of Pennsylvania, and privately with Ernest Bloch and Vincent d'Indy. He was born in Russia, March 26, 1900, and was brought to America at the age of three.

His orchestral works number two Suites published in Paris, *Jeux de Timbres* (1931) and *Triptyque* (1932); an earlier Suite *Vibrations* (1928); a symphonic rhapsody *Pygmalion* (1926); a *Ballad* for piano and small orchestra (1925); a Suite *Pastorales* (1936); and a Symphony (1937). He has also written two String Quartets, a Quartet for piano and strings published in 1944 by the Society for the Publication of American Music, and other chamber music works.

If the life of CHARLES NAGINSKI (1909–1940) had been spared, he might have become one of our most distinguished composers, for the relatively few works he composed showed great promise. He was born in Cairo, Egypt, and came to America in 1927. He studied with Rubin Goldmark at the Juilliard School, and did some further work with Roger Sessions. In 1938 he received a fellowship of the American Academy in Rome. He became an American citizen, and was just gaining recognition when he was drowned in a lake near Lenox, Massachusetts while attending the Berkshire Festival, August 4, 1940. His works included a Sinfonietta, a *Children's Suite*, a ballet entitled *The Minotaur*, and a number of highly individual songs.

*   *   *

It was not easy to take GEORGE ANTHEIL (1900——) seriously after the production in New York of his *Ballet mécanique* in 1927, with its score calling for several player pianos and all sorts of mechanical contraptions, all calculated to produce what to uninitiated ears was nothing but rhythmic noise and din. And since that time the man's career has been so varied that it is difficult to characterize him.

He was born in Trenton, New Jersey, July 8, 1900. He studied with Constantin von Sternberg in Philadelphia, and had some lessons from Ernest Bloch. At the age of twelve he began to compose, and played modern music in public. For many years he lived abroad and his works were first played there. His *Zingareska*, a symphony in which jazz was used, was played in Berlin in 1922, and a String Quartet was heard in Paris in 1926. His Symphony in F was played in 1926 in Paris under Golschmann, and his Piano Concerto under the same auspices the next year. For the Berlin State Theatre he wrote incidental music to Sophocles's *Oedipus*, and in 1929 he became assistant musical director there. His ballet *Fighting the Waves*, to a text by W. B. Yeats, was produced in the same year at the Abbey Theatre in Dublin, Ireland.

In 1930 his opera *Transatlantic* was performed at the State Theatre in Frankfort. Among other ingredients it employed jazz of an old-fashioned type, in the service of a libretto that presented a caricature of American life. The plot had to do with a beautiful woman of doubtful origin named Helen who tried to decoy Hector, the hero, candidate for the presidency. There was a feverish struggle for power and for love; scenes at dances, booze parties, political meetings, attempts at murder, until finally Hector rescued Helen from suicide on Brooklyn Bridge and was elected president.

In 1932, and again in 1933, the jury for awarding Guggenheim Fellowships took Antheil seriously enough to include him on their list of beneficiaries, and John Erskine collaborated with him in an opera *Helen Retires*, produced by the Juilliard School in February, 1934. Lawrence Gilman called Antheil's music for this opera "disheartening . . . with its blend of Puccini and Strauss, musical comedy and sophisticated jazz, its plebeian humors and its almost unrelieved banalties."

In recent years Antheil has been in Hollywood composing scores for Paramount Pictures. Among them have been *Once in a Blue Moon, The Plainsman,* and *The Buccaneer.* In addition he signs a syndicated newspaper column containing advice to the lovelorn. These activities, however, have not removed Antheil from the concert field. His Fourth Symphony received what was announced as its "world première" in a broadcast by the NBC Symphony Orchestra under Leopold Stokowski, February 13, 1944. The advance announcement of the event stated that "the new symphony brings a change in Antheil's style. It is more impulsive, more emotional than his previous compositions. Architectonically it follows a modernized symphony style and the instruments are the conventional ones of the standard orchestra." In other words, no more player pianos.

COLIN McPHEE (1901——) was at one time known principally as a member of the experimentalist group. Following a visit to Bali in 1931, which was extended from the originally intended six months to six years, he became a specialist in Balinese music. In 1942 and 1943 he was granted a Guggenheim Fellowship to pursue his researches further and to prepare a book on the subject.

Born in Montreal, Canada, March 15, 1901, McPhee studied composition with Strube, LeFlem, and Varèse, and piano with Friedheim and Philipp. His music was introduced by the now defunct International Composers' Guild in the 1920's, and has been heard on the programs of the Copland-Sessions Concerts, the Pan-American Association of Composers, and the League of Composers. He was quoted in Wallingford Riegger's article in *American Composers on American*

Music as saying he had been trying to convey through music "an emotion resulting from contact with daily life—its noise, rhythm, energy, and mechanical daring." It was not program music that he had in mind, but a "tonal structure," which, "while orderly and complete," should be "as complex as the structure of a large bridge." "My output has been small for the past few years," he wrote in 1932, "as I have . . . mistrusted my natural facility."

McPhee's works from these years included a Concerto for piano and orchestra; a *Sarabande* for orchestra; a one-movement Symphony; a Concerto for piano and eight wind instruments, published by *New Music;* a Sonatina for two flutes, clarinet, trumpet, and piano; and scores for two very interesting "modernistic" films: *Mechanical Principles* and H_2O.

The years in Bali gave a new impetus to McPhee's music, and directed his talent into fresh and rewarding channels. In 1936 he produced a symphonic work *Bali,* and later transcribed a set of three pieces of *Balinese Ceremonial Music* for two pianos. In response to a League of Composers commission he wrote a choral work *From the Revelation of St. John the Divine,* for men's chorus, two pianos, three trumpets, and timpani, first sung by the Princeton Glee Club. In the summer of 1940 he furnished incidental music for Paul Robeson's performance of Eugene O'Neill's *Emperor Jones.*

RUTH PORTER CRAWFORD (1901———) is a graduate of the American Conservatory of Chicago where she studied with Adolf Weidig, Heniot Levy, and others. She was born in East Liverpool, Ohio, July 3, 1901. In 1930 she received a Guggenheim Fellowship for study in Berlin and Paris, and during the late thirties settled in Washington, where the work of her husband Charles Seeger, in the Resettlement Administration and in the Federal Music Project of the Work Projects Administration, brought her into contact with American folk music. In this connection she collaborated with John and Alan Lomax in the editing of the second volume of *American Folk Songs and Ballads.*

Miss Crawford is very much the modernist, and her original works are designed primarily for what her husband has described as a "particular group of people who are interested in that sort of thing." In 1933, her *Three Songs* for contralto, oboe, piano, and percussion, with orchestral ostinato, were chosen as one of two American works on the programs of the Festival of the International Society for Contemporary Music in Amsterdam. Her works include also a Violin Sonata; a String Quartet; *Three Movements* for wind instruments and piano; *Two Movements* for chamber orchestra; four *Diaphonic Suites* for flute, oboe, clarinets, and celli; and numerous other pieces.

GERALD STRANG (1908——) has been assistant to Arnold Schoenberg in the Music Department of the University of California in Los Angeles since 1935. He was born in Claresholm, Alberta, February 13, 1908, and was graduated from Leland Stanford University. He has interested himself particularly in comparative musicology, an interest he shared with Henry Cowell, with whom he became associated in 1933 as director of the New Music Workshops, and whom he succeeded in 1936 as director of the New Music Society and managing editor of the New Music Edition. In composition Strang has confined himself largely to chamber music, much of it based on elaborate canonic devices. He has composed numerous pieces for woodwind instruments, a Quintet for clarinet and strings, two String Quartets and a *Passacaglia* for string quartet, a choral work, *Vanzetti in the Death House, Incidental Music for a Satirical Play* and a piano piece *Mirrorrorrim.*

MARC BLITZSTEIN (1905——) belonged for a time among the experimenters, and to some it seemed that his brilliant musical talents did not belong in the field of composition. But like numerous other artists of recent years, the march of political and social events caught him up and persuaded him to place his music at the service of a cause. Blitzstein cast his lot with the political left, and whatever the effect on politics, the effect on his music was to give it a function and a direction which until then it had seemed to lack. *The Cradle Will Rock,* a play with music (originally written for the W.P.A. Theatre, and later produced in 1937 by the Mercury Theatre with Blitzstein himself presiding as pianist and narrator), was a powerful and biting allegory. It made a deep impression on its audiences and achieved a Broadway run of several months.

Blitzstein was born in Philadelphia, March 2, 1905. He studied at the University of Pennsylvania and at the Curtis Institute. He studied piano with Siloti, composition with Scalero, and abroad with Boulanger and Schoenberg. His early works included a Concerto for piano and orchestra; a set of Variations for orchestra; and numerous pieces of chamber music which were played at the Copland-Sessions concerts, the League of Composers concerts, and at the first Yaddo Festival. A sketch *Triple Sec* was included in the Garrick Gaieties, and then came *The Cradle Will Rock*.

In 1940 he composed a "radio song play" on commission from the Columbia Broadcasting System. Its title was *I've Got the Tune*, and it proved to be an allegory on Blitzstein's own career as a composer. Its moral was that the mission of the modern composer is to write music for the masses. To quote his own words: "The accepted and conventional audience of upper- and middle-class music lovers is being augmented by the untutored, fresh and yet amazingly critical public of working people, who until now have been unable to satisfy their hunger and love for music. My music is conditioned upon this observation. I know for whom I am writing, whom I would wish to please, stir, educate."

In 1940, Blitzstein was awarded a Guggenheim Fellowship, and in the following year he was ready with another opera, which, like *The Cradle Will Rock*, was concerned with the class struggle between trade-unionism and social injustice. Entitled *No for an Answer*, and produced at the Mecca Auditorium in New York, January 5, 1941, it portrayed a love scene, a labor-party meeting, an arrest, a fight, a fire, and the death of a union organizer. Virgil Thomson wrote of the opera in the New York *Herald Tribune* (January 12, 1941): "What makes the Blitzstein work . . . pungent just now . . . is the fact that its locale is here and that its language is our own. It is also of some impact that Mr. Blitzstein's musical style, as contrasted with the morass of respected, academic American music writing that bogged down our opera houses annually, until these institutions got tired of losing money and stopped it, is itself pretty pungent and deep."

Blitzstein composed music for the documentary film *Valley Town*, and he supplied the incidental music for the Orson Welles production of *Julius Caesar* at the Mercury Theatre, New York.

*   *   *

And now the rest of the composers from the 1900–1909 decade are presented briefly in the following list:

MARTHA ALTER

Born, New Bloomfield, Pennsylvania, 1904.

Orchestral Introduction and song from *Bill George* (American Composers' Concerts, Eastman School, 1932). Ballet: *Anthony Comstock* (same, 1932); Suite for violin, piano, and percussion (same, 1934).

WILLIAM AMES

Born, Cambridge, Massachusetts, 1901.

Two Symphonies; Rhapsody for orchestra; Sonata for violin and piano; Sonata for cello and piano; Two String Quartets; Quintet for piano and strings; Quintet for clarinet and strings; short instrumental pieces, songs, and choral music.

PARKER BAILEY

Born, Kansas City, Missouri, 1902.

Sonata for flute and piano, published by Society for Publication of American Music, 1929; compositions for organ, choruses, songs.

DAVID BARNETT

Born, New York, 1907.

Pianist, teacher, and composer.

Divertimento for orchestra.

EVELYN BERCKMAN

Born, Brooklyn, New York, 1900.

Ballets: *County Fair*, and *A Page from Homer;* Suite for harp, flute, and cello; *Swans* for orchestra; *Dr. Johnson's Tour to the Hebrides*, Suite for voice and flute; *Archangels*, Suite for three harps.

ANTON BILOTTI

Born, New York, 1904.

Pianist-composer.

Concerto for piano and orchestra; *Danse Macabre* for piano and orchestra; numerous piano pieces.

RADIE BRITAIN

Born, Amarillo, Texas, 1903.

Heroic Poem for orchestra; *Southern Symphony; Light,* and *Canyon,* for orchestra; *Theme and Variations on the Old Gray Mare;* choral and chamber music works.

MARK BRUNSWICK

Born, New York, 1902.

Ballet Suite *Lysistrata; Fantasia* for viola solo; Sonata for viola solo; Symphony for chorus and orchestra.

ELLIOTT CARTER

Born, New York City, 1908.

Two one-act operas: *Tom and Lily* and *One-act Opera;* two ballets: *Pocahontas* and *The Ballroom Guide;* Concerto for English horn and orchestra; two String Quartets; Flute Sonata; *Madrigal Book* for mixed voices; *The Bridge,* an oratorio; *Tarantella,* for male chorus and orchestra; an *a cappella* chorus *Heart Not So Heavy as Mine;* and *To Music,* a choral work.

ANTHONY DONATO

Born, Prague, Nebraska, 1909.

Three Imitations for string quartet (American Composers' Concerts, Eastman School, 1939); *Divertimento* for strings.

FILIPPI, AMADEO DE

Born, Ariano, Italy, 1900. Came to America in 1905.

Conductor, violinist, composer.

Overture to Shakespeare's Twelfth Night; Medieval Court Dances for orchestra; *Diversions* for string orchestra; Concerto for flute, bassoon, horn, trumpet, and strings; *Raftsman's Dance* for orchestra (based on Mississippi folk tunes, and commissioned by Columbia Broadcasting System); Suite for brass quartet; *Music for Recreation,* string orchestra; Piano Quintet; String Quartet; Sonata for viola and piano.

FLORENCE GRANDLAND GALAJIKIAN

Born, Maywood, Illinois, 1900.

Teacher, composer.

Symphonic Intermezzo (winner of fourth prize, NBC Orchestral Contest, 1932); *Tragic Overture* for orchestra (1934); Fantasie for violin and piano (1930); *Andante and Scherzo* for string quartet; Ballet, *Transitions* (1937); choral works.

RAY GREEN

Born, Cavendish, Missouri, 1908.

Composer, teacher; head of composition department, San Francisco Conservatory.

Concertino for piano and orchestra; Prelude and Fugue for orchestra; Music for *The Birds* of Aristophanes; Chamber music and choral works.

ARTHUR HENDERSON

Born, Caledonia, New York, 1908.

Sonata for violin and piano (American Composers' Concerts, Eastman School, 1937).

DOROTHY JAMES

Born, Chicago, Illinois, 1901.

Opera, *Paolo and Francesca* (performed in part, American Composers' Concerts, Eastman School, 1931); *Three Orchestral Fragments* (same, 1932); *The Jumblies* (Ann Arbor Festival, 1935).

HUNTER JOHNSON

Born, Benson, North Carolina, 1906.

Fellow, American Academy in Rome, 1933; Guggenheim Fellowship, 1941.

Prelude for orchestra (1929); Symphony (1931); Concerto for pianoforte and small orchestra (1935); *Andante* for flute and strings (1939); *Elegy* for clarinet and strings (1937); Sonatina for violin and piano (1937); Piano Sonata (1934).

GERALD KEENAN

Born, Hornell, New York, 1906.

Andante, Interlude, and Finale, for horn and strings (American Composers' Concerts, Eastman School, 1935).

GORDON KINNEY

Born, Rochester, New York, 1905.

Concert Piece for piano and orchestra (Rochester Symposium, 1936).

SOLOMON PIMSLEUR

Born, Paris, France, 1900; came to America in 1903.

Dynamic Overture; Impetuous Toccata and Fugal Fantasia; Fiery Sonata for Trio; Impetuous Sonata for violin and piano; *Symphonic Ballade* for orchestra.

HERMAN RUDIN

   Born, Rochester, New York, 1906.

   Prelude and Dance from an Impressionistic Suite (American Composers' Concerts, Eastman School, 1932); Suite for strings (same, 1934); *Symphonic Fragments* (same, 1934); String Quartet (same, 1937).

ALEXANDER SEMMLER

   Born, Germany, November 12, 1900; came to America, 1923. Composer and conductor for Columbia Broadcasting System since 1923.

   American Indian Suite; Sinfonietta; Times Square Overture (1942); *Pastoral Suite* for strings (1943). Arrangements: *Deep River; Habanera* from Carmen (1937); Moszkowski *Waltz,* Op. 34, No. 1.

TIBOR SERLY

   Born, Hungary, 1900; came to America in childhood.

   Composer; violist in Cincinnati Symphony (1927–28); Philadelphia Orchestra (1928–36); NBC Symphony Orchestra.

   Sonata for violin and piano (1923); Symphony (1937); String Quartet (1924); Viola Concerto (1929); *Two Symphonic Movements* for winds and percussion (1932).

MEREDITH WILLSON

   Born, Mason City, Iowa, 1902.

   Composer, flutist, conductor.

   Symphony; *O. O. McIntyre Suite* for orchestra; *The Jervis Bay,* Symphonic Poem; popular songs.

ALLAN A. WILMAN

   Born, Hinckley, Illinois, 1909.

   Winner of Paderewski Prize, 1935.

   Ballade of the Night, for voice and string quartet (American Composers' Concerts, Eastman School, 1937); Symphonic Poem *Solitude* (Boston Symphony, 1936); Symphonic Overture (1935); Piano Sonata (1930); Suite for violin and piano (1937).

5. COMPOSERS BORN SINCE 1910

Of the composers who have made their appearance since this volume was first issued, few have made faster progress than WILLIAM SCHUMAN (1910———). Born in New York City, August 4, 1910, he organized a jazz band in high school and started to compose popular songs. He studied harmony with Max Persin and associated himself with Tin-Pan Alley, as a song writer, arranger, and song-plugger. Meanwhile, he was becoming interested in symphonic music, and studied counterpoint with Charles Haubiel. He entered Columbia University and took Bachelor's and Master's degrees in music. In 1935 he went to Salzburg to study conducting, and in 1939 and 1940 he was awarded a Guggenheim Fellowship. Upon his return from Salzburg, in 1935, he became instructor at Sarah Lawrence College in Bronxville, New York, and in 1945 was appointed publication director of G. Schirmer, Inc. In the fall of 1945 he became president of the Juilliard School of Music. He remains on the staff of Schirmer's as special consultant.

Unlike George Gershwin, Schuman made a complete break with popular songs and has since devoted himself exclusively to serious works. He has returned to Broadway on occasion (he wrote the music for a sketch in Billy Rose's Revue *The Seven Lively Arts*, 1944), but not as a Tin-Pan Alley composer. Jazz has its place in his major works, but there is also present the influence of Roy Harris, who, while not one of Schuman's teachers in a formal sense, was his adviser and candid critic for a number of years. Nathan Broder, in an article "The Music of William Schuman" stated that the most prominent traits of Schuman's music are "boldness, originality, freshness, resourcefulness, and intensity of feeling." "There is little," Broder continued, "of what the average listener would be inclined to regard as grace or charm, but humor may be found, either of the burlesque sort . . . or of a subtler kind. But what strikes the listener most of all in this music is its complete honesty and integrity, its deep seriousness—even at its gayest— its unswerving fidelity to the highest aims. Schuman can be light and unpretentious but he is seldom trivial." [1]

[1] *Musical Quarterly*, January, 1945.

Schuman has composed four Symphonies. The First was written in 1935 and is scored for eighteen instruments. It was performed for the first time by the Gotham Orchestra, October 1, 1936. The Second was composed in 1937, and was first performed by the Greenwich Orchestra, May 25, 1938. Both works were later withdrawn by the composer for revision. The Third Symphony was completed in January of 1941 and presented by the Boston Symphony, October 17 of that year. In the following spring it received the award of the New York Music Critics' Circle. In this work the composer showed what Robert Lawrence, writing in the New York *Herald Tribune* (November 23, 1941), called a "superb rhythmical equipment." "One had only to hear the subject of his fugue," wrote Lawrence, "to recognize a composer who can accomplish anything he wants in the field of technique." Schuman's Fourth Symphony, completed the following August, was introduced January 22, 1942, by the Cleveland Orchestra, and was subsequently played by the Philadelphia Orchestra, April 4 and 6, 1942 in Philadelphia, and April 7 in New York.

Others of Schuman's orchestral works are the *American Festival* Overture (introduced by the Boston Symphony, October 6, 1939), based on a three-note theme which the composer describes as a New York boys' street-call; a Concerto for piano and small orchestra (1942); *Prayer in Time of War* (1943); Symphony for strings (1943); *William Billings Overture* (1943); and *Side Show* (1944). His *Newsreel, in Five Shots* (1941) was originally composed for band, but has been arranged also for orchestra.

Schuman has written much choral music. *Pioneers*, an eight-part *a cappella* chorus to a Walt Whitman text, was first sung by the Westminster Festival Chorus, May 23, 1938. *This Is Our Time*, designated as Secular Cantata No. 1, was presented by the People's Philharmonic Choral Society and the Philharmonic-Symphony Society at the Lewisohn Stadium, July 4, 1940. Secular Cantata No. 2 was *A Free Song*, also to a Whitman poem, and introduced March 26, 1943, by the Boston Symphony with the Harvard Glee Club and the Radcliffe Choral Society. This won a Pulitzer Prize of $500. There are also numerous other choral works, and three String Quartets composed, respectively, in 1936, 1937, and 1939. In 1944, Schuman composed the music for an Office of War Information film *Steeltown*.

SAMUEL BARBER (1910——) is one of the more widely played of the composers from this decade; two of his works—*Adagio for Strings* and *Essay for Orchestra*—were selected by Toscanini as the first American works to be played under his leadership by the NBC Symphony Orchestra in 1938. Shortly after the entry of the United States in the second World War, Barber entered the Army, and for the duration of the war many of his works had a military background, or indicated in some way his experiences at the time. His Second Symphony was dedicated to the Army Air Force. There were also a *Commando March*, introduced by the Boston Symphony, October 29 and 30, 1943, and *A Stop Watch and an Ordnance Map*, played by the Columbus (Ohio) Philharmonic, October 24, 1944.

Barber is a nephew of Louise Homer and was born in West Chester, Pennsylvania, March 9, 1910. He studied at The Curtis Institute (composition with Rosario Scalero), and by the time he was twenty-five years old had won several prizes: in 1928 and in 1933 the Bearns Prize from Columbia University, and in 1935 both the Pulitzer Scholarship and the American *Prix de Rome*. He won the Pulitzer Award again the next year. The work that won the 1933 Bearns Prize was the Overture to *The School for Scandal*, composed in 1932.

Barber's next major orchestral work, written in the following year, was entitled *Music for a Scene from Shelley*, taking for its inspiration certain lines from *Prometheus Unbound*. It was given its first performance in March, 1935, by the New York Philharmonic-Symphony under Werner Janssen. The composer's First Symphony was his *Symphony in One Movement*, composed while he was a Fellow at the American Academy in Rome, and first performed in Rome by the orchestra of the Augusteo under Molinari late in 1936. Artur Rodzinski introduced it to the United States with the Cleveland Orchestra in Cleveland in January, 1937, and in New York during the following month. In the summer of the same year Rodzinski conducted the Symphony at Salzburg and in London, announcing that he considered Barber one of the greatest of American composers. The work had a performance also by the New York Philharmonic-Symphony Orchestra in March of the same year.

After Toscanini's introduction of the *Adagio for Strings* in 1938, the work was performed by the New York Philharmonic-Symphony

Society, January 25 and 26, 1940. The *Essay for Orchestra* was subsequently performed by the Philadelphia Orchestra (1940) and the Boston Symphony (1943). The latter was followed by a *Second Essay for Orchestra*, which was played first by the New York Philharmonic-Symphony, April 16, 17, and 19, 1942, and by the Philadelphia Orchestra, the following October 23 and 24. In reviewing the performance by the New York Philharmonic, Jerome D. Bohm remarked in the New York *Herald Tribune:* "I received a definite impression that it has its roots in his [Barber's] reactions to the war. The thematic substance is strong and somewhat austere and is developed resourcefully and economically. It builds to a cannily constructed climax and the orchestration is masterly. It is an affirmative, closely knit score, emanating a courageous atmosphere."

The Second Symphony, dedicated to the Army Air Force, is descriptive in its content. It is not so much heroic in its intention, however, as it is seemingly reflective of the serene detachment and calm which fliers say they experience while in the air. The second movement, *Andante,* utilizes an electrical instrument which imitates the reiterated radio signal which keeps aviators on their course in flight. The work was first performed by the Boston Symphony in Boston, March 3 and 4, and in New York, March 11, 1942.

Barber's Concerto for violin and orchestra was performed for the first time by Albert Spalding and the Philadelphia Orchestra in 1941 in Philadelphia at the February 7 and 8 pair of concerts, and in New York, February 11. The following year (March, 1942) Ruth Posselt played it with the Boston Symphony; it was heard at the Eastman Festival, April 27, 1944; and it was later featured on a program of the New York Symphony, Stokowski conducting, with Roman Totenberg as soloist.

When Spalding played the work with the Philadelphians in New York, Virgil Thomson described it in the New York *Herald Tribune* (February 12, 1941) as "tenderly poetic in melody and disarmingly straightforward in its general make-up. . . . It cannot," he continued, "fail to charm by its gracious lyrical plenitude and its complete absence of tawdry swank."

Barber has written a number of chamber music works: a *Serenade* for string quartet; a String Quartet in B Minor; a Sonata for cello and piano; a *Capricorn Concerto* for flute, oboe, trumpet, and strings; and *Dover Beach*, for medium voice and string quartet. A choral work *God's Grandeur*, written in free, dissonant, polyphonic style, was performed at the Westminster Festival in Princeton, New Jersey in May, 1938.

GIAN-CARLO MENOTTI (1911——) is the composer of two operas produced at the Metropolitan Opera House—*Amelia Goes to the Ball* and *The Island God;* and of a radio opera *The Old Maid and the Thief*, commissioned by the National Broadcasting Company. Menotti was born in Milan, Italy, July 7, 1911, and grew up in an atmosphere of opera. In 1928 he came to America to study composition with Rosario Scalero at the Curtis Institute in Philadelphia. He has lived in this country since that time.

Amelia al Ballo ("Amelia Goes to the Ball") was first started in 1933 when the composer was twenty-two, and finished two and a half years later. It was first produced by the opera department of the Curtis Institute, in Philadelphia and in New York, and in March of 1938 it was presented by the Metropolitan in New York. Lawrence Gilman in the New York *Herald Tribune* (March 4, 1938) called it "an astonishing piece of work." "Its score," he wrote, "is written with a sense of the stage, an innate awareness of what will be effective in the theatre, a wit and gusto and deftness that are the product of two centuries or so of operatic tradition and inheritance."

The success of *Amelia* led to the commission from the National Broadcasting Company, and *The Old Maid and the Thief* was first broadcast in April of 1939. Again there was sparkling humor, and skill and craftsmanship. The libretto, like that of *Amelia*, was written by Menotti himself. In February of 1941 the work was given a stage performance by the Philadelphia Opera Company.

The Island God was produced for the first time by the Metropolitan on February 20, 1942. It is a one-act tragedy which has so little stage action that it could almost be considered a cantata. It showed, too, that Menotti's talents are more happily expressed in merry wit and jollity. As Virgil Thomson remarked in the New York *Herald Tribune* (February 21, 1942): "He [Menotti] proved in *Amelia at the Ball* his sense of theatrical values, but he has not proved in *The Island God* that he can do without a plot."

Aside from his operas, Menotti has composed a piano composition *Variations on a Theme of Robert Schumann,* which won the Carl F. Lauber Music Award in 1931; and a *Pastorale* for string orchestra and piano which was performed by the Philadelphia Chamber String Sinfonietta in 1935, and at the Saratoga (New York) Spa Music Festival in 1937.

BERNARD HERRMANN (1911——) became known as a composer of large ambitions when his dramatic cantata for male chorus, soloists, and orchestra, *Moby Dick,* was first produced by the New York Philharmonic-Symphony, April 11, 1940. His works had been performed previously, but this was something far more immense than anything he had tried before. On the whole, it was a successful attempt. Francis D. Perkins, writing in the New York *Herald Tribune* (April 12, 1940), announced that the work "reveals a remarkable command of the resources of instrumental color and timbre, an exceptional ability to depict with convincing vividness a wide variety of emotional hues and atmosphere." The libretto of *Moby Dick* was written by Clark Harrington.

Herrmann was born in New York City, June 29, 1911, and studied with Albert Stoessel, Philip James, and Bernard Wagenaar at the Juilliard Graduate School. His principal activities, aside from composing, have been the conducting of various programs over the Columbia Broadcasting System, where he has been a staff conductor since 1938. In 1943 he was appointed symphonic director. He has conducted the Columbia Workshop programs, the American School of the Air, and "Invitation to Music," and is known as a pioneer in presenting the first American performances of little known works.

The titles of many of Herrmann's compositions are based on native American subjects: *Moby Dick;* a *Currier and Ives Suite—The Skating Pond* for orchestra (1935); a tone poem, *The City of Brass* (1934), and Orchestral Variations on *Deep River* and *Water Boy* (1933).

In addition to the pieces with descriptive titles, his earlier works include a Sinfonietta for string orchestra (1935); a *Nocturne and Scherzo* for orchestra (1936), performed at the American Composers' Concerts in Rochester in January, 1938; a Violin Concerto (1937); a String Quartet (1932); and numerous shorter works.

On July 27, 1941, Herrmann's First Symphony was performed by the Columbia Symphony Orchestra under the composer's direction, and on December 16, 17, and 19, 1943, the New York Philharmonic-Symphony played a brief orchestral work *To the Fallen*. In addition to composing for radio, Herrmann also wrote the score for the motion picture *Citizen Kane*. In 1942 he received a $1,000 award from the American Academy of Arts and Letters.

One of the major events of the 1943-44 concert season in New York was the sudden prominence of LEONARD BERNSTEIN (1918——), a twenty-six year old musician who overnight found himself famous. Since that time he has continued his career in a manner to justify the acclaim he received on his debut. The previous summer Bernstein had been appointed assistant conductor of the New York Philharmonic-Symphony Society. In November, Bruno Walter became ill during his term as guest conductor, and Bernstein was called upon to take his place. With little preparation Bernstein led the concert so well that he not only received an ovation from the audience and the praise of the critics, but he was immediately assigned several further concerts by Artur Rodzinski, permanent conductor of the orchestra. Then followed numerous invitations to appear as guest conductor with orchestras in other cities.

Bernstein was born in Lawrence, Massachusetts, August 25, 1918. At first he intended to become a pianist, but at Harvard he studied composition with Walter Piston and Edward Burlingame Hill. Then he spent two years at the Curtis Institute in Philadelphia, and his summers at Tanglewood in the Berkshires, studying conducting with Koussevitzky. In the summer of 1942, Bernstein settled in New York, and endured the traditional hardships of young musicians. He gave music lessons at small fees and did some arranging for a music publisher who was sufficiently impressed with his talents to give him a weekly salary. Then came his appointment as assistant conductor of the Philharmonic-Symphony and his chance to show his abilities as a substitute for Walter at the concert of November 14, 1943. This was a Sunday afternoon affair, broadcast over the Columbia Broadcasting network, so the young man's success became a national rather than a local event. Within a short time the Bernstein career had become an Horatio Alger success story, with the hero requiring a secretary to handle his fan mail, to arrange appointments, and to protect him from the curious.

It was not long before he had a chance to establish himself as a composer, for at the Philharmonic-Symphony concert of March 29, 1944, he conducted the orchestra in a performance of his Symphony *Jeremiah*, which had been previously performed by the Pittsburgh Symphony. This is a work based on the Book of Lamentations and requiring a soprano soloist. The first movement is *Prophecy;* the second, *Profanation;* and the third, *Lamentation.* The following spring the work received the Music Critics' Circle Award as the best orchestral work by an American composer heard in New York that season.

During the same season Bernstein showed himself in a less serious, and altogether joyous, vein when his ballet *Fancy Free* was produced by the Ballet Theatre at the Metropolitan Opera House, New York, April 11, 1944. This was so entertaining that it achieved the status of a Broadway hit, and the house was sold out whenever it was announced on the company's bill. For the following season Bernstein incorporated some of the material from *Fancy Free* in a score for the musical comedy *On the Town,* and added to it a number of gay, sparkling songs. That, too, became an immediate success, and was one of the most popular musical comedies of the 1944–45 season.

With all this Bernstein found himself faced with a success so sudden and so great that it could easily destroy him. As Mark A. Schubart remarked at the conclusion of an article in the Magazine Section of *The New York Times* (January 28, 1945): "Bernstein's friends and well-wishing critics realize full well that the youthful musician's success represents, in a sense, the most serious obstacle he must overcome in maturing as a composer and as a conductor. His *Jeremiah* Symphony, for example, was generally regarded as the work of a talented young man, rather than that of a finished musician; and it is no easy feat for Bernstein, in view of his spectacular career, to give such opinion serious consideration. Yet it is generally agreed that Bernstein must overcome his success in order to achieve a position in the world of music which will be less striking, perhaps, but much more durable."

Others of Bernstein's works include a Sonata for clarinet and piano; a String Quartet; a humorous song cycle *I Hate Music;* and a Suite for piano *Seven Anniversaries.*

MORTON GOULD (1913——) is one of the most American of our composers because he brings to his symphonic scores a flavor of the American popular idiom in a manner which is never "arty," but which is simultaneously both Broadway and concert-hall. His product is a bit theatrical and in the Hollywood and radio manner, but it has proved immensely popular and is wholly sincere.

Gould was born in Richmond Hill, New York, December 10, 1913. He was a prodigy in childhood and started to compose at the age of four. When he was fifteen he was graduated from New York University. He studied music privately, and might easily have come to be an eccentric, for he enjoyed amazing his friends by being "an elbow pianist." Economic reverses made it necessary for the young man to earn his living, so he sought the thoroughly practical and remunerative Tin-Pan Alley. Eventually he found a place on the music staff of the Radio City Music Hall as arranger, and later with the National Broadcasting Company. He also became a conductor, and is now one of our leading directors of commercial radio programs.

All of this activity has given Gould a ready outlet for his own music, and he is, accordingly, one of the most frequently performed of our composers, not only on the radio but in the concert halls as well. His *Chorale and Fugue in Jazz* was played by Stokowski and the Philadelphia Orchestra in January, 1936; he has played his Piano Concerto with various leading orchestras; and Fritz Reiner commissioned his *Foster Gallery*, a work based on melodies by the immortal Stephen. His first *American Symphonette*, particularly its *Pavane* movement, is a radio and concert favorite. There is also a second *American Symphonette* composed in 1940. *A Lincoln Legend* was introduced by the NBC Symphony Orchestra, November 1, 1942; Spirituals in *Five Movements* by the New York Philharmonic-Symphony, November 18, 1942, and *Symphony on Marching Tunes* by the same orchestra June 4, 1944. Others of Gould's works are a Cantata; a Symphony; a *New China March*; a *Red Cavalry March*, and an *American Salute;* and for piano, three Sonatas; an *Americana Suite;* and a *Boogie-Woogie Etude.*

DAVID DIAMOND (1915——) has been a frequent prize winner. In 1935 he won an Elfrida Whiteman Scholarship; in 1938, and in 1941, Guggenheim Fellowships; then a prize from the American Academy in Rome (1942); the Paderewski Prize in 1943; and a $1,000 award from the American Academy of Arts and Letters in 1944.

Diamond was born in Rochester, New York, July 9, 1915. He studied at the Cleveland Institute, at the Eastman School, with Roger Sessions and Paul Boepple at the New Music School, and with Nadia Boulanger in Paris. His orchestral works include a Sinfonietta (1934); two Symphonies (1935 and 1944), a Violin Concerto (1936), a *Serenade* for strings (1937); a *Psalm* for orchestra (1937); an *Elegy in Memory of Ravel* (1938); a *Heroic Piece* (1939); a *Concert Piece* written for the New York High School of Music and Art, and a Concerto for chamber orchestra which figured in the September, 1940, programs at Yaddo. His Sonata for cello and piano, composed in 1936, was published three years later in an issue of *New Music*. Other chamber music works are a Piano Sonata (1936), a Violin Sonatina (1937), a Trio (1937), a Quintet for flute, three strings, and piano (1937) published in 1942 by the Society for the Publication of American Music; a *Divertimento* for piano and small orchestra (1936), a Chamber Symphony (1936), and a Sonatina for piano, published in 1937. In April, 1940, the Eastman Festival programs included his *Variations on an Original Theme,* for orchestra.

DANA SUESSE (1911——) came to the concert halls by way of Broadway. At one time she was an arranger for T. B. Harms and Famous Music, publishers of popular music. In addition to numerous popular songs, she composed the music for two of the *Casa Mañana Revues* which Billy Rose produced in Fort Worth, Texas, in 1936 and 1937, and the music for the World's Fair Aquacade, 1939. Earlier than these was the *Concerto in Three Rhythms* for piano and orchestra which Paul Whiteman commissioned from her in 1932.

Miss Suesse was born in Kansas City, Missouri, December 3, 1911. Aside from piano lessons with Siloti and some composition study with Rubin Goldmark, she is largely self-taught in music, having composed since childhood. In recent years she has decided that she has said almost all she has to offer in the jazz medium, and does not intend to restrict herself to its limitations. Her later compositions include a Concerto for two pianos and orchestra, played by Bartlett and Robinson with the Cincinnati Orchestra, December 10 and 11, 1943; a

Suite for orchestra bearing the title *Three Cities: Vienna, Warsaw, Paris;* a Suite for harp and orchestra, originally entitled *Young Man with a Harp;* a Concertino for piano and orchestra; and a *Cocktail Suite* for piano. She is now working on an *Antique Symphony,* using archaic material. She also plans to compose an opera based on the life of Isadora Duncan, and hopes to have it ready in 1947 for the twentieth anniversary of the famous dancer's death.

PAUL FREDERIC BOWLES (1911——) is a native New Yorker, and for several years has been a music reviewer for the New York *Herald Tribune.* He was born in the metropolis, and is a pupil of Aaron Copland and Virgil Thomson. His interest in exotic folk music has taken him to Spain, Northern Africa, the Sahara, the Antilles, and South and Central America. The Philadelphia Orchestra played his *Yankee Clipper* ballet music in 1937, and in 1938 the work was presented in its full form by the Ballet Caravan in New York. It is an imaginative score, describing the adventures of a young farmer who voyages around the world. At every port, music appropriate to the native locale establishes the atmosphere and color.

Bowles has written other music for the stage, particularly the incidental music for WPA productions of *Horse Eats Hat* and Marlowe's *Doctor Faustus* and for the Helen Hayes–Maurice Evans *Twelfth Night.* He has also composed a Suite for small orchestra; a piece for nine instruments entitled *Melodia;* a Trio; a three-act opera *Denmark Vesey;* a Cantata; and several shorter pieces. His more recent works include the score for the documentary film *The Congo,* and a musical setting for a play by García Lorca, *The Wind Remains.* Bowles was awarded a Guggenheim Fellowship in 1941.

The titles of several pieces by ROBERT GUYN MCBRIDE (1911——) show where his youthful interests lay, and demonstrate that he has by no means turned his back on them now that he has become a teacher at Bennington College, a Guggenheim Fellow (1937), and a recipient of a $1,000 award from the American Academy of Arts and Letters (1942). One of his most recent works is *Strawberry Jam (Home Made)* which was played by the National Orchestral Association in New York March 16, 1942. Others in a similar vein are *Wise-Apple Five; Jungle Jangle; Swing Stuff; Workout;* the *Go Choruses*

(1936), based on the adventures of a jazz band where each player in turn takes a chorus of the tune and "goes" with it; and *Fugato on a Well-known Theme*. And the music is as jazzy as the titles.

McBride was born in Tucson, Arizona, February 20, 1911, and was educated at the University of Arizona. His musical career, however, had started long before he entered college. At ten he began playing the clarinet, then the oboe, the saxophone, and the piano. He was constantly busy in school bands, local theatre orchestras, and jazz bands. At the University he specialized in public school music, and received his Bachelor's degree in 1933. Two years later he took his Master's degree in composition, and then joined the faculty of Bennington College in Vermont.

Others of McBride's works, some of them with more somber titles, are *Depression* (1934), a Sonata for violin and piano; *Prelude to a Tragedy*, performed by the New York Philharmonic-Symphony, November 20, 1935; a *Mexican Rhapsody* for orchestra (1934); a ballet *Show Piece* (1937); and a *Prelude and Fugue* for string quartet.

The First Symphony of GARDNER READ (1913——) won the first prize of $1,000 awarded by the New York Philharmonic-Symphony in its 1937 contest, and in 1943 his Second Symphony won the Paderewski Prize of equal amount. Read was only twenty-four years old when his First Symphony was accorded this honor. Born in Evanston, Illinois, January 2, 1913, he studied at Northwestern University and at the Eastman School of Music. In 1938 and 1939 he was given a Cromwell Fellowship for travel in Europe, and in 1943 he was appointed to the music faculty of the Kansas City (Missouri) Conservatory of Music.

His orchestral works include the First Symphony, which had its première by the New York Philharmonic-Symphony, November 4 and 5, 1937; the Second Symphony, introduced by the Boston Symphony, November, 1943; a symphonic poem *The Lotus-Eaters* (1932); a Symphonic Suite *The Painted Desert* (1933); another Symphonic Suite *Sketches of the City* (1933), performed by the Rochester, Chicago, and Cincinnati Orchestras, and published by the Juilliard Foundation; a *Fantasy* for viola and orchestra (1935); a *Prelude and Toccata* (1937); a First Overture (1943); and *Night Flight* (1944). There are also a Piano Sonata (1935); a *Passacaglia and Fugue* for organ (1936); and a set of songs for mezzo-soprano and thirty-eight instruments, *From a Lute of Jade* (1935).

GAIL KUBIK (1914———) was the winner of a $1,000 prize offered in 1941 by Jascha Heifetz for a new Violin Concerto. In addition, the composer received for his work $500 from the RCA-Victor Company. His earlier Violin Concerto was performed by the New York Civic Orchestra in 1938.

Kubik was born in South Coffeyville, Oklahoma, September 5, 1914, and studied at the American Conservatory in Chicago and at the Eastman School of Music. During the second World War his work as composer was devoted to several branches of the Armed Services. As music consultant for the Motion Pictures Bureau of the Office of War Information, he composed the score for the documentary film *The World at War*. For the United States Maritime Commission's documentary film *Men and Ships*, he provided a score which was also heard as a concert piece on the radio, and as a corporal of the Army Air Force he has composed music for its motion pictures.

Several of Kubik's works have been presented at the American Composers' Concerts at the Eastman School: a Trio (1935); a Suite for orchestra (1939); and *Whoopee Ti-Yi-Yo* (1942). For piano he has composed a *Sonatina* (1942), and a *Dance Soliloquy* (1943). In 1944 his Sonatina for violin and piano was published by the Society for the Publication of American Music, and in the following year he was awarded a postwar Guggenheim Fellowship.

EARL ROBINSON (1910———) became one of the most frequently heard of American composers through a single composition, his *Ballad for Americans*, first introduced in 1939 in the WPA production *Sing for Your Supper*. It was then broadcast by Paul Robeson on the "Pursuit of Happiness" radio program, and it brought such a deluge of fan mail that it continued its career in movies, on phonograph records, and on symphony orchestra programs. Then, in 1940 and 1941, Robinson was awarded a Guggenheim Fellowship to work on a musical setting of Carl Sandburg's *The People, Yes*. The *Ballad for Americans* used a text by John La Touche which is given highly dramatic treatment, alternating song and speech, and scored for chorus, solo voice, and orchestra. It was first heard at a time when Americans were becoming increasingly conscious of the blessings of democracy, and it became one of our most widely used patriotic concert pieces during World War II.

Robinson was born in Seattle, Washington, July 2, 1910, and was educated at the University of Washington. He has composed several songs and choruses in a vein similar to *Ballad for Americans*, and he wrote the music for several Federal Theatre plays.

WAYNE BARLOW (1912——) was educated at the Eastman School, and has since become a member of its faculty. He studied also with Schoenberg. He was born in Elyria, Ohio, September 6, 1912. His most played work, *The Winter's Past*, is based on an Appalachian Mountain tune and is scored for oboe and strings. Others of his compositions are *Three Moods for Dancing* (orchestra); a Poem for orchestra—*De Profundis;* a String Quartet; a choral ballet *False Faces;* a cantata *Zion in Exile;* a Sonata for violin and piano; and a number of songs.

A. LEHMAN ENGEL (1910——) is known as a choral conductor. He organized and directed the Madrigal Singers, a unit of the WPA Music Project in New York, and conducted the premières of numerous modern works under other auspices. He was born in Jackson, Mississippi, September 14, 1910. In addition to his studies at the Cincinnati College, the Cincinnati Conservatory, and the Juilliard School, he worked with Lora and Trucco in New York, and with Roger Sessions.

His works include four orchestral pieces—*Jungle Dance* (1930), *Introduction and Allegretto* (1932), *Scientific Creation* (1935), and *Traditions* (1935); a number of choral pieces; a String Quartet (1934); and a Piano Sonata (1936). He has also composed much for the stage—incidental music to Eliot's *Murder in the Cathedral* (1936), O'Casey's *Within the Gates* (1934), Aristophanes's *Birds* (1935), Shakespeare's *Macbeth* (1941), and other plays. He has written two operas—*Medea* (1935) and *Pierrot of the Minute* (1927); and a ballet *Phobias* (1933).

RICHARD FRANKO GOLDMAN (1910——) is the son of the band conductor Edwin Franko Goldman. Born in New York City, December 7, 1910, he studied piano with Ralph Leopold and Clarence Adler, and composition with Pietro Floridia. He was graduated with honors from Columbia University in 1930 and was awarded a Fellowship in Fine Arts which had been created especially for him. After a post-graduate year at Columbia he went to Paris for further study in composition with Nadia Boulanger. Upon his return he became assistant conductor of the Goldman Band in 1937, and during World War II entered the office of Strategic Services of the United States Army.

Goldman's compositions include *A Curtain Raiser and Country Dance* for band; a *Hymn for Brass Choir;* a setting for orchestra of the old American tune *The Lee Rigg;* a Sonatina for piano; a *Divertimento* for flute and piano; and two *Monochromes* for flute alone. He is also the compiler of *Landmarks of Early American Music,* a collection of songs and pieces dating from 1760 to 1800. These works are arranged by Goldman and Roger Smith for orchestra or band or small instrument groups, or for mixed chorus, with or without accompaniment. His book *The Band's Music* was published in 1938.

ROBERT ELMORE (1913———) was born of American parents in India, and was brought to America when he was a year old. He began studying the piano when he was six and the organ when he was nine. In 1933 he received the degree of Licentiate of the Royal Academy of Music, London, in three different subjects—organ, piano, and piano accompaniment. In the United States he studied organ under Pietro Yon and composition under Harl McDonald. He attended the University of Pennsylvania where he received his Bachelor of Music degree in 1937. In 1940 he began teaching composition at the University of Pennsylvania, and since 1942 he has been organist at the Church of the Holy Trinity in Philadelphia. His other works are a tone poem for orchestra, *Valley Forge—1777,* which had its première in Philadelphia in 1937; a Concerto in C Minor for organ and orchestra, performed by the Philadelphia Orchestra in 1938; *Three Colors,* a Suite of *Green, Blue, and Orange,* performed in Philadelphia in 1941; and some songs. Recently he produced a choral work entitled *The Prodigal Son* (A Sermon in Swing).

SYDNEY FOSTER's (1917———) Trio had its New York première in 1945. He was born in South Carolina in 1917, and was educated at the Curtis Institute of Music where he studied with Walter Goldstein and David Saperton. In 1939 he made his debut as a pianist with the Dallas Orchestra, and appeared in Philadelphia and New York the same year. In 1945 he was appointed head of the piano department at the University of Texas.

STANLEY BATE (1912———) has won many awards which have given him opportunity for extensive training in Europe with Nadia Boulanger, Paul Hindemith, and others. He was born in Devonshire, England, in 1912, and first studied under Vaughan Williams at the Royal College of Music in London. In 1941 he toured Australia, lecturing on contemporary music and appearing as soloist in his own Piano Concerto. After settling in America, he was awarded a Guggenheim Fellowship in 1942. He played his Piano Concerto at Carnegie Hall in that year and was soloist in a performance of his *Concertante* for piano and strings with the New York Philharmonic-Symphony Orchestra in 1943. His Sinfonietta No. 1 was first heard at the 1942 International Festival for Contemporary Music. He has written two String Quartets, and composed the incidental music for *The Patriots,* a play based on the life of Thomas Jefferson—a production of 1943.

HAROLD SHAPERO (1920———) won the 1941 *Prix de Rome* with his *Nine-Minute Overture* which was performed by CBS Symphony Orchestra in 1941. Shapero was born in Massachusetts in 1920 and studied with Nicolas Slonimsky and Ernst Křenek. He majored in music at Harvard, and later worked with Piston, Hindemith, and Copland. His other works include: Piano Sonatina (1939); *Three Pieces for Three Pieces*—for flute, clarinet, and bassoon (1939); Trumpet Sonata, for trumpet and piano (1940); and String Quartet (1941).

*   *   *

HENRY DREYFUS BRANT (1913———) belongs with the avowed experimenters. Henry Cowell, in *American Composers on American Music,* has pointed out some original features of Brant's music. One of them, Cowell says, is Brant's interest in "oblique harmony"; not the mere sound of two or more voices at the same time satisfies him, nor yet the contrast of two or more melodic lines, but the relations between one voice at one point and another at another. If in the process of working out such "intellectual" systems, Brant's music "happens to sound well," he does not mind, we are told.

Brant was born September 15, 1913, in Montreal, Canada, and studied at McGill University's School of Music where his father taught the violin, and at the Juilliard School. He also studied with

George Antheil, whom he acknowledges as his principal teacher. He has won several prizes, has acted as secretary of the Pan-American Association of Composers, has done some orchestrating for the films, and has received commissions from the Yaddo Festival and from the American Ballet Company.

Brant's works include *Variations in Oblique Harmony*, to be played by "any four instruments"; *Miss O'Grady*, an opera; *Entente cordiale*, a satire with music; a *Lyric Cycle*, for soprano, three violas and piano; *Crying Jag*, for military band; a Symphony in B-flat Minor; a Quintet for oboe and strings; a Concerto for eleven flutes; a Concerto for double bass and orchestra; a *Sonata Sacra* for hardware and piano; a Violin Concerto; a Clarinet Concerto which was awarded a $100 prize by the Society of Professional Musicians; a *Whoopee Overture*; and a ballet *The Great American Goof*.

In commenting on his works and his idiom, Brant himself once said: "No two of my works have any surface resemblance in technique and style."

A specialist in the use of percussive sounds, JOHN CAGE (1913——) succeeded in producing tones that have probably never before been heard in concert-halls, and has demonstrated his unique ideas at the New School for Social Research. He was born in Seattle, Washington, trained for the ministry, and went to New York in 1942. He has a repertoire of fifty compositions for "prepared piano," meaning the placing in the piano of small pieces of anything from metal to leather at certain distances between the strings. With this battery he produces his "twelve-tone maneuvers." His compositions have been presented by groups of players using everything from flower pots to electric buzzers, depending upon the sounds he wishes to produce. His works include *The Perilous Night* and *Imaginary Landscape, No. 3*.

* * *

The concluding list of symphonic composers is as follows:

RUSSELL BAUM
    Born, Buffalo, New York, 1912.
    Variations on a Theme of Paganini for piano and orchestra, (American Composers' Concerts, Eastman School, 1935); *Passacaglia and Fugue*, and *Choreographic Sketches* (same, 1938).

WILLIAM BERGSMA

Born, Oakland, California, 1921.

Pioneer Saga, for orchestra (American Composers' Concerts, Eastman School, 1939).

NORMAN CAZDEN

Born, New York, 1915.

String Quartet; Sonata for flute and piano.

ARTHUR COHN

Born, Philadelphia, 1910.

Four String Quartets; *Four Documents,* for orchestra; *Music for Ancient Instruments.*

WILLIAM D. DENNY

Born, Seattle, Washington, 1910.

Winner of *Prix de Rome,* 1939.

Sinfonietta for string orchestra; Suite for small orchestra; Concertino for orchestra; Incidental Music for *A Horace Festival.*

ALVIN ETLER

Born, Battle Creek, Iowa, 1913.

Guggenheim Fellow, 1940 and 1941.

Music for Chamber Orchestra (American Composers' Concerts, Eastman School, 1939); *Five Speeds Forward.*

WILLIAM P. GRANT

Born, Cleveland, Ohio, 1910.

Symphony in D Minor (American Composers' Concerts, Eastman School, 1936).

EDMUND HAINES

Born, Ottumwa, Iowa, 1914.

Symphony; Poem for viola and orchestra; *Symphony in Miniature* (American Composers' Concerts, Eastman School, 1940).

DAVID HOLDEN

Born, 1912.

Composer, teacher; instructor at Boston Conservatory of Music.

Chamber Music for Piano and Strings, published by the Society for the Publication of American Music, 1939.

SOL KAPLAN

Born, Philadelphia, 1919.

Suite for string quartet, Hollywood, 1940.

HOMER KELLER

Born, Oxnard, California, 1915.

Symphony in A Minor (awarded $500 prize, Henry Hadley Foundation Contest, 1939); *Serenade* for clarinet and strings (American Composers' Concerts, Eastman School, 1939, 1942); Chamber Symphony (same, 1941).

ROBERT KELLY

Born, 1916.

Adirondack Suite, National Broadcasting Company, 1941.

KENT KENNAN

Born, Milwaukee, Wisconsin, 1913.

Winner of *Prix de Rome,* 1936.

Night Soliloquy for flute and strings (American Composers' Concerts, Eastman School, 1938 and 1939); Symphony No. 1, *Promenade* for orchestra, Nocturne, for viola and orchestra, and *Il Campo di Fiori* for trumpet and orchestra (same, 1939, 1940 and 1942); *Andante* for oboe and small orchestra (same, 1941); Suite for orchestra (same, 1943).

IRVING LANDAU

Born, New York City, 1911.

Free Variations for Orchestra (American Composers' Concerts, Eastman School, 1933); Sinfonietta (same, 1934).

JEROME MOROSS

Born, Brooklyn, New York, 1913.

Composer; member of music staff, Paramount Pictures, Hollywood.

For orchestra: Symphony; *Paeans* (1931); *Biguine* (1934); *Paul Bunyan* (1935); *Tall Story* (commissioned by Columbia Broadcasting System, 1938); two ballets—*Memorials* (1935) and *American Pattern* (1936); an opera *Requiem for Johnnie* (1937).

WALTER MOURANT

Born, Chicago, Illinois, 1910.

Five Inhibitions (American Composers' Concerts, Eastman School, 1937); Quintet for strings (same, 1942); *Three Dances* (Rochester Symposium, 1939).

ROBERT PALMER
> Born, Syracuse, New York, 1915.
> *Poem* for violin and orchestra (American Composers' Concerts, Eastman School, 1939); Piano Sonata.

OWEN REED
> Born, Odessa, Missouri, 1910.
> Symphony (American Composers' Concerts, Eastman School, 1939).

JULIA SMITH
> Born, Texas, 1911.
> Opera *Cynthia Parker*, produced at Denton, Texas, 1939; *Little Suite*, and *Episodic Suite*, for orchestra.

JOSEPH WOOD
> Born, Pittsburgh, 1915.
> Opera *The Mother*, winner of Juilliard Opera Competition and produced at Juilliard Graduate School, New York, 1942.

WYNN YORK
> Born, Claremore, Oklahoma, 1914.
> *Night Clouds*, for orchestra (American Composers' Concerts, Eastman School, 1939, 1942, 1943).

6. COMPOSERS BEST KNOWN BY THEIR SMALLER WORKS

At this point we present those composers who are most widely known for short works—songs, piano pieces, and, in some cases, teaching material. Many of them have composed also in the larger forms, but they are best known to the public for their briefer compositions.

One of the most beloved ballads of the early twentieth century was *Absent*, which was popularized by the tenor Evan Williams, in concert and on early phonograph records. *Absent* was composed by JOHN W. METCALF (1856–1926), a colleague and close friend of George W. Chadwick. He is said to have been the first music instructor at Stanford University in California. *Absent* was published in 1899, and was followed by a *Persian Serenade; Hark, as the Twilight Fades; O Sing Ye Birds* (1903); *The Cares of Yesterday* (1908); *Love and Springtime* (1911); *The Sunset Glow* (1916); *Watching* (1917); and *Niawasa: an American Indian Idyl* (1922).

Perhaps the artistic parent of all our present-day song composers was ETHELBERT NEVIN (1862–1901), who left us *The Rosary* and *Mighty Lak' a Rose*. Edward MacDowell once said that long after many composers of symphonies are forgotten, the lilting tunes of Ethelbert Nevin will be cherished and remembered. Since his death, Nevin has been sentimentalized on the one hand, and scoffed at on the other. Neither is a fair estimate. He needs no sentimentalizing to establish his worth, and it is impossible to brush aside with a sneer songs and piano pieces that have achieved such popularity and have held their place in the public esteem. *The Rosary* is nearly fifty years old, and it is still sung wherever there is music.

The Rosary has had to stand much abuse; it has suffered from the onslaughts of many admirers. Yet it is one of the most ingeniously contrived songs that has ever been written. Coated with sugar, yes; but its telling climax is a bit of theatre that never fails to reach its mark, even when badly sung. Performed sincerely and with restraint by a true artist, the little song is an almost perfect work of art. Made maudlin by a tyro, with dripping obbligato, it seems like mushy trash. When this happens, and it is often, blame the singer and not the song.

Comparison of the careers of Stephen Foster and Nevin is startling in the similarities it reveals. Both came from the environs of Pittsburgh. Both were born of parents of superior education and culture. Each encountered opposition when he wanted to become a musician. Both tried business first. Neither had long life; Foster died when he was thirty-seven, and Nevin at thirty-eight. Foster ended in the gutter; and Nevin finished his days in a nervously unstrung state, with his productive years behind him.

Yet the few years of life that were granted to Nevin were probably all he needed to have his say, for as a miniaturist of mood and fancy he had no doubt spent his powers when he passed away. Again, as with Foster, death may have been merciful in ending what was already finished, a short life of song. Louis Campbell-Tipton pondered this question shortly after Nevin's death. Writing in 1901, in the magazine *Music,* he said:

I have been reflecting over the Nevin subject, recalling how, when I first began to hear his songs, I felt an instinctive impress of a great power, greater in its possibilities than shown in the moment, and I have been wondering if its lack of fulfillment has proven my intuition as playing me false, or whether circumstance has been less kind to him, after all, than he deserved; and if, had he been involved in other conditions of life than the ones seemingly laid out for him, he would have developed potentialities beyond those realized.

This I am inclined to doubt. In my opinion his rare gifts had had their flowering, and could not have blossomed much further. His friends have told me that in his latter years he was working spasmodically on an opera based on the Nathan Hale episode, using leitmotifs in Wagnerian fashion. But Nevin was never one who could write on broad outlines; the larger forms were beyond him. A talent like Nevin's and Foster's can go so far, and then no farther. For proof examine a few of the posthumous songs. In Nevin's case, especially in his setting of Shelley's *I Fear Thy Kisses*, they are sadly inferior to his earlier works. Yet again there is always the exception. *Mighty Lak' a Rose* was published a few months after his death.

Nevin was born November 25, 1862, at "Vineacre," his father's country place near Pittsburgh. There are many Nevins in this part of the country, so many that churchgoers in Sewickley are said to grow confused and murmur—"Our Father who art a Nevin." Ethelbert was the fifth child in a family of eight. His father, Robert Peebles Nevin, was a literary man. He wrote for the *Atlantic Monthly*, the *Knickerbocker Magazine*, and *Lippincott's*. He helped to found the Pittsburgh *Evening Leader* and later the *Pittsburgh Times*. He was a poet and also a musician. He wrote several songs, one of them, *Our Nominee*, a campaign song that helped Polk into the presidency. Ethelbert's mother was a cultured musician. The first grand piano that had ever been hauled over the Alleghenies was brought for her use. In his childhood and youth Nevin enjoyed a cultured and gracious home life.

He showed his musical talent when he was hardly more than a baby. When he was five he used to sit on the piano stool and improvise accompaniments to the songs he knew. When he was eight he was given piano lessons, first by Von der Heide at the Williams Conservatory in Pittsburgh, and a year or so later by William Guenther. In 1877 the Nevin family spent a year abroad, and Ethelbert had piano lessons from Franz Boehme in Dresden. He heard much music in

Berlin, Leipzig, Dresden, and Vienna. When the family returned to America, Ethelbert entered the Western University at Pittsburgh; he was never an academic student, but was the kind who absorbed culture and education from travel and from his own reading. And so he stayed in college for only a year.

He was making progress with his music. He had given a number of concerts in Pittsburgh, one of them with orchestra. He had written some music of his own which had been highly complimented. But when it came to being a musician, his father, an amateur musician himself, opposed him. Music was not a profession for those in the Nevins' walk of life. The church, law, and medicine were the accepted vocations for those who did not want business. So Ethelbert had a few unhappy months in the Pittsburgh offices of the Pennsylvania Railroad. Then he went to his father and begged that he let him be poor all his life, if he could only be a musician. There was no further argument, and the next winter was spent at home practicing and taking counterpoint lessons by mail with a teacher in New York, Dr. S. Austin Pearce.

The next year, 1881, he went to Boston to study with B. J. Lang, who put him to work on scales and exercises that would have frightened away any but a real talent. He had harmony lessons with Stephen A. Emery. His teachers worked him hard, but he stood the grind for two years before he went back to Pittsburgh to settle down as a pianist and teacher. A year later he realized he needed still more training, so in 1884 he went to Klindworth in Berlin, and after a year graduated with highest honors from the Klindworth school, and was invited by von Bülow to have some lessons with him. He studied theory with Carl Bial, who encouraged him to give more time to writing. Nevin had not started his career with the idea of being a composer; it was only after some of his little pieces became popular that he realized he would do best to concentrate on composition.

He returned to America in the fall of 1886, and in December made his debut as a pianist in Pittsburgh. The papers were loud in their praise, but Nevin did not intend to settle down in Pittsburgh and become a local musician. He wanted to try Boston, and he went there to live in January, 1887.

A year later he married Anne Paul of Pittsburgh. He wrote more songs, and they were warmly received by the Manuscript Club in

Boston. One of them was *Oh, That We Two Were Maying,* published that year in his Opus 2, the *Sketch Book,* a collection of songs and piano pieces. When the book came out there were thirteen numbers altogether; a lucky number, for its success was one of the factors that determined Nevin to spend most of his time writing music.

Some of his best songs came from this period: *Herbstgefühl; Wynken, Blynken and Nod;* and *Little Boy Blue.* His piano Suite *Water Scenes* was published in 1891. The fourth of these five pieces was *Narcissus,* destined to be his most popular piano piece—so popular that Nevin came to hate it with all his heart. *Narcissus* is Nevin at his most facile. Trivial, but agreeable and flowing—and sincere.

From 1891 the next six years were spent mostly in Europe. In 1892 he wrote his Suite *In Arcady,* for piano, and in 1895 the Nevins settled in Italy. In Montepiano, near Florence, Ethelbert wrote *May in Tuscany,* a piano Suite with a fanciful little program. In Venice he wrote his popular Suite *A Day in Venice.* In the fall of 1897 the Nevins came home again, this time to an apartment on 57th Street in New York. Nevin rented a studio in Carnegie Hall, where in those days many notable painters, writers, and musicians worked.

It was in February, 1898 that Nevin wrote *The Rosary,* and Francis Rogers, who sang it for the first time in public, has described the event in the article in the *Musical Quarterly* (July, 1917):

A few days before the concert I was dining with the Nevins in New York. . . . After dinner Nevin sat down at the piano, as was his custom, and began to play. After a little, he handed me a slip of music-paper with the voice part and the words of a song scribbled on it in pencil, saying as he did so, "Here is a song I want you to sing at our concert next week." I deciphered my part as best I could, while Nevin played the accompaniment from memory. Except for the pencil manuscript then in my hand, I doubt whether any part of the song had been committed to writing. The song was "The Rosary."

. . . The following week, February 15, 1898, in Madison Square Garden Concert Hall, we gave "The Rosary" its first public performance. It made, as one paper puts it, "the hit of the afternoon."

The text of "The Rosary" had been sent by some correspondent to Nevin, who recognized at once its fine lyric quality, and, with my voice in mind, set to music. He knew nothing at the time about the author, Robert Cameron Rogers, nor did Mr. Rogers know anything about him. The life of the song has been one of great and undiminishing prosperity. Soon after its publication, I sang it in England to appreciative ears, and I am told that it has retained its popularity there just as it has here.

These latter years were far from ideal for Nevin. He was highly nervous, and his health was breaking. In June of 1898 he went to Vineacre and stayed there for almost a year, struggling against ill health. He recovered partially, and late in the fall of 1900 the family went to New Haven, Connecticut. It was not for long. Nevin was taken ill Saturday, February 16, 1901, and passed quietly away the afternoon of the next day.

He was buried in Sewickley. His music was performed at the funeral services: *The Rosary; Jesu, Jesu, Miserere;* and the *Ave Maria* from *A Day in Venice*. His life was done, and his work was finished. Not as a master of great things, but as a poet of beautiful little verses.

Many of our song composers have written art-songs of the highest type; and have really interpreted the texts they have chosen for their settings. Carpenter and Griffes have already been discussed, and many of our symphonists have been happy in their song composing. There are others who are known chiefly for their songs.

ALICE BARNETT brings a delicately feminine touch to her graceful writing. Born in Lewistown, Illinois, in 1888, she studied with Weidig, Borowski, Middelschulte, and Ganz in Chicago, and with Hugo Kaun in Berlin. She first attracted serious attention with her setting of Clinton Scollard's *Serenade* in 1916. Several songs followed, most important a cycle of eight poems from Browning—*In a Gondola*. Here she added dramatic power to her lyric gifts. Then came settings of verses by Sara Teasdale, John Vance Cheney, and others, and in 1924 Cale Young Rice's *Chanson of the Bells of Oseney*. In this song each bell has its own carillonlike motive; an air of mysticism pervades the whole work. Her setting of Le Gallienne's *A Caravan from China Comes* is one of the best of the many that have been made by our composers.

WINTTER WATTS is another composer of sensitive songs. He is less subjective than Miss Barnett, rarely as subtle; but his directness, his sincerity, and above all his independence, raise him above the crowd. Born in Cincinnati in 1884, he studied at the Institute of Musical Art. His symphonic poem *Young Blood* won the Morris Loeb Prize of

$1,000 in 1919; also the Pulitzer Prize in 1923, and the *Prix de Rome* which enabled him to live at the American Academy in Rome from 1923 to 1925. He remained in Europe until 1931 and then returned to New York. His larger works include a *Bridal Overture* (1916), a Suite *Etchings* (1921), and three songs with string orchestra (1924).

Possibly his best-known songs are *The Poet Sings*, and *Wings of Night* (both to poems by Sara Teasdale); *The Little Page's Song* (thirteenth century), *Wild Tears*, *Alone*, *With the Tide*, *Joy*, and a cycle of nine songs—*Vignettes of Italy*, to a text by Sara Teasdale.

The death of EDWARD HORSMAN (1873–1918) was a loss to American song literature, for he showed a rare talent in *Bird of the Wilderness* and the few of the songs he left us.

BAINBRIDGE CRIST has experimented with Oriental texts, and has been particularly happy in his *Chinese Mother Goose Rhymes*, *Drolleries from an Oriental Doll's House*, and *Coloured Stars* (four songs to translations from the Oriental by E. Powys Mathers). Possibly his best songs are the exquisite *Into a Ship Dreaming* (de la Mare), and the joyous *April Rain*. In *Queer Yarns*, Crist matches the whimsy of Walter de la Mare. He was born in Indiana in 1883, educated in Cincinnati and Boston, and now lives in Washington, D.C. He has written a number of instrumental works, available as piano solos and in many cases for various orchestral combinations: *Egyptian Impressions*; *Oriental Dances*; *Hymn to Nefertiti* (1936); *Fête Espagnole* (1937); a Javanese ballet *Pregiwa's Marriage*; and others.

MARY TURNER SALTER (1856–1938) was the wife of Sumner Salter, a composer of church and choral music who appears in the following chapter. Born in Illinois, she studied with John O'Neil in Boston and Hermine Rudersdorff in New York. She was a soprano soloist in churches in Boston, New York, Buffalo, Syracuse, and Atlanta. She was successful in concert and oratorio appearances, and taught at Wellesley College for two years. After 1893 she centered all her attention on composition and teaching, and published nearly a hundred songs, duets, part-songs, and church music. *The Pine Tree* and *The Cry of Rachel* are fine specimens of her gift of melody. In her eightieth year she wrote *A Christmas Song*, one of the best of her works.

JESSIE L. GAYNOR (1863–1921) was a specialist in children's songs.

Her *Slumber Boat*, to Alice C. D. Riley's verses, has been sung so much that it is almost a folk song. Her collections of *Songs to Little Folks, Songs and Scissors, Mother Goose Songs*, and her operettas and entertainments have amused the children of two generations. She wrote songs for adults, too. She was born in St. Louis, and though she was educated in Boston she spent most of her life in the Middle West. Her daughter DOROTHY GAYNOR BLAKE is a composer also.

MARGARET RUTHVEN LANG is the daughter of Benjamin J. Lang, the eminent Boston conductor and teacher of the latter nineteenth century. She was born in Boston in 1867; as a child she was a pupil of her father and later of Chadwick and MacDowell. She has written many songs, some piano pieces, choral music, and a few works for orchestra.

GENA BRANSCOMBE was born in Ontario, Canada, in 1881, but she was educated in the United States and has lived here for many years. Her principal music teachers were Felix Borowski in Chicago, and Engelbert Humperdinck abroad. As a song writer she is known for her cycles: *A Lute of Jade, Songs of the Unafraid*, and for her delightful *Unimproving Songs for Enthusiastic Children*. Her *Festival Prelude* for orchestra has been played at Peterboro, and in New York and San Francisco. The symphonic Suite *Quebec* was first played in Chicago by the Women's Symphony Orchestra, with the composer conducting. *Pilgrims of Destiny*, for soli, chorus, and orchestra, was awarded a prize in 1928 by the National League of American Pen Women. *The Phantom Caravan*, for men's chorus and orchestra, was first produced in 1932. Her *Procession* for orchestra was first heard in 1935. Other choral works include *Youth of the World* (1932), *A Wind from the Sea, Dancer of Fjaard, Mary at Bethlehem, Hail Ye Tyme of Holiedayes*, and *Sun and the Warm Brown Earth* (1935). Other well-known songs are *The Morning Wind, Across the Blue Aegean Sea*, and *At the Postern Gate*. She has written a String Quartet, a number of piano pieces and a few for violin. She has made a choral arrangement of the *Fair Scene* from Delius's *A Village Romeo and Juliet*.

MANA-ZUCCA is one of the best known of the contemporary women composers. She was born in New York in 1891, and studied under Alexander Lambert, Godowsky, Busoni, and Max Vogrich. Her songs are widely sung: *Rachem, If Flowers Could Speak, The Big Brown*

Bear, Mirror of My Soul, Memory, What Is a Kiss, Retribution (1945), and over a hundred others. She has published a Piano Concerto which she played with orchestras in New York and Chicago. Her piano pieces are used for recitals and for teaching.

LILY STRICKLAND may be famous for her *Lindy Lou,* but she has written much else besides: the *Bayou Songs,* the song cycles—*From a Sufi's Tent, Songs of India, A Beggar at Love's Gate*—and others. She was born in South Carolina in 1887 and went to New York in 1910. She studied there with A. Mildenberg (piano) and A. J. Goodrich (theory); also at the Institute of Musical Art (1909–1911). She has lived in many parts of the world, in India from 1920 to 1930, and her music is a travelog, for she has always been successful in catching the spirit of native melodies, and carrying their idiom into tunes of her own. She has written instrumental music: piano pieces; a symphonic Suite *Carolina;* and a Piano Concerto. Her most recent song is *Herald of Spring.*

FAY FOSTER made her reputation during the first World War, when she published *The Americans Come* in 1918. It was precisely what concert singers needed for a timely number on their programs, and besides, it was really dramatic and thrilling when well sung. The composer was born in Leavenworth, Kansas, in 1886, and studied in Chicago with Sherwood, F. G. Gleason, and Madame Voitte. In Leipzig she was a pupil of Reisenauer and Jadassohn; at Munich a pupil of H. Schwartz; and she continued her piano studies with Rosenthal and Sophie Mentor. She won a prize at the International Waltz Competition in Berlin in 1910; and first prize in the American Composers' Contest in New York in 1913. She has composed three operettas; over a hundred songs; choral works; chamber music; and works for the piano. Among her songs are *Dusk in June, My Menagerie, One Golden Day, Your Kiss, Maria Mia,* and *Serenade in Seville.*

PEARL CURRAN (1875–1941), another of the successful women composers, did not begin to write music until she was thirty-five. *Life,* one of her forty songs, was first sung by Caruso. She was born in Denver, the daughter of James H. Gildersleeve, a Civil War veteran. Some of her best-known songs are *Dawn, Rain, Nocturne,* and *The Best Is Yet to Come.* She also produced a number of sacred songs: *The Lord's Prayer, The Lord Is My Shepherd, The Crucifixion and*

Resurrection. She composed several children's songs for her grand-children.

HARRIET WARE is known for her setting of Edwin Markham's *The Cross.* She was born in Wisconsin in 1877 and studied in New York with William Mason; then went to Paris and became a pupil of Sigismund Stojowski in piano and composition. In 1906 she settled in New York. Her *Women's Triumphal March* was made the national song of the Federation of Women's Clubs in 1927. Her tone poem *The Artisan* was performed by the New York Symphony Orchestra in 1929. She has written two cantatas, and the choral cycle *Trees;* also the songs *Joy of the Morning, Stars, Sunlight, Hindu Slumber Song,* and others.

MARIA GREVER, born in Mexico City in 1894, was educated in Spain in a convent, then studied with Debussy, and has since made her home in New York. She has won a number of prizes with her works, which include the songs—*Jurame, Lamento Gitana, Make Love With a Guitar,* and *Tipitin.*

KATHLEEN LOCKHART MANNING, born in California in 1890, stud-ied with Moszkowski, Elizabeth Eichelberger, and Regina de Sales (Paris). Her many songs include two cycles—*Sketches of Paris* and *Sketches of New York.* Other numbers are *Autumn Leaves, Nostalgia, The Truant,* and *Chinois.*

CLARA EDWARDS, born in Minnesota in 1887, was active as an ac-companist and then began to compose. She studied at the State Nor-mal School in Minnesota; and later in Vienna. She made several recital tours in Europe and in 1914 returned to the United States. In 1934 she organized her own Chautauqua Concert Company, with which she toured the country. She has written children's music, in-cidental music to *Alice in Wonderland,* and many songs—*By the Bend of the River, Into the Night, The Fisher's Widow,* and others. In 1940 an early song of hers, *With the Wind and the Rain in Her Hair,* was made into a popular song, and for several weeks it held top place on the "Hit Parade."

The works of many of our older composers are still heard. One of the most respected of the elder men was ADOLPH M. FOERSTER (1854–1927), who was born in Pittsburgh and lived there most of his life. His songs seem to have been influenced chiefly by Robert Franz, and possibly his own German ancestry. *The Daisy, At Night, Love Seemeth Terrible,* and *The Robin's Lullaby* are among the best of them. He also wrote for orchestra; some chamber music, and shorter instrumental pieces.

HALLETT GILBERTÉ is another of the older song writers. He has had much success with his songs, and his setting of Browning's *Ah, Love But a Day* has rivaled Mrs. Beach's in popularity. He was born in Maine in 1875, and was a pupil of John Orth, C. Barmann, and Ethelbert Nevin. He has written about two hundred and fifty songs, several choral works, and piano and violin compositions.

FREDERICK FIELD BULLARD (1864–1904) published some forty songs; the best known *A June Lullaby, From Dreams of Thee,* and the rousing *Stein Song.*

SIDNEY HOMER has a nice gift of melody; one that has caught the popular fancy. His *Banjo Song, The Song of the Shirt, Sing to Me, Sing,* and the *Songs from Mother Goose* are but a few of the many songs that are known to singers and their audiences all over the country. Homer was born in Boston in 1864; he studied with Chadwick, and with Rheinberger in Munich. His wife is Louise Homer, the eminent contralto. Besides his songs he has composed a Sonata and an *Introduction and Fugue* for organ; a Quintet for piano and strings (1932), a Violin Sonata (1936), a String Quartet (1937), a Piano Trio (1937), and a set of *Twenty Little Piano Pieces.* Some of his songs were scored for orchestra by Frederick Stock—*Sweet and Low, Sing to Me, Sing, A Banjo Song,* and *From the Brake the Nightingale.*

WILLIAM ARMS FISHER is one of the Dvořák pupils. He studied with both Dvořák and Horatio Parker at the National Conservatory in New York. He was born in San Francisco in 1861, and since 1897 has lived in Boston. From 1897 to 1937 he was editor and publication manager for the Oliver Ditson Company, and from 1926 to 1937, its vice-president. His editorial work has been significant, and in addition to bringing out the work of many composers, he has developed several editions of classics—*The Musician's Library,* the *Music Student's Library,* and others. He has been a student of American music from the early days to the present, and is now publishing the results of his research in this field.

As a composer, Fisher has been concerned chiefly with song writing.

He has made many settings of Negro spirituals, and his famous *Goin'* *Home* is a vocal adaptation of the *Largo* melody from the slow movement of Dvořák's *New World Symphony*. He has written many original songs.

There are other editors who have been composers themselves, but whose work in other fields has overshadowed their own music. OSCAR G. SONNECK (1873–1928) will no doubt always be known first as a musicologist, a pioneer research worker in early American music. He was born in Jersey City and educated in Germany. From 1902 to 1917 he was in charge of the Music Division of the Library of Congress. He developed one of the great music libraries of the world from what had been a mere accumulation of music in the copyright division of the government. From 1917 until his death he was music editor for the publishing house of G. Schirmer in New York. He founded the *Musical Quarterly* in 1915.

Sonneck wrote a number of songs, highly original, thoughtful and scholarly. *To Helen* is for singers the most grateful of them. *Studies in Song*, Opus 19, were frankly experiments in the use of flexible rhythms in setting poems.

CARL ENGEL (1883–1944) was known chiefly as an editor and scholar, but he was also a highly individual composer. His compositions include a *Triptych* for violin and piano; many songs—among them *The Sea-Shell; The Trout; The Conspirator; My Heart, I Said*—and a number of piano pieces. Engel was born in Paris and was educated at the Universities of Strassburg and Munich. In 1905 he came to America, and from 1909 to 1921 he was editor and musical adviser of the Boston Music Company. In 1922 he was appointed chief of the Music Division of the Library of Congress, to succeed O. G. Sonneck. In 1929 he became president of G. Schirmer, Inc., and succeeded Sonneck as editor of the *Musical Quarterly*. He was instrumental in establishing the Archives of American Folksong at the Library of Congress, and he was one of the founders of the American Musicological Society.

CHARLES FONTEYN MANNEY was a vocal pupil of William Arms Fisher, and was associated with him as music editor of the Oliver Ditson Company, from 1898 to 1930. He was born in Brooklyn, New York, in 1872, and studied counterpoint with Wallace Goodrich and composition with Percy Goetschius. He has composed an opera, three cantatas, songs, and piano pieces. Among his works are a song cycle— *A Shropshire Lad,* and songs—*At Evenfall, And Let Me the Canakin Clink,* and others.

Before RUPERT HUGHES became a novelist he was a musician, composer, and writer on musical subjects. His first songs were published in 1892: *Tears, Idle Tears,* and *In a Gondola.* Then he became something of a modernist, showing investigation of dissonance in his dramatic monologue *Cain,* and in his *Free Verse Songs.* He was born in Missouri in 1872, and though he had some lessons with Edgar Stillman Kelley, he was largely self-taught in music. His writings include a volume devoted to *Contemporary American Composers; Love Affairs of Great Musicians; The Music Lover's Encyclopedia,* and others.

A. WALTER KRAMER is a prolific composer who has been active also in editorial fields. Born in New York in 1890, he was on the staff of *Musical America* from 1910 to 1922 and became its editor-in-chief in 1929. Since 1936 he has been managing director of the Galaxy Music Corporation, New York. For several years he represented that firm as a publisher-member of the ASCAP Board of Directors, and in 1943 he was elected a composer-member of the board.

He has composed in many forms, but he has achieved the widest distinction in his songs. He is versatile in his style—from the quiet, subjective contemplation of his sonnet cycle—*Beauty of Earth* (C. H. Towne), Sara Teasdale's *Swans,* or *Green* (D. H. Lawrence), to the directness and simplicity of the *lied*-like *Bitte* of Hermann Hesse, or Christina Rossetti's *Christmas Carol.* He showed dramatic powers in setting Louis Untermeyer's *The Faltering Dusk,* and *The Last Hour* (Jessie C. Brown).

He has written a number of piano pieces. His *Symphonic Rhapsody* for violin and orchestra was performed at the Stadium Concerts in New York; and Kathleen Parlow played it in recital to piano accompaniment. His *Elizabethan Days* is a favorite with small orchestras. The *Eklog* for violin and piano (originally for cello), and the *Chant Nègre* are featured by violinists.

He has composed also two *Symphonic Sketches;* a *Gavotte* and a *Night Song* for orchestra; a symphonic poem *The Tragedy of Man,* a cantata *The Lady of Ceret;* a choral cycle *In Normandy* (*A Rococo Romance*); and has made a transcription of Bach's *Chaconne* for orchestra (1931).

In 1945, JOHN TASKER HOWARD, the author of this volume, became associated with Kramer and Deems Taylor as one of the so-called standard composer-members of the Board of Directors of the American Society of Composers, Authors and Publishers. Howard is perhaps known more widely for his books on American music than he is as a composer, but he has nevertheless composed a *Fantasy on a Choral Theme* for piano and orchestra; *Mosses from an Old Manse* for string orchestra; *From Foster Hall,* for string quartet; a *Foster Sonatina* for violin and piano (also scored as a Sinfonietta for orchestra); numerous piano pieces; songs and choral works; and a number of settings of Stephen Foster songs and works by early American composers. He was born in Brooklyn, New York, November 30, 1890, received his academic education at Williams College, and studied music privately with Paul Tidden, Howard Brockway, and Mortimer Wilson. His books, in addition to *Our American Music,* include *Stephen Foster, America's Troubadour; Ethelbert Nevin; Our Contemporary Composers;* and *This Modern Music.* Since 1940 he has been curator of the Americana Music Collection at the New York Public Library.

GEORGE ALFRED GRANT-SCHAEFER (1872–1939) was born in Williamstown, Ontario, and was head of the vocal department of the Music School at Northwestern University from 1908 to 1920. His *Cuckoo Clock* has long been a favorite encore song. He has composed operettas, many songs, and moderately difficult piano pieces, and has made some unusual arrangements of French-Canadian folk songs.

ARTURO BUZZI-PECCIA was born in Milan in 1854 and died in New York August 29, 1943. His father was Antonio Buzzi, a composer of operas and ballets, and at one time head of the Moscow Conservatory. Arturo studied under Massenet and Saint-Saëns in Paris. In 1898 he came to the United States and taught in Chicago for a few years. Then he moved to New York where he lived as a teacher and composer. Among his pupils were Alma Gluck and Sophie Breslau. He wrote an opera *Forza d'Amore;* an orchestral work *Saturnale;* many songs, such as *Lolita, Gloria, Under the Greenwood Tree,* and *Faith;* also chamber music and choral works.

Louis Edgar Johns, born in Pittsburgh, 1886, has written in many forms, and has had success with songs in the style of the German romanticists. His *Lyrics from the German*, in five volumes, show that he is at home in painting various emotions. He has written some piano pieces, orchestral works, and some chamber music.

Claude Warford is a singing teacher who was born in New Jersey in 1877. He has published more than forty songs, among them *Pietà*, *Earth is Enough*, *Dream Song*, and *Three Ghosts*. He has composed a number of choruses also.

Heinrich Gebhard was a German, born in 1878, who came to America when a boy and was educated in Boston. He became a talented pianist and a composer of distinguished songs, as well as chamber music. He has written a *Fantasy* for piano and orchestra, performed by the New York Philharmonic-Symphony Orchestra in 1925; a *Divertimento* for piano and chamber orchestra, presented by the Boston Symphony in 1927; a String Quartet; *Waltz Suite* for two pianos; a song cycle—*The Sun, Cloud and the Flower;* a Sonata for piano and violin; also many piano pieces. He has arranged Loeffler's *A Pagan Poem* for two pianos. He was the pianist who played the solo part in this work when it was first performed in Boston, and he has always been considered its most authentic interpreter.

Henry Purmont Eames, born in Chicago in 1875, is a musical missionary and lecturer, who received his Music Doctor's degree at Cornell College, Iowa, in 1906. He studied with Sherwood, and later in Europe with Clara Schumann and Paderewski. He has toured the United States and Europe several times; has taught in several colleges; and since 1928 has been the music director of Scripps College in Claremont, California. He has written many songs, including *Sweetest and Dearest*, and *Irish Croon-song;* some choruses, a few works for orchestra, and a light opera that won the David Bispham Medal in 1925.

Robert Huntington Terry is another of our song writers. He was born in Hudson, New York, in 1867. Among his well-known songs are *The Answer, At Twilight, Song Is So Old*, and *Which Flower I Love*.

Ralph Cox (1884–1941), a native of Ohio, left a song list to his credit with such songs as *To a Hilltop, Sylvia, Somebody Loves Me,*

At the End of the Day, Garden Gossips, Madame April, and *My Love Comes Soon.*

CHARLES GILBERT SPROSS is an accompanist whose experience on the concert platform has stood him in good stead in writing songs that are effective, and grateful to the singer. He was born in Poughkeepsie, New York, in 1874. He studied piano under Scharwenka and theory under Carol Lachmund in New York. He was organist at St. Paul's, Poughkeepsie, for seven years; at Rutgers Presbyterian Church, New York, for four years; at the Second Presbyterian Church, Paterson, New Jersey, for eight years; at the Presbyterian Church in Poughkeepsie from 1912 to 1929; later at the First Congregational Church in Poughkeepsie. He has published cantatas, anthems, songs, a Sonata for violin and piano, and piano pieces. Among his well-known songs are *Abide with Me, The Conquest, I Do Not Ask, O Lord, Forever and a Day, When Winds Are Raging,* and *Asleep.*

FRANK LA FORGE is another accompanist who writes brilliant and stunningly effective songs: *Song of the Open, Hills, I Came with a Song,* and others. He was born in Illinois in 1879, studied in Chicago, and with Leschetizky in Vienna, and is now resident in New York as accompanist and coach to singers. For ten years he was accompanist to Sembrich, and he has toured with Schumann-Heink, Matzenauer, Frances Alda, and others. He was one of the first to play accompaniments from memory. Recently he has written a *Fledermaus Fantasy* for voice and flute, and has made an arrangement of Alabieff's *Nightingale.*

WALTER GOLDE is much in demand as an accompanist, and his songs have found favor with a number of singers. His setting of Rossetti's *Sudden Light* is one of his best art-songs, and *To an Invalid* and *A Lad Went a-Wooing* are typical of his lyricism. Golde was born in Brooklyn in 1887, and studied at the Imperial Conservatory in Vienna. He has accompanied many prominent artists, and has been guest conductor for orchestras.

RICHARD HAGEMAN, a Hollander born in 1882, has lived in America since 1907. He has been prominent both as an opera conductor and as an accompanist for singers. He studied at the Brussels and Amsterdam Conservatories. In 1907 he was appointed assistant conductor at the Metropolitan Opera House, and from 1916 to 1921 he was one of its regular conductors. For a number of years he was head of the voice department of the Chicago Musical College. He has conducted orchestras in many of the larger cities in the United States. His opera *Caponsacchi* was performed at the Metropolitan Opera House in 1937. He has written music for the films; also piano pieces and many songs, among them *At the Well, May Night, Do Not Go, My Love, Lift Thou the Burdens, Father*, and the currently successful *Miranda*.

BRUNO HUHN is famous for his setting of Henley's *Invictus*, but he has published also many other songs. He was born in England in 1871, and came to New York when he was twenty years old. He is an exceptional accompanist. As an organist he is self-taught and has held several positions in New York. He has written many choral works: *Te Deum Laudamus, Blest Pair of Sirens, The Message, Christ Triumphant, Meditation, Jubilate Deo*; many secular songs; the cycle *The Divan*, for mixed quartet; and organ and piano pieces.

HOWARD McKINNEY became known for his whimsical *Crumbs from Peacock Pie*. He was born in Pine Bush, New York, in 1890. He is an organist and teacher and the coauthor of a widely used book on music appreciation. He is also music editor for the publishing firm of J. Fischer and Brother.

JOHN DENSMORE (1880–1943), a native of Massachusetts, wrote songs of the ballad type. He studied composition and orchestration at Harvard. He wrote a cantata for chorus and orchestra—*Hail, Ceres, Hail*; many choral works; and the songs—*All to Myself, Roadways, I Must Down to the Seas Again, A Village Romance*, and others.

JOHN PRINDLE SCOTT (1877–1932) composed sacred and secular songs, quartets, and some piano music, and wrote the words to nearly all of his own songs. Born in New York, he received his chief musical training at Oberlin Conservatory. He directed choruses, lectured on folk music, and taught. His first important song was *The Secret*. Among later songs that became popular are *Wind's in the South, A Sailor's Love Song, Nocturne*, and *The Old Road*. Two of his well-known church songs are *The Voice in the Wilderness* and *He Maketh Wars to Cease*. He also wrote piano pieces, including three *Irish Sketches*.

And then we have the composers of lyric ballads and songs with a distinctly popular appeal, but destined to longer life than ordinary popular music. CARRIE JACOBS-BOND heads the list. *A Perfect Day*, her "best seller," rivals Nevin's *Rosary* in popularity. Some of her songs have a true folk-song quality in their simplicity—*Just a-Wearyin' for You*, *I Love You Truly*, *A Little Bit o' Honey*, and others. She was born in Wisconsin in 1862.

OLEY SPEAKS is of a different type. Most of his songs are best sung by men—*On the Road to Mandalay*; the war song *When the Boys Come Home*; the tender *Sylvia*; or the effective *Morning*. He has published over two hundred songs. He was born in Ohio in 1876, and for many years was a concert singer as well as composer.

GEOFFREY O'HARA's songs are sometimes more elaborate than those of Speaks, but they have the same popular appeal. The French Canadian songs, *Leetle Bateese* and *The Wreck of the Julie Plante* are dramatic narratives that singers can use with telling effect. *Give a Man a Horse He Can Ride* may be akin to the opening phrase of *Yip I Yaddy*, made famous by Blanche Ring some years back, but it improves the original. O'Hara's songs have become so well known by their first lines that he has found it necessary to print a catalogue listing the misnamed titles opposite the correct ones. He was born in Canada in 1882. He has had an active life, as instructor of native Indian music for the government, song leader in the army camps, and as an entertainer.

FREDERICK VANDERPOOL was born in New York in 1877. He studied organ with R. Huntington Woodman, and voice with Koemmenich, Carl Dufft, and Frank Dossert, and traveled with various musical and theatrical companies. He published his first song in 1900, and has written many lyric ballads: *If*, *Values*, *I Did Not Know*, *Ma Little Sunflower*, and others of their type.

FRANK H. GREY was born in Philadelphia in 1883. He was a pupil of Walter Spaulding and John Knowles Paine at Harvard, and of Charles Dennée and Frederick S. Converse at the New England Conservatory in Boston. He has been a radio director in New York, and formerly conducted Broadway musical comedies. He has composed orchestral works and many songs and piano pieces. His piano pieces include *Ten Aquarelles* and *Winter Scenes*. His musical comedies include *Sue, Dear* (1922), *Matinee Girl* (1926), and *Happy* (1927).

JAMES MACDERMID, composer and accompanist, has called himself a writer of "plain songs." He was born in Ontario, Canada, in 1875. He studied in Canada and in Chicago. He himself published the first ten of his songs—with success. Others followed, and have been on the programs of famous singers. Finally he turned over his compositions to a publishing house, and gave his full time to composing and accompanying. He made a number of tours with his wife, Sybil Sammis MacDermid. Among his fifty or more songs are *If I Knew You and You Knew Me; Fulfillment;* and *The Song My Heart Is Singing.*

For many years the song *Trees* was as widely sung as many a "popular" song of Broadway. It was composed by Oscar Rasbach, who was born in Dayton, Kentucky, in 1888. He studied in Los Angeles; then went to Vienna to study piano with Leschetizky. Later he established himself as a private teacher in San Marino, California. Among his songs are *April, The Look,* and *Mountains.* His piano compositions include *Scherzo, Valse Charlene,* and *You and You—* the latter a transcription of Strauss's Waltzes from *The Bat.* He has published three unusual *Folksong Sonatinas* for piano. The first *Sonatina,* entitled *Early California,* is based on such tunes as *La Cucaracha* and *Juanita,* but also involves *Dixie, Nobody Knows the Trouble I've Seen,* and *Oh! Susanna.* The second of the series is called *From Dixieland.* The third, published in 1944, is *In Colonial Days,* with *Money Musk* and *Yankee Doodle* among its themes.

For current popularity, the counterpart of Rasbach's *Trees* in the 1940's is *The Lord's Prayer* by Albert Hay Malotte. The sales of this song have been phenomenal, and are said to surpass those of any other items in its publisher's catalogue—the same publisher, incidentally, that issued *Trees.* There is hardly a concert singer who does not include Malotte's setting of *The Lord's Prayer* in his or her repertoire, and singers from the entertainment field have taken it up, among them Gracie Fields.

Malotte was born in Philadelphia, in 1895. He became a theatre organist in Chicago and in London, and for several years was a member of the music staff in the Walt Disney Studios in Hollywood. During this engagement he composed the scores for several of the "Silly Symphonies," and for *Ferdinand the Bull.* In addition to *The Lord's Prayer,* Malotte has made settings of the *23rd Psalm* and other scriptural texts.

ERNEST CHARLES has composed songs which have been widely used by concert and radio singers. He was born in Minneapolis, in 1895. His songs include *Clouds, The House on the Hill, Spendthrift, Sweet Song of Long Ago,* and *When I Have Sung My Songs. Summer Night,* and the Waltz-Interlude *Let My Song Fill Your Heart,* are among his piano pieces.

A composer and arranger, JOHN CHARLES SACCO distinguished himself with his tenderly appealing song *Johnny the One.* He was born in New York City in 1905, and was a captain in the Army during World War II. Others of his songs are: *That's Life, Never the Nightingale, Let It Be Forgotten, Revelation, When the Lilac Grows,* and the *Rag Picker.*

A number of our composers have proved able writers of instrumental pieces, for concert and for teaching. CECIL BURLEIGH is one of the best known. A violinist himself, he has written principally for his own instrument. He was born in Wyoming, New York, in 1885. His family moved to Omaha when he was nine years old, and he had his early music lessons there, and later in Bloomington, Illinois. Then he went abroad and studied violin with Anton Witek and Max Grunberg, and composition with Leichtentritt; after that in Chicago with Emil Sauret and Felix Borowski. Since his student days he has been active as a violinist and teacher; since 1921 teacher of violin at the University of Wisconsin.

His teaching pieces have been much used, for they are distinguished by the combination of practical usefulness and real musical interest. His concert pieces are well known, too; his three Violin Concertos are published, as well as his two Violin Sonatas—*The Ascension,* and *From the Life of St. Paul.* He has written a number of piano pieces and many songs.

EASTWOOD LANE is an intense individualist, a man who prides himself on his lack of musical training and is content to let his natural talent find its own outlet. He is truly creative; some of his short pieces have enough ideas for a symphony. In some cases he would have done better to have fewer ideas, and to give them some development. Yet there is an Americanism about Lane's music that makes it important, and maybe formal training would have stifled his natural exuberance.

He has written several sets of piano pieces—*Sleepy Hollow, Five*

American Dances, Adirondack Sketches, and others. Ferde Grofé scored some of them for Paul Whiteman's Orchestra—among them *Sea Burial* and *Persimmon Pucker.* He was born in the early eighties in a small town near Syracuse, New York. He is largely self-educated, academically and musically.

FANNIE CHARLES DILLON is a composer whose piano music has been featured on recital programs. When Josef Hofmann played an American program on his concert tours a few years ago, one of the pieces was Miss Dillon's *Birds at Dawn,* in which she wove together the notes of the vireo, the wren-tit, and the chickadee. She again went to nature for her Suite *Melodic Poems of the Mountains—Heights Sublime, Birds at Dusk, Harp of the Pines,* and *Brooklets and Quiet Pools.* She was born in Denver in 1881, and studied with Godowsky and Hugo Kaun in Berlin, and later with Rubin Goldmark in New York. In 1908 she made her debut as a pianist. She taught at Pomona College for three years, and since 1918 has been teaching in Los Angeles. For orchestra she has written *Celebration of Victory, The Cloud, A Letter of the Southland, Mission Garden, The Alps,* and *Chinese Symphonic Suite.* In 1918 she gave a concert of her own music in New York at the invitation of the Beethoven Society. She has composed also songs and chamber music.

Hofmann's American program had as its *pièce de résistance* a sonata by ALEXANDER MACFADYEN (1879–1936), a composer who was born in Milwaukee. He was trained principally at the Chicago Musical College, and was active as a teacher in New York and Milwaukee. He published about a hundred works, piano pieces and songs. The *Cradle Song* and *Inter Nos* have been widely sung.

The *Introduction and Fugue* of CLAYTON JOHNS (1857–1932) was another of the pieces on the Hofmann program. Johns was one of the older composers and was born in Delaware. He studied architecture in Philadelphia before he decided to make music his career. He studied in Boston with John K. Paine, then went to Berlin to work with Rummel and Kiel. He came back to Boston as a recitalist, teacher, and composer in 1884, and in 1912 joined the staff of the New England Conservatory. He left many piano pieces, and some for violin, among them a *Melody, Berceuse, Intermezzo, Romance,* and *Scherzino.* He wrote books on music, and published his *Reminiscences of a Musician.*

JOHN ORTH (1850–1932) was born in Bavaria and brought to America as an infant. From 1875 he was prominent in Boston as a teacher, and as an authority on Liszt, with whom he studied. He wrote many piano pieces, and did considerable editorial work. CONSTANTIN VON STERNBERG (1852–1924) was a Russian who came here in 1880 and became a citizen in 1886. From 1890 he lived in Philadelphia and founded the Sternberg School of Music there. He wrote over a hundred works for piano, many of them played by Hofmann, Fannie Bloomfield-Zeisler, Godowsky, and others. RICHARD BURMEISTER (1860——) was younger. He was born in Germany and settled in America when he was twenty-five. In 1903 he returned to Europe. During his eighteen years in America he taught at the Peabody Conservatory in Baltimore, and was director of the Scharwenka Conservatory in New York. Probably the best known of his many pieces was the *Persian Song* for piano. He wrote an impressive Piano Concerto.

CAMILLE ZECKWER (1875–1924) was a native of Philadelphia, the son of Richard Zeckwer, a musician who came to America in 1869. The son was educated at the Philadelphia Musical Academy, studied with Dvořák in New York, then with Scharwenka in Berlin. He later returned to Philadelphia to teach at the Academy; for many years he was its codirector with Frederick E. Hahn. Zeckwer was a prolific composer of songs, pieces, and many works in larger forms—a Symphonic Poem, a Piano Concerto, cantatas, an opera, and some chamber music.

FELIX BOROWSKI is famous for his *Adoration*, if for nothing else in his long list of achievements. Its melodic sweep is Wagnerian in its continued impulse, and yet it is unlike Wagner. The piece is best known as a violin solo, but it is also available for piano, and has been played in various instrumental combinations. Borowski was born in England in 1872, the son of a Polish nobleman who had settled in England after the Polish Revolution in the 1860's. He made quite a reputation abroad as a composer, and in 1897 he was invited to America to be the head of the theory and composition department of the Chicago Musical College. He has been an eminent music critic for newspapers, and since 1907 has written the program notes of the Chicago Symphony Orchestra. He has written much in the larger forms: a Piano Concerto, tone poems, overtures, rhapsodies, ballets, and pantomimes for orchestra, three Organ Sonatas, a Piano Sonata, and many pieces in smaller forms.

GUSTAV SAENGER (1865–1935) was one of the music editors who was a composer himself. Born in New York, he was for many years a violinist, then a conductor, at the Empire Theatre in New York. In 1897 he became associated with the firm of Carl Fischer, first as arranger, then as editor of publications; and from 1904 to 1929 he was the editor of the *Musical Observer*. He arranged standard works for the violin, but wrote many original pieces as well; a Concertino for violin, and many smaller pieces.

GIUSEPPE FERRATA (1865–1928) was born in Italy, and came to America when he was twenty-seven. He was active as a teacher and music director in a number of schools and colleges—one of them the Newcomb College at New Orleans. He wrote many piano pieces, works for violin and piano, songs, organ pieces, a String Quartet, a Piano Concerto, a Symphony for orchestra and chorus, and some Catholic church music—a *Messe Solennelle*, a *Missa* in G Major, and others.

ANNA PRISCILLA RISHER was born in Pennsylvania in 1875. She was educated principally at the New England Conservatory, where she studied with Goetschius and Chadwick. Aside from composing, her principal activities have been teaching and organ playing. In recent years she has been in California. Altogether she has published some three hundred compositions—piano pieces, trios for piano, violin, and cello, and songs. Much of her work is for teaching; she has three books on piano technique. Her *Indian Lament* for piano won one of the Presser prizes.

FRANCES TERRY writes principally for the piano. A number of her works are often on recital programs—among them the *Impromptu Appassionato;* the *Three Impromptus;* the Suite *Idyls of an Inland Sea;* the *Six Recital Etudes;* the *Ballade Hongroise,* and others. She also has a Sonata for violin and piano, and a *Theme and Variations* for string quartet. She is a native of Connecticut, and now lives in Massachusetts. Her music teachers were Scharwenka, Louis Victor Saar, and Mr. and Mrs. Edmund Severn.

CECIL COWLES was born in San Francisco in 1901. She was a child prodigy and made her debut as a pianist when she was six years old.

Her works for piano include an *Arabesque, In a Ricksha, Song of Persia, Lotus Flower, The Ocean,* and others. Her song *Hey Nonny, Oh* has been popular. She has slightly modern tendencies, but never forgets her melodic line. Another of the young women, HELEN DALLAM, is a native of Illinois, educated in Chicago. The bulk of her work is for instructive purposes—violin and piano pieces. She has also written for orchestra; notably her *Sea Pictures.*

There have been excellent pieces by other composers—the witty *Outlandish Suite* for violin and piano by SUSAN DYER; the *St. Lawrence Sketches* for organ by ALEXANDER RUSSELL. Russell deserves mention not only for his work as a composer but for his many activities—first as a pianist, then for his lectures and choral conducting at Princeton University, and finally for his work as director of concerts at the Wanamaker stores in New York and Philadelphia. He was born in Tennessee in 1881, and in addition to his organ pieces and works for chorus he has written a number of charming songs. CHARLES BOCHAU (1870–1932) became a teacher at the Peabody Conservatory in Baltimore in 1912 and wrote many violin pieces, some anthems, and songs. He was born in Germany, but was brought to this country in his youth. JAMES FRANCIS COOKE, known chiefly as editor of *The Etude,* and for many years in charge of the publications of the Presser firm in Philadelphia, has a number of compositions—many of them for piano. *Sea Gardens* is one of his most popular pieces. Cooke was born in Michigan in 1875. THORVALD OTTERSTRÖM, the Chicago professor of composition and theory, has been an active composer himself. His piano pieces have been played by such pianists as Fannie Bloomfield-Zeisler and Rudolph Ganz, and his orchestral works by the Chicago Symphony. He was born in Denmark in 1868, and came to America when he was twenty-four.

Although LEE PATTISON is best known as a pianist and music educator, he is also a composer of piano pieces. He was born in Grand Rapids, Wisconsin, in 1890. His musical training was at the New England Conservatory in Boston, and later in Berlin. He studied with Chadwick, Baermann, Juon, and Schnabel. He made his debut in Boston in 1913. Then for several years he and Guy Maier appeared in recitals as a two-piano team, during a period when very little duo work was being done. They toured the United States, Australia, and played in many European cities. Pattison has taught in Chicago and New York. Since 1937 he has been on the faculty of Columbia University. His compositions for piano include *Florentine Sketches* and a Suite called *Told in the Hills*.

ELIZABETH GEST specializes in two-piano arrangements of standard works, but she has written also original piano solos, violin pieces, and songs. She was born in New Jersey and studied at the Peabody Conservatory in Baltimore, the Institute of Musical Art, and with Nadia Boulanger in Paris. She is an active lecturer, pianist, and composer, and lives in Philadelphia. Her arrangements for two pianos include the chorale *Jesu, Joy of Man's Desiring,* by Bach; *The Little Windmills,* by Couperin; the Strauss Waltz *Vienna Life; Bamboula,* by Gottschalk; and others.

Many composers have specialized in piano teaching pieces. Among them: ERNEST R. KROEGER (1862–1934), CHARLES DENNÉE (1863——), WILLIAM HENRY BERWALD (1864——), FREDERICK A. WILLIAMS (1869——), LOUIS ADOLPHE COERNE (1870–1922), CARL WILHELM KERN (1874——), BERT R. ANTHONY (1876–1923), STANLEY R. AVERY (1879——), J. FRANK FRYSINGER (1878——), CEDRIC W. LEMONT (1879——), ROY S. STOUGHTON (1884——), CHARLES HUERTER (1885——), ERNEST HARRY ADAMS (1886——), L. LESLIE LOTH (1888——). And among the women: FLORENCE NEWELL BARBOUR, THEODORA DUTTON, CARRIE WILLIAM KROGMAN, and MATHILDE BILBRO. Miss Bilbro was born in Alabama and began studying the piano at six. Her entire education was acquired in the United States. She has written hundreds of compositions for piano students.

The development of class piano instruction led many composers and editors to devise methods and to write attractive pieces adapted to the new ways of teaching: HELEN CURTIS, ANGELA DILLER, MARTIN HAAKE, LEON ILTIS, HAZEL GERTRUDE KINSCELLA, GUY MAIER, OSBOURNE MCCONATHY, OTTO MIESSNER, and others. Miessner has also written many choral works, a Piano Sonata, and songs. He was a pupil of Edgar Stillman Kelley; born in Indiana in 1880.

JOHN M. WILLIAMS is one of the most successful with piano teaching material. He was born on a plantation in Texas in 1884. His musical studies were in Chicago and New York. Since 1913 he has taught and lectured in the United States and abroad. His Piano Books probably have a wider distribution than the works of any composer of similar numbers. His methods for beginners and his collections of solo and duet material cover more than forty volumes. He also conducts classes in teacher training.

Mrs. Crosby Adams is a specialist in music for children. She was born Juliette A. Graves at Niagara Falls, New York, and studied with local instructors. She and her husband lived successively in Buffalo, Kansas City, Chicago, and Montreat, North Carolina, teaching for more than twenty years in Chicago. In Montreat their busy careers are continuing today. Mrs. Adams's better-known piano works for beginners are *Graded Studies, Five Tone Sketches,* and *Thirty Improvisations.*

One group of our composers has specialized in choral writing. Elmer Samuel Hosmer, born in Massachusetts in 1862, a pupil of J. C. D. Parker and Percy Goetschius, has written many anthems, solos, and duets for church use, and three cantatas—*The Man Without a Country, Columbus,* and *Pilgrims of 1620.* He taught music at the Rhode Island College of Education in Providence.

Nathaniel Clifford Page (San Francisco, 1866——) has made hundreds of arrangements of other composers' music for chorus, and for orchestra, but he has also been a composer on his own account. His first ventures were light operas. He composed several of them, as well as cantatas, incidental music for plays, orchestral music, songs, and pieces. As a member of the editorial staff of the Oliver Ditson Company in Boston, Carl Fischer in New York, and then Ditson again, he has revised and edited many publications of songs.

Daniel Protheroe (1866–1934) was born in Wales and came to America in 1886. He was a talented chorus conductor and led many of our choral organizations. He wrote many pieces for chorus; also cantatas, a Symphonic Poem, and two String Quartets. He compiled the *Hymnal* for the Welsh Presbyterian Church, and four books of ritual music for the Scottish Rite.

William Rhys-Herbert (1868–1921) was also born in Wales, but was identified with music in this country for many years. His specialty was operettas for schools. He published part-songs and cantatas, and a number of songs. Mark Andrews (1875–1939) was an

Englishman who was identified with choral and church music. His setting for male voices of the hunting song *John Peel* has probably been used by every glee club in the country. For many years he was an organist in Montclair, New Jersey, and was the conductor of several glee clubs in surrounding towns.

SAMUEL RICHARDS GAINES is of Welsh parentage, born in Michigan in 1869. His *Salutation* for chorus is probably his best-known work. In 1928 he conducted the first performance of his oratorio *The Vision*, in Texas. His *Fantasy on Russian Folk Songs* won him a prize, and he was invited to conduct its performance at the Maine Festival in 1930. He has been a choral conductor in several cities, among them Detroit and Columbus, Ohio. At present he is organist and choirmaster of the Old Shawmut Church in Boston.

HENRY CLOUGH-LEIGHTER (Washington, D.C., 1874——) has been active as a composer for chorus, and as an editor. He has edited and prepared for publication approximately four thousand compositions and literary works on music, by American and foreign composers and authors. From 1901 to 1908 he was with Ditson; from 1908 to 1921 with the Boston Music Company; and after 1921 editor-in-chief of the E. C. Schirmer Music Company in Boston. His own works include the cantatas *The Righteous Branch*, and *Christ Triumphant;* a symphonic ode *Christ of the Andes*, for double chorus, soli, and orchestra; several songs and song cycles for solo voice and orchestra, some hundred shorter choral works, and an equal number of songs.

F. FLAXINGTON HARKER (Scotland, 1876–1936) came to this country when he was twenty-five, and from 1914 was a choral conductor and organist in Richmond, Virginia. He wrote cantatas, anthems, choruses, sacred and secular songs, and organ pieces.

KURT SCHINDLER (Germany, 1882——) came to New York in 1905 to be an assistant conductor at the Metropolitan. He founded the MacDowell Chorus in 1909, which became the Schola Cantorum in 1912. He was a specialist in choral arrangements of folk songs— Russian, Spanish, and Finnish, and he composed many original choruses and songs.

WILLIAM LESTER (England, 1889——) was brought to America when he was thirteen. He was educated in Chicago, chiefly by Adolf Brune, and has since been active there as a teacher, choral conductor, and organist. His oratorios include *Everyman, The Manger Babe, The Coming of the King,* and *The Golden Legend.* His grand opera *Manabozo* was performed at the Covent Garden in London. This was the first of a trilogy of operas on the tribal legends of the Iroquois Indians, the libretto by Francis Neilson. In addition to his cantatas, part-songs, and songs, he has written Suites for piano, for organ, and for chamber music combinations; a String Quartet; and a Violin Sonata.

JOSEPH WADDELL CLOKEY (1890——) is known principally for choral works. He was a pupil of Edgar Stillman Kelley and was born in New Albany, Indiana, August 28, 1890.

His works include a Symphony, five operas, numerous part-songs, cantatas, sacred choruses, organ music, and an orchestral Ballet Suite. He has also made some highly effective choral transcriptions of early American songs: an anthem by Billings, Stephen Foster songs, and two choice examples of gutter-balladry—*Cocaine Lil* and *Frankie and Johnnie.*

Clokey is skillful in using sharp contrasts, sudden changes of tonality, and cannily planned dissonance. In late years a more serious study of the nature of church music, liturgies, medieval music, and plain song has made his style more objective, modal rather than chromatic.

A number of our composers have been identified with the early days of the phonograph. VICTOR YOUNG was for eight years music director for Thomas A. Edison and his experimental laboratory in Orange, New Jersey. He arranged and conducted orchestral accompaniments for singers on many of the Edison records.

He was born in Bristol, Tennessee, in 1889, and had his early music training with Romeo Gorno and Louis Victor Saar in Cincinnati. In New York he studied composition with Mortimer Wilson and Frederick Schlieder, and orchestration with Adolf Schmid. He appeared with the Russian Symphony Orchestra as piano soloist, and made recital tours both as soloist and accompanist in the United States, Canada, and England.

He has published operettas, orchestral works, and about seventy songs. For orchestra he has written *In the Great Smokies, Arizona Sketches* which he conducted at its première in the Hollywood Bowl (1936), and a novelty entitled *Jeep.* He composed a ballet *Charm*

Assembly Line, and *A Fragment* for string orchestra. Popular among his songs are *A Winter Rose, Land of Evangeline, Flowers and You, Red Rosey Bush,* and *The Song of the Teakettle.*

ARTHUR BERGH was another specialist in conducting orchestras for phonograph records. He was born in St. Paul, Minnesota in 1882, and was educated in America as a violinist. He wrote two melodramas with orchestra—*The Raven,* and *The Pied Piper of Hamelin;* a symphonic chorale *The Unnamed City;* a romantic opera *Niorada; Festival March* for orchestra; and *Honor and Glory,* March for orchestra (1939); two operettas—*In Arcady* and *The Goblin Fair;* a chorus *O Captain, My Captain;* a song cycle *The Congo;* about eighty songs; pieces for violin and for piano.

For several years, RICHARD KOUNTZ was affiliated with the pioneer radio station KDKA in Pittsburgh, writing weekly feature programs. He is a composer of songs and has written some pieces for organ and for piano. He was born in Pittsburgh in 1896. In 1928 he wrote *Lady Divine* for motion pictures. From 1927 to 1939 he was manager of the Standard and Educational Publications Department of M. Witmark and Sons. He composed a *Pastorale* for organ. His songs include *The Sleigh* (as solo, and also arranged for choral combinations), *Lilac, Cossack Love Song,* and *Prayer of the Norwegian Child.*

CLARENCE OLMSTEAD is another song composer who has been associated with radio. An advertising executive for many years, he has in recent years been in Hollywood in charge of major programs for advertising agencies. His songs include *Deep in My Heart* (1922); *Tears* (1923); *Thy Sweet Singing* (1922); *I Am Thy Harp* (1925); *The Ladies of St. James's* (1925); *Pirate Song* (1925); *Today* (1927); *Until the Day* (1926); and, more recently, a *Time Suite.* He was born in Minneapolis in 1892.

Among the composers who have specialized in Negro music, the name of HENRY THACKER BURLEIGH is prominent because he was one of the pioneers in arranging spirituals for concert use, and also because as a singer, himself a Negro, he has sung the songs of his people throughout the country. He was born in Erie, Pennsylvania, December 2, 1866, and as a young man he was active principally as a church singer. In 1892 he was awarded a scholarship at the National Conservatory in New York, where he studied with Dvořák, who be-

Ethelbert Nevin
(See pages 559–563)

Albert Hay Malotte
(See page 576)

Oley Speaks
(See page 575)

came enthusiastic over the Negro songs that Burleigh sang for him. Since 1894, Burleigh has been the baritone soloist at St. George's Church in New York, and on Palm Sunday in 1944 sang *The Palms* for the fiftieth time in that church. For many years he appeared frequently in concert, and has acted as music editor for a publishing house.

Burleigh has made arrangements of dozens of the spirituals, generally without development or alteration of the melodies. His setting of *Deep River* has enjoyed as great a popularity as any of the Negro songs. Strange to say, though he is a Negro, his harmonizations and treatment are often far from Negroid. He brings to the melodies a sophistication of treatment, chromatic harmonies and the like, which sometimes lifts them from their native element.

CLARENCE CAMERON WHITE (1880——) is one of the Negroes who was educated at the Oberlin, Ohio, Conservatory of Music. Later he went abroad to study with the famous English Negro, Coleridge-Taylor. Born in Clarksville, Tennessee, in 1880, he has been principally active as a violinist, but his *Bandanna Sketches*, for violin and piano, have attracted attention to his gifts as a composer. Kreisler, Spalding, and other famous violinists have found his setting of *Nobody Knows the Trouble I've Seen* a highly effective program number. White has published a book of forty Negro spirituals, and he has composed a String Quartet on Negro themes, and a Negro Rhapsody for orchestra.

WILLIAM J. REDDICK (1890——) first came to the attention of a wide public through his characteristic settings of the Negro spirituals: *Standin' in the Need of Prayer, Leanin' on de Lawd*, and *Wait till I Put on My Crown*. He was born in Paducah, Kentucky, in 1890, and studied at the Cincinnati College of Music. From 1920 to 1937 he was organist of the Central Presbyterian Church, New York. For several years he taught at the Master Institute of United Arts and at the Brooklyn Music School Settlement. In 1926 he founded the Little Theatre Opera, which he conducted for four years. From 1936 to 1942 he was musical director and producer of the Ford Sunday Evening Hour, and in 1943 he became manager of the Licensing Division of Associated Music Publishers. In 1945 he again became director of the Ford concerts.

Reddick's major works include *Espanharmlem* for orchestra, and *Armistice Day* for orchestra, men's chorus, and tenor and baritone soli. Among his songs are *Velvet Darkness, Red Bombay, Since You Are Gone, Your Love and Mine, In the Darkness of Night,* and *I'm Goin' to Hitch My Mule.* He has also compiled and edited an album of *Roustabout Songs of the Ohio River.*

ROBERT MACGIMSEY knows the idiom of the Louisiana Negro so well that it is difficult to distinguish between his settings of Negro folk songs and the songs which are entirely of his own composing. *Shadrach, Daniel in the Lion's Den, The Old Home, To My Mother, Roofs, The Old Slave, Sweet Little Jesus Boy, Jonah and the Whale,* and *Abraham* are only a few of the MacGimsey songs which have become tremendously popular in concert and on the radio.

MacGimsey started life as a boy soprano. He was born in Pineville, Louisiana, in 1898, the son of a professor of mathematics at Centenary College in Shreveport, and a mother who was a pianist and singer. After studying in his home state he came to New York and worked with Oscar Seagle and Frank Damrosch. In Louisiana he has been a lawyer, a real estate dealer, and a cotton planter. He was a Senatorial secretary in Washington for three years, and is now living in Hollywood.

JACQUES WOLFE has made a specialty of Negro-like songs which are remarkable for their authentic racial flavor. He was born in Botoshani, Roumania, in 1896, and came to the United States as a small boy. He studied at the Institute of Musical Art in New York with Percy Goetschius and Franklin Robinson, and was graduated in 1915. He became a United States citizen, and has taught music in the New York High Schools for many years. His setting of the folk song *Shortnin' Bread* has become a great favorite. His original songs include *De Glory Road, Gwine to Hebb'n, Betsy's Boy,* and *God's World.* He also wrote the music for the play *John Henry,* produced in 1939 and starring Paul Robeson.

DAVID GUION (1895———) is important among the group of white composers who have turned to Negro songs, even though he has become equally well known for his settings of cowboy songs, particularly *Home on the Range.* His concert transcription for piano of *Turkey in the Straw* ranks with Dett's *Juba Dance* as one of the most characteristic arrangements of native music. His polyphonic subtleties never interfere with the melodic outline of the original, or destroy its delicious impertinence. Guion has classified his piano pieces into several groups. First there are the "Cowboys' and Old Fiddlers' Breakdowns"—*Turkey in the Straw; Sheep and Goat Walkin' to Pasture;* and the *Arkansas Traveler.* (Be sure to pronounce it Arkansaw.) Next on his list comes the group of "Alley Tunes"—*Brudder Sinkiller and His Flock of Sheep; The Lonesome Whistler;* and *The Harmonica Player.* He has made piano settings of traditional Mother Goose rhyme tunes, and in his list of drawing room and concert pieces are a *Negro Lament;* a *Pickaninny Dance; The Scissors Grinder;* and a *Jazz Scherzo.*

For voice he has arranged many of the spirituals, as well as a number of cowboy songs, and he has written a group of *Imaginary Early Louisiana Songs of Slavery.* In the larger forms he has composed a Suite for Orchestra, and a primitive African ballet *Shingandi.*

Primarily a nationalist, Guion interprets his observations in terms of the part of the country he came from—the Southwest. He knew the real Southern darkey—he can preserve his native accent. And as for his kinship with the cowboys, he grew up in the saddle. To quote Charles Finger, he can sit there with as much case as he can sit on the piano stool.

He was born in Ballinger, Texas, in 1895. He had some musical training in America, and then went abroad to study in Vienna. He has held a number of teaching positions in Texas, and also at the Chicago Musical College. Percy Grainger, always a lover of folk music, has termed *Turkey in the Straw* a cosmopolitan masterpiece, and John Powell has ranked the settings of the Old Fiddlers' Breakdowns higher than Beethoven's Country Dances.

JOSEPHINE MCGILL (1877–1919), was one of the first collectors of Appalachian Mountain ballads, but she also composed several original songs. *Duna* was made famous by Reinald Werrenrath, and by hundreds of other singers. She was born in Louisville, Kentucky; studied with Alexander Lambert in New York. She collected and published *Folk Songs of the Kentucky Mountains,* and wrote a number of articles on American music.

JOHN JACOB NILES (1892——) is a collector and arranger of both

Negro folk songs and the Anglo-American ballads of the Southern Appalachians. He was born in 1892 in Louisville, Kentucky, and studied at the Cincinnati Conservatory of Music and at the Schola Cantorum in Paris. In addition to collecting folk material, he constructs his own instruments for accompanying his singing (traditional dulcimers and lutes) and has concertized extensively, both alone and in collaboration with Marion Kirby. Niles's publications include: *Seven Kentucky Mountain Songs* (1929); *Seven Negro Exaltations* (1929); *Songs of the Hill-Folk* (1934); *Ten Christmas Carols* (1935); *More Songs of the Hill-Folk* (1936); *Ballads and Tragic Legends* (1937); *Singing Soldiers* (1927); and *Songs My Mother Never Taught Me* (1929).

Oscar J. Fox was one of the first to make concert arrangements of cowboy songs, chiefly those found in the Lomax collections. He has set the "dogie song," *Whoopee ti yi yo; Old Paint;* the *Old Chisholm Trail; Rounded Up in Glory;* and others; as well as three desperado songs—*Sam Bass; Prisoner for Life;* and *Jesse James.* Fox was born in Texas, October 11, 1879.

Harvey Worthington Loomis (1865–1930) was a specialist in catching the spirit of Indian music, and preserving it in his arrangements of the melodies. His *Lyrics of the Red Man,* settings for piano, first issued by the Wa-Wan Press, are altogether remarkable in the way they emphasize native, primitive traits. Loomis did not appear as a white man, presenting in civilized fashion a European version of Indian music; he achieved the true distinction of clothing his material in appropriate dress.

He was born in Brooklyn, New York, in 1865. He won a three years' scholarship at the National Conservatory, and became one of Dvořák's favorite pupils. His Indian settings gained him a considerable reputation, and he was also successful in writing music for children. He composed an opera *The Traitor Mandolin;* four comic operas; a number of musical pantomimes; incidental music to plays; a Piano Sonata and a Sonata for violin. He died at Roxbury, Massachusetts, in 1930.

Thurlow Lieurance (1878——) is known to the public principally for his song *By the Waters of Minnetonka,* which has rivaled Cadman's *Sky-Blue Water* in popularity. Lieurance has adapted an

Indian melody for his song, and placed against it a harplike accompaniment which is effective, even though it may not be authentic. He was born in 1878 in Oskaloosa, Iowa, trained at the Cincinnati College of Music, and spent altogether some twenty years in research work among the Indians, studying their life and recording their songs. In addition to his many settings of Indian songs he has composed an opera *Drama of the Yellowstone*. For many years he was associated with the University School of Music at Lincoln, Nebraska, and later became dean of the Music Department, Municipal University of Wichita, Kansas.

CHAPTER THIRTEEN

Latter-Century and Present-Day Religious Music

I. DUDLEY BUCK (1839–1909) AND HIS SUCCESSORS

IN previous chapters the growth of religious music has been traced from colonial days, through the work of Lowell Mason and his colleagues in the first half of the nineteenth century. The first psalmodists and hymn-tune writers were succeeded by men of better training, some of whom studied in Europe. Many wrote tunes which are still in wide use. Few of them, however, attempted the larger forms of choral writing. In this field the name of DUDLEY BUCK stands out as a pioneer, just as John K. Paine rises above his colleagues as the first of our symphonists to achieve success. Buck wrote for the orchestra, and Paine wrote some choral music, but each is known best in his own field.

In many ways Buck's missionary work in giving organ recitals was as educational as that of Theodore Thomas with his orchestra. His musicianship was combined with the ability to catch and hold popular attention. As a choir director and composer he helped to develop our literature for the church, and since he was fond of the mixed quartet which has been a feature of American worship, and sometimes its curse, he had a profound influence on our choir music. In his larger choral works he had due regard for the requirements of the texts he chose, and he was inventive and versatile in attaining appropriate effects. As a teacher he trained many church composers of the next generation—Harry Rowe Shelley, John Hyatt Brewer, Frederick Grant Gleason, and others.

Buck and Paine were close contemporaries—both were born in the same year—1839. Buck studied in Europe when Paine was there, and both returned to take up their work at home in 1862. Both were commissioned by Thomas to write works for our important expositions —Philadelphia in 1876 and Chicago in 1893. Both lived to see the twentieth century—Paine died in 1906 and Buck in 1909.

Dudley Buck was born in Hartford, Connecticut, March 10, 1839. His father was a shipping merchant, and even though the son showed an early taste for music, his father intended that he should become a business man. He had no music lessons until he was sixteen, but he made up for lost time and became so ardent a music pupil that his father changed his plans, allowed his son to become a musician, and determined that he should have the best possible training for his profession. Dudley went to Leipzig in 1858, where he studied with Hauptmann, Richter, Plaidy, and Moscheles. Then he went to Dresden to take organ lessons with Friedrich Schneider. He later spent a year in Paris, and then came home in 1862 to become the organist of Hartford's Park Church.

In 1864 he published his first *Motette Collection*, at a time when such motets were much needed. In 1869 he was called to Chicago as organist of St. James's. When the church burned in the great fire of seventy-one, many of his manuscripts were lost, including a setting of Drake's poem *The Culprit Fay*. Then he went to Boston to take charge of the music at St. Paul's. In 1872 he composed a *Festival Hymn for Gilmore's* second jubilee; a year later his setting of the 46th Psalm was performed by the Handel and Haydn Society. In 1874 he published *The Legend of Don Munio*, a setting of a metrical version of Irving's *Alhambra*, for small orchestra and chorus. The work was well adapted to the choral resources of small cities, and it became very popular.

Theodore Thomas invited Buck to come to New York in 1875, to act as assistant conductor of the Central Park Garden Concerts. He also appointed him assistant conductor of the Cincinnati Festival. Buck moved his family to Brooklyn, and after a short term at St. Ann's in New York, he became the organist of Holy Trinity in Brooklyn. In 1876 he wrote the *Centennial Meditation of Columbus*, which was performed under Thomas at the inaugural ceremonies of the centennial in Philadelphia. The poem was written for the occasion by Sidney Lanier, the poet-musician who deserves a place in our music history.

In 1877, Buck published a work which has been of great help to organists and choir masters: *Illustration in Choir Accompaniment, with Hints on Registration.* This handbook enjoyed many editions, and is still in use. In the same year he published his second Organ Sonata. *The Nun of Nidaro* (1879) was from Longfellow's poems, as were the *Scenes from the Golden Legend,* the symphonic cantata that won the $1,000 prize at the Cincinnati Festival in 1880. In the same year Theodore Thomas introduced Buck's symphonic overture to Scott's *Marmion* at one of the concerts of the Brooklyn Philharmonic.

In the *Golden Legend,* and in the *Marmion* Overture, Buck attempted the use of the leit-motif for identifying characters and emotions; yet he never became particularly Wagnerian, for he loved too well the Italian style of declamation and *bel canto.* His gift of agreeable melody was almost too suave at times, yet there was generally substance behind his facility.

In 1881, Buck published settings of more of Longfellow's *Saga of King Olaf,* from which he had taken the *Nun of Nidaro.* The later work was *King Olaf's Christmas.* Like the *Nun,* it was scored for male chorus with solos, to accompaniment of piano obbligato, reed organ, and string quartet ad lib. The composer knew what was practical in the way of accompaniment in his day.

His reputation abroad was strengthened in 1885 by the London performance of a dramatic cantata *The Light of Asia.* Lillian Nordica was one of the soloists. For the text of *The Voyage of Columbus,* Buck again turned to Washington Irving and adapted a libretto from the *Life of Columbus.* Buck's cantata presents six scenes—*The Chapel of St. George at Palos, On the Deck of the Santa Maria, The Vesper Hymn, Mutiny, In Distant Andalusia,* and *Land and Thanksgiving.* The work has had frequent performances in America and in Germany. Buck made his own German translation of the libretto.

Church choirs have found most useful the series of short cantatas depicting the prophecy, the birth, the death, resurrection, and ascension of Christ. There are three works in the cycle—*The Coming of the King, The Story of the Cross,* and *Christ the Victor.* All contain music that is mellifluous, not difficult to perform, and any one of them may be performed in connection with a Christmas or Easter service. *A*

Midnight Service for New Year's Eve has seen many old years out and many new years in.

He wrote a number of shorter songs and ballads, sacred and secular. Some are a trifle cloying in their sweetness. Sometimes, too, in his writing for the organ, he made transcriptions of familiar songs—*Home, Sweet Home* and *The Last Rose of Summer*, but many congregations would rather hear these as an offertory than music of Bach or Handel. Buck wrote for his market, and his work as a whole represents a compromise between the public taste and the composer's own ideals. Yet he constantly worked to raise standards, and he succeeded.

Buck's pupils made names for themselves. Of Frederick Grant Gleason we have already learned. CHARLES BEACH HAWLEY (1858–1915) was the son of a Massachusetts farmer who appreciated good music. Hawley had a musical education, and before he came to Buck for study in composition he had been a church organist and had directed the music at the Cheshire Military Academy. He was also a singer, and at eighteen was a soloist at the Calvary Episcopal Church. Then he was made assistant organist at St. Thomas's Episcopal Church. For many summers he took charge of the music at St. James's Chapel in Elberon, New Jersey, attended by Presidents Grant and Garfield. Hawley's principal compositions were songs, for he had a pretty gift for lyric melody. Through his connection with the Mendelssohn Glee Club he wrote many part-songs for men's voices, many of them of a "bullfrog on the bank" variety. Male quartets of several generations sang *They kissed! I Saw Them Do It*. There were sacred songs, too—no pupil of Dudley Buck could have avoided writing them. His *Trisagion and Sanctus* was perhaps the best known.

WILLIAM HAROLD NEIDLINGER (1863–1924) was an organist and conductor, but he specialized in child psychology, and wrote many delightful songs for children. Born in Brooklyn, he had his musical training with Dudley Buck. Besides his songs, he wrote a cantata *Prayer, Promise and Praise*, as well as two comic operas.

Three of Buck's most prominent pupils have had Brooklyn as their home and their principal scene of activity. JOHN HYATT BREWER (1851–1931) was organist at the Lafayette Avenue Presbyterian Church from 1881. Born in Brooklyn in 1856 he was for several years famous as a boy soprano in Brooklyn and New York. He studied with

Dudley Buck, and then became organist at the City Park Chapel (Brooklyn), when he was fifteen. He was prominent as a choral conductor. While Buck was conductor of Brooklyn's Apollo Club, Brewer was accompanist. When Buck retired in 1903, Brewer was made conductor. He was one of the founders of the American Guild of Organists, and in 1916, New York University made him a Doctor of Music.

Brewer wrote over two hundred compositions, many of them for chorus. Some have won prizes—*Up with the Flag*, the Brooklyn City Prize in 1894; *Lord of the Dunderberg*, a cantata for men's voices and orchestra, the Schubert Glee Club prize in 1905; *Bedouin Love-Song*, for mixed voices *a cappella*, the Chicago Madrigal Club prize in 1906. He wrote much for instruments—a String Quartet, a Suite for orchestra, an orchestral *Fantasie*, and some pieces for string quintet and flute.

HARRY ROWE SHELLEY was born in New Haven in 1858. He began his career as an organist at the Center Church in that city and studied music first at Yale College, and then later with Dudley Buck. He studied with Dvořák at the National Conservatory. He has lived in Brooklyn, and has been organist of two of her leading churches— Plymouth Church and the Church of the Pilgrims. For many years he was the organist at the Fifth Avenue Baptist Church in New York. Like his teacher Buck, Shelley has been successful with sacred oratorios and cantatas—*The Inheritance Divine; Death and Life; Vexilla Regis;* and *Lochinvar's Ride*. His anthems are singable and effective, for he knows his church choir from experience. His orchestral works include two Symphonies; a *Santa Claus* Overture; an orchestral Suite *Souvenir de Baden-Baden;* a Violin Concerto; and a *Fantasia* for piano and orchestra.

RAYMOND HUNTINGTON WOODMAN (1861–1943) was the third of Buck's pupils to be identified with Brooklyn. In 1930 he celebrated his fiftieth anniversary as organist of the First Presbyterian Church. His father had been an organist before him. Brooklyn was his birthplace in 1861, and his father was his teacher. He studied with Dudley Buck, and then with César Franck in Paris. His works include anthems and cantatas, a few works for organ, and many songs. His setting of Christina Rossetti's *The Birthday* has helped many a song recitalist to an encore. He was straightforward in his music, always to the point, and sparing in his use of irrelevant elaborations.

At the celebration of his fiftieth year as organist of the First Church, the combined choirs of nine churches came together to do him tribute by singing his music. Fellow organists came to play—William C. Carl, Clarence Dickinson and others; and Dr. Morgan Noyes, then pastor of the church, spoke of Woodman's leadership in the ministry of music, and his distinguished contribution to the beauty of public worship.

So much for the pupils of Dudley Buck. There are many others who have contributed to the literature of worship music. Homer Newton Bartlett had a long and respected career—from 1846 to 1920. For thirty-three years he was organist of the Madison Avenue Baptist Church in New York. He came from New York State, born in a village named Olive and schooled in Ellenville. His music teachers were S. B. Mills and O. F. Jacobsen. He wrote over two hundred and fifty compositions; for organ a *Toccata*, a Suite, a *Festival Hymn*, *De Profundis*, and a *Méditation sérieuse*. He composed an opera and an operetta; a symphonic poem and a *Legende* for orchestra; a Concerto and a *Ballade* for violin and orchestra. Like Shelley and Woodman, Bartlett was one of the founders of the American Guild of Organists.

Music pupils of a past generation knew Bartlett through his Opus 1, a *Grande Polka de Concert*. Rupert Hughes called it "one of the most outrageously popular piano pieces ever published in America," and it was indeed both outrageous and popular. It gained a facile reputation that needed many better works to balance it. These Bartlett supplied, for much of his music is thoughtful as well as agreeable. He occasionally tried stunts that did not come off, such as imitating Gounod by adding a vocal part to a Cramer *Etude* and calling the result *Lord God, Hear My Prayer*. His *Jehovah Nissi*, a sacred march chorus, was a stirring, effective piece of writing.

Lucien Gates Chaffin (1846–1927) lived to be more than eighty years old. He was born in Worcester, Massachusetts, graduated from Brown University, and then gave himself to teaching, composing, and work as a concert organist, music critic, and editor. His works include a setting of the 23rd Psalm, a cantata *Holy Night*, many anthems, organ pieces, and songs.

Sumner Salter (1856–1944) was one of the most prolific of our composers for the church. For nearly twenty years choirmaster at Williams College, he wrote many anthems for men's voices. *Tarry with Me, O My Saviour* has long been a favorite, largely because of its restful melodic line and its warm harmonies in the register of male singers. He made hundreds of vocal arrangements for various combinations—he knew what voices could do and how they would blend effectively. His responses and choir services are both musical and devotional.

Salter was born in Iowa in 1856. He began his career as an organist while a student at Amherst College, where he was graduated in 1877. His music teachers were Eugene Thayer and J. C. D. Parker; he also had some lessons in theory with J. K. Paine. For a couple of summers he was assistant teacher to Sherwood. He held many church and teaching positions in various parts of the country. For two years he was at Cornell University, and then in 1905 he went to Williams. For three years he was editor of the *Pianist and Organist*. His wife, Mary Turner Salter, was a song writer. Her work is discussed in the preceding chapter.

HAMILTON CRAWFORD MACDOUGALL (1858–1945) was organist, choirmaster, and professor of music at Wellesley College for almost thirty years. Pupil of Sherwood, Lang, and J. C. D. Parker, he was by tradition well equipped in both organ playing and choir training. Some of his choral works and anthems have achieved distinction and wide use. His festival setting of *Onward, Christian Soldiers* almost sings itself in its stirring melody and rhythm. He published music for the Masonic ritual, and made a setting of the 85th Psalm for tenor, bass, chorus, and organ. He wrote many articles and several books on organ playing and church music.

PETER CHRISTIAN LUTKIN (1858–1931), from 1897 dean of the School of Music in Northwestern University, was an active composer of church music. He wrote a Communion Service, several *Te Deums*, a number of settings of the *Magnificat* and *Nunc Dimittis*, and many anthems.

JAMES HOTCHKISS ROGERS (1857–1940) was born in Connecticut, but from 1883 was identified with the musical life of Cleveland, where he was organist of the Euclid Avenue Temple and the First Unitarian Church. Rogers studied first with Towne and Clarence Eddy in Chicago, then went abroad and worked with Haupt and Loeschorn in Germany, and with Guilmant and Widor in Paris. For organ, Rogers wrote a Sonata, two Suites, a Concert Overture, a grand *chœur*, a Christmas *Pastorale*, and a *Processional March*. He composed morning and evening services, two cantatas, and many anthems. Among his songs the best known are *The Star* and *Wind-Song*. He was an able teacher, and for many years was music critic of the Cleveland *Plain-Dealer*.

GEORGE WARING STEBBINS (1869–1930) was the son of George C. Stebbins, the singing evangelist, but his love for good music and his foreign training with Guilmant and Henschel made a respectable musician of him. He was one of the founders of the American Guild of Organists, and was organist at several Brooklyn churches—including Emmanuel Baptist and Plymouth. His compositions number many organ pieces, anthems, choruses, and songs.

GEORGE BALCH NEVIN (1859–1933), a cousin of Ethelbert Nevin, was long known as a composer of church music. He wrote several cantatas: *The Crown of Life, the Incarnation*, and others. Like Chadwick he made a setting of Lanier's *Into the Woods My Master Went*. Nevin was born in Pennsylvania and spent most of his life in Easton, Pennsylvania. For nearly thirty years he divided his time between a wholesale paper business and music.

His son, GORDON BALCH NEVIN (1892–1943) made music his profession, and was organist at churches in Easton, Pennsylvania, Cleveland, and latterly at Johnstown, Pennsylvania. He published a number of works, principally for the organ. Chief among them are a *Sonata Tripartite* and a *Pageant Triumphale*. There are also a number of secular songs. He published effective concert versions of three Stephen Foster songs: *I Dream of Jeanie, Carry Me 'Long*, and *De Camptown Races*.

CHARLES WHITNEY COOMBS (1859–1940), was prolific in both sacred and secular music. Born in Bucksport, Maine, of New England parentage, he encountered as a youth the Puritan prejudice against making music his profession. It was not until he had proved beyond all doubt that this was the career for which he was fitted that his mother consented to his studying music seriously. He went abroad in 1878, first studying at Stuttgart and Dresden, and finally in 1887 becoming the organist and choirmaster of the American Church at Dresden. He held this position for years, and returned to America in 1891 to become organist of the Church of the Holy Communion in New York. This position he occupied for seventeen years, and in 1908 became organist at St. Luke's in New York, remaining until 1928 when he retired from active professional life.

Of Coombs's many works the most important are his cantatas: *The Vision of St. John, The First Christmas, Ancient of Days, Sorrows of Death,* and *Light Eternal.* He wrote many anthems and songs, sacred and secular. *Her Rose* is perhaps the best known of the songs.

LOUIS RAPHAEL DRESSLER (1861–1932) was born in New York and spent practically all of his life there. For many years he was organist at All Souls', and was active as choral conductor, accompanist, composer of church music, and music editor for a publishing house.

WALTER HENRY HALL (1862–1935), though born in England, lived in this country after he was twenty-one years old. He was organist in Germantown, Pennsylvania, and Albany, New York, and after 1896 in New York City. In 1893 he founded the Brooklyn Oratorio Society. In 1913 he was made professor of Choral and Church Music at Columbia University. His compositions include a Communion Service in G, a *Magnificat* and *Nunc Dimittis,* a *Festival Te Deum,* and many anthems, canticles, and hymn-tunes. In 1919 he was a member of the committee on the Episcopal *Hymnal.*

After thirty years' service as organist and choirmaster of St. Thomas's Church in New York, T. TERTIUS NOBLE (1867——) retired his post in 1943. Since then he has been giving his time to composition. He feels that the purpose of church music is to stimulate a devotional attitude in the congregation—and that the answer to this is the creating of more beautiful and more inspiring music.

Born in Bath, England in 1867, Noble was a scholarship pupil at the Royal Conservatory where he studied organ with Parratt, harmony and counterpoint with Bridge, and composition with Stanford. He became the organist at All Saints' Church at Colchester in 1881 and remained until 1889. From 1890 to 1892 he was assistant organist at Trinity College, Cambridge. He was organist at Ely Cathedral from 1892 to 1898, and at York Minster from 1898 to 1913. In 1910 he revived the once celebrated York Festival, after they had lapsed for seventy-five years.

Noble came to the United States in 1913 and centered his musical activities in St. Thomas's Church, where he not only played the organ and directed the choir, but also established a choir school which has been training choristers since 1918.

He has concertized extensively in the United States, Canada, and England. He has written orchestral works, services, hymns, choruses, songs, and pieces for piano and for violin. He composed a comic opera *Killibegs* (1911); for orchestra he has written *Introduction and Passacaglia* (1934), and a *Morris Dance;* for organ, a Concerto in G Minor, *Toccata and Fugue* in F Minor, *Solemn March* in E Minor, *Theme in D flat with Variations;* also a festival cantata *Gloria Domini;* and songs, including *Winter, A Birthday Song,* and *Waiting for the May.*

Noble's distinguished New York colleague CLARENCE DICKINSON (1873——) is a native of Indiana. Trained in Chicago, and then with Guilmant, Vierne, and Moszkowski in Paris, he was active in Chicago until 1909—organist of St. James's Church, conductor of the Chicago English Opera Company and several choral societies. When he came to New York he was appointed organist of the Brick Presbyterian Church, and the Temple Beth-El. In 1912 he became associated with the Union Theological Seminary; from 1928, the director of its School of Sacred Music. He succeeded Frank Damrosch as conductor of the Mendelssohn Glee Club and helped found the American Guild of Organists.

Dickinson's compositions include vocal solos and choruses, a Symphony for organ, and shorter works for organ and stringed instruments. He has edited a series of *Sacred Choruses, Ancient and Modern,* a *Book of Eighty Anthems,* and a *Book of Forty Antiphons.* In 1945 he published *90 Interludes* for organ (arrangements).

Canon CHARLES WINFRED DOUGLAS (1867–1944) was a High Churchman who devoted much of his life to the restoration of plain song in the Episcopal Church. In fact, he was the most important advocate of a revival of both plain song and of later medieval music. As one of the editors of the music edition of the 1940 *Hymnal* of the

Episcopal Church he introduced about forty tunes of plain song or polyphonic type into that *Hymnal*. He composed a number of original hymn-tunes, notably one for John Bunyan's words: "He would valiant be, let him come hither."

After many years as organist in several churches Canon Douglas became director of music for the Sisterhood of St. Mary and instructor in plain chant at the General Theological Seminary in New York. His works include a *Missa de Angelis, Asperges me, Cantica Eucharistica, Compline, Missa Marialis, Missa Penitentialis, Missa Paschalis,* the *Canticles at Evensong,* the *St. Dunstan Psalter and Kyrial,* and a Mass in G for women's voices and small orchestra.

T. CARL WHITMER, born in Pennsylvania in 1873, is an organist and choirmaster who has done much creative work. He considers that his life work has been the writing and composing of a series of *Spiritual Music Dramas* which have been produced at *Dramamount,* an artistic colony Whitmer has founded near the Hudson River in New York State. His published works include songs, pieces for piano and for organ, anthems and choruses, a *Syrian Ballet* for orchestra, and a *Choral Rhapsody* for soli, chorus, and orchestra, to a text by Walt Whitman. He has in manuscript several works for chamber music combinations. Whitmer was organist of the Sixth Presbyterian Church of Pittsburgh from 1916 to 1932. He is now teaching in New York.

JAMES ROBERT GILLETTE (1886——) was a professor of music at Wesleyan College, Macon, Georgia, from 1914 to 1919. He was city organist in Evansville, Indiana, from 1919 to 1923, and organist and teacher at Carleton College, Northfield, Minnesota, from 1923 to 1937. He founded the Carleton Symphonic Band in 1923, the Gillette Chamber Orchestra in 1937, and has made several tours as organist and conductor of chamber music. He has published two cantatas; two Symphonies for modern band: *Pagan,* first performed by the Goldman Band in New York in 1934, and *Sinfonietta in Olden Style,* heard at the Eastman School in 1937; about forty organ pieces, including *Chanson de Matin, Toccatina, Pastorale,* and *Grand Choeur;* also band compositions and songs. He is now teaching in Lake Forest, Illinois.

HARVEY BARTLETT GAUL (1881–1945) was a prolific composer who produced instrumental as well as vocal music in almost every form, but he became so well known as a choir and choral conductor that he seemed most closely associated with church music. He was born in New York in 1881, and was a resident of Pittsburgh from 1910— as organist at Calvary Church, music teacher at Carnegie Institute of Technology, and music critic for the *Post* and *Sun*. At seventeen he was assistant organist at St. John's Chapel, New York, and later became organist at St. Luke's Chapel in Paris. He studied and played in France and England, as well as in America. His foreign teachers were Widor, d'Indy, and Guilmant, and in New York he studied with Dudley Buck and Le Jeune.

Gaul composed overtures, suites, and tone poems for orchestra, including *Pere Marquette* and *New England Prelude*. His *Fosteriana* is a Suite featuring Stephen Foster's melodies, for string orchestra. His best-known choruses are, perhaps, *Prayer of Thanksgiving* and *Appalachian Mountain Melodies*. He published cantatas, oratorios, songs, and organ pieces. He died in Pittsburgh, December 1, 1945.

EDWIN SHIPPEN BARNES (1887———) studied with Horatio Parker at Yale, and then with d'Indy in Paris. He came to New York in 1911 and was organist first at the Church of the Incarnation and then at the Rutgers Presbyterian Church. He went to Philadelphia in 1924 to become organist at St. Stephen's Church. In 1938 he became organist and choirmaster at the First Presbyterian Church in Santa Monica, California. His works include: three cantatas—*The Comforter, Remember Now Thy Creator*, and *Christmas;* three Suites and two Symphonies for organ; *Fantasia* for chorus and organ; many organ solos and piano pieces; anthems and sacred songs. His recent compositions are *Scherzo* for organ; and the songs—*In April, The Master Soul, Thou Hast My Heart, The Fatherland, My Guide*, and *In Bethlehem's Manger Lowly*.

From 1915 to 1940, HAROLD VINCENT MILLIGAN (1888———) was organist of the Park Avenue Baptist Church which became the famous Riverside Church on Riverside Drive, New York, and of which Harry Emerson Fosdick was the pastor. Before going to Dr. Fosdick's church, Milligan had been organist at Plymouth Church in Brooklyn, the Fifth Avenue Baptist Church in New York, and the West End Synagogue. He has written a number of choral works, sacred and secular, some organ pieces, and two operettas; but he is perhaps best known to the general public for his arrangements of songs by Francis Hopkinson and other early American composers. He is the author of a biography of Stephen Foster.

In recent years CARL MUELLER (1892——) has achieved a nation-wide reputation, chiefly as a skilled arranger of works for *a cappella* chorus. He was born in Sheboygan, Wisconsin, and was educated at Elmhurst College in Illinois and at Westminster Choir College, Princeton, New Jersey. He studied music with private teachers in Saint Louis, Milwaukee, Chicago, and New York. He has been the choral director at the State Teachers College, Upper Montclair, New Jersey, and was on the faculty of Union Theological Seminary, New York. Since 1927 he has been organist and choirmaster of the Central Presbyterian Church in Montclair, and has organized in that city an excellent *a cappella* choir. He has composed more than a hundred works for voice, chorus, organ, and piano. He has written also *The Junior Chorister* and the *Junior Choir Anthem Book*.

NOBLE CAIN (1896——) is another *a cappella* specialist. Born in Aurora, Indiana, in 1896, he was a piano pupil of Allen Spencer, and studied theory with Adolf Weidig and Leo Sowerby. He was graduated from Friends' University, the University of Chicago, the American Conservatory, and received an Honorary Music Doctor's degree from Lawrence College. For ten years he conducted the choral work for a high school. Then in 1930 he organized the Chicago *A Cappella* Choir, and presented this choir in various parts of the country. He has conducted over NBC since 1933, specializing in arrangements of Negro spirituals. And he has made lecture tours for several years.

His cantatas include *The King and the Star, Evangeline*, and *Paul Revere's Ride*. Among his *cappella* choruses are *Rarely Comest Thou, Watchers of the Stars, Offering of the Soul*, and *Wake Up, Sweet Melody*. He has written an oratorio *Christ in the World*. He has composed more than a hundred other part-songs and has written a textbook on choral music.

ROBERT LEECH BEDELL (1909——) has become a prominent organist, and has given many organ recitals in New York City and the East. He has written about fifty original organ numbers and more than a hundred organ transcriptions and arrangements. Perhaps the best known of his original compositions is *Legende*, which he has recorded and has written also for full orchestra. Among his anthems are *Sing We This Day, 'tis Gladsome Easter* and *March On, Ye Soldiers True.* His latest piano piece is *Arabesque.* He has made piano arrangements of standard classics, such as works of Bach, Brahms, Handel, and others.

To return to the older composers, EDWARD JULIUS BIEDERMANN (1849–1933) was chiefly concerned with music for the Catholic Church. He was the son of A. J. Biedermann, piano teacher and composer. The younger Biedermann wrote several masses and considerable choral music.

EDUARDO MARZO (1852–1929) was another of the composers of Catholic Church music. He was an Italian who came to New York in 1867 as a prodigy pianist. For several years he traveled as accompanist for soloists; Carlotta Patti, Annie Louise Cary, Sarasate, and others. From 1878 he lived in New York, as a vocal teacher, as organist at the Church of the Holy Name, and as a music editor and composer. He wrote nine Masses, four vespers, forty songs and anthems for the Catholic service, as well as three *Te Deums,* forty anthems and sacred solos for the Protestant church. He wrote much secular music, too. Operettas and cantatas and songs.

NICOLA ALOYSIUS MONTANI (1880——) is the organizer of the Society of St. Gregory to promote Gregorian music in the Roman Catholic Church. He has written much church music: two masses, a *Stabat Mater,* and motets.

PIETRO YON (Italy, 1886–1943) was substitute organist at the Vatican before he came to America. In 1907 he became organist at St. Francis Xavier's in New York, and in 1926 began his seventeen years of service at St. Patrick's Cathedral. He wrote many Masses and several motets; a Sonata and a number of pieces for organ. His *Gesù Bambino* has become famous as an organ piece and as a song. His most recent work was *Pater Noster,* for mixed chorus and organ.

2. FOLK HYMNS AND THE GOSPEL SONG

Conservative churchgoers, and the members of liturgical congregations, are apt to raise their eyebrows at the so-called "gospel songs." They feel that if religion is to be held as a noble part of our daily or weekly lives, music better fitted to the dance hall will hardly preserve its nobility.

The songs, of course, have a distinct mob value, and have been highly useful in swaying crowds at revival meetings. Some of them have shown amazing endurance—we still gather at the river, "the beautiful, the beautifu-hul river," and some of our children, in Sunday School at least, continue to "fight with sin bravely," in waltz time. Basses and tenors still echo sopranos and altos in singing, "In the sweet —(in the sweet)—By and By—(by and by)" and for a full quarter-century, Billy Sunday brought the repentant up the sawdust trail to the strains of Homer Rodeheaver's *Brighten the Corner Where You Are*.

Actually the gospel song, as a type, has a long history. It has been, perhaps, the most stirring, even disturbing, phenomenon in religious music. It appeared as revival song, Sunday School song, or gospel hymn less than one hundred years ago and its production line is still moving rapidly.

A fact less widely recognized is that the gospel songs are not an "original" but a side sprout or "sucker growth" from an older, sturdier stem; sturdier because its roots reached into the rich soil of American folk song and British folk song, too. This earlier music remained long unwritten and was unrevealed to the literate, musical person, and since it was purely "country" music, was completely strange to urban ears. The uncovering of this honest American religious folk-song tradition is all but exclusively the work of George Pullen Jackson, whose research has been accomplished during the past twenty years. Dr. Jackson found that throughout the Gulf States there is still a hoary, rural community-singing activity indulged in by the *Sacred Harp* singers, who took their name from the title of a fat, oblong, hundred-year-old volume of part-song. This has been their sole musical manual. Jackson observed this folkway at firsthand and gave a description of it in *White Spirituals in the Southern Uplands* (1933). He coined the name as a temporary term to avoid confusion with the Negroes' similarly named songs. In two subsequent volumes—*Spiritual Folk Songs of Early America* (1937) and *Down East Spirituals and Others* (1942)—he edited and published the bulk of the tunes, five hundred and fifty from *The Sacred Harp* (first edition, 1844), *The Southern Harmony* (1835), and a score of other all-but-forgotten country handbooks of a similar nature. Jackson's diggings into origins, nature, and habitat gradually lighted up the whole growth period of country religious song, beginning some two hundred years ago.

This peculiar song innovation accompanied or followed a peculiar religious outburst, the "New Awakening" which began with Jonathan Edwards and other religious ecstatics. For it became apparent that psalm singing was too sedate to suit this fiery upheaval of hell-fire and heaven-storming. What was this song? Well, it had to be *different*. It had to be suited to the countryside and frontier and frontiersman. And under such circumstances what was more natural than that these religious leftists (rural Baptists, chiefly, then Methodists, New Side Presbyterians, and others) should begin to sing their favorite folksy hymns (Watts, Newton, Stennett, Cennick), as well as many religious lyrics which were homemade, to the well-known tunes of the old secular ballads—*Barbara Allen, Little Hugh, Captain Kidd, Lord Lovel*, and scores of others? This process went on briskly during the decades following the Revolutionary War. Jackson's five hundred and fifty songs just mentioned are the product; and his latest book *White and Negro Spirituals, Their Life Span and Kinship* (1943), tells the two hundred years' story in detail. The songs are a time-tested body of melody of, for, and by the very people who brought them into a new environment in which they expressed religious folk emotions.

Around the year 1800 the all-denominational camp meetings took up these songs, livened them, filled out partially remembered texts with much repetition, refrains, and choruses, and thus made them over into a rather roistering type of song which took its place by the side of the comparatively quieter variety, and went under the various names —spiritual songs, camp meeting songs, revival songs, and chorus songs.

Both of these closely related folksy song types grew in popularity throughout the first half of the nineteenth century; this, despite the frowns (and worse) of the more cultured church folk and their musical mentors. The songs grew, but they remained for almost that whole period essentially "unwritten music." And when they did appear in printed form gradually during the 1830's to the 1860's they were dressed up in a notation as different from the usual symbolism as were the tunes from those of the regular ecclesiastic tradition. It was a modification of the "shape notation" which we have noted in the opening pages of Chapter III as Andrew Law's experiment. It had become by mid-century the "God's music" of all pious rurals from Pennsylvania onward south and west, where it remains surprisingly widespread to this day.

To be sure, as early as 1805 one semiliterate enthusiast, Jeremiah Ingalls, had dared to publish a book of the tunes—*The Christian Harmony*—in New Hampshire. But the book was shunned in its region as an illegitimate, and it had no progeny there. The really successful, and in time complete, recording of the unwritten songs took place to the southward, first in Pennsylvania (*Beauties of Harmony*, 1813?), then in Virginia (*The Kentucky Harmony*, before 1815), and in still later and further Southern books. The old tradition lives today only among the deep-Southern *Sacred Harp* singers.

This country music had hardly come into full light before what some have called "the religious section of Tin-Pan Alley" recognized it as a trend which could be capitalized. The result of this recognition was the personally fabricated and signatured, and thus copyrightable, songs of the 1850's. The earliest publications showed the most obvious cribbing of folk-melody ideas. Dadmun's *Revival Melodies* (1859) is an example. Then the light gait, the refrain-and-chorus technic, and the textual repetitivity of the earlier anonymous folk material flowed further and naturally, but mechanically, into the productions of the Sankeys and their kind.

There were, of course, men of lesser and greater gifts who contributed songs of corresponding quality. One of the oldest of the gospel song writers was CHARLES CROZAT CONVERSE (1832–1918). His best-known hymn was *What a Friend We Have in Jesus*, a pretty melody that has been widely used. Converse was a well-educated musician. He studied with Richter and Hauptmann in Germany; then became a lawyer and practiced both music and law in Erie, Pennsylvania. He wrote a song that he hoped would become a national hymn—*God for Us*. He composed an *American Concert Overture* (based on *Hail Columbia*), a *Festouvertüre*, and he left in manuscript two symphonies, two oratorios, several overtures, string-quartets, and quintets. He spent his last years in Highwood, New Jersey.

WILLIAM HOWARD DOANE (1832–1915) was one of the most prolific of the gospel hymn writers. Born in Connecticut, a pupil of

B. F. Baker in Boston, he spent his life principally in business—a manufacturer of woodworking machinery. His musical activities date from his thirtieth year, and he was awarded the Doctor of Music degree by Denison University in 1875. *Saved by the Blood, My Faith Still Clings, This I Know,* and *Sound the Alarm* are among Doane's favorite hymns.

WILLIAM GUSTAVUS FISCHER (1835–1912) was a Philadelphia bookbinder who became interested in music, and developed his gifts as a teacher and choral leader. For thirty years from 1868 he was a successful piano dealer. He is best known to Sunday Schools through his ballad-hymn *I Love to Tell the Story,* and the somewhat maudlin *Whiter than Snow.*

HART PEASE DANKS (1834–1903) is known to fame as the composer of *Silver Threads Among the Gold,* yet he, too, devoted his saccharine talents to the church. His first composition, the tune *Lake Street,* appeared in Bradbury's *Jubilee Collection.* He wrote a sacred song *Not Ashamed of Christ,* and in 1892 he published a set of what he or his publishers modestly termed *Superior Anthems for Church Choirs.* Danks was born in New Haven. When he was eight the family moved to Saratoga Springs, where he attended the district school and had some music lessons. While he was still a youth, his family moved again, this time to Chicago, and he helped his father in his trade as a builder. When he was nineteen he became a carpenter, but his interest in music led him into various musical pursuits: bass singer, choir leader, and conductor of musical societies. He was largely self-taught in music, but he struck the popular taste and was successful. It is said that he published over 1,300 compositions, mostly songs. In its day, *Don't Be Angry with Me, Darling* ranked with *Silver Threads* in popularity.

The name of THOMAS PHILANDER RYDER (1836–1887) is seldom heard today, but this New Englander made something of a name for himself, first as organist at Hyannis, and later at the Tremont Temple in Boston. He was a popular teacher and choir leader, and his hymns were used considerably. He was the compiler of *Golden Treasure,* "a collection of hymn tunes, anthems, chants, etc. for public worship, together with part-songs and glees, for mixed and male voices, for musical conventions."

PHILIP PAUL BLISS (1838–1876) was a protégé of George F. Root, who, incidentally, belongs in this chapter as well as in the discussion of Civil War songs. In his later years Bliss was connected with the gospel meetings of Major D. W. Whittle, and it was his task to lead the singing and put life into it. He helped Root and his partner Cady conduct music conventions. His experience taught him the psychology of religious mass meetings, and his songs reflected his experience. *Hold the Fort, Only an Armor Bearer, Pull for the Shore, Rescue the Perishing* were among his exhortations. Nor can we laugh too much at the Negro, when Bliss told the story of the Ark with a waltz. He compiled many hymnbooks: *The Joy;* "a collection of new and carefully selected music for classes, choirs and conventions"; *Sunshine for Sunday Schools;* and he contributed to the standard Bigelow and Main collection of *Gospel Hymns.* Bliss had a tragic end; he was killed in the Ashtabula train wreck in 1876.

HUBERT PLATT MAIN (1839–1925) wrote hundreds of hymns. He was musically a practical person; he knew what people liked to sing. He was brought up on the music of Bradbury and Woodbury, and when he was ten he could read their songs by note or syllable. After several years of clerical and editorial work in New York, he went to work for Bradbury. When his father, Silvester Main, helped to organize Bradbury's successors, Bigelow and Main, Hubert Main stayed with the firm and eventually became one of its partners.

He spent the rest of his long life as a writer and compiler of hymns, and he met with great success. *Search Me, O Lord; Our Refuge; Wonderful Love,* are typical of his style. Main looked at his art somewhat through the dollar sign. When I was studying composition, my teacher told him that I was writing fugues. "He'll never sell 'em!" was Main's prompt reply. He was right.

One of the leading latter-century composers was IRA DAVID SANKEY (1840–1908), best known of all the musical evangelists in latter years. Sankey was for years the musical partner of Dwight L. Moody, one of the most famous of our revivalists. From 1871 until 1899, Sankey toured with Moody through the United States and Great Britain. "Moody and Sankey songs" became an almost generic term, representing to many musicians the lowest depths to which music can descend. Yet there was something moving in Sankey's tunes, maybe a matter of association to one who went to Sunday School in the nineties;

something that grips in spite of their obvious banality and sentimental-ism. The tunes are pretty cheap, yet they were favorites for many years. *Shine on, O Star!; He Is Coming; Not Far from the Kingdom; O Brother, Life's Journey Beginning; The Ninety and Nine; A Soldier of the Cross* were among the hundreds of hymns that Sankey wrote.

There were other composers who should be mentioned—especially GEORGE C. STEBBINS (1846–1945) who outlived his son George Waring Stebbins, and who composed until his death at the age of ninety-nine. He wrote over fifteen hundred hymn-tunes.

HOMER RODEHEAVER (1880——) is one of the most active of the gospel hymn group, as leader of singing at revival meetings, as com-poser of gospel songs, and as a publisher of songbooks. He has already been mentioned as the composer of *Brighten the Corner Where You Are,* which became famous as the theme song of Billy Sunday's mam-moth tent sessions. For more than twenty years (1909–1931) Rode-heaver had charge of the music at Billy Sunday's revival meetings, and was a trombone player as well as a singer. He made a tour of the world with the evangelist William Edward Biederwolf in 1923–24. He was born in Union Furnace, Ohio, and was a nongraduate student at Ohio Wesleyan University.

Rodeheaver has led the singing of the largest community groups ever congregated in this country. He directed the 62,000 at the open-ing of the Atlantic City Auditorium; the 85,000 for the Chicagoland Festival in Soldiers' Field; and the 250,000 at Elwood, Indiana, for the Willkie notification. Over KDKA he presented the first gospel song program ever heard over the radio, when that station was a pioneer. He has written a number of hymn-tunes, edited several hymn-books, and founded a school of evangelistic singing. As a publisher he is president of the Rodeheaver-Hall-Mack Company.

In view of the comments on the character of gospel songs which were made at the beginning of this chapter, it seems only fair to end with what Rodeheaver once wrote in response to an invitation to speak in their behalf:

The gospel song is a declaration of God's plan of salvation and his prom-ises, addressed to the people. We can bring you thousands of illustrations of individuals whose lives have actually been changed by the message of the gospel song, and who have become assets in their communities where they were liabilities before. These songs are not written for prayer meetings, but to challenge the attention of people on the outside who have not been interested in any form of church work or worship. They are used simply as a step from nothing to something. If critics knew how some of these songs were loved by many people, they would never refer to the "saccharine talents" of great and good men who have blessed the world with their songs.

Another influence of the gospel songs is apparent. Many of the older of these songs are reflected in the spiritual songs of the Negro, and it may be that the writers of our gospel songs have had far more to do with Negro spirituals than have African tribesmen. This matter is more fully discussed in the next chapter, under the heading "Negro Folk Music."

CHAPTER FOURTEEN

Our Folk Music

I. THE MUSIC OF THE NORTH AMERICAN INDIAN

1

THE folk music of the United States is a controversial topic among musicians. What is it? Where did it come from? Which part of it is truly American? These are matters that are easily decided by those who think superficially; but scholars hesitate to answer such questions. It all depends on what we consider to be American in our surroundings. If Americanism is a matter of geography, or residence, the distinction is clear. But if sources and distinguishing traits are to be considered, the subject of American folk song offers a puzzle that is not easy to solve.

There are many definitions of folk song. It is obviously a song of the people, not the street tune that is sung for a few months and then forgotten, but a song that lives for generations. Generally its origin is unknown, as far as the individual who composed it is concerned. To be a true folk song it must be typical of the people who sing it, part of their daily lives. Most important of all, the song itself must be more important than its composer. *Dixie* is better known than Dan Emmett; *Old Folks at Home*, than Stephen Foster.

We have many groups of folk songs in this country, yet few of them belong to the United States as a whole. The Negro songs are a characteristic utterance of those who were our slaves. The cowboy songs belong to the West; mountain ballads to the mountaineers; hillbilly songs come from the Ozarks; and the music of the American Indian is a primitive expression which has little to do with the art forms of a civilized people. There is folk music in America, but the overworked melting pot has much to do before any part of our folk song literature becomes a characteristic utterance of the entire nation.

The music of the Indians is a case in point. It is as far from our way of musical thinking as Chinese music. Although the Indians inhabited America for centuries before our ancestors came here, who are the Americans today: the white men or the red men? A brutally asked question, but pertinent. In their mode of life the primitive Indians who sang the songs that have since been collected from the remnants of the original tribes, are as foreign to the various white groups that compose America now as the Eskimos or South Sea Islanders. Can it then be said that primitive Indian music is American folk song?

Some say that Indian music is as much the heritage of Americans, as the music of the barbaric hordes of Russia is the heritage of cultured Russians. Not at all; the Russians of today are the descendants of those barbaric ancestors. Relatively few of us have Indian blood in our veins. Furthermore, as soon as composers attempt to idealize the songs of the Indian, and reduce them to a white man's harmonization, their whole character is lost in the process. For there is a long distance between savage music and folk music. Folk song is a relatively polished product, and while it may be composed of the same basic material, this material is presented in coherent sentences instead of in ejaculations and recurrence of unchanging rhythms.

Then, too, the term *Indian*, as applied to all primitive peoples who lived on the North American continent, is too general. There were over fifty basic linguistic stocks, all of whom were divided into separate tribes. At the present time the Office of Indian Affairs is dealing with three hundred and forty-two tribes, not including the subtribes and rancheria. These separate races all had different customs and ways of living. Some were highly organized socially and politically, while others were simply constituted. Each had its own legends, and presumably its own music. It is more exact, therefore, to speak of Chippewa, Hopi, or Blackfoot music, than Indian music, even though it all may sound the same to the novice. There are traits that all tribes seem to have in common musically, but these are probably characteristics that would be common to savage music in general.

II

It would be impossible in a chapter on the music of the American Indian to give anything approaching a comprehensive account of the songs of the many tribes. All that can be presented is a brief survey of the research that has been done in the field, and a short review of some of the things that these investigators have found. The earliest settlers in America spoke of the Indian's music, and there were many remarks on its peculiarities. When William Wood visited Plymouth and Massachusetts Bay he published an account of what he heard and saw. (London, 1634.)

Their musick is lullabies to quiet their children, who generally are as quiet as if they had neither spleene or lungs. To hear one of these Indians unseene, a good eare might easily mistake their untaught voyce for the warbling of a well tuned instrument. Such command have they of their voices.

Being unmusical themselves, the colonists made little attempt to study the music of the Indians, or to make any notation of their songs. In the latter eighteenth century there were several publications that attempted to reproduce occasional Indian songs in music notation. William Beresford printed an Indian tune when he published in 1789 his record of *A voyage around the world; but more particularly to the northwest coast of America.* Somewhere around 1800, George Gilfert published in New York, and P. A. Van Hagen in Boston, a song that purported to be a genuine Indian melody. This was *Alknomook, the Death Song of the Cherokee Indians.* It had been sung in Mrs. Hatton's *Tammany,* for which James Hewitt had arranged the music (1794). The song became very popular, and was known in almost every American drawing room in the early nineteenth century.

It was published in London first. It was issued there in 1784 under the title *Alknomook,* "The death song of the Cherokee Indians, An Original Air, brought from America by a gentleman long conversant with the Indian tribes, and particularly with the Nation of the Cherokees. The Words adapted to the Air by a Lady." Frank Kidson, in the *Musical Antiquary,* said that this "lady" was Anne Hone Hunter, the wife of a famous surgeon, and Haydn's hostess when he was in London. She wrote verses for a number of Haydn's settings, notably "My mother bids me bind my hair." Whatever Cherokee or primitive traits *Alknomook* may have had, it appeared in wholly conventional dress in both the English and American editions.

When George Catlin published the report of his "eight years travel [1832–39] amongst the wildest tribes of Indians in North America," he included a description of Indian music and dances. Henry Rowe Schoolcraft, in 1851, gave an account of the rites and symbolic notation of the songs of the Walbeno, and showed how these people used mnemonic symbols to refresh their memories for traditional songs.

The first serious attempt by a musician to make a scientific study of the music of the Indians was undertaken by THEODORE BAKER, in 1880. Baker, a German who later made his permanent residence in this country, was at the time a student at Leipzig University. He chose the music of the North American Indians as the subject of a thesis for his doctorate, and he visited the Seneca Reservation in New York State and the Indian school at Carlisle, Pennsylvania. He collected a number of songs, studied and analyzed them, but since his essay was published in Germany, it has had less influence than those by others which followed it.

ALICE C. FLETCHER came next. Her treatise on Omaha songs, various articles on the music of the Sioux and Pawnee Indians, and her book *The Indian in Song and Story*, were among the first authoritative works on the subject. Miss Fletcher was a Fellow in the Peabody Museum of Harvard University. Among her collaborators was Francis La Flesche, who made a study of the customs of the Osage and Omaha Indians. JOHN COMFORT FILLMORE assisted Miss Fletcher in harmonizing and analyzing the characteristics of the tunes she had collected. Fillmore was a well-trained musician, founder of the Milwaukee School of Music, and later director of music at Pomona College in California. His arrangements of the Omaha melodies are adequate from a musical standpoint, yet they are so conventional that they make the tunes seem not the real thing, even to the ears of the layman. He went so far as to state that the Indians have a subconscious sense of harmony and that their tunes are harmonic melodies.

When the Hemenway Southwestern Expedition was at work among the Zuñi, Hopi, and other Pueblo Indians, BENJAMIN IVES GILMAN had charge of the study of their music. Gilman was very scientific. He studied certain songs from the acoustic standpoint, and by using a mechanical device, sought to measure the exact intervals the Indians used in their songs. He invented a system of notation to show minute deviations from diatonic pitch.

Probably the first investigator to use the phonograph in recording the songs of the Indian was JESSE WALTER FEWKES, who first studied the songs of the Passamaquoddy Indians in Maine in 1889. He later joined the Hemenway Expedition, and it was from his records of Zuñi songs that Gilman made his analysis.

FREDERICK R. BURTON commenced his study of Ojibway music in 1901. While at Harvard in 1882 he wrote music for *Hiawatha*. This was later developed into a dramatic cantata and published in 1898. After this he lived among the Indians for long periods. His study of their music culminated in his book *American Primitive Music,* published shortly after his death in 1909.

NATALIE CURTIS started her work with the Hopis and Zuñis in the Southwest about the same time that Burton began his study of the Ojibways in Minnesota and Wisconsin. Miss Curtis, later Mrs. Burlin, published her observations of over eighteen tribes in *The Indian's Book*. She did not harmonize the songs, but offered them as faithfully to their original form as music notation could present them. Her work is especially valuable in showing the Indians' attitude toward their music.

FRANCES DENSMORE has for many years been collaborator of the Bureau of American Ethnology of the Smithsonian Institution. Her researches have led her to study the music and customs of many Indian tribes—Chippewa, Teton Sioux, Northern Ute, Mandan Hidatsa, and others. She has used the phonograph in recording native singing, and her records have been preserved for students. She is one of the outstanding authorities on the subject of Indian music, and her views are based on a common sense attitude that not only demands facts, but distinguishes between the logical and the purely romantic point of view.

III

Although it is rarely accurate to speak of Indian music and customs as such, there are a few traits common to all tribes. Few Indians make music for its own sake. Every song is associated with some tribal custom, and is used only for the performance of that custom. There is a song for almost everything—friends, enemies, gods, animals, forests, lakes, clothing, and sometimes whiskey. As Densmore puts it, "the Indians used song as a means of accomplishing definite results"—to treat the sick, to have success in war or in the hunt, to accomplish anything the Indian felt was beyond his power as an individual. Songs are so closely associated with the ceremonies they accompany that Indians do not like to sing them on other occasions, even when they are showing the white man the songs of their tribe. One old Indian refused to sing a hunting song for Burton because it was not hunting season at the time.

Indians sing differently from white men, and there has been much discussion of their relative musical abilities. Some hold that the Indian has a far greater developed sense of rhythm than the white man, shown by his ability to beat his drum in one rhythm while he sings his song in another. Some think that the Indian's scale is far in advance of ours; that his divisions into smaller intervals than we use give him far greater flexibility and expressiveness in his melodies. Yet there are cynics who say that these phenomena merely show that the Indian cannot keep time nor sing in tune. Maybe they are right, for it is but logical to believe that our musical scale, evolved through centuries, has been formalized by natural acoustic laws. Primitive music is no doubt an early groping for these natural effects.

Of course, it is often true that an Indian singer will render a song many times over in exactly the same way that he sang it first. Miss Densmore has had songs recorded in the summer and again in the following winter by the same singer. Comparison of the two records shows the performances to be exactly alike in melody, pitch, and tempo. Often a song has been sung eight or ten times on a single phonograph record and the repetitions have been uniform in every respect. Burton took issue with Gilman on the question of the Indian's intonation. Gilman devised an elaborate notation to show exactly what intervals the Indians sang. Burton believed that deviations from pitch were caused, not by the singers' instinctive feeling for smaller intervals than those of the diatonic scale, but by their inability to hold an accurate pitch. He pointed out that this inability was by no means confined to

ASCAP

Jerome Kern
(See pages 666–667)

Photo by *Underwood & Underwood*

Victor Herbert
(See pages 653–654)

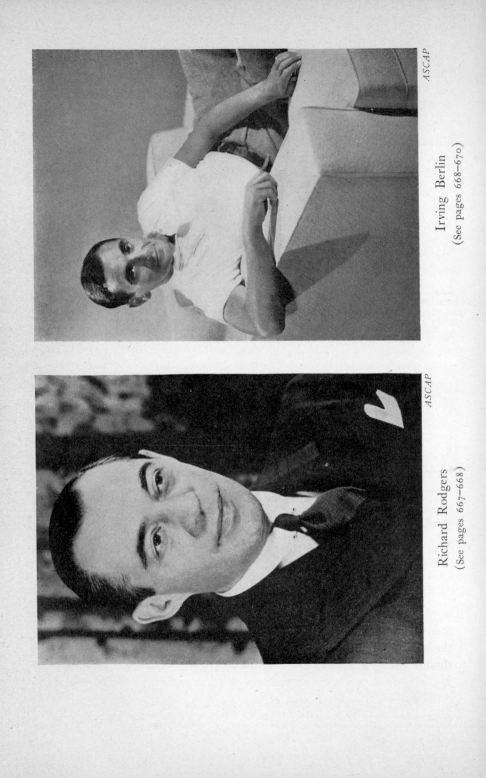

Irving Berlin
(See pages 668–670)

Richard Rodgers
(See pages 667–668)

the Indian, and that if we were to make phonographic records of civilized chorus rehearsals, when the singers were unaccompanied, we would find many curious intervals, if we undertook to measure them accurately. Also records of opera singers. He cited an experience that Fillmore had had with the Indians: [1]

In one case, Mr. Fillmore observed that the second part of a song was sung in a key a semitone lower than the first part. There was an upward skip of an octave and the singers fell short of it. They proceeded, however, from their false start and sang the second part relatively like the first; but when Mr. Fillmore played the song to them on the pianoforte and carried through the second part, his Indian listeners were displeased. When he played the piece throughout in the same key, they were satisfied.

Many Indians sing with a vibrato, and one of their favorite tricks is to attack a tone by beginning it sharp and immediately sliding down to the sustained tone. Descending melodies are a characteristic of all savage music. Often an Indian tune will descend steadily from the first note to the last. Sometimes there is an ascent in the middle, but then it starts to go down again. Miss Densmore found that in eight hundred and twenty songs, 67 per cent began with a downward progression, and in 87 per cent, the last note was the lowest tone occurring in the melody.

Reduced to an approximation of the accepted scale, many Indian melodies are found to utilize the five-tone, or pentatonic, major and minor modes. This is true of much folk music, for these modes involve the most natural intervals. Many of the songs seem to be in no particular key, although Miss Densmore has found that the majority of them seem to end on a tone that proved a satisfactory keynote to the ear. She found this true of 67 per cent of three hundred and forty Chippewa songs.

Then there is the question of multiple rhythms. When a civilized musician sings a song, his audience expects that song and accompaniment shall have some relation to each other. When the Indian sings, the arm that wields his drumstick has never heard of his voice, even though they both belong to the same person. When Burton began to study Indian music he had the conviction that the Indian had de-

[1] Frederick R. Burton, *American Primitive Music*, Moffat, Yard & Co.

veloped rhythm more highly than the white man. Intensive study made him change his mind, and brought him to the conclusion that the Indian is not aware that his drum beat is in conflict with the scheme of accents he invents for his song.[2]

Both, drum beat and song, are ingenuous expressions of his nature. One is extremely primitive, the other comparatively advanced, and, as he is still primitive, he clings to his cheerful noise, understanding it, aroused by it, while his musical soul toils darkly on toward an expression that aims ever at, and sometimes attains, symmetry. All of which is to say that he drums as he does because he knows no better.

IV

The collector of Indian songs has to be a discriminating person, to choose between what is traditional and real and what is new and synthetic. Much passes for Indian music that is quite modern, composed by comparatively civilized Indians. There are three classes of songs, as far as collectors are concerned. First, the old songs, sung by the old singers. These are now growing scarce, but many have been preserved on records. Second, the old ceremonial and medicine songs belonging to men now dead, but which can still be sung with reasonable correctness by Indians who heard their owners sing them. Third, the comparatively modern songs, representing a transitional culture, and showing the influence of civilization.

There are many kinds of Indian songs, each tribe having not only its own songs, but its own types as well. Many of the tribes have lullabies and children's songs. Some have comparatively few of these, for the mothers were busy in the fields all day, and babies were left to lie in their hammocks. Yet the Chippewa, Yuma, Makah, Mandan, Ute, and Hopi tribes are notable for their children's songs. Many of them accompany games which teach the young how to do essential things.

Songs are often the property of individuals. Those received in dreams may generally be sung only by their owners. Some songs may be purchased from their owners, generally with magic power for heal-

[2] Frederick R. Burton, *American Primitive Music*, Moffat, Yard & Co.

ing the sick. There are songs praising a man's virtues, his success in war or in hunting, or maybe his generosity.

Miss Densmore claims that love songs were not sung by the old-time Indians except in working love charms. Marriages among Indians were usually arranged by parents, and were confined to groups who had no blood relationship. Except with the Makahs, love songs are modern, and generally associated with disappointments. Playing the flute at dusk is a custom common to nearly every tribe, although it may not always be for the romantic purpose that poets would have us believe. Yet no doubt it has often helped the bashful lover to say his little speech.

The musical instruments of the Indians were flutes, whistles, drums, and rattles. In some form these were common to all tribes in North America. Miss Densmore has said that the Tule Indians of Panama were the only Indians who did not use a drum or pound anything. Flutes were often played by the youth of the village to please the maidens, but sometimes they were used to warn against the approach of an enemy in wartime. Whistles were used by magicians and by doctors when attending patients.

The drum was essential to all Indian music. Many Indians could not sing without it. There were hand drums, big drums which took several men to play, and drums that looked like kegs and were partly filled with water. They accompanied ceremonial dances, religious rites, and the singing of all sorts of songs. Rattles were generally regarded as sacred objects to be used only on religious occasions. There were different kinds of rattles. Some were receptacles containing small objects that hit against each other; some were sticks with objects that hit together suspended from them; and some were wooden clappers. Then there was the notched stick, which was laid by one end on a hollow gourd, while the performer ran a smaller stick over the notches.

In the bulletins of the Bureau of American Ethnology, Miss Densmore has given a detailed account and analysis of Chippewa songs. There were the Mĭdè, or Medicine songs, for the expression of religious ideas. Some were for direct ceremonial use (initiations, to secure success in hunting, and so on), and others were connected with the use of medicine (for healing or working charms). Many of these songs were taught only to those who would pay for the privilege of learning them.

The Chippewas were firm believers in dream songs, learned in visions while fasting. Some of these were the songs of the doctor, which could never be bought or sold. There were also the songs of the juggler, who did a sort of Houdini act in freeing himself from all sorts of ropes and knots before the assembled tribe. There were of course the war songs—some to incite war, some, songs of the warpath, and others of the scalp dance. Many of them had a religious significance; the "God with us" idea is by no means the sole property of the white man in wartime.

Game songs were found in many tribes; often each side sang them to invoke victory. The Indians were great gamblers and the stakes sometimes ran high. In the moccasin game of the Chippewas, four bullets or balls were hidden under four moccasins. The man or side that guessed which bullet was marked got the jack pot. Some of the songs showed a true sporting instinct. One is translated—"I will go home if I am beaten, after more articles to wager."

There is indeed a rich literature in the traditional music of the various Indian tribes. Much of it is interesting and some of it is beautiful. As interpretations of the Indian the songs are invaluable. As specimens of primitive art they are choice. American composers (way back to the time of Father Heinrich) have given us interesting examples of what can be done with these songs in larger compositions. We have already heard of MacDowell's *Indian Suite,* and there are many others who have sought to tap the melodic source of the primitive savages. There is an exotic flavor about them that is tempting; there is a haunting loveliness in some of the melodies that is very beautiful. Yet not all of them can be reduced to our conception of harmony and survive the process with any degree of appropriateness.

To select Indian tunes because they are useful is one thing. To choose them for nationalistic purposes is a different matter entirely, for they are American in the geographic sense alone. Mrs. H. H. A. Beach commented on the matter with much common sense when I asked her what she thought of using Indian themes. "I see no harm in it, if you want to do it," she replied.

2. NEGRO FOLK MUSIC

I

The songs of the American Negro form one of the choicest groups of folk song found in this country. Whatever their origin, or their ultimate significance to us, they are as rich, as colorful, and as warm in their melodic phrases as any songs that have ever been born here, or have been brought to our shores from abroad. For the Negro likes to sing, and whether he is singing a tune he inherited from his ancestors, or something he has picked up from the white man, he puts all of himself into his performance, gay or sad.

The songs are vital because they are sincere—they speak the Negro's real nature. Some of them fervent, some superstitious, others shiftless and irresponsible, they all show some phase of the undeveloped black man's childlike temperament. And when songs truly reflect the character of the people who sing them, they are folk songs, beyond all question of their origin. Everything the Negro sings about —"Norah" and the Ark, Daniel in the Lion's Den, or the ribald tale of Frankie and Johnnie (*Albert* with the Negroes)—he invariably reduces to his own experience.

Negro music has probably made a deeper impression on American life than has any other class of songs. First, through its cousin the minstrel song, then by way of ragtime, and later through the blues and jazz, the Negroid manner has permeated our popular music. The intelligentsia has so glorified this element that serious composers have been able to stay respectable while they experiment with its idiom. Side by side has come our welcome to the "spirituals," the Negro's religious songs. They have been invited to our concert halls, whether clothed in the trappings of Debussy and sometimes of Stravinsky, or in more appropriate costumes.

General recognition of the artistic value of Negro songs is comparatively modern. Singing on the plantations has long been a tradition, but the vogue of the "spiritual" has come with the present century. Thomas Jefferson spoke of the natural musical talents of the Negro in his *Notes on Virginia*, way back in 1784, and there were some airs from Virginia, one a Negro Jig, in Aird's *Selection of Scotch, Eng-*

lish, Irish and Foreign Airs, published in Glasgow in 1782. (It was this collection that contained the first known printing of *Yankee Doodle.*) We have seen how the minstrel shows, from the 1830's, were direct imitations of Negro singing. But serious consideration of Negro songs, as anything better than comedy dialect, did not come until after the Civil War, and not too quickly even then.

Negro singing, somewhat formalized, first became known to the country at large through the travels of Negro singers, first from Fisk University, and then from Hampton, Tuskegee, and other industrial schools. Fisk University was founded in Nashville, Tennessee in 1866, a pioneer institution to educate the freed slaves. Its early years saw bitter struggles; it was hard to raise money for a project not altogether popular at the time. Finally George L. White, who had been in charge of singing at the school, started on a concert tour with thirteen members of his choir. This was in 1871, and, though the first months were discouraging, before the little band of singers had finished three years' travel, they had raised $150,000 for the University—chiefly through voluntary collections among their audiences. Moreover, they had been a feature of Pat Gilmore's 1872 Jubilee in Boston, they had been abroad, received by Queen Victoria in England, and by the Emperor in Germany.

As other Negro institutes were founded, this became one of the favorite ways of raising funds for their maintenance. The Hampton and Tuskegee quartets have sung in churches in the winter, and at resort hotels in the summer, and through their singing have gained money for their cause, and have helped create the vogue of the Negro spiritual.

At the end of the century a few serious composers experimented with Negro music. Years before, Gottschalk had used Creole songs from Louisiana (in his *Bananier, Bamboula,* and other piano pieces), but it was not until our guest composer of the nineties, the Bohemian Dvořák, wrote his *New World* Symphony, that the idea of using Negro music took hold. At that, there is considerable dispute as to whether Dvořák intended to use actual Negro tunes, or whether he merely meant to catch their spirit. But what Dvořák accomplished was to create our respect for the folk songs that existed in our own country. Since then we have had hundreds of concert settings of Negro songs, some sophisticated and others simple in treatment; choral arrangements; and developments and elaborations of Negro material in symphonic works.

II

The origin of these songs is a matter that has troubled many a student, and caused much discussion. The more seriously students study the question, the less they are inclined to venture dogmatic theories. One supposition is that their idiom is African; that the ancestors of the Negroes brought their songs with them in the slave ships. Their peculiarities were adapted to English words when the Negroes learned the language of their masters, and heard the Bible stories of the missionaries and evangelists. Comparisons are made between the music of African savages and that of the American Negro. The pentatonic scale is common to both; each has a decided tendency to syncopation. Both seem to have an instinct for part-singing. Specific songs are brought forth to prove a connection. One writer claimed that *Go Down, Moses* so resembles an old Jewish Chant *Cain and Abel*, that Hebrews think the Negro song is theirs, and that Negroes claim the Jewish song. This has led to a theory that there was an ancient relation between Negro and Semitic races on the African continent. And yet again it may only explain why the Jew becomes an expert at jazz.

Of course, the pentatonic scale is found in folk songs the world over, and syncopation is the exclusive property of no race in particular. Yet it is only logical to assume that there are the relics of an African background in the music of the American Negro. Disputes today center around the question of how much of the Negro music we hear is African, and how much is learned from the white man. Some say that none of the spirituals, or at least very few, really belong to the colored man. They are merely his version of songs he heard from revivalists and missionaries. Those who know the gospel songs of the white folk are in accord with this view. It is known that the Negro did adopt many scores of his religious tunes and texts from the white people, especially the Baptist white people. He resang them with that perfect freedom which led to much unconscious revision according to his abilities, racial preferences, and individual hunches (just as all real folk singers do). The adoptive process was comparatively late, beginning not much before the middle of the nineteenth century.

Yet, even though gospel hymns are the parents of many of the spirituals, it may be admitted that the Negro has improved them musically, and has treated them according to his African heritage.

Testimony on the makings of many of these spirituals is forthcoming from those who have witnessed them. Baptisms, camp meetings, spiritual orgies are supposed to give birth to new songs. One starts to intone a phrase, another joins him, and soon the whole crowd is answering and swaying to the rhythm. A folk song is born, then and there. Natalie Curtis Burlin described such a scene in the *Musical Quarterly*, January, 1919:

On a suffocatingly hot July Sunday in Virginia, in a little ramshackle meeting-house that we had approached over a blinding road nearly a foot deep in dust, a number of rural Negroes had gathered from an outlying farm, dressed all in their dust-stained Sunday best for the never-to-be-omitted Sabbath service. . . . Service had already begun before we came and the congregation, silent and devout, sat in rows on the rough backless benches. The preacher now exhorted his flock to prayer and the people with one movement surged forward from the benches and down onto their knees, every black head deep-bowed in an abandonment of devotion. Then the preacher began in a quavering voice a long supplication. Here and there came an uncontrollable cough from some kneeling penitent or the sudden squall of a restless child; and now and again an ejaculation, warm with entreaty, "O Lord!" or a muttered "Amen, Amen"—all against the background of the praying, endless praying.

Minutes passed, long minutes of strange intensity. The mutterings, the ejaculations, grew louder, more dramatic, till suddenly I felt the creative thrill dart through the people like an electric vibration, that same half-audible hum arose—emotion was gathering atmospherically as clouds gather—and then, up from the depths of some "sinner's" remorse and imploring, came a pitiful little plea, a real Negro "moan," sobbed in musical cadence. From somewhere in that bowed gathering another voice improvised a response: the plea sounded again, louder this time and more impassioned: then other voices joined in the answer, shaping it into a musical phrase; and so, before our ears, as one might say, from this molten metal of music a new song was smithied out, composed then and there by no one in particular and by everyone in general.

Collectors of Negro songs tell of many individual bards who are reputed to have composed their songs. C. W. Hyne, in the introduction to *Utica Jubilee Singers Spirituals* [1] gives an account of "Singing" Johnson, who sang his way from community to community.

His coming was eagerly anticipated. The congregation hung on his voice, alert to learn a new song. As they listened, some would join in uncertainly, the keener ears soon catching the melody and words. The whole congregation easily learned the response, which is generally unvarying. Always the strong voice of the leader corrected errors until the song was learned perfectly. Singing Johnson undoubtedly derived his support in somewhat the same way as the preachers: part of a collection, food and lodging. He spent his leisure time in originating new words and melodies and new lines for old songs. A maker of songs and a man with a delicate sense of when to come to the preacher's support after a climax in the sermon, by breaking in with a line or two of a song that expressed a certain sentiment, often just a single line.

Odum and Johnson, in *Negro Workaday Songs*,[2] tell the story of "Left Wing" Gordon, of the *species hobo*, who never stayed in any place more than three weeks, "leastwise never mo' 'n fo'." Gordon was a great songster.

"Wing" claimed a blues for every state and more; if there was none already at hand, he would make one of his own. . . . Wing had practically no variation in his tunes and technique of singing. A high-pitched voice, varied with occasional low tones, was the most important part of his repertoire. But what variation in words and scenes, phrases and verses, the recording of which would exhaust the time and endurance of the listener and call for an ever-recording instrument!

It is not always safe to trust the Negro's claim to authorship. William Francis Allen and Lucy McKim Garrison, when they published their collection of *Slave Songs* in 1867, often found songs in Methodist Hymn Books, which Negroes said they had composed themselves. *Climb Jacob's Ladder* proved to be a song from a Northern book, as did *Give Me Jesus*, and *I'll Take the Wings of the Morning*.

Discussion regarding the origin of Negro songs is after all an aca-

[1] *Utica Jubilee Singers Spirituals*, taken down by J. R. Johnson, introduction by C. W. Hyne: Oliver Ditson Co.

[2] Odum and Johnson, *Negro Workaday Songs*, University of North Carolina Press.

demic matter. The important fact is that they are the Negro's inter- pretations of his surroundings, his superstitions, his beliefs, his legendry. If he has derived, even copied, a small part or most of this from the white man, it makes little difference. The songs are beautiful, and there is a wealth of them. If they have been shaped by the Negro's American surroundings and influences, they have far more claim to being American than if they were pure importations from Africa.

III

In one respect, the singing groups from Fisk and Hampton have given a false, or at least one-sided, emphasis to our idea of Negro music. The traveling quartets, which have sung principally in churches, have confined themselves to the spirituals, or religious songs. When a Negro "gets religion" he turns his back to his "wicked" secular songs. It is largely through Tin-Pan Alley that the nonreligious type of Negro song is generally known, and then largely formalized and stripped of most of its native charm. For this reason some of the latest collections of authentic Negro secular songs are most valuable.

Although all the songs of the colored man have much in common, musically and temperamentally, his music may be separated into religious and secular groups. Of course, the religion of the Negro is partly superstition. Also, in the slave days, he seized upon the idea of an after life as his release from bondage. He interpreted many Bible stories in terms of his own experience. The children of Israel were in a predicament similar to his own; he looked to a black Moses for his deliverance. If the Lord had delivered Daniel, he certainly wouldn't forget the poor black man in America.

The religious songs include the spirituals and the shout songs. Allen and Garrison claimed that the shout songs, or "Running Sper-chels" were confined to the Baptists, and were to be heard mostly in South Carolina and the states south of it. A typical "shout" was described by a writer in the New York *Nation* in 1867.

The true "shout" takes place on Sundays or on "praise-nights" through the week, and either in the praise-house or in some cabin in which a regular religious meeting has been held. . . . The benches are pushed back to the wall when the formal meeting is over, and old and young, men and women, sprucely-dressed young men, grotesquely half-clad field-hands . . .

boys with tattered shirts and men's trousers, young girls barefooted, all stand up in the middle of the floor, and when the "sperchil" is struck up, begin first walking and by-and-by shuffling round, one after the other, in a ring. The foot is hardly taken from the floor, and the progression is mainly due to a jerking, hitching motion, which agitates the entire shouter, and soon brings out streams of perspiration. Sometimes they dance silently, sometimes as they shuffle they sing the chorus of the spiritual, and sometimes the song itself is also sung by the dancers. But more frequently a band, composed of some of the best singers and of tired shouters, stand at the side of the room to "base" the others, singing the body of the song and clapping their hands together or on the knees. Song and dance are alike extremely energetic, and often, when the shout lasts into the middle of the night, the monotonous thud, thud of the feet prevents sleep within half a mile of the praise house.

Some of the spirituals are sad, some are happy. Generally the sad ones express a hope for the future, or a childlike faith in the hereafter: "Nobody knows the trouble I see, Nobody knows but Jesus"; "Swing low, sweet chariot, Comin' for to carry me Home." Often lively rhythms and tunes were used for the most devout songs: "Couldn' hear nobody pray"; "Roll, Jordan, roll"; "I want to be ready."

The precentor idea was common among the Negroes. Hundreds of the spirituals, and the secular songs, too, had their verses lined out by the leader, while the congregation of worshipers waited to join in the oft-repeated refrain. The leader would start:

> I got a robe, you got a robe;

then the chorus:

> All God's chillun got a robe,
> When I get to heab'n, gonna put on my robe,
> Gonna shout all over God's heab'n.

In the next verse the leader had a harp, in the third, wings, and in the fourth, somewhat in anticlimax, shoes.

Obviously the spirituals may be subdivided into many smaller groups. Funeral songs and chants, songs of a semireligious nature, sung in a comic vein, but with Bible stories for their text. Slave songs and sorrow songs form a definite group, although many fall into several classifications.

IV

The secular songs cover a far greater field than is commonly appreciated. Not only are there the songs that date back to the slave days—plantation melodies and cabin songs—but many of more modern origin, which show outside influences, but nevertheless seem authentically of the Negro. Work songs, for cotton picking, corn shucking, stevedoring; railroad songs of the section gang; steamboat songs; prison songs of the chain gang and the rock pile. Bad men's songs; devil songs (many unprintable); and then, of course, the "blues," which have been carried into our modern jazz.

The Negro has a love of balladry, of the true narrative type. Many of these songs are his versions of the white man's ballads—*Casey Jones*, and others of its kind; and some of the English ballads from the mountaineers in the Appalachians are sung by the Negroes. Yet many of them seem to be of his own making. He loves the bad-man ballads—the tale of the *Travelin' Man*, who made a "livin' stealin' chickens"; or *Bad Man Lazarus* (not the one of Bible fame), who "broke in de commissary"; and finally was shot down with a "forty-five." The Negro often violates the impersonal tradition of balladry by using the first personal pronoun, thus injecting his imaginary self into the story. "I'm de hot stuff man from de devil's lan' "; or "I'm de rough stuff of dark-town alley."

In his music the Negro is often filled with self-pity. Like many white men, he loves to think how people will mourn for him after he is dead, maybe by his own hand, by jumping into the sea, or by laying his head on a railroad track. Then he will be understood and appreciated, when it is too late. He sings "Ship my po' body home, If I die long way from home"; or "I wish I was dead," in which he borrows a phrase from the white man—"Over de hill is de po' house."

This self-pity element has been partly responsible for the "blues," a type of the sorrow songs. This kind of song has forced its way into our modern jazz, and into polite musical circles. It was popularized largely through the efforts of W. C. Handy, who published the *Memphis Blues* in 1912. Of its development and its part in our popular music of the day we shall learn later, for we are concerned here only with how the Negro enjoys his music in its native state. The blues are based on self-pity, yet often in happy-go-lucky fashion they express the singer's knowledge, or hope, that maybe things are not so bad after all. Handy once summed the matter up in these words:

Why the happy character in a plaintive mood? Why call it the blues when the music is joyous? It happens in this way: Rastus owes his rent. He is going to be ejected to-morrow if he does not pay. He has part of the money. He tries in vain to get the rest. Defying his fate, he goes to a party—dances joyously, spends generously, camouflaging perfectly his heavy heart. That's why the blues are joyous.

Yet the real blues are often lonely and melancholy. In most of them the trouble is caused by the relationship of man and woman, so rarely satisfactory, according to the Negro bard. "The man I love he has done lef' this town"; or "I laid in jail, back to the wall, Brown skin gal cause of it all."

Since Handy popularized the blues, they have been sung by whites as well as blacks. Many have been written by sophisticated composers, yet the originals are no doubt genuine, and thoroughly characteristic of a predominant phase of the uneducated Negro's make-up. Odum and Johnson, in *Workaday Songs*, discuss at length the question of authentic and modern blues, especially in view of the millions of phonograph records that have been sold in the past ten or fifteen years. They have found a surprising similarity between the words and titles of recent popular blues, and those of the songs collected more than twenty-five years ago. Explaining the present relationship between folk blues and the formal, or composed, variety, they write: [3]

When a blues [phonograph] record is issued it quickly becomes the property of a million Negro workers and adventurers who never bought it and perhaps never heard it played. Sometimes they do not even know that the song is from a record. They may recognize in it parts of songs long familiar to them and think that it is just another piece which some songster has put together. Their desire to invent a different version, their skill at adapting stanzas of old favorites to the new music, and sometimes their misunderstanding of the words of the new song, result in the transformation of the song into many local variants. In other words, the folk creative process operates upon a song, the origin of which may already be mixed,

[3] Odum and Johnson, *Negro Workaday Songs*, University of North Carolina Press.

and produces in turn variations that may later become the bases of other formal blues. . . .

Whether the formal blues have come to stay or not, it is impossible to tell at present. Possibly they will undergo considerable modification as the public becomes satiated and the Negro takes on more and more of the refinements of civilization. . . .

The folk blues will also undergo modification, but they will always reflect Negro life in its lower strata much more accurately than the formal blues can. For it must be remembered that these folk-blues were the Negro's melancholy song long before the phonograph was invented. Yet the formal songs are important. In their own way they are vastly superior to the cruder folk productions, since they have all of the advantages of the artificial over the natural. They may replace some of the simpler songs and thus dull the creative impulse of the common Negro folk to some extent, but there is every reason to suppose that there will be real folk blues as long as there are Negro toilers and adventurers whose naïveté has not been worn off by what the white man calls culture.

v

And now for the significance of all this Negro music to America. It has been protested that it is the song of the Negro alone, who represents but a single part of our population. Those of us who are not black cannot share the ownership of this literature with the Negro, because it is characteristic of him, and not of us. The Americanism of Negro song involves questions that are beyond the scope of a book on music; social and political questions, involving segregation of races, or admixtures not pleasant to discuss. In the case of mixtures, one Southern gentleman has said that the melting pot would become a witches' cauldron, and there are many Northerners who would sympathize with him. Obviously, the Negro songs are nearer our musical comprehension than the savage chants of the Indian. The Negro has been long enough in contact with the white man to acquire his musical scale.

There is a universality of appeal about the Negro music that makes it something more than the chant of a single race. The songs are so fundamentally human that they have already outlived the generation and conditions that produced the oldest of them. As Alain Locke writes in *The New Negro*:[4]

[4] *The New Negro*, edited by Alain Locke: A. & C. Boni.

They have survived in turn the contempt of the slave owners, the conventionalizations of formal religion, the repressions of Puritanism, the corruptions of sentimental balladry, and the neglect and disdain of second-generation respectability. They have escaped the lapsing conditions and the fragile vehicle of folk art, and come firmly into the context of formal music.

We have seen in foregoing chapters how many of these Negro songs have been used by serious composers. Some have been treated in type, and some have been garbed in a dress that is incongruous. Though the Negro songs are nearer our own expression than the music of the Indians, they nevertheless have to be treated appropriately to preserve their native appeal, otherwise their original flavor is lost. As MacDowell said when discussing Indian music, the problem of Americanism in music is not so easily solved as by taking folk songs born in America and harmonizing them haphazardly.

Some feel that the strongest impress of Negro music has come by way of jazz, now the sport of the musically polite. Rather than the naïve idealism of the spiritual, the restless syncopation, the discordant shriekings of the primitive black man, more nearly voice the fever of modern American life. Maybe they do, but all of these are questions that time alone can answer. We know that in America we have the songs of the Negro, some of them his own, and some his version of what he has learned from us. If the Negro is American, his songs are American. If we like his songs, we are welcome to use them, even though we may be borrowing them from a tenant who is none of our relation.

3. OTHER SOURCES OF FOLK SONGS

I

Throughout America there are sources of folk songs that have been appreciated by collectors only in recent years. It is good for our literature that we have at last awakened to the fact that we have valuable folk songs in hitherto unsuspected places, for as primitive customs and manners disappear, the songs associated with these traditions will vanish also. Civilization—and especially its age of machinery—does not provide fertile soil for folk songs. With our modern standardization of living, and such mediums as the radio and the talking pictures setting artificial standards in even the remotest places, the most rural countryman may soon acquire the manners and speech of the city dweller. Then he will sing the latest jazz hits instead of his own songs.

Folk songs are generally common to people whom civilization has touched the least, where society and life in general is the least organized. Isolation from other people, hand labor, and lack of printed literature are factors that nourish and perpetuate folk music. A certain naïveté is essential to the true people's song; sophistication is its deadliest enemy. True folk music is found among the Negroes, the mountaineers in the Southeast Appalachians, the cowboys, the lumberjacks and shanty boys, in the New England farm districts, among the wandering tribe of hoboes, with sailors and longshoremen, and often in the jails.

Not that each group has an exclusive, individual literature. There is much interrelation of songs. The cowboy sings, "Bury me not on the lone prai-rie," and the sailor chants, "O bury me not in the deep, deep sea." *The Dying Hobo* is heard in West Virginia, among the Maine lumberjacks, and in Texas. *Turkey in the Straw*, originally known as *Zip Coon*, is native to the minstrel show, indigenous to the South and Southwest, it is the authentic accompaniment to the Virginia Reel, and it is used for barn dances in Maine. It is probably the nearest approach to a truly national folk tune that we have.

II

The mountain regions of Kentucky, Tennessee, the Carolinas, and Virginia offer a splendid example of preservation of folk song by isolation. British settlers came into these mountains in the latter eighteenth or early nineteenth century. The region is secluded and inaccessible. Few roads have been built into the mountains, and railroads are miles away. The people have been dependent on themselves alone. Each family has raised its own vegetables, and had its own cattle and sheep. Money was unnecessary; when they traded, the mountaineers bartered in kind. For liquor they had their own stills, and made their own moonshine; hence, the feuds with revenue officers of the government. When disputes arose with neighbors, justice was a private matter, often requiring a gun. Then revenge was in order, and blood feuds between families and clans were carried on for generations.

Otherwise, they are a leisurely people, sociable and kindly when they are not suspicious. Hospitable to anyone they are not afraid is a "revenoo-er," they are cordial to strangers, courteous and dignified. Cecil Sharp found them somewhat like English peasants, with one essential difference. They had none of the obsequiousness common to the English villager.

Most of the mountain songs are traditional English ballads, brought from England by the ancestors of the present inhabitants. Civilization has not touched the singers or the songs, and even though those who sing today may understand little of what they are singing, they tell of knights and ladies, of courtships and tragedies, of a time and place far different from their own. Cecil Sharp, when he published his collection of *English Folk Songs from the Southern Appalachians*, included in his work an appendix that shows where various of the songs have been noted in England. Thirty-seven of the ballads are to be found, for example, in Child's *English and Scottish Ballads*. Among them are the tales of *Barbara Allen; The Maid Freed from the Gallows* (known also as *The Hangman's Song*, and sung in various forms in many corners of the globe); *The Two Brothers; Lord Randal; Earl Brand;* and many others. The songs include *My Boy Billy* (generally known as *Billie Boy*); *Sourwood Mountain; The Farmyard* (seemingly an ancestor of the Rotarians' *Old MacDonald Had a Farm*); *Frog Went a-Courtin';* and so on.

Other collectors have noted some of these and other songs. Josephine McGill published a collection, and Howard Brockway and Loraine Wyman gathered a number into their set of *Lonesome Tunes* and *Twenty Kentucky Mountain Songs*. In his *Folk Songs of the South*, John H. Cox presented songs he had collected in West Virginia.

While most of the songs were obviously brought by the first settlers from England, some of them make references to more modern events. *Brother Green* speaks of the "Southern foe," who "laid him low." The story evidently refers to the Civil War, though in its present form the song may be a variant of an older version. *The Wreck on the C. & O., The Boston Burglar,* and others of their kind are the mountaineers' versions of American ballads.

Generally the mountain people sing without accompaniment, in a straightforward manner, unconscious of an audience. The folk singer thinks of the story he is telling rather than the effect he is producing on a listener. In some quarters, visitors to the mountains have found instruments. Occasionally a fiddle, and sometimes a guitar. Some of the folk singers accompany themselves on the dulcimer, a shallow wooden box, with four sound-holes—a sort of elongated violin. Generally three strings are stretched over this box. Two are used as drones, and the third for the melody. The effect is either that of an ancient drone, or a sound like the twanging of a banjo or guitar.

III

The cowboys of the Southwest have had their song literature, some of it preserved by such ardent collectors as John A. Lomax. Railroads and other modern forms of transportation, and the cutting up of the huge ranches into small farms, have dimmed the romance of the time-honored profession of cow punching. The old-time roundup has almost disappeared, and the cattle trails to Kansas and to Montana are covered with grass. In the seventies and eighties large forces of men were needed to take care of the cattle in the winter season, to round them up in the spring and to brand the calves. Then they had to be driven to market, up the long trails from Texas, sometimes as far north as Montana, where the grass made better grazing.

The cowboys had to provide their own entertainment; so they sang, sometimes songs they had learned elsewhere, and often those they composed themselves. Many of their songs were useful—rhythmic yells to stir up lagging cattle, or cattle "lullabies" to quiet the restless animals at night. Sometimes the "dogie" songs were used to halt stampedes. Aside from songs connected with his business, the cowboy's taste ran to opposites. He liked songs and ballads of the desperado—*Jesse James* (found in many parts of the country); *Billy the Kid;* or the story of *The Hell-Bound Train.* He could grow sentimental and sing of *The Dying Cowboy; his Home on the Range;* or the religious *Rounded Up in Glory.* He also shared many ballads and songs with frontiersmen and ballad singers generally. Some of these were pretty much unchanged by the cowboy: *The Boston Burglar;* the tale of *MacAfee's Confession,* and others. Sometimes he adapted songs to his own surroundings, and occasionally he included in his

song-words, stanzas that are found elsewhere. For example, the cowboy refrain

> Jack o' diamonds, Jack o' diamonds,
> I know you of old,
> You've robbed my pockets
> Of silver and gold,

is similar to the refrain of a totally different song—the Negro convict
song *Water-Boy*, known chiefly through Avery Robinson's concert
arrangement.

The cowboy literature is colorful; some of the melodies he sang are
very beautiful. On the whole, his ballads are typical of himself, and
like all folk song literature they show the temperament and life of
those who sing them. As Lomax has written in his volume of *Cowboy
Songs:* [1]

> The changing and romantic West of the early days lives mainly in song
> and story. The last figure to vanish is the cowboy, the animating spirit of the
> vanishing era. He sits his horse easily as he rides through a wide valley, en-
> closed by mountains, clad in the hazy purple of the coming night,—with his
> face turned steadily down the long, long road, "the road that the sun goes
> down." Dauntless, reckless, without the unearthly purity of Sir Galahad,
> though as gentle to a pure woman as King Arthur, he is truly a knight of the
> twentieth century. A vagrant puff of wind shakes a corner of the crimson
> handkerchief knotted loosely at his throat; the thud of his pony's feet
> mingling with the jingle of his spurs is borne back; and as the careless,
> gracious, lovable figure disappears over the divide, the breeze brings to the
> ears, faint and far yet cheery still, the refrain of a cowboy song:

> Whoopee ti yi yo, git along little dogies;
> It's your misfortune and none of my own.
> Whoopee ti yi yo, git along little dogies;
> For you know Wyoming will be your new home.

IV

Lumberjack songs from the woods of Michigan, Wisconsin, and
Minnesota have been collected by Franz Rickaby, and published in a
volume of *Ballads and Songs of the Shanty-Boy*.[2] Some of these seem

---

[1] John A. Lomax, *Cowboy Songs and other Frontier Ballads*, Macmillan Co.
[2] Franz Rickaby, *Ballads and Songs of the Shanty-Boy*, Harvard University Press.

to be original and others are adaptations. Rickaby found that the shanty boy makes no general use of his songs while he is actually at work. He is not by nature a gang worker, and so his songs do not have the place that other songs have had in labors where efforts are timed in unison, or the general rhythm of the work is maintained by the singing of the group, or an individual in the group. But, as Rickaby wrote,

. . . back in the shanty, particularly on Saturday evenings, secure from the outer cold,—his supper stowed safely within him, the old iron stove throwing out its genial heat, and the mellowing ministrations of tobacco well begun,—the shanty-boy became story-teller and singer. The emotional thaw set in; and a great many of his songs were, in the words of an old shanty-boy, "as fine as any you'll hear."

Many of his favorite songs tell of his own type of life:

> Oh, a shanty-man's life is a wearisome life,
>   Altho' some think it void of care.
> Swinging an axe from morning till night
>   In the midst of the forests so drear.

Or the *Shanty-man's Alphabet*, in which

> A is for axe as you all very well know,
> B is for boys that can use them just so.
> C is for chopping, and now I'll begin;
> And D is for danger we ofttimes run in.

Rickaby believes that the woods songs were composed by individuals who set out definitely to compose. There has been little communal writing of songs and ballads, similar to that attributed to the Negro. New stanzas might often have been added, but the songs themselves rarely if ever originated with the group. Generally the words were fitted to a tune the author had in mind when he wrote them.

Roland Palmer Gray collected the *Songs and Ballads of the Maine Lumberjacks*. His volume presents a number of the songs that Rickaby found in the Midwest: *The Alphabet Song*, and a version of the *Shanty Man's Life*—the *Lumberman's Life* in Maine. There are a few of the old English ballads—*The Twa Sisters*; *The Dark-Eyed Sailor*, and some historical ballads. Some of these, culled from broadsides, record local historical events of recent date—*The Bangor Fire*, of 1911. One is a tribute to President Wilson.

v

Origin of folk songs and ballads will always provide material for discussion and controversy, and it is difficult and dangerous to be arbitrary in such matters. Sometimes a publisher has issued a sheet music edition of a traditional ballad, and many people have thought it a new song. There was a recent vogue of *Ain' gonna rain no more*, and not all who heard it for the first time realized how old it really was. *Frankie and Johnnie* has been attributed to various sources, and has known countless versions. The incident it relates has been credited to various localities—from New Orleans to the North. Recently a story in the New York *World* stated positively that it occurred in St. Louis, as recently as 1889; that the man's name was Albert and that Frankie is still living. Moreover, that the actors in the tragedy were not white, but colored.

Sometimes a recently composed and published song achieves such currency that it is commonly considered a traditional ballad. *The Blue and the Gray* was issued before the Spanish War as coming from the pen of Paul Dresser, brother of Theodore Dreiser, the novelist, yet it is included in Louise Pound's *American Ballads and Songs*, with the meager information that the compiler found the text in a manuscript book.

The perpetuation of these songs is as interesting as their origin. Some were introduced into plays, and were sung nightly all over the country. *In the Baggage Coach Ahead* was used in vaudeville, its dreary story illustrated by lantern slides. Then there were broadsides, or song sheets (a relic of an English custom dating back to the time of Queen Elizabeth), which were sold at fairs and circuses, or by traveling sellers of patent medicines. Of course, in isolated sections, such as the mountain districts, songs were handed down from father to son by word of mouth, especially where the people were illiterate. Then there was another way in which families have helped to preserve songs through several generations—the manuscript books, into which were written the words of songs heard orally.

We have already learned something of the extent of the overlapping of songs in different sections of the country; how some lyrics and ballads are the common property of cowboys and lumberjacks, Negroes and mountain whites. The more general anthologies are valuable in showing types of songs which have had widespread use. In *The American Songbag*, Carl Sandburg groups the songs as "Dramas and Portraits," "Minstrel Songs," "The Ould Sod" (those of an Irish flavor), "Pioneer Memories," Kentucky Songs, songs commemorating "The Lincolns and Hankses," the "Great Lakes and Erie Canal," "Hobo Songs," tales of "The Big Brutal City," "Prison and Jail Songs," "Blues, Mellows and Ballets," songs of "The Great Open Spaces," "Mexican Border Songs," ballads and lyrics of the "Southern Mountains," "Picnic and Hayrack Follies, Close Harmony, and Darn Fool Ditties," "Railroad and Work Gangs," songs of "Lumberjacks," and of the "Sailorman," "Bandit Biographies," songs of the "Five Wars," about "Lovely People," and the "Road to Heaven."

VI

What effect all this folk music, and the songs of the Indian and the Negro, will have on American music of the future is impossible to determine. It is hard to say just which of it is truly American. Some has been born here, and some brought from abroad. There are people who hold that whatever folk songs of the many European races or nationalities which make up the American nation have survived the transplantation on American soil, are legitimately to be considered as forming part of the body of American folk music. And there are others who say that nothing is American that does not have its origin here.

Yet in folk music, as in the formal music of the concert hall, Americanism is a more subtle thing than a mere question of geographic origin. As in spoken or written language, there are certain habits of speech and certain points of view that are peculiar to us. Not mere reference to local events and scenes, but the manner of referring to them and looking at them. So in music; it is a question of association and traits inherent in the music itself.

In America, as elsewhere, some people say that a composer shows his poverty of ideas if he cannot invent his own tunes. Yet it is surely better to hear a good folk song, admirably handled, than a mediocre

theme of the composer's own making. For even great composers sometimes write undistinguished melodies. Music makers the world over
have made frequent use of folk tunes almost since music began, just
as poets have based their poems on traditional legends, and painters
have taken their subjects from life and nature. Haydn's music was
filled with Croatian melodies; the first phrases of the *Austrian Hymn*
were taken literally from a folk song. Weber, Brahms, Liszt, Grieg,
the Russian nationalists since Glinka have drawn heavily on the songs
of their people.

The American composers who have used the folk songs heard in
this country have generally done so for one of two reasons—sometimes for both. Often they have had no purpose other than to take
melodies, which they thought were beautiful, and treat them in a way
that would emphasize their beauty or their native character. Sometimes
they have aimed to make their compositions describe the people who
sing the songs.

The other motive has been a desire to throw off the European yoke,
to cease imitating the styles and traditions of the Old World. So much
of our early music has been in imitation of foreign models that American musicians have developed an inferiority complex, which has made
some of them take desperate measures to cut the cord as quickly as
possible. Even though they must have known that such a condition was
inevitable in a country that had been a nation for little more than a
century, composed of people from all races, and of our composers who
had gone to European masters for their training, they nevertheless
grew self-conscious about our lack of nationalism in music, and took
stern measures to acquire a native speech. They preferred provincial-
ism to a diluted internationalism. Some of them used traditional musical formulae in handling the folk songs, and employed accepted
forms and harmonies. Others made sincere attempts to devise a harmonic dress that would clothe primitive themes in robes to emphasize
their native flavor.

Although the problem of musical nationalism is far too complex
to solve by the use of such obvious devices, and though many of the
ardent nationalists have shot wide of their mark, the interest in folk
music has stimulated composition in this country. It has put into our
music a more vital note than it had before. And the intense sincerity

of the leaders in the movement has rendered it something that cannot be brushed aside by cynicism. Though we cannot admire all we hear, we must needs respect the pioneer spirit at the bottom of it all, and take off our hats to the man who wants to be himself and not a mere reflection of someone else.

We have learned that American composers experimented with folk music, Indian melodies, and the like, way back into the eighteenth century. Father Heinrich was the first to use Indian themes in orchestral works of the larger variety. But the idea never took strong hold or aroused much interest until Antonin Dvořák spent almost four years in this country, from 1892 to 1895. An intense nationalist, his work is filled with the folk spirit of his native Bohemia. In his work at the National Conservatory of Music in New York he tried to develop a nationalistic school of music among his American pupils. The works he wrote in this country were intended as examples of what our own composers could do with the material at hand. He expressed the impressions he received during his visits to various parts of the country. He studied the folk songs in America and used and imitated them in his works. The *New World* Symphony, played first by the New York Philharmonic in 1893, has the benefit of being the greatest of Dvořák's several symphonies; and because it is a great work, and a highly popular one, it focused attention on the use of American folk songs. Whether or not Dvořák actually used *Swing Low, Sweet Chariot*, or whether he himself composed Negro-like themes for his symphony, he did try to express America. He tried to embody the same spirit in a string quartet and in a quintet. Probably all he accomplished was to give a Bohemian's impression of America, and in plaintive moments to voice his own homesickness. But he started the vogue, and most of the serious effort to harness American folk song dates from the visit of the Bohemian Dvořák.

Arthur Farwell, Henry F. B. Gilbert, Harry Burleigh, Harvey Worthington Loomis, Charles Wakefield Cadman, Charles S. Skilton, Carl Busch, all were among the pioneers who turned to folk music of the North American continent around the turn of the century. Some of them lost their enthusiasm in later years, or at least decided that they did not care to limit themselves to folk material. They came to realize the subtlety of Americanism in art, and that while the essence of folk music is native, it alone cannot produce a nationalist idiom.

CHAPTER FIFTEEN

Our Lighter Musical Moments

I. YESTERDAY

MOST of the popular music of the day has been transitory; here today and gone tomorrow, with something new to take its place. And not always so new, either. Often the latest songs are old ideas rehashed and modernized. Yet with each generation the type of popular music changes; as people become sophisticated their songs do likewise. Of course, much of the music discussed in our early chapters has been popular music, especially the early balladry and minstrel songs. Stephen Foster's songs were, and still are, songs that people everywhere sing. The only difference has been that Foster's songs have been the real thing, and have endured. They have passed from the category of popular music into that of true folk songs.

In the middle of the nineteenth century, when Foster was writing his immortal songs, the minstrel shows were entering their prime. These entertainments naturally produced later composers, and the one whose name is best known today is JAMES A. BLAND (1854–1911), who has lived to our day, and perhaps for all time, through just one of the many songs he composed—*Carry Me Back to Old Virginny*. Bland was himself a Negro, and one of the ironic features of his career was the difficulty he had in realizing his ambition to become a minstrel performer. Minstrel companies were for the most part composed of white men who blacked their faces and imitated colored men. There was no place in these troupes for a genuine Negro, and it was not until a real "colored minstrel" company came along that Bland found his place in his chosen profession.

He was the son of a Charleston, South Carolina, father who was one of the first college-bred Negroes in America. James Bland was born in Flushing, New York, October 22, 1854. Then his parents moved to Washington, D.C. where his father was appointed examiner in the United States Patent Office—the first colored man to hold such a position.

James received his education in the Washington public schools, and later was graduated from Howard University, at the age of nineteen. He was not particularly brilliant in his academic subjects, but was considered a musical prodigy. He was always energetic, and his affability made friends for him wherever he went. As a boy he was a page in the House of Representatives. Then his talents became known, and he was frequently engaged to entertain prominent guests in Washington. He could sing, play the banjo, and compose songs for any occasion.

He was famous as a song writer before he was able to perform with minstrel troupes. He appeared first with a colored troupe in New York in 1879 and then toured the Pacific Coast with them. In 1882 he went to England and Scotland where he made a great success and remained for nearly twenty years. He is said to have earned ten thousand dollars a year in those days. King Edward, then Prince of Wales, attended his performances and honored him on several occasions.

Returning from England in 1901, Bland arrived in Washington, destitute. The only work he could find was a job in the office of a friend. He became discouraged and moved to Philadelphia, where he died May 5, 1911.

He wrote about seven hundred songs, of which not many are remembered today. Among them are *Christmas Dinner, Dem Golden Slippers* (which sold over 100,000 copies before 1888), *De Golden Wedding*, and *In the Evening by the Moonlight*.

During Stephen Foster's lifetime WILLIAM SHAKESPEARE HAYS (1837–1907), popularly known as "Will Hays," was one of his strongest rivals. Hays was the composer of one of the most maudlin self-pity songs ever written—*Driven from Home*, which is today revived by song antiquarians as a curiosity. The rivalry with Foster was so strong at one time that some of Hays's admirers claimed that he, and not Foster, was the real author of some of Foster's songs.

Hays wrote his first ballad when he was sixteen. After that he pub-

lished nearly three hundred songs, which in their day had a sale total-
ing several millions. He was born in Louisville, Kentucky, in 1837,
and died there July 22, 1907. Some of his best-known songs were
Evangeline, My Southern Sunny Home, Mollie Darling, and *Write
Me a Letter from Home.*

There are others who contributed at least one significant song to our
popular music (even if that significance rests chiefly on an unquestionably wide appeal), and their words and melodies are still remembered,
although their names may be forgotten.

GEORGE COOPER (1840–1927) whose collaboration with Foster has
been mentioned earlier, became one of our most important writers
of lyrics that people love to sing. His best-known song text was that
of *Sweet Genevieve,* inspired by his first and only love who died
shortly after their marriage in 1869. Cooper wrote his poem from an
aching heart, but during one of his habitual periods of financial difficulty he sold it for five dollars to HENRY TUCKER, who supplied the
tune that has become a permanent favorite with informal harmoniz-
ers. (Tucker has already received credit for the music of *Weeping
Sad and Lonely or When This Cruel War Is Over.* He wrote many
songs, among them a setting of Bret Harte's *The Heathen Chinee,*
and was famous also as an editor and arranger of music, including the
famous *Star of the Evening* by James M. Sayles.)

As a result of his association with Foster, George Cooper for many
years remained the pet lyricist of our popular tunesmiths. His partnership with JOHN ROGERS THOMAS (1829–1896) was particularly fruit-
ful, with *Rose of Killarney* as a climax (1876). With T. BRIGHAM
BISHOP (1835–1925) he wrote *Pretty as a Picture* (1872), popularized by the minstrel Billy Emerson whose best-known song was
The Big Sunflower (by Bobby Newcombe). As late as 1883, Cooper
had an immense hit in *Strolling on the Brooklyn Bridge,* which he
wrote with J. P. SKELLY. He lived until 1927, a gold mine of information on American popular song writing from Foster to Tin-Pan
Alley.

An earlier song, with a history similar to that of *Sweet Genevieve,*
was *When You and I Were Young, Maggie,* published by its composer JAMES AUSTIN BUTTERFIELD (1837–1891) in 1866. The words
were by a Canadian schoolteacher, George W. Johnson, who had

fallen in love with one of his pupils, Maggie Clark. His poem was inspired by the actual scenes of their courting, and represented what he hoped would be the memories of their old age together. But, like Cooper's Genevieve, Maggie died soon after her marriage. Johnson's words were published in a collection called *Maple Leaves,* where they attracted the attention of Butterfield, a trained musician, who was born in England in 1837. For many years a musical leader in Chicago, Butterfield was active as a composer, publisher, teacher, singer, and conductor. Both men live today in the one song *When You and I Were Young, Maggie.*

Many of America's most popular songs, both before and after Stephen Foster's day, came from England or were written by English composers in this country. A successful song writer of the 1860's was MRS. CHARLOTTE ALINGTON BARNARD (1830–1869) known by the pseudonym "Claribel," a woman of some musical education, who depended chiefly on her own reliable instinct for sentimentality. Claribel's *Take Back the Heart That Thou Gavest* (1864) is remembered today for its lush lines and solid waltz rhythm. But her best song was unquestionably *Come Back to Erin,* which has often been regarded as a piece of actual Irish folk music.

Far more important to America's popular music was the visit of WILLIAM HORACE LINGARD (1839–1927) who came here from London in 1868. He was an accomplished comedian, heading his own company on Broadway, and he wrote at least the words of a number of successful songs. Best remembered today is *Captain Jinks of the Horse Marines,* for which T. MACLAGAN supplied the tune. Lingard was also the lyricist of *Walking Down Broadway* (music by CHARLES E. PRATT, 1841–1902), which was honored by both imitations and parodies. (Its chorus contains an early example of the slang expression "O.K.") Another Lingard song, for which he seems to have written the music as well as the words, was *On the Beach at Brighton,* and this was immediately copied by American versions which substituted Cape May and Newport for the English resort.

Another Englishman to score an American success both as actor and as song writer was GEORGE LEYBOURNE, who deserves credit for the words of *The Flying Trapeze* (later prefixed by *The Man on*), with music by ALFRED LEE, also of English birth. This famous song, brought out piratically and anonymously by at least three publishers in 1868, has had the doubtful compliment of a modern revival in highly garbled form. The combination of Leybourne and Lee also produced the popular *Champagne Charlie,* with the former as its greatest interpreter.

Leybourne may have had a hand also in that early aviation song *Up in a Balloon,* which was introduced to New York by Mrs. Lingard, professionally known as Alice Dunning. The probable composer was G. W. HUNT (another Englishman), and, as usual, there were several American versions. Hunt was responsible for a number of other hits, including the utterly British *Awfully Clever* and *The Bell Goes a-Ringing for Sai-rah.*

The musical director of Lingard's company was a young Englishman named DAVID BRAHAM (1838–1905), who was soon to make American history as composer and conductor for the immortal team of Harrigan and Hart. He had come to this country as a violinist, playing in various theatre orchestras and conducting Harry Leslie's show at Tony Pastor's Theatre as early as 1865.

The song which made Braham famous was *The Mulligan Guard.* This was likewise the first great Harrigan and Hart success, the foundation for several of their complete shows, and forerunner of a technique which was to contribute something quite new to the musical stage. *The Mulligan Guard* was originally nothing more than a conventional comedy number, with a lively tune in march time (mentioned in Kipling's *Kim* as the favorite band piece of the English soldiers in India). It was gradually built up into something like a vaudeville sketch, and its absurd satire on the pseudomilitary organizations of the day, existing chiefly for political and convivial reasons, practically put those clubs out of business.

But it was a long time before America saw what is now regarded as a typical Harrigan and Hart show. The growth of this unique fulllength entertainment, combining the best features of minstrelsy, vaudeville, and musical comedy, was very gradual, and it is impossible to fix upon any title as actually representing the first of its kind. Edward Harrigan and Tony Hart (ten years his junior) were vaudeville partners as early as 1871, and by 1876 they had acquired the Theatre Comique on Broadway and developed a large company of their own.

Harrigan was the guiding spirit of the enterprise, creating the shows, writing the dialogue and song lyrics, acting the principal roles, and serving as stage director and manager of the theatre. Hart specialized in feminine parts, possessing a sweet singing voice and a most attractive personality.

It was 1879 before Harrigan and Hart introduced the full evening's entertainment known as *The Mulligan Guard Ball*, which ran right through the rest of the season. This show contained, in addition to the parent song, a Negro parallel *The Skidmore Fancy Ball* (whose ancestor was *The Skidmore Guard*), and *The Babies on Our Block*, definitely pointing toward the later *Sidewalks of New York*. Dave Braham was responsible for all of the tunes.

The adventures of the Mulligans and the Skidmores were good for three years of Harrigan and Hart activity. Then came *The Major*, with Ned Harrigan playing a mid-Victorian English fop and singing the hit song *Major Gilfeather*. Braham, who had become Harrigan's son-in-law, continued to supply the music for the shows, besides conducting the orchestra in the pit.

Squatter Sovereignty, which opened in 1882, contained such popular Harrigan-Braham songs as *Paddy Duffy's Cart* and *The Widow Nolan's Goat*. The Mulligans came back nearly two years later in *Cordelia's Aspirations*, whose outstanding song was *My Dad's Dinner Pail*.

Tony Hart left the partnership in 1885, for reasons never explained, but Harrigan and Braham carried on with *Old Lavender*, one of their greatest hits, containing the honestly pathetic song *Poverty's Tears Ebb and Flow*. As late as 1890 they had a big success in *Reilly and the Four Hundred*, with the popular waltz *Maggie Murphy's Home*.

The Harrigan-Braham song hit of 1891 was *Danny by My Side*, from *The Last of the Hogans*. Tony Hart died that year, and the type of entertainment he had helped to create gradually became a nostalgic memory, although Harrigan himself lived until 1911. David Braham died in 1905, and his son George wrote the music for the final Harrigan show *Under Cover*, which was a failure. A new audience had arisen, too sophisticated for the simple jokes and songs of the seventies.

But much of the popular music of the days of Harrigan, Hart, and Braham is still in circulation. The passage of time has had little effect on such a song as *Silver Threads Among the Gold*, written in 1872 by HART PEASE DANKS and EBEN E. REXFORD. It sold more than two million copies before the end of the century, and another million after its revival in 1907. Other popular songs of the early seventies were the still current *Reuben and Rachel*, by HARRY BIRCH and WILLIAM GOOCH (1871), WILLIAM SCANLAN's *Jim Fisk* (1872), which whitewashed one of the most notorious swindlers of the time, and *Bonnie Sweet Bessie, the Maid of Dundee* (1873), by BELLA ROOT and J. L. GILBERT.

I'll Take You Home Again, Kathleen, still appearing on our community song sheets, was written in 1876 by THOMAS PAINE WESTENDORF, a Virginian, who had moved to Louisville, Kentucky with his wife, after the death of their son. Mrs. Westendorf, prosaically christened Jane but nicknamed Kathleen, had been ill and unhappy in their new surroundings, and her husband realized that a change was needed. A poem by George Parsely, *Barney, I'll Take You Home Again*, gave him the idea for the song, and within an hour he had written both the words and the music of *I'll Take You Home Again, Kathleen*.

In 1877 the Reverend ROBERT LOWRY (1826–1899), composer of the successful hymn-tune *I Need Thee Every Hour*, created the words and music of *Where Is My Wandering Boy Tonight*, which millions of Americans have heard sung in *The Old Homestead*. The same year produced the contrastingly lively *Whoa, Emma*, of English origin.

The early eighties were not marked by many popular songs beyond those of Harrigan and Braham. A certain JENNIE LINDSAY wrote the moralizing *Always Take Mother's Advice* in 1884, and the same year saw the publication of BANKS WINTER's *White Wings*, whose lilting melody is still familiar. The perennial *Rock-a-bye, Baby*, by EFFIE I. CANNING (who died in 1940) is dated 1887. And in 1888, Frank Harding published the rousing *Drill, Ye Tarriers, Drill*, while Monroe H. Rosenfeld announced *With All Her Faults I Love Her Still*.

Then came those sturdy Irish ditties—*Down Went McGinty*, by JOSEPH FLYNN (1889), and J. W. KELLY's *Throw Him Down, Mc-*

Closkey (1890), popularized by the Amazonian Maggie Cline. When HENRY SAYERS (1854–1929) picked up the nonsensical *Ta-ra-ra-boom-deré* in a St. Louis brothel, turning the dusky Babe Connors into a "sweet Tuxedo girl," the Gay Nineties had definitely arrived.

There were, of course, thousands of songs of sentiment. They are always with us. As Sigmund Spaeth says in the title of his recent book, "They Still Sing of Love"; and they probably always will. It was in the nineties that the story-telling song came into its greatest vogue. CHARLES K. HARRIS (1865–1930) gave it a tremendous boost with *After the Ball.* His autobiography is one of the best accounts of the song-writing business in existence. It tells how a natural melodist thinks of his songs and then has an arranger write them down for him; and of how songs were promoted and made popular in the days before the radio and the sound pictures. Harris was smart enough to realize that the vogue of his songs depended on the popularity of the actors and singers who sang them in public, and he wrote songs to fit various situations in the plays they acted in. Among his best-known lyrics were *Break the News to Mother; Hello, Central, Give Me Heaven* (one of the first telephone songs); *Can You Pay for a Broken Heart; Kiss and Let's Make Up; Why Don't They Play with Me; No One to Kiss You Good-night; My Mother's Kiss* (*The Sweetest Kiss of All*), and many others. He was also influential in having the copyright bill of 1909 passed. This enabled song writers and composers to collect royalties from the sale of phonograph records and other reproducing devices.

PAUL DRESSER was an older man than Harris—he lived from 1857 to 1911—but his songs were of the same type. He was best known for a song that has been almost a folk song—*On the Banks of the Wabash, Far Away;* but he wrote many of the story songs too: *The Letter That Never Came; Just Tell Them That You Saw Me; She Went to the City;* and others. *The Blue and the Gray* was first copyrighted in 1890, but it became popular in the days of the Spanish War, with a line changed (or added) to the chorus, telling that one of the sons was laid away at Santiago. The others lay at Appomattox and Chickamauga.

These years produced many songs by contemporaries of Dresser and Harris. Among the comics—*Has Anybody Here Seen Kelly; Tammany.* From the Spanish War songs—*A Hot Time in the Old Town*

To-night; Good-by, Dolly Gray. And among the sentimental songs such gems as *The Little Lost Child* (which Spaeth claims was the first to be illustrated with lantern slides); *My Mother Was a Lady, or If Jack Were Only Here,* and others equally effective in drawing tears. The song writer of the nineties was somewhat in the position of the minister who must find ideas for his sermons from daily occurrences. The lyricist developed song stories from characters he met on the streets, or from homely incidents of everyday life.

We discussed many of the ballad writers in our chapter on song composers, but ERNEST R. BALL (1878–1927) really belongs here, because his sentimental songs achieved a popularity equal to any of the songs of the day. For several years *Love Me and the World Is Mine* decorated the music desks of pianos in parlors all over the country, and was sung in all kinds of places. Ball wrote it in 1906, and then in 1910 followed its success with *Mother Machree* which he wrote with Chauncey Olcott to words by Rida Johnson Young. He tried to follow its success a few years later with *She's the Daughter of Mother Machree,* but it never took hold of the public fancy the way the first one had. He also wrote *'Till the Sands of the Desert Grow Cold; Let the Rest of the World Go By; West of the Great Divide; A Little Bit of Heaven;* and others. He was born in Cleveland, and in addition to being a song writer he was a professional entertainer. His songs were highly sentimental, but they nevertheless had something of an individuality, and a number of them are still sung.

PATRICK SARSFIELD GILMORE (1829–1892) has already made his appearance in our book. We heard of his Peace Jubilees when we discussed Matthias Keller's National Hymn.[1]

He was something of a composer, too, and claimed the authorship of *When Johnny Comes Marching Home* (1863), a song that was popular for years after the Civil War. Gilmore was best known as a bandmaster. His was the crack band of his day; it was really the first of our concert bands. He was born in Ireland in 1829, came first to Canada and then to Massachusetts, where he organized and conducted a band of his own. During the Civil War he was bandmaster of the Union Army. After the Jubilee Festivals he moved to New York, got together another band, and made tours all over the country.

[1] Page 297.

JOHN PHILIP SOUSA (1854-1932) was Gilmore's successor, and carried the concert band to heights it had never achieved before. He devised an instrumentation that allows of effects as soft as those of a symphony orchestra. Moreover, his marches earned him the title of the "March King," for he was to the march what Johann Strauss was to the waltz. *The Stars and Stripes Forever; The Washington Post; The High School Cadets; The Gladiator,* are only a few of the many that bear the indelible Sousa trade-mark. He wrote ten comic operas—the most successful *The Bride Elect; El Capitán;* and *The Free Lance.* There are many other compositions of a miscellaneous variety; and as a writer he not only wrote the lyrics and librettos of some of his operas, but he published three novels, and an autobiography *Marching Along* which is one of the most readable books of memoirs in American literature.

He had a remarkable career, bringing recognition from all over the world. He was born November 6, 1854, in Washington, the son of a Portuguese father and a Bavarian mother. When he was ten he had violin lessons with a local teacher named John Esputa, and later studied theory and composition with G. F. Benkert. He learned to play band instruments, and his father had him enlist in the Marine Band when he was thirteen. He also played in civilian orchestras. Later he got a discharge from the Marine Band, and in 1872, at eighteen, became the director of the orchestra at Washington's Theatre Comique, a variety house. Later he led the orchestra in a comedy company, and for Morgan's Living Pictures. This was in the days when undraped ladies were rarer on the stage than they are today, and there were several encounters with the authorities in various cities.

In 1876 he went to Philadelphia, played under Offenbach, and at several of the theatres. In 1880 he was appointed director of the Marine Band in Washington, and in the twelve years he held the position he served under five presidents—Hayes, Garfield, Arthur, Cleveland, Harrison. He made a new band of what had been a mere routine organization; built up its library, changed its instrumentation, and raised its morale. In 1892 he formed his own band, which gave its first concert in Plainfield, New Jersey, September 26. The first season was not too successful financially, owing to the manager's poor judgment in selecting the towns the band was to visit. Sousa had more courage than his manager, and he insisted that they keep on; with the result that after the first season the band became an immense success. There were annual tours through the United States and Canada, four to Europe, and one around the world. The band was engaged for almost all of our important expositions, starting with the Chicago World's Fair in 1893. In 1917, when America had entered the first World War, Sousa became a lieutenant in the Naval Reserve. He was decorated by crowned heads and by various academies and societies, and lived until March 6, 1932.

EDWIN FRANKO GOLDMAN (1878——) has carried on the concert-band tradition of Sousa. His band has become the leading group of its kind, and has specialized in playing symphonic band works, many of them written especially for it. Since 1922, the Goldman Band has given nightly summer concerts in New York's principal parks. Goldman was born in Louisville, Kentucky, January 1, 1878. He studied in New York with Dvořák, and from 1895 to 1905 was a trumpet player in the orchestra of the Metropolitan Opera House. As a composer he has written a long list of popular marches, the best known being the lilting *On the Mall*.

The United States has made important contributions to the light opera stage, and the leading figure in that field is undoubtedly VICTOR HERBERT (1859–1924). He was a magnificently equipped musician, at home in composing for any medium or in any form, but he will always be best known for his lighter music. He was born in Dublin, Ireland, February 1, 1859, and came to this country when he was twenty-seven. He was the grandson of Samuel Lover, the famous Irish novelist, playwright, and composer—author and composer of *Rory O'More* and *The Low Backed Car*. Herbert was trained in Germany at the Stuttgart Conservatory, and became an able cellist. In 1886 he married a Viennese opera singer, Therese Foerster. She had been engaged for the Metropolitan in New York, and Herbert came to America with her and became first cellist in the orchestra at the opera house. He was soon engaged for several appearances with the Thomas and Seidl orchestras, and in 1887 introduced his own Concerto and Suite for cello. He produced a second Cello Concerto in 1894, and dedicated it to the New York Philharmonic. From 1894 to 1898 he was bandmaster of the Twenty-second Regiment of the New York National

Guard. Then he went to Pittsburgh, where he was conductor of the symphony orchestra until 1904. After that he came back to New York and devoted most of his time to composition until his death May 26, 1924.

He made two attempts at grand opera—in 1911 *Natoma*, based on an Indian theme, and in 1914 in *Madeleine*. Both were produced. *Natoma* by the Philadelphia-Chicago Opera Company in Philadelphia, New York, Chicago, and on tour (thirty-five performances); and in 1914 by the Aborn Company at New York's Century Theatre. *Madeleine* was produced at the Metropolitan in New York, and had four performances. But Herbert was never happy in his choice of librettos for his grand operas; he lacked the literary and dramatic judgment and taste necessary to selecting a work suited to serious treatment on the opera stage.

So it is always as a composer of light operas that we will know and love him, and without doubt hear his music for many years to come. There is a sparkle and a freshness about his tunes that is all too rare in light music. He had few failures; most of his operettas enjoyed long runs wherever they were produced, and they are being constantly revived today. He wrote almost forty, among them *The Fortune Teller* (1898); *Babes in Toyland* (1903); *It Happened in Nordland* (1904); *Mlle. Modiste* (1905); *The Red Mill* (1906); *The Rose of Algeria* (1908); *Little Nemo* (1908); *Naughty Marietta* (1910); *The Lady of the Slipper* (1912); *The Madcap Duchess* (1913); and *Eileen* (1917).

The songs from these operettas are still whistled by those who remember the plays, and by those who have heard them sung and played since they were first produced. *Kiss Me Again*, from *Mlle. Modiste*; *Because You're You*, from *The Red Mill*; *Italian Street Song* from *Naughty Marietta*; *Toyland* from *Babes in Toyland*; and dozens of others. It may be that in the change of musical fashions and the coming of jazz we are growing away from the music of Victor Herbert; yet it seems to be holding its own, for there are certainly millions of people who still like to hear it. He was a musician who knew his medium, and while he undoubtedly had ambitions for his works in more pretentious forms, he was never ashamed to be known for what he could do best. For in that field he was very great.

Another composer known for light opera was REGINALD DE KOVEN (1859–1920), whose *Robin Hood* has become a standard work. De Koven, like Herbert, was a serious musician, and wrote two grand operas—*The Canterbury Pilgrims*, produced at the New York Metropolitan in 1917, and *Rip Van Winkle*, presented by the Chicago company in Chicago and in New York in 1920.

He was born in Middletown, Connecticut, April 3, 1859, the son of a clergyman who moved to England when his son was thirteen. Consequently, De Koven had his university training at Oxford, and graduated from St. John's College when he was twenty. Then he went to the Continent to study music—piano with Speidel and Leibert, and harmony with Pruckner at Stuttgart; composition with Hauff at Frankfort; singing with Vannuccini at Florence; and finally composition with Genée and Delibes in Vienna and Paris. Then he came back to America and was active as a music critic and as a composer. For the season of 1889–90 he wrote music reviews for the Chicago *Evening Post*. The next year he came to New York and was music critic for the *World* for seven years; then for two years for the *Journal*. From 1902 to 1905 he was conductor of a Philharmonic Orchestra in Washington, which he organized. Then he came back to New York and from 1907 to 1912 he wrote for the *World* again. In his last years he had resumed the role of critic, and was music editor of the New York *Herald* until his death, January 16, 1920.

He had an agreeable flow of melody, and a facile gift for scoring, which give him a place somewhat akin to the English Sullivan. He published over four hundred songs, many piano pieces, an orchestral suite, and ballets. But his fame rests chiefly on his operettas. *Robin Hood* (1890) was one of the earliest, and by all odds the best of them. Of the almost twenty he wrote and produced, the best known are *The Knickerbockers* (1893), *The Algerian* (1893), *The Highwayman* (1897), *Red Feather* (1903), *The Golden Butterfly* (1907), *The Beauty Spot* (1909), and *Her Little Highness* (1913).

One of the leading popular-music figures of the early twentieth century was GEORGE MICHAEL COHAN (1878–1942). The song that brought him the greatest distinction was *Over There*, the most widely sung song of World War I. For this song Congress awarded Cohan a medal which was presented to him by President Franklin D. Roosevelt. Cohan had a remarkable career in the theatre as song-and-dance man, actor, producer, director, playwright, and composer of songs which had a certain ragtime flavor, but were never in the modern jazz style. He always claimed to have been born on the Fourth of July, in Providence, Rhode Island, and boasted of it in one of his songs. But his friend and later biographer, Ward Morehouse, dug up the birth certificate and found that the date was actually July 3. Cohan's songs included many that are still sung: *I'm a Yankee Doodle Dandy; Give My Regards to Broadway; Mary,* and the never-to-be-forgotten *Over There.* He lived until November 5, 1942.

The first World War inevitably produced hundreds of songs, and many have survived, not only among members of the American Legion, but with Americans generally and the boys of World War II. Sometimes it has seemed as though the soldier of the second World War preferred the songs of the preceding war to those of the one in which he himself was fighting. And so Zo ELLIOTT's *Long, Long Trail* is still winding at sing-fests of all sorts, GEOFFREY O'HARA's *K-K-K-Katy* still makes many of us stammer willingly, the *Smiles* of LEE ROBERTS have not come off yet, and today's soldiers still want to murder the bugler when they sing Irving Berlin's *Gee, How I Hate to Get Up in the Morning.*

Many of the songs of the first World War were borrowed from our Allies—*Tipperary* and *Keep the Home Fires Burning* from England; and our soldiers made ardent love to the French *Madelon.* Most of the American songs were in a light, adventurous strain. There was nothing of hate in them; they were all cheerful and philosophic. Even when they told the Kaiser what they would do to him they joked about it.

To get closest to the life of the soldier in camp, it is best to study the songs he actually sang on his way to the front—the innumerable parodies on published versions. These are presented in several anthologies—Dolph's *Sound Off,* Niles's *Singing Soldiers* and *Songs My Mother Never Taught Me,* and others.

The serious song writers contributed concert songs during the first war. There were dozens of settings of John McRae's poem *In Flanders Fields,* while Fay Foster's *The Americans Come* and Oley Speaks's

When the Boys Come Home had their vogue when people were thinking in terms of war and of their sons at the front.

The first World War songs are not the historical documents that those of the Civil War have proved to be, probably because of the state of mind of the American soldier—his adventurous attitude in going over, and the ability of his humor to save him from bitterness and rancor. Judged from its songs, the first World War would seem a joyous pilgrimage; which perhaps was just as well, for the singing of the soldiers was one of the things that sustained their courage and kept them going.

2. RAGTIME TO JAZZ AND SWING

Even though much of our modern popular music is only a more sophisticated treatment of earlier ballad patterns, the main stream of our people's music has followed an evolutionary pattern of ragtime—jazz—swing. Jazz is quite different and more elaborate than ragtime, but it is its child nevertheless. Ragtime was a form of syncopation that became popular about 1895. Kerry Mills's *The Georgia Camp Meeting* (1897) was one of the first well-known ragtime pieces, and after that almost all of the so-called "coon" songs were in ragged rhythm. Learned scholars are still arguing as to whether the syncopated elements of ragtime were originally of African origin, and found their way to our present-day jazz through the Negro spirituals, or whether they just happened. Of course, syncopation is common to all music, and was used by classic masters over a century ago. Yet the way it has been developed in this country is at least novel, even if it did originate somewhere else.

The early ragtime was very simple. It consisted of a regular accompaniment, and a melody whose rhythmic accent fell on a weak rather than a strong beat. And that is the basis of jazz, for jazz is primarily a matter of rhythm. To some it means a music that is lively—pepped up—and colored by a bizarre instrumentation of its own peculiar orchestra. To others it means a contrapuntal weaving of irregular rhythmic patterns.

Jazz was developed by extemporizing musicians who would improvise counter melodies on the clarinet (if the first of them could be called melodies), while a pianist or cornetist played the tune. Then when such noises became a favorite indoor sport of expensive cafés, musicians started to write on paper what each player should do, and jazz became a highly sophisticated form of light music, developed to such a point that it attracted the attention of serious musicians the world over.

One of the first of the authoritative books on the subject was Henry O. Osgood's *So This Is Jazz*, published in 1926.[1] This gave considerable information on the beginnings of jazz. The author examined the various legends on the origin of the word itself, as verb, noun, and adjective and, with the true instinct of the scholar, came to no conclusion. He traced the careers of the earliest known jazz bands, and told the story of *Razz's Band* in New Orleans; the doings of *Chas.* ("Chaz") *Washington* in Vicksburg; and how Joseph K. Gorham started the jazz craze in the country by bringing one of the bands to a café in Chicago in the winter of 1915–16.

The vogue of jazz really dates from that season. It spread through the country from coast to coast in an incredibly short time, and became a favorite topic of discussion—pro and con. At first the cons had everything on their side, for most of the jazz was pretty crude stuff. Then when the skilled arrangers got busy and really created a new sonority with muted brass and saxophones, they won many converts to the new music.

In the early days of jazz, the real pioneers, such groups as the Memphis Five and the Dixieland Jazz Band, did not come to the attention of a wide public. It was the more commercially minded type of jazz player who created the vogue of jazz in the high-priced cafés and restaurants. Men like TED LEWIS were quick to sense the novelty and to imitate it.

Lewis came from Circleville, Ohio, where his name was Theodore Lewis Friedman. He learned to play the clarinet and was promptly ousted from the boys' band of the city when he improvised a genuine ragtime break in a performance of the *Poet and Peasant* Overture. He ultimately landed at Coney Island as a clarinetist of Earl Fuller's band, and because he was so agile with his clarinet, the whole band

---

[1] Boston: Little, Brown & Co.

was engaged for Rector's in New York, with Lewis as star performer. He started his own band in 1917, and after that his way has been prosperous, even though hard on the ears of some of his listeners.

Lewis was a fair copy of jazz in all its primitive urge. There were only a few men in his band at first. He played his clarinet; and had for his helpers a piano player, a cornetist, a trombonist, and a drummer who included in his battery frying pans, rattles, tin cans, cowbells, and whistles. The cornetist and pianist were principally concerned with playing the tune. The trombonist added color with glissandos and all sorts of amazing outbursts. The drummer was always busy, throwing his traps in the air, pounding his bass drum with his feet, and holding his whistle in his teeth. Ted was comedian. He stood, or rather pranced, in front of his men, battered top hat on one side of his head, as he made his faithful clarinet squeal like a pig, and do other things that seemed to have little to do with the music.

That embodied the public's idea of "hot" jazz. It had a considerable popularity for a time, and then went into a temporary eclipse when the arrangers got hold of it and created what eventually became known as "sweet" jazz. PAUL WHITEMAN was the first to make jazz "respectable." In some ways he did for the jazz band what Gilmore, and later Sousa, did for the military band—he made a concert organization out of it.

Whiteman was born in Denver, Colorado, March 28, 1890. His father was supervisor of music in the public schools, and one of the pioneers in developing high school orchestras. Paul was drafted as a violinist, and later became first viola player in the Denver Symphony Orchestra. When he was twenty-two he left Denver and went to San Francisco. He played there in the World's Fair Orchestra in 1915, and later he became a member of the San Francisco Symphony under Alfred Hertz. This was the time when jazz came to the Coast, and Whiteman was interested. He left the symphony and got a job in Tait's orchestra, from which he was fired after one night because he couldn't play jazz. So he decided to learn, and gradually gathered around him a group of six or seven who wanted to learn too.

Then the war came along, and Whiteman's little band fell apart. Paul weighed three hundred pounds at the time. He couldn't get into the Army as a soldier, but enlisted as a band leader instead. When the war was over, he became leader of the orchestra at the Fairmont Hotel in San Francisco. Later he organized a band of his own, which had several ups and downs—from being regularly hired, to playing in a dance hall at a Southern California Beach where a tin can was hung in front of the orchestra to catch the silver dollars of those who were naturally generous.

Then he was engaged for the Hotel Alexandria in Los Angeles, and his real career dates from that time. The next engagement was at the Hotel Ambassador in Atlantic City; thence to the Palais Royal in New York; to England; and back home to a glory that has not yet dimmed. For all the while he had been having ideas, and either putting them into effect himself or entrusting them to such adept arrangers as Ferde Grofé, the pianist who was with him in Los Angeles, and who is discussed as a composer elsewhere in this book. The first shock the music world had from Whiteman was the colorful jazzing of such bits of musical literature as Rimsky-Korsakoff's *Song of India*. When he jazzed some of the classics in England one of the critics publicly asked him to stick to jazz and "keep his hands off his musical betters." Which wasn't altogether nice, even though it did crystallize the opinions of some musicians. For no matter what they thought of the ethics of the proceeding, it must be admitted that the result was voluptuously beautiful, that it introduced a new instrumental coloring, and that a lot of people heard fine tunes who might not have heard them otherwise.

It was in 1924 that Whiteman made his first gesture in the grand manner, when he took jazz to the concert halls and, as Osgood says, made an honest woman of her. All this was done in a concert at Æolian Hall, in New York, on the afternoon of February 12. The affair was called "An Experiment in Modern Music." It showed what jazz could do to conventional music, and what symphonic treatment could do for popular tunes. The most important part of the concert, of course, was the introduction of George Gershwin and his *Rhapsody in Blue*, which was commissioned for the concert.

From that time the highly arranged, sweet type of jazz became the fashion and reigned supreme through the rest of the prosperous twenties. But in the early thirties the original hot variety, which the pioneers had been playing for their own enjoyment and that of a select few, burst forth once more with renewed vigor, aided by a younger group of musicians who had learned to play it almost as well as the originators. And this time it had a new name—"swing."

The word "swing" has almost as many definitions as definers. The most generally accepted meaning seems to be a style of free improvisation around a given tune, as opposed to "arrangements" planned and written out in advance. The idea is not new, and it has apparently been with us since the beginning of jazz, particularly among Negro musicians. But in the last few years it has blossomed forth as a popular cult, with aesthetic canons that are strict and exclusive, and a characteristic jargon that calls nothing by its right name. The mere musician is as helpless and bewildered by a page of professional comment from *The Metronome*, the jazzist's trade paper, as an Englishman would be by the *Daily News* account of a baseball game.

The various "Kings of Swing" are highly successful in the exploitation of their talents through radio, recordings, films, and personal appearances. Yet the word "commercial" is a term of severe reproach in referring to their playing. Your swing fan is satisfied only with the genuine inspiration of the moment—no mere playing of the printed notes, no matter how skillfully arranged or executed, interests him.

On the whole, he wants his music loud, fast, and highly ornamented in its melodic line, though these qualities are perhaps valued less in themselves than as symptoms that the player is "going to town." "Sweet," sentimental playing, with vibrato, in close harmony, is "out" —"corny." "Swing" is more hard boiled, more nasal in quality, more polyphonic. Above all, it must be spontaneous. The swing lover's dream is a "jam-session" when several of his favorite players are "in the groove."

One does not need to be a one hundred per cent enthusiast to recognize in swing certain vital elements. Improvisation has always been a feature of a healthy musical life. Perhaps its almost complete disappearance from our "serious" music is as significant as its reappearance in our folk music. For if the claim of jazz to the title of folk music has serious flaws, there can be no doubt that swing strengthens that claim. The radio and sound film have tended to stereotype jazz styles. In broadcasts timed to the minute there is little leeway for spontaneity. The "special arrangements" heard on the most popular programs have very much the same virtues and vices as the programs themselves. They are smooth and expert to the point of slickness, but they have a sort of mechanized, mass-production uniformity. The same is true to some extent of the popular tunes of the day. Time was when a tune "caught on" through an unpredictable combination of circumstances in which luck played a large part. The fate of a popular tune was as little to be foreseen as that of the musical show in which it was featured. But to a certain extent, anyway, the laws of natural selection were operative, and there was at least a partial survival of the fittest. The radio and the sound film have combined to reduce greatly the element of chance and popular selection. A tune has to be pretty bad not to catch on when it is heard in thousands of movie theatres and from millions of loud-speakers every night. The tendency, then, is for popular music to become almost as standardized as the cosmetics and cigarettes and foods it is used to advertise.

Swing represents a natural and essentially healthy reaction against this standardization. In contrast to "commercial" jazz, which has reached a point of relative and perhaps temporary stagnation, swing pursues the ideal of eternal change. The swing band not only must sound different from any other—it must never play in just the same way that it has ever played before. This attitude embodies healthy elements. But that does not mean that all the music produced in this way is high art, or even worth listening to. As usual, a good thing is being overpraised, which often makes it seem less good than it is.

Among the top-notch names of swing are Louis Armstrong (whose autobiography is one of the testaments of swing, and a very interesting book), Red Nichols, Stuff Smith, Frank Trumbauer, Bunny Berigan, Jack Teagarden, Count Basie, Artie Shaw, the Dorsey brothers, the lamented Bix Beiderbecke, Fats Waller and Benny Goodman.

3. TWENTIETH-CENTURY COMPOSERS OF POPULAR MUSIC

A number of our popular song writers have helped to unite the folk elements of Negro music and the commercial product of Broadway. The popularization of the Negro "blues" by WILLIAM CHRISTOPHER HANDY (1873——) is discussed in the chapter on Negro Folk Music. Handy was born in Florence, Alabama, November 16, 1873, the son of a Negro preacher. He has justly earned his title of "Father of the Blues" not only by popularizing the classic *St. Louis Blues,* but also with the *Memphis Blues,* the *Beale Street Blues,* the *Yellow Dog Blues,* and hundreds of others. In spite of failing eyesight, Handy has established and successfully developed a publishing house which for many years has been known as the "home of the blues." Recognition has come to him, and he is invariably honored at all gatherings of musicians and song writers.

Handy's colleague JOHN ROSAMOND JOHNSON (1873——) was born in Jacksonville, Florida, and was first known as a Negro composer of light music. He wrote the music for Cole and Johnson's *Shoo-Fly Regiment,* and for some of the productions of Bert Williams. One of his songs was the famous *Under the Bamboo Tree.* He toured in vaudeville. Later he turned his attention to more serious matters, and has made several collections of Negro spirituals. For many years he was director of the Music School Settlement for Colored People in New York. And in 1942 he returned to the stage to play the part of the lawyer in the revival of Gershwin's *Porgy and Bess.* He is the composer of a song that has become known as the Negro National Anthem—*Lift Every Voice and Sing.* The words were written by his brother, James Weldon Johnson.

WILL MARION COOK (1869–1944) was a Negro composer a few years older than Rosamond Johnson, and, like his colleague, he was one who started his career in the age of ragtime, and lived to see it grow into jazz and swing. Cook trained an all-Negro band in New York in 1905, and in 1919 when jazz was taking hold, he organized the American Syncopated Orchestra, which toured Europe as well as America.

He was a well-educated musician. Born in Washington, D.C., January 27, 1869, he was the son of a professor of law at Howard University. He went to Oberlin Conservatory to study the violin when he was thirteen. Two years later he won a scholarship which took him to Berlin where he studied with Joachim and remained for several years. Later he studied with Dvořák at the National Conservatory in New York.

When Cook first returned to the United States he found ragtime's popularity spreading from coast to coast. He began writing choruses and songs, and composed the operetta *Clorinda*, sometimes called *The Origin of the Cake-Walk*. This created a sensation in New York when it was produced on Broadway in 1898, and the songs *That's How the Cake-Walk Is Done* and *Emancipation Day* were in great demand.

His "popular" songs included *I May Be Crazy but I Ain't No Fool; Red, Red Rose; Mandy Lou;* and *I'm Comin' Virginia*. He wrote the music for the Williams and Walker shows *Dahomey* (1902), *Abyssinia* (1906), *Bandanna Land* (1907). He also wrote the music for *Darkeydom* (1912), *The Traitor*, and *The Casino Girl*.

A number of Cook's songs have been used extensively by recitalists in concert, some of them also arranged for chorus: *Swing Along, Exhortation*, and the *Rain Song*. He wrote also an opera, *St. Louis 'ooman*, a drama of Negro life on the Mississippi in the nineties. He lived to be seventy-five years old, and died in New York, July 19, 1944.

A number of white composers have been signally successful in catching the Negroid spirit of the blues. With *Blues in the Night*, HAROLD ARLEN (1905——) made a contribution to American popular music that established him as one of our most gifted light composers. His work is typically an expression of the age he lives in; it contains some of the sophistication that has been popularized by such men as Cole Porter, and it also catches an authentic Negroid flavor that is characteristic of the folk element of jazz. Arlen was born in Buffalo, New York, February 15, 1905. He came to New York intending to be an actor, but on being engaged as a rehearsal pianist for a Vincent Youmans production (*Great Day*) he became interested in song writing for the theatre.

He wrote the music for many *Cotton Club Revues*, Earl Carroll's *Vanities*, and other stage shows. Many of his songs were introduced by the Negro orchestra of Cab Calloway: *Kickin' the Gong Around, I've Got the World on a String*, and *Between the Devil and the Deep Blue Sea*. The most famous of his earlier songs is *Stormy Weather*. He wrote the music for the Broadway show *Life Begins at 8:40* and for *Bloomer Girl*.

He has composed also for motion pictures—*Blues in the Night*, in the film of the same name; *Over the Rainbow*, from *The Wizard of Oz*; and *Ac-cent-tchu-ate the Positive*, from *Here Come the Waves*.

The lyrics for many of Arlen's songs are written by E. Y. Harburg. ZEZ CONFREY (1895——) was a pioneer in developing piano jazz. His *Kitten on the Keys* is something of a classic. His song *Stumbling* was an early popularization of *Cross Rhythms*. Moreover, he wrote and published an honest-to-goodness instruction book on "Novelty Piano Playing"—in other words, jazz piano playing. It told all the tricks of the trade, and one hundred and fifty thousand copies were sold in the first two months it came from the press. Confrey was born in Illinois, April 3, 1895. He went to study at the Chicago Musical College, so that he might be a concert pianist, but he found that jazz was easier for him, and more profitable.

* * *

There is, of course, another main stream of popular music which has been affected either not at all or only partially by jazz and swing. Prominent in this field are a number of composers of operettas and musical comedies who follow in direct descent from Victor Herbert and Reginald De Koven. Two of them, Rudolf Friml and Sigmund Romberg, stem from the Viennese tradition of Franz Lehar and Oskar Straus.

RUDOLF FRIML was born in Prague, December 7, 1881. He was a pupil of Dvořák, and in 1901 came to America as accompanist for the violinist Jan Kubelík. Then he appeared frequently as a concert pianist and played his own Piano Concerto with the New York Symphony Orchestra. He composed many piano teaching pieces with great success, but found his most profitable field in the operetta stage, and subsequently in the motion picture adaptations that have since been made from works originally produced in the theatre. *The Firefly, Katinka, High Jinks, The Vagabond King,* and *Rose Marie* are romantic works which enjoyed extended runs when first produced, and are still played by repertory companies and by amateurs.

SIGMUND ROMBERG was born in Hungary, July 29, 1887. Until he came to America in 1909 music was his avocation, for he had been trained as an engineer to build bridges. On his arrival in this country he switched to music for a livelihood. After playing the piano in several light orchestras he wrote the music for his first show in 1913—a New York Winter Garden production *Whirl of the World*. From then on he kept writing; first the popular *revue* type of music, and from 1919, operettas.

He has a warm melodic gift, which he uses with taste and discretion. He brought out *Blossom Time* in 1924, an adaptation of Schubert melodies which caused much discussion, especially for the waltz treatment of a theme from the *Unfinished* Symphony. He followed this with *The Student Prince;* then *My Maryland, The Desert Song,* and *The New Moon* which presented that lusciously crooning song *Lover, Come Back to Me.*

For a number of years Romberg produced no new works, but busied himself with the founding and organization of the Song Writers' Protective Association. Then he returned to the theatre in 1945 with *Up in Central Park,* an operetta with book by Herbert and Dorothy Fields, based on the activities of the notorious Tweed ring in the 1870's. The work proved to be a streamlined Romberg—not jazzy, and still highly romantic; but up to date in its utilization of modern ballet techniques. Like many of its predecessors, the newest Romberg work was an immense box-office success.

JEROME KERN's *Showboat* was first produced in 1928, and it remains a legend in the American theatre. It was revived a few years after its original run, then it was made into a movie, and today its songs—*Why Do I Love You, Can't Help Lovin' That Man of Mine, My Bill,* and *Old Man River,* all with charming lyrics by Oscar Hammerstein II—are in the standard repertoire of American ballads. Based upon Edna Ferber's book of the same title, *Showboat* was almost a folk opera, with folk music of Kern's composing. Seldom has any subject been treated with better taste, musical and dramatic, than in this unpretentious classic. Some have gone so far as to say that if there is ever to be an American school of opera, this is the model upon which it must be based.

Kern was born in New York City, January 27, 1885, and studied with Paolo Gallico and Alexander Lambert. Although he started composing in 1903, he first became known to Broadway in 1911 when he wrote the music for *The Red Petticoat. The Girl from Utah* came in 1914, with Julia Sanderson singing her way to fame with *They Didn't Believe Me.* Then followed the series of Princess Theatre operettas—*Oh, Boy!; Very Good Eddie; Oh, Lady, Lady;* and others;

Stepping Stones, for Fred Stone and his family at the Globe; *Sally* at the New Amsterdam in 1920; and *Sunny* at the same theatre in 1925.

Sweet Adeline, The Cat and the Fiddle, Music in the Air, and *Roberta* are among those that came in the 1930's. In recent years Kern had been in Hollywood, concerned principally with composing the score for Hollywood "musicals."

Lately the concert halls have been hearing Kern music. In 1941, Artur Rodzinski, then conductor of the Cleveland Symphony, asked the composer to prepare a symphonic version of the *Showboat* music. The *Scenario for Orchestra on Themes from Showboat* was accordingly arranged, and presented for the first time by the Cleveland Orchestra in October, 1941. The following December the work was heard in New York when Rodzinski was appearing as guest conductor with the Philharmonic-Symphony Society.

In 1942 André Kostelanetz commissioned Kern, along with two other composers (Aaron Copland and Virgil Thomson), to compose an entirely original work. Kern accordingly provided a *Portrait of Mark Twain for Orchestra,* which had its première when Kostelanetz was guest conductor with the Cincinnati Symphony May 14, 1942. On June 7 it was performed on a CBS network by Kostelanetz's own orchestra. The first section of the work is *Hannibal Days;* the second, *Gorgeous Pilot House;* the third, *Wandering Westward;* and the finale, *Twain in His Career.* Robert Lawrence, in commenting on the piece in the New York *Herald Tribune* (June 8, 1942), wrote, in part:

" 'Twain' offered much that made for good basic listening. This seemed not to be music aimed at the intellect. It avoided contrapuntal forms, placing its reliance on melodic, harmonic and emotional appeal. . . . It is pleasant, once in a while, not to be fugally overwhelmed, and Mr. Kern's approach for its own purposes must be accounted a success."

Kern lived to be sixty years old. He died in New York, November 11, 1945, where he had come from his home in California to work as joint producer with Oscar Hammerstein II, on a revival of *Show Boat.*

RICHARD RODGERS has lately stepped into a place alongside of Jerome Kern as a composer of operetta-type musical comedies which are truly works of art. He was born in New York City, June 28, 1902. When he was a student at Columbia he wrote music for the 'Varsity shows, but before that he had had a Broadway production for a show he had written when he was sixteen—*The Poor Little Ritz Girl*. He wrote his early musical comedies with the same lyricist, Lorenz Hart: *Dearest Enemy; The Girl Friend; Peggy Ann; Present Arms; The Connecticut Yankee; Chee-Chee; Spring Is Here; Heads Up;* and *Simple Simon*. And until Hart died, in 1943, the team of Rodgers and Hart was as seemingly indissoluble as that of George and Ira Gershwin.

Shortly before Hart's death Rodgers had started collaborating with Oscar Hammerstein II, the librettist who had furnished some of their best lyric material to Jerome Kern, Sigmund Romberg, and others. The first Rodgers and Hammerstein work was an adaptation of Lynn Riggs's play *Green Grow the Lilacs*, which was renamed *Oklahoma*. It was produced by the Theatre Guild at the St. James Theatre, New York, early in 1943, and was played for several years to sold-out houses in New York, and by a number of traveling companies in various parts of the country.

Oklahoma is a triumph of collaboration. Rodgers's music is highly individual, easily remembered, and of lasting quality. Hammerstein's lyrics are filled with poetic imagery, but avoid oversophistication; and his adaptation of the original Riggs play to operetta purposes is a miracle in achieving a unity of plot, dialogue, songs, ballet numbers, and ensembles.

The success of *Oklahoma* was followed two years later by the second Rodgers-Hammerstein collaboration. This time, again under the auspices of the Theatre Guild, the partners adapted Ferenc Molnar's play *Liliom*, and produced a work they called *Carousel*. The foreign locale was brought home to New England, and the characters were changed to Americans. Musically, the score of *Carousel* was more ambitious than that of *Oklahoma*. Rodgers attempted and achieved truly operatic effects, particularly in such extended numbers as his hero's soliloquy. In the spring of 1945 the new musical play moved into the Majestic Theatre on 44th Street, New York, directly opposite the St. James Theatre where *Oklahoma* was still playing.

IRVING BERLIN, a highly individual lyricist and melodist, is actually a throwback to the sentimental songs of a past day. It is not unusual to hear Berlin referred to as a composer of "jazz," but that is not accurate, even though his first hit-song *Alexander's Ragtime Band* (1912) was one of the first songs that the jazz bands seized upon and made their own. The song itself is distinctly not jazz; it is scarcely ragtime.

Berlin's real name was Izzy Baline. Born in Russia, May 11, 1888, he was brought to America by his family when he was little more than a baby, and he has on his forehead today a scar that was caused by a knife, dropped by someone in a higher bunk of the steerage when he crossed on the steamer. He grew up on the lower East Side and the Bowery in New York, and started singing as a "busker." Alexander Woollcott, in *The Story of Irving Berlin*, explains that the buskers are the American relatives of the comedians who sing in the Paris cafés, or on the sidewalks outside the London theatres. Little Izzy Baline was one of the buskers who haunted the Bowery saloons. Later he had a job as singing waiter at Nigger Mike's in Chinatown, reputed to be the gathering place of gangsters, thieves, and gunmen, but more likely a show place for slumming parties from uptown.

Berlin wrote his first song while he was at Nigger Mike's—*Marie from Sunny Italy*, words by I. Berlin, music by N. Nicholson. Nicholson was the pianist at Nigger Mike's. At first Berlin wrote only the words of songs: his gift of melody was not apparent until later. He played the piano a little himself, enough to piece together the tunes he wrote, and then an arranger took them down and fixed up their harmonies for him. When he was fired from Nigger Mike's, because the boss found him asleep one morning when he was supposed to be watching the cash register, and found it short a few dollars which he, the boss, had himself borrowed from it the previous evening, Berlin went uptown and got to know the song publishers.

Then followed a series of songs, hundreds of them, "words and music" by Irving Berlin, which are part of the folk literature of our country. Songs with luscious melodic intervals, with words and melody wedded in an inseparable rhythmic pattern. To mention only a few of them—there were *My Wife's Gone to the Country; Alexander's Ragtime Band; Everybody's Doin' It; When That Midnight Choo-Choo Leaves for Alabam'; A Pretty Girl Is Like a Melody; When My Baby Smiles at Me; Who; What'll I Do; All Alone; Russian*

Lullaby; Always; Blue Skies; Remember; Pack Up Your Sins. In time, Berlin came to have his own publishing business; he became a theatrical producer, bringing out principally musical comedies and revues for which he had written the music; and he became one of the highest paid and most sought after composers of songs for motion pictures.

During the first World War, as a private at Camp Upton, Berlin wrote and produced the soldier show *Yip! Yip! Yaphank,* containing in its score the later famous song *Gee! How I Hate to Get Up in the Morning.* At the beginning of World War II he immediately set to work writing and producing another soldier show—*This Is the Army.* It had a long Broadway run, toured the country, went abroad, and was made into a sound picture. His song *God Bless America* became widely used shortly before America entered the second World War. It had been written and laid aside many years earlier, but Kate Smith started singing it on the radio, and it became almost an unofficial national anthem. Berlin donated all of his royalties on the song to the Boy Scouts and Girl Scouts of America, and set up a board of trustees to administer the proceeds. Many other topical songs came from the Berlin pen during the war years—songs devoted to the Bond Drives, to the Red Cross, and even to the paying of income taxes.

In the 1920's, VINCENT YOUMANS (1898——) was one of the brightest lights in the musical comedy field. His songs for *No, No, Nanette* (*I Want to Be Happy; Tea for Two*), for *Hit the Deck* (*Hallelujah,* and others), his *Bambolina,* and the score of *Great Day,* were among the choicest bits of gayety that graced the Broadway stage and found their way to phonograph records and the radio. They are still standard songs, as is Youmans's ballad *Without a Song,* and it is much to be regretted that the composer's ill health interrupted his steady stream of buoyant songs. Youmans was born in New York City, September 27, 1898.

COLE PORTER (1892——) represents the height of sophistication in song writing. The author of both words and music of his songs, he deals with the primal instincts of love in typically twentieth-century fashion; never hesitating to use many-syllabled words, even though he is actually writing for the masses. He often rhymes whole phrases, such as "a certain fear in me, wakes the pioneer in me; or "under the hide of me; burning inside of me." In this practice he has created a fashion, and has many imitators. And being a versatile fellow, he has written an authentic imitation of cowboy ballads in his recent *Don't Fence Me In.*

Porter was born in Peru, Indiana, June 9, 1892. He became a law student at Yale, then in 1915 went to the Harvard Music School for study in harmony. Later he studied at the Schola Cantorum in Paris. Many of his songs have been incorporated into his scores for musical comedies, which include *Fifty Million Frenchmen, Gay Divorcee, Anything Goes, Jubilee, Red Hot and Blue, Panama Hattie,* and many others. Among his best-known songs are *In the Still of the Night, Night and Day, Begin the Beguine, Rosalie,* and many others of Hit Parade standing which have outlasted their first popularity.

Like Porter, HOAGY CARMICHAEL (1903———) gave up the law to be a composer. *Stardust* is the song which brought him his first fame, and he has continued his success with *Lazybones, Georgia on My Mind, Rockin' Chair,* and dozens of others in the "hit" class. Carmichael was born in Bloomington, Indiana, November 22, 1903. After starting to practice law in Florida, he found the career of musician more to his liking and returned to Indiana where he organized a dance orchestra. Recently he has been making personal appearances in motion pictures.

ARTHUR SCHWARTZ (1900———) is another ex-lawyer. He is also a member of Phi Beta Kappa, holds four University degrees, and has been an English teacher. His erudition, however, does not prevent him from writing songs which have a wide appeal, and are as melodious and as singable as anything that has come out of this century's popular music. *Dancing in the Dark, You and the Night and the Music,* and *Something to Remember You By* are typical of the haunting tunes he has written for Broadway productions and for motion pictures. His musical comedy scores include the intimate revues: *The Grand Street Follies, The Little Show,* and *Three's a Crowd;* and the more elaborate *Flying Colors, Revenge with Music, Band Wagon,* and *American Jubilee.* Schwartz was born in Brooklyn, New York, November 25, 1900.

PETER DE ROSE (1896———) has become identified with a type of song which bridges the gap between the so-called "popular" type and the ballad. His *Deep Purple* has become what is known as a "standard" in the radio repertoire, and he has composed sacred songs which have an appeal equal to that of some of the hit-songs. De Rose was born in New York City, March 10, 1896. In 1923 he formed a professional partnership with May Singhi Breen, and the two became popular on the radio as the "Sweethearts of the Air." The romantic implication was not only for the benefit of the public, however, for they were married in 1929. The De Rose songs include *Tiger Rose, Wagon Wheels, Somebody Loves You, Muddy Water,* and many others which have had wide popularity.

RAY HENDERSON (1896——) has been both a composer and publisher; for a number of years he was a member of the firm of De Sylva, Brown and Henderson. Born in Buffalo, New York, December 1, 1896, he had musical training at the Chicago Conservatory and from private teachers. His best-known songs include *My Sin, Sonny Boy, Bye Bye, Blackbirds, Follow the Swallow,* and others. He is a member of the Board of Directors of the American Society of Composers, Authors and Publishers (ASCAP).

GEORGE W. MEYER (1884——), secretary and a director of the American Society of Composers, Authors and Publishers, is known best for a song composed many years ago, but which provided the hit-song, and the title, for a motion picture in the early 1940's—*For Me and My Gal.* He is the composer of many sentimental songs characteristic of an earlier day—*I Believe in Miracles, Tuck Me to Sleep in My Old Kentucky Home, Everything Is Peaches Down in Georgia,* and others of their kind.

Meyer's companion on the ASCAP Board of Directors, FRED E. AHLERT (1892——), is a native of New York City. Like many of the song writers, he intended to be a lawyer before he abandoned his studies at Fordham Law School. He is known for many "hit-songs": *I'll Get By, Mean to Me, I'm Going to Sit Down and Write Myself a Letter,* Bing Crosby's theme-song *Where the Blue of the Night Meets the Gold of the Day,* and others.

IRVING CAESAR (1895——), another ASCAP director, is perhaps best known as a lyricist, being the author of the words of George Gershwin's *Swanee,* the songs from Vincent Youmans's *No, No, Nanette,* and dozens of other popular songs. But he also composes the music to songs which have met popular favor. In the field of utilitarian music, Caesar compiled a volume of songs for children entitled *Sing a Song of Safety,* offering practical advice on avoiding the traffic hazards of city streets.

The name of MABEL WAYNE (1898———) is synonymous with her song *Romona,* but she has achieved an almost equal success with several other songs, including *In a Little Spanish Town,* and *Chiquita.* She was born in New York City, July 16, 1898, and in addition to writing songs has been a singer, dancer, and vaudeville entertainer.

LOUIS ALTER (1902———) is the composer of a type of instrumental piece which is distinctly in the popular idiom, but which is actually a modern type of salon music. *Manhattan Serenade* and *Metropolitan Nocturne* are perhaps the best known of them, and like the others they are marked by urban sophistication and make polite use of modern dissonance. Often they reflect a jazz and blues influence. Alter has also written popular songs: *Morning, Noon and Night; Twilight on the Trail, Blue Shadows,* and a long list of others composed for Broadway shows and Hollywood musicals. He was born in Haverhill, Massachusetts, June 18, 1902, and studied music at the New England Conservatory in Boston.

HAROLD J. ROME (1908———) started life as an architect, but he achieved such fame with some of the songs he wrote for the labor revue *Pins and Needles,* that he found himself in great demand for similar productions, many of them for workers in industrial plants during World War II. The songs: *Sunday in the Park, One Big Union for Two, Sing Me a Song of Social Significance,* and *Nobody Makes a Pass at Me* are as melodious as they are witty. Rome was born in Hartford, Connecticut, May 27, 1908.

Holiday for Strings, a gay, sparkling instrumental piece, established DAVID ROSE (1910———) as one of the genuinely talented of our popular composers. Born in London, June 15, 1910, Rose was brought to Chicago at the age of four. He studied at the Chicago College of Music, and began playing the piano in dance bands. He became an arranger, a conductor of radio orchestras, and finally music director of the Mutual Don Lee West Coast radio network. In 1942 he interrupted his music activities to enter the Armed Forces, and soon found himself appointed composer of the music and director of the Army

Air Force Show *Winged Victory*. His compositions include a collection of piano pieces called *Music for Moderns*.

Another musician born in England, and in the same year as David Rose, is ALEC TEMPLETON (1910——), a most clever musical satirist. His witty irony in his pianologue parodies have made him one of the nation's most popular entertainers—on the radio, in night clubs, and on the lecture platform. Totally blind since birth, he seems to have been helped rather than handicapped by his affliction, for his sense of hearing is so sharp that he detects characteristics in the performances of others that might easily escape those whose sense of sight would prevent the close concentration on sound.

Templeton was born in Cardiff, Wales, July 4, 1910, and was educated musically at the Royal Academy of Music in London. He came to America in the 1930's, and has made his permanent home with us. His best compositions are his satires: *Bach Goes to Town, Mozart Matriculates, Mendelssohn Mows 'em Down*, and dozens of others with equally interesting titles.

ALEC WILDER (1907——) composes songs and orchestral works, many of them in popular vein. He was born in Manchester, New York, and studied at the Eastman School of Music. He has written a ballet *Juke Box*, produced by the American Ballet. His works include a series of piano solos entitled *Seldom the Sun, A Debutante's Diary*, and *Neurotic Goldfish*. Among his songs are *Who Can I Turn To, Song to Spring, Moon and Sand, I'll Be Around*, and· *Psalm 137 (By the Rivers of Babylon)*.

ERNEST GOLD (1921——), a pianist and composer of popular music, was born in Vienna. He was educated at the Music Academy in Vienna. He has written an opera and orchestral works, including *American Miniature* (1940) and *Instrumentals*, symphonic jazz. He wrote *The Shining Hour* for piano and orchestra, *Pied Piper, Jr.*, for solo clarinet and orchestra, and the popular songs: *Here in the Velvet Night, Boogie Woogie to You, Montevideo, Practice Makes Perfect*, and others. His latest work is a Piano Concerto.

FRANK LOESSER (1910——) had been achieving a distinguished reputation as a lyricist for popular songs, when he came into prominence also as a tunester, by writing both words and music for *Praise the Lord and Pass the Ammunition* (1942); *What Do You Do in the Infantry*

(1943), and several others including *Rodger Young,* and *First Class Private Mary Brown.*

Loesser comes of a musical family. His brother is well known as a pianist and as a teacher at the Cleveland Institute of Music. Frank Loesser was born in New York City, June 29, 1910, and came to Tin-Pan Alley by a circuitous route of journalism and business. He commenced writing songs with William Schuman, and the two of them wrote a song called *In Love with a Memory of You.* Schuman, as we have found, left the "popular" field, but Loesser has made a prosperous profession of writing hit-songs. In 1942 he enlisted in the Infantry, and was assigned to the special services principally to provide songs for specific purposes. *Praise the Lord and Pass the Ammunition,* based on a phrase actually uttered by Lieutenant Colonel Howell E. Forgy at Pearl Harbor, may prove to be one of the outstanding songs of the second World War.

*   *   *

This brings us again to the subject of war songs. It is still too early to judge the lasting value of songs that were inspired by the second World War; therefore, it is not possible to write a complete, or even a comprehensive, account of our war music, or of the influence the war has had on our American music. When a final survey can be made, it will perhaps be found that music has played a greater part in the conduct of this war, a more utilitarian part, than it has ever played in past wars. Many of the compositions relating to World War II, and inspired by it, are discussed in the pages and paragraphs devoted to those who have composed such works. They may be found by consulting in the Index the list under the heading "World War II."

There are some things, however, which are already apparent. Our popular music, and some of our more serious efforts, which were composed in the years preceding America's entry into the war, reflect accurately the public state of mind. Most of them were works which made us more aware of the dangers to democracy, and which emphasized its blessings. Earl Robinson's *Ballad for Americans* was the most widely known of them, and exerted the strongest influence. There were also isolationist songs, some of them sincere; some, perhaps, prompted by sinister propagandists. Even after we entered the war, the "Peace

Now" group was represented by a song bearing that title. The great bulk of the music, however, was intensely patriotic in spirit, and violently anti-Fascist.

Immediately after Pearl Harbor, the songsmiths came into action. Hundreds of hastily written songs were published almost overnight, to subjects ranging from Pearl Harbor itself to General MacArthur, Tokyo, Yokohama (*Goodbye, Mamma, I'm Off to Yokohama*), to Singapore and all points in the South Pacific. Sap was rhymed with Jap, Axis with taxes, and the total output was typical of American high-pressure, mass production. Nothing of lasting quality seemed to be forthcoming, and the song writers themselves became so concerned about the situation that it was the principal subject for discussion at a dinner of the Song Writers' Protective Association. President Sigmund Romberg urged the members present to "create songs to be sung by the fighting forces, rather than at them." That presented a problem, for soldiers are notoriously capricious about what they want to sing. Old favorites, and songs popular in the first World War seemed to be filling their needs very nicely. When a prominent officer expressed the average soldier's taste in songs, one of the song writers, Edward Laska, gave him exactly what he suggested and even incorporated the officer's statement in his title and chorus—*We Want to Sing About Women*.

At the SPA dinner Romberg stated that "the country needs songs that will arouse the nation's armed forces and not soothe them, songs to inspire the fighting mood rather than dreams of the girls they left behind." But the soldiers themselves had considerable to say on that subject, and the singing they did was more for relaxation and temporary escape than for battlecries under fire.

Some of the songs became increasingly popular at home, and they had a telling effect on civilians, regardless of whether they were sung by the members of the armed forces. *Coming In on a Wing and a Prayer*, and *Praise the Lord and Pass the Ammunition* were heard many times each day on the radio, but they were played so much in such a short space of time, that for the present, at least, they have suffered the eclipse that is the fate of a modern popular song which is "plugged" to death.

A serious effort to provide the type of songs needed, and then to promote the distribution and popularity of such songs, was made by the Music Committee of the Writers' War Board. The various branches of the armed services, the Red Cross, the Treasury Department, and the recruiting agencies, were invited to send requests to the committee for whatever songs they felt would be helpful. Then the committee asked for volunteers, or assigned to professional members the task of writing such songs. The utilitarian results were good. Whether songs of lasting merit have been forthcoming from this clearing house is another matter, and perhaps not altogether important if the immediate results were helpful.

Anyway, each branch of the armed services had its own songs, some of them official. The Bond Drives, the Red Cross, the income tax collections have all had songs written for them urging the public to take its part in the war effort. And the production of these songs was organized on a systematic basis comparable to our major industries. For the home front, musical revues were written for production in industrial plants, *Lunchtime Follies*, and such, and many songs were composed urging civilians to enter war industries and to stick at their jobs.

Sometime in the future, let us hope not too far off, the story of these songs and the part of music in the war, can be written. Then the thousands of ballads can be sorted and evaluated and we shall see which of them, and what composers of them, will have become a part of our permanent music. We may then determine what effect the greatest of all wars has had on the music of our country.

CHAPTER SIXTEEN

Conclusion

WE are at the end of our story. In the year 1945, with more than three hundred and twenty-five years of our American music behind us. And much of it still with us. At a place where maybe we can have a bit of perspective, and take stock of what we have amassed in our musical inventory. Three and a quarter centuries—not a very long time as the world looks at things; but ages in terms of American history.

The three periods of our musical growth have been suggested by the divisions of our book. The first, from 1620 to 1800, produced very little that has lived to our day—Holden's *Coronation, Yankee Doodle,* and *Hail Columbia* are about the only bits of music that have preserved themselves, for Hopkinson's songs and Billings's anthems were discovered and revived. Yet these formative years produced the seeds of things that would bear fruit later.

The second period, 1800 to 1860, gave us Lowell Mason and the hymn writers, as well as Gottschalk and Stephen Foster, but it is only since 1860 that we have had our important serious composers, starting with John K. Paine and Dudley Buck. Yet the two hundred and forty years before their productive years must be known and understood if we are to know our present-day composers, even if it is only to appreciate them by contrast with what went before them. For composers rarely happen; they are generally produced by environment or heredity. Or in some cases by tradition.

Especially interesting have been our foreign relations. In art we were not able to sign a declaration of independence and to pursue a policy of isolation. It is doubtful if it would have been desirable anyway. We had to depend on Europe for culture, until we had been here long enough to develop an art of our own. And that was not as easy as planting corn and watching it sprout in the same season. We have had to import, before we could manufacture and export.

There have been three distinct periods of intensive immigration. The 1780's and 1790's, following our independence, and the French Revolution abroad; the influx of 1848, when there was unrest in Central Europe; and that of our own time, from the days of the first World War to the present. The first two periods of immigration had a profound effect on our few native composers. In the last quarter of the eighteenth century the foreigners took the center of the stage, and Billings and his colleagues retired to the background. After the turn of the century the native composer returned with Lowell Mason, but again in 1848 the foreigners, principally Germans, took matters into their own hands. There were few musicians here who could compare in ability with those from abroad. So most of the natives took a rear place. Some were a bit sensitive about foreign domination, and we met Fry and Bristow as early champions of the American composer. We started to grow self-conscious in the middle of the nineteenth century.

In the twentieth century, particularly during the last decade, immigrations from Europe have had a different effect from those of the preceding centuries. In the late nineteenth century, or even in the early 1900's, we would have been completely overwhelmed by the arrival of so many hundreds of foreigners. When racial persecution menaced Central Europe in the early 1930's, and refugees packed every ship coming to our shores, we would no doubt have been forced to turn over to them the entire conduct of our music life, had our native musicians, particularly our composers, been in the same position, and as comparatively few in numbers, as their predecessors were a half, or even a quarter century before. But this time the newcomers did not press our native composers into their own mold, and make our music little more than an imitation of their own. The Americans and the foreigners both realized that each had something important to learn from the other, and to teach to each other. American music had established itself by that time, and the newcomers recognized the fact; many of them were as much influenced by their new environment as the nineteenth-century American composers had been affected by European surroundings.

Obviously, this state of affairs did not just happen. Much conscious effort, and a great deal of propagandizing, some of it wise and some of it misguided, had been necessary to gain for the American composer the three essentials of his existence: publication of his music, particularly of his larger compositions; performances of his important works; and adequate payment when his music is performed for profit.

As the first half of the century nears its end, the publishing of larger works by American composers is assuming major proportions. It has been materially aided by new methods of offset printing which have reduced the cost considerably. And in cases where the printing of orchestral parts is not warranted, publishers have instituted rental service of parts photographically duplicated from manuscript copies. Publishers have also been alert to develop new markets for orchestral music among amateur and school and college orchestras.

But even if the American publisher has done as much and more than could have been expected of him, he has not been able to print all that should be published. Many of the excellent scores that have been composed and performed, have had to remain in manuscript form, simply because there has been a limit to what our publishers can handle.

Back in 1901, Arthur Farwell sensed this problem. He felt that publishers were interested only in works in conventional mold; that they were afraid of anything that seemed too new, especially if written by Americans who had not yet established their reputations. He felt that the only way to remedy the evil was to start a new publishing venture, and he founded the Wa-Wan Press which was the first to introduce several talented composers to the music lovers of their own country. To secure regular distribution, subscribers were solicited who would receive in periodical form the publications of the Press as they were issued quarterly each year.

The Society for the Publication of American Music adopted a similar method of distribution when it was founded by Burnet Corwin Tuthill in 1919. In this case the object was to issue chamber music. This was published not only as a philanthropic gesture, but also was wisely put into the hands of musicians and music lovers who would play it at home and in public. Subscriptions were solicited and sold. The membership fee entitles the subscriber to the works issued each year by the society.

By this method the buyer agrees in advance to take what is published, and the society in turn is assured of a certain sale for the works it brings out. The Society for the Publication of American Music has achieved permanence, and by 1943 had issued no less than forty-five publications.

Several philanthropists have taken an interest in the publication of orchestral works. George Eastman, of Kodak fame, who founded and endowed the Eastman School of Music at Rochester, established a fund for the annual publication of orchestral scores by American composers. The works published are selected from those performed at the American Composers' Concerts at the Eastman School. They are issued by a commercial publishing house and distributed through regular trade channels, but all costs of publication are paid by the Eastman fund, and the commercial publisher takes no risk.

The Juilliard Musical Foundation subsidizes publication of orchestral works by Americans in a similar manner. The printing and distribution is attended to by a regular publishing house, but the Juilliard Foundation pays all the bills and gets no return. Of the gross returns from the sale of printed copies and from performance fees, the composer gets sixty per cent and the publisher forty.

Yet publication is not all of the problem. If printed music is never performed it remains just so much paper and ink. In the case of the Eastman publications, they have already had performance at Rochester before they are selected for publication, and the Juilliard Foundation undertakes to secure major performances for the works issued under its subsidy. As far as our regular symphony orchestras are concerned, we still hear echoes of Fry's complaint against the New York Philharmonic almost eighty years ago. The situation has changed, however. Fifty years ago few American compositions were played by orchestras because there were few American compositions. Today there are so many that it would be impossible for our orchestras to give all the worthy ones an adequate hearing even if all the conductors wanted to. We have already learned that agitation for the American composer's rights began early in the nineteenth century. The Bohemian Heinrich felt himself entitled to recognition because he was an American, and a naturalized one at that. Fry and Bristow bewailed the plight of their fellows and themselves. With the turn of the century many more took up the cudgels, and by the time of the first World War, the thing became an organized propaganda with slogans—The American Composer First, and others.

Way back in 1856, Edward Jerome Hopkins started an American Music Association to promote works by American composers. There were several sporadic attempts after that to form organizations that would help our writers, for some people were beginning to realize that if we were to have serious composers, they must have their day in the concert hall. The Manuscript Society of New York was organized in 1889, to meet once a month for hearing compositions written by its members. In 1899 it was reorganized as the Society of American Musicians and Composers. The meetings introduced many interesting works, but the society was never successful in its ambition to interest the general public in its activities. A Manuscript Society was organized in Philadelphia in 1892, with William Wallace Gilchrist as its first president. Like the New York society, the Philadelphia group held monthly meetings for performances of original works by its members, and it also arranged public concerts with the Philadelphia Orchestra and the choral societies of the city. It held a number of prize contests for new works. In 1896 a Manuscript Society was organized in Chicago, and Frederick Grant Gleason was the first president. There have been similar organizations in other cities.

Arthur Farwell was interested in performances of American works as well as in their publication. He was one of the organizers of the American Music Society, and its moving spirit. The society was formed first in Boston, and by the time Farwell joined the staff of *Musical America* in New York (1910) and had to give up the traveling that the organization entailed, there were chapters, or centers, as they were called, in twenty cities. The objects of the society were the study and performance of the works of American composers; the study of all folk music touching the development of music in the United States; and the publication of articles, discussions, or any significant matter relative to American music. It disclaimed any intention of urging acceptance of American music simply because it is American; it must be good music.

The young American composer needs a laboratory for his experiments. The major symphony orchestras can play only his finished works, when he has gained a command of his technique. Before that he needs to hear what he has written so that he will know what his ideas for instrumental combinations sound like. The growth of orchestras in smaller cities, of conservatory orchestras and amateur groups is helping to provide a workshop for our composers. When the short-lived State Symphony Orchestra was established in New York (1923), one of its functions was to hold special rehearsals to which composers could bring their manuscripts and hear them performed. This was valuable, but of course a finished performance was not possible, as the works were merely read through by conductor and players.

The American Composers' Concerts at the Eastman School in Rochester overcame this difficulty. They provide carefully rehearsed performances of works that have for the most part never before been played in public. The composer is invited to come to Rochester to hear the rehearsals and the performances.

It is often an expensive matter for a composer to have an unpublished work performed. When his music has been accepted for performance, he has had to provide not only a copy of the score, but copies of the individual parts for the players, generally at his own expense. The Juilliard School of Music offers assistance to a limited number of composers whose manuscript works have been accepted for major performance, by paying the cost of a copyist to prepare the parts.

The League of Composers, established in New York in 1923, is concerned chiefly with the modernists of America and the world. Whereas the average symphony orchestra devotes its smallest percentage of performances to American works, the League of Composers reversed this process in the first six years of its career. At its concerts it presented in all, one hundred and ten works. Of these, thirty-five were American, eighteen Russian, seventeen Italian, fourteen German, eight English, five Hungarian, three Polish, two Czechoslovakian, four Spanish, two Dutch, one Mexican, and one Swedish.

Shortly before his death in 1937, Henry Hadley founded the National Association for American Composers and Conductors. Since his passing, the organization has continued an active career, offering programs of American music, awarding annually a medal and citations for distinguished service to American music, and sponsoring the Henry Hadley Memorial Library in the Americana Music Room of the New York Public Library.

It is interesting to learn what share of the programs of our major orchestras has been devoted to American works during the past twenty-five years. Howard Hanson analyzed the record for the years from 1919 to 1925. He found that in a period of six and a half seasons, from the fall of 1919 to the fall of 1925, the thirteen most important orchestras of the country gave something over four hundred and fifty performances of works by ninety-five native-born American composers. This was an average of 5.3 per cent American works each season by each of the thirteen orchestras.

Fifteen years later a survey made by the National Music Council told a different story. This time fifteen orchestras were surveyed. In the season 1939–40 these organizations played 134 compositions by native-born or naturalized American composers (9.7 per cent of the entire works played during the season); in 1940–41, these compositions numbered 206 (14.5 per cent); in 1941–42 the total was 232 (17.1 per cent); and in 1942–43 it increased to 257 (20.8 per cent). In the four-year period, these fifteen orchestras performed a total of 829 American works, or an average of 13.8 per cent of the total by each of the orchestras each season. Some of the larger orchestras, of course, played more concerts a season than did their colleagues in smaller cities. Consequently, we find the following well above the average: in the 1942–43 season the New York Philharmonic-Symphony played 32 American works; the Cincinnati Symphony, 29; Chicago Symphony, 24; Philadelphia Orchestra, 22; St. Louis Symphony, 21; Boston Symphony, 16; and Los Angeles Philharmonic, 16.

The comparison between the 1919 to 1925 figures and those of 1939 to 1943 is not altogether fair, since the latter included naturalized and native-born composers. But even considering that factor, the increase in American works was notable.

We are insisting that the music of our American contemporaries has as much right to be heard in our concert halls and on our radio programs as that of any of their European colleagues. And it is apparent from the foregoing statistics that we are hearing it—even in such formerly impregnable citadels as the concerts of the Philharmonic-

Symphony Orchestra. Commissions, once very scarce treasures indeed, and usually reserved for foreign notables, are offered in increasing number to Americans—by the symphony societies, the broadcasting companies, the music festivals, the League of Composers—and prizes for American compositions by the Philharmonic-Symphony itself.

We are also getting away from the idea that a composer must be content with the honor and prestige he gains from a major performance. We are coming to realize that unless he can some day make a living by composing, he is engaged in an economically unsound profession. The vigilance of the American Society of Composers, Authors and Publishers (ASCAP), and kindred organizations, is securing for our composers a more just share of the profits which accrue through their efforts to the broadcasting, recording, and motion picture companies, and to the concert field. Our symphony orchestras are becoming more used to the fact that a composer is as much entitled to a performing fee for having written a work, as a pianist or a violinist is for playing it, and they have agreed to pay license fees to ASCAP, which represents the composers.

The American Society of Composers, Authors and Publishers deserves a chapter by itself. Founded in 1914, it resulted from a composer's realizing that while performers were paid for playing and singing his music, he was getting nothing. One evening in 1913, Victor Herbert was sitting in Shanley's Restaurant in New York when he noticed that the band was playing music from his *Sweethearts*, which was at that time enjoying a run on Broadway. Herbert knew that the copyright law of 1909 established minimum damages of two hundred and fifty dollars and costs for the unauthorized performance for profit of copyrighted music. Was this performance for profit? Herbert said it was. Shanley's said it wasn't. It took Herbert four years to get a final, favorable determination of the issues, and when it came it was from Justice Oliver Wendell Holmes, voicing a unanimous opinion of the United States Supreme Court.

Herbert's claim had been fought bitterly by an association of hotel and restaurant owners, and he had realized early in the proceedings that an individual composer could not possibly afford to collect his due under the copyright law if he were to be opposed by the combined forces of all the interests who wished to withhold it from him. So he banded together with Sousa, Nathan Burkan (an attorney), Gene Buck (author of many Ziegfeld *Follies* books), and a few others, to form the American Society of Composers, Authors and Publishers— that is, a society of all those interested in maintaining their rights under the provisions of the law covering public performance of copyrighted music for profit.

By so doing, these pioneers founded an organization which does far more than seek recognition and fame for the composer and the song writer; it has come to provide for their material needs by collecting and turning over to them payment for the use and performance of their music. With the coming of radio, ASCAP established through litigation the fact that a radio performance was actually a performance for profit, even though the broadcasters had claimed it was not because the listener paid nothing for it. And so the society protected those who provided the music for the radio, and saw to it that they were paid for their contribution. Today the American Society of Composers, Authors and Publishers collects from users of music, and distributes among its members, several millions of dollars annually.

There are many prize contests open to American composers. Many years before his death, Ignace Paderewski established a fund to award from time to time two prizes: one of $1,000 for an orchestral work; and the other of $500 for a piece of chamber music. The Hollywood Bowl Association (California) offers $1,000 yearly for a symphonic poem. Columbia University offers two prizes annually under the will of Lillia M. Bearns: $1,200 for a composition in large form, and $900 for a smaller work. The RCA-Victor Company and the National Broadcasting Company have awarded generous prizes for American works, and the Columbia Broadcasting System and the Blue Network (American Broadcasting Company) have inaugurated a policy of commissioning works from American composers. Several of the symphony orchestras are giving commissions to our composers. Koussevitzky has been a leader in this movement, and has earned the lasting gratitude of the profession.

One of the organizations that has most consistently had at heart the good of the American composer has been the National Federation of Music Clubs, not only by offering prizes for compositions, but also by urging its members (now 300,000 from 4,867 local clubs) to give intelligent support to American music. The Federation had its first national meeting in 1899, and since that time has had a national gathering every two years, in various centers of the country. Since 1909 it has fostered prize contests open to American composers, and the prizes have ranged from $100 to the $10,000 that was awarded to Horatio Parker's opera *Fairyland* in 1915.

A number of prize awards have been devoted to providing composers with the leisure necessary for devoting their attention to composition, to let them have a few years respite from the necessity of earning a living. The American Academy in Rome has for many years awarded fellowships in music. There are three of them; one provided by the Frederick A. Juilliard Fund, another by the Walter Damrosch Fund, and the third by the Horatio Parker Fund. Each allows an annual payment of $1,500 a year for three years, and a traveling allowance of $500 a year. The John Simon Guggenheim Memorial Fellowships include music. Each fellowship allows $2,500 a year, and carries no restrictions. Under the will of the late Joseph Pulitzer an annual scholarship is awarded to the student of music "who is deemed to be the most talented and deserving, in order that he may continue his studies with the advantage of European instruction." The student is expected to devote a sufficient amount of his time to composition, during the year he holds the scholarship, to produce a serious work in one of the larger forms.

The MacDowell Colony at Peterboro has already been mentioned in the chapter on Edward MacDowell. Creative artists in all fields of art and literature, as well as music, are invited to spend all or part of their summers at the colony, to work undisturbed in peaceful surroundings. The colony has been successful because it has never been the plaything of faddists. The artists are not on display for tourists to look at; they go to Peterboro for an opportunity to work, and they get it. The fulfillment of Peterboro's promise is best shown by the high character of the works that have been produced there.

The colony suffered a crushing blow in 1938. In September of that year a wildly destructive hurricane swept over the New England States, laying waste enormous acreages of woodland as far north as the upper White Mountains. The Peterboro Colony was a most heavy sufferer, and the damage sustained has as yet by no means been fully repaired. But Mrs. MacDowell's efforts in behalf of the colony were only redoubled, and as was expected by all who knew her, they were fully successful.

Naturally, the first World War, and the years which led to the economic depression of the 1930's, had a tremendous effect on our music life. Fortunately, some of the results were beneficial.

The depression hit all forms of musical activities and hit them hard. Performing musicians, already displaced in large numbers by the radio and the sound film, found opportunities for employment growing steadily scarcer. Music teachers lost many of their pupils, and had to reduce their fees to those who remained. Music publishers, recording companies, instrument manufacturers—all of the music industries —suffered an immense reduction of their profits, or even sustained heavy losses.

Yet by 1940, at the close of the same decade, we saw that music in America had grown beyond our fondest hopes of ten years ago. The number of people studying music was far greater than ever before. The amount of good music broadcast, in response to popular demand, was growing steadily. Music teachers were busy again. The music industries had revived to a degree that would have seemed fantastic a short time ago. America had never yet been so musical a nation, never had so many orchestras and bands, so much music in the schools, so many composers, conductors, singers, violinists, pianists, teachers, and scholars really equipped to do their jobs and do them well.

What was the explanation? How did it happen that less than ten years after the American people touched bottom, both in their commerce and industry and in their general morale, music had bounded back to a place far higher than it ever held before?

There were many reasons. The same situation that underlies the unemployment of thousands of musicians—the steady advance of technology, which provides machines to do the work that men used to do—provided the whole population, employed as well as unemployed, with hours of leisure unknown to earlier generations. That was not a new situation, or one whose advent had not been foreseen by thinking men and women. Educators, in particular, had been working for many years at the problems involved, and it was largely their work that bore the fruit we were harvesting.

The first World War had caused a countrywide sprouting of community activities and community consciousness. In the great swarm of patriotic meetings and assemblies, music played a large part. Music undoubtedly helped to win that war. And if world events sometimes made us question the value of the fruits of victory, we could not doubt for a moment that the surge of national unity caused by the war immensely helped the cause of music.

The pleasures of community singing and playing were not to be laid aside with the guns and the uniforms. On the contrary, music, as perhaps the most social of the arts, was cultivated with more enthusiasm than ever when the tenseness of war was over. Choruses sprang up all over the country, and it was not too long before they inevitably turned to the treasures of the Golden Age of choral music—the polyphonic masters of the pre-Bach periods. A genuine and countrywide rebirth of choral singing and choral writing took place, especially in the *a cappella* style.

The spread of choral singing continues right up to the present, with ever increasing momentum. It has been a wholesome influence upon composers. The limitations of the human voice, for one thing, have tended to encourage them to be practical in their writing, while the virtuosity of the modern orchestra has been in a way a contributor to the stylistic disorder of our age. And since there are many people who can sing, for every one who can play an instrument, a composer finds it relatively easy to get his choral music sung, while he may wait years for a single performance of an orchestral work.

But that situation, too, is changing. Community orchestras had begun to spring up in the 1920's. And their growth was greatly encouraged by the spread of instrumental instruction in the schools. It is estimated that there were between 150,000 and 200,000 school bands and orchestras in the United States, a number that is increasing at a tremendous rate. Each year, then, schools and colleges pour forth into the general stream of population an increasing proportion of young men and women trained for musical performance. One result has been the rise of professional symphony orchestras in many of our smaller cities. Another has been a great increase in amateur music making, in the field of chamber music as well as orchestra music.

A third has been what has at times seemed an oversupply of musicians, leading in times of depression to widespread unemployment. But insofar as unemployment among musicians exceeds that in other fields, it would seem to be a passing phase. For the spread of musical training is accompanied or quickly followed by a corresponding spread of public interest in music. The Federal Music Project was a great help in "taking up the slack" caused by the lag of the latter after the former.

When the continuance and deepening of the depression in the early 1930's made it clear that as many as 10,000,000 or more of our population had no hope of gaining employment in private industry in the immediate future, the Federal Government found it necessary to set up a work relief program. Fortunately for the cause of music, this program was not confined to manual workers. It made provision for the white-collar class as well. Politicians and economists will continue to argue about the wisdom of the Works Progress Administration program and the efficiency of its organization. But from a narrowly musical point of view, at least, there can be no doubt that it gave our development an immense impetus.

The WPA's Federal Music Project was active in many directions. It put performing musicians to work in bands and orchestras, and in chamber music, choral, and operatic groups throughout the country. Through these organizations the participants were enabled to keep up their morale, and to maintain and develop their technique. Audiences were offered music which they showed themselves eager to hear, at prices they could afford to pay. And composers saw their opportunities for performance multiply by the score. Performances by WPA organizations were counted in the hundred thousands, total audiences in the hundred millions, American composers represented on the programs in the thousands. Musical instruction was given to millions who could not have paid for it, by teachers who represented the oversupply of the moment. Hundreds of copyists, arrangers, and librarians were put to work making the manuscript and out-of-print treasures of our libraries available to the borrowing public. New activities and opportunities for the composer were developed. Composers' Forum Laboratories—sessions at which the works of a composer were played in his presence, and he was questioned or challenged about them by the audience at the end of the playing—were inaugurated in many cities.

The effect of all this upon our development as a musical nation was incalculable. The wide dissemination of music by radio, which both preceded and accompanied the activities of the Federal Music Project, worked in conjunction with it, and with the increasing emphasis on music in the schools, toward making us a truly musical nation. Perhaps in this sense, and to this extent, we are becoming the first such nation. For music is being democratized in these United States. Every city and every town is bringing forth its own native musicians. Yes, and composers, too. And a wide musical culture such as we are developing is a prerequisite to that great and high period of musical creation toward which we have all, perhaps a little too impatiently, been looking forward.

The ordeal through which the nation passed during the depression brought forth still other benefits. In the period of partly exaggerated and artificial prosperity we had been often too busy, each with his own affairs, to think much of the problems and purposes we had in common. The lean years made us realize that our individual fates depend upon our common destiny. They deepened our feeling of unity. They tried and strengthened our faith in what has come to be known as the American Way. The dissensions and disturbances that continually upset and threaten the Old World have reminded us of our good fortune in belonging to the New. And they hardened us and united us for the trials of the second World War.

A further gain from the depression and the war that followed it has been a general sobering of the musical language. In the first hilarious years of release after the tension of the first war, it was widely considered to be the most appropriate aim of art to amuse, to startle, to shock. Indeed, the desire to *épater les bourgeois* is a good deal older than that. It was originally a reaction to the earnest, stuffy optimism of the end of the nineteenth century and the beginning of the twentieth. But the events of the past ten years have to a large extent taken the point out of practical jokes on the musical public. There is little complacency left in any of us, and it is only the complacent who are fun to shock. Composers have not escaped the conviction that has overtaken most artists and thinkers in all fields—that we live in a critical era, and that this is no time for fooling. Questions of "style" and "idiom," which monopolized attention in the 1920's, are retiring to their proper places. There is less faddism, less following of aesthetic cults, and a more general desire to do a good job at writing whatever kind of music one has a talent for. That, surely, is progress.

Bibliography

GENERAL

(This section is arranged chronologically in order of publication.)

Ritter, Frédéric Louis. *Music in America.* New York: Charles Scribner's Sons, 1884. (Revised, 1890.)

Mathews, W. S. B., associate editor. *A Hundred Years of Music in America.* Chicago: G. L. Howe, 1889.

Hughes, Rupert. *American Composers.* Boston: The Page Company, 1900. (Revised to 1914 by Arthur Elson.)

Paine, J. K., Theodore Thomas, and Karl Klauser. *Music in America,* Vol. II of Famous Composers and Their Works. Boston: J. B. Millet and Company, 1901.

Elson, Louis C. *The History of American Music.* New York: The Macmillan Company, 1904. (Revised to 1925 by Arthur Elson.)

Hubbard, W. L. *History of American Music,* Volume in the American History and Encyclopedia of Music. Toledo, Ohio: Irving Squire, 1908.

Farwell, Arthur, and W. Dermont Darby. *Music in America,* Vol. IV of The Art of Music. New York: The National Society of Music, 1915.

Pratt, Waldo Selden, editor. *Grove's Dictionary of Music and Musicians.* American Supplement, Vol. VI. New York: The Macmillan Company, 1920 and 1928.

Lahee, H. C. *Annals of Music in America.* Boston: Marshall Jones Company, 1922.

"Fifty Years of Music in America, 1876–1926." *Music Teachers' National Association Proceedings, 1928,* pp. 1–263.

Tuthill, Burnet C. *Fifty Years of Chamber Music in the United States.* Reprinted from *Music Teachers' National Association Proceedings, 1928.*

Rosenfeld, Paul. *An Hour with American Music.* Philadelphia: J. B. Lippincott Company, 1929.

Pfleiderer, Elizabeth. *The Music of the United States—Guide Map to Its Sources and History.* New York: J. H. H. Muirhead, 1930.

Howard, John Tasker. *A Program Outline of American Music.* New York: Thomas Y. Crowell Company, 1931.

— Stringfield, Lamar. *America and Her Music.* Chapel Hill, North Carolina: University of North Carolina Press, 1931.

Fisher, William Arms. *One Hundred and Fifty Years of Music Publishing in the United States.* Boston: Oliver Ditson Company, 1933.

Morris, Harold. *Contemporary American Music.* Rice Institute Pamphlets, Vol. XXI. Houston, Texas: Rice Institute of Liberal and Technical Learning, 1934.

Barnes, Edwin N. C. *American Music: from Plymouth Rock to Tin Pan Alley.* Washington, D.C.: Music Education Publications, 1936.

Despard, Mabel H. *The Music of the United States, Its Sources and Its History. A Short Outline.* New York: J. H. H. Muirhead, 1936.

Kaufmann, Helen L. *From Jehovah to Jazz; Music in America from Psalmody to the Present Day.* New York: Dodd, Mead and Company, 1937.

"American Composers' Forum." *National Federation of Music Clubs Book of Proceedings,* Vol. III. Ithaca, New York, 1939.

Kinscella, Hazel Gertrude. *History Sings. Backgrounds of American Music.* Lincoln, Nebraska: The University Publishing Company, 1940.

Bio-bibliographical Index of Musicians in the United States of America from Colonial Times. Washington, D.C.: Music Division, Pan-American Union, 1941.

Howard, John Tasker. *Our Contemporary Composers: American Music in the Twentieth Century.* New York: Thomas Y. Crowell Company, 1941.

List of American Orchestral Works Recommended by WPA Music Project Conductors. Washington, D.C.: Work Projects Administration, 1941.

Ewen, David. *Music Comes to America.* New York: Thomas Y. Crowell Company, 1942.

MISCELLANEOUS COMMENTARIES

Clarke, Eric. *Music in Everyday Life.* New York: W. W. Norton and Company, Inc., 1935.

Copland, Aaron. "Serge Koussevitzky and the American Composer." *Musical Quarterly,* July, 1944.

Engel, Carl. *An Introduction to the Study of National Music.* London: Longmans, Green and Dyer, 1866.

Farwell, Arthur. *A Letter to American Composers.* Newton Center, Massachusetts: The Wa-Wan Press, 1903.

Fisher, William Arms. "The American Music Publisher and His Relationship to the Music Teacher and the Composers." *Music Teachers' National Association Proceedings, 1918.*

—— "The Great American Symphony." *Music Teachers' National Association Proceedings, 1929.*

Gilbert, Henry F. "The American Composer." *Musical Quarterly,* April, 1915.

Gruenberg, Louis. "For an American Gesture." *Modern Music,* June, 1924.

Hanson, Howard. "A Forward Look in American Composition." *Music Teachers' National Association Proceedings, 1925* (Reprinted by the Eastman School of Music, Rochester).

Hopkins, Edward Jerome. *Music and Snobs, or a Few Funny Facts Regarding the Disabilities of Music in America.* New York: R. A. Saalfield, 1888.

Manchester, Arthur L. "Music Education; A Musical America; The American Composer." *Musical Quarterly,* October, 1928.

Mason, Daniel Gregory. *The Dilemma of American Music.* New York: The Macmillan Company, 1928.

—— *Music in My Time.* New York: The Macmillan Company, 1938.

—— *Tune In, America!* New York: Alfred A. Knopf, 1931.

Pettis, Ashley. "The WPA and the American Composer." *Musical Quarterly,* January, 1940.

Phillips, H. D. "The Musical Psychology of America." *Musical Quarterly*, October, 1923.

Salter, Sumner. "Early Encouragements to American Composers." *Musical Quarterly*, January, 1932.

Simpson, Eugene E. *America's Position in Music*. Boston: The Four Seas Company, 1920.

Sonneck, O. G. "The American Composer and the American Music Publisher." *Musical Quarterly*, January, 1923.

―――― *Miscellaneous Studies in the History of Music* (Chapter on The History of Music in America). New York: The Macmillan Company, 1921.

―――― *Suum Cuique* (Chapter on a Survey of Music in America). New York: G. Schirmer, Inc., 1916.

Spalding, Walter R. "The War in Its Relation to American Music." *Musical Quarterly*, January, 1918.

Thorpe, H. C. "Interpretative Studies in American Songs." *Musical Quarterly*, January, 1929.

Upton, William Treat. *Art-Song in America*. Boston: Oliver Ditson Company, 1930.

Whitmer, T. Carl. "The Energy of American Crowd Music." *Musical Quarterly*, January, 1918.

REFERENCES TO AMERICAN MUSIC IN OTHER BOOKS

Bauer, Marion. *Twentieth Century Music*. New York: G. P. Putnam's Sons, 1933.

Bauer, Marion, and Ethel Peyser. *How Music Grew*. New York: G. P. Putnam's Sons, 1925.

Elson, Arthur. *Music Club Programs from All Nations*. Boston: Oliver Ditson Company, 1928.

―――― *Woman's Work in Music*. Boston: L. C. Page and Company, 1913.

Finck, H. T. *Songs and Song Writers*. New York: Charles Scribner's Sons, 1900.

Howard, John Tasker. *This Modern Music*. New York: Thomas Y. Crowell Company, 1942.

Jones, Howard Mumford. *America and French Culture, 1750–1848*.

(Chapter on French Music in America.) Chapel Hill, North Carolina: University of North Carolina Press, 1927.

Keppel, Frederick P., and R. L. Duffus. *The Arts in American Life.* New York: McGraw-Hill Book Company, Inc., 1933.

Lavignac, Albert. *Music and Musicians,* with Chapters on Music in America by H. E. Krehbiel. New York: Henry Holt and Company, 1899.

Levant, Oscar. *A Smattering of Ignorance.* New York: Doubleday, Doran, 1940.

Mather, Morey and Henderson. "The American Spirit in Art" (Vol. VI, of *The Pageant of America*). New Haven: Yale University Press, 1927.

Odell, George C. D. *Annals of the New York Stage,* Vols. I–XIII. New York: Columbia University Press, 1927–40.

Pannain, Guido. *Modern Composers.* London: J. M. Dent and Sons, 1932.

Slonimsky, Nicolas. *Music Since 1900.* New York: W. W. Norton and Company, 1937.

Smythe, J. Henry, editor. *The Amazing Benjamin Franklin* (Chapter on Franklin: The Patron Saint of the Music Industries, by Dewey Dixon). New York: Frederick A. Stokes and Company, 1929.

Stearns, H. E., editor. *Civilization of the United States* (Chapter on Music by Deems Taylor). New York, 1922.

Wagenknecht, Edward Charles. *Jenny Lind.* Boston: Houghton, Mifflin Company, 1931.

EARLY MUSIC AND MUSICAL LIFE

(see also "Sacred Music," and "Regional History")

Brooks, Henry M. *Olden-Time Music.* A compilation from newspapers and books. Boston: Ticknor and Company, 1888.

Brown, Francis. *An Address on Music,* delivered before the Handel Society, Dartmouth College, August, 1809. Hanover, New Hampshire: C. and W. S. Spear, 1810.

Burnham, C. G. "Olden Time Music in the Connecticut Valley." *New England Magazine,* 1900.

Drummond, Robert Rutherford. *Early German Music in Philadelphia*. New York: D. Appleton and Company, 1910.

Earle, Alice M. *The Sabbath in Puritan New England*. New York: Charles Scribner's Sons, 1896.

Engel, Carl, compiler. *Music from the Days of George Washington*. Washington, D.C.: United States George Washington Bicentennial Commission, 1931.

Fisher, William Arms. *Notes on Music in Old Boston*. Boston: Oliver Ditson Company, 1918.

————— *Ye Olde New England Psalm Tunes (1620–1820)*, with historical sketch. Boston: Oliver Ditson Company, 1930.

Gay, Julius. *Church Music in Farmington in the Olden Time*. Hartford, Connecticut: Lockwood and Brainard Company, 1891.

Goldman, Richard Franko. *Landmarks of Early American Music, 1760–1800*. A Collection of 32 compositions. New York: G. Schirmer, Inc., 1943.

Hood, George. *History of Music in New England*. Boston: Wilkins, Carter and Company, 1846.

Howard, John Tasker. *The Music of George Washington's Time*. Washington, D.C.: United States George Washington Bicentennial Commission, 1931.

————— *A Program of Early American Piano Pieces*. (Works by Reinagle, Taylor, Pelissier, Carr, and others.) New York: J. Fischer and Brother, 1931.

————— *A Program of Early and Mid-Nineteenth Century American Songs*. New York: J. Fischer and Brother, 1931.

Howard, John Tasker, and Eleanor S. Bowen. *Music Associated with the Period of the Formation of the Constitution and the Inauguration of George Washington*. Washington, D.C.: United States Constitution Sesquicentennial Commission, 1937.

Jackson, George S. *Early Songs of Uncle Sam*. Boston: Bruce Humphries, Inc., 1933.

Johnson, H. Earle. "Early New England Periodicals Devoted to Music." *Musical Quarterly*, April, 1940.

Learned, Marion Dexter. *Life of Francis Daniel Pastorius, the Founder of Germantown*. Philadelphia: W. J. Campbell, 1908.

Madeira, L. C. *Annals of Music in Philadelphia*. Philadelphia: J. B. Lippincott Company, 1896.

Memoirs of a New England Village Choir. Atkinson, New Hampshire, 1829.

Milligan, Harold V. *Pioneer American Composers*. A Collection of Early American Songs. Boston: The Arthur P. Schmidt Company, 1921.

Parker, Mrs. A. A. *Church Music and Musical Life in Pennsylvania in the Eighteenth Century* (3 vols.). Philadelphia: Pennsylvania Society of the Colonial Dames in America, 1926–27.

Parker, John R. *A Musical Biography*. Boston: Stone and Farwell, 1825.

Pierce, Edwin Hall. "The Rise and Fall of the 'Fugue-Tune' in America." *Musical Quarterly*, April, 1930.

Pratt, Waldo Selden. *The Music of the Pilgrims*. Boston: Oliver Ditson Company, 1921.

Sachse, Julius Friedrich. *Music of the Ephrata Cloister*. Lancaster, Pennsylvania: For the author, 1903.

Scholes, Percy A. *The Puritans and Music in England and New England*. New York: Oxford University Press, 1934.

Sewall, Samuel (1652–1730). *Diary*. Three-volume edition. Boston: Massachusetts Historical Society, 1878–82. One-volume edition, edited by Mark Van Doren, New York: Macy-Masius, 1927.

Sonneck, O. G. *Bibliography of Early Secular American Music*. Washington, D.C.: H. L. McQueen, 1905. (Revised and enlarged by William Treat Upton. Washington, D.C.: The Library of Congress, 1945.)

——— *Early Concert Life in America*. Leipzig: Breitkopf and Haertel, 1907.

Standish, L. W. *The Old Stoughton Musical Society*. Stoughton, Massachusetts, 1929.

Staples, Samuel E. *The Ancient Psalmody and Hymnology of New England*. Worcester, Massachusetts: C. Jillson, 1880.

SACRED MUSIC

(see also "Early Music and Musical Life")

Foote, Henry Wilder. *Three Centuries of American Hymnody*. Cambridge, Massachusetts: Harvard University Press, 1940.

Gould, Nathaniel D. *History of Church Music in America*. Boston: A. N. Johnson, 1853.

Hall, Jacob Henry. *Biography of Gospel Songs and Hymn Writers*. New York: Fleming H. Revell Company, 1914.

Hastings, Thomas. The History of Forty Choirs. New York: Mason Brothers, 1854.

MacDougall, Hamilton C. *Early New England Psalmody, 1620–1820*. Brattleboro, New Hampshire: Stephen Daye Press, 1940.

Metcalf, Frank J. *American Psalmody (1721–1820)*. New York: C. F. Heartmann, 1917.

—— *American Writers and Compilers of Sacred Music*. New York: The Abingdon Press, 1925.

—— *Stories of Hymn Tunes*. New York: The Abingdon Press, 1928.

Pierce, Edwin H. "Gospel Hymns and Their Tunes." *Musical Quarterly*, July, 1940.

Warrington, James. *Short Titles of Books Relating or Illustrating the History and Practice of Psalmody in the United States*. Philadelphia: Privately printed, 1898.

OPERA

Armstrong, W. G. *Record of the Opera at Philadelphia*. Philadelphia: Porter and Coates, 1884.

Da Ponte, Lorenzo. *Memoirs*. Boston: Houghton Mifflin Company, 1929.

Dunlap, William. *A History of the American Theatre*. New York: J. and J. Harper, 1832.

Hackett, Karleton. *The Beginning of Grand Opera in Chicago (1850–1859)*. Chicago: The Laurentian Press, 1913.

Hipsher, Edward Ellsworth. *American Opera and Its Composers*. Philadelphia: Theodore Presser Company, 1927.

The History of Opera in San Francisco. San Francisco: Work Projects Administration, 1938.

Ireland, J. N. *Records of the New York Stage, from 1750 to 1860*. New York: T. H. Marell, 1866–67.

Krehbiel, Henry E. *Chapters of Opera.* New York: Henry Holt and Company, 1909.

—— *More Chapters of Opera.* New York: Henry Holt and Company, 1919.

Lahee, H. C. *Grand Opera in America.* Boston: L. C. Page and Company, 1902.

Maretzek, Max. *Crochets & Quavers; or Revelations of an Opera Manager in New York.* New York, 1855.

—— *Sharps & Flats; a Sequel to Crochets & Quavers.* New York: American Musician Publishing Company, 1890.

Mattfield, Julius. *A Hundred Years of Grand Opera in New York (1825–1925).* New York: New York Public Library, 1927.

Memoirs of Lorenzo Da Ponte, translated by Elisabeth Abbott, edited by Arthur Livingston. Philadelphia: J. B. Lippincott Company, 1929.

Seilhamer, George O. *History of the American Theatre (1749–1797).* Philadelphia: Globe Printing House, 1888–91.

Sonneck, O. G. *Early Opera in America.* New York: G. Schirmer, Inc., 1915.

—— *Miscellaneous Studies in the History of Music* (Chapter on Early American Operas). New York: The Macmillan Company, 1921.

Vernon, Grenville. *Yankee Doodle-Doo; A Collection of Songs of the Early American Stage.* New York: Payson and Clarke, 1927.

REGIONAL HISTORY

(see also "Early Music and Musical Life"
and "Regional Folk Songs")

Alabama
Thomas, Margaret F. *Musical Alabama.* Montgomery: The Paragon Press, 1925.

California
—Alverson, Margaret Blake. *Sixty Years of California Songs.* San Francisco: Sunset Publishing House, 1913.

Art and Music in California. Reprinted from News-Notes of California Libraries. Sacramento: W. W. Shannon, Superintendent State Printing, 1908.

Celebrities in Eldorado, 1850–1906. A biographic record of 111 prominent musicians who visited San Francisco. San Francisco: Work Projects Administration, 1940.

Fredricks, Jessica M. *California Composers.* San Francisco: California Federation of Music Clubs, 1934.

Northern California Musicians' Directory. San Francisco: Donaldson Printing Company, 1916–17.

Pacific Coast Musical Review (Panama-Pacific Exposition Souvenir and Historical Edition). San Francisco: September 25, 1915.

Pacific Coast Musical Review. 17th Anniversary Edition, Vol. XXXIII, No. 3, 1917.

Pacific Coast Musicians' Year Book. Los Angeles: F. H. Colby, 1926–27.

Rodríguez, José. *Music and Dance in California.* Hollywood, California: Bureau of Musical Research, 1940.

Southern California Musicians' Directory. Los Angeles: H. A. Horwitz, 1916.

Colorado

Music in Denver and Colorado. Denver: *The Lookout,* Vol. I, No. 1, 1927.

Connecticut

Burnham, C. G. "Olden Time Music in the Connecticut Valley." *New England Magazine,* 1900.

Johnson, Frances Hall. *Musical Memories of Hartford.* Hartford, Connecticut: Witkower's, 1931.

Vaill, J. H., compiler. *Litchfield County Choral Union (1900–1912).* Norfolk, Connecticut: Litchfield County University Club, 1912.

Illinois

Ffrench, Florence. *Music and Musicians in Chicago.* Chicago: F. F. Ffrench, 1899.

Hackett, Karleton. *The Beginning of Grand Opera in Chicago (1850–1859).* Chicago: The Laurentian Press, 1913.

Otis, Philo A. *The Chicago Symphony Orchestra (1891–1924).* Chicago: Clayton F. Summy Company, 1924.

—— "The Development of Music in Chicago; an Historical

Sketch." *Music Teachers' National Association Proceedings,*
1920.

Russell, Charles Edward. *The American Orchestra and Theodore Thomas.* New York: Doubleday, Page and Company,
1927.

Upton, George P. *Musical Memories.* Chicago: A. C. McClurg
and Company, 1908.

Indiana

Music by Indiana Composers and About Indiana. Indianapolis:
State Library, 1942.

Seebirt, Elizabeth E. Gunn. *Music in Indiana.* South Bend, Indiana: For the author, 1928.

Kansas

Reinbach, Edna, compiler. *Music and Musicians in Kansas.*
Topeka: Kansas State Historical Society, 1930.

Louisiana

Fischer, D. B. "The Story of New Orleans's Rise as a Music
Center." *Musical America,* Vol. XIX, No. 19, 1914.

Maine

Berry, Ira. *Sketch of the History of the Beethoven Musical Society of Portland, Maine (1819–1825).* Portland: S. Berry,
1888.

Edwards, George Thornton. *Music and Musicians of Maine.*
Portland: The Southworth Press, 1928.

Maine Musical Festivals: Programs, 1897–1928.

Maryland

Hewitt, John Hill. *Shadows on the Wall.* Baltimore: Trumbull
Brothers, 1877.

Scharf, John Thomas. *History of Baltimore City and County*
(chap. xxxviii). Philadelphia: L. H. Everts, 1881.

Massachusetts

Apthorp, William Foster. *Musical Reminiscences of Boston
Thirty Years Ago.*

Barton, E. M. *History of the Worcester Choral Union.* Worcester: West and See, 1875.

Boston Academy of Music. *Annual Reports.* Boston: Perkins and
Marvin, 1833–46.

Boston School Committee; *Report* upon the petition that instruction in vocal music be introduced into the public schools of the city. Boston, 1837.

Fernald, John P. *History of the Salem Oratorio Society, 1868–91*. Salem: Barry and Lufkin, 1891.

Fisher, William Arms. *Notes on Music in Old Boston.* Boston: Oliver Ditson Company, 1918.

Hood, George. *History of Music in New England.* Boston: Wilkins, Carter and Company, 1846.

Howe, Mark Anthony De Wolfe. *The Boston Symphony Orchestra, An Historical Sketch.* Boston: Houghton Mifflin Company, 1914. (Sesquicentennial Edition, revised and extended by John N. Burk, 1931.)

Johnson, Harold Earle. *Musical Interludes in Boston, 1795–1830.* New York: Columbia University Press, 1943.

Lucas, G. W. *Remarks on the Musical Conventions in Boston.* Northampton: For the author, 1844.

Perkins, Charles C., and John S. Dwight. *History of the Handel & Haydn Society of Boston.* Boston: A. Mudge and Sons, 1883.

Proceedings of the Musical Convention Assembled in Boston, August 16, 1838. Boston: Kidder and Wright, 1838.

Sonneck, O. G. *Early Concert Life in America* (Chapter on Boston). Leipzig: Breitkopf and Haertel, 1907.

Standish, L. W. *The Old Stoughton Musical Society.* Stoughton, 1929.

White, G. H., editor. *The Boston Musical Year Book.* Boston: George H. Ellis, 1883–86.

Winsor, Justin, editor. *The Memorial History of Boston, 1630–1880*, Vol. IV, chap. vii. Boston: J. R. Osgood and Company, 1880–81.

Worcester County Musical Festival Programs. Worcester, 1873.
Michigan
Ling, Louis. "Music in Detroit." *Music Teachers' National Association Proceedings, 1921.*

Michigan Federation of Music Clubs: Year Book. Issued annually.

Michigan Library Bulletins, March and December, 1926 (Biographical Sketches of Michigan Composers with Lists of Their Works). Lansing: Michigan State Library.

Minnesota

Minnesota Music. Minneapolis: Publication of Minnesota State Music Teachers' Association, 1913–20.

Simpson, Eugene E. *A History of St. Olaf Choir.* Minneapolis: Augsburg Publishing House, 1921.

Wascher, A. E., and T. C. Ingham. *Who's Who in Music and Dramatic Art in the Twin Cities* (containing histories of Minneapolis Symphony Orchestra and various St. Paul and Minneapolis musical organizations). Minneapolis: Associated Publishers' Bureau, 1925.

Missouri

Krohn, Ernst C. *A Century of Missouri Music.* St. Louis: Privately printed, 1924.

—— "The Development of the Symphony Orchestra in St. Louis." *Music Teachers' National Association Proceedings, 1924.* (Reprinted, St. Louis, 1924.)

Scharf, John Thomas. *History of St. Louis City and County,* Vol. II, chap. xxxviii. Philadelphia: L. H. Everts and Company, 1883.

New York

Andrus, Helen Josephine. *A Century of Music in Poughkeepsie, 1802–1911.* Poughkeepsie, New York: F. B. Howard, 1912.

The Directory of New York State Musicians. New York: New York Federation of Music Clubs, 1931.

Howe, Mabel Almy. *Music Publishers in New York City Before 1850.* New York: New York Public Library, 1917.

Huneker, James Gibbons. *The Philharmonic Society of New York and Its 75th Anniversary.* New York: The Society, 1917.

Ireland, J. N. *Records of the New York Stage, from 1750 to 1860.* New York: T. H. Marell, 1866–67.

Krehbiel, H. E. *Chapters of Opera,* New York: Henry Holt and Company, 1909.

Krehbiel, H. E. *More Chapters of Opera*, New York: Henry Holt and Company, 1919.

—— *Notes on the Cultivation of Choral Music and the Oratorio Society in New York*. New York: Edw. Schuberth and Company, 1884.

—— *The Philharmonic Society of New York*. New York and London: Novello, Ewer and Company, 1892.

—— *Review of the New York Musical Season, 1885–86 to 1889–90*. New York and London: Novello, Ewer and Company, 1886–90.

Manuscript Society of New York; Constitution and Bylaws. New York: The Lotus Press, 1895.

Mattfeld, Julius. *A Hundred Years of Grand Opera in New York (1825–1925)*. New York: New York Public Library, 1927.

New York Philharmonic Journal (edited by Edward Jerome Hopkins). New York: The Society, 1868–1885.

Redway, Virginia Larkin. *Music Directory of Early New York City*. A file of musicians, music publishers, and musical instrument makers . . . from 1786 through 1835. New York: New York Public Library, 1941.

—— "A New York Concert in 1736." *Musical Quarterly*, April, 1936.

Saerchinger, César. "Musical Landmarks in New York." *Musical Quarterly*, 1920.

Sonneck, O. G. Early Concert Life in America (Chapter on New York). Leipzig: Breitkopf and Haertel, 1907.

Ohio

Ellis, F. R. "Music in Cincinnati." *Music Teachers' National Association Proceedings, 1913*.

Frank, Leonie C. *Musical Life in Early Cincinnati*. Cincinnati: The author, 1932.

Huntington, P. W. "Old-time Music of Columbus, Ohio." Columbus: *Old Northwest Genealogical Quarterly*, Vol. VIII, No. 2, 1905.

Mathews, W. S. B. "Art Music in the Middle West" (Cleveland, Cincinnati), *The Etude*, Vol. XXIII, No. 3, 1905.

Osburn, Mary. *Ohio Composers and Musical Authors*. Columbus, Ohio: Heer Printing Company, 1942.

Tunison, Frank. *Presto! From the Singing School to the May Festival*. Cincinnati: E. H. Beasley Company, 1888.

Pennsylvania

Armstrong, W. G. *Record of the Opera at Philadelphia*. Philadelphia: Porter and Coates, 1884.

Campbell, Jane. *Old Philadelphia Music*. Philadelphia: City History Society, 1926.

Drummond, Robert Rutherford. *Early German Music in Philadelphia*. New York: D. Appleton and Company, 1910.

Durang, Charles. *History of the Stage in Philadelphia*.

Gerson, Robert A. *Music in Philadelphia*. Philadelphia: Theodore Presser Company, 1940.

Good, Marian Bigler. *Some Musical Backgrounds of Pennsylvania*. Carrolltown, Pennsylvania: Carrolltown News Press, 1932.

Grider, Rufus A. *Historical Notes on Music in Bethlehem, Pennsylvania (1741–1871)*. Philadelphia: J. A. Martin, 1873.

Hoban, C. F. *Pennsylvania in Music*. Harrisburg, Pennsylvania: Public Instruction Department, 1926.

Learned, Marion Dexter. *Life of Francis Daniel Praetorius, the Founder of Germantown*. Philadelphia: W. J. Campbell, 1908.

Madeira, L. C. *Annals of Music in Philadelphia*. Philadelphia: J. B. Lippincott Company, 1896.

Musical Attractions at Willow Grove Park, with a Short History of Music's Development in Philadelphia, from Colonial Days Up to the Present Time. Philadelphia: John Winston Company, 1910.

Parker, Mrs. A. A. *Church Music and Musical Life in Pennsylvania in the Eighteenth Century* (3 vols.). Philadelphia: Pennsylvania Society of the Colonial Dames in America, 1926–27.

Pennsylvania in Music. Harrisburg: Department of Public Instruction, 1927.

Rau, Albert George, and Hans T. David. *A Catalogue of Music by American Moravians*. Bethlehem, Pennsylvania: The Moravian Seminary, 1938.

Rohrer, Gertrude Martin. *Music and Musicians of Pennsylvania*. Philadelphia: Theodore Presser Company, 1940.

Sachse, Julius Friedrich. *Music of the Ephrata Cloister*. Lancaster: The author, 1903.

Scharf, J. T., and Thompson Wescott. *History of Philadelphia*. Philadelphia: L. H. Everts and Company, 1884.

Sonneck, O. G. *Early Concert Life in America* (Chapter on Philadelphia). Leipzig: Breitkopf and Haertel, 1907.

Swope, R. H. *Items of Music in the Annals of Harrisburg*. Paper read before Dauphin County Historical Society, 1928.

Walters, Raymond. *The Bethlehem Bach Choir*. Boston: Houghton Mifflin Company, 1918.

South Carolina

Sonneck, O. G. *Early Concert Life in America* (Chapter on Charleston and the South). Leipzig: Breitkopf and Haertel, 1907.

Texas

Spell, Lota May. *Music in Texas*. Austin, Texas, 1936.

Wisconsin

Mathews, W. S. B. "Art Music in the Middle West" (Milwaukee). *The Etude*, Vol. XXIII, No. 3, 1905.

Mendel, Henry M. *History of Milwaukee from Its First Settlement to the Year 1895*, edited by H. L. Conrad, Vol. II (Chapter on Music and Musical Societies). Chicago and New York: American Bibliographical Publishing Company, 1925.

Miller, Winifred V. "Wisconsin's Place in the Field of Music." *Wisconsin Blue Book*. Madison: State Printing Board, 1929.

Wisconsin Music Teacher. Official Publication of Wisconsin Music Teachers' Association, quarterly since 1912. Madison.

Pacific Northwest

Pacific Northwest Musical Directory (Music and Musicians), annually since 1915. Seattle, Washington.

INDIVIDUAL COMPOSERS AND MUSICIANS

George Antheil

  Copland, Aaron. "George Antheil." *Modern Music,* January, 1925.

  Antheil, George. *Bad Boy of Music.* Garden City: Doubleday, Doran & Company, 1945.

  Thompson, Randall. "George Antheil." *Modern Music,* May–June, 1931.

Frederick Ayres

  Upton, William Treat. "Frederick Ayres." *Musical Quarterly,* January, 1932.

Samuel Barber

  Horan, Robert. "Samuel Barber." *Modern Music,* March–April, 1943.

Mrs. H. H. A. Beach

  Tuthill, Burnet C. "Mrs. H. H. A. Beach." *Musical Quarterly,* July, 1940.

Nicolai T. Berezowsky

  Berezowsky, Alice. *Duet with Nicky.* Philadelphia: J. B. Lippincott Company, 1943.

Irving Berlin

  Woollcott, Alexander. *The Story of Irving Berlin.* New York: G. P. Putnam's Sons, 1925.

Leonard Bernstein

  Schubart, Mark A. "Triple-Note Man of Music." *New York Times Magazine,* January 28, 1945.

William Billings

  Goldberg, Isaac. "The First American Musician." *American Mercury,* Vol. XIV, pp. 67–75.

  Lindstrom, Carl E. "William Billings and His Times." *Musical Quarterly,* October, 1939.

  Pierce, Edwin Hall. "The Rise and Fall of the 'Fugue-Tune' in America." *Musical Quarterly,* April, 1930.

Arthur Bird

  Loring, William C., Junior. "Arthur Bird, American." *Musical Quarterly,* January, 1943.

Philip Paul Bliss
Whittle, Daniel W., editor. *Memoirs of Philip P. Bliss.* New York: A. S. Barnes and Company, 1877.

Marc Blitzstein
Blitzstein, Marc, "Towards a New Form." *Musical Quarterly,* April, 1934.

Ernest Bloch
Gatti, G. M. "Ernest Bloch." *Musical Quarterly,* January, 1921.
Rosenfeld, Paul. *Musical Chronicle.* New York: Harcourt, Brace and Company, 1923.
——— *Musical Portraits.* New York: Harcourt, Brace and Company, 1923.
Sessions, Roger. "Ernest Bloch." *Modern Music,* November, 1927.
Stackpole, Ralph. "Portraits of Ernest Bloch." *Modern Music,* November, 1927.

Dudley Buck
A Complete Bibliography of His Works. New York: G. Schirmer, Inc., (ca.) 1910.

Ole Bull
Bull, Sara Chapman. *Ole Bull, A Memoir.* Boston: Houghton Mifflin Company, 1883.
Smith, Mortimer B. *The Life of Ole Bull.* Princeton, New Jersey: Princeton University Press, 1943.

Cecil Burleigh
Howard, John Tasker. *Cecil Burleigh.* New York: Carl Fischer, Inc., 1929.

Charles Wakefield Cadman
Sanford-Tefft, Lulu. *Little Intimate Stories of Charles Wakefield Cadman.* Hollywood, California: David Graham Fischer Corporation, 1926.

John Alden Carpenter
Borowski, Felix. "John Alden Carpenter." *Musical Quarterly,* October, 1930.
Downes, Olin. "John Alden Carpenter." *Musical Quarterly,* October, 1930.
Howard, John Tasker. "John Alden Carpenter." *Modern Music,* November–December, 1931.

Rosenfeld, Paul. *Musical Chronicle*. New York: Harcourt, Brace and Company, 1923.

Benjamin Carr

Redway, Virginia Larkin. "The Carrs, American Music Publishers." *Musical Quarterly*, January, 1932.

George W. Chadwick

Engel, Carl. "George W. Chadwick." *Musical Quarterly*, July, 1924. (Reprinted in pamphlet form by the New England Conservatory of Music, Boston.)

Langley, Allen Lincoln. "Chadwick and the New England Conservatory of Music." *Musical Quarterly*, January, 1935.

Aaron Copland

French, Alfred. "Aaron Copland, a Portrait." *Modern Music*, March, 1926.

Hill, Edward Burlingame. "Copland's Concerto in Boston." *Modern Music*, May, 1927.

Kirkpatrick, John. "Aaron Copland's Piano Sonata." *Modern Music*, May–June, 1942.

Thomson, Virgil. "Aaron Copland." *Modern Music*, January–February, 1932.

Bainbridge Crist

Howard, John Tasker. *Bainbridge Crist*. New York: Carl Fischer, Inc., 1929.

Walter Damrosch

Damrosch, Walter. *My Musical Life*. New York: Charles Scribner's Sons, 1923.

Henderson, W. J. "Walter Damrosch." *Musical Quarterly*, January, 1932.

Reginald De Koven

De Koven, Mrs. Reginald. *A Musician and His Wife*. New York: Harper and Brothers, 1926.

Paul Dresser

Dreiser, Theodore, editor. *The Songs of Paul Dresser*. New York: Boni and Liveright, 1927.

James P. Dunn

Howard, John Tasker. *James P. Dunn*. New York: J. Fischer and Brother, 1925.

John Sullivan Dwight

Waters, Edward N. "John Sullivan Dwight, First American Critic of Music." *Musical Quarterly*, January, 1935.

Stephen Foster

Foster, Morrison. *My Brother Stephen*. Indianapolis, Indiana: Privately printed for the Foster Hall Collection, 1932.

—— *Songs and Musical Compositions of Stephen Collins Foster*. Pittsburgh, 1896.

Howard, John Tasker. "Newly Discovered Fosteriana." *Musical Quarterly*, January, 1935.

—— *Stephen Foster, America's Troubadour*. New York: Thomas Y. Crowell Company, 1934. (Reprint edition, Tudor Publishing Company, New York.)

Jackson, George Pullen. "Stephen Foster's Debt to American Folk-Song." *Musical Quarterly*, April, 1936.

Milligan, Harold V. *Stephen Collins Foster, A Biography*. New York: G. Schirmer, Inc., 1920.

Morneweck, Evelyn Foster. *Chronicles of Stephen Foster's Family*; 2 volumes. Pittsburgh, Pennsylvania: Pittsburgh University Press, 1944.

Purdy, Claire Lee. *He Heard America Sing; the Story of Stephen Foster*. New York: Julian Messner, Inc., 1940.

Songs, Compositions and Arrangements by Stephen Collins Foster. Foster Hall Reproductions. Indianapolis: Privately printed, 1933.

Sonneck, O. G., and Walter Whittlesey. *Catalogue of the First Editions of Stephen C. Foster*. Washington: Library of Congress, Government Printing Office, 1915.

Walters, Raymond W. *Stephen Foster: Youth's Golden Gleam; a Sketch of His Life and Background in Cincinnati, 1846–1850*. Princeton, New Jersey: Princeton University Press, 1936.

George Gershwin

Armitage, Merle. *George Gershwin*. New York: Longmans, Green and Company, 1938.

Ewen, David. *The Story of George Gershwin*. New York: Henry Holt and Company, 1943.

Gershwin, George. *George Gershwin's Song Book.* New York: Simon and Schuster, 1930.

Goldberg, Isaac. *George Gershwin, A Study in American Music.* New York: Simon and Schuster, 1931.

Jacobi, Frederick. "The Future of Gershwin." *Modern Music,* November–December, 1937.

Thomson, Virgil. "George Gershwin." *Modern Music,* November–December, 1935.

Henry F. Gilbert

Carter, Elliott. "American Figure, with Landscape." *Modern Music,* May–June, 1943.

Downes, Olin. "An American Composer." *Musical Quarterly,* January, 1918.

Patrick Gilmore

Gilmore, P. S. *History of the National Peace Jubilee and Great Musical Festival.* Boston: For the author, 1871.

Louis Moreau Gottschalk

Arpin, Paul. *Life of Louis Moreau Gottschalk,* translated from the French by H. C. Watson. New York, 1852.

Fors, Luis Ricardo, *Louis Moreau Gottschalk.* Havana, 1880.

Hensel, Octavia. *Life and Letters of Louis Moreau Gottschalk.* Boston: Oliver Ditson Company, 1870.

Howard, John Tasker. "Louis Moreau Gottschalk, as Portrayed by Himself." *Musical Quarterly,* January, 1932.

Peterson, Robert Evans, translator. *Notes of a Pianist by Louis Moreau Gottschalk.* Philadelphia: J. B. Lippincott Company, 1881.

Percy Grainger

Hughes, Charles W. "Percy Grainger, Cosmopolitan Composer." *Musical Quarterly,* April, 1937.

Gottlieb Graupner

Stone, Mrs. George Whitefield. Manuscript *Biography of Graupner* in Public Library of the city of Boston.

Charles Tomlinson Griffes

Bauer, Marion. "Charles T. Griffes as I Remember Him." *Musical Quarterly,* July, 1943.

Howard, John Tasker. *Charles Tomlinson Griffes.* New York:
G. Schirmer, Inc., 1923.
Maisel, Edward M. *Charles T. Griffes; The Life of an American
Composer.* New York: Alfred A. Knopf, 1943.
Upton, William Treat. "The Songs of Charles T. Griffes." *Musical Quarterly,* July, 1923.

Louis Gruenberg
Kramer, A. Walter. "Louis Gruenberg." *Modern Music,* November–December, 1930.

Henry K. Hadley
Boardman, Herbert R. *Henry Hadley, Ambassador of Harmony.* Emory University, Georgia: Banner Press, 1932.

William C. Handy
Handy, William C. *Father of the Blues; An Autobiography.*
New York: The Macmillan Company, 1941.

Howard Hanson
Alter, Martha. "Howard Hanson." *Modern Music,* January–February, 1941.
Tuthill, Burnet C. "Howard Hanson." *Musical Quarterly,* April,
1936.

Charles K. Harris
Harris, Charles K. *After the Ball, Forty Years of Melody; An
Autobiography.* New York: Frank-Maurice, Inc., 1926.

Roy Harris
Farwell, Arthur. "Roy Harris." *Musical Quarterly,* January,
1932.
Piston, Walter. "Roy Harris." *Modern Music,* January–February, 1934.

Anton Philip Heinrich
Upton, William Treat. *Anthony Philip Heinrich.* New York:
Columbia University Press, 1939.

Victor Herbert
Kaye, Joseph. *Victor Herbert.* New York: G. H. Watt, 1931.
Purdy, Claire Lee. *Victor Herbert, American Music Master.*
New York: Julian Messner, Inc., 1945.

Edward Burlingame Hill
Smith, George H. L. "Edward Burlingame Hill." *Modern
Music,* November–December, 1938.

Sidney Homer

Homer, Sidney. *My Wife and I; The Story of Louise and Sidney Homer.* New York: The Macmillan Company, 1939.

Thorpe, Henry Colin. "The Songs of Sidney Homer." *Musical Quarterly*, January, 1931.

Francis Hopkinson

Hastings, George E. *The Life and Works of Francis Hopkinson.* Chicago: The University Press, 1926.

Milligan, Harold V. *Colonial Love Lyrics: Six Songs by Francis Hopkinson.* Boston: The Arthur P. Schmidt Company, 1919.

—— *The First American Composer: Six Songs by Francis Hopkinson.* Boston: The Arthur P. Schmidt Company, 1918.

Sonneck, O. G. *Francis Hopkinson and James Lyon.* Washington: H. L. McQueen, 1905.

Charles Ives

Bellamann, Henry. "Charles Ives: The Man and His Music." *Musical Quarterly*, January, 1933.

—— "The Music of Charles Ives." *Pro-Musica Quarterly*, March, 1927.

Carter, Elliott. "Ives Today: His Vision and Challenge." *Modern Music*, May–June, 1944.

Cowell, Henry. "Charles Ives." *Modern Music*, November–December, 1932.

Rosenfeld, Paul. "Ives' Concord Sonata." *Modern Music*, January–February, 1939.

Frederick Jacobi

Diamond, David. "Frederick Jacobi." *Modern Music*, March–April, 1937.

Carrie Jacobs-Bond

Jacobs-Bond, Carrie. *The Roads of Melody.* New York: D. Appleton and Company, 1927.

Louis Antoine Jullien

Jullien's Concert Book. New York: J. Darcie, 1853.

Jerome Kern

Adams, Franklin P. "Words and Music." *The New Yorker*, February 8, 1930.

Simon, Robert. "Jerome Kern." *Modern Music*, January, 1929.

A. Walter Kramer
    Howard, John Tasker. *A. Walter Kramer.* New York: J. Fischer and Brother, 1926.

Eastwood Lane
    Howard, John Tasker. *Eastwood Lane.* New York: J. Fischer and Brother, 1925.

Jenny Lind
    Werner, M. R. *Barnum.* New York: Harcourt, Brace and Company, 1923.

Charles Martin Loeffler
    Engel, Carl. "Charles Martin Loeffler." *Musical Quarterly,* July, 1925.
    Gilman, Lawrence. *Phases of Modern Music.* New York: Harper and Brothers, 1904.
    Hill, Edward Burlingame. "Charles Martin Loeffler." *Modern Music,* November–December, 1935.
    Rosenfeld, Paul. *Musical Portraits.* New York: Harcourt, Brace and Company, 1923.

James Lyon
    Alexander, Samuel Davies. *Princeton College During the 18th Century.* New York: A. D. F. Randolph and Company, 1872.
    Edwards, George Thornton. *Music and Musicians of Maine.* Portland: The Southworth Press, 1928.
    Sonneck, O. G. *Francis Hopkinson and James Lyon.* Washington: H. L. McQueen, 1905.

Edward MacDowell
    Brown, Abbie Farwell. *The Boyhood of Edward MacDowell.* New York: Frederick A. Stokes and Company, 1924.
    Brown, Rollo Walter. *Lonely Americans.* New York: Coward-McCann, Inc., 1929.
    Butler, Nicholas Murray. "Columbia and the Department of Music." New York: The University, 1904. (Reprinted from the *New York Times,* February 8, 1904.)
    Currier, T. P. "MacDowell as I Knew Him." *Musical Quarterly,* January, 1915.

Erskine, John. "MacDowell at Columbia: Some Recollections." *Musical Quarterly*, October, 1942.

Garland, Hamlin. "Roadside Meetings of a Literary Nomad." *The Bookman*, March, 1930.

Gilbert, Henry F. "Personal Recollections of Edward Mac-Dowell." *New Music Review*, Vol. II, No. 132, 1912.

Gilman, Lawrence. *Edward MacDowell, A Study*. New York: John Lane Company, 1908.

—— *Phases of Modern Music*. New York: Harper and Brothers, 1904.

Hier, Ethel G. *The Boyhood and Youth of Edward MacDowell*. Peterboro, New Hampshire: The Nubanusit Press, 1926.

Humiston, William H. *MacDowell*. New York: Breitkopf and Haertel, 1921.

MacDowell, Edward. *Critical and Historical Essays*. Boston: The A. P. Schmidt Company, 1912.

MacDowell, Marian. "MacDowell's 'Peterboro Idea.'" *Musical Quarterly*, January, 1932.

McWhood, Leonard. "Edward MacDowell at Columbia University." *Music Teachers' National Association Proceedings, 1923*.

Matthews, James Brander. *Commemorative Tributes to Edward MacDowell*. New York: American Academy of Arts and Letters, 1922.

Page, Elizabeth Fry. *Edward MacDowell, His Work and Ideals*. New York: Dodge Publishing Company, 1910.

Porte, John F. *Edward MacDowell, A Great American Tone Poet*. London: K. Paul, Trench, Trubner and Company, 1922.

Sinclair, Upton. "MacDowell." *American Mercury*, Vol. VII, pp. 50–54, 1926.

Sonneck, O. G. *Catalogue of the First Editions of Edward MacDowell*. Washington: Library of Congress, Government Printing Office, 1917.

—— *Suum Cuique* (*MacDowell vs. MacDowell*). New York: G. Schirmer, Inc., 1916.

Lowell Mason

Birge, Edward Bailey. *History of Public School Music in the United States.* Boston: Oliver Ditson Company, 1928.

Boston Academy of Music. *Annual Reports.* Boston: Perkins and Marvin, 1833–46.

Boston School Committee. Report (upon the petition praying that music be introduced into the public schools of the city). Boston, 1837.

Lucas, G. W. *Remarks on the Musical Conventions in Boston.* Northampton: The author, 1844.

Mason, Henry L. *Hymn-Tunes of Lowell Mason; A Bibliography.* Cambridge, Massachusetts: The University Press, 1944.

Proceedings of the Musical Convention Assembled in Boston, August 16, 1838. Boston: Kidder and Wright, 1838.

Seward, T. F. *The Educational Work of Lowell Mason.* 1879.

William Mason

Mason, William. *Memories of a Musical Life.* New York: The Century Company, 1902.

Douglas Moore

Luening, Otto. "Douglas Moore." *Modern Music,* May–June, 1943.

Ethelbert Nevin

Howard, John Tasker. *Ethelbert Nevin.* New York: Thomas Y. Crowell Company, 1935.

Rogers, Francis. "Some Memories of Ethelbert Nevin." *Musical Quarterly,* July, 1917.

Thompson, Vance. *The Life of Ethelbert Nevin.* Boston: Boston Music Company, 1913.

Leo Ornstein

Buchanan, C. L. "Ornstein and Modern Music." *Musical Quarterly,* April, 1918.

Martens, Frederick L. *Leo Ornstein.* New York: Breitkopf and Haertel, 1918.

Rosenfeld, Paul. *Musical Chronicle.* New York: Harcourt, Brace and Company, 1923.

———— *Musical Portraits*. New York: Harcourt, Brace and Company, 1923.

John Knowles Paine

Howe, Mark Anthony De Wolfe. "John Knowles Paine." *Musical Quarterly*, July, 1939.

Horatio Parker

A Brief Tribute to the Life and Work of Dr. Horatio Parker. New York: Silver, Burdett Company, 1925.

Chadwick, George W. *Horatio Parker*. New Haven: Yale University Press, 1921.

"Horatio Parker." *Musical Times*, London, September 1, 1902.

Krehbiel, H. E. "Parker's Hora Novissima and Bach's Magnificat in D." *New Music Review*, Vol. IX, pp. 146–7, 1914.

Rosenfeld, Paul. *Musical Chronicle* ("The Fate of Mona"). New York: Harcourt, Brace and Company, 1923.

Semler, Isabel Parker. *Horatio Parker*. New York: G. P. Putnam's Sons, 1942.

Smith, David Stanley. "A Study of Horatio Parker." *Musical Quarterly*, April, 1930.

John Frederick Peter

Rau, Albert G. "John Frederick Peter." *Musical Quarterly*, July, 1937.

Walter Piston

Atkowitz, Israel. "Walter Piston, Classicist." *Modern Music*, January–February, 1936.

Silas G. Pratt

"Silas G. Pratt, American Composer." New York: *American Art Journal*, Vol. LXVII, No. 6. J. Fischer and Brother, 1925.

Alexander Reinagle

Krohn, Ernst C. "Alexander Reinagle as Sonatist." *Musical Quarterly*, January, 1932.

Bernard Rogers

Hanson, Howard. "Bernard Rogers." *Modern Music*, March–April, 1945.

George Frederick Root

Root, George F. *The Story of a Musical Life*. Cincinnati, Ohio: The John Church Company, 1891.

Carl Ruggles
 Seeger, Charles. "Carl Ruggles." *Musical Quarterly*, October, 1932.
Alexander Russell
 Howard, John Tasker. *Alexander Russell*. New York: J. Fischer and Brother, 1925.
Henry Russell
 Russell, Henry. *Cheer! Boys, Cheer! Memories of Men and Music*. London: John MacQueen, 1895.
 ——— *The Passing Show*. Boston: Little, Brown and Company, 1926.
Lazare Saminsky
 Lazare Saminsky. New York: Bloch Publishing Company, 1930.
 Saleski, Gdal. *Famous Musicians of a Wandering Race*. New York: Bloch Publishing Company, 1927.
 Slonimsky, Nicolas. "Lazare Saminsky." *Modern Music*, January–February, 1935.
Ira D. Sankey
 Sankey, Ira D. *My Life and Sacred Songs*. London: Hodder and Houghton, 1906.
Daniel Schlesinger
 Biographical Notices of Daniel Schlesinger. Extracts from the *New York Mirror* (1839) in the New York Public Library.
William Schuman
 Bernstein, Leonard. "Young American—William Schuman." *Modern Music*, January–February, 1942.
 Broder, Nathan. "The Music of William Schuman." *Musical Quarterly*, January, 1945.
 Frankenstein, Alfred. "William Schuman." *Modern Music*, November–December, 1944.
Roger Sessions
 Brunswick, Mark. "Roger Huntington Sessions." *Modern Music*, May–June, 1933.
 Welch, Roy D. "A Symphony Introduces Roger Sessions." *Modern Music*, May, 1927.
Oliver Shaw
 Memorial of Oliver Shaw. Providence, Rhode Island: Veteran Citizens' Historical Association, 1884.

William, Thomas. *A Discourse on the Life and Death of Oliver Shaw.* Boston: C. C. P. Moody, 1851.

Arthur Shepherd

Leedy, Denoe. "Arthur Shepherd." *Modern Music,* January–February, 1939.

Charles Sanford Skilton

Howard, John Tasker. *Charles Sanford Skilton.* New York: Carl Fischer, Inc., 1929.

David Stanley Smith

Tuthill, Burnet C. "David Stanley Smith." *Musical Quarterly,* January, 1942.

O. G. Sonneck

Putnam, Herbert, and Rubin Goldmark. "Remarks at the Funeral Services." *Musical Quarterly,* January, 1929.

John Philip Sousa

Lewiton, Mina. *John Philip Sousa, the March King.* New York: Didier, 1944.

Sousa, John Philip. *Marching Along, An Autobiography.* Boston: Hale, Cushman and Flint, 1928.

Leo Sowerby

Tuthill, Burnet C. "Leo Sowerby." *Musical Quarterly,* July, 1938.

Albert Spalding

Spalding, Albert. *Rise to Follow, an Autobiography.* New York: Henry Holt and Company, 1943.

William Grant Still

Arvey, Verna. *William Grant Still.* New York: J. Fischer and Brother, 1939.

Deems Taylor

Howard, John Tasker. *Deems Taylor.* New York: J. Fischer and Brother, 1927.

Theodore Thomas

Rice, Edwin T. "Thomas and Central Park Garden." *Musical Quarterly,* April, 1940.

Russell, Charles Edward. *The American Orchestra and Theodore Thomas.* New York: Doubleday, Page and Company, 1927.

Thomas, Rose Fay. *Memoirs of Theodore Thomas.* New York: Moffat, Yard and Company, 1911.

Thomas, Theodore. *A Musical Autobiography* (2 vols.), edited by G. P. Upton. Chicago: A. C. McClurg and Company, 1905.

Randall Thompson

Porter, Quincy. "Randall Thompson." *Modern Music*, May–June, 1942.

Virgil Thomson

Barlow, S. L. M. "Virgil Thomson." *Modern Music*, May–June, 1941.

Rudy Vallée

Vallée, Rudy. *Vagabond Dreams Come True*. New York: E. P. Dutton and Company, 1930.

Edgar Varèse

Cowell, Henry. "The Music of Edgar Varèse." *Modern Music*, January, 1928.

Hirsch, Stefan. "Portrait of Varèse." *Modern Music*, January, 1928.

Bernard Wagenaar

Fuller, Donald. "Bernard Wagenaar." *Modern Music*, May–June, 1944.

Emerson Whithorne

Hammond, Richard. "Emerson Whithorne." *Modern Music*, January–February, 1931.

Howard, John Tasker. *Emerson Whithorne*. New York: Carl Fischer, Inc., 1929.

Arthur Whiting

Mason, Daniel G. "Arthur Whiting." *Musical Quarterly*, January, 1937.

Septimus Winner

Claghorne, Charles Eugene. *The Mocking Bird; the Life and Diary of Its Author, Septimus Winner*. Philadelphia: The Magee Press, 1937.

Henry Clay Work

Work, Bertram G., compiler. *Songs of Henry Clay Work*. New York: J. J. Little and Ives Company, 1920.

COLLECTIVE BIOGRAPHY

Bakeless, Katharine. *Story-Lives of American Composers.* New York: Frederick A. Stokes, 1941.

Baker, Theodore, editor. *Biographical Dictionary of Musicians.* New York: G. Schirmer, Inc., 1919. (Revised edition, 1940.)

Barnes, Edwin N. C. *American Women in Creative Music.* Washington, D. C.: Music Education Publications, 1936.

Cowell, Henry, editor. *American Composers on American Music.* Stamford University, California: Stamford University Press, 1933.

Cuney-Hare, Maud. *Negro Musicians and Their Music.* Washington, D.C.: The Associated Publishers, 1936.

Grove's Dictionary of Music and Musicians (American Supplement edited by W. S. Pratt). New York: The Macmillan Company, 1920 and 1928.

Handy, William C. *Negro Authors and Composers of the United States.* New York: Handy Brothers Music Company, 1938.

Johnson, Allen, and Dumas Malone, editors. *Dictionary of American Biography.* 20 volumes. New York: Charles Scribner's Sons, 1928-1936.

Jones, F. O. *A Handbook of American Music and Musicians.* Buffalo, New York: C. W. Moulton and Company, 1887.

Key, Pierre, editor. *Pierre Key's Musical Who's Who.* New York: Musical Publications, Inc., 1930.

Knippers, Ottis J. *Who's Who Among Southern Singers and Composers.* Lawrenceburg, Tennessee: J. D. Vaughn, 1937.

Reis, Claire. *Composers in America, 1912-1937.* New York: The Macmillan Company, 1938.

Slonimsky, Nicolas. "Composers of New England" (principally Gilbert, Allen, Ruggles, Ives, Sessions). *Modern Music,* February-March, 1930.

Thompson, Oscar, editor. *The International Cyclopedia of Music and Musicians.* New York: Dodd, Mead and Company, 1939.

Trotter, James M. *Music and Some Highly Musical People: Containing . . . Sketches of the Lives of Remarkable Musicians of the Colored Race.* Boston: Lee and Shepard, 1878.

Upton, William Treat. "Our Musical Expatriates" (Strong, Fairchild, Campbell-Tipton, Spellman). *Musical Quarterly*, January, 1928.

MEMOIRS

Apthorp, William Foster. *Musicians and Music Lovers*. New York: Charles Scribner's Sons, 1908.

Arditi, Luigi. *My Reminiscences*. New York: Dodd, Mead and Company, 1896.

Aronson, Rudolph. *Theatrical and Musical Memoirs*. New York: McBride, Nast and Company, 1913.

Bispham, David. *A Quaker Singer's Recollections*. New York: The Macmillan Company, 1921.

Da Ponte, Lorenzo. *Memoirs*. Boston: Houghton Mifflin Company, 1929.

Finck, Henry T. *My Adventures in the Golden Age of Music*. New York: Funk and Wagnalls Company, 1926.

Foote, Arthur. "A Bostonian Remembers." *Musical Quarterly*. January, 1937.

Franko, Sam. *Chords and Discords; Memoirs and Musings of an American Musician*. New York: The Viking Press, 1938.

Freer, Eleanor Everest. *Recollections and Reflections of an American Composer*. New York: Musical Advance Publishing Company, 1929.

Hewitt, John Hill. *Shadows on the Wall*. Baltimore: Trumbull Brothers, 1877.

Hoffman, Richard. *Some Musical Recollections of Fifty Years*. New York: Charles Scribner's Sons, 1910.

Johns, Clayton. *Reminiscences of a Musician*. Cambridge: Washburn and Thomas, 1929.

Jordan, Jules. *The Happenings of a Musical Life*. Providence, Rhode Island: Palmer Press, 1922.

Maretzek, Max. *Crotchets & Quavers; or Revelations of an Opera Manager in America*. New York, 1855.

—— *Sharps & Flats; a Sequel to Crotchets & Quavers*. New York: American Musician Publishing Company, 1890.

Memoirs of Lorenzo De Ponte. Translated by Elisabeth Abbott, edited by Arthur Livingston. Philadelphia: J. B. Lippincott Company, 1929.

Offenbach, Jacques. *Offenbach in America.* New York: G. W. Carleton and Company, 1877.

Rogers, Clara Kathleen. *Memories of a Musical Career.* Boston: Little, Brown and Company, 1919.

Ryan, Thomas. *Recollections of an Old Musician.* New York: E. P. Dutton and Company, 1899.

Samaroff Stokowski, Olga. *An American Musician's Story.* New York: W. W. Norton and Company, 1939.

Schoen-René, Anna Eugenie. *America's Musical Inheritance; Memories and Reminiscences.* New York: G. P. Putnam's Sons, 1941.

Upton, George P. *Musical Memories (1850–1900).* Chicago: A. C. McClurg and Company, 1908.

INDIAN MUSIC

Baker, Theodore. *Über die Musik der nordamerikanischen Wilden.* Leipzig: Breitkopf and Haertel, 1882.

Boas, F. "The Central Eskimo." Washington: Bureau of Ethnology, *6th Annual Report,* 1888.

Burton, Frederick R. *American Primitive Music.* New York: Moffat, Yard and Company, 1909.

Cadman, Charles Wakefield. "The Idealization of Indian Music." *Musical Quarterly,* July, 1915.

Catlin, George. *Letters and Notes on the Manners, Customs, and Condition of the North American Indians.* London: For the author, 1841.

Cringan, Alexander T. *Iroquois Folk Songs.* Toronto: Toronto Educational Department, 1903.

Curtis, Natalie. "American Indian Cradle-Songs." *Musical Quarterly,* October, 1921.

—— *The Indian's Book.* New York: Harper and Brothers, 1907.

Densmore, Frances. *The American Indians and Their Music.* New York: The Woman's Press, 1926.

—— "Chippewa Music" and "Chippewa Music No. 2." *Bulletins* 45 and 53 of the Bureau of American Ethnology. Washington, 1910 and 1913.

Densmore, Frances. *Indian Action Songs*. Boston: C. C. Birchard and Company, 1921.

────── "Mandan and Hidatsa Music." *Bulletin 80* of the Bureau of American Ethnology. Washington, 1923.

────── "Northern Ute Music." *Bulletin 75* of the Bureau of American Ethnology. Washington, 1922.

────── "The Study of Indian Music." *Musical Quarterly*, April, 1915.

────── "Teton Sioux Music." *Bulletin 61* of the Bureau of American Ethnology. Washington, 1918.

Drake, F. S., editor. *The Indian Tribes of the United States*. Philadelphia, 1884.

Farwell, Arthur. *American Indian Melodies*, harmonized by Arthur Farwell. Newton Center, Massachusetts: The Wa-Wan Press, 1901.

Fewkes, J. W. *Additional Studies of Zuñi Songs and Rituals with the Phonograph*. 1890.

────── "A Contribution to Passamaquoddy Folk-lore." *Journal of American Folk-Lore*, Vol. III, 1890.

────── *On the Use of the Phonograph Among the Zuñi Indians*. 1890.

Fillmore, John Comfort. *The Harmonic Structure of Indian Music*. New York: G. P. Putnam's Sons, 1899.

Fletcher, Alice C. "The Hako: A Pawnee Ceremony." Washington: Bureau of American Ethnology, *22nd Annual Report*, 1904.

────── *Indian Games and Dances with Native Songs*. Boston: C. C. Birchard and Company, 1915.

────── *Indian Story and Song from North America*. Boston: Small, Maynard and Company, 1900.

Fletcher, Alice C., with Francis La Flesche. "The Omaha Tribe." Washington: Bureau of American Ethnology, *27th Annual Report*, 1911.

Fletcher, Alice C., with John Comfort Fillmore. *A Study of Omaha Indian Music*. Cambridge: Peabody Museum of American Archæology and Ethnology, 1893.

Gilman, Benjamin Ives. "Hopi Songs." *Journal of American Ethnology and Archæology*, Vol. V, 1908.

────── "Zuñi Melodies." *Journal of American Ethnology and Archæology*, Vol. I, 1891.

Griggs, John Cornelius. *Studien über die Musik in Amerika.* Leipzig: Breitkopf and Haertel, 1894.

Hoffman, Walter James. "The Mide'-wiwin or 'Grand Medicine Society' of the Ojibway." Washington: Bureau of American Ethnology, *7th Annual Report*, 1891.

La Flesche, Francis. "The Osage Tribe." Washington: Bureau of American Ethnology, *36th Annual Report*, 1921.

Lieurance, Thurlow. *Songs of the North American Indians.* Philadelphia: Theodore Presser Company, 1920.

Loomis, Harvey Worthington. *Lyrics of the Red Man.* Newton Center, Massachusetts: The Wa-Wan Press, 1903-4.

Matthews, Washington. *Navaho Legends.* Boston: Houghton Mifflin Company, 1897.

Nevin, Arthur. "Two Summers with the Blackfeet Indians of Montana." *Musical Quarterly*, April, 1916.

Schoolcraft, Henry Rowe. *Information Respecting the History, Condition, and Prospects of the Indian Tribes in the United States.* Philadelphia: Lippincott, Grambo and Company, 1851-57.

Speck, F. G., and J. D. Sapir. *Ceremonial Songs of the Creek and Yuchi Indians.* Philadelphia: University of Pennsylvania Anthropological Publications, Vol. I, 1911.

Troyer, Carlos. *Indian Music Lecture: The Zuñi Indians and Their Music.* Philadelphia: Theodore Presser Company, 1913.

Wallaschek, Richard. *Primitive Music.* (Chap. I, "America"). London: Longman's, Green & Co., 1893.

NEGRO FOLK MUSIC

Allen, William Francis, Charles P. Ware, and Lucy McKim Garrison. *Slave Songs of the United States.* New York: A. Simpson and Company, 1867. (Reprinted 1929 by Peter Smith, New York.)

Armstrong, Mrs. F. W., and Helen W. Ludlow. *Hampton and Its Students.* New York: G. P. Putnam's Sons, 1875.

Ballanta, C. J. S. *St. Helena Spirituals.* New York: G. Schirmer, Inc., 1925.

Brawley, Benjamin. *The Negro in Literature and Art in the United States.* New York: Duffield and Company, 1929.

Burleigh, Harry T. *Negro Folk Songs*. New York: G. Ricordi and Company, 1921.

—— *Negro Spirituals* (2 vols.). New York: G. Ricordi and Company, 1917–22.

Burlin, Natalie Curtis. "Black Singers and Players." *Musical Quarterly*, October, 1919.

—— *Hampton Series of Negro Folk-Songs* (4 books). New York: G. Schirmer, Inc., 1918–19.

—— "Negro Music at Birth." *Musical Quarterly*, January, 1919.

Christensen, Abigail M. H. "Spirituals and Shouts of Southern Negroes." *Journal of American Folk-Lore*, Vol. III, 1890.

Cohen, Lily Young. *Lost Spirituals*. New York: W. Neale, 1928.

Coleridge-Taylor, Samuel. *Twenty-four Negro Melodies*. Transcribed for the piano. Boston: Oliver Ditson Company, 1905.

Curtis, Natalie. *Songs and Tales from the Dark Continent*. New York: G. Schirmer, Inc., 1920.

Dann, Hollis, and H. W. Loomis. *Fifty-eight Spirituals for Choral Use*. Boston: C. C. Birchard and Company, 1924.

Dett, R. Nathaniel. *Negro Spirituals*. (3 vols.) Cincinnati: John Church Company, 1919.

Diton, Carl R. *Thirty-six South Carolina Spirituals*. New York: G. Schirmer, Inc., 1930.

Edwards, Charles L. *Bahama Songs and Stories*. Boston: Houghton Mifflin Company, 1895.

Fenner, T. P., and F. G. Rathbon. *Cabin and Plantation Songs as Sung by the Hampton Students*. New York: G. P. Putnam's Sons, 1874.

Fisher, William Arms, editor. *Seventy Negro Spirituals*. Boston: Oliver Ditson Company, 1926.

Gellert, Lawrence. *Negro Songs of Protest*. New York: American Music League, 1936.

Grissom, Mary Allen. *The Negro Sings a New Heaven*. Chapel Hill, North Carolina: University of North Carolina Press, 1930.

Guion, David. *Darkey Spirituals*. New York: M. Witmark and Sons, 1918.

Hallowell, Emily. *Calhoun Plantation Songs*. Boston: C. W. Thompson and Company, 1901.

Johnson, Guy B. *John Henry; Tracking Down a Negro Legend.* Chapel Hill, North Carolina: University of North Carolina Press, 1929.

Johnson, Hall. *The Green Pastures Spirituals.* New York, 1930.

Johnson, J. Rosamond. *Rolling Along in Song; a Chronological Survey of American Negro Music.* New York: The Viking Press, 1937.

—— *Sixteen New Negro Spirituals.* New York: Handy Brothers Music Company, 1939.

—— *Utica Jubilee Singers' Spirituals,* taken down by J. Rosamond Johnson. Introduction by C. W. Hyne. Boston: Oliver Ditson Company, 1930.

Johnson, James Weldon, and J. Rosamond Johnson. *The Book of American Negro Spirituals.* New York: The Viking Press, 1940.

Kennedy, R. Emmet. *Black Cameos.* New York: A. and C. Boni. 1924.

—— *Mellows: Negro Work Songs, Street Cries, and Spirituals.* New York: A. and C. Boni, 1925.

—— *More Mellows.* New York: Dodd, Mead and Company, 1931.

Kirby, Percival R. "A Study of Negro Harmony." *Musical Quarterly,* July, 1923.

Krehbiel, Henry E. *Afro-American Folk Songs.* New York: G. Schirmer, Inc., 1914.

Laubenstein, Paul Fritz. "Race Values in Aframerican Music." *Musical Quarterly,* July, 1930.

Lee, George W. *Beale Street, Where the Blues Began.* New York: R. O. Ballou, 1934.

Locke, Alain. *The Negro and His Music.* Washington, D.C.: The Associates in Negro Folk Education, 1936.

Locke, Alain, editor. *The New Negro.* New York: A. and C. Boni, 1927.

Lomax, John A. " 'Sinful Songs' of the Southern Negro." *Musical Quarterly,* April, 1934.

Lomax, John A., and Alan Lomax. *Negro Folk Songs as Sung by Lead Belly.* New York: The Macmillan Company, 1936.

Ludlow, Helen W. *Tuskegee Normal and Industrial Institute; Its Story and Songs.* Hampton, Virginia: Institute Press, 1884.

McIlhenny, Edward A. *Befo' de War Spirituals*. Boston: The Christopher Publishing House, 1933.

Marsh, J. B. T. *The Story of the Jubilee Singers, with Their Songs.* Boston: Houghton Mifflin Company, 1880.

Monroe, Mina. *Bayou Ballads, Twelve Folk-Songs from Louisiana.* New York: G. Schirmer, Inc., 1921.

The Negro Singer's Own Book. Philadelphia: Turner and Fisher, 1846.

Niles, John J. *Seven Negro Exaltations*. New York: G. Schirmer, Inc., 1929.

—— "Shout, Coon, Shout!" *Musical Quarterly*, October, 1930.

Odum, H. W., and G. B. Johnson. *The Negro and His Songs*. Chapel Hill, North Carolina: University of North Carolina Press, 1925.

—— *Negro Workaday Songs*. Chapel Hill, North Carolina: University of North Carolina Press, 1926.

Parrish, Lydia. *Slave Songs of the Georgia Sea Islands*. New York: Creative Age Press, 1942.

Parsons, Elsie Clews. *Folk-Lore of the Sea Islands, South Carolina.* Cambridge, Massachusetts: American Folk-Lore Society, 1923.

Peterson, Clara Gottschalk. *Creole Songs from New Orleans*. New Orleans: Gruenewald and Company, 1902.

Pike, G. D. *The Jubilee Singers and Their Campaign for Twenty Thousand Dollars*. Boston: Lee and Shepard, 1873.

Religious Folk-Songs of the Negro as Sung on the Plantations. Hampton, Virginia: Institute Press, 1909. (Revised and enlarged edition by R. Nathaniel Dett. New York: G. Schirmer, Inc., 1926.)

Roberts, Helen M. "Possible Survivals of African Song in Jamaica." *Musical Quarterly*, July, 1926.

Rodeheaver, Homer A. *Rodeheaver's Spirituals*. Chicago: The Rodeheaver Company, 1923.

Scarborough, Dorothy. *On the Trail of Negro Folk-Songs*. Cambridge: Harvard University Press, 1925.

Scherpf, John C. *African Quadrilles, Selected from the Most Admired Negro Melodies and Arranged for the Pianoforte*. New York: E. Riley, 1844.

Seward, Theodore F. *Jubilee Songs, as Sung by the Jubilee Singers of Fisk University*. New York: Biglow and Main, 1872.

Smith, N. Clark. *New Plantation Melodies as Sung by the Tuskegee Students*. Tuskegee, Alabama, 1909.

Still, William Grant. *Twelve Negro Spirituals*. New York: Handy Brothers Music Company, 1937.

Turner, Harriet. *Folk Songs of the American Negro*. Boston: Boston Music Company, 1925.

White, Clarence Cameron. *Negro Folk Melodies*. Philadelphia: Theodore Presser Company, 1927.

White, Newman I. *American Negro Folk-Songs*. Cambridge: Harvard University Press, 1928.

Work, Frederick Jerome. *Some American Negro Folk-Songs*. Boston, 1909.

Work, John Wesley. *American Negro Songs*. New York: Howell, Soskin and Company, Inc., 1940.

—— *Folk Song of the American Negro*. Nashville, Tennessee: Fisk University Press, 1915.

REGIONAL FOLK MUSIC

California

Black, Eleanora, and Sidney Robertson. *The Gold Rush Song Book*. San Francisco: The Colt Press, 1940.

Check List of California Songs. Berkeley, California: University of California, 1940.

De Silva, Owen Francis. *Mission Music of California*. Los Angeles, California: W. F. Lewis, 1941.

Hague, Eleanor. *Early Spanish-Californian Folk Songs*. New York: J. Fischer and Brother, 1922.

Lummis, Charles F. *Spanish Songs of Old California*. Los Angeles: The author, 1923.

McCoy, William J. *Folk-Songs of the Spanish California*. San Francisco: Sherman Clay and Company, 1926.

Music of the Gold Rush Era. San Francisco: Work Projects Administration, 1939.

Illinois

Neely, Charles. *Tales and Songs of Southern Illinois*. Menasha, Wisconsin: George Banta Publishing Company, 1938.

Indiana

Brewster, Paul G. *Ballads and Songs of Indiana.* Bloomington, Indiana: Indiana University, 1940.

Iowa

Stout, Earl J. *Folklore from Iowa.* New York: The American Folk-Lore Society, 1936.

Kentucky

McGill, Josephine. *Folk Songs of the Kentucky Mountains.* New York: Boosey and Company, 1917.

—— "Following Music in a Mountain Land." *Musical Quarterly*, July, 1917.

—— "Old Ballad Burthens." *Musical Quarterly*, April, 1918.

Niles, John J. *Seven Kentucky Mountain Songs.* New York: G. Schirmer, Inc., 1929.

Shearin, A. M., and J. H. Coombs. *Syllabus of Kentucky Folk-Songs.* Transylvania University Studies in English, 1911.

Sulzer, Elmer G. *Twenty-five Kentucky Folk Ballads.* Lexington, Kentucky: Transylvania Printing Company, 1936.

Thomas, Jean. *Devil's Ditties, Being Stories of the Kentucky Mountain People.* Chicago: W. W. Hatfield, 1931.

Wyman, Loraine, and Howard Brockway. *Lonesome Tunes; Folksongs from the Kentucky Mountains.* New York: H. W. Gray Company, 1916.

—— *Twenty Kentucky Mountain Songs.* Boston: Oliver Ditson Company, 1920.

Louisiana

Whitfield, Irène Thérèse. *Louisiana French Folk Songs.* University, Louisiana: Louisiana State University Press, 1939.

Maine

Barry, Philips. *British Ballads from Maine.* New Haven, Connecticut: Yale University Press, 1929.

—— *The Maine Woods Songster.* Cambridge, Massachusetts: The Powell Printing Company, 1939.

Eckstorm, Fannie Hardy, and Mary Winslow Smyth. *Minstrelsy of Maine.* Boston: Houghton Mifflin Company, 1927.

Gray, Robert P. *Songs and Ballads of the Maine Lumberjacks.* Cambridge: Harvard University Press, 1924.

Mitchell, Edwin Valentine. "Music on the Maine Coast." (In *Anchor to Windward*, pp. 87–101.) New York: Coward-McCann, Inc., 1940.

Michigan

Beck, Earl Clifton. *Songs of the Michigan Lumberjacks*. Ann Arbor, Michigan: University of Michigan Press, 1941.

Gardner, Emelyn E., and Geraldine J. Chickering. *Ballads and Songs of Southern Michigan*. Ann Arbor, Michigan: University of Michigan Press, 1939.

Missouri

Belden, H. M. *A Partial List of Song Ballads and Other Popular Poetry Known in Missouri*, 1910.

Randolph, Vance. *Ozark Mountain Folks*. New York: The Vanguard Press, 1932.

New Mexico

Van Stone, Mary R. *Spanish Folk Songs of New Mexico*. Chicago: R. F. Seymour, 1926.

Ohio

Eddy, Mary Olive. *Ballads and Songs from Ohio*. New York: J. J. Augustin, 1939.

Pennsylvania

Shoemaker, Henry W. *Mountain Minstrelsy of Pennsylvania*. Philadelphia: J. F. McGirr, 1931.

—— *Music and Musical Instruments of Pennsylvania Mountaineers*. Altoona, Pennsylvania: Mountain City Press, 1924.

South Carolina

Smith, Reed. *South Carolina Ballads*. Cambridge: Harvard University Press, 1928.

Texas

Dobie, James Frank. *Texas and Southwestern Lore*. Austin, Texas: Texas Folk-Lore Society, 1927.

Vermont

Flanders, Helen. *The New Green Mountain Songster; Traditional Folk Songs of Vermont*. New Haven: Yale University Press, 1939.

Flanders, Helen, and George Brown. *Vermont Folk-Songs and Ballads*. Brattleboro, Vermont: Stephen Daye Press, 1931.

Sturgis, Edith B., and Robert Hughes. *Songs from the Hills of Vermont*. New York: G. Schirmer, Inc., 1919.

Virginia

Davis, Arthur K. *Traditional Ballads of Virginia*. Cambridge: Harvard University Press, 1929.

Washington

Roberts, H. H. "Some Songs of the Puget Sound Salish." *Journal of American Folk-Lore*, Vol. XXXI, 1918.

United States: Appalachians

Campbell, Olive D., and Cecil J. Sharp. *English Folksongs from the Southern Appalachians*. New York: G. P. Putnam's Sons, 1917.

Henry, Mellinger Edward. *Folk-Songs from the Southern Highlands*. New York: J. J. Augustin, 1938.

Mark, Jeffrey. "Recollections of Mountaineers." *Musical Quarterly*, April, 1930.

McMeekin, I. M. *Melodies and Mountaineers*. Boston: Stratford, 1921.

Niles, John J. *Songs of the Hill-Folk; Twelve Ballads from Kentucky, Virginia, and North Carolina*. New York: G. Schirmer, Inc., 1934.

Richardson, Ethel Park, and Sigmund Spaeth. *American Mountain Songs*. New York: Greenberg, Publisher, 1927.

Scarborough, Dorothy. *A Song Catcher in the Southern Mountains*. New York: Columbia University Press, 1937.

Sharp, Cecil J. *American-English Folk Songs*. New York: G. Schirmer, Inc., 1918.

—— *Folk-Songs of English Origin from the Appalachian Mountains*. London: Novello and Company, 1921.

—— *Nursery Songs from the Appalachian Mountains*. London: Novello and Company, 1921–23.

Thomas, Jean. *The Singin' Fiddler of Lost Hope Hollow*. New York: E. P. Dutton and Company, 1938.

Thomas, Jean, and Joseph A. Leeder. *The Singin' Gatherin'; Tunes from the Southern Appalachians*. New York: Silver Burdett Company, 1939.

United States: New England

Linscott, Eloise Hubbard. *Folk Songs of Old New England.* New York: The Macmillan Company, 1939.

United States: South

Cox, John H. *Folk Songs of the South.* Cambridge: Harvard University Press, 1925.

Weedon, Miss Howard. *Songs of the Old South.* New York: Doubleday, Page and Company, 1900.

MISCELLANEOUS FOLK MUSIC
(see also "Popular Music")

Andrews, Edward D. "Shaker Songs." *Musical Quarterly,* October, 1937.

Buchanan, Annabel Morris. *Folk-Hymns of America.* New York: J. Fischer and Brother, 1938.

Burchenal, Elizabeth. *American Country Dances.* New York: G. Schirmer, Inc., 1918.

Burlin, Natalie Curtis. "A Plea for Our Native Art." *Musical Quarterly,* April, 1920.

Carmer, Carl. *America Sings; Stories and Songs of America's Growing.* New York: Alfred A. Knopf, 1942.

—— *Songs of the Rivers of America.* New York: Farrar and Rinehart, Inc., 1942.

Check-List of Recorded Songs in the English Language in the Archive of American Folk Song, to July, 1940. Washington, D.C.: Library of Congress, 1942.

Davis, A. K., Junior. "Some Problems of Ballad Publication." *Musical Quarterly,* April, 1918.

Downes, Olin, and Elie Siegmeister. *A Treasury of American Song.* New York: Alfred A. Knopf, 1943.

Farwell, Arthur. *Folk-Songs of the West and South: Negro, Cowboy and Spanish California.* Newton Center, Massachusetts: The Wa-Wan Press, 1905.

—— *From Mesa and Plain; Indian, Cowboy and Negro Sketches.* Newton Center: The Wa-Wan Press, 1905.

Finger, C. J. *Frontier Ballads*. New York: Doubleday, Page and Company, 1927.

Ford, Ira W. *Traditional Music of America*. New York: E. P. Dutton and Company, 1940.

Gordon, R. W. "American Folk-Music"; series of eighteen articles in *New York Times Magazine*, 1926–27.

Jackson, George Pullen. *A Directory of Sacred Harp Singers and Singing Conventions*. Nashville, Tennessee: Privately printed, 1945.

—— *Down-East Spirituals*. New York: J. J. Augustin, 1943.

—— *Spiritual Folk-Songs of Early America*. New York: J. J. Augustin, 1937.

—— *The Story of the Sacred Harp, 1844–1944*. Nashville, Tennessee: Vanderbilt University Press, 1944.

—— *White and Negro Spirituals, Their Life Span and Kinship*. New York: J. J. Augustin, 1944.

—— *White Spirituals in the Southern Uplands*. Chapel Hill, North Carolina: University of North Carolina Press, 1933.

Korson, George. *Coal Dust on the Fiddle; Songs and Stories of the Bituminous Industry*. Philadelphia: University of Pennsylvania Press, 1943.

—— *Minstrels of the Mine Patch; Songs and Stories of the Anthracite Industry*. Philadelphia: University of Pennsylvania Press, 1938.

Lomax, John A. *Cowboy Songs and Other Frontier Ballads*. New York: The Macmillan Company, 1929.

Lomax, John A., and Alan Lomax. *American Ballads and Folk Songs*. New York: The Macmillan Company, 1934.

—— *Our Singing Country; a Second Volume of American Ballads and Folk Songs*. New York: The Macmillan Company, 1941.

Mason, Daniel Gregory. "The Folk-Songs and American Music." *Musical Quarterly*, July, 1918.

Mattfeld, Julius. *The Folk Music of the Western Hemisphere*. A List of References in the New York Public Library. New York: New York Public Library, 1925.

Pound, Louise. *American Ballads and Songs*. New York: Charles Scribner's Sons, 1922.

Powell, John. *Twelve Folk Hymns.* New York: J. Fischer and Brother, 1934.

Provisional Check List of Disks (excluding primitive music) in the Archive of American Folk Song in the Library of Congress. Washington, D.C.: Library of Congress, 1937.

Rickaby, Franz. *Ballads and Songs of the Shanty Boy.* Cambridge: Harvard University Press, 1926.

Smith, C. Alphonso. "Ballads Surviving in the United States." *Musical Quarterly,* January, 1916.

Smith, Reed. *American Anthology of Old World Ballads.* New York: J. Fischer and Brother, 1937.

Wheeler, Mary, and William J. Reddick. *Roustabout Songs; a Collection of Ohio River Valley Songs.* New York: Remick Music Corporation, 1939.

POPULAR MUSIC AND MINSTREL SONGS
(see also "Folk Music")

Hopkins, John. *Hopkins' New Orleans 5-cent Songster* (Confederate Songs). New Orleans, 1861.

Johnson, Helen Kendrick. *Our Familiar Songs and Those Who Made Them.* New York: Henry Holt and Company, 1907.

Jordan, Phillip D., and Lillian Kessler. *Songs of Yesterday.* Garden City, New York: Doubleday, Doran, 1941.

Jubilee and Plantation Songs. Boston: Oliver Ditson Company, 1887.

Loesser, Arthur. *Humor in American Song.* New York: Howell Soskin, Inc., 1942.

Luther, Frank. *Americans and Their Songs.* New York: Harper and Brothers, 1942.

Marks, Edward B. *They All Had Glamour. From the Swedish Nightingale to the Naked Lady.* New York: Julian Messner, Inc., 1944.

—— *They All Sang, from Tony Pastor to Rudy Vallée.* New York: The Viking Press, 1934.

Mitchell, Mrs. A. L. *Songs of the Confederacy and Plantation Melodies.* Cincinnati, Ohio: The G. B. Jennings Company, 1901.

Paskman, Dailey, and Sigmund Spaeth. *Gentlemen, Be Seated; A*

Parade of the Old-time Minstrels. New York: Doubleday, Doran, 1928.

Plantation Songs and Jubilee Hymns. Chicago: White, Smith and Company, 1881.

Posselt, Eric. *Give Out! Songs of, by, and for the Men in Service.* New York: Arrowhead Press, 1943.

A San Francisco Songster, 1849–1939. San Francisco: Work Projects Administration, 1939.

Shay, Frank. *My Pious Friends and Drunken Companions.* New York: The Macaulay Company, 1927.

—— *More Pious Friends and Drunken Companions.* New York: The Macaulay Company, 1928.

—— *Drawn from the Wood; Consolations in Words and Music for Pious Friends and Drunken Companions.* New York: The Macaulay Company, 1929.

Spaeth, Sigmund. *Read 'em and Weep.* New York: Doubleday, Page and Company, 1926.

—— *Weep Some More, My Lady.* New York: Doubleday, Page and Company, 1927.

—— *They Still Sing of Love.* New York: Horace Liveright, Inc., 1929.

Witmark, Isidore. *The Story of the House of Witmark: from Ragtime to Swingtime.* New York: L. Furman, 1939.

JAZZ AND SWING
(see also "Folk Music")

Armstrong, Louis. *Swing That Music.* New York: Longmans, Green and Company, 1926.

Copland, Aaron. "Jazz Structure and Influence." *Modern Music,* January, 1927.

Goffin, Robert. *Jazz, from the Congo to the Metropolitan.* Garden City, New York: Doubleday, Doran, 1944.

Goldberg, Isaac. *Tin Pan Alley.* New York: The John Day Company, 1930.

Goodman, Benny, and Irving Kolodin. *The Kingdom of Swing.* New York: Stackpole Sons, 1939.

Handy, William C. *Blues; an Anthology*. New York: A. and C. Boni, 1926.

—— *Collection of Blues*. New York: Robbins-Engel, Inc., 1925.

Handy, William C., and E. A. Niles. *Blues; an Anthology of Jazz Music from the Early Negro Folk Blues to Modern Music*. New York: A. and C. Boni, 1926.

Hobson, Wilder. *American Jazz Music*. New York: W. W. Norton and Company, 1939.

Laubenstein, Paul Fritz. "Jazz—Debit and Credit." *Musical Quarterly*, October, 1929.

Levy, Newman. "The Jazz Formula." *Modern Music*, June, 1924.

Miller, Eduard Paul. *Miller's Year Book of Popular Music*. Chicago: Pen Publications, 1943.

Osgood, Henry O. *So This Is Jazz*. Boston: Little, Brown and Company, 1926.

Panassié, Hugues. *Hot Jazz*. New York: M. Witmark and Sons, 1936.

—— *The Real Jazz*. New York: Smith and Durrell, 1942.

Ramsey, Frederic, and Charles Edward Smith, editors. *Jazzmen*. New York: Harcourt, Brace and Company, 1939.

Sargeant, Winthrop. *Jazz: Hot and Hybrid*. New York: Arrow Editions, 1939.

Stringham, E. J. "Jazz—An Educational Problem." *Musical Quarterly*, April, 1926.

Whiteman, Paul, and Mary Margaret McBride. *Jazz*. New York: J. H. Sears and Company, 1926.

NATIONAL AIRS AND SOLDIER SONGS

Browne, C. A. *The Story of Our National Ballads*. New York: Thomas Y. Crowell Company, 1919.

A Check List of the Literature and Other Material in the Library of Congress on the European War (List of Music prepared by Walter R. Whittlesey). Washington: Library of Congress, Government Printing Office, 1918.

Dolph, Edward Arthur. *Sound Off! Soldier Songs from the Revolution to World War II*. New York: Farrar and Rinehart, 1942.

Elson, Louis C. *The National Music of America*. Boston: The Page
    Company, 1899. (Revised to 1924 by Arthur Elson.)
Kidson, Frank. "Some Guesses About Yankee Doodle." *Musical Quar-
    terly*, January, 1917.
Kobbé, Gustav. *Famous American Songs*. New York: Thomas Y.
    Crowell Company, 1906.
Maginty, Edward A. " 'America': The Origin of Its Melody." *Musi-
    cal Quarterly*, July, 1934.
Moore, Frank. *Lyrics of Loyalty*. New York: G. P. Putnam, 1864.
—— *Rebel Rhymes and Rhapsodies*. New York: G. P. Putnam,
    1864.
—— *Songs and Ballads of the American Revolution*. New York:
    D. Appleton and Company, 1856.
—— *Songs of the Soldiers*. New York: G. P. Putnam, 1864.
Muller, Joseph. *The Star-Spangled Banner; Words and Music Is-
    sued Between 1814–1864*. An annotated bibliographical list. New
    York: G. A. Baker and Company, 1935.
Nason, Reverend Elias. *Our National Song, a Monogram*. Albany,
    New York: J. Munsell, 1869.
Nathan, Hans. "Two Inflation Songs of the Civil War." *Musical
    Quarterly*, April, 1943.
Niles, John J. *Singing Soldiers*. New York: Charles Scribner's Sons,
    1927.
Niles, John J., and Douglas Moore. *Songs My Mother Never Taught
    Me*. New York: The Macaulay Company, 1929.
Preble, George Henry. *History of the Flag of the United States*
    (Chapter on National and Patriotic Songs). Boston: A. Williams
    and Company, 1880.
Salisbury, Stephen. *An Essay on the Star-Spangled Banner and
    National Songs*. Worcester, Massachusetts: C. Hamilton,
    1873.
Smith, Nicholas. *Stories of Great National Songs*. Milwaukee: The
    Young Churchman Company, 1899.
Sonneck, O. G. *Miscellaneous Studies in the History of Music* (Chap-
    ter on The First Edition of *Hail Columbia*). New York: The
    Macmillan Company, 1921.
Report on *The Star-Spangled Banner, Hail Columbia, America, Yan-*

kee Doodle. Washington: Library of Congress, Government Printing Office, 1909.

The Star-Spangled Banner. Revised and enlarged from the Report of 1909. Washington: Library of Congress, Government Printing Office, 1914.

Weybright, Victor. *Spangled Banner; The Life of Francis Scott Key.* New York: Farrar and Rinehart, 1935.

White, Richard Grant. *National Hymns—How They Are Written, and How They Are Not Written.* New York: Rudd and Carleton, 1886.

MUSIC PERIODICALS

(Arranged in chronological order, according to their founding. Those still published are marked with an asterisk [*].)

Euterpeiad: or Musical Intelligencer. Devoted to the Diffusion of Musical Information and Belles Lettres. Boston, 1820 to 1823.

Lyre: The New York Musical Journal. New York, 1824 to 1825.

Euterpeiad, an Album of Music, Poetry and Prose. New York, 1830 to 1831.

The Musical Review and Record of Musical Science, Literature, and Intelligence. New York, 1838.

Boston Musical Gazette. Boston, 1838 to 1846.

Musical Magazine. Boston, 1839 to 1842.

Musical World. New York, 1849 to 1860.

American Monthly Musical Review. New York, 1851 to 1852.

The American Musical Almanac for 1852. New York, 1851.

Musical Review and Choral Advocate. New York, 1852 to 1853.

The Musical World and Journal of Fine Arts. New York, 1852 to 1856.

Dwight's Journal of Music. Boston, 1852 to 1881.

Boston Musical Journal. Boston, 1853 to 1854.

New York Musical Review and Choral Advocate. New York, 1854 to 1855.

New York Musical Pioneer and Chorister Budget. New York, 1855 to 1871.

New York Musical Review and Gazette. New York, 1855 to 1860.

The Musical Review and Musical World. New York, 1860 to 1864.

American Art Journal. New York, 1863 to 1905.

Folio; a Journal of Music, Art, Drama and Literature. Boston, 1871 to 1895.

Ditson & Co.'s Musical Record. Boston, 1878 to 1903.

Musical Review. New York, 1879 to 1881.

Southern Musical Journal. 1879 to 1882.

* *Musical Courier.* New York, 1880 to the present.

* *The Etude.* Philadelphia, 1883 to the present.

The Boston Musical Year-Book. Boston, 1883 to 1886.

* *Metronome.* New York, 1885 to the present.

The Musical Year-Book of the United States. Boston, 1886 to 1893.

Music. Chicago, 1891 to 1902.

Music Review. Chicago, 1892 to 1894.

* *The Musical Leader.* Chicago, 1895 to the present.

* *The Musician.* Boston (now New York), 1896 to the present.

Concert-goer. New York, 1897 to 1903.

* *Musical America.* New York, 1898 to the present.

Pacific Coast Musical Review. San Francisco, 1901 to 1933.

* *New Music Review and Choral Advocate.* New York, 1901 to the present.

* *Music Teachers' National Association Book of Proceedings.* 1906 to the present.

The Musical Observer. New York, 1904 (absorbed by *Musical Courier*, 1931).

* *Music Supervisors' Journal:* official organ of the Music Supervisors' National Conference, 1914 to 1934; became *Music Educators' Journal*, 1934, to the present.

* *Music News.* Chicago, 1908 to the present.

Wisconsin Music Teacher. Madison, 1912 to 1919.

The Musical Monitor. New York, 1912 to 1921; official organ of the National Federation of Music Clubs.

Minnesota Music. Minneapolis, 1913 to 1920.

* *The Musical Quarterly.* New York, 1915 to the present.

* *Music and Musicians.* Seattle, 1915 to the present.

Pacific Coast Musician. Los Angeles, 1919 to 1937.

* *Official Bulletin of the National Federation of Music Clubs*. 1922 to 1928. Became *Music Clubs' Magazine,* 1928 to the present.

* *Musical Digest*. New York, 1921 to the present.

Pro-Musica Quarterly. New York, 1923 to 1929.

* *Modern Music*. New York, 1924 to the present.

Pierre Key's International Music Year Book. New York, 1925–26, 1926–27, 1929–30, 1935, 1938.

Singing. New York, 1926 to 1927; became *Singing & Playing*, New York, 1927 to 1930; became *Encore*, 1930 to 1933.

Northwest Musical Herald. Minneapolis, 1926 to 1934.

* *American Record Guide*. New York, 1935 to the present.

* *Music Publishers' Journal*. New York, 1943 to the present.

Index

(The names of the chief composers appear in capitals; the pages at which appears the main discussion of each are set in italics.)

Pastorales, 529
Pygmalion, 529
Triptyque, 529
Vibrations, 529
other works, 529
Freedom Train (Siegmeister), 524
Free Lance, The (Sousa), 652
FREEMAN, HENRY LAWRENCE
(1875-), 400
Freeman's Journal, 40
"free music," 416
FREER, ELEANOR EVEREST (1864-
1943), 361
Free School for Spreading the Knowl-
edge of Vocal Music, 105
Free Song, A (Schuman), 540
Free Variations for Orchestra (Landau),
557
Free Verse Songs (Hughes), 570
FRENCH, JACOB (1754-?), 64
Harmony of Harmony, 64
New American Melody, 64
Psalmodist's Companion, 64
French-Canadian folk songs, 571, 575
French Genevan Psalter, 5, 6
French Revolution, 118
Friedheim, Arthur, 531
Friedman, Theodore Lewis (see Lewis,
Ted)
Friends and Enemies of Modern Music,
467
Friends of Music, 413, 434
Friends (see Quakers)
Fries, August, 215
Fries, Wulf, 215
FRIML, RUDOLF (1881-), 665
Firefly, The, 665
High Jinks, 665
Katinka, 665
Rose Marie, 665
Vagabond King, The, 665
Frog Went a Courtin', 635
From a Log Cabin (MacDowell), 330
From a Lute of Jade (Read), 551
From a Sufi's Tent (Strickland), 566
From Dixieland (Rasbach), 576
From Dreams of Thee (Bullard), 568
From Foster Hall (Howard), 571
From Greenland's Icy Mountains (Ma-
son), 137
From Grieg to Brahms (Mason, D. G.),
376
From Mount Rainier (Reiser), 435
From My Youth (Wilson), 387-388

From Old New England (Severn), 363
From the Brake the Nightingale (Ho-
mer), 568
From the Canebreak (Gardner), 494
From the Garden of Hellas (Ballantine),
435
From the Journal of a Wanderer (Still),
465
From the Land of the Sky Blue Water,
The (Cadman), 407, 409
From the Life of St. Paul (Burleigh),
577
From the Mountain Kingdom of the
Great North West, Suite (Saar),
361
From the Northland (Sowerby), 470
From the Plains (Ayres), 391
From the Revelation of St. John the Di-
vine (McPhee), 532
From These States (Bacon), 500
From Vernon's Mount Behold the Hero
Rise (Holden), 61
FRY, WILLIAM HENRY (1815?-
1864), 238-247, 250, 681
Breaking Heart, The, 245
Childe Harold, 245
Day in the Country, 245
Leonora, 239-242, 250
Notre Dame de Paris, 252
Santa Claus Symphony, 245-247
FRYSINGER, J. FRANK (1878-),
582
Fuchs, Robert, 427
Fugato on a Well-known Theme (Mc-
Bride), 550
fugue, Tans'ur on, 56
Fugue Fantasia (Farwell), 383
Fugue for Eighteen Violins (Dubensky),
489
Fuguing pieces (Billings), 49, 55-57
Fugue with Chorale (Leidzen), 511
Fuji in the Sunset Glow (Rogers, B.),
480
FULEIHAN, ANIS (1900-), 520
Calypso, 520
Fiesta, 520
Mediterranean, 520
Preface to a Child's Storybook, 520
Symphonic Episode, 520
Symphony Concertante
other works, 520
Fulfillment (MacDermid), 576
Fuller, Earl, 658
funds (see Fellowships in Music)

812 INDEX